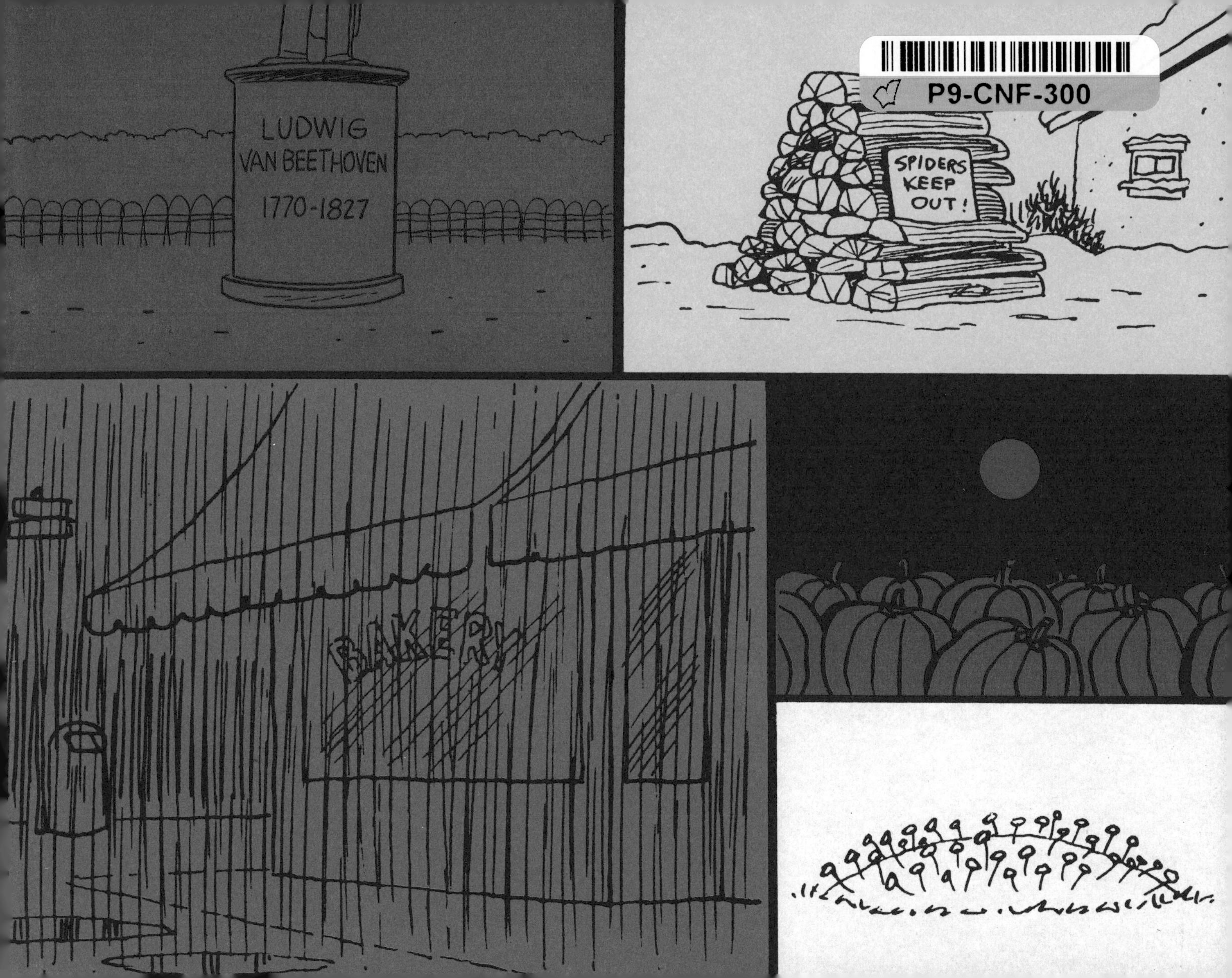
LUDWIG
VAN BEETHOVEN
1770-1827
SPIDERS KEEP OUT!
BAKERY

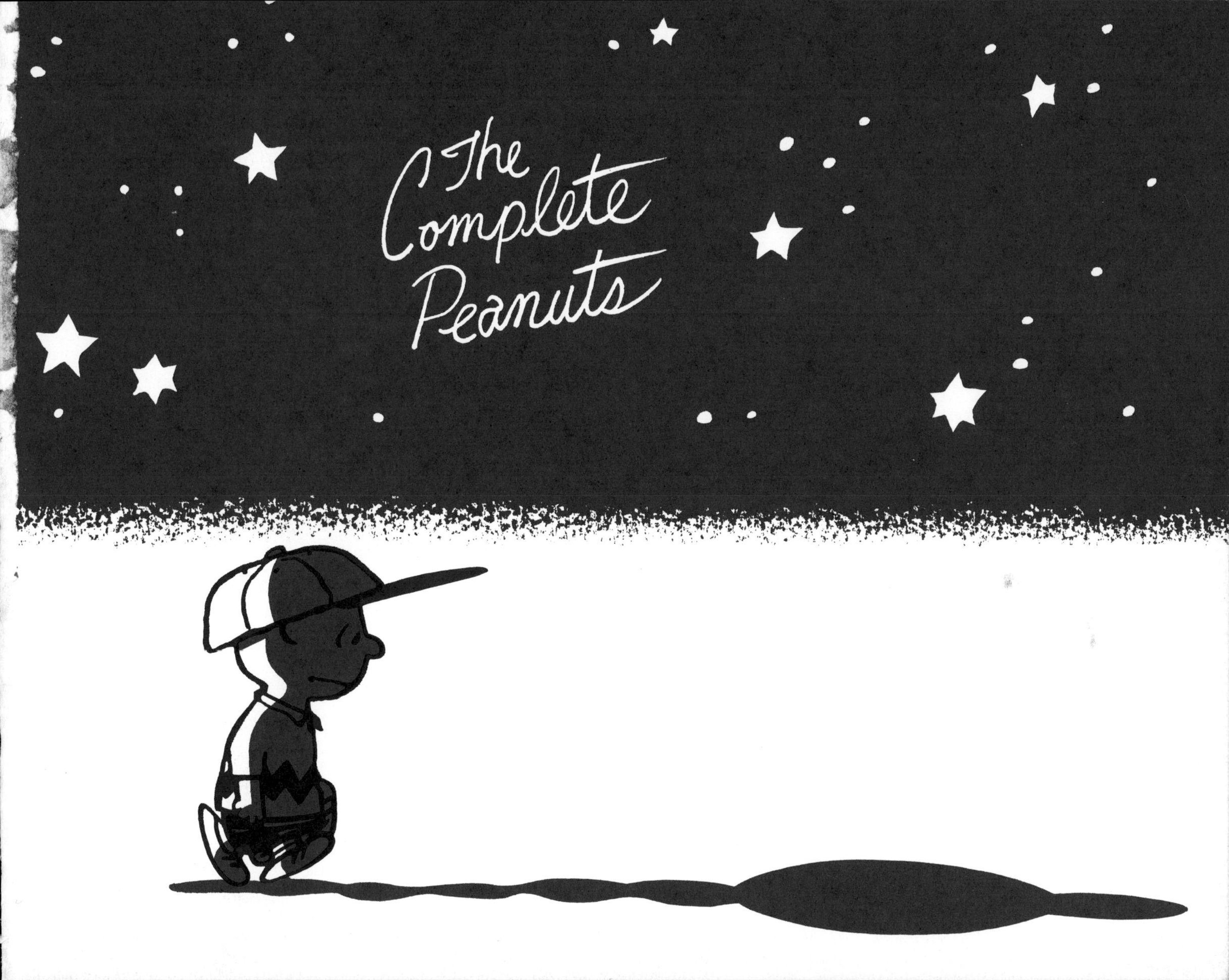
The Complete Peanuts

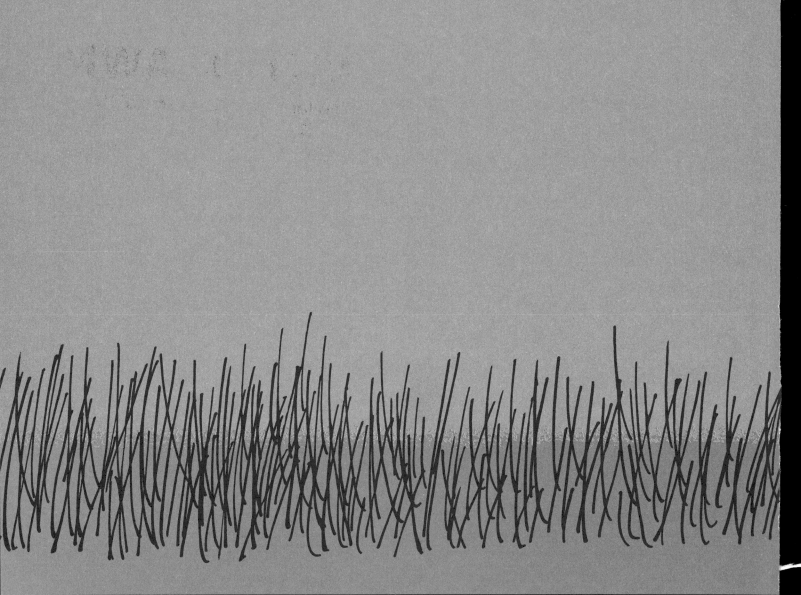

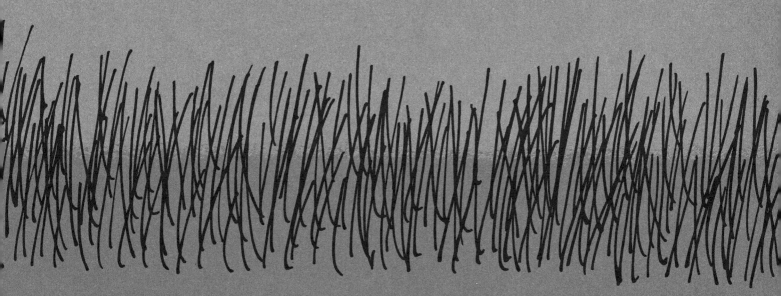

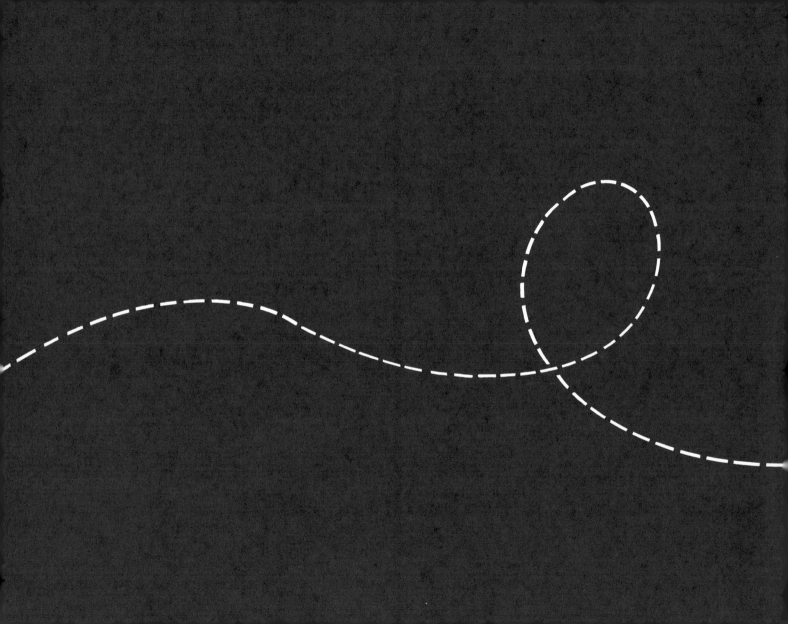

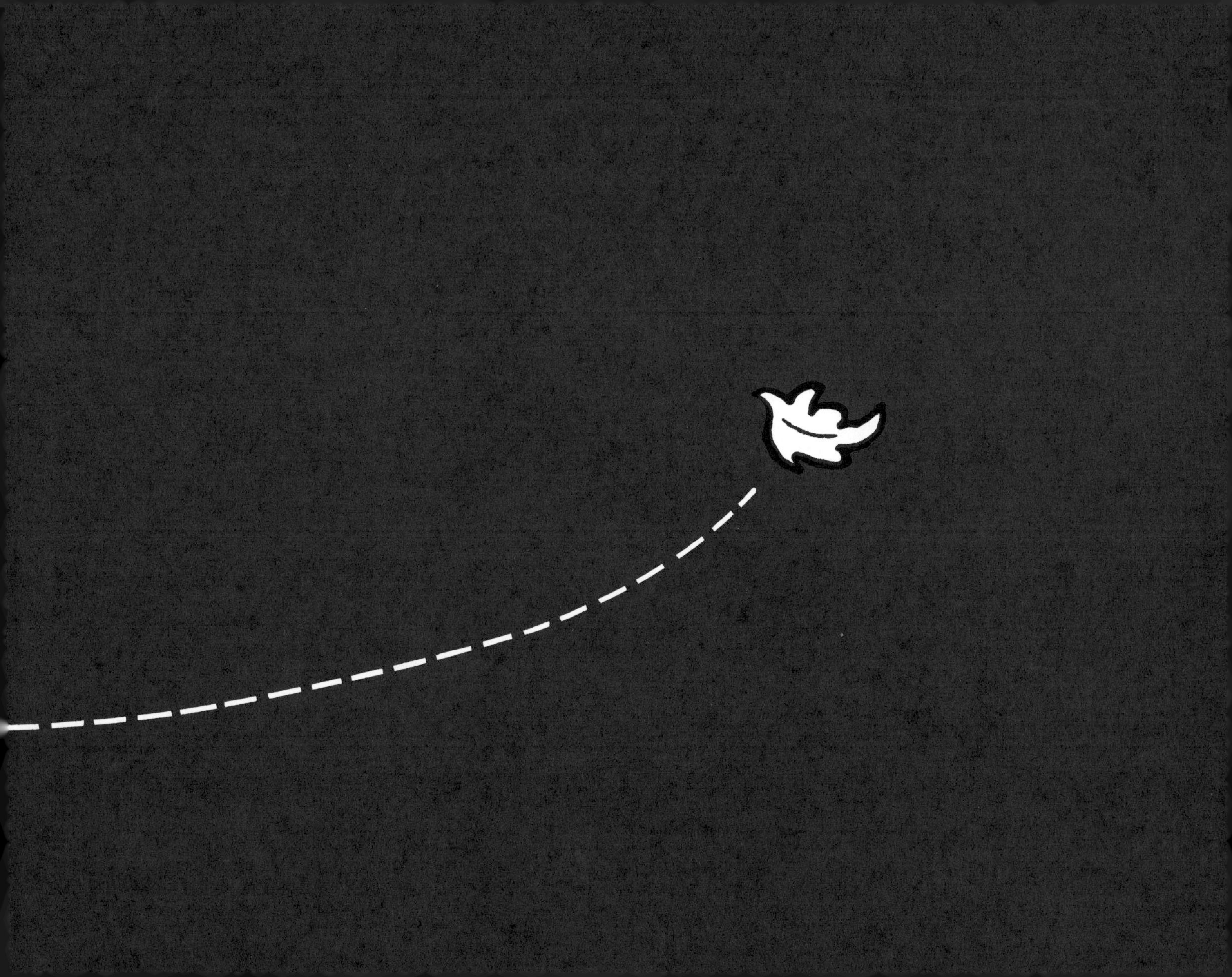

THE COMPLETE PEANUTS
by Charles M. Schulz
published by
Fantagraphics Books

Editor: Gary Groth
Designer: Seth
Production Manager: Kim Thompson
Production, assembly, and restoration: Paul Baresh, Adam Grano, and Angela Stork
Archival and production assistance: Nat Gertler & Marcie Lee
Index compiled by Houria Kerdioui
Promotion: Eric Reynolds
Publishers: Gary Groth & Kim Thompson

Special thanks to Jeannie Schulz, without whom
this project would not have come to fruition.
Thanks also to the
Charles M. Schulz Creative Associates,
especially Paige Braddock and Kim Towner.
Thanks for special support from United Media.

Fantagraphics Books, 7563 Lake City Way, Seattle, WA 98115, USA. For a free full-color catalogue of comics,
call 1-800-657-1100. Our books may be viewed on our website at www.fantagraphics.com.

Distributed to the book trade by:

USA: W.W. Norton and Company, Inc.
500 Fifth Avenue, New York, NY 10010
212-354-5500
Order Department: 800-233-4830

CANADA: Raincoast Books
9050 Shaugnessy Street, Vancouver, British Columbia V6P 6E5
Customer Service: 800-663-5714

ISBN-13: 978-1-56097-672-1   ISBN-10: 1-56097-672-1
First printing: August 2006   Printed in China

CHARLES M. SCHULZ

THE COMPLETE PEANUTS

1961 TO 1962

" THOSE "NYAHS" GET DOWN
INTO YOUR STOMACH, AND THEN
THEY JUST LAY THERE AND BURN "

▪ FANTAGRAPHICS BOOKS ▫

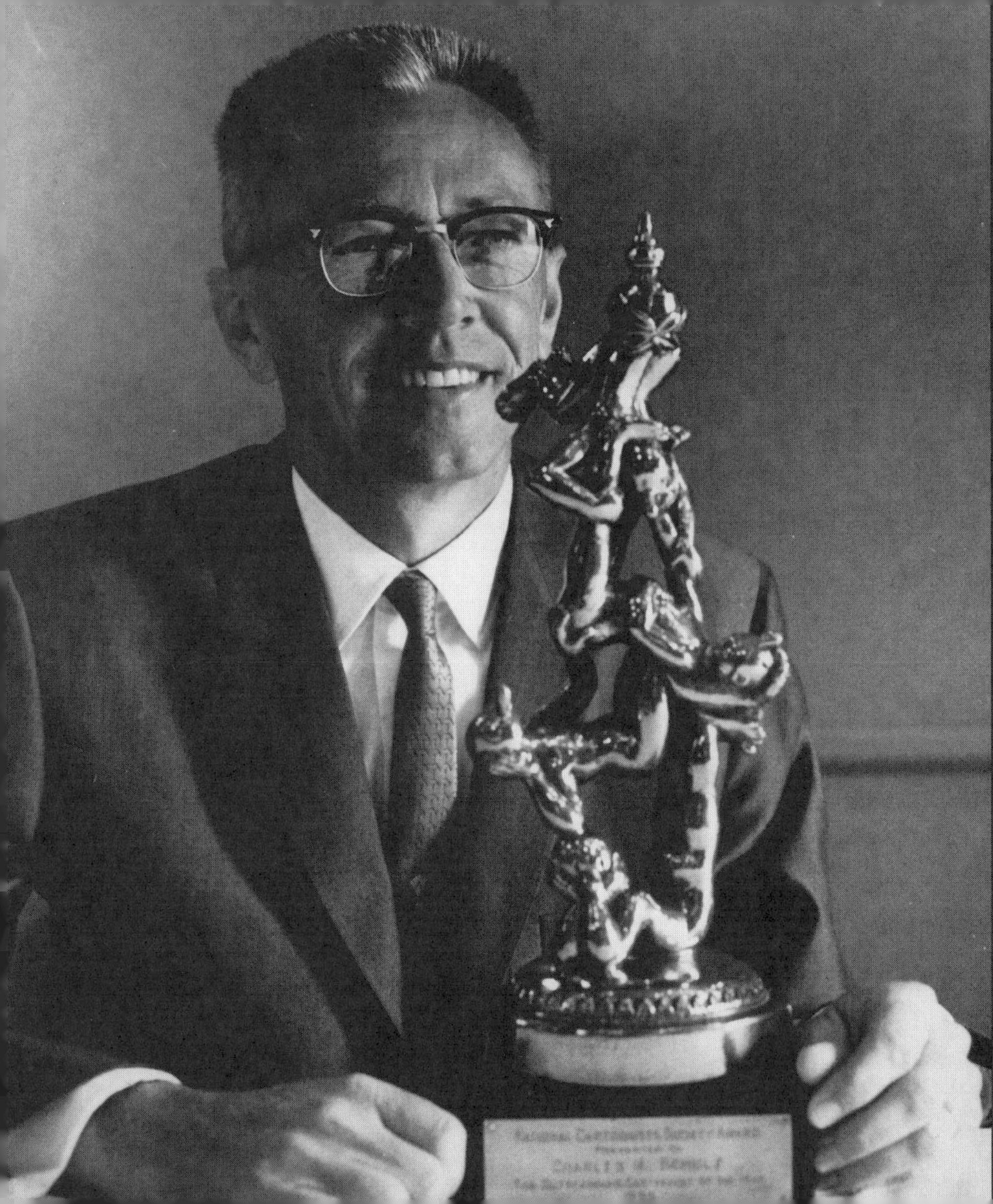

Charles Schulz with his second Reuben award, circa 1964.

FOREWORD by DIANA KRALL

I was a little girl when I discovered *Peanuts*. One of my earliest memories is of my Dad drawing "Snoopy" on my T-shirt in indelible ink. My favorite uniform when I was around 4 years old was a Charlie Brown sweatshirt; there's a picture somewhere at my Dad's. It wasn't all glamour.

I suppose I related to Charlie Brown. The expression "I got a rock" is part of my language as an adult — not that I'm cynical. I think the first time I heard little kids, or anyone for that matter, use words like "sarcasm," "cynical," and "depressed" was in the world of Charlie Brown, a world where the kids were smart and the adults were merely *blah blah bla blah blah*. "Please put 5 cents in the can," for when the psychiatrist Lucy was in to discuss your problems, still exists in my language — although the price has gone up slightly now.

The Charlie Brown gang was certainly not without its hang-ups. Although Charlie

Brown was the anchor of the strip, all his pals had their own distinct personalities and tenderly expressed neuroses. We all knew a Lucy, a Linus, a Peppermint Patty, a Sally, and a Snoopy. In fact, my husband claims that he most resembles Pig-Pen. I hope that what we learned for ourselves from these characters was a sense of compassion and forgiveness.

However, Charles Schulz didn't portray children as pious, or as little innocents waiting to be instructed by adults. They ask their own questions and have their own sense of wonder, whether through a belief in the Great Pumpkin or the Easter Beagle. These gentle parables have a light and joyful spirituality.

It is only in the television film, *A Charlie Brown Christmas,* that Schulz has Linus read the Nativity story directly from the gospels.

He does this to console Charlie Brown after he apparently fails in his assignment to purchase the centerpiece of the children's Christmas party by choosing a puny, threadbare tree over the more glittering offerings of a commercialized Christmas. Schulz, who, like myself, was raised Lutheran, would later describe himself as a "secular Humanist." He clearly sought answers in other beliefs, while retaining the value of those initial teachings.

Music is another recurring motif and value in *Peanuts.* Needless to say, I identify most of all with the occasionally exasperated pianist, Schroeder. I had a head start when going to my childhood piano lessons because Schroeder had already made me familiar with the names Beethoven and Chopin, even though I probably would have preferred a bust of Fats Waller.

After so many musical allusions and references in the comic strips, the melodies were finally made audible in the Emmy-winning film *A Charlie Brown Christmas*. It turned out to be some of the hippest and most charming jazz ever, composed by Vince Guaraldi and performed by his trio. Hey, as a kid who loved jazz, that music was the best. It proves that you don't have to play that cutesy stuff for children. They can definitely handle it. The dancing scene in *A Charlie Brown Christmas* is the grooviest. We see young hipsters who only drink chocolate-milk and can still groove to some jazz, baby!

Schroeder's running musical commentary could also be heard. I especially love the scene where Lucy is asking Schroeder to play *Jingle Bells* and, to her disappointment, he runs through every grand version including one

on the pipe organ until you hear Schroeder's exasperated toy piano... "plink plink plink, plink plink plink, plink plink plink plink pliiiiiiiiiiinkkkkkkkkkk!!!!," then the revelatory "That's it!" from Lucy. That happens quite often in real life to me.

My family and I have lived the characters every day, quotes pop up in conversation to illustrate a point, if only to face the realization that sometimes you only "get a rock." Charlie Brown and his friends endure because Charles Schulz trusted the intelligence and instinct of even his youngest readers to understand subtly illustrated dilemmas and simple truths expressed in a cartoon strip. His creations appeal to you as a child and speak to you as an adult. I look forward to the day when I might share these books with my own children.

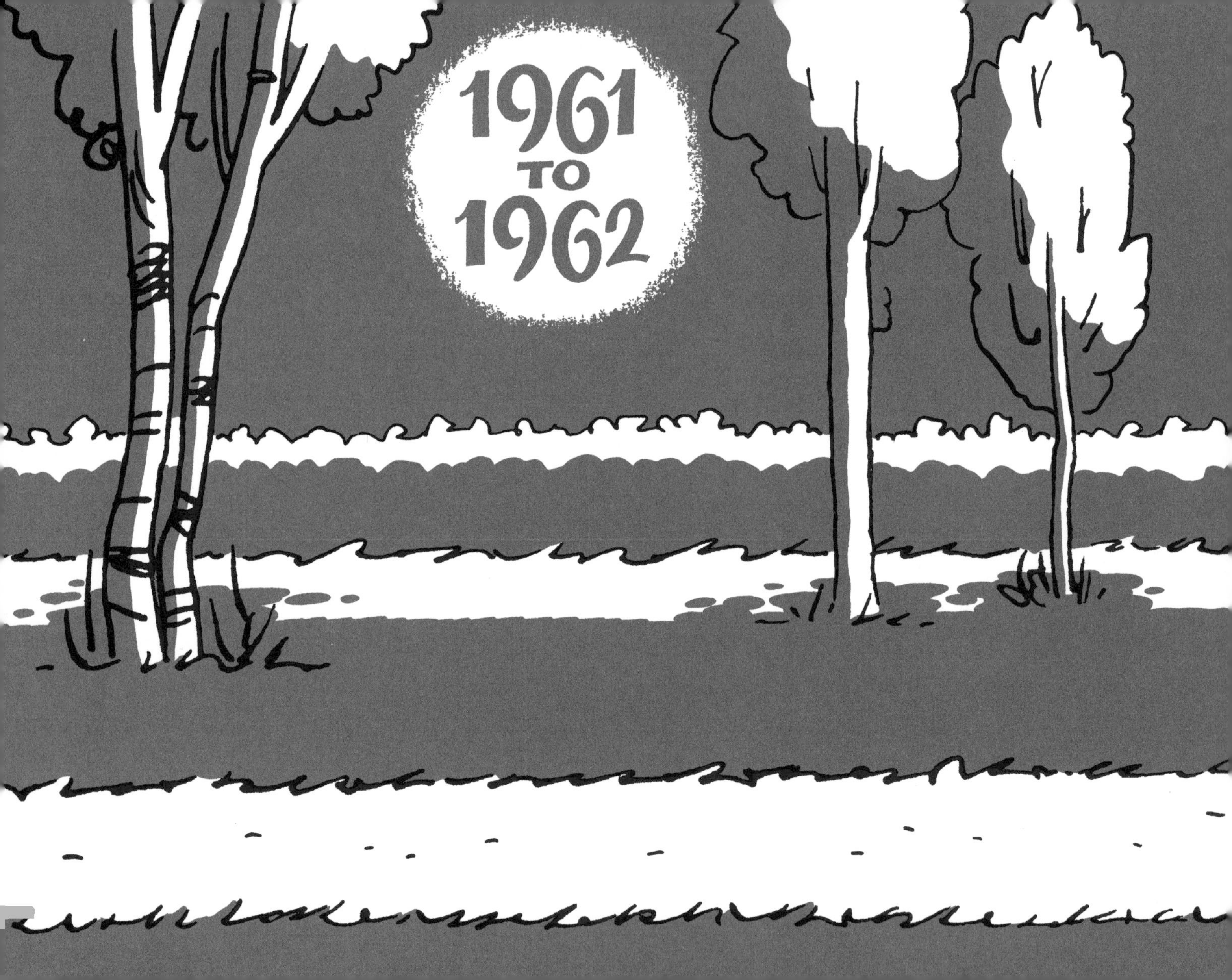
1961
TO
1962

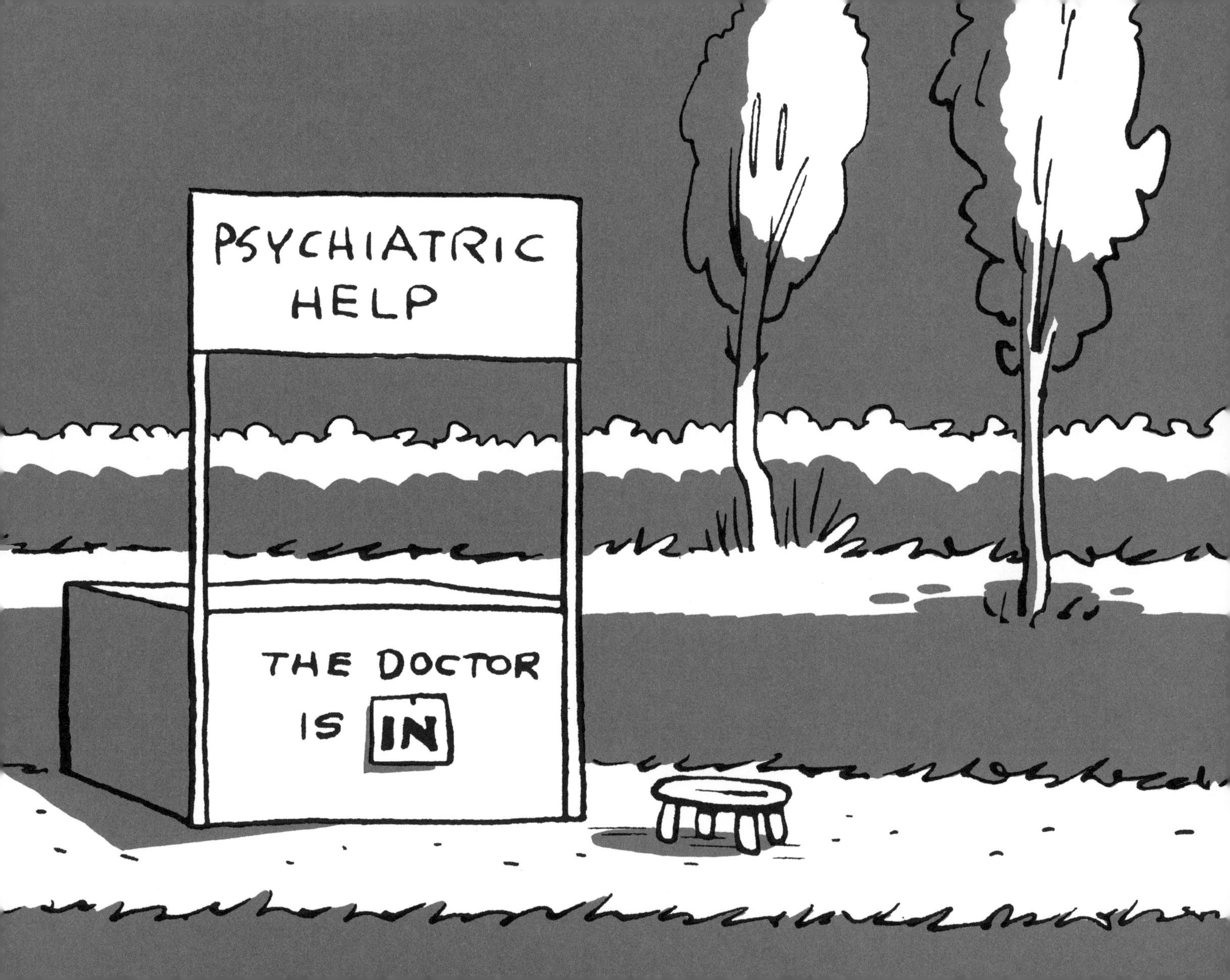
PSYCHIATRIC HELP
THE DOCTOR IS IN

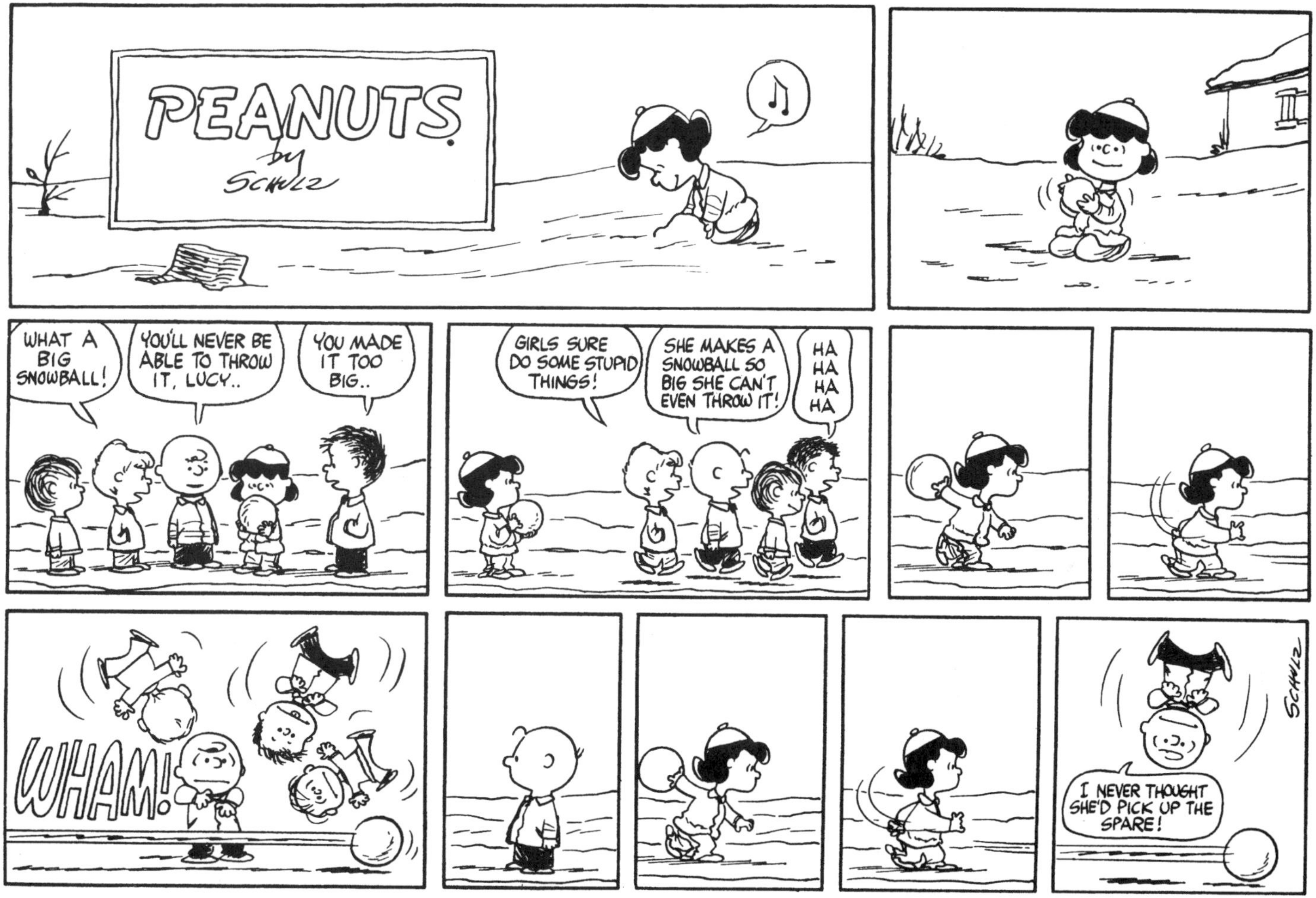
PEANUTS
by SCHULZ
WHAT A BIG SNOWBALL!
YOU'LL NEVER BE ABLE TO THROW IT, LUCY..
YOU MADE IT TOO BIG..
GIRLS SURE DO SOME STUPID THINGS!
SHE MAKES A SNOWBALL SO BIG SHE CAN'T EVEN THROW IT!
HA HA HA HA
WHAM!
SCHULZ
I NEVER THOUGHT SHE'D PICK UP THE SPARE!

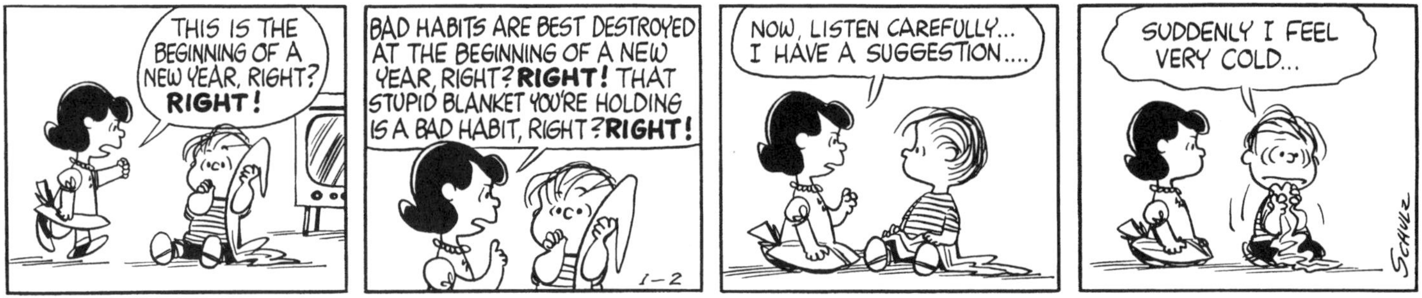
THIS IS THE BEGINNING OF A NEW YEAR, RIGHT? RIGHT!
BAD HABITS ARE BEST DESTROYED AT THE BEGINNING OF A NEW YEAR, RIGHT? RIGHT! THAT STUPID BLANKET YOU'RE HOLDING IS A BAD HABIT, RIGHT? RIGHT!
1-2
NOW, LISTEN CAREFULLY... I HAVE A SUGGESTION....
SUDDENLY I FEEL VERY COLD...
SCHULZ

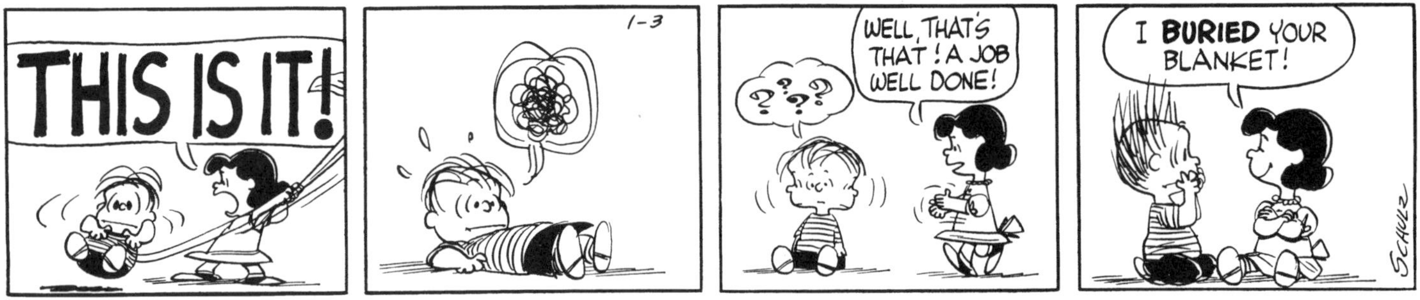
THIS IS IT!
1-3
WELL, THAT'S THAT! A JOB WELL DONE!
I BURIED YOUR BLANKET!
SCHULZ

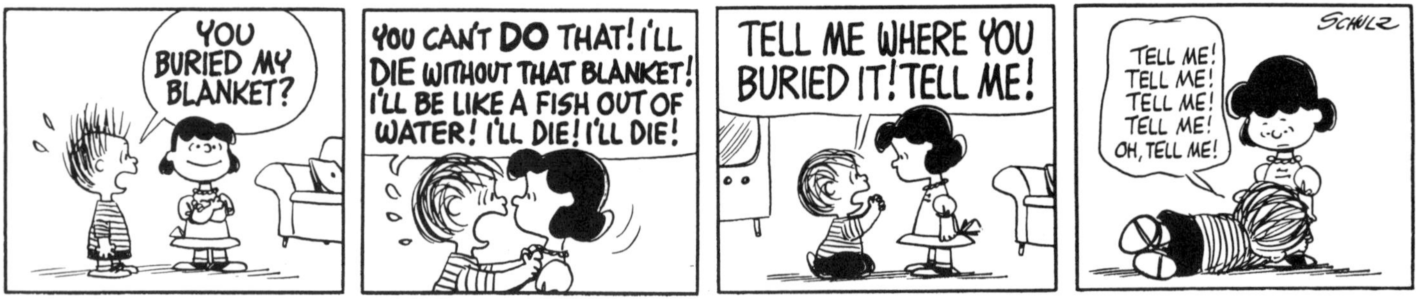
YOU BURIED MY BLANKET?
YOU CAN'T DO THAT! I'LL DIE WITHOUT THAT BLANKET! I'LL BE LIKE A FISH OUT OF WATER! I'LL DIE! I'LL DIE!
TELL ME WHERE YOU BURIED IT! TELL ME!
SCHULZ
TELL ME! TELL ME! TELL ME! TELL ME! OH, TELL ME!

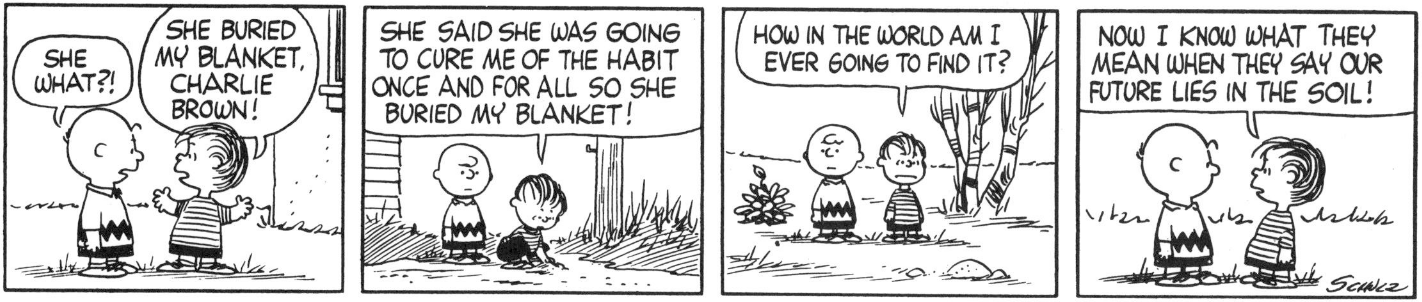
SHE WHAT?!
SHE BURIED MY BLANKET, CHARLIE BROWN!
SHE SAID SHE WAS GOING TO CURE ME OF THE HABIT ONCE AND FOR ALL SO SHE BURIED MY BLANKET!
HOW IN THE WORLD AM I EVER GOING TO FIND IT?
NOW I KNOW WHAT THEY MEAN WHEN THEY SAY OUR FUTURE LIES IN THE SOIL!
SCHULZ

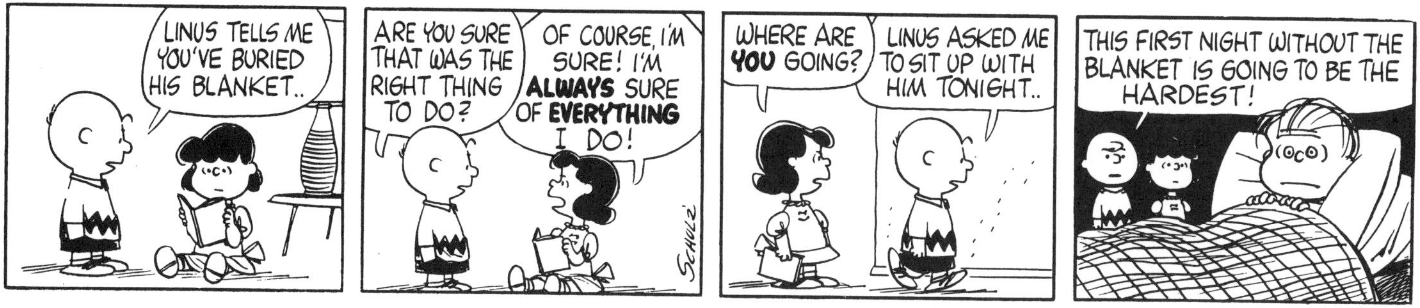
LINUS TELLS ME YOU'VE BURIED HIS BLANKET..
ARE YOU SURE THAT WAS THE RIGHT THING TO DO?
OF COURSE, I'M SURE! I'M **ALWAYS** SURE OF **EVERYTHING** I DO!
SCHULZ
WHERE ARE **YOU** GOING?
LINUS ASKED ME TO SIT UP WITH HIM TONIGHT..
THIS FIRST NIGHT WITHOUT THE BLANKET IS GOING TO BE THE HARDEST!

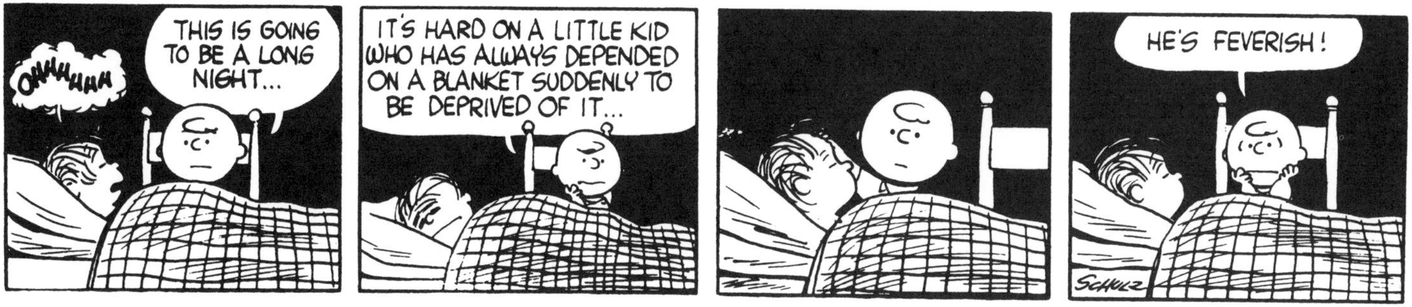
OHHHHHH
THIS IS GOING TO BE A LONG NIGHT...
IT'S HARD ON A LITTLE KID WHO HAS ALWAYS DEPENDED ON A BLANKET SUDDENLY TO BE DEPRIVED OF IT...
HE'S FEVERISH!
SCHULZ

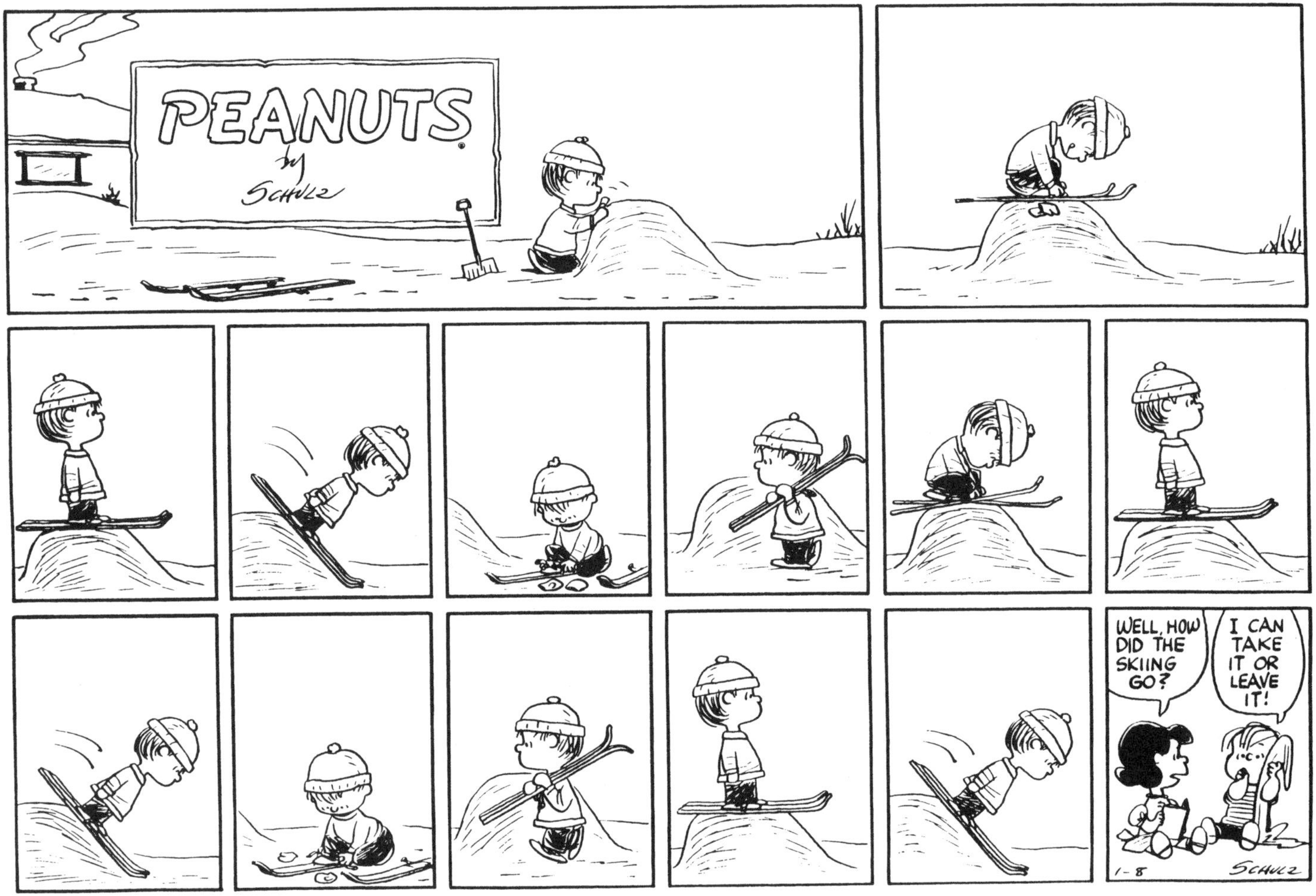
PEANUTS
by
SCHULZ
WELL, HOW DID THE SKIING GO?
I CAN TAKE IT OR LEAVE IT!
1-8
SCHULZ

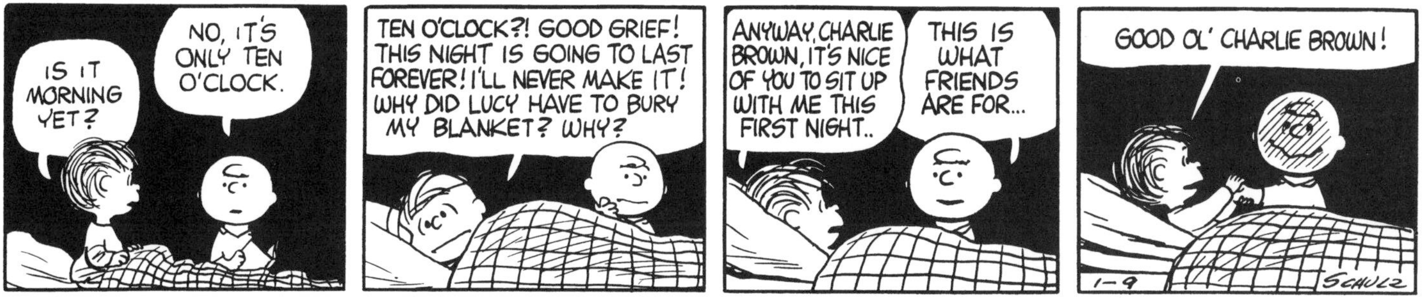
IS IT MORNING YET?
NO, IT'S ONLY TEN O'CLOCK.
TEN O'CLOCK?! GOOD GRIEF! THIS NIGHT IS GOING TO LAST FOREVER! I'LL NEVER MAKE IT! WHY DID LUCY HAVE TO BURY MY BLANKET? WHY?
ANYWAY, CHARLIE BROWN, IT'S NICE OF YOU TO SIT UP WITH ME THIS FIRST NIGHT..
THIS IS WHAT FRIENDS ARE FOR...
GOOD OL' CHARLIE BROWN!
1-9
SCHULZ

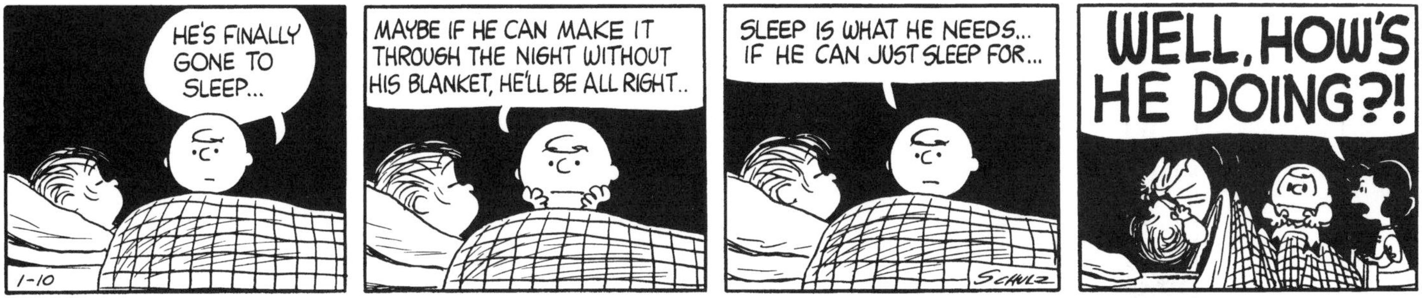
HE'S FINALLY GONE TO SLEEP...
1-10
MAYBE IF HE CAN MAKE IT THROUGH THE NIGHT WITHOUT HIS BLANKET, HE'LL BE ALL RIGHT..
SLEEP IS WHAT HE NEEDS... IF HE CAN JUST SLEEP FOR...
SCHULZ
WELL, HOW'S HE DOING?!

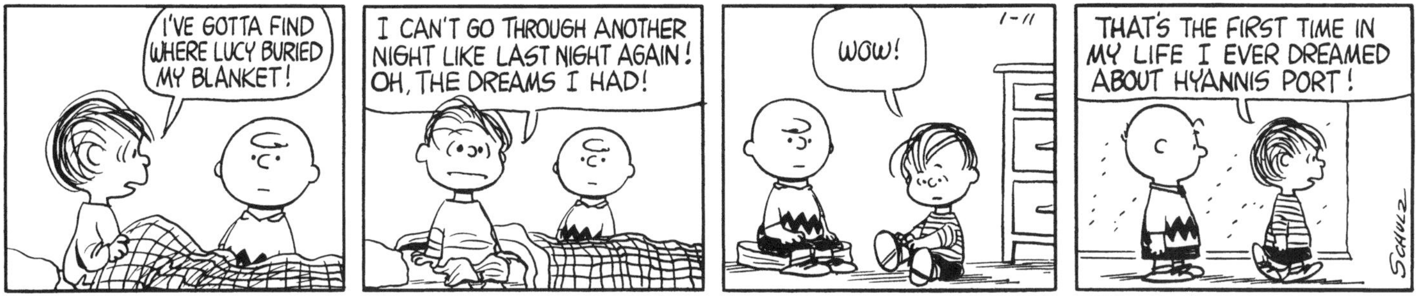
I'VE GOTTA FIND WHERE LUCY BURIED MY BLANKET!
I CAN'T GO THROUGH ANOTHER NIGHT LIKE LAST NIGHT AGAIN! OH, THE DREAMS I HAD!
1-11
WOW!
THAT'S THE FIRST TIME IN MY LIFE I EVER DREAMED ABOUT HYANNIS PORT!
SCHULZ

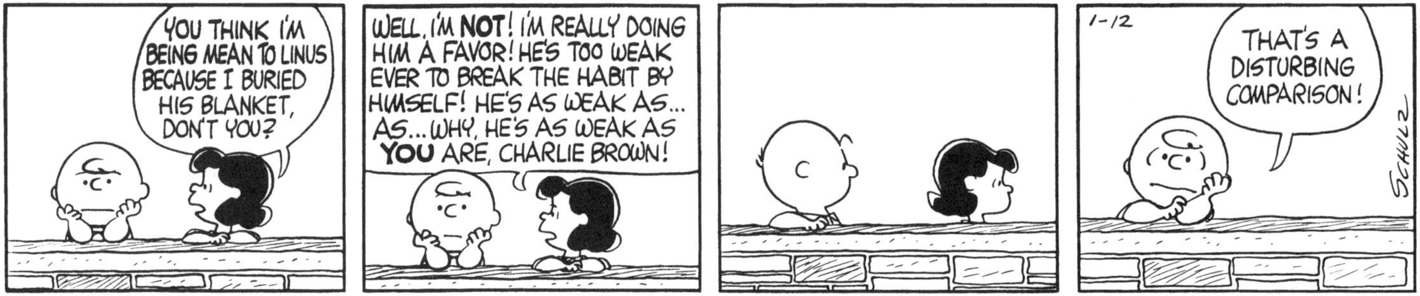
YOU THINK I'M BEING MEAN TO LINUS BECAUSE I BURIED HIS BLANKET, DON'T YOU?
WELL, I'M **NOT**! I'M REALLY DOING HIM A FAVOR! HE'S TOO WEAK EVER TO BREAK THE HABIT BY HIMSELF! HE'S AS WEAK AS... AS... WHY, HE'S AS WEAK AS **YOU** ARE, CHARLIE BROWN!
1-12
THAT'S A DISTURBING COMPARISON!
SCHULZ

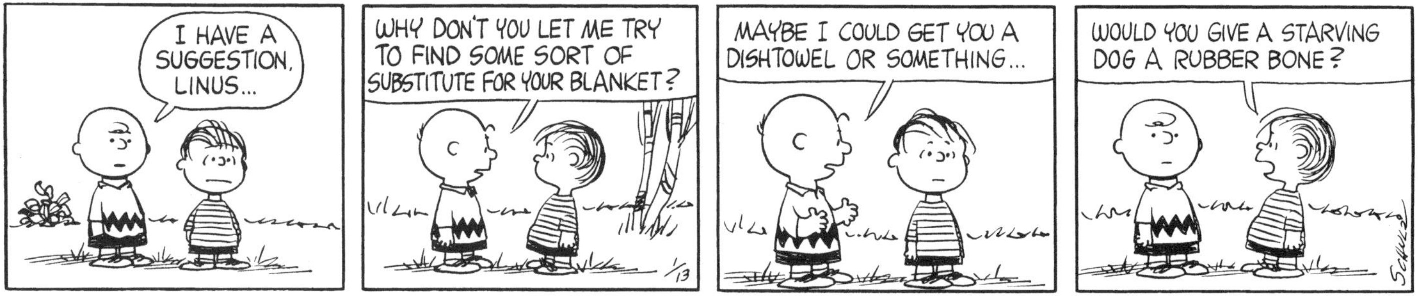
I HAVE A SUGGESTION, LINUS...
WHY DON'T YOU LET ME TRY TO FIND SOME SORT OF SUBSTITUTE FOR YOUR BLANKET?
1/13
MAYBE I COULD GET YOU A DISHTOWEL OR SOMETHING...
WOULD YOU GIVE A STARVING DOG A RUBBER BONE?
SCHULZ

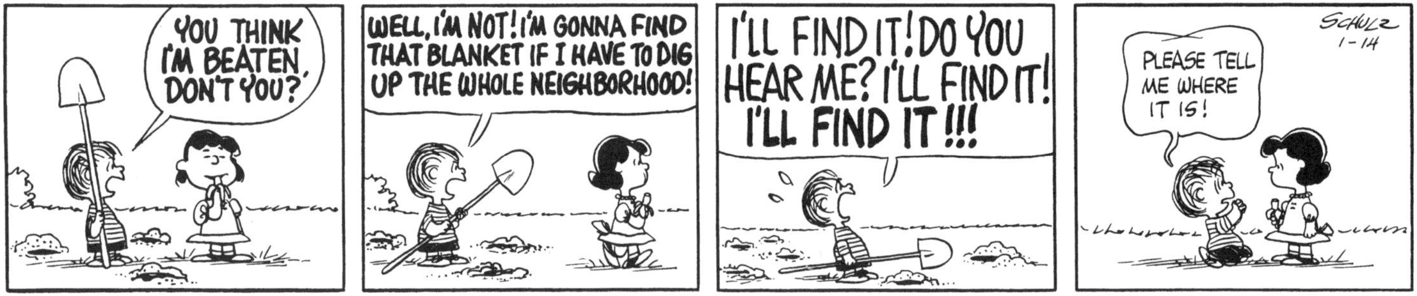
YOU THINK I'M BEATEN, DON'T YOU?
WELL, I'M NOT! I'M GONNA FIND THAT BLANKET IF I HAVE TO DIG UP THE WHOLE NEIGHBORHOOD!
I'LL FIND IT! DO YOU HEAR ME? I'LL FIND IT! I'LL FIND IT!!!
SCHULZ 1-14
PLEASE TELL ME WHERE IT IS!

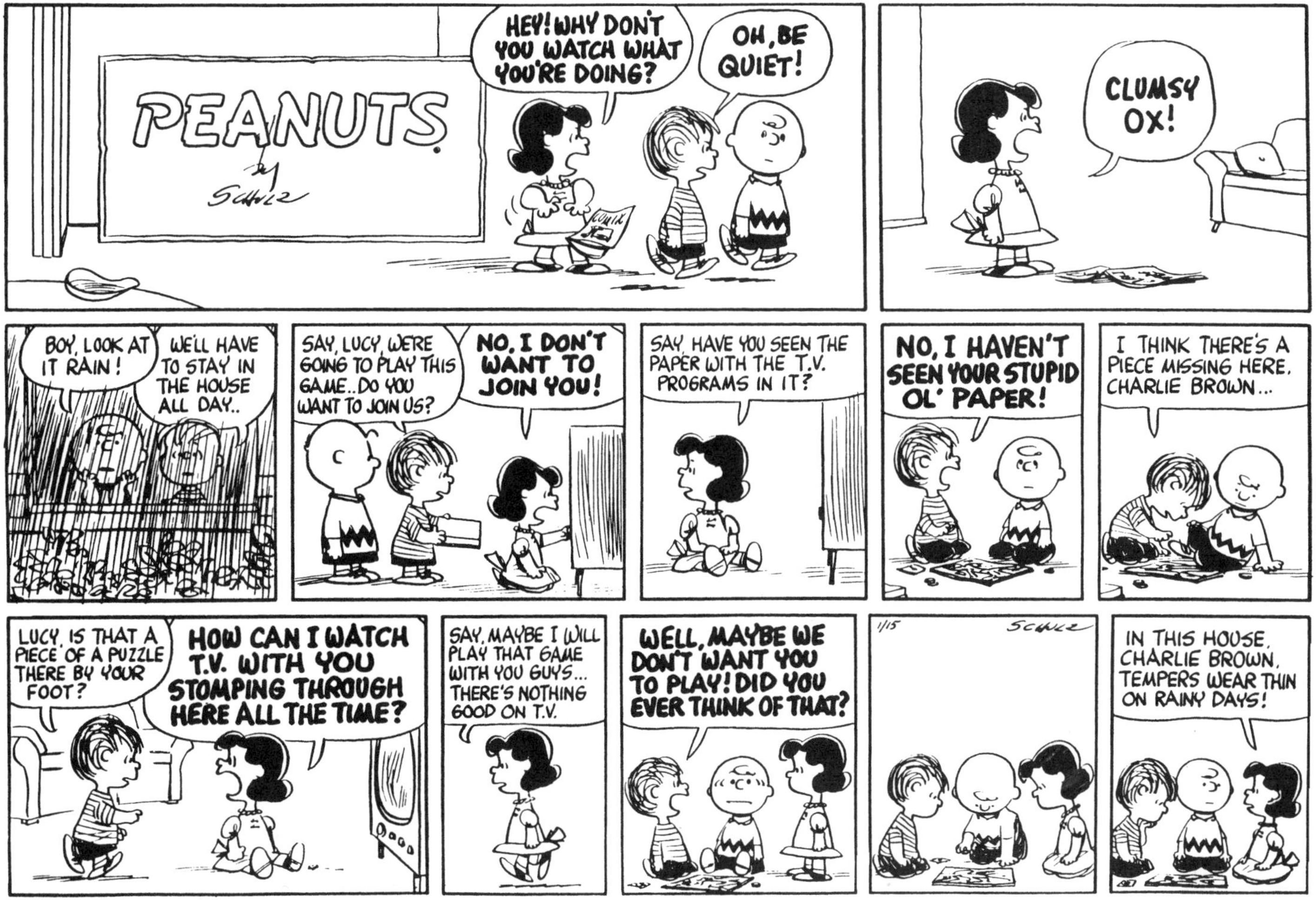
PEANUTS
by SCHULZ
HEY! WHY DON'T YOU WATCH WHAT YOU'RE DOING?
OH, BE QUIET!
CLUMSY OX!
BOY, LOOK AT IT RAIN!
WE'LL HAVE TO STAY IN THE HOUSE ALL DAY..
SAY, LUCY, WE'RE GOING TO PLAY THIS GAME..DO YOU WANT TO JOIN US?
NO, I DON'T WANT TO JOIN YOU!
SAY, HAVE YOU SEEN THE PAPER WITH THE T.V. PROGRAMS IN IT?
NO, I HAVEN'T SEEN YOUR STUPID OL' PAPER!
I THINK THERE'S A PIECE MISSING HERE, CHARLIE BROWN...
LUCY, IS THAT A PIECE OF A PUZZLE THERE BY YOUR FOOT?
HOW CAN I WATCH T.V. WITH YOU STOMPING THROUGH HERE ALL THE TIME?
SAY, MAYBE I WILL PLAY THAT GAME WITH YOU GUYS... THERE'S NOTHING GOOD ON T.V.
WELL, MAYBE WE DON'T WANT YOU TO PLAY! DID YOU EVER THINK OF THAT?
1/15
SCHULZ
IN THIS HOUSE, CHARLIE BROWN, TEMPERS WEAR THIN ON RAINY DAYS!

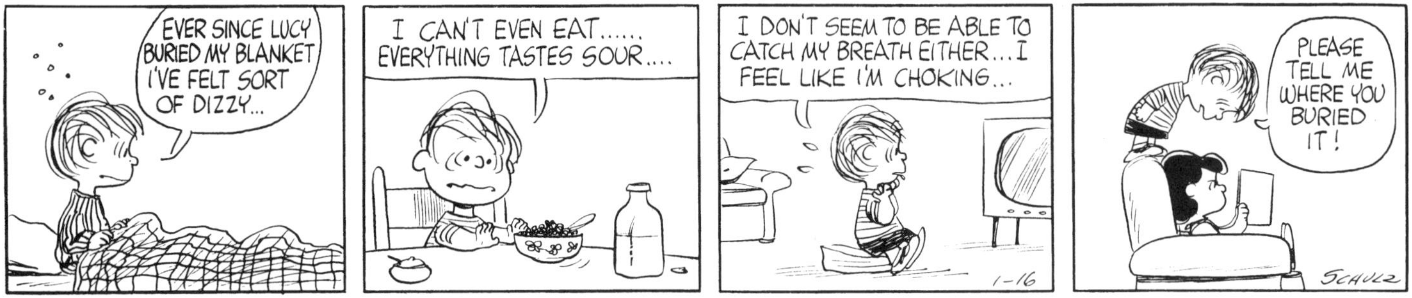
EVER SINCE LUCY BURIED MY BLANKET I'VE FELT SORT OF DIZZY...
I CAN'T EVEN EAT...... EVERYTHING TASTES SOUR....
I DON'T SEEM TO BE ABLE TO CATCH MY BREATH EITHER...I FEEL LIKE I'M CHOKING...
PLEASE TELL ME WHERE YOU BURIED IT!

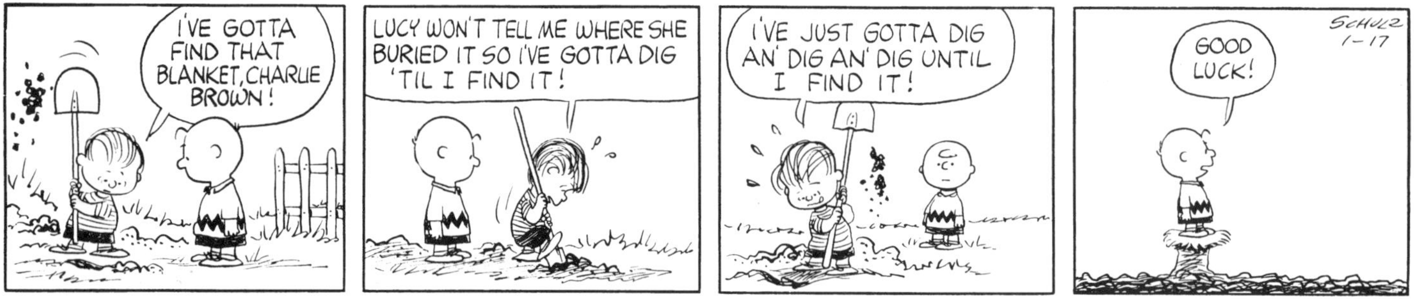
I'VE GOTTA FIND THAT BLANKET, CHARLIE BROWN!
LUCY WON'T TELL ME WHERE SHE BURIED IT SO I'VE GOTTA DIG 'TIL I FIND IT!
I'VE JUST GOTTA DIG AN' DIG AN' DIG UNTIL I FIND IT!
GOOD LUCK!

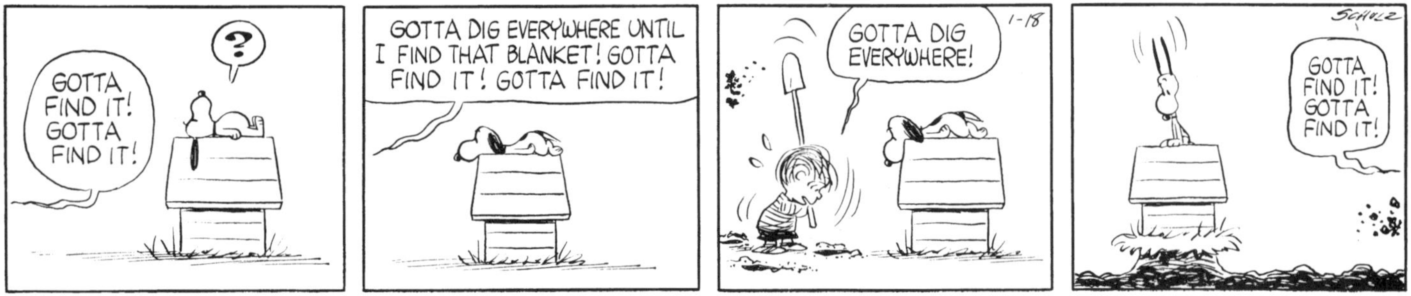
GOTTA FIND IT! GOTTA FIND IT!
?
GOTTA DIG EVERYWHERE UNTIL I FIND THAT BLANKET! GOTTA FIND IT! GOTTA FIND IT!
GOTTA DIG EVERYWHERE!
GOTTA FIND IT! GOTTA FIND IT!

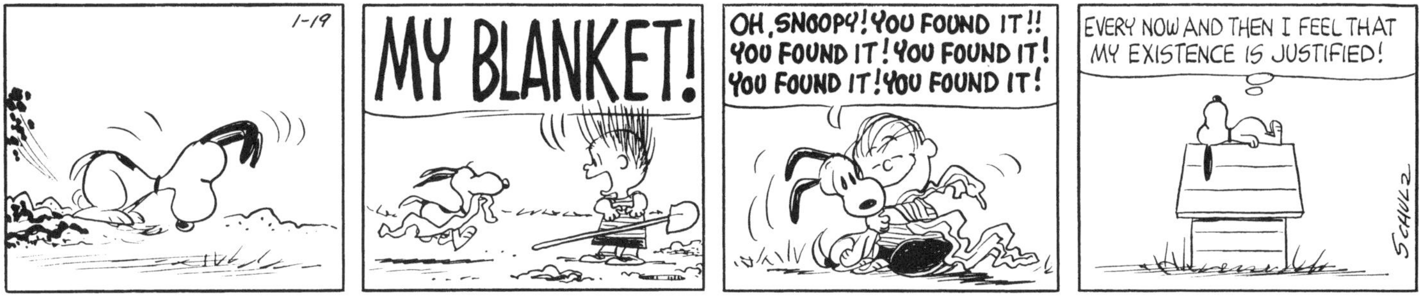
1-19
MY BLANKET!
OH, SNOOPY! YOU FOUND IT!! YOU FOUND IT! YOU FOUND IT! YOU FOUND IT! YOU FOUND IT!
EVERY NOW AND THEN I FEEL THAT MY EXISTENCE IS JUSTIFIED!
SCHULZ

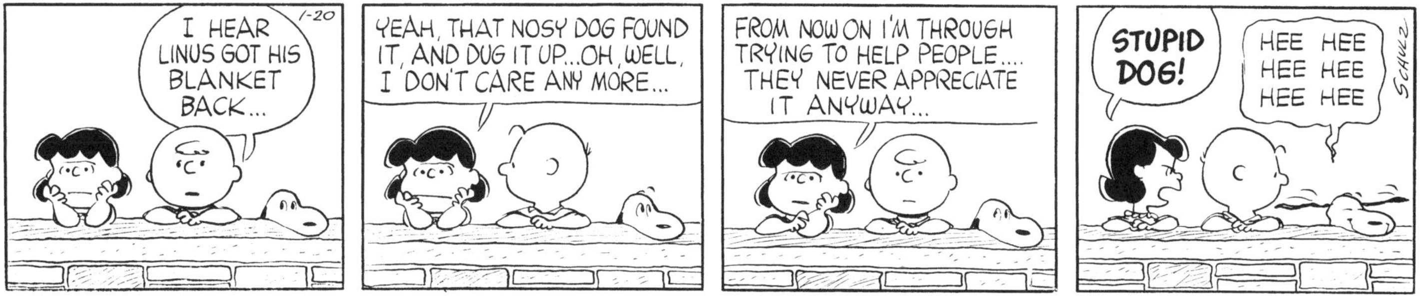
1-20
I HEAR LINUS GOT HIS BLANKET BACK...
YEAH, THAT NOSY DOG FOUND IT, AND DUG IT UP...OH, WELL, I DON'T CARE ANY MORE...
FROM NOW ON I'M THROUGH TRYING TO HELP PEOPLE.... THEY NEVER APPRECIATE IT ANYWAY...
STUPID DOG!
HEE HEE HEE HEE HEE HEE
SCHULZ

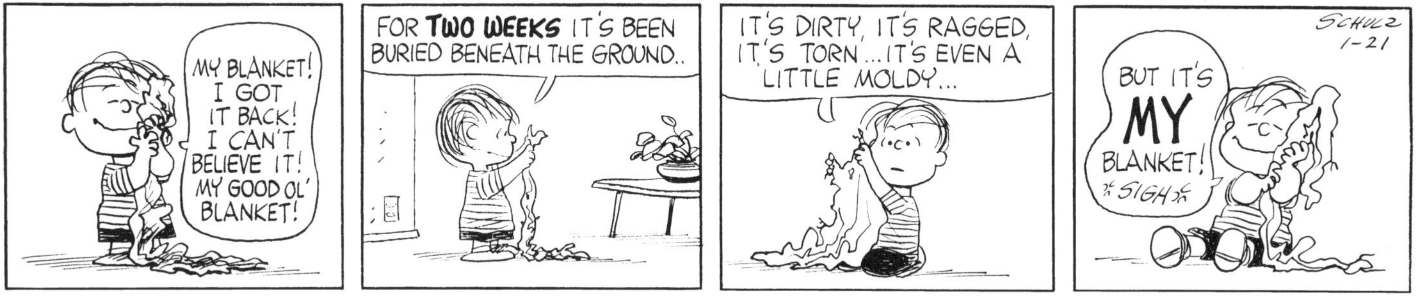
MY BLANKET! I GOT IT BACK! I CAN'T BELIEVE IT! MY GOOD OL' BLANKET!
FOR TWO WEEKS IT'S BEEN BURIED BENEATH THE GROUND..
IT'S DIRTY, IT'S RAGGED, IT'S TORN...IT'S EVEN A LITTLE MOLDY...
SCHULZ 1-21
BUT IT'S MY BLANKET!
SIGH

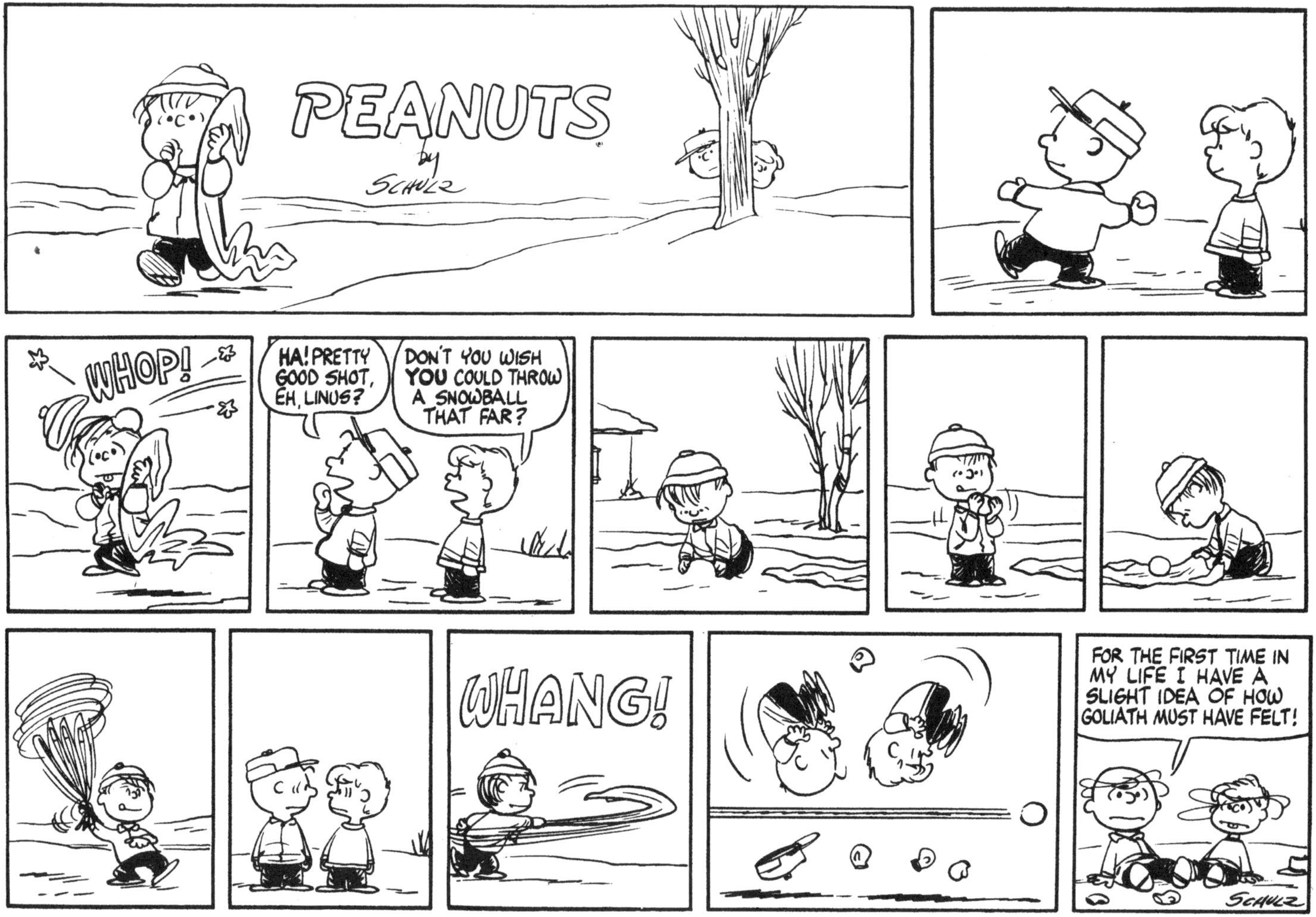
PEANUTS
by
SCHULZ
WHOP!
HA! PRETTY GOOD SHOT, EH, LINUS?
DON'T YOU WISH YOU COULD THROW A SNOWBALL THAT FAR?
WHANG!
FOR THE FIRST TIME IN MY LIFE I HAVE A SLIGHT IDEA OF HOW GOLIATH MUST HAVE FELT!
SCHULZ

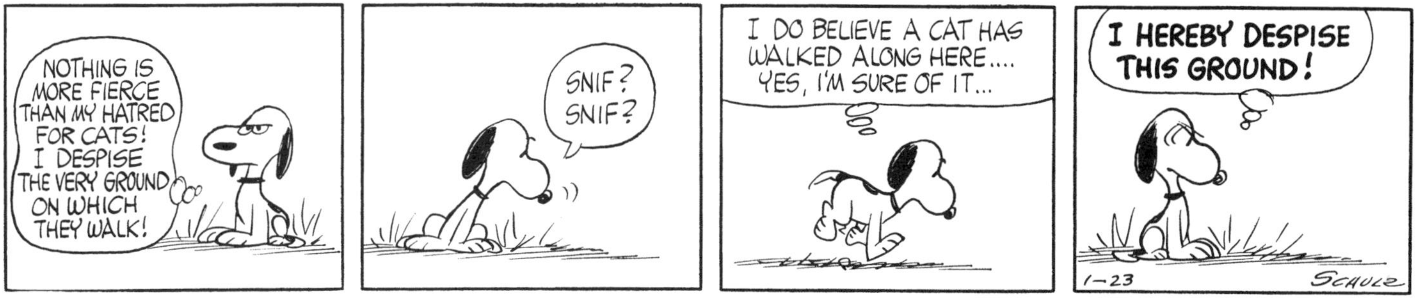
NOTHING IS MORE FIERCE THAN MY HATRED FOR CATS! I DESPISE THE VERY GROUND ON WHICH THEY WALK!
SNIF? SNIF?
I DO BELIEVE A CAT HAS WALKED ALONG HERE.... YES, I'M SURE OF IT...
I HEREBY DESPISE THIS GROUND!
1-23
SCHULZ

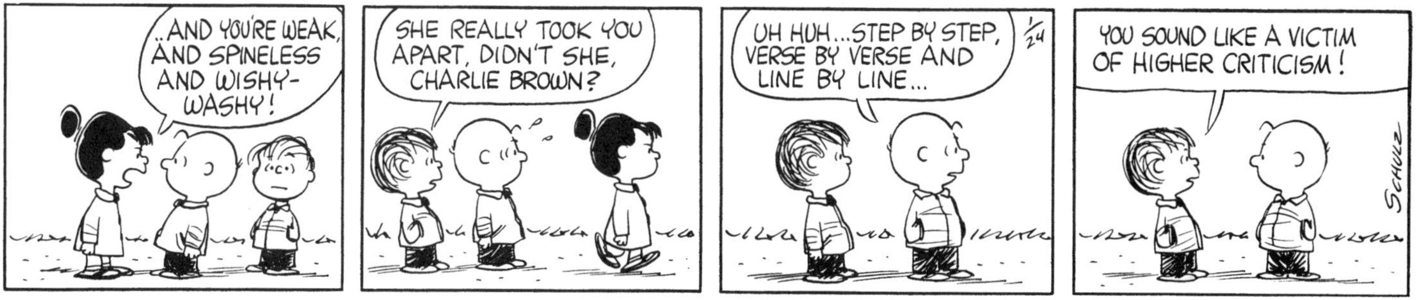
..AND YOU'RE WEAK, AND SPINELESS AND WISHY-WASHY!
SHE REALLY TOOK YOU APART, DIDN'T SHE, CHARLIE BROWN?
UH HUH...STEP BY STEP, VERSE BY VERSE AND LINE BY LINE...
1/24
YOU SOUND LIKE A VICTIM OF HIGHER CRITICISM!
SCHULZ

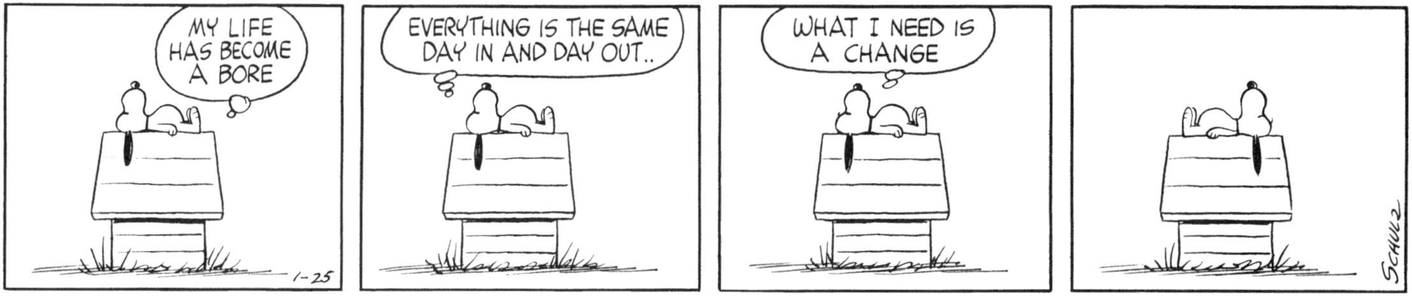
MY LIFE HAS BECOME A BORE
1-25
EVERYTHING IS THE SAME DAY IN AND DAY OUT..
WHAT I NEED IS A CHANGE
SCHULZ

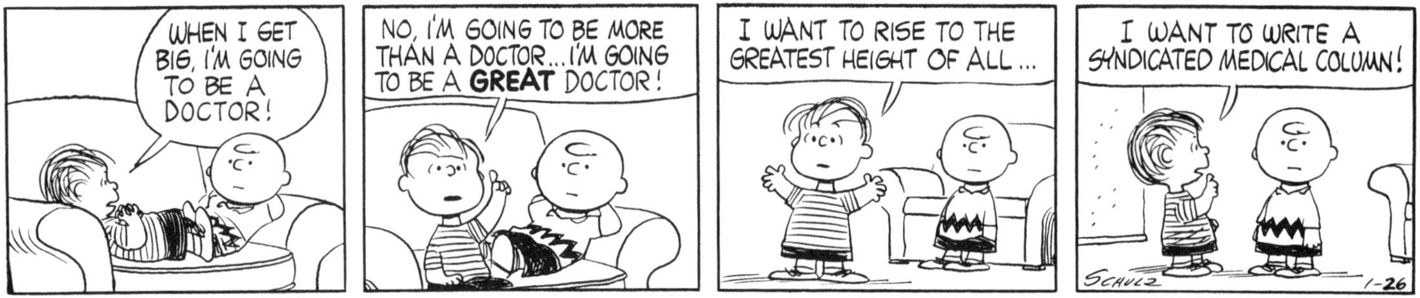
WHEN I GET BIG, I'M GOING TO BE A DOCTOR!
NO, I'M GOING TO BE MORE THAN A DOCTOR...I'M GOING TO BE A **GREAT** DOCTOR!
I WANT TO RISE TO THE GREATEST HEIGHT OF ALL...
I WANT TO WRITE A SYNDICATED MEDICAL COLUMN!
SCHULZ
1-26

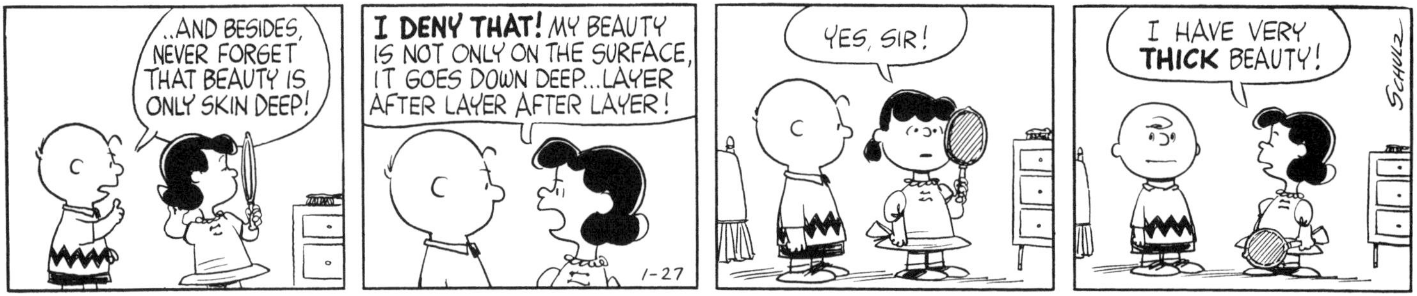
..AND BESIDES, NEVER FORGET THAT BEAUTY IS ONLY SKIN DEEP!
I DENY THAT! MY BEAUTY IS NOT ONLY ON THE SURFACE, IT GOES DOWN DEEP...LAYER AFTER LAYER AFTER LAYER!
1-27
YES, SIR!
I HAVE VERY **THICK** BEAUTY!
SCHULZ

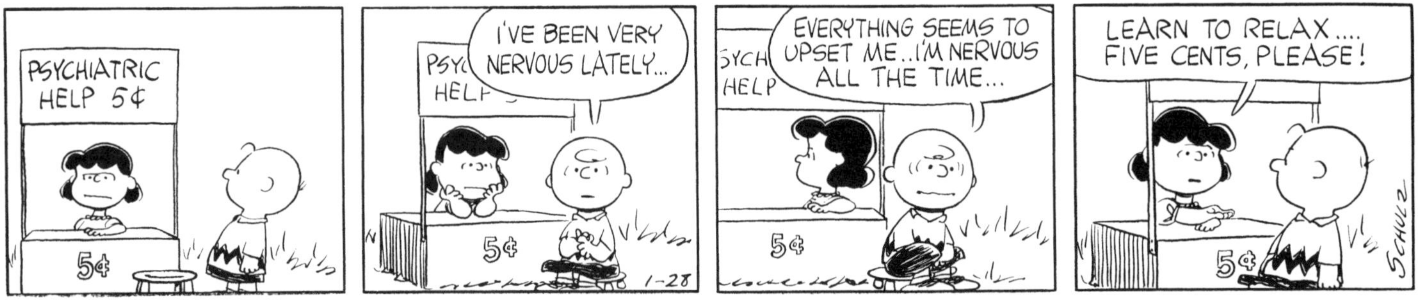
PSYCHIATRIC HELP 5¢
5¢
I'VE BEEN VERY NERVOUS LATELY...
1-28
EVERYTHING SEEMS TO UPSET ME..I'M NERVOUS ALL THE TIME...
LEARN TO RELAX.... FIVE CENTS, PLEASE!
SCHULZ

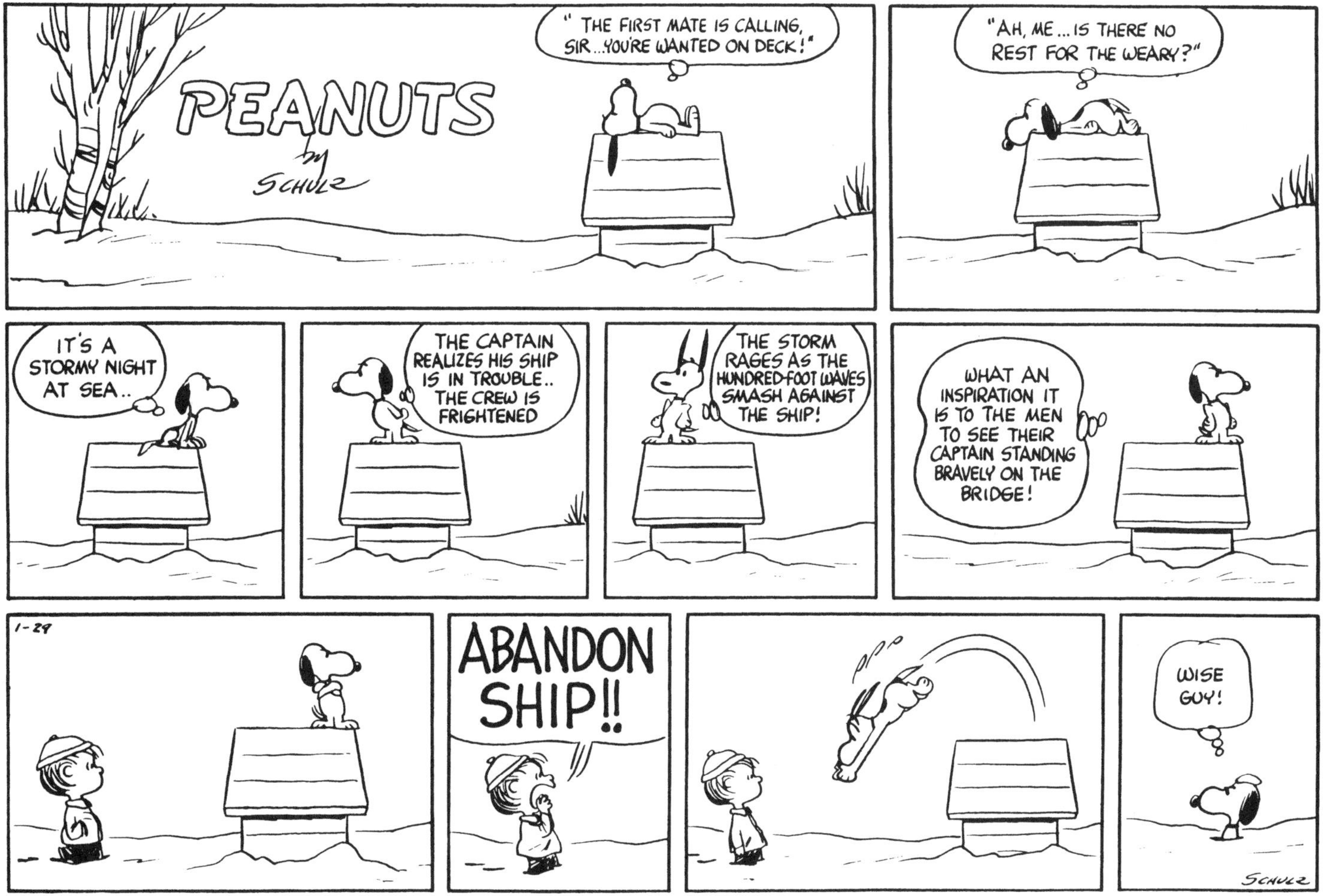
PEANUTS
by SCHULZ
" THE FIRST MATE IS CALLING, SIR...YOU'RE WANTED ON DECK!"
"AH, ME...IS THERE NO REST FOR THE WEARY?"
IT'S A STORMY NIGHT AT SEA..
THE CAPTAIN REALIZES HIS SHIP IS IN TROUBLE.. THE CREW IS FRIGHTENED
THE STORM RAGES AS THE HUNDRED-FOOT WAVES SMASH AGAINST THE SHIP!
WHAT AN INSPIRATION IT IS TO THE MEN TO SEE THEIR CAPTAIN STANDING BRAVELY ON THE BRIDGE!
1-29
ABANDON SHIP!!
WISE GUY!
SCHULZ

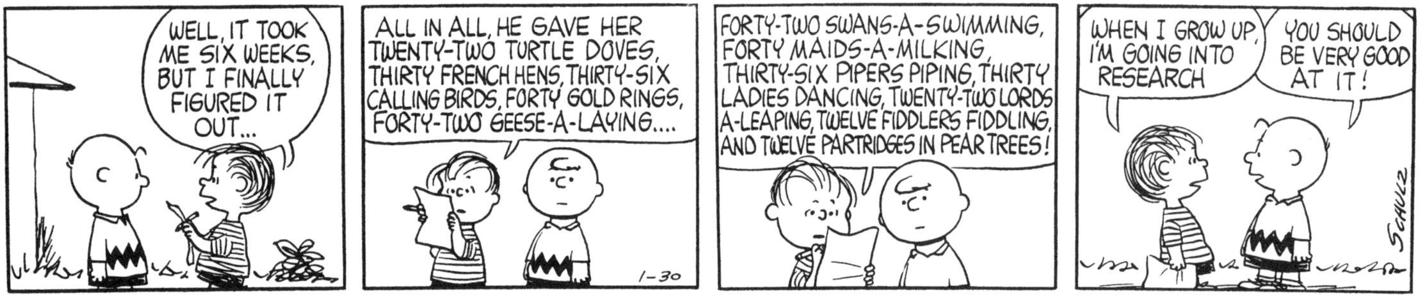
WELL, IT TOOK ME SIX WEEKS, BUT I FINALLY FIGURED IT OUT...
ALL IN ALL, HE GAVE HER TWENTY-TWO TURTLE DOVES, THIRTY FRENCH HENS, THIRTY-SIX CALLING BIRDS, FORTY GOLD RINGS, FORTY-TWO GEESE-A-LAYING....
1-30
FORTY-TWO SWANS-A-SWIMMING, FORTY MAIDS-A-MILKING, THIRTY-SIX PIPERS PIPING, THIRTY LADIES DANCING, TWENTY-TWO LORDS A-LEAPING, TWELVE FIDDLERS FIDDLING, AND TWELVE PARTRIDGES IN PEAR TREES!
WHEN I GROW UP, I'M GOING INTO RESEARCH
YOU SHOULD BE VERY GOOD AT IT!
SCHULZ

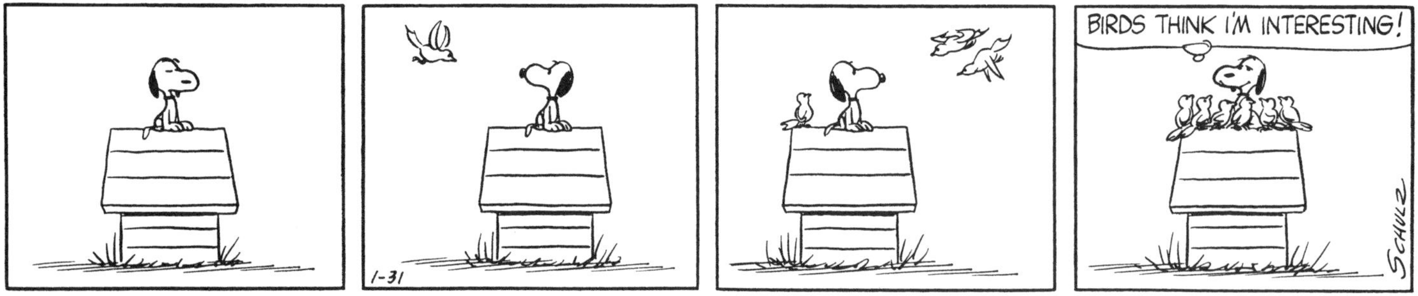
1-31
BIRDS THINK I'M INTERESTING!
SCHULZ

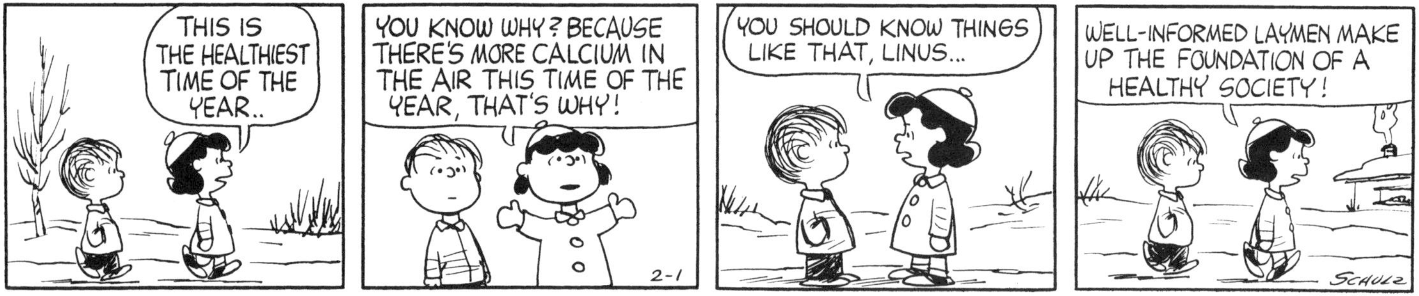
THIS IS THE HEALTHIEST TIME OF THE YEAR..
YOU KNOW WHY? BECAUSE THERE'S MORE CALCIUM IN THE AIR THIS TIME OF THE YEAR, THAT'S WHY!
2-1
YOU SHOULD KNOW THINGS LIKE THAT, LINUS...
WELL-INFORMED LAYMEN MAKE UP THE FOUNDATION OF A HEALTHY SOCIETY!
SCHULZ

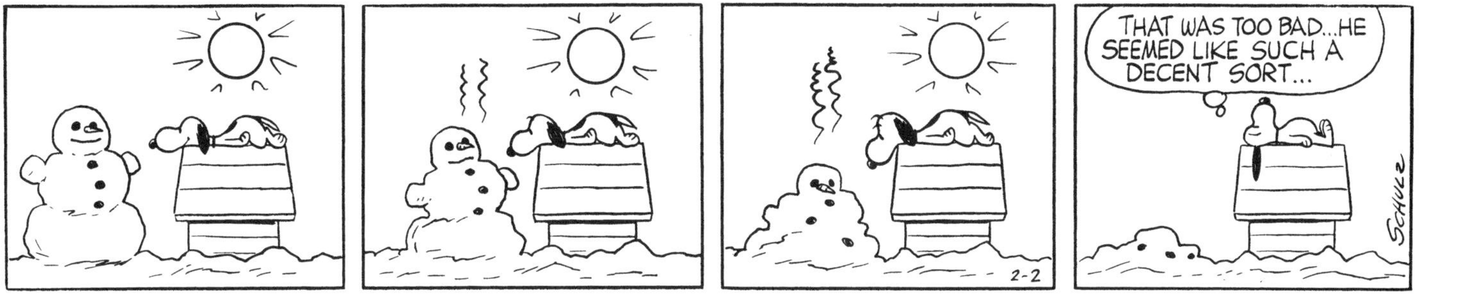
2-2
THAT WAS TOO BAD...HE SEEMED LIKE SUCH A DECENT SORT...
SCHULZ

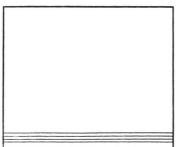

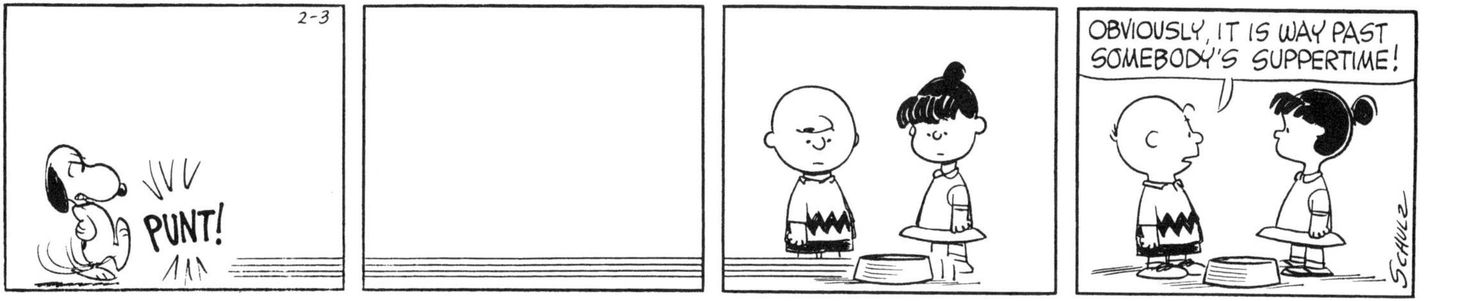
2-3
PUNT!
OBVIOUSLY, IT IS WAY PAST SOMEBODY'S SUPPERTIME!
SCHULZ

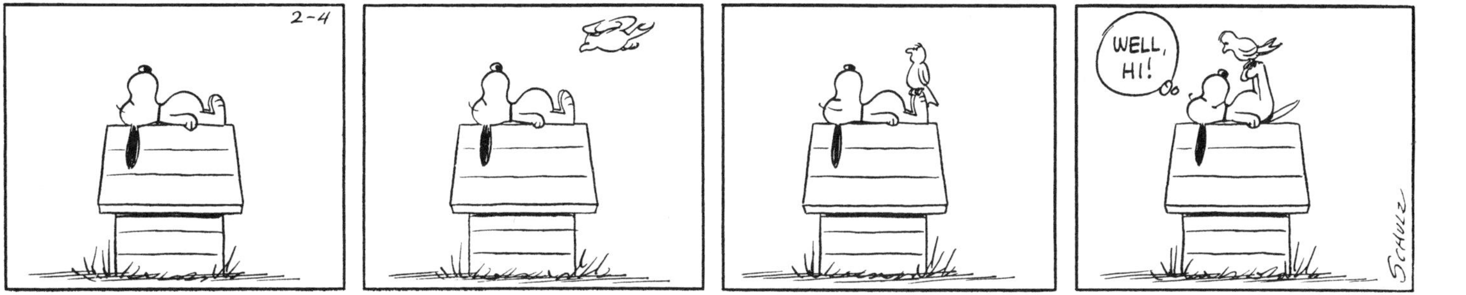
2-4
WELL, HI!
SCHULZ

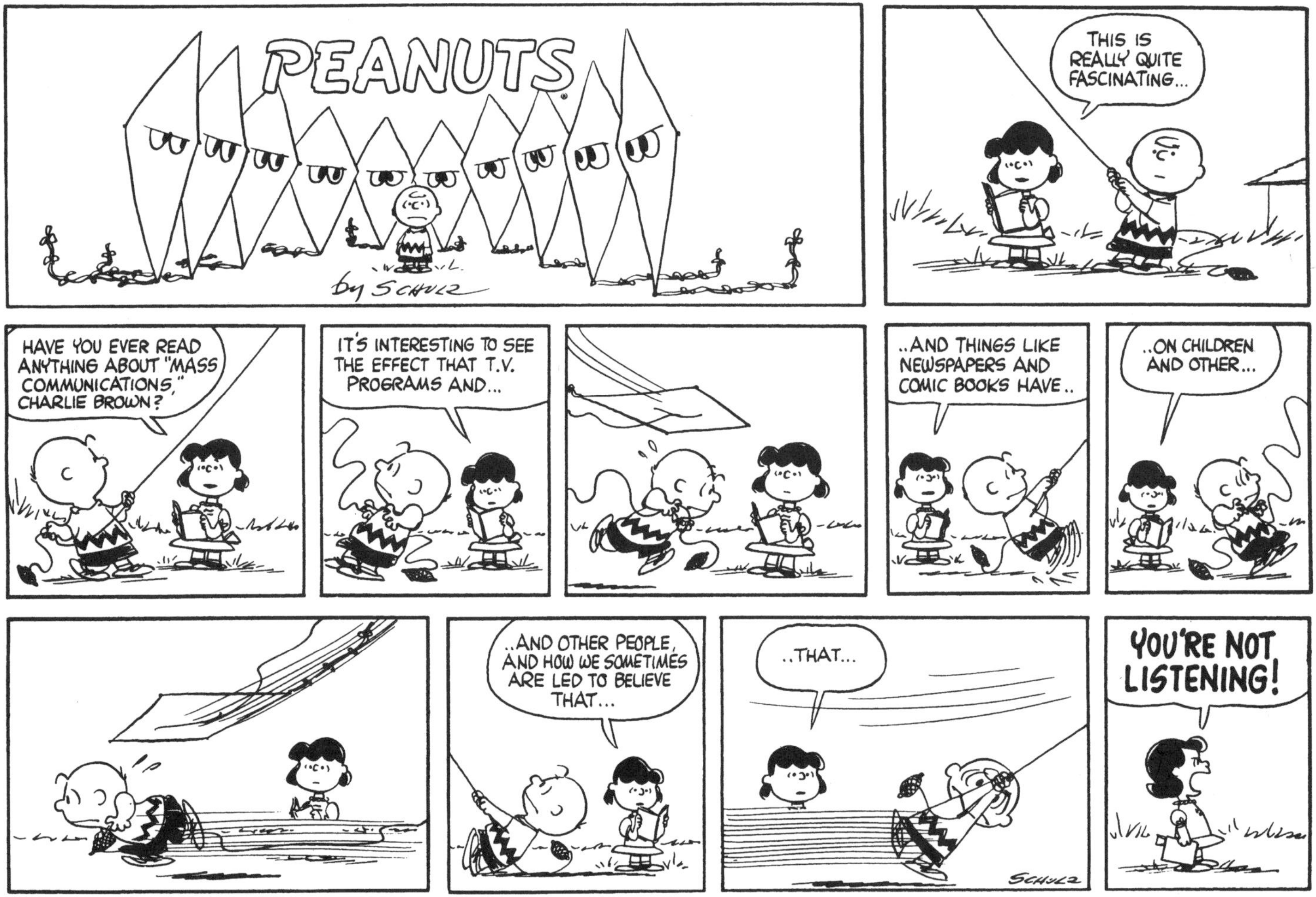
PEANUTS
by SCHULZ
THIS IS REALLY QUITE FASCINATING...
HAVE YOU EVER READ ANYTHING ABOUT "MASS COMMUNICATIONS," CHARLIE BROWN?
IT'S INTERESTING TO SEE THE EFFECT THAT T.V. PROGRAMS AND...
..AND THINGS LIKE NEWSPAPERS AND COMIC BOOKS HAVE..
..ON CHILDREN AND OTHER...
..AND OTHER PEOPLE, AND HOW WE SOMETIMES ARE LED TO BELIEVE THAT...
..THAT...
SCHULZ
YOU'RE NOT LISTENING!

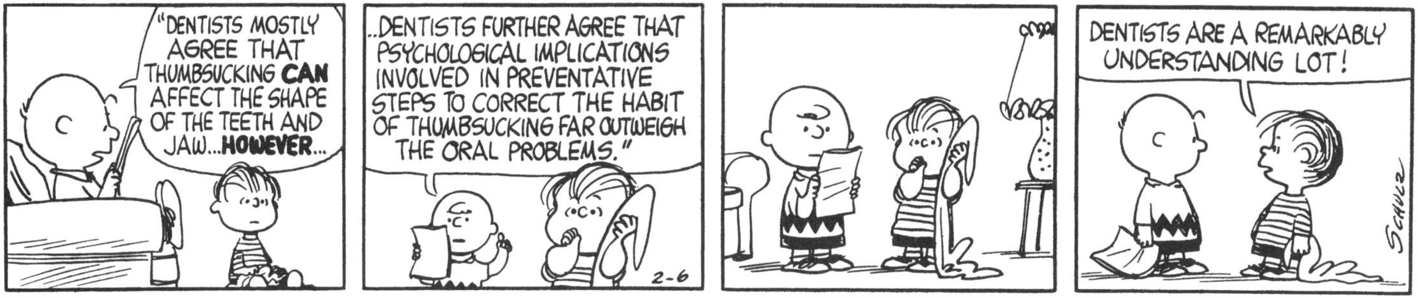
"DENTISTS MOSTLY AGREE THAT THUMBSUCKING **CAN** AFFECT THE SHAPE OF THE TEETH AND JAW...**HOWEVER**...
..DENTISTS FURTHER AGREE THAT PSYCHOLOGICAL IMPLICATIONS INVOLVED IN PREVENTATIVE STEPS TO CORRECT THE HABIT OF THUMBSUCKING FAR OUTWEIGH THE ORAL PROBLEMS."
2-6
DENTISTS ARE A REMARKABLY UNDERSTANDING LOT!
SCHULZ

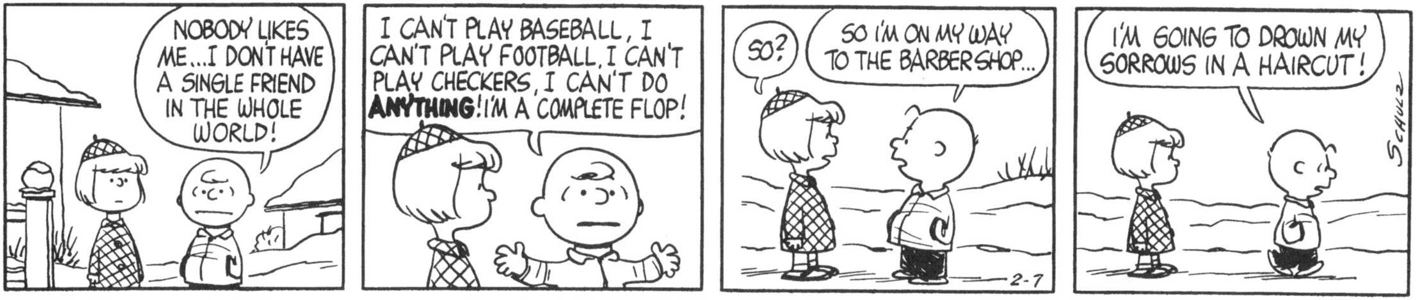
NOBODY LIKES ME...I DON'T HAVE A SINGLE FRIEND IN THE WHOLE WORLD!
I CAN'T PLAY BASEBALL, I CAN'T PLAY FOOTBALL, I CAN'T PLAY CHECKERS, I CAN'T DO **ANYTHING**! I'M A COMPLETE FLOP!
SO?
SO I'M ON MY WAY TO THE BARBERSHOP...
2-7
I'M GOING TO DROWN MY SORROWS IN A HAIRCUT!
SCHULZ

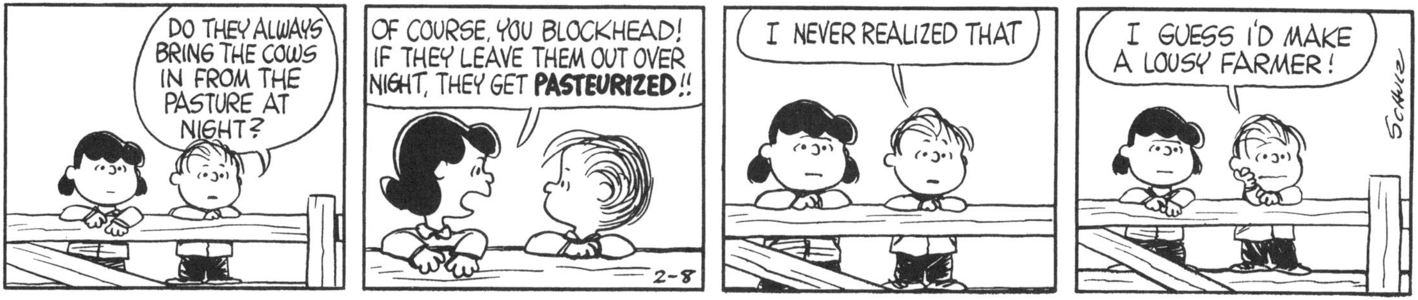
DO THEY ALWAYS BRING THE COWS IN FROM THE PASTURE AT NIGHT?
OF COURSE, YOU BLOCKHEAD! IF THEY LEAVE THEM OUT OVER NIGHT, THEY GET **PASTEURIZED**!!
2-8
I NEVER REALIZED THAT
I GUESS I'D MAKE A LOUSY FARMER!
SCHULZ

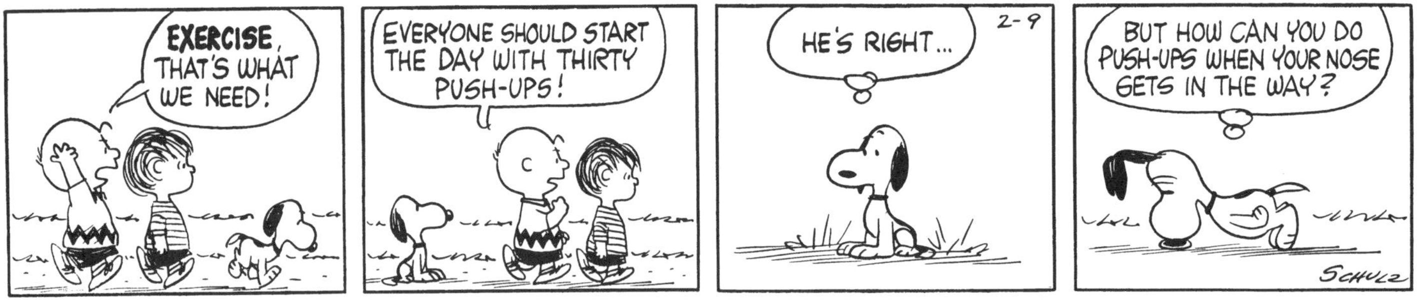
EXERCISE, THAT'S WHAT WE NEED!
EVERYONE SHOULD START THE DAY WITH THIRTY PUSH-UPS!
HE'S RIGHT...
2-9
BUT HOW CAN YOU DO PUSH-UPS WHEN YOUR NOSE GETS IN THE WAY?
SCHULZ

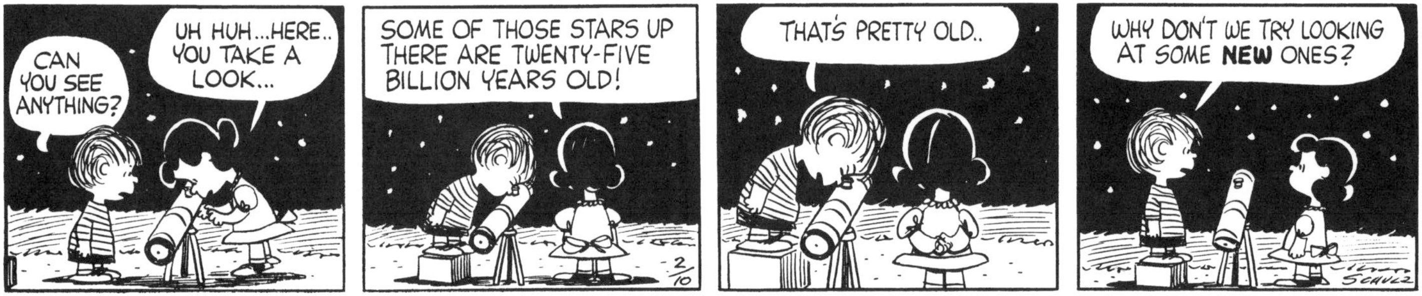
CAN YOU SEE ANYTHING?
UH HUH...HERE.. YOU TAKE A LOOK...
SOME OF THOSE STARS UP THERE ARE TWENTY-FIVE BILLION YEARS OLD!
2/10
THAT'S PRETTY OLD..
WHY DON'T WE TRY LOOKING AT SOME **NEW** ONES?
SCHULZ

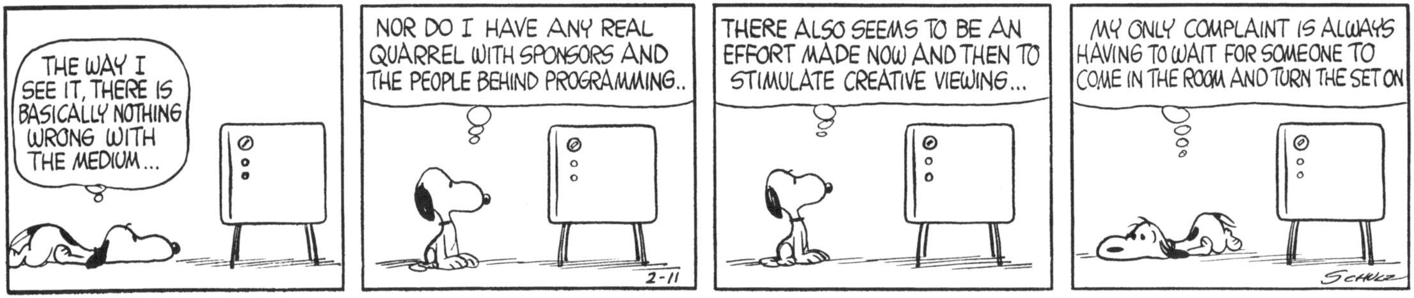
THE WAY I SEE IT, THERE IS BASICALLY NOTHING WRONG WITH THE MEDIUM...
NOR DO I HAVE ANY REAL QUARREL WITH SPONSORS AND THE PEOPLE BEHIND PROGRAMMING..
2-11
THERE ALSO SEEMS TO BE AN EFFORT MADE NOW AND THEN TO STIMULATE CREATIVE VIEWING...
MY ONLY COMPLAINT IS ALWAYS HAVING TO WAIT FOR SOMEONE TO COME IN THE ROOM AND TURN THE SET ON
SCHULZ

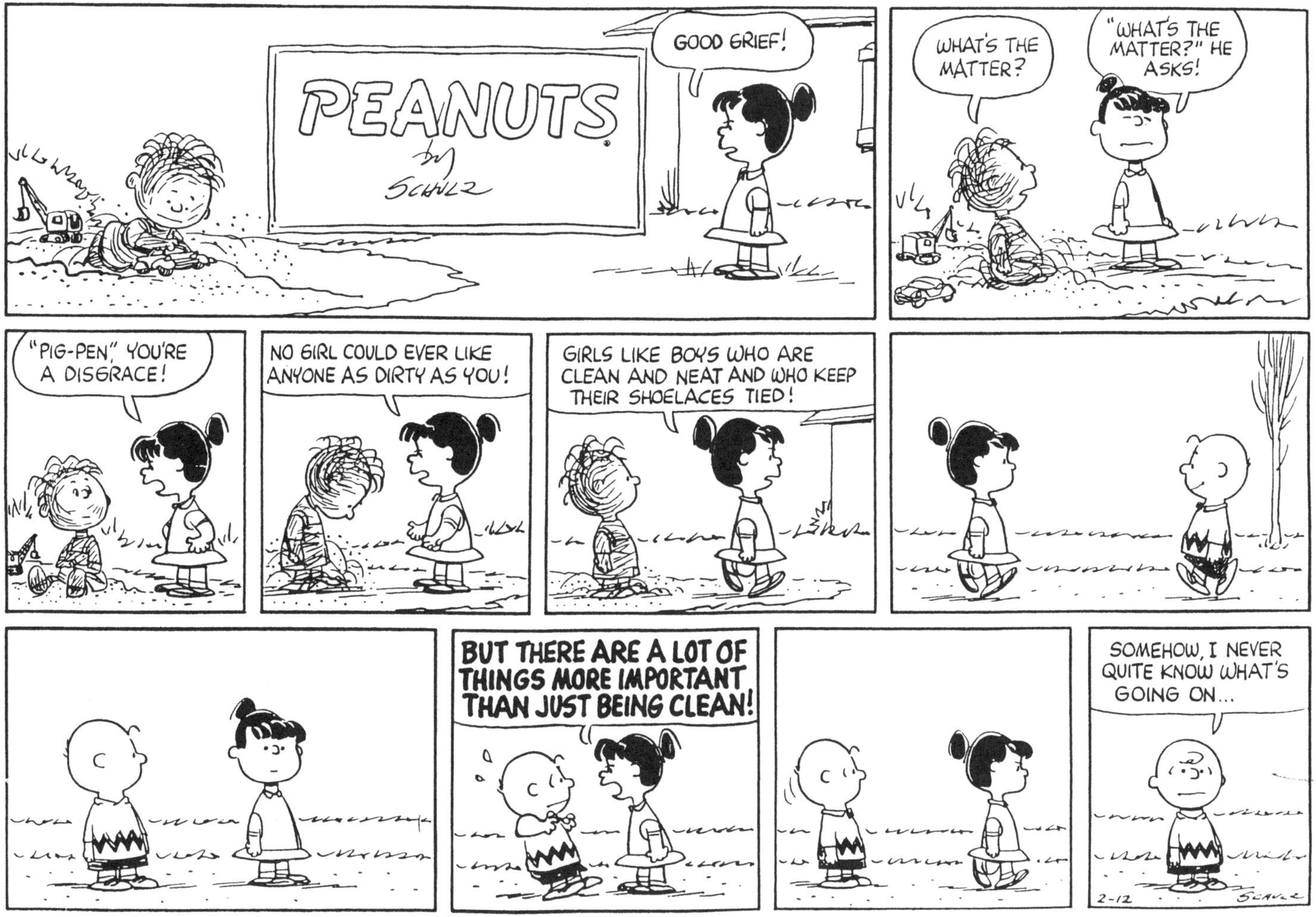
PEANUTS
by SCHULZ
GOOD GRIEF!
WHAT'S THE MATTER?
"WHAT'S THE MATTER?" HE ASKS!
"PIG-PEN," YOU'RE A DISGRACE!
NO GIRL COULD EVER LIKE ANYONE AS DIRTY AS YOU!
GIRLS LIKE BOYS WHO ARE CLEAN AND NEAT AND WHO KEEP THEIR SHOELACES TIED!
BUT THERE ARE A LOT OF THINGS MORE IMPORTANT THAN JUST BEING CLEAN!
SOMEHOW, I NEVER QUITE KNOW WHAT'S GOING ON...
2-12
SCHULZ

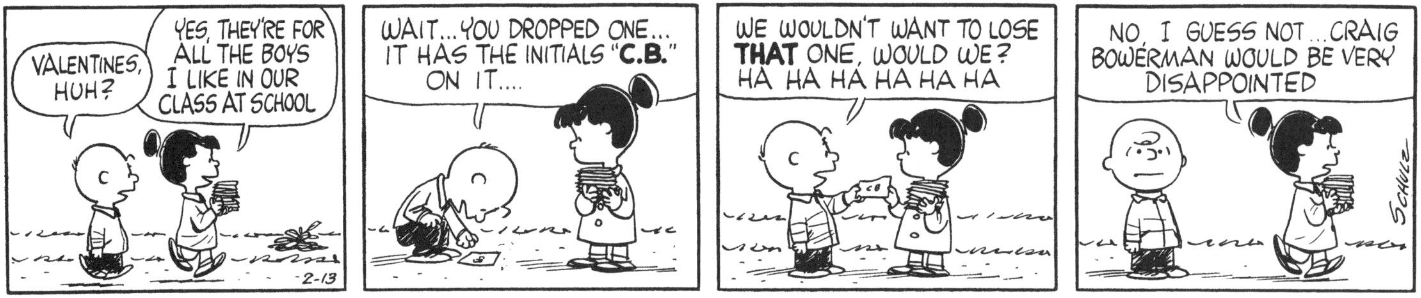
VALENTINES, HUH?
YES, THEY'RE FOR ALL THE BOYS I LIKE IN OUR CLASS AT SCHOOL
2-13
WAIT...YOU DROPPED ONE... IT HAS THE INITIALS "C.B." ON IT....
WE WOULDN'T WANT TO LOSE THAT ONE, WOULD WE? HA HA HA HA HA HA
NO, I GUESS NOT...CRAIG BOWERMAN WOULD BE VERY DISAPPOINTED
SCHULZ

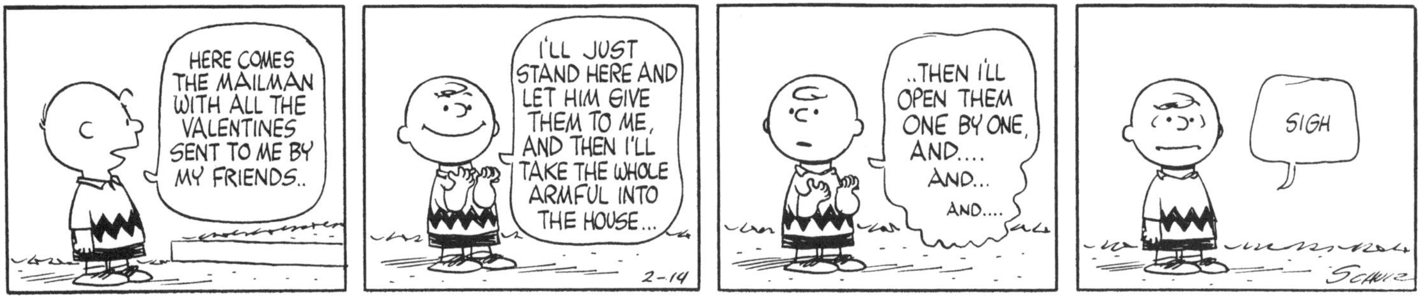
HERE COMES THE MAILMAN WITH ALL THE VALENTINES SENT TO ME BY MY FRIENDS..
I'LL JUST STAND HERE AND LET HIM GIVE THEM TO ME, AND THEN I'LL TAKE THE WHOLE ARMFUL INTO THE HOUSE...
2-14
..THEN I'LL OPEN THEM ONE BY ONE, AND.... AND... AND....
SIGH
SCHULZ

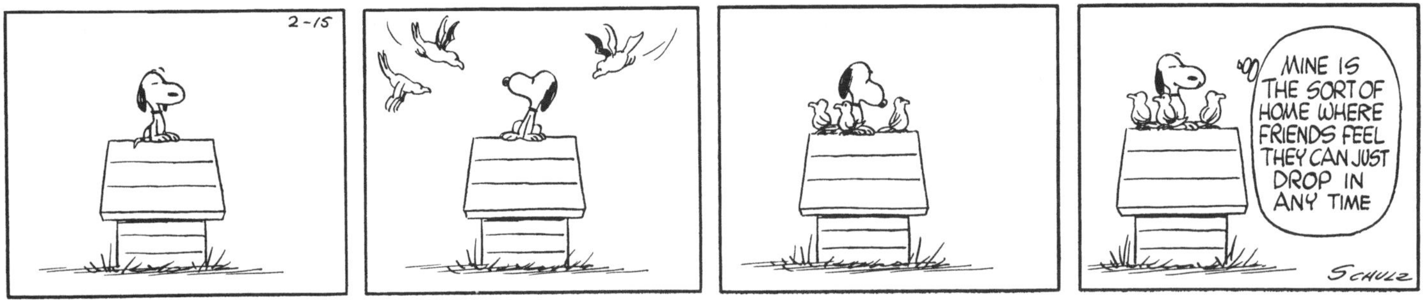
2-15
MINE IS THE SORT OF HOME WHERE FRIENDS FEEL THEY CAN JUST DROP IN ANY TIME
SCHULZ

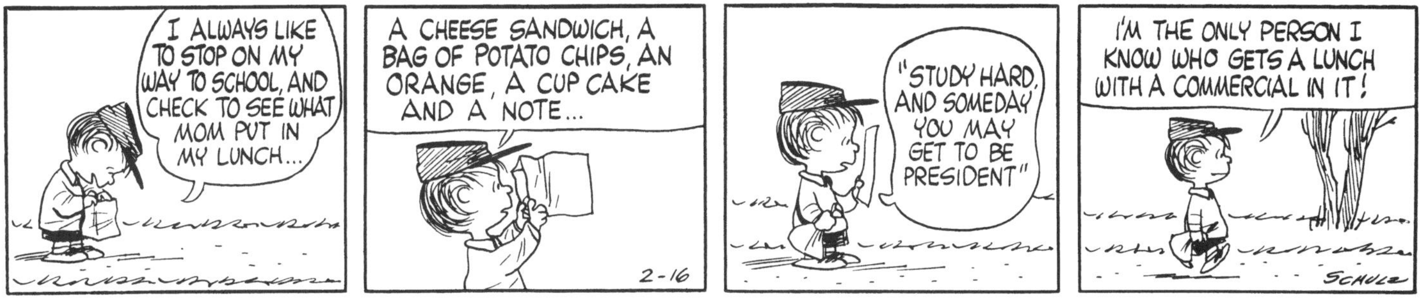
I ALWAYS LIKE TO STOP ON MY WAY TO SCHOOL, AND CHECK TO SEE WHAT MOM PUT IN MY LUNCH...
A CHEESE SANDWICH, A BAG OF POTATO CHIPS, AN ORANGE, A CUP CAKE AND A NOTE...
2-16
"STUDY HARD, AND SOMEDAY YOU MAY GET TO BE PRESIDENT"
I'M THE ONLY PERSON I KNOW WHO GETS A LUNCH WITH A COMMERCIAL IN IT!
SCHULZ

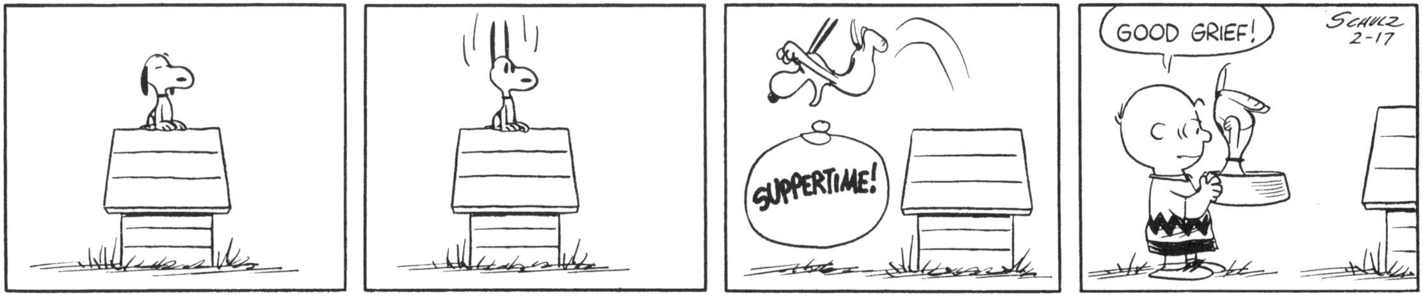
SUPPERTIME!
GOOD GRIEF!
SCHULZ 2-17

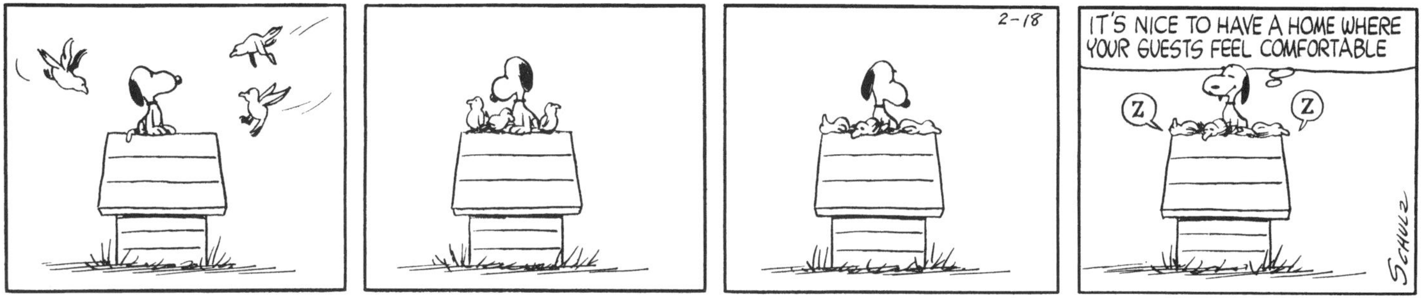
2-18
IT'S NICE TO HAVE A HOME WHERE YOUR GUESTS FEEL COMFORTABLE
Z
Z
SCHULZ

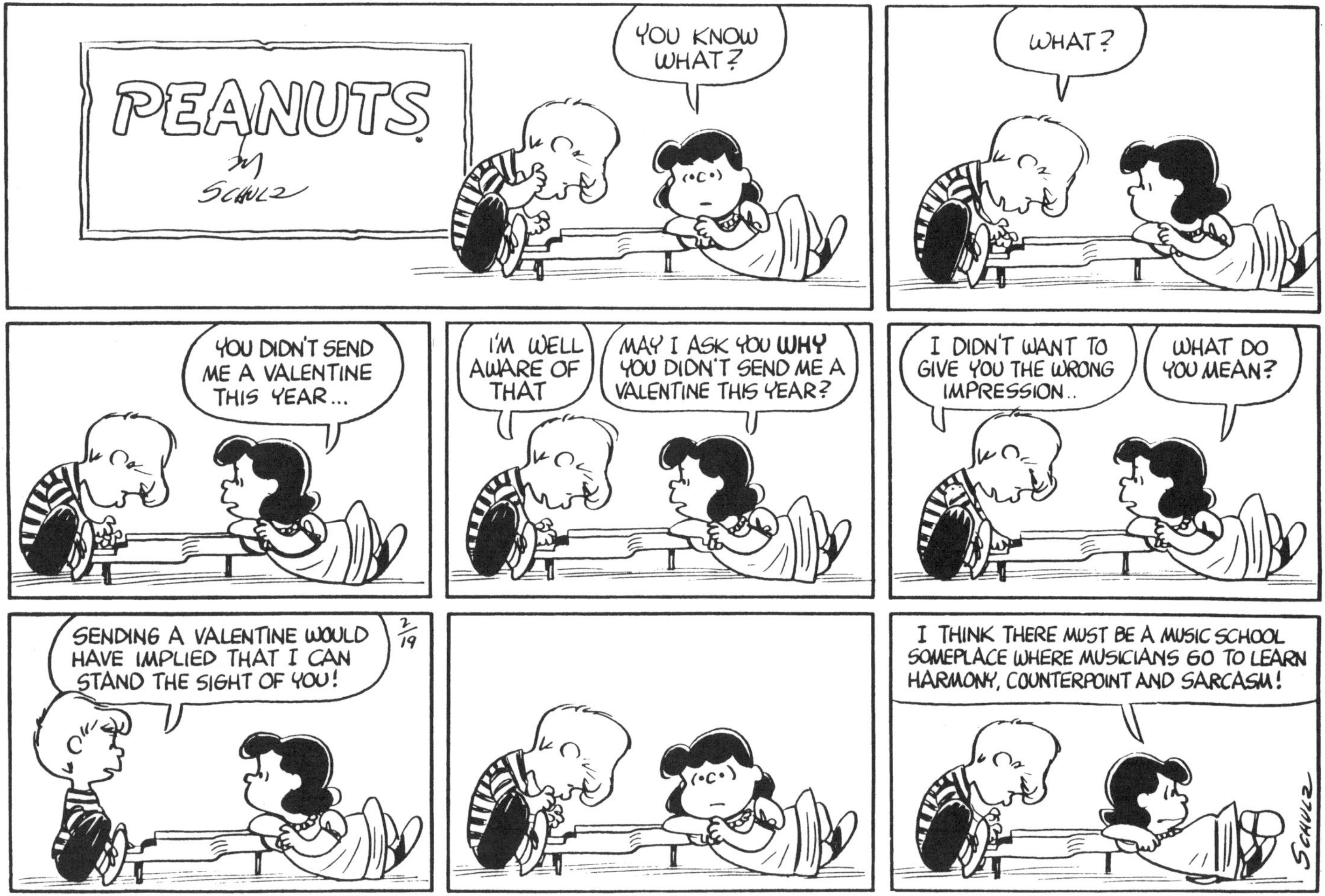
PEANUTS
SCHULZ
YOU KNOW WHAT?
WHAT?
YOU DIDN'T SEND ME A VALENTINE THIS YEAR...
I'M WELL AWARE OF THAT
MAY I ASK YOU WHY YOU DIDN'T SEND ME A VALENTINE THIS YEAR?
I DIDN'T WANT TO GIVE YOU THE WRONG IMPRESSION..
WHAT DO YOU MEAN?
SENDING A VALENTINE WOULD HAVE IMPLIED THAT I CAN STAND THE SIGHT OF YOU!
2/19
I THINK THERE MUST BE A MUSIC SCHOOL SOMEPLACE WHERE MUSICIANS GO TO LEARN HARMONY, COUNTERPOINT AND SARCASM!
SCHULZ

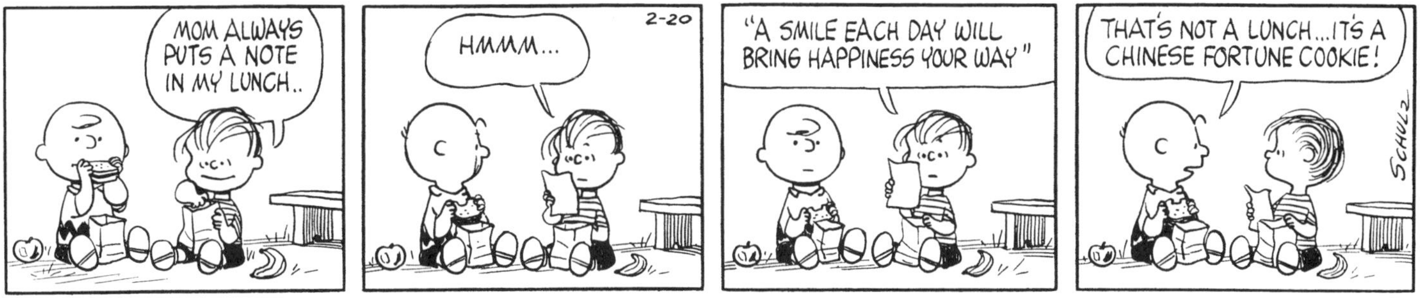
MOM ALWAYS PUTS A NOTE IN MY LUNCH..
2-20
HMMM...
"A SMILE EACH DAY WILL BRING HAPPINESS YOUR WAY"
THAT'S NOT A LUNCH...IT'S A CHINESE FORTUNE COOKIE!
SCHULZ

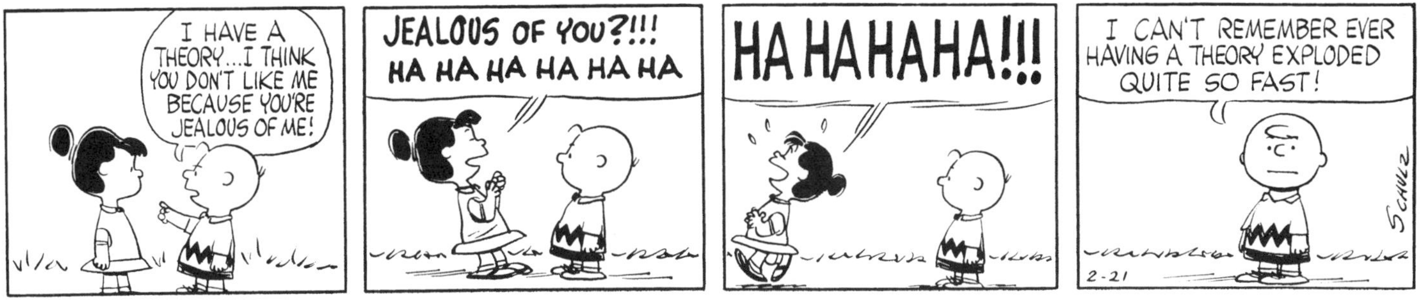
I HAVE A THEORY...I THINK YOU DON'T LIKE ME BECAUSE YOU'RE JEALOUS OF ME!
JEALOUS OF YOU?!!! HA HA HA HA HA HA
HA HA HA HA!!!
I CAN'T REMEMBER EVER HAVING A THEORY EXPLODED QUITE SO FAST!
SCHULZ
2-21

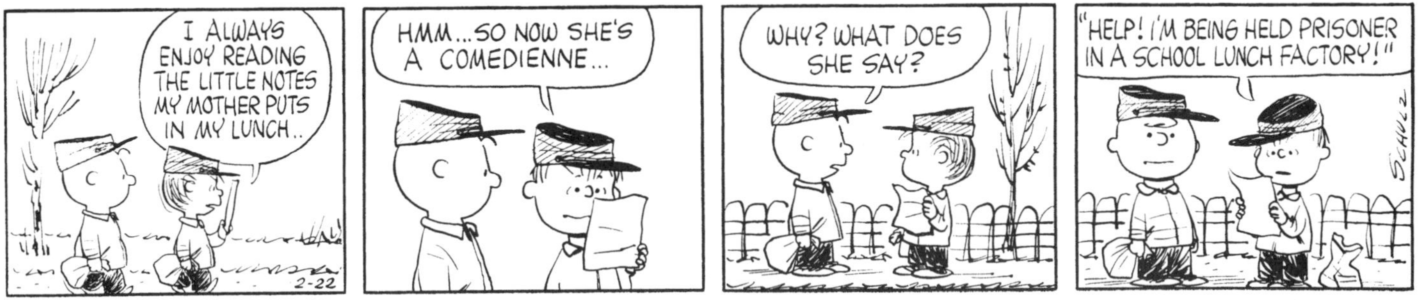
I ALWAYS ENJOY READING THE LITTLE NOTES MY MOTHER PUTS IN MY LUNCH..
2-22
HMM...SO NOW SHE'S A COMEDIENNE...
WHY? WHAT DOES SHE SAY?
"HELP! I'M BEING HELD PRISONER IN A SCHOOL LUNCH FACTORY!"
SCHULZ

Panel 3: 2-23

Panel 4: SCHULZ

I'VE ALWAYS WANTED ONE OF THOSE!

Signs: BEWARE OF THE DOG!

Panel 5: MY DAD HATES ME...

Panel 6: MONDAY NIGHT HE WENT TO A PTA MEETING, TUESDAY NIGHT IT WAS THE SCHOOL BOARD, WEDNESDAY NIGHT IT WAS THE BOARD OF DEACONS AND LAST NIGHT IT WAS BOWLING! 2-24

Panel 7: SO THIS MORNING HE SAYS TO ME, "HI, THERE!" AND I SAID, "WHO ARE YOU? I DON'T RECOGNIZE YOU!"

Panel 8: HE DOESN'T ACTUALLY HATE ME... HE JUST THINKS I'M TOO SARCASTIC!

Panel 9: "BEWARE OF THE FROG"... WHAT DOES THAT MEAN?

Sign: BEWARE OF THE DOG

Panel 10: IT DIDN'T SAY "FROG" YOU BLOCKHEAD, IT SAID, "DOG"!

Sign: WARE OF THE DOG

Panel 11: OH..

Panel 12: GOOD GRIEF! 2-25

Sign: BEWARE OF THE DOG

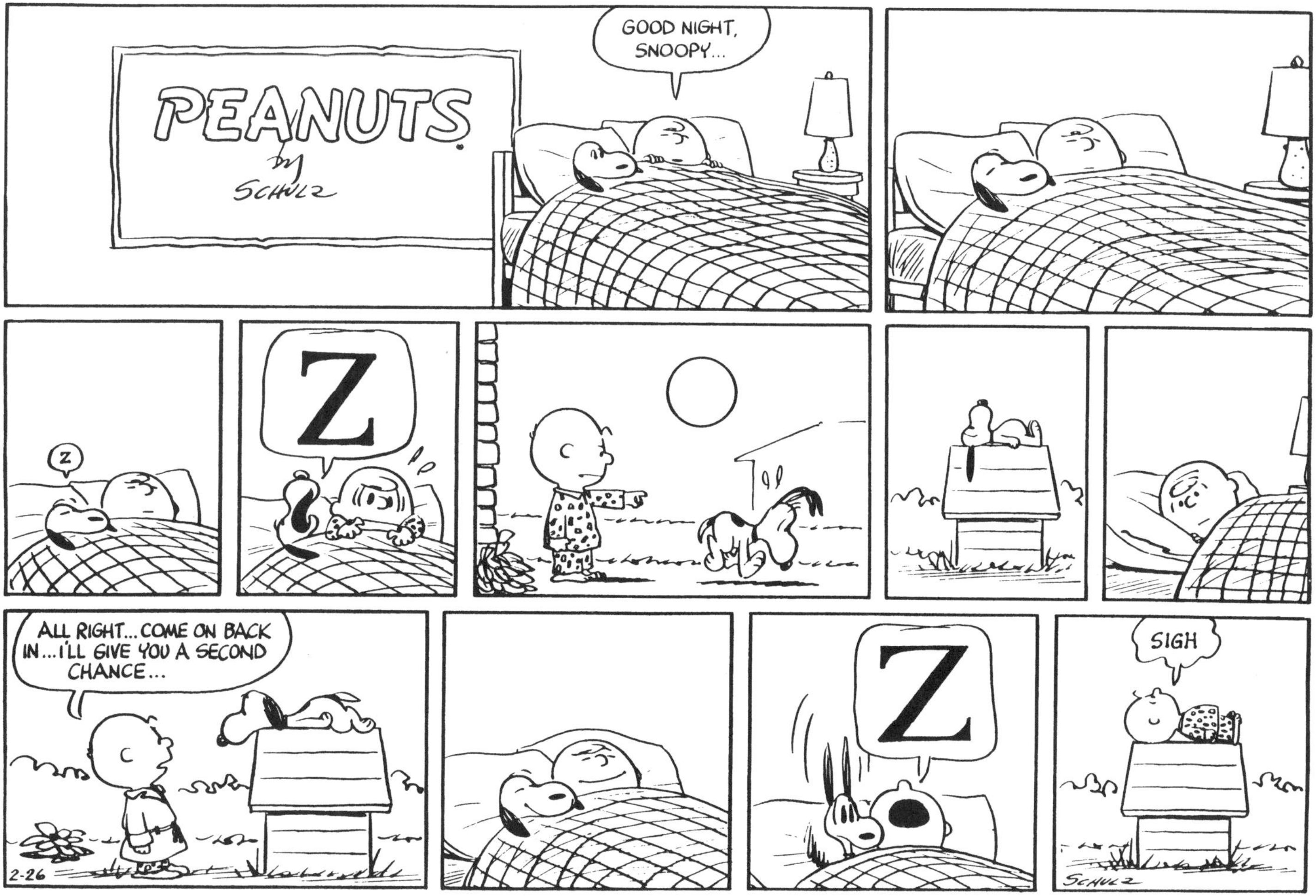
PEANUTS
by SCHULZ
GOOD NIGHT, SNOOPY...
Z
Z
ALL RIGHT...COME ON BACK IN...I'LL GIVE YOU A SECOND CHANCE...
2-26
Z
SIGH
SCHULZ

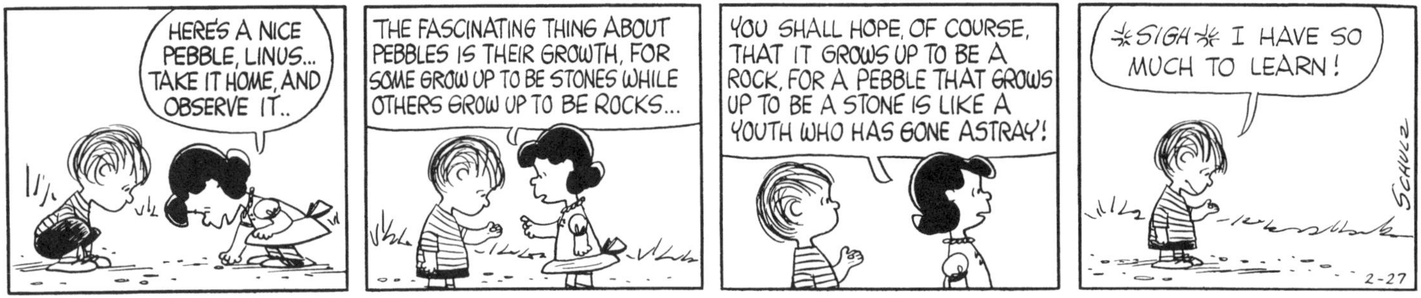
HERE'S A NICE PEBBLE, LINUS... TAKE IT HOME, AND OBSERVE IT..
THE FASCINATING THING ABOUT PEBBLES IS THEIR GROWTH, FOR SOME GROW UP TO BE STONES WHILE OTHERS GROW UP TO BE ROCKS...
YOU SHALL HOPE, OF COURSE, THAT IT GROWS UP TO BE A ROCK, FOR A PEBBLE THAT GROWS UP TO BE A STONE IS LIKE A YOUTH WHO HAS GONE ASTRAY!
SIGH I HAVE SO MUCH TO LEARN!
SCHULZ
2-27

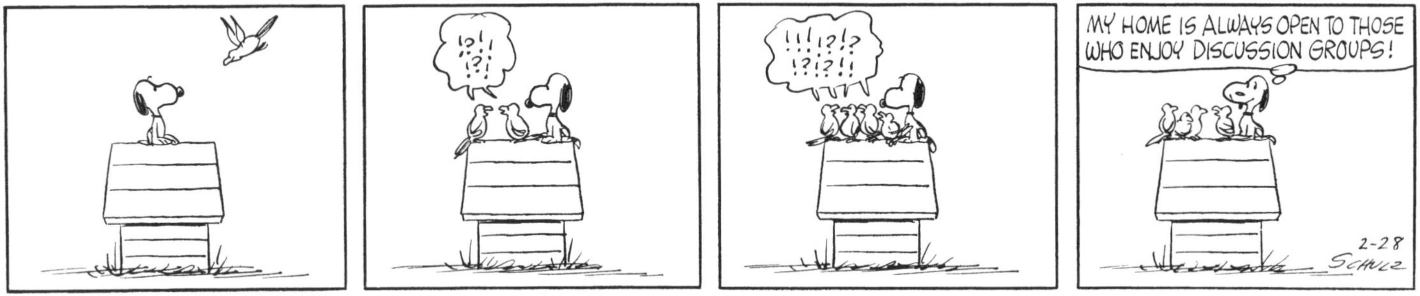
!?!! !?!
!!!!?!? !?!?!!
MY HOME IS ALWAYS OPEN TO THOSE WHO ENJOY DISCUSSION GROUPS!
2-28
SCHULZ

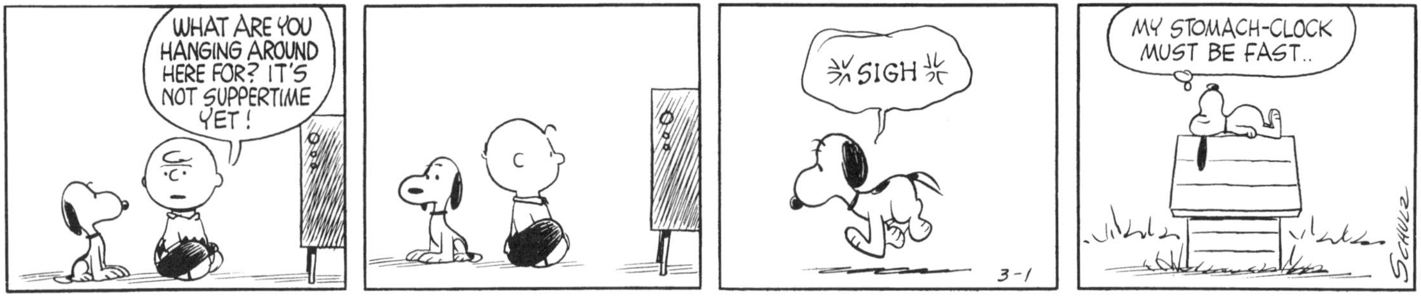
WHAT ARE YOU HANGING AROUND HERE FOR? IT'S NOT SUPPERTIME YET!
SIGH
3-1
MY STOMACH-CLOCK MUST BE FAST..
SCHULZ

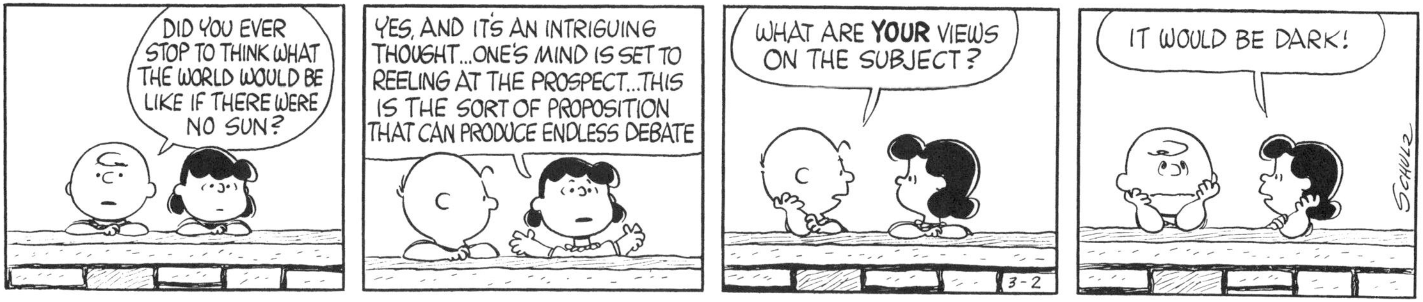
DID YOU EVER STOP TO THINK WHAT THE WORLD WOULD BE LIKE IF THERE WERE NO SUN?
YES, AND IT'S AN INTRIGUING THOUGHT...ONE'S MIND IS SET TO REELING AT THE PROSPECT...THIS IS THE SORT OF PROPOSITION THAT CAN PRODUCE ENDLESS DEBATE
WHAT ARE YOUR VIEWS ON THE SUBJECT?
3-2
IT WOULD BE DARK!
SCHULZ

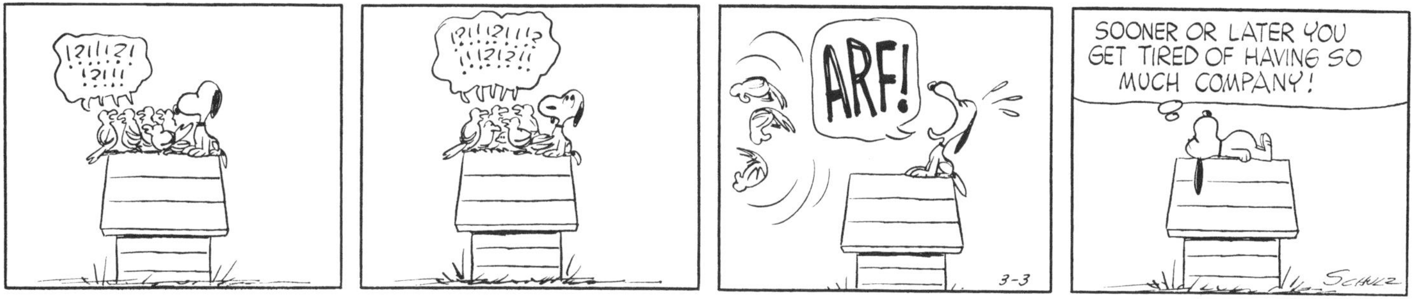
ARF!
3-3
SOONER OR LATER YOU GET TIRED OF HAVING SO MUCH COMPANY!
SCHULZ

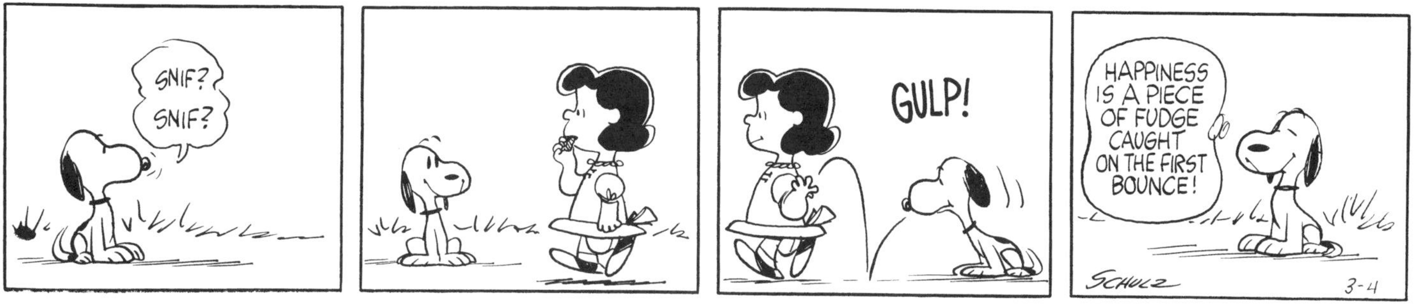
SNIF? SNIF?
GULP!
HAPPINESS IS A PIECE OF FUDGE CAUGHT ON THE FIRST BOUNCE!
SCHULZ
3-4

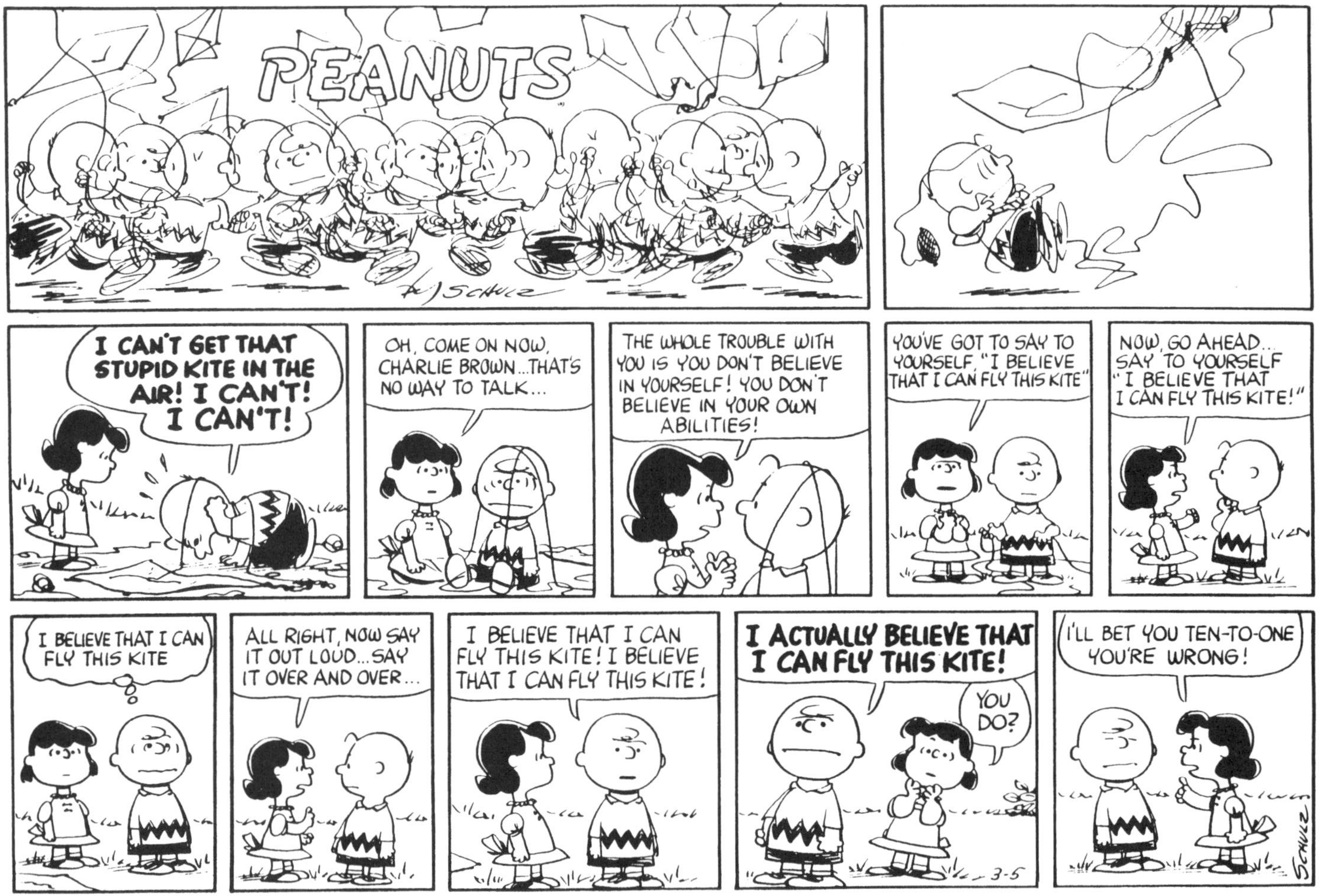
PEANUTS
I CAN'T GET THAT STUPID KITE IN THE AIR! I CAN'T! I CAN'T!
OH, COME ON NOW, CHARLIE BROWN...THAT'S NO WAY TO TALK...
THE WHOLE TROUBLE WITH YOU IS YOU DON'T BELIEVE IN YOURSELF! YOU DON'T BELIEVE IN YOUR OWN ABILITIES!
YOU'VE GOT TO SAY TO YOURSELF, "I BELIEVE THAT I CAN FLY THIS KITE"
NOW, GO AHEAD... SAY TO YOURSELF "I BELIEVE THAT I CAN FLY THIS KITE!"
I BELIEVE THAT I CAN FLY THIS KITE
ALL RIGHT, NOW SAY IT OUT LOUD...SAY IT OVER AND OVER...
I BELIEVE THAT I CAN FLY THIS KITE! I BELIEVE THAT I CAN FLY THIS KITE!
I ACTUALLY BELIEVE THAT I CAN FLY THIS KITE!
YOU DO?
3-5
I'LL BET YOU TEN-TO-ONE YOU'RE WRONG!
SCHULZ

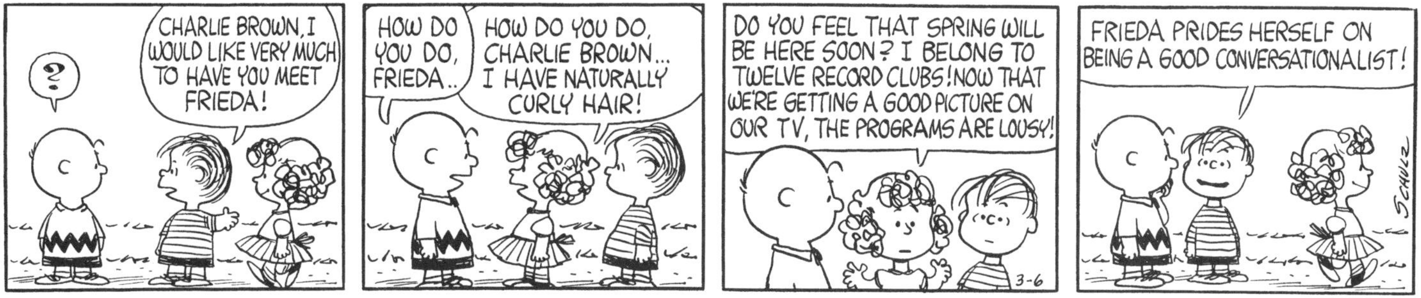
?
CHARLIE BROWN, I WOULD LIKE VERY MUCH TO HAVE YOU MEET FRIEDA!
HOW DO YOU DO, FRIEDA..
HOW DO YOU DO, CHARLIE BROWN... I HAVE NATURALLY CURLY HAIR!
DO YOU FEEL THAT SPRING WILL BE HERE SOON? I BELONG TO TWELVE RECORD CLUBS! NOW THAT WE'RE GETTING A GOOD PICTURE ON OUR TV, THE PROGRAMS ARE LOUSY!
3-6
FRIEDA PRIDES HERSELF ON BEING A GOOD CONVERSATIONALIST!
SCHULZ

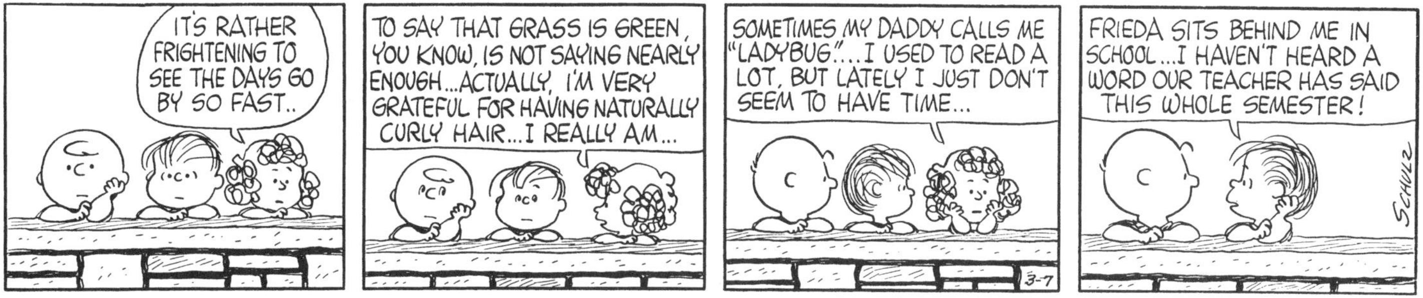
IT'S RATHER FRIGHTENING TO SEE THE DAYS GO BY SO FAST..
TO SAY THAT GRASS IS GREEN, YOU KNOW, IS NOT SAYING NEARLY ENOUGH...ACTUALLY, I'M VERY GRATEFUL FOR HAVING NATURALLY CURLY HAIR...I REALLY AM...
SOMETIMES MY DADDY CALLS ME "LADYBUG"... I USED TO READ A LOT, BUT LATELY I JUST DON'T SEEM TO HAVE TIME...
3-7
FRIEDA SITS BEHIND ME IN SCHOOL...I HAVEN'T HEARD A WORD OUR TEACHER HAS SAID THIS WHOLE SEMESTER!
SCHULZ

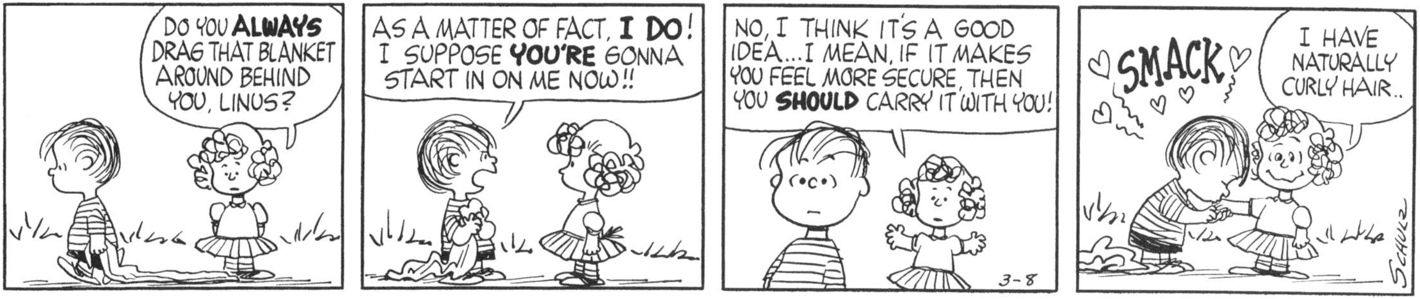
DO YOU ALWAYS DRAG THAT BLANKET AROUND BEHIND YOU, LINUS?
AS A MATTER OF FACT, I DO! I SUPPOSE YOU'RE GONNA START IN ON ME NOW!!
NO, I THINK IT'S A GOOD IDEA...I MEAN, IF IT MAKES YOU FEEL MORE SECURE, THEN YOU SHOULD CARRY IT WITH YOU!
3-8
SMACK
I HAVE NATURALLY CURLY HAIR..
SCHULZ

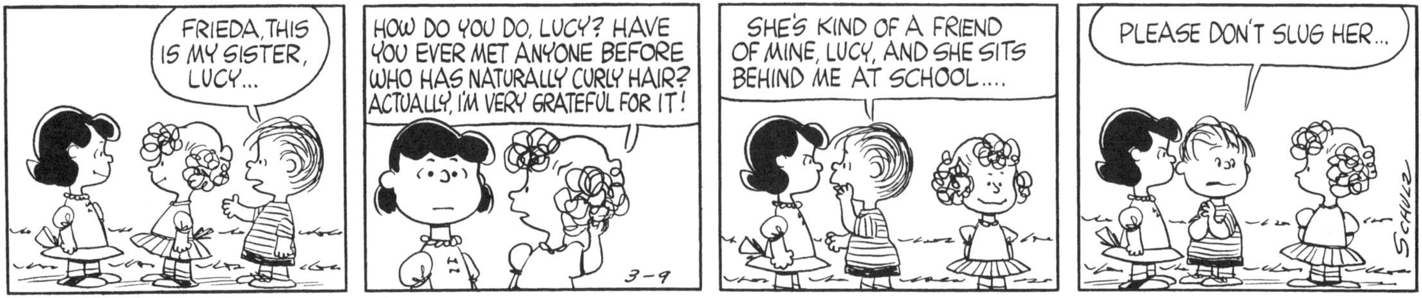
FRIEDA, THIS IS MY SISTER, LUCY...
HOW DO YOU DO, LUCY? HAVE YOU EVER MET ANYONE BEFORE WHO HAS NATURALLY CURLY HAIR? ACTUALLY, I'M VERY GRATEFUL FOR IT!
3-9
SHE'S KIND OF A FRIEND OF MINE, LUCY, AND SHE SITS BEHIND ME AT SCHOOL....
PLEASE DON'T SLUG HER...
SCHULZ

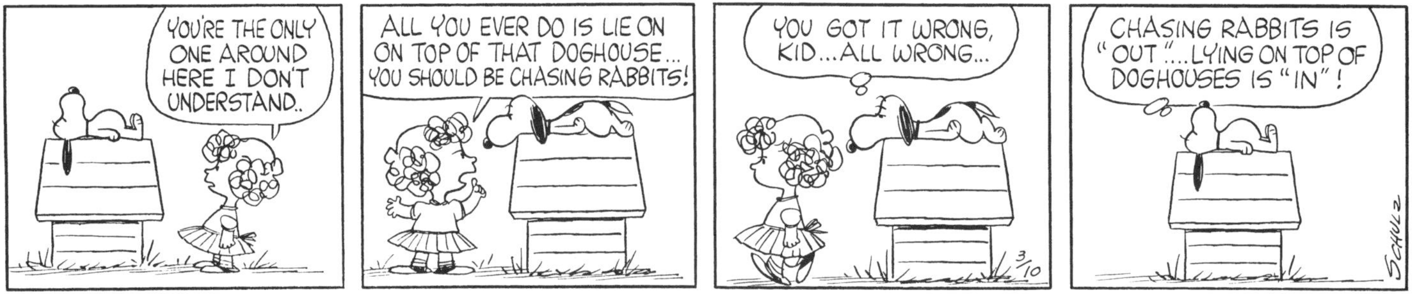
YOU'RE THE ONLY ONE AROUND HERE I DON'T UNDERSTAND..
ALL YOU EVER DO IS LIE ON ON TOP OF THAT DOGHOUSE... YOU SHOULD BE CHASING RABBITS!
YOU GOT IT WRONG, KID...ALL WRONG...
3/10
CHASING RABBITS IS "OUT"....LYING ON TOP OF DOGHOUSES IS "IN"!
SCHULZ

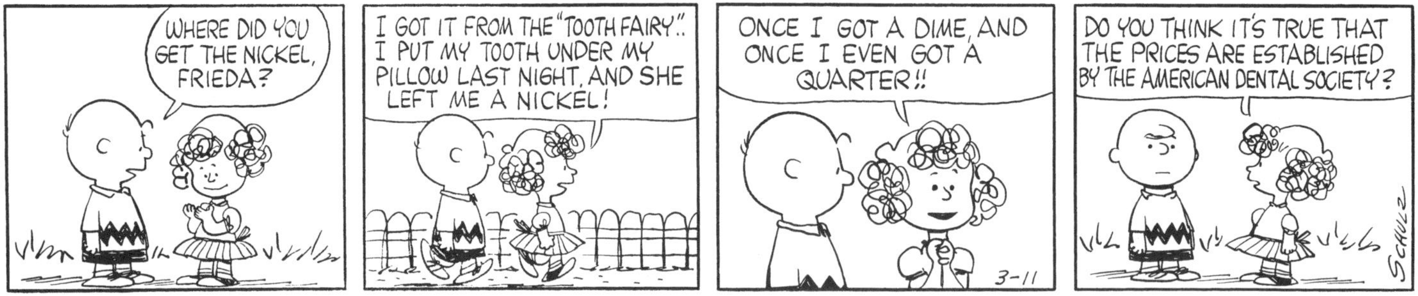
WHERE DID YOU GET THE NICKEL, FRIEDA?
I GOT IT FROM THE "TOOTH FAIRY".. I PUT MY TOOTH UNDER MY PILLOW LAST NIGHT, AND SHE LEFT ME A NICKEL!
ONCE I GOT A DIME, AND ONCE I EVEN GOT A QUARTER!!
3-11
DO YOU THINK IT'S TRUE THAT THE PRICES ARE ESTABLISHED BY THE AMERICAN DENTAL SOCIETY?
SCHULZ

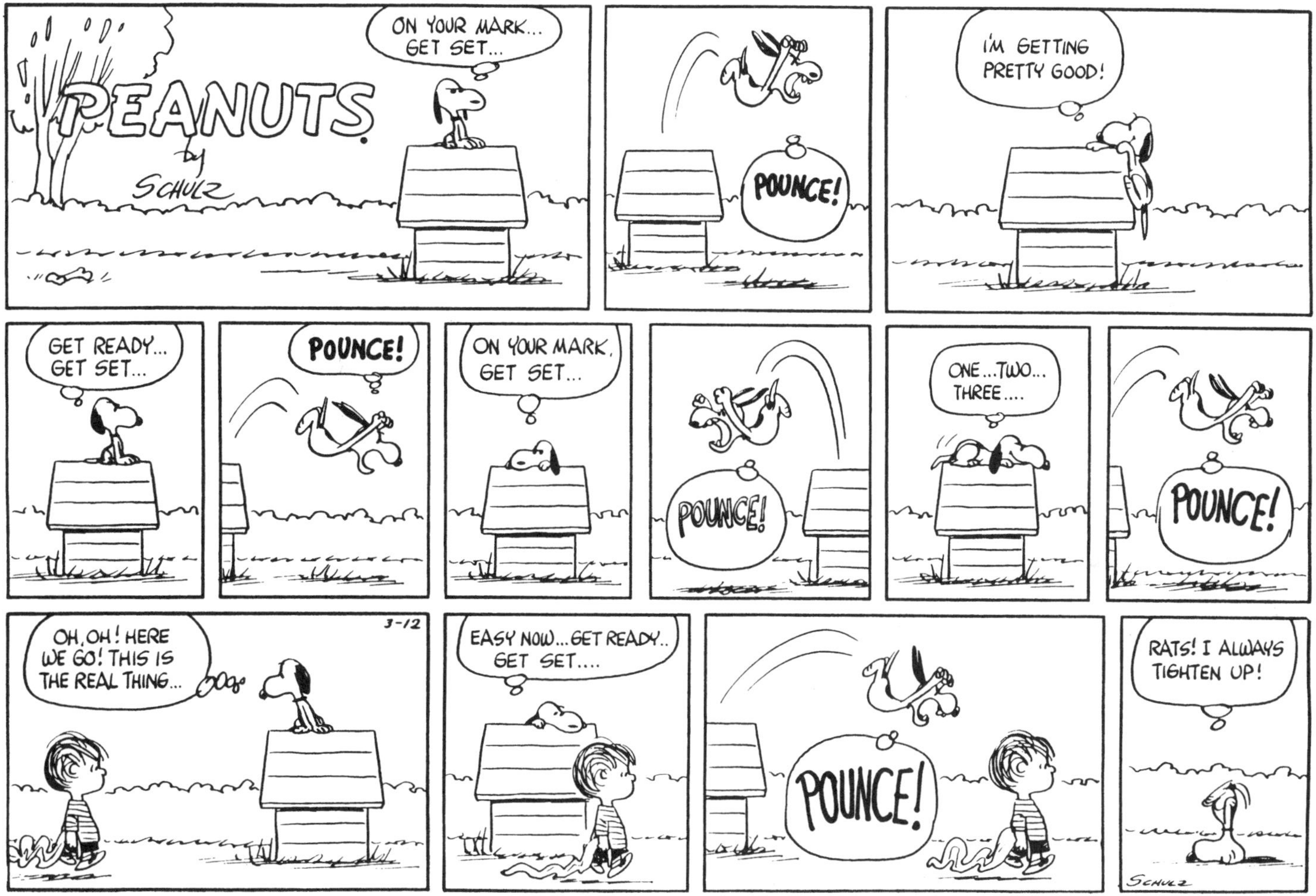
PEANUTS
by SCHULZ
ON YOUR MARK... GET SET...
POUNCE!
I'M GETTING PRETTY GOOD!
GET READY... GET SET...
POUNCE!
ON YOUR MARK, GET SET...
POUNCE!
ONE...TWO... THREE....
POUNCE!
3-12
OH, OH! HERE WE GO! THIS IS THE REAL THING...
EASY NOW...GET READY.. GET SET....
POUNCE!
RATS! I ALWAYS TIGHTEN UP!
SCHULZ

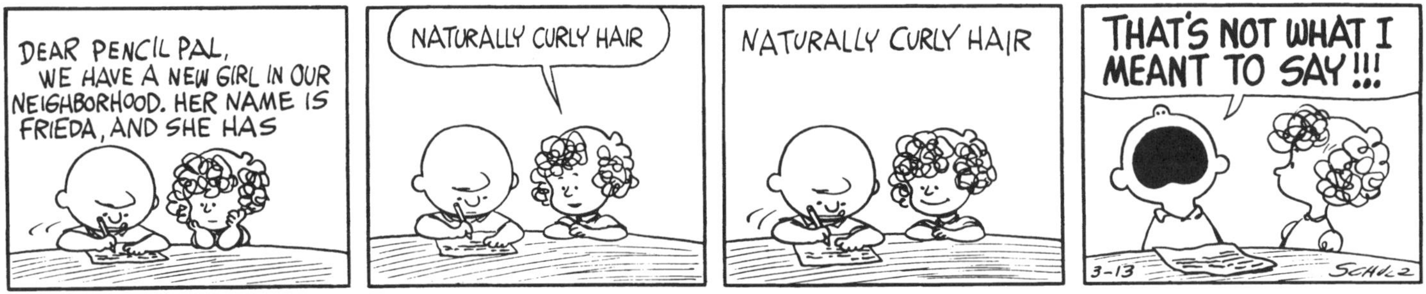
DEAR PENCIL PAL,
WE HAVE A NEW GIRL IN OUR NEIGHBORHOOD. HER NAME IS FRIEDA, AND SHE HAS
NATURALLY CURLY HAIR
NATURALLY CURLY HAIR
THAT'S NOT WHAT I MEANT TO SAY!!!
3-13
SCHULZ

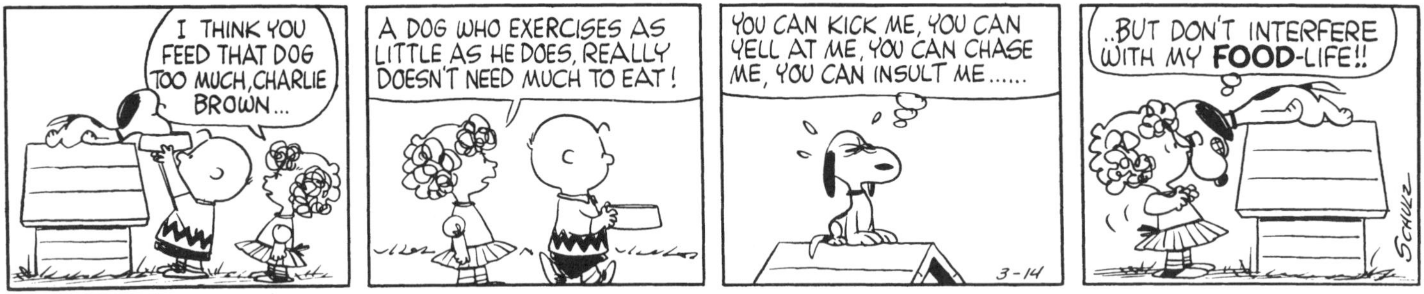
I THINK YOU FEED THAT DOG TOO MUCH, CHARLIE BROWN...
A DOG WHO EXERCISES AS LITTLE AS HE DOES, REALLY DOESN'T NEED MUCH TO EAT!
YOU CAN KICK ME, YOU CAN YELL AT ME, YOU CAN CHASE ME, YOU CAN INSULT ME......
3-14
..BUT DON'T INTERFERE WITH MY **FOOD**-LIFE!!
SCHULZ

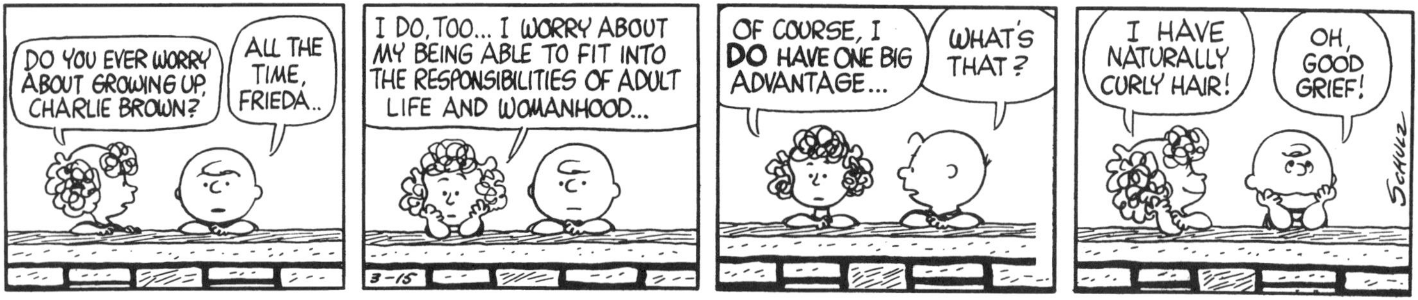
DO YOU EVER WORRY ABOUT GROWING UP, CHARLIE BROWN?
ALL THE TIME, FRIEDA..
I DO, TOO... I WORRY ABOUT MY BEING ABLE TO FIT INTO THE RESPONSIBILITIES OF ADULT LIFE AND WOMANHOOD...
3-15
OF COURSE, I **DO** HAVE ONE BIG ADVANTAGE...
WHAT'S THAT?
I HAVE NATURALLY CURLY HAIR!
OH, GOOD GRIEF!
SCHULZ

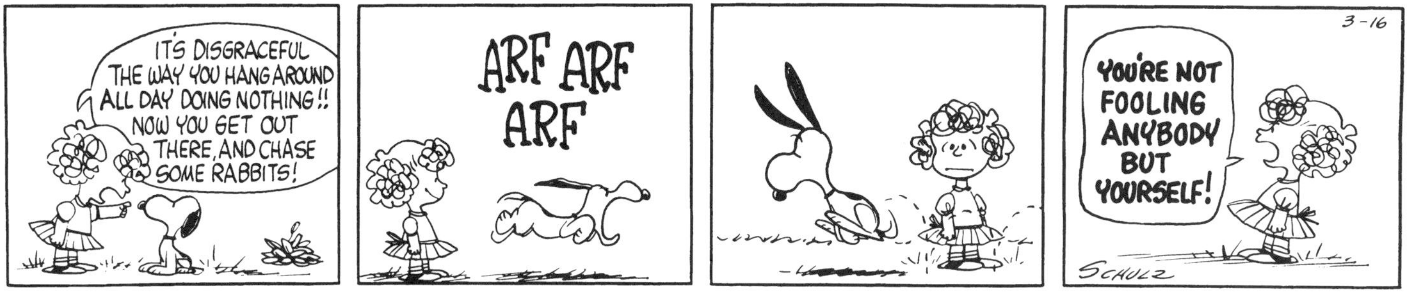
IT'S DISGRACEFUL THE WAY YOU HANG AROUND ALL DAY DOING NOTHING!! NOW YOU GET OUT THERE, AND CHASE SOME RABBITS!
ARF ARF ARF ARF
3-16
YOU'RE NOT FOOLING ANYBODY BUT YOURSELF!
SCHULZ

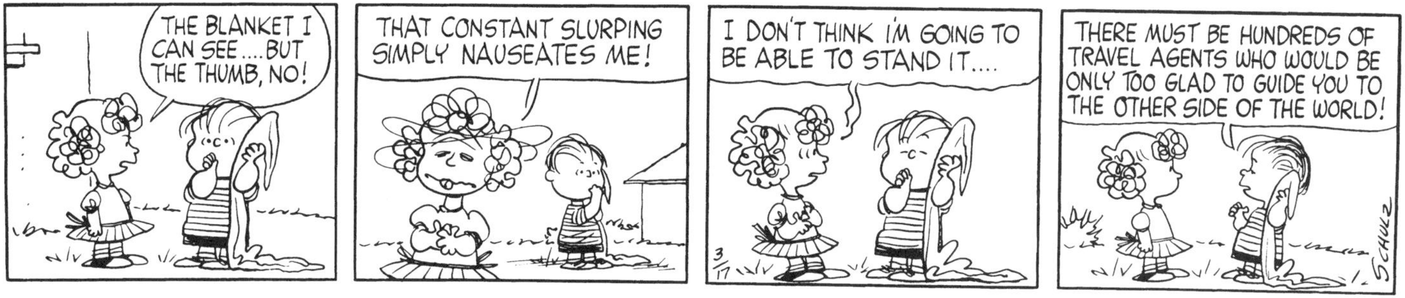
THE BLANKET I CAN SEE....BUT THE THUMB, NO!
THAT CONSTANT SLURPING SIMPLY NAUSEATES ME!
I DON'T THINK I'M GOING TO BE ABLE TO STAND IT....
3/17
THERE MUST BE HUNDREDS OF TRAVEL AGENTS WHO WOULD BE ONLY TOO GLAD TO GUIDE YOU TO THE OTHER SIDE OF THE WORLD!
SCHULZ

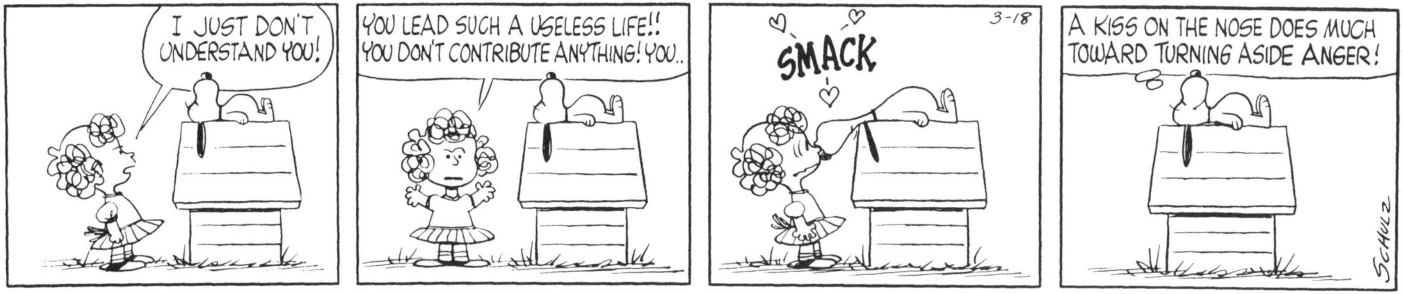
I JUST DON'T UNDERSTAND YOU!
YOU LEAD SUCH A USELESS LIFE!! YOU DON'T CONTRIBUTE ANYTHING! YOU..
3-18
SMACK
A KISS ON THE NOSE DOES MUCH TOWARD TURNING ASIDE ANGER!
SCHULZ

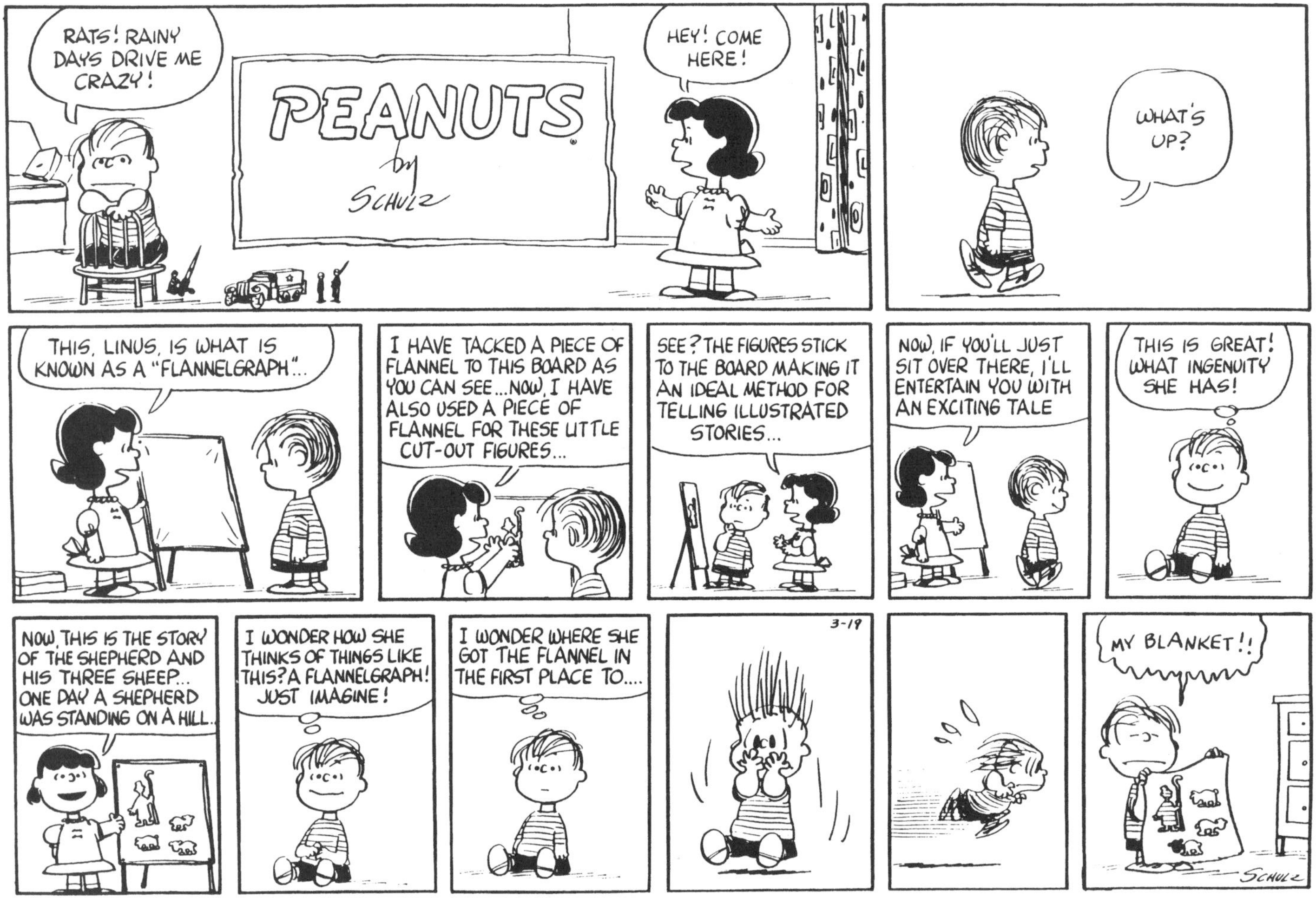
RATS! RAINY DAYS DRIVE ME CRAZY!
PEANUTS
by SCHULZ
HEY! COME HERE!
WHAT'S UP?
THIS, LINUS, IS WHAT IS KNOWN AS A "FLANNELGRAPH"...
I HAVE TACKED A PIECE OF FLANNEL TO THIS BOARD AS YOU CAN SEE...NOW, I HAVE ALSO USED A PIECE OF FLANNEL FOR THESE LITTLE CUT-OUT FIGURES...
SEE? THE FIGURES STICK TO THE BOARD MAKING IT AN IDEAL METHOD FOR TELLING ILLUSTRATED STORIES...
NOW, IF YOU'LL JUST SIT OVER THERE, I'LL ENTERTAIN YOU WITH AN EXCITING TALE
THIS IS GREAT! WHAT INGENUITY SHE HAS!
NOW, THIS IS THE STORY OF THE SHEPHERD AND HIS THREE SHEEP... ONE DAY A SHEPHERD WAS STANDING ON A HILL..
I WONDER HOW SHE THINKS OF THINGS LIKE THIS? A FLANNELGRAPH! JUST IMAGINE!
I WONDER WHERE SHE GOT THE FLANNEL IN THE FIRST PLACE TO....
3-19
MY BLANKET!!
SCHULZ

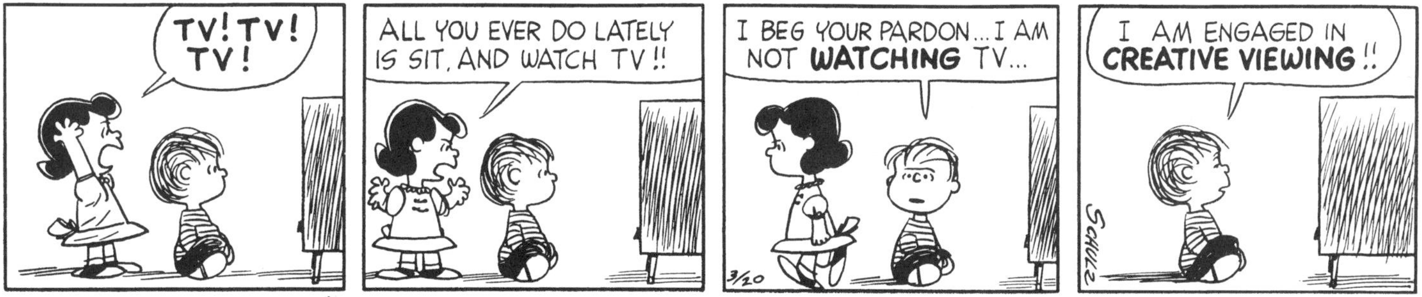
TV! TV! TV!
ALL YOU EVER DO LATELY IS SIT, AND WATCH TV!!
I BEG YOUR PARDON... I AM NOT **WATCHING** TV...
3/20
I AM ENGAGED IN **CREATIVE VIEWING**!!
SCHULZ

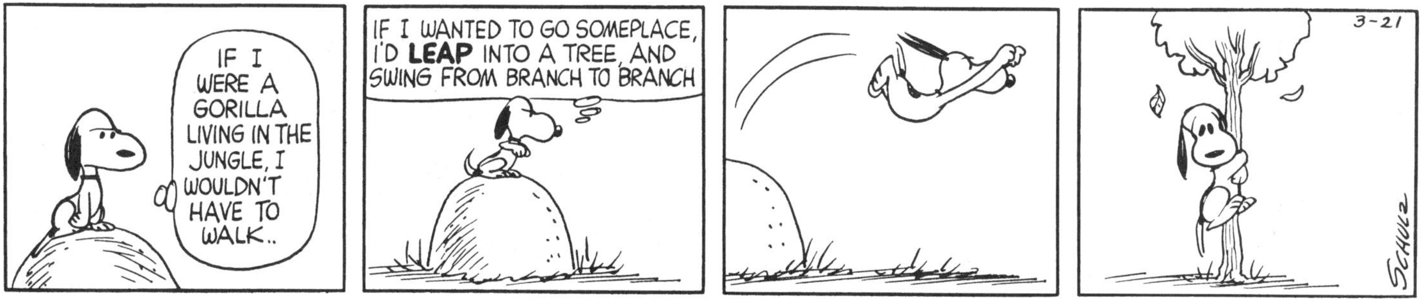
IF I WERE A GORILLA LIVING IN THE JUNGLE, I WOULDN'T HAVE TO WALK..
IF I WANTED TO GO SOMEPLACE, I'D **LEAP** INTO A TREE, AND SWING FROM BRANCH TO BRANCH
3-21
SCHULZ

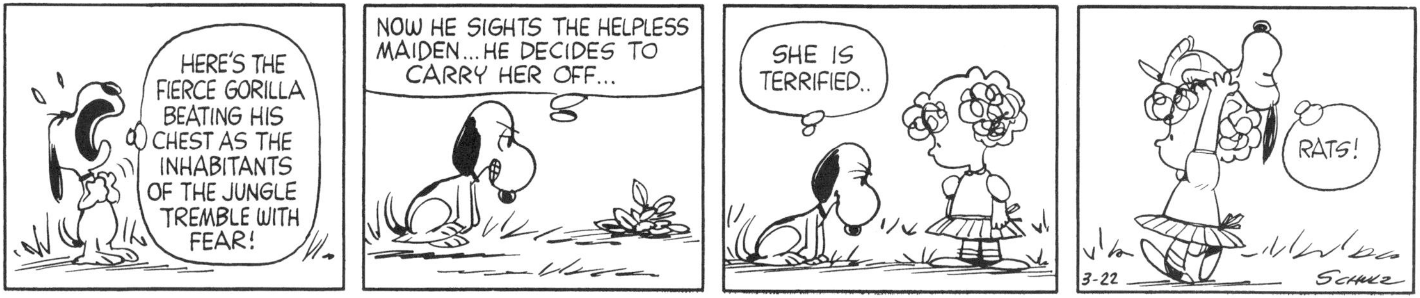
HERE'S THE FIERCE GORILLA BEATING HIS CHEST AS THE INHABITANTS OF THE JUNGLE TREMBLE WITH FEAR!
NOW HE SIGHTS THE HELPLESS MAIDEN... HE DECIDES TO CARRY HER OFF...
SHE IS TERRIFIED..
RATS!
3-22
SCHULZ

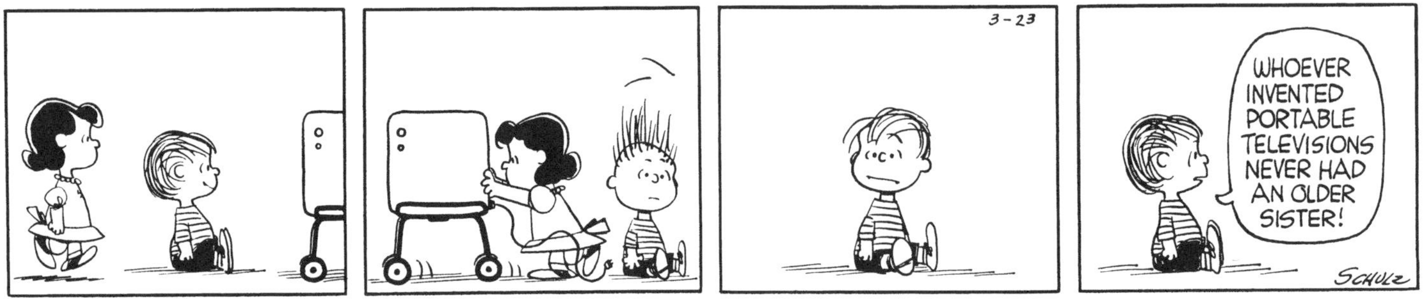
3-23
WHOEVER INVENTED PORTABLE TELEVISIONS NEVER HAD AN OLDER SISTER!
SCHULZ

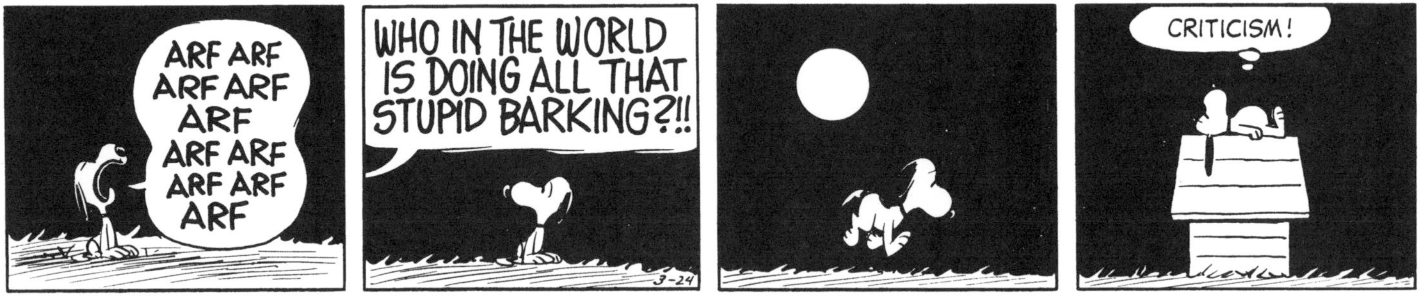
ARF ARF ARF ARF ARF ARF ARF ARF ARF ARF
WHO IN THE WORLD IS DOING ALL THAT STUPID BARKING?!!
3-24
CRITICISM!

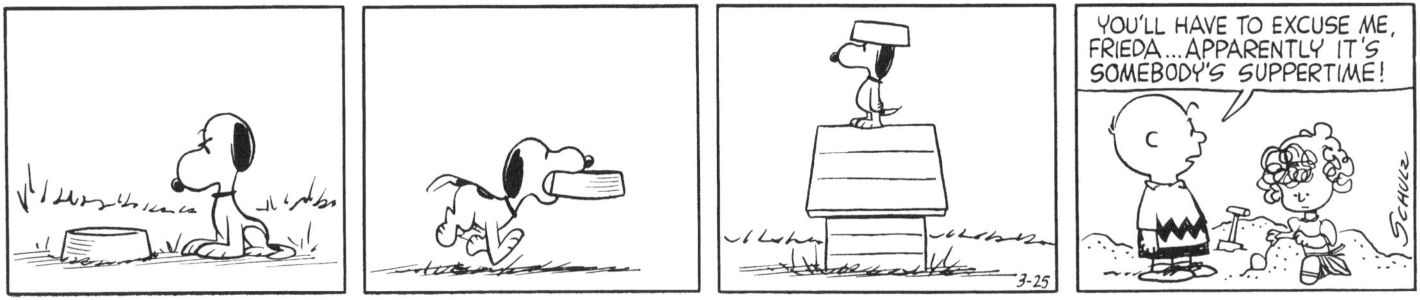
3-25
YOU'LL HAVE TO EXCUSE ME, FRIEDA... APPARENTLY IT'S SOMEBODY'S SUPPERTIME!
SCHULZ

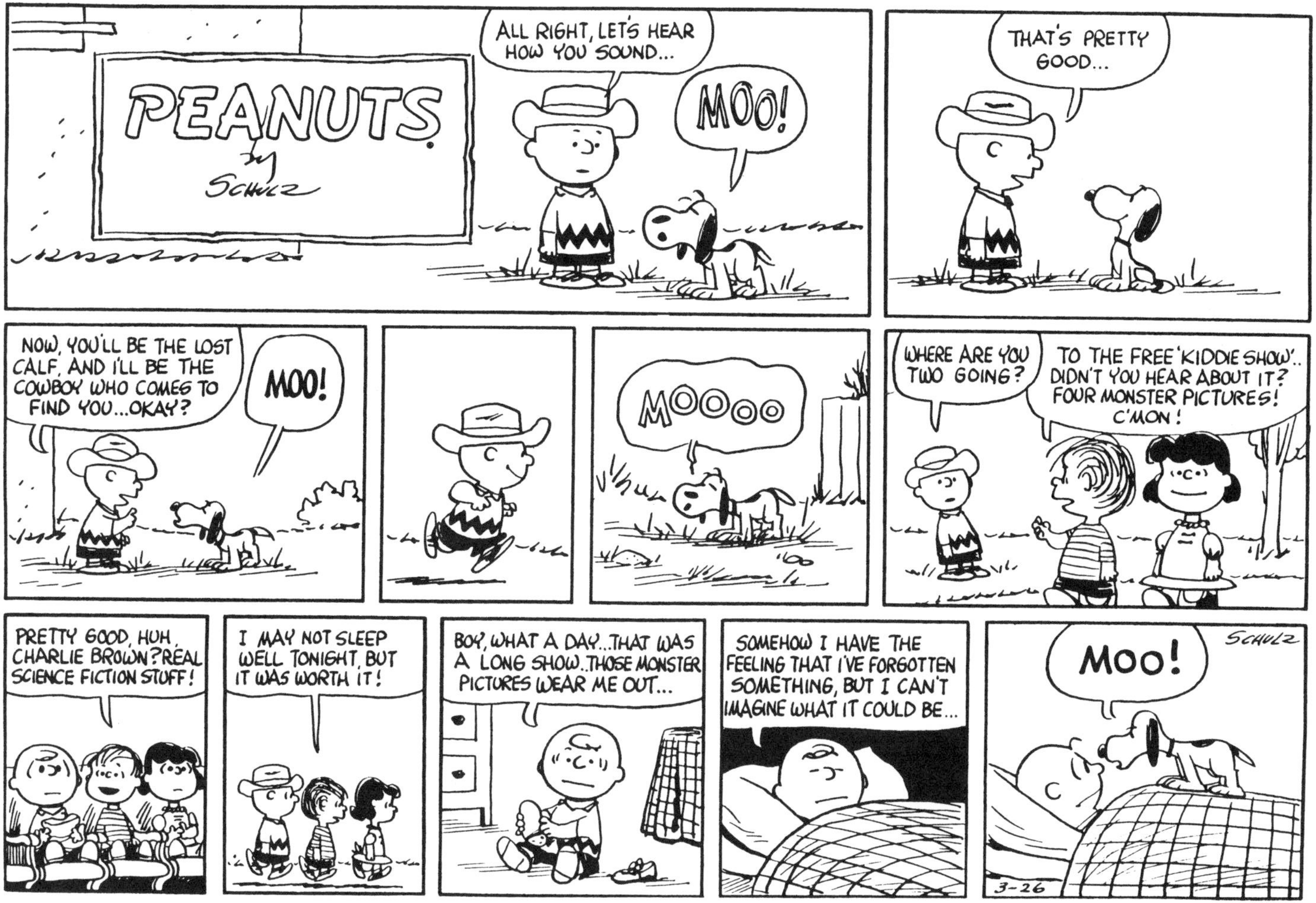
PEANUTS
by SCHULZ
ALL RIGHT, LET'S HEAR HOW YOU SOUND...
MOO!
THAT'S PRETTY GOOD...
NOW, YOU'LL BE THE LOST CALF, AND I'LL BE THE COWBOY WHO COMES TO FIND YOU...OKAY?
MOO!
MOOOOO
WHERE ARE YOU TWO GOING?
TO THE FREE 'KIDDIE SHOW'.. DIDN'T YOU HEAR ABOUT IT? FOUR MONSTER PICTURES! C'MON!
PRETTY GOOD, HUH, CHARLIE BROWN? REAL SCIENCE FICTION STUFF!
I MAY NOT SLEEP WELL TONIGHT, BUT IT WAS WORTH IT!
BOY, WHAT A DAY...THAT WAS A LONG SHOW..THOSE MONSTER PICTURES WEAR ME OUT...
SOMEHOW I HAVE THE FEELING THAT I'VE FORGOTTEN SOMETHING, BUT I CAN'T IMAGINE WHAT IT COULD BE...
SCHULZ
MOO!
3-26

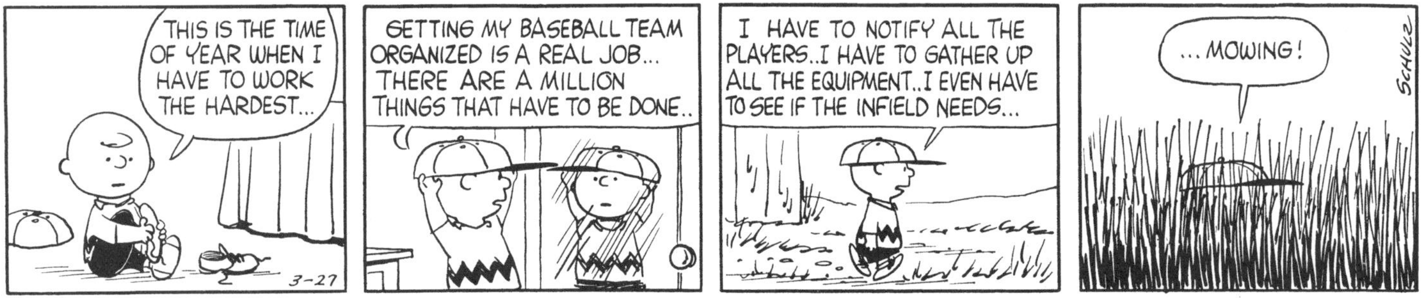

THIS IS THE TIME OF YEAR WHEN I HAVE TO WORK THE HARDEST...
3-27
GETTING MY BASEBALL TEAM ORGANIZED IS A REAL JOB... THERE ARE A MILLION THINGS THAT HAVE TO BE DONE..
I HAVE TO NOTIFY ALL THE PLAYERS..I HAVE TO GATHER UP ALL THE EQUIPMENT..I EVEN HAVE TO SEE IF THE INFIELD NEEDS...
...MOWING!
SCHULZ

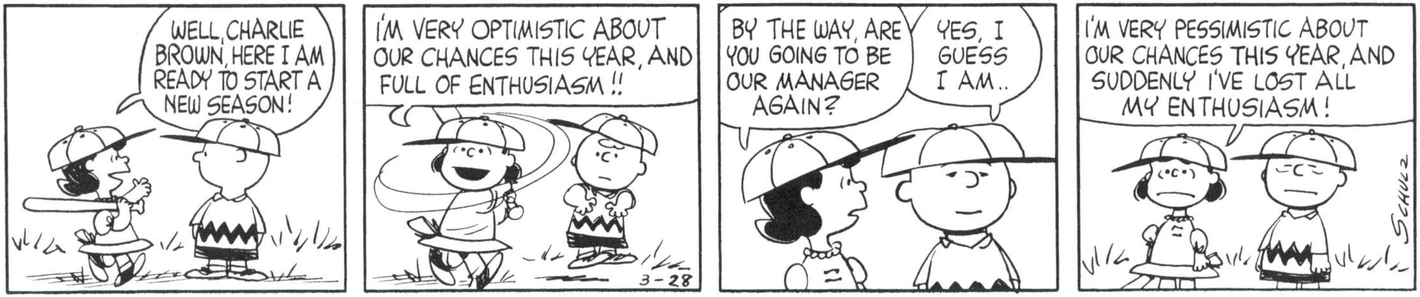

WELL, CHARLIE BROWN, HERE I AM READY TO START A NEW SEASON!
I'M VERY OPTIMISTIC ABOUT OUR CHANCES THIS YEAR, AND FULL OF ENTHUSIASM!!
3-28
BY THE WAY, ARE YOU GOING TO BE OUR MANAGER AGAIN?
YES, I GUESS I AM..
I'M VERY PESSIMISTIC ABOUT OUR CHANCES THIS YEAR, AND SUDDENLY I'VE LOST ALL MY ENTHUSIASM!
SCHULZ

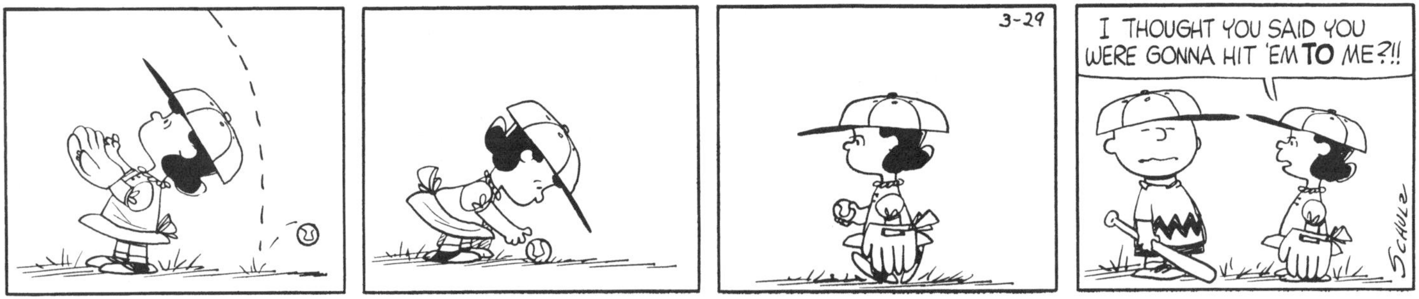

3-29
I THOUGHT YOU SAID YOU WERE GONNA HIT 'EM **TO** ME?!!
SCHULZ

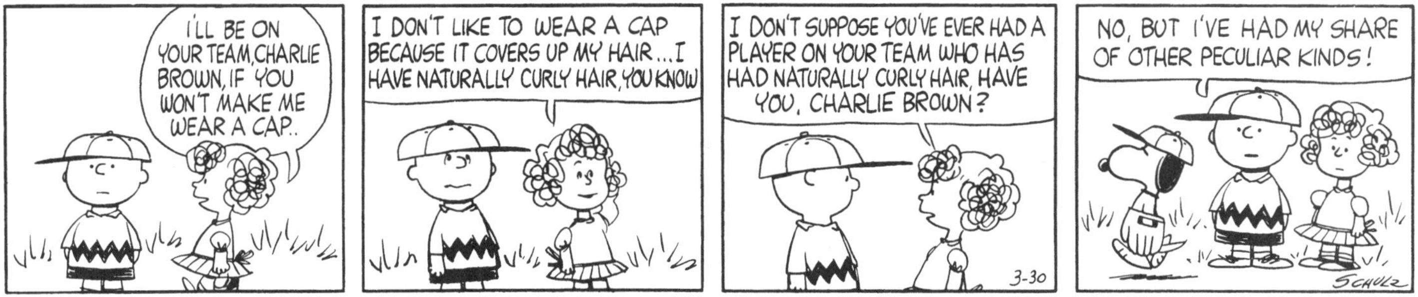
I'LL BE ON YOUR TEAM, CHARLIE BROWN, IF YOU WON'T MAKE ME WEAR A CAP..
I DON'T LIKE TO WEAR A CAP BECAUSE IT COVERS UP MY HAIR...I HAVE NATURALLY CURLY HAIR, YOU KNOW
I DON'T SUPPOSE YOU'VE EVER HAD A PLAYER ON YOUR TEAM WHO HAS HAD NATURALLY CURLY HAIR, HAVE YOU, CHARLIE BROWN?
3-30
NO, BUT I'VE HAD MY SHARE OF OTHER PECULIAR KINDS!
SCHULZ

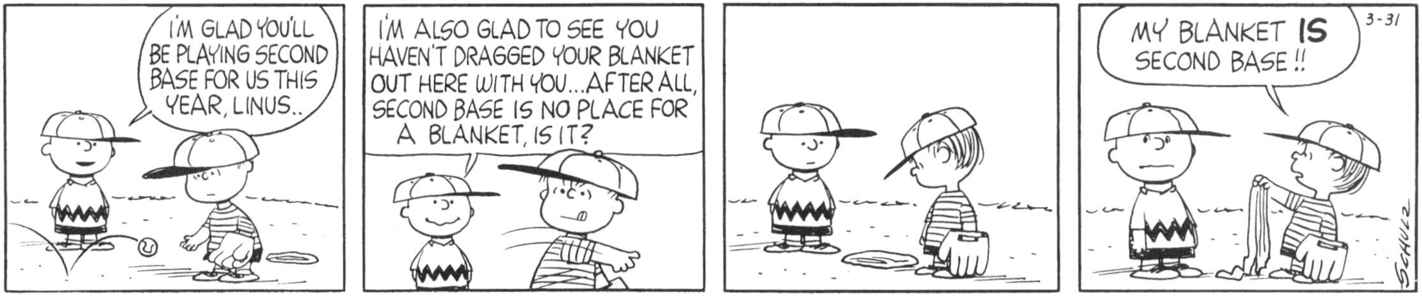
I'M GLAD YOU'LL BE PLAYING SECOND BASE FOR US THIS YEAR, LINUS..
I'M ALSO GLAD TO SEE YOU HAVEN'T DRAGGED YOUR BLANKET OUT HERE WITH YOU...AFTER ALL, SECOND BASE IS NO PLACE FOR A BLANKET, IS IT?
MY BLANKET **IS** SECOND BASE!!
3-31
SCHULZ

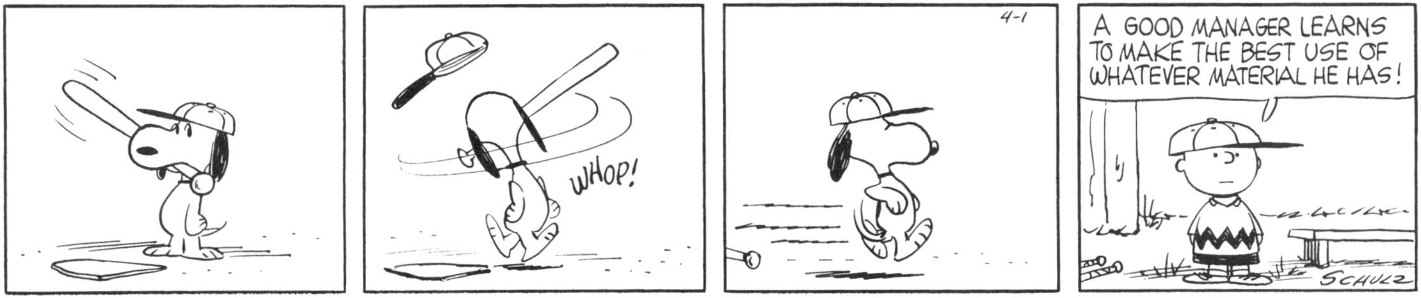
WHOP!
4-1
A GOOD MANAGER LEARNS TO MAKE THE BEST USE OF WHATEVER MATERIAL HE HAS!
SCHULZ

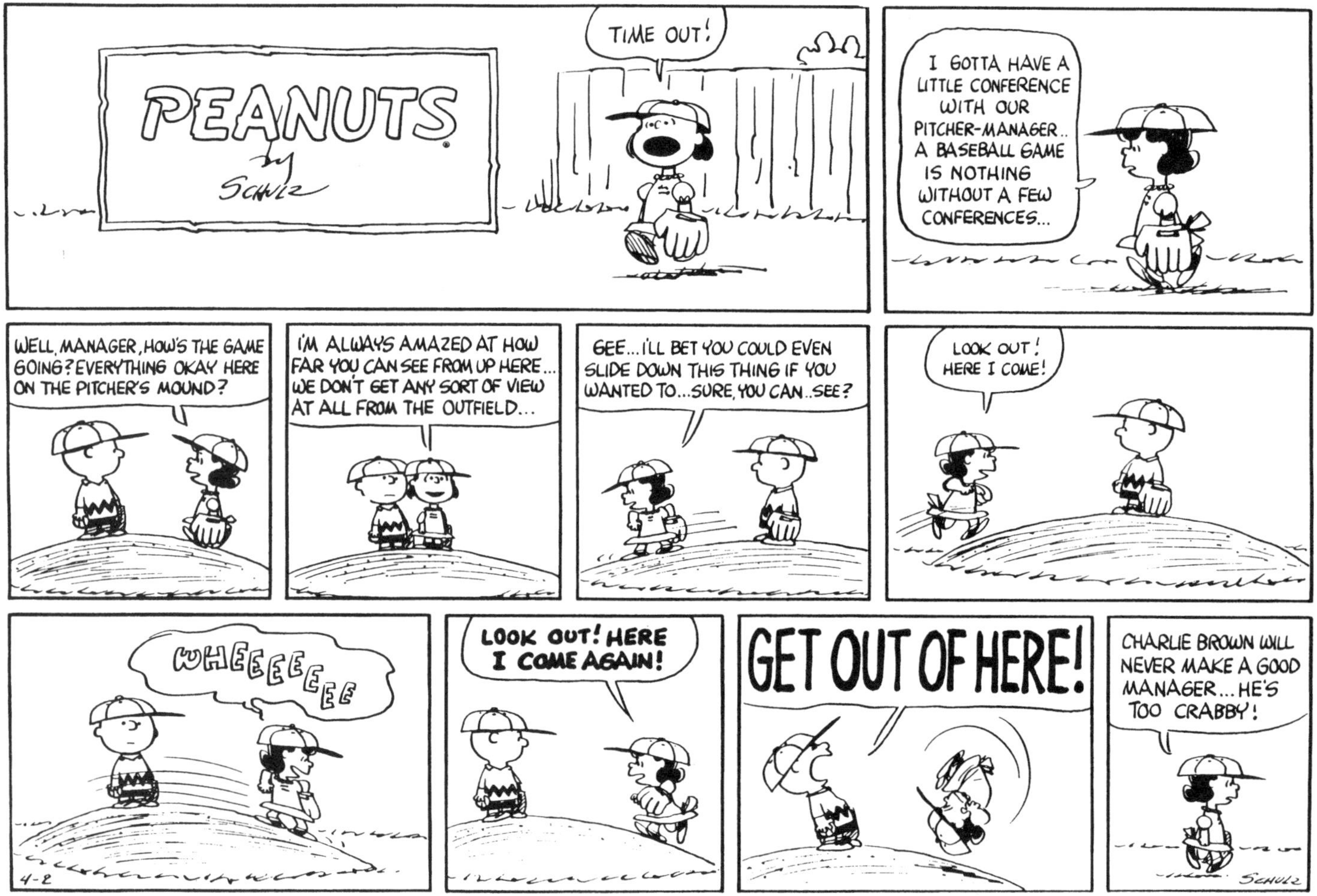
PEANUTS
by
SCHULZ
TIME OUT!
I GOTTA HAVE A LITTLE CONFERENCE WITH OUR PITCHER-MANAGER.. A BASEBALL GAME IS NOTHING WITHOUT A FEW CONFERENCES...
WELL, MANAGER, HOW'S THE GAME GOING? EVERYTHING OKAY HERE ON THE PITCHER'S MOUND?
I'M ALWAYS AMAZED AT HOW FAR YOU CAN SEE FROM UP HERE... WE DON'T GET ANY SORT OF VIEW AT ALL FROM THE OUTFIELD...
GEE... I'LL BET YOU COULD EVEN SLIDE DOWN THIS THING IF YOU WANTED TO... SURE, YOU CAN.. SEE?
LOOK OUT! HERE I COME!
WHEEEEEEEEE
4-2
LOOK OUT! HERE I COME AGAIN!
GET OUT OF HERE!
CHARLIE BROWN WILL NEVER MAKE A GOOD MANAGER... HE'S TOO CRABBY!
SCHULZ

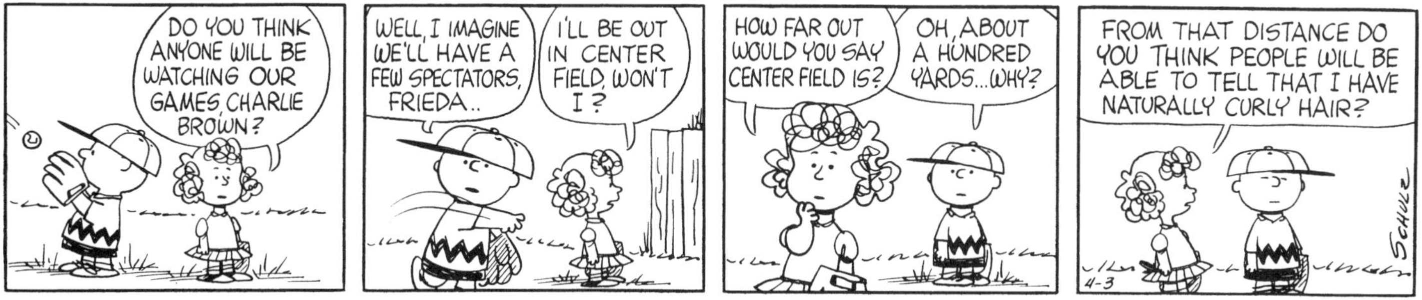
DO YOU THINK ANYONE WILL BE WATCHING OUR GAMES, CHARLIE BROWN?
WELL, I IMAGINE WE'LL HAVE A FEW SPECTATORS, FRIEDA..
I'LL BE OUT IN CENTER FIELD, WON'T I?
HOW FAR OUT WOULD YOU SAY CENTER FIELD IS?
OH, ABOUT A HUNDRED YARDS...WHY?
FROM THAT DISTANCE DO YOU THINK PEOPLE WILL BE ABLE TO TELL THAT I HAVE NATURALLY CURLY HAIR?
SCHULZ
4-3

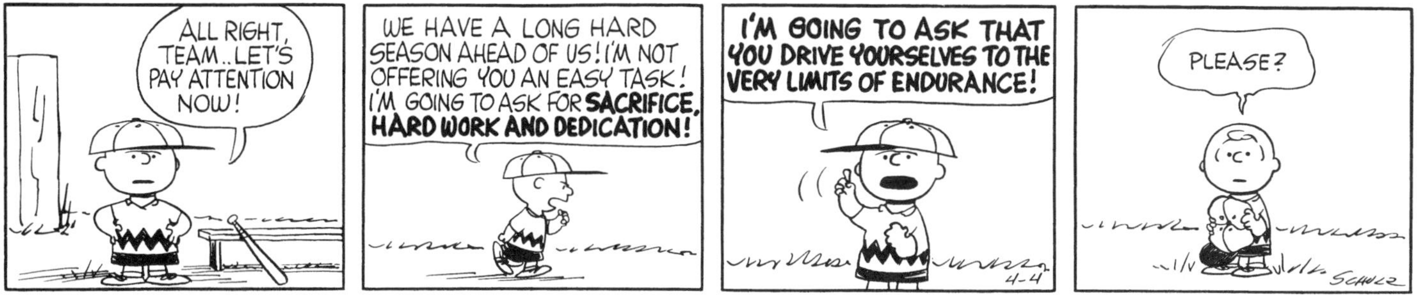
ALL RIGHT, TEAM..LET'S PAY ATTENTION NOW!
WE HAVE A LONG HARD SEASON AHEAD OF US! I'M NOT OFFERING YOU AN EASY TASK! I'M GOING TO ASK FOR SACRIFICE, HARD WORK AND DEDICATION!
I'M GOING TO ASK THAT YOU DRIVE YOURSELVES TO THE VERY LIMITS OF ENDURANCE!
4-4
PLEASE?
SCHULZ

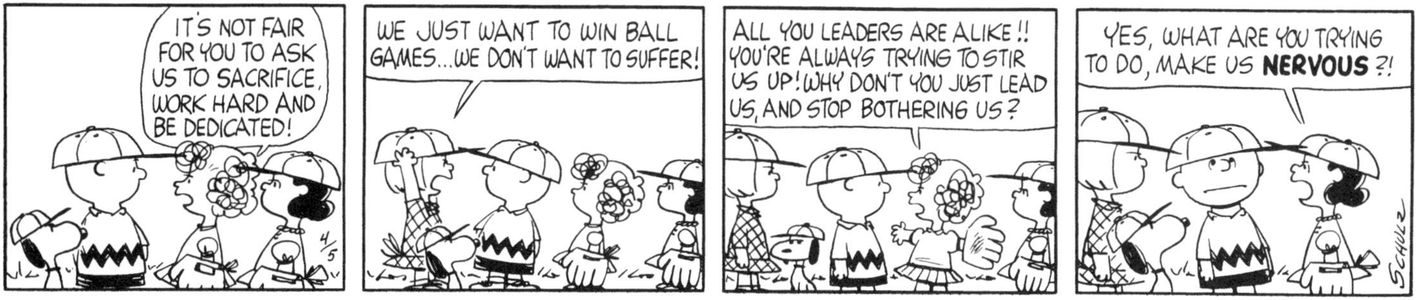
IT'S NOT FAIR FOR YOU TO ASK US TO SACRIFICE, WORK HARD AND BE DEDICATED!
4/5
WE JUST WANT TO WIN BALL GAMES...WE DON'T WANT TO SUFFER!
ALL YOU LEADERS ARE ALIKE!! YOU'RE ALWAYS TRYING TO STIR US UP! WHY DON'T YOU JUST LEAD US, AND STOP BOTHERING US?
YES, WHAT ARE YOU TRYING TO DO, MAKE US NERVOUS?!
SCHULZ

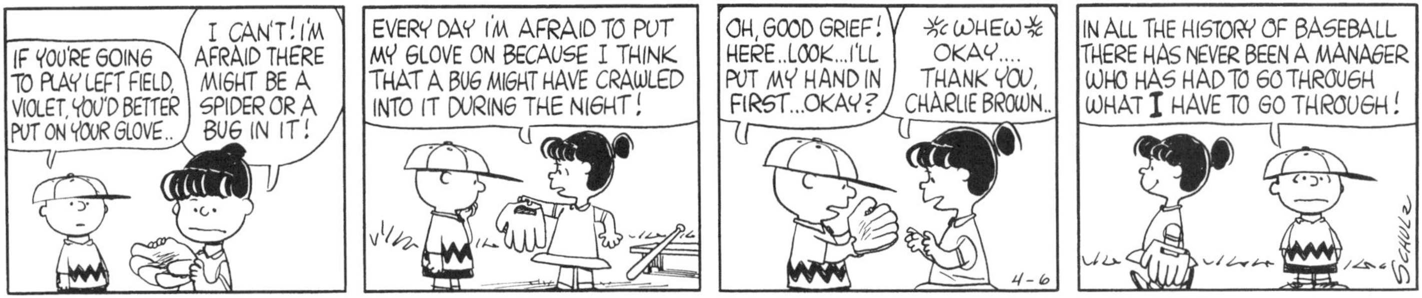
IF YOU'RE GOING TO PLAY LEFT FIELD, VIOLET, YOU'D BETTER PUT ON YOUR GLOVE..
I CAN'T! I'M AFRAID THERE MIGHT BE A SPIDER OR A BUG IN IT!
EVERY DAY I'M AFRAID TO PUT MY GLOVE ON BECAUSE I THINK THAT A BUG MIGHT HAVE CRAWLED INTO IT DURING THE NIGHT!
OH, GOOD GRIEF! HERE..LOOK...I'LL PUT MY HAND IN FIRST...OKAY?
WHEW OKAY.... THANK YOU, CHARLIE BROWN..
IN ALL THE HISTORY OF BASEBALL THERE HAS NEVER BEEN A MANAGER WHO HAS HAD TO GO THROUGH WHAT I HAVE TO GO THROUGH!
4-6
SCHULZ

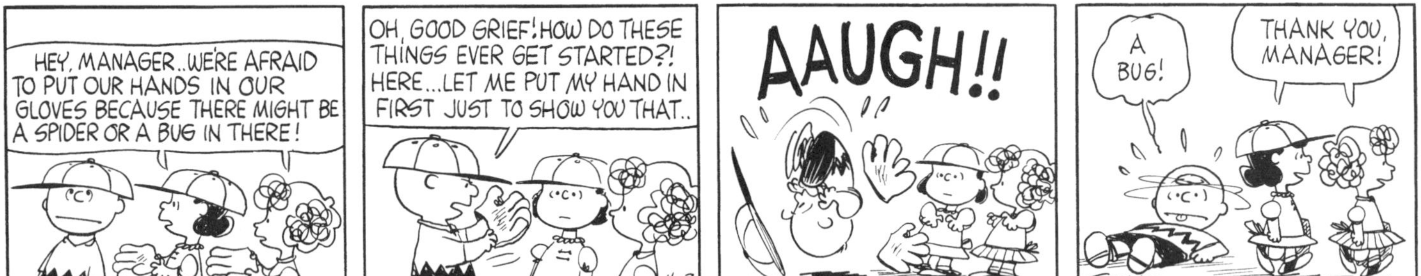
HEY, MANAGER..WE'RE AFRAID TO PUT OUR HANDS IN OUR GLOVES BECAUSE THERE MIGHT BE A SPIDER OR A BUG IN THERE!
OH, GOOD GRIEF! HOW DO THESE THINGS EVER GET STARTED?! HERE...LET ME PUT MY HAND IN FIRST JUST TO SHOW YOU THAT..
4-7
AAUGH!!
A BUG!
THANK YOU, MANAGER!
SCHULZ

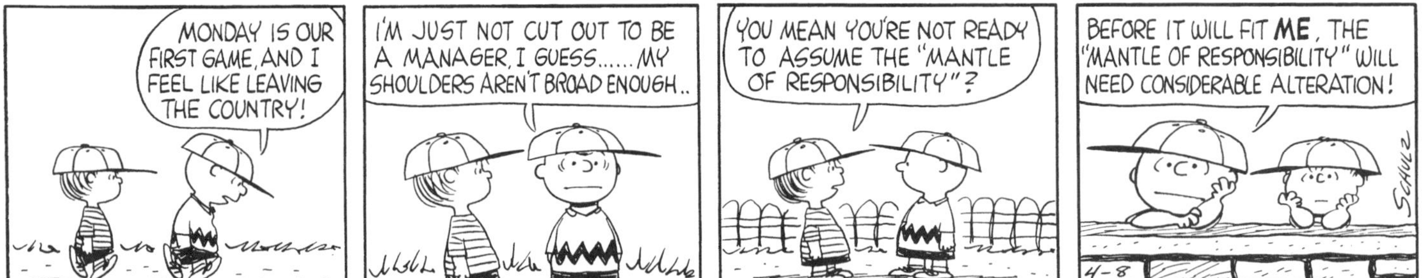
MONDAY IS OUR FIRST GAME, AND I FEEL LIKE LEAVING THE COUNTRY!
I'M JUST NOT CUT OUT TO BE A MANAGER, I GUESS...... MY SHOULDERS AREN'T BROAD ENOUGH..
YOU MEAN YOU'RE NOT READY TO ASSUME THE "MANTLE OF RESPONSIBILITY"?
BEFORE IT WILL FIT ME, THE "MANTLE OF RESPONSIBILITY" WILL NEED CONSIDERABLE ALTERATION!
SCHULZ
4-8

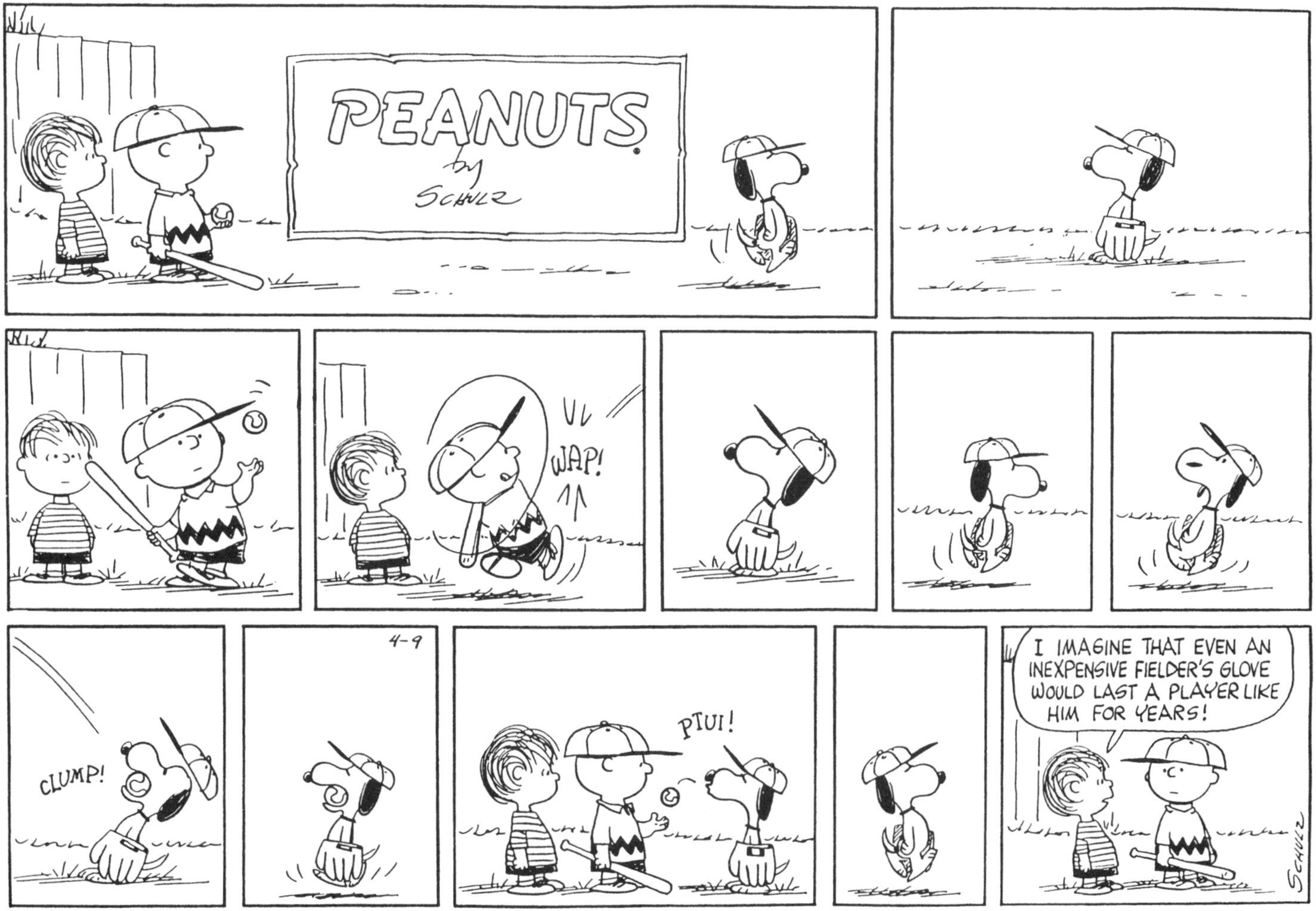
PEANUTS
by SCHULZ
WAP!
CLUMP!
4-9
PTUI!
I IMAGINE THAT EVEN AN INEXPENSIVE FIELDER'S GLOVE WOULD LAST A PLAYER LIKE HIM FOR YEARS!
SCHULZ

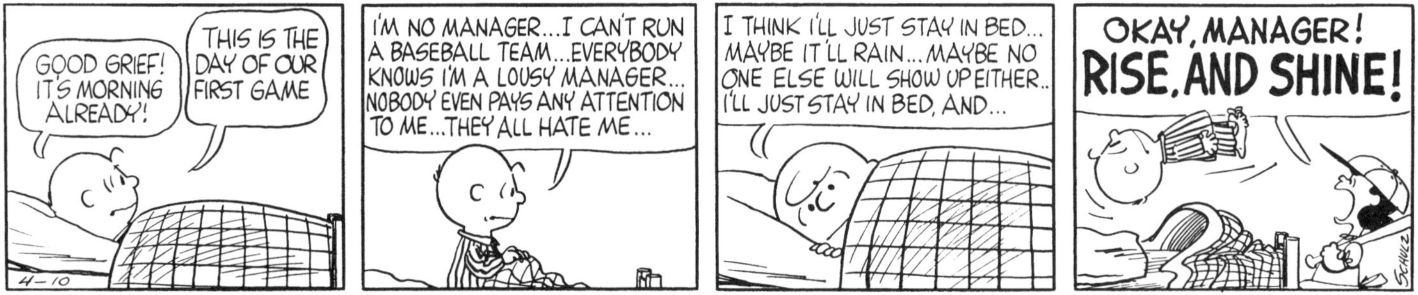
GOOD GRIEF! IT'S MORNING ALREADY!
THIS IS THE DAY OF OUR FIRST GAME
I'M NO MANAGER...I CAN'T RUN A BASEBALL TEAM...EVERYBODY KNOWS I'M A LOUSY MANAGER... NOBODY EVEN PAYS ANY ATTENTION TO ME...THEY ALL HATE ME...
I THINK I'LL JUST STAY IN BED... MAYBE IT'LL RAIN... MAYBE NO ONE ELSE WILL SHOW UP EITHER.. I'LL JUST STAY IN BED, AND...
OKAY, MANAGER! RISE, AND SHINE!

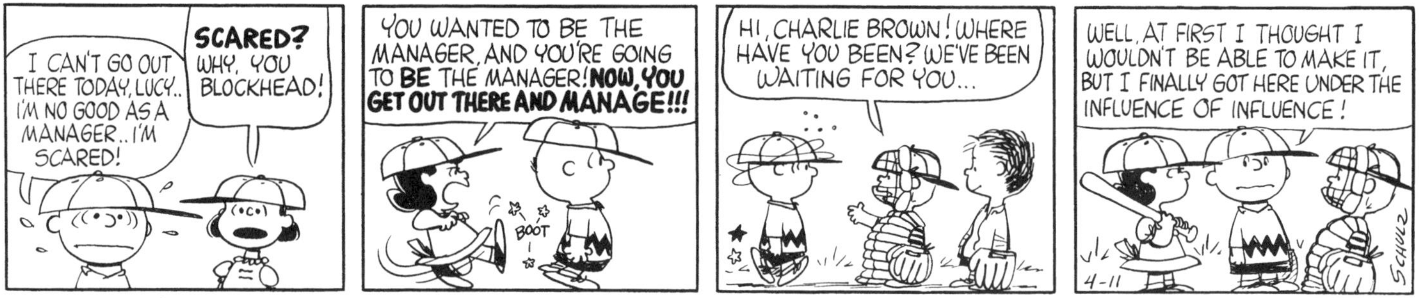
I CAN'T GO OUT THERE TODAY, LUCY.. I'M NO GOOD AS A MANAGER.. I'M SCARED!
SCARED? WHY, YOU BLOCKHEAD!
YOU WANTED TO BE THE MANAGER, AND YOU'RE GOING TO BE THE MANAGER! NOW, YOU GET OUT THERE AND MANAGE!!!
BOOT
HI, CHARLIE BROWN! WHERE HAVE YOU BEEN? WE'VE BEEN WAITING FOR YOU...
WELL, AT FIRST I THOUGHT I WOULDN'T BE ABLE TO MAKE IT, BUT I FINALLY GOT HERE UNDER THE INFLUENCE OF INFLUENCE!

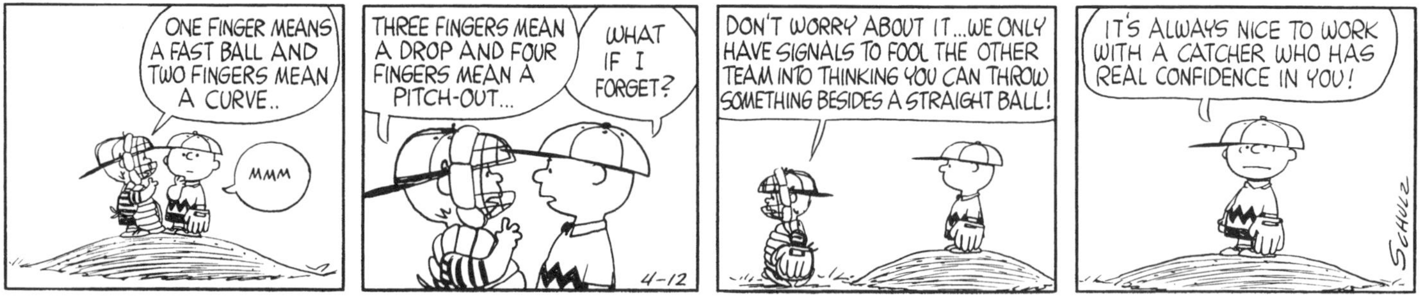
ONE FINGER MEANS A FAST BALL AND TWO FINGERS MEAN A CURVE..
MMM
THREE FINGERS MEAN A DROP AND FOUR FINGERS MEAN A PITCH-OUT...
WHAT IF I FORGET?
DON'T WORRY ABOUT IT...WE ONLY HAVE SIGNALS TO FOOL THE OTHER TEAM INTO THINKING YOU CAN THROW SOMETHING BESIDES A STRAIGHT BALL!
IT'S ALWAYS NICE TO WORK WITH A CATCHER WHO HAS REAL CONFIDENCE IN YOU!

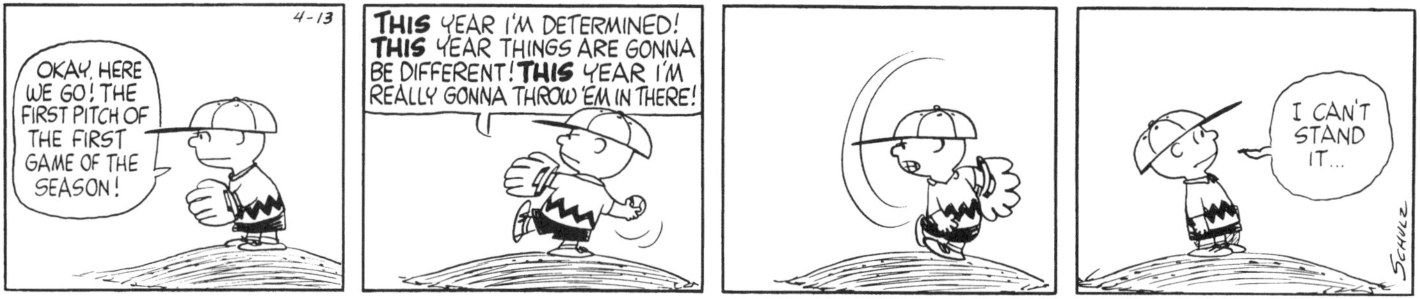
4-13
OKAY, HERE WE GO! THE FIRST PITCH OF THE FIRST GAME OF THE SEASON!
THIS YEAR I'M DETERMINED! THIS YEAR THINGS ARE GONNA BE DIFFERENT! THIS YEAR I'M REALLY GONNA THROW 'EM IN THERE!
I CAN'T STAND IT...
SCHULZ

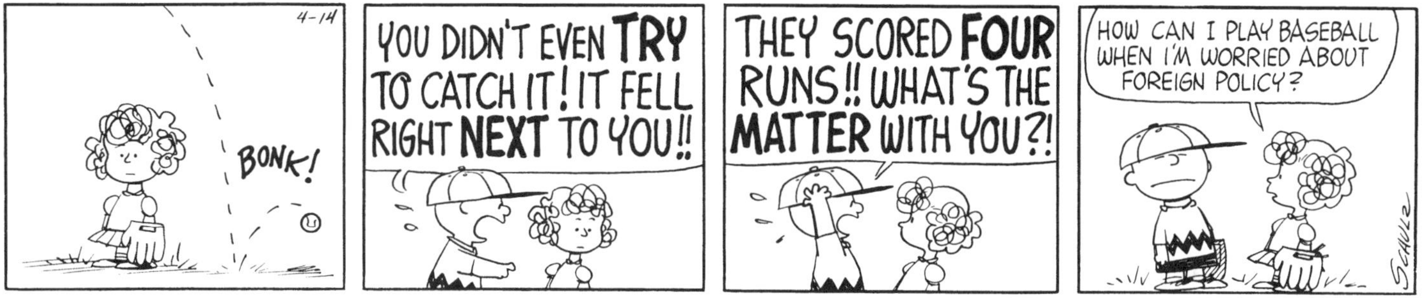
4-14
BONK!
YOU DIDN'T EVEN TRY TO CATCH IT! IT FELL RIGHT NEXT TO YOU!!
THEY SCORED FOUR RUNS!! WHAT'S THE MATTER WITH YOU?!
HOW CAN I PLAY BASEBALL WHEN I'M WORRIED ABOUT FOREIGN POLICY?
SCHULZ

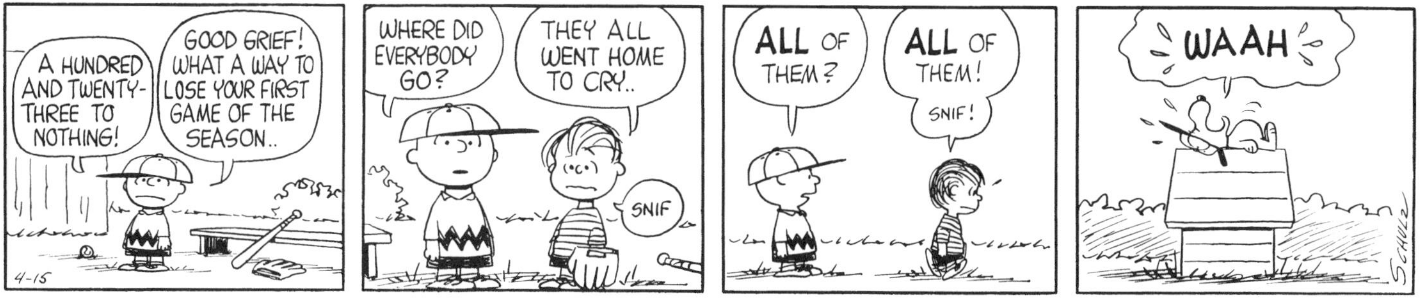
A HUNDRED AND TWENTY-THREE TO NOTHING!
GOOD GRIEF! WHAT A WAY TO LOSE YOUR FIRST GAME OF THE SEASON..
4-15
WHERE DID EVERYBODY GO?
THEY ALL WENT HOME TO CRY..
SNIF
ALL OF THEM?
ALL OF THEM!
SNIF!
WAAH
SCHULZ

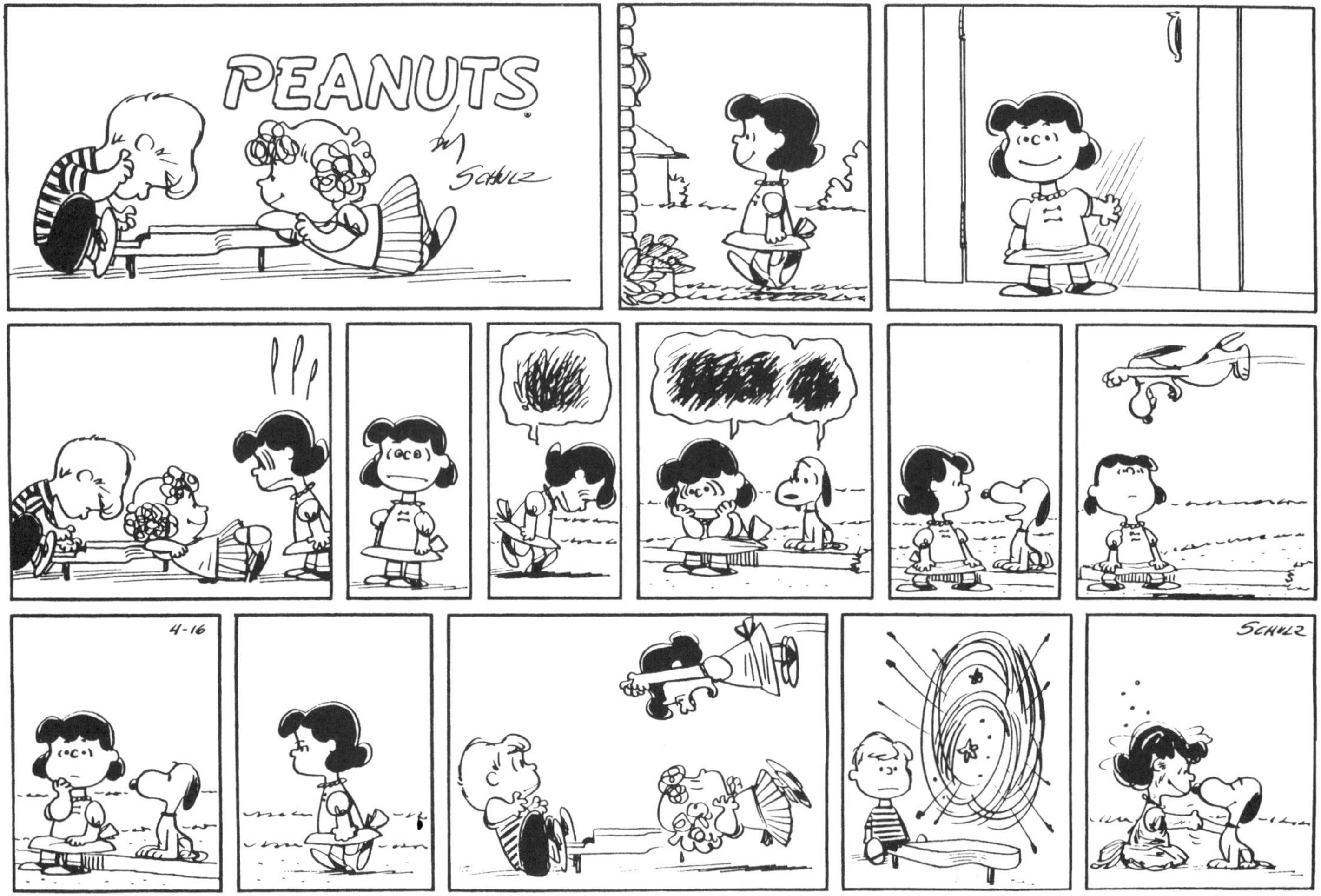
PEANUTS
SCHULZ
4-16
SCHULZ

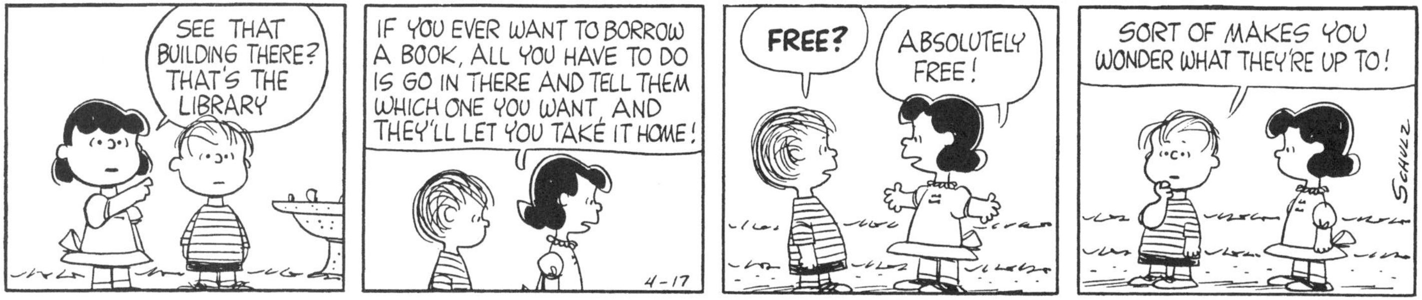
SEE THAT BUILDING THERE? THAT'S THE LIBRARY
IF YOU EVER WANT TO BORROW A BOOK, ALL YOU HAVE TO DO IS GO IN THERE AND TELL THEM WHICH ONE YOU WANT, AND THEY'LL LET YOU TAKE IT HOME!
4-17
FREE?
ABSOLUTELY FREE!
SORT OF MAKES YOU WONDER WHAT THEY'RE UP TO!
SCHULZ

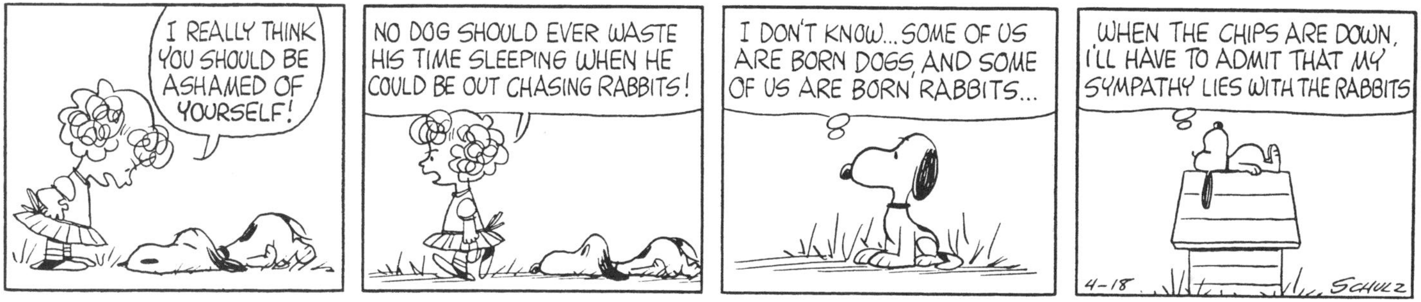
I REALLY THINK YOU SHOULD BE ASHAMED OF YOURSELF!
NO DOG SHOULD EVER WASTE HIS TIME SLEEPING WHEN HE COULD BE OUT CHASING RABBITS!
I DON'T KNOW...SOME OF US ARE BORN DOGS, AND SOME OF US ARE BORN RABBITS...
WHEN THE CHIPS ARE DOWN, I'LL HAVE TO ADMIT THAT MY SYMPATHY LIES WITH THE RABBITS
4-18
SCHULZ

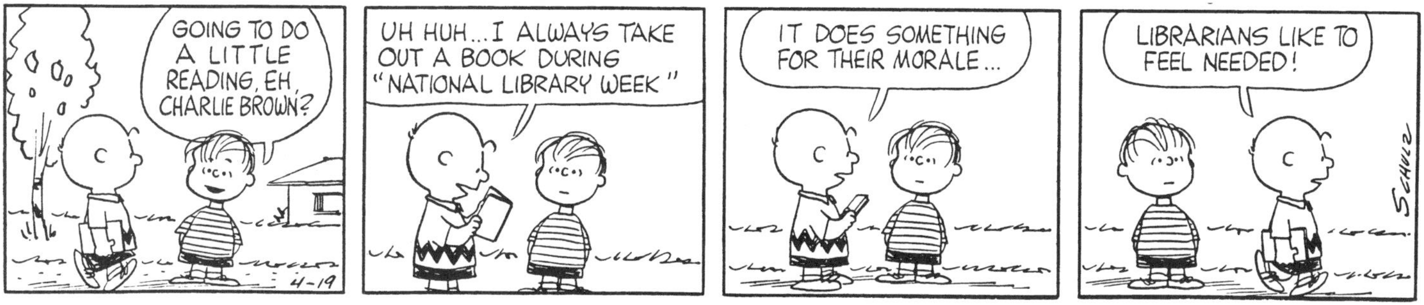
GOING TO DO A LITTLE READING, EH, CHARLIE BROWN?
4-19
UH HUH...I ALWAYS TAKE OUT A BOOK DURING "NATIONAL LIBRARY WEEK"
IT DOES SOMETHING FOR THEIR MORALE...
LIBRARIANS LIKE TO FEEL NEEDED!
SCHULZ

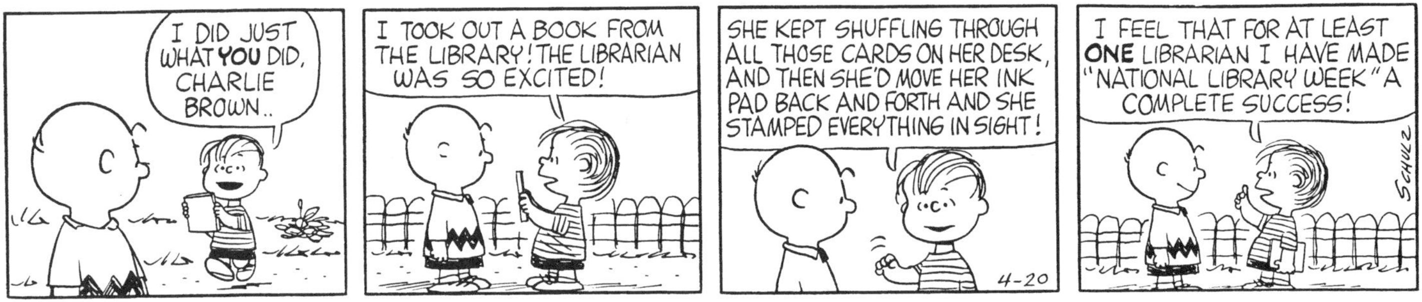
I DID JUST WHAT YOU DID, CHARLIE BROWN..
I TOOK OUT A BOOK FROM THE LIBRARY! THE LIBRARIAN WAS SO EXCITED!
SHE KEPT SHUFFLING THROUGH ALL THOSE CARDS ON HER DESK, AND THEN SHE'D MOVE HER INK PAD BACK AND FORTH AND SHE STAMPED EVERYTHING IN SIGHT!
4-20
I FEEL THAT FOR AT LEAST ONE LIBRARIAN I HAVE MADE "NATIONAL LIBRARY WEEK" A COMPLETE SUCCESS!
SCHULZ

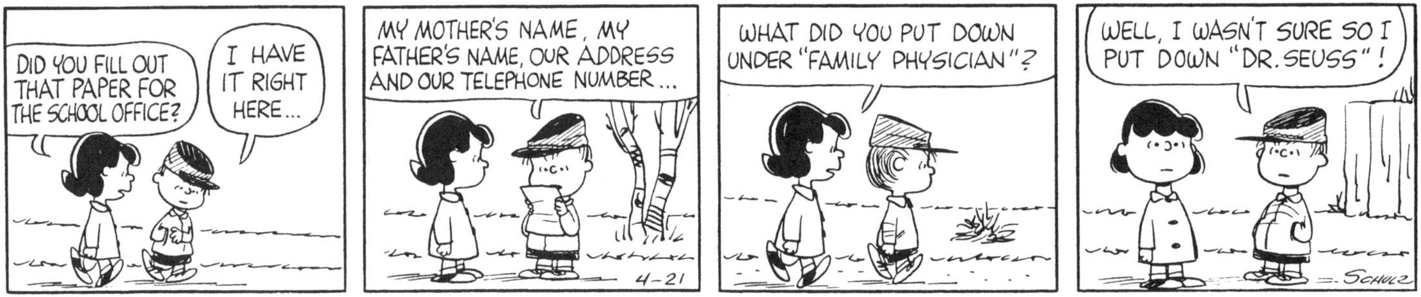
DID YOU FILL OUT THAT PAPER FOR THE SCHOOL OFFICE?
I HAVE IT RIGHT HERE...
MY MOTHER'S NAME, MY FATHER'S NAME, OUR ADDRESS AND OUR TELEPHONE NUMBER...
4-21
WHAT DID YOU PUT DOWN UNDER "FAMILY PHYSICIAN"?
WELL, I WASN'T SURE SO I PUT DOWN "DR. SEUSS"!
SCHULZ

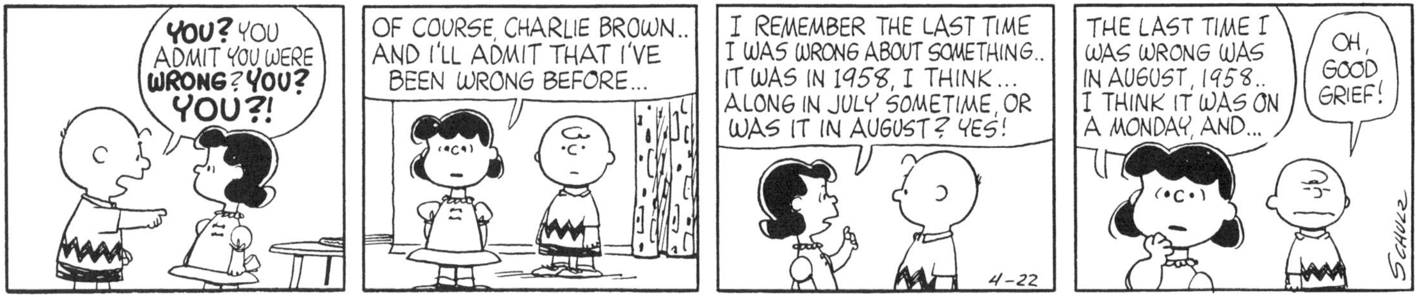
YOU? YOU ADMIT YOU WERE WRONG? YOU? YOU?!
OF COURSE, CHARLIE BROWN.. AND I'LL ADMIT THAT I'VE BEEN WRONG BEFORE...
I REMEMBER THE LAST TIME I WAS WRONG ABOUT SOMETHING.. IT WAS IN 1958, I THINK... ALONG IN JULY SOMETIME, OR WAS IT IN AUGUST? YES!
4-22
THE LAST TIME I WAS WRONG WAS IN AUGUST, 1958.. I THINK IT WAS ON A MONDAY, AND...
OH, GOOD GRIEF!
SCHULZ

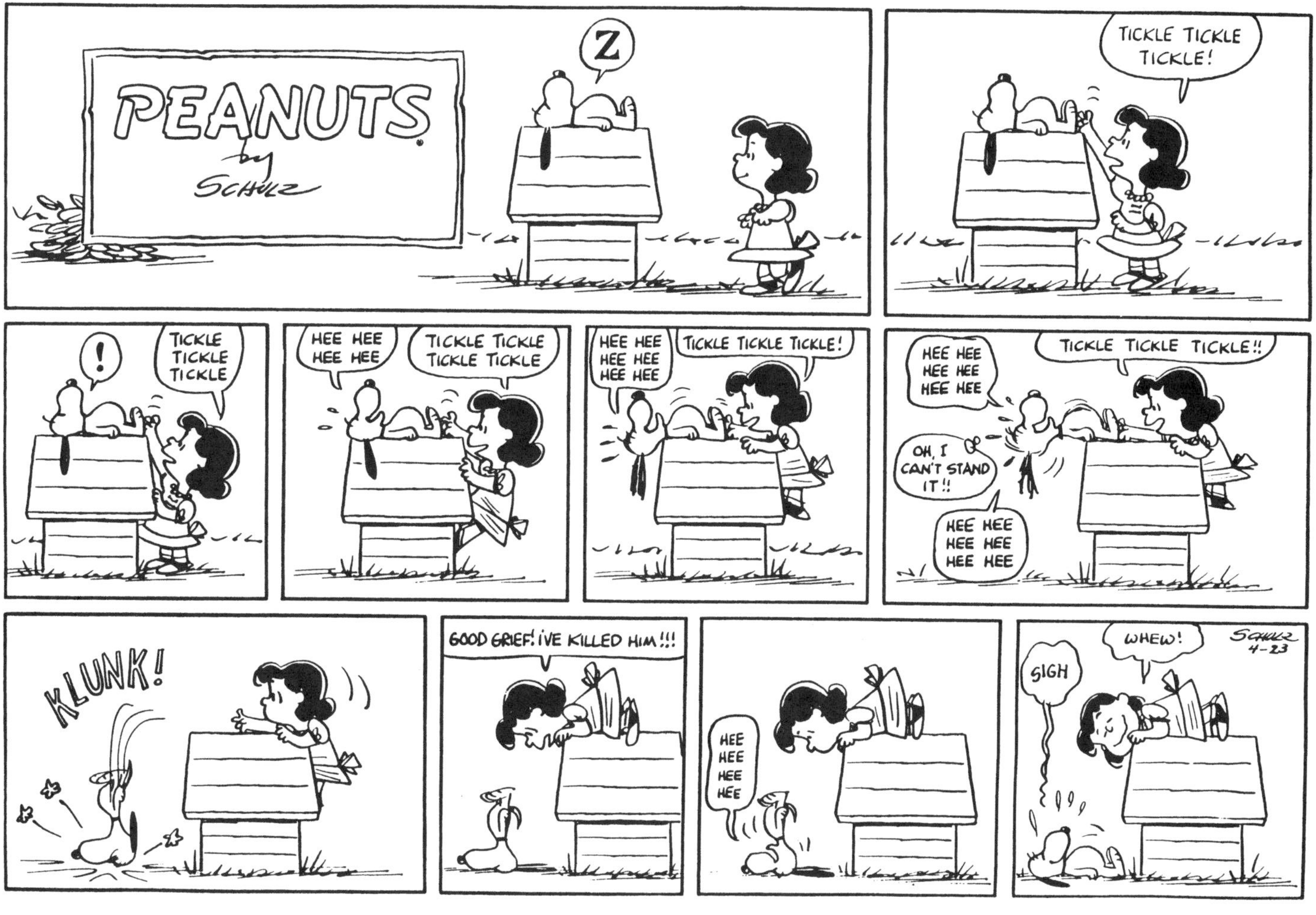
PEANUTS
by SCHULZ
Z
TICKLE TICKLE TICKLE!
!
TICKLE TICKLE TICKLE
HEE HEE HEE HEE
TICKLE TICKLE TICKLE TICKLE
HEE HEE HEE HEE HEE HEE
TICKLE TICKLE TICKLE!
HEE HEE HEE HEE HEE HEE
TICKLE TICKLE TICKLE!!
OH, I CAN'T STAND IT!!
HEE HEE HEE HEE HEE HEE
KLUNK!
GOOD GRIEF! I'VE KILLED HIM!!!
HEE HEE HEE HEE
SIGH
WHEW!
SCHULZ 4-23

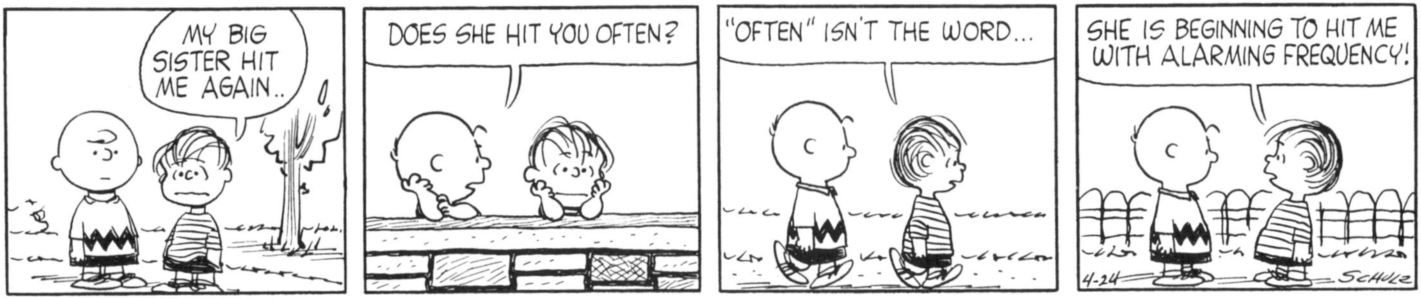
MY BIG SISTER HIT ME AGAIN..
DOES SHE HIT YOU OFTEN?
"OFTEN" ISN'T THE WORD...
SHE IS BEGINNING TO HIT ME WITH ALARMING FREQUENCY!
4-24

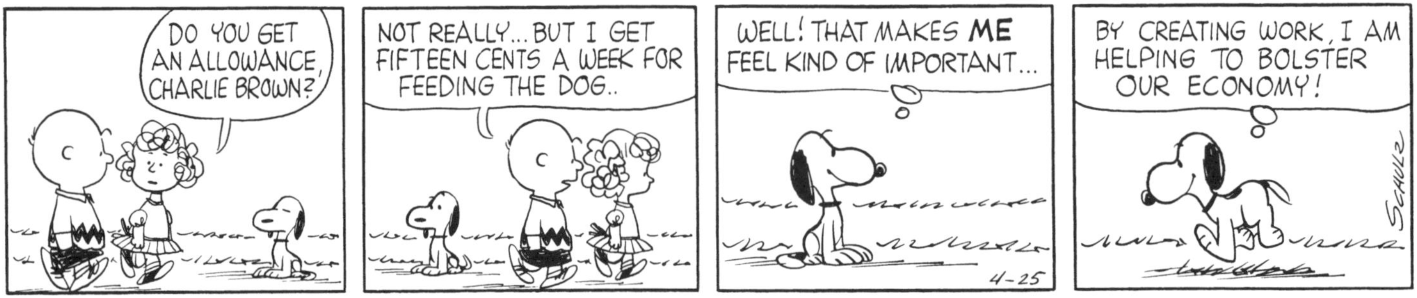
DO YOU GET AN ALLOWANCE, CHARLIE BROWN?
NOT REALLY... BUT I GET FIFTEEN CENTS A WEEK FOR FEEDING THE DOG..
WELL! THAT MAKES ME FEEL KIND OF IMPORTANT...
4-25
BY CREATING WORK, I AM HELPING TO BOLSTER OUR ECONOMY!

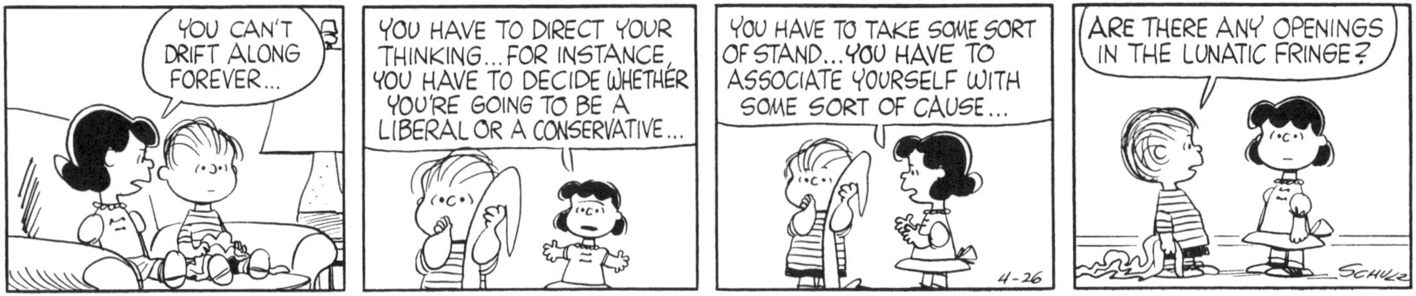
YOU CAN'T DRIFT ALONG FOREVER...
YOU HAVE TO DIRECT YOUR THINKING...FOR INSTANCE, YOU HAVE TO DECIDE WHETHER YOU'RE GOING TO BE A LIBERAL OR A CONSERVATIVE...
YOU HAVE TO TAKE SOME SORT OF STAND...YOU HAVE TO ASSOCIATE YOURSELF WITH SOME SORT OF CAUSE...
4-26
ARE THERE ANY OPENINGS IN THE LUNATIC FRINGE?

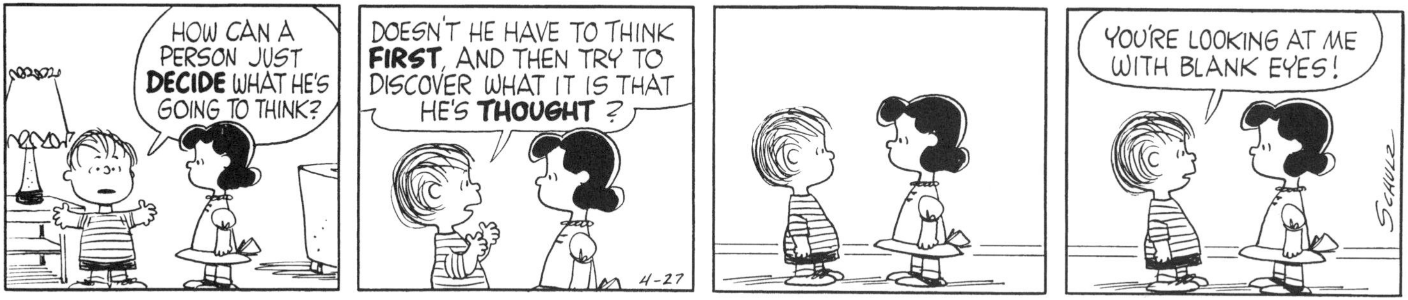
HOW CAN A PERSON JUST DECIDE WHAT HE'S GOING TO THINK?
DOESN'T HE HAVE TO THINK FIRST, AND THEN TRY TO DISCOVER WHAT IT IS THAT HE'S THOUGHT ?
4-27
YOU'RE LOOKING AT ME WITH BLANK EYES!
SCHULZ

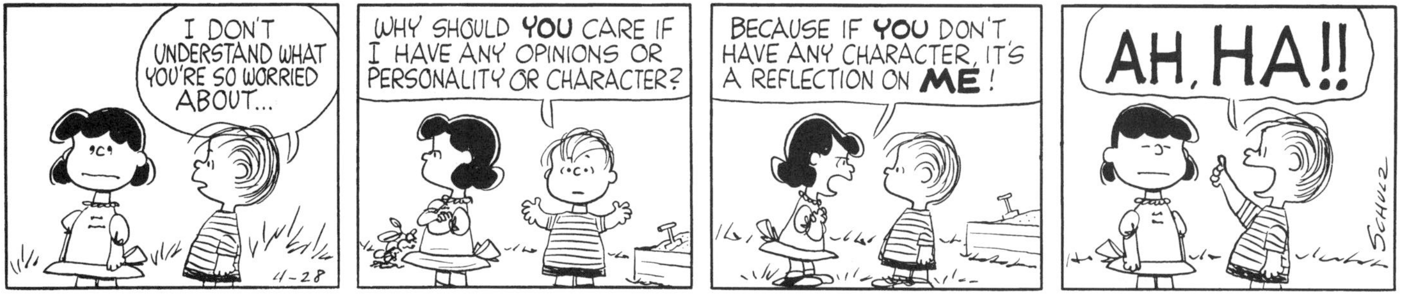
I DON'T UNDERSTAND WHAT YOU'RE SO WORRIED ABOUT...
4-28
WHY SHOULD YOU CARE IF I HAVE ANY OPINIONS OR PERSONALITY OR CHARACTER?
BECAUSE IF YOU DON'T HAVE ANY CHARACTER, IT'S A REFLECTION ON ME!
AH, HA!!
SCHULZ

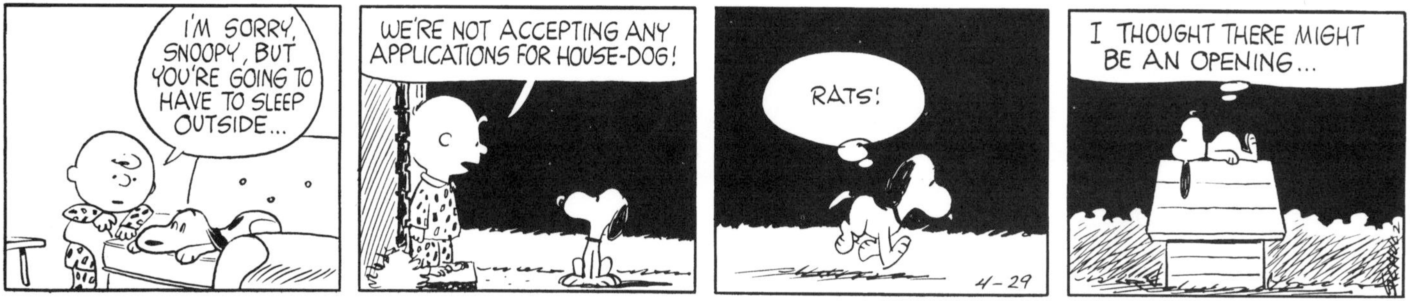
I'M SORRY, SNOOPY, BUT YOU'RE GOING TO HAVE TO SLEEP OUTSIDE...
WE'RE NOT ACCEPTING ANY APPLICATIONS FOR HOUSE-DOG!
RATS!
4-29
I THOUGHT THERE MIGHT BE AN OPENING...

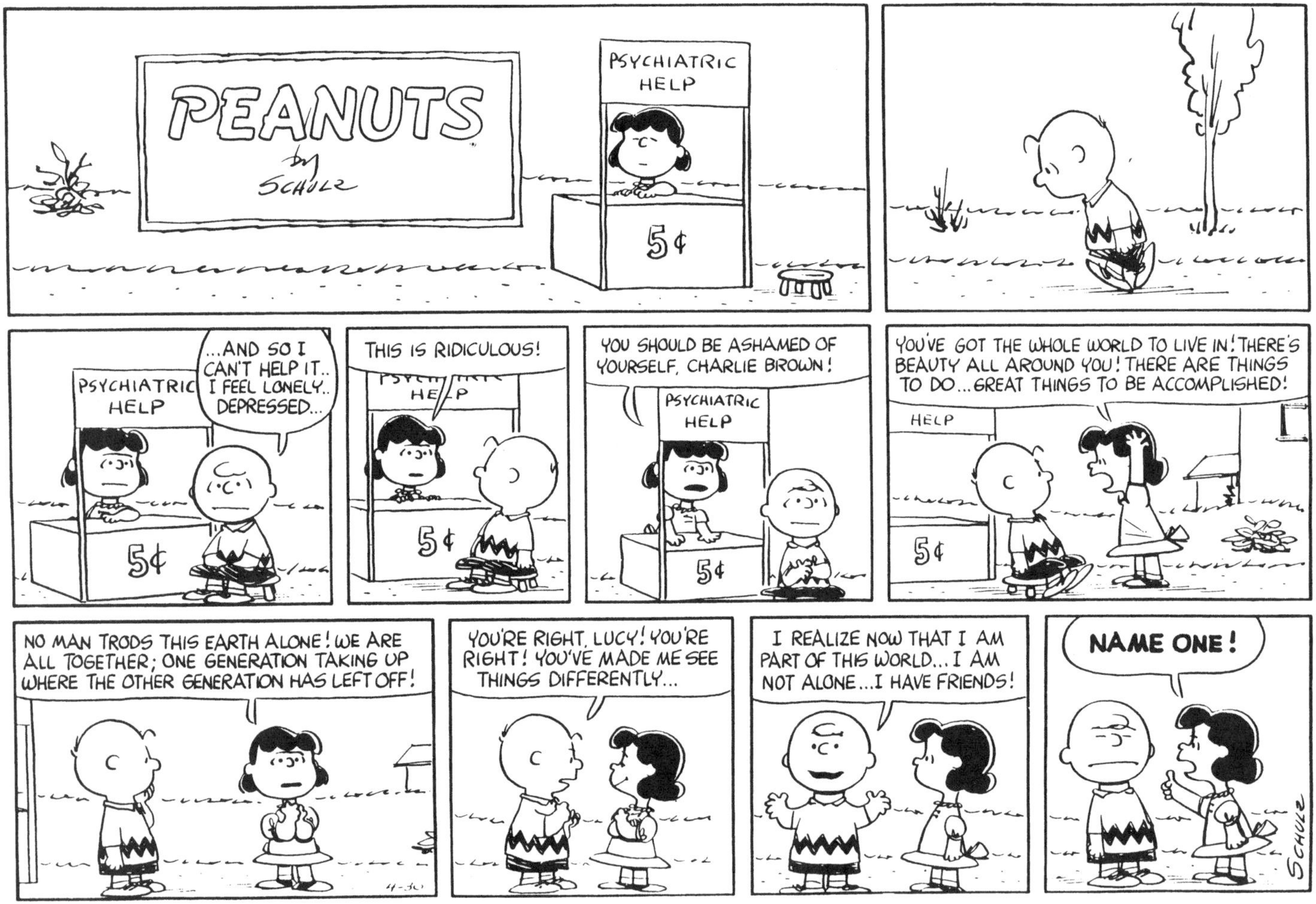
PEANUTS
by SCHULZ
PSYCHIATRIC HELP
5¢
PSYCHIATRIC HELP
...AND SO I CAN'T HELP IT.. I FEEL LONELY.. DEPRESSED...
5¢
THIS IS RIDICULOUS!
5¢
YOU SHOULD BE ASHAMED OF YOURSELF, CHARLIE BROWN!
PSYCHIATRIC HELP
5¢
YOU'VE GOT THE WHOLE WORLD TO LIVE IN! THERE'S BEAUTY ALL AROUND YOU! THERE ARE THINGS TO DO...GREAT THINGS TO BE ACCOMPLISHED!
HELP
5¢
NO MAN TRODS THIS EARTH ALONE! WE ARE ALL TOGETHER; ONE GENERATION TAKING UP WHERE THE OTHER GENERATION HAS LEFT OFF!
YOU'RE RIGHT, LUCY! YOU'RE RIGHT! YOU'VE MADE ME SEE THINGS DIFFERENTLY...
I REALIZE NOW THAT I AM PART OF THIS WORLD... I AM NOT ALONE...I HAVE FRIENDS!
NAME ONE!
SCHULZ

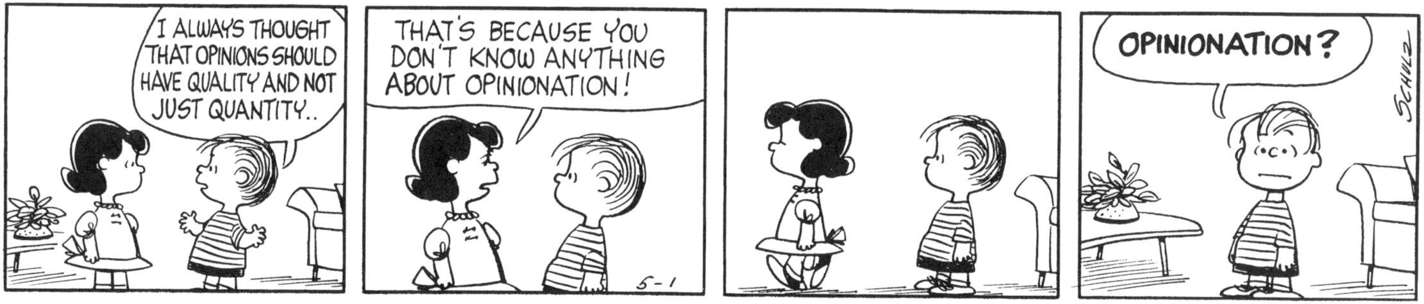
I ALWAYS THOUGHT THAT OPINIONS SHOULD HAVE QUALITY AND NOT JUST QUANTITY..
THAT'S BECAUSE YOU DON'T KNOW ANYTHING ABOUT OPINIONATION!
OPINIONATION?
SCHULZ

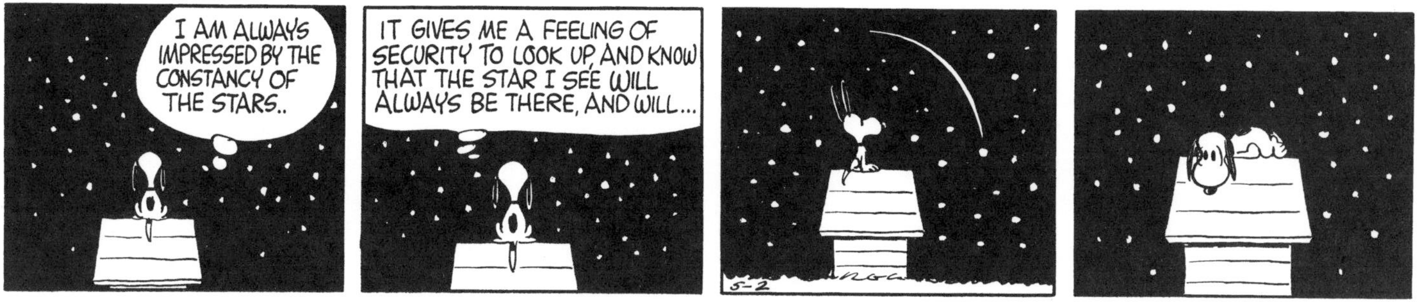
I AM ALWAYS IMPRESSED BY THE CONSTANCY OF THE STARS..
IT GIVES ME A FEELING OF SECURITY TO LOOK UP, AND KNOW THAT THE STAR I SEE WILL ALWAYS BE THERE, AND WILL...

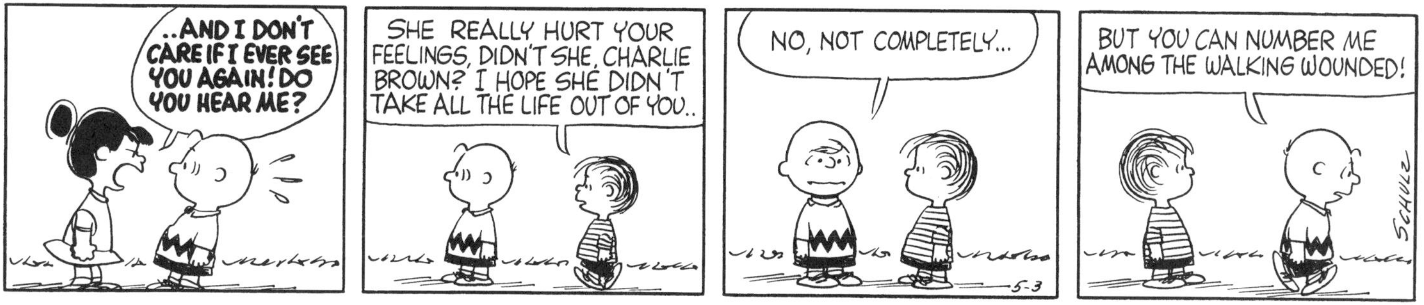
..AND I DON'T CARE IF I EVER SEE YOU AGAIN! DO YOU HEAR ME?
SHE REALLY HURT YOUR FEELINGS, DIDN'T SHE, CHARLIE BROWN? I HOPE SHE DIDN'T TAKE ALL THE LIFE OUT OF YOU..
NO, NOT COMPLETELY...
BUT YOU CAN NUMBER ME AMONG THE WALKING WOUNDED!
SCHULZ

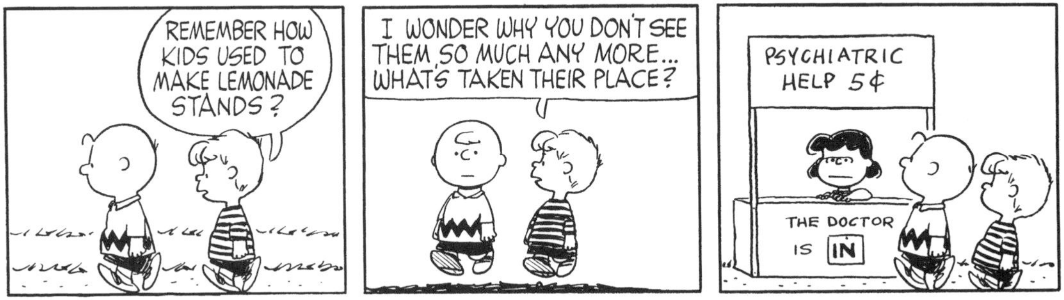
REMEMBER HOW KIDS USED TO MAKE LEMONADE STANDS?
I WONDER WHY YOU DON'T SEE THEM SO MUCH ANY MORE... WHAT'S TAKEN THEIR PLACE?
PSYCHIATRIC HELP 5¢
THE DOCTOR IS IN
NOW YOU KNOW!
SCHULZ
5-4

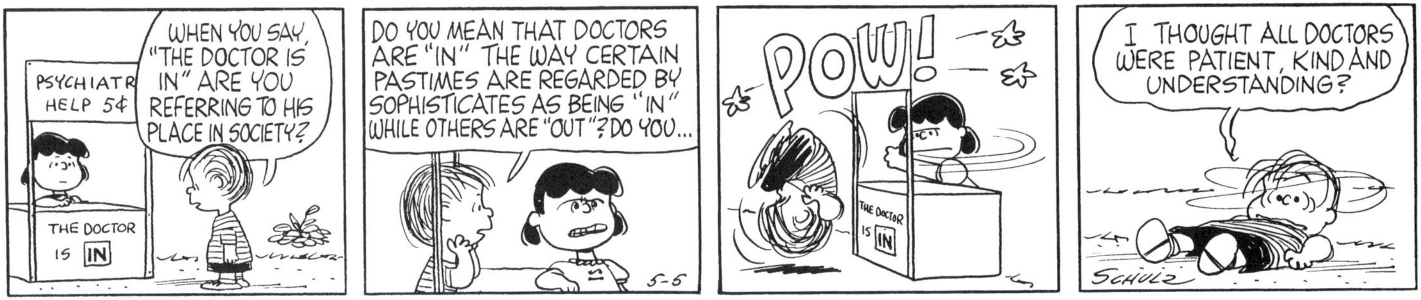
PSYCHIATR HELP 5¢
THE DOCTOR IS IN
WHEN YOU SAY, "THE DOCTOR IS IN" ARE YOU REFERRING TO HIS PLACE IN SOCIETY?
DO YOU MEAN THAT DOCTORS ARE "IN" THE WAY CERTAIN PASTIMES ARE REGARDED BY SOPHISTICATES AS BEING "IN" WHILE OTHERS ARE "OUT"? DO YOU...
5-5
POW!
THE DOCTOR IS IN
I THOUGHT ALL DOCTORS WERE PATIENT, KIND AND UNDERSTANDING?
SCHULZ

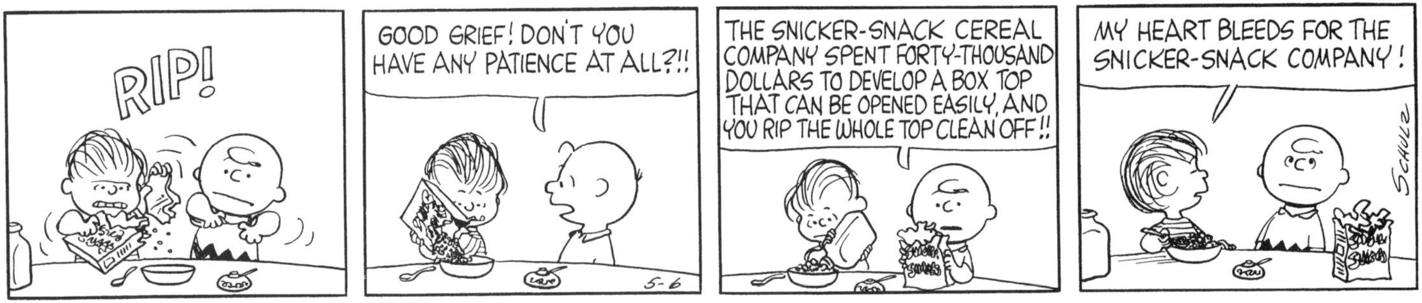
RIP!
GOOD GRIEF! DON'T YOU HAVE ANY PATIENCE AT ALL?!!
5-6
THE SNICKER-SNACK CEREAL COMPANY SPENT FORTY-THOUSAND DOLLARS TO DEVELOP A BOX TOP THAT CAN BE OPENED EASILY, AND YOU RIP THE WHOLE TOP CLEAN OFF!!
MY HEART BLEEDS FOR THE SNICKER-SNACK COMPANY!
SCHULZ

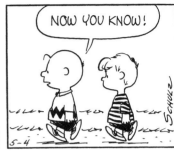

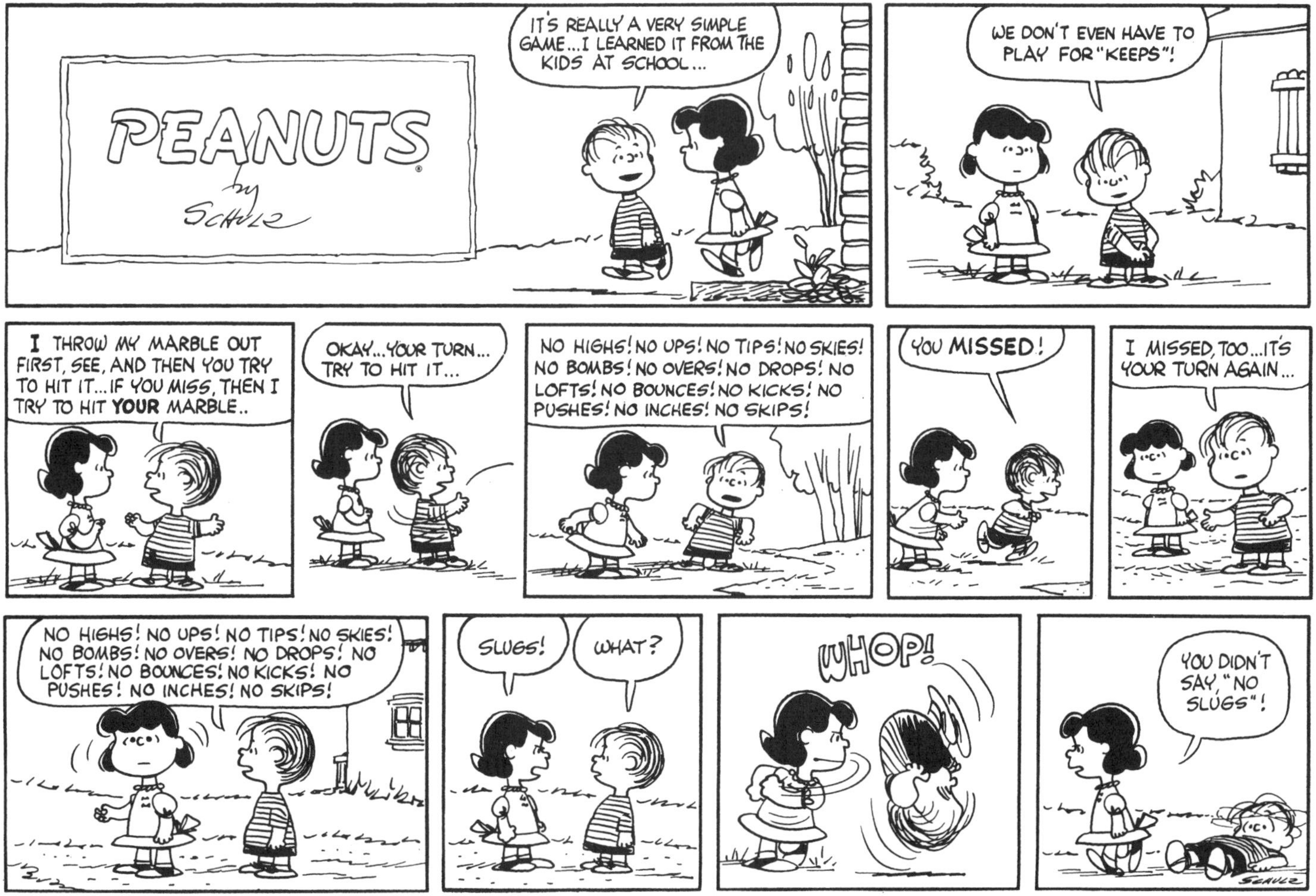
PEANUTS
by SCHULZ
IT'S REALLY A VERY SIMPLE GAME...I LEARNED IT FROM THE KIDS AT SCHOOL...
WE DON'T EVEN HAVE TO PLAY FOR "KEEPS"!
I THROW MY MARBLE OUT FIRST, SEE, AND THEN YOU TRY TO HIT IT...IF YOU MISS, THEN I TRY TO HIT YOUR MARBLE..
OKAY...YOUR TURN... TRY TO HIT IT...
NO HIGHS! NO UPS! NO TIPS! NO SKIES! NO BOMBS! NO OVERS! NO DROPS! NO LOFTS! NO BOUNCES! NO KICKS! NO PUSHES! NO INCHES! NO SKIPS!
YOU MISSED!
I MISSED, TOO...IT'S YOUR TURN AGAIN...
NO HIGHS! NO UPS! NO TIPS! NO SKIES! NO BOMBS! NO OVERS! NO DROPS! NO LOFTS! NO BOUNCES! NO KICKS! NO PUSHES! NO INCHES! NO SKIPS!
SLUGS!
WHAT?
WHOP!
YOU DIDN'T SAY, "NO SLUGS"!
SCHULZ

GET ON YOUR MARK, GET SET....

GO!!

5-8

HOW'S THAT FOR SPEED?

?

HE'S BACK ALREADY!

MY DAD IS A BETTER BOWLER THAN YOUR DAD!

HE HAS A 185 AVERAGE IN HIS MONDAY NIGHT LEAGUE, A 170 AVERAGE IN HIS THURSDAY NIGHT LEAGUE...

5-9

AND A 204 AVERAGE IN HIS FRIDAY NIGHT LEAGUE!

MY DAD STAYS HOME NIGHTS!

I DREAMED ABOUT YOU LAST NIGHT, SCHROEDER..

I DREAMED THAT YOU GAVE UP THIS STUPID PIANO, AND WENT TO TRADE SCHOOL TO LEARN HOW TO MAKE A LIVING SO YOU COULD SUPPORT ME AFTER WE GOT MARRIED!

THE ONLY WAY I WOULD EVER MARRY YOU WOULD BE IF YOU WERE THE LAST GIRL ON EARTH, AND IN THAT CASE ALL THE TRADE SCHOOLS WOULD PROBABLY BE GONE, TOO!

5/10

I'LL HAVE TO ADMIT THAT SOUNDS LOGICAL!

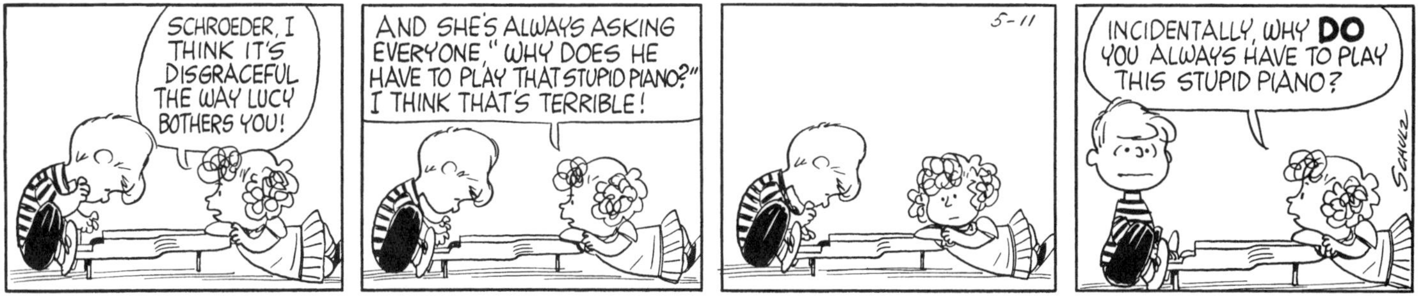
SCHROEDER, I THINK IT'S DISGRACEFUL THE WAY LUCY BOTHERS YOU!
AND SHE'S ALWAYS ASKING EVERYONE, "WHY DOES HE HAVE TO PLAY THAT STUPID PIANO?" I THINK THAT'S TERRIBLE!
5-11
INCIDENTALLY, WHY **DO** YOU ALWAYS HAVE TO PLAY THIS STUPID PIANO?
SCHULZ

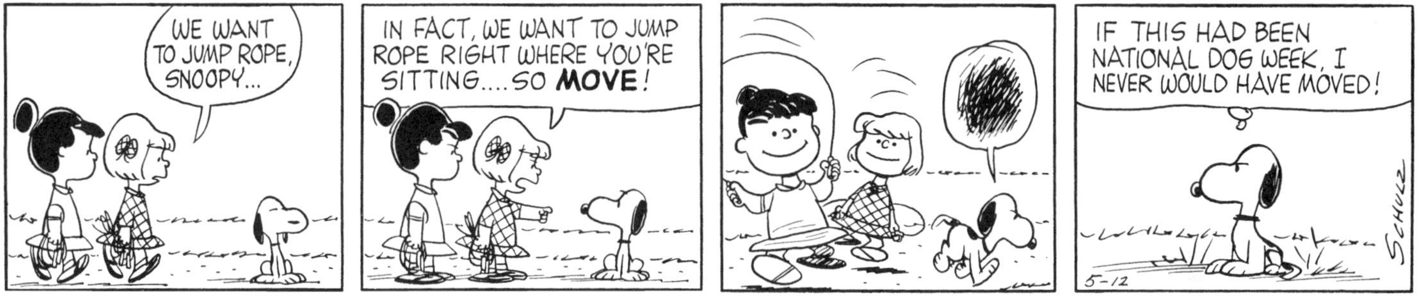
WE WANT TO JUMP ROPE, SNOOPY...
IN FACT, WE WANT TO JUMP ROPE RIGHT WHERE YOU'RE SITTING....SO **MOVE**!
IF THIS HAD BEEN NATIONAL DOG WEEK, I NEVER WOULD HAVE MOVED!
SCHULZ
5-12

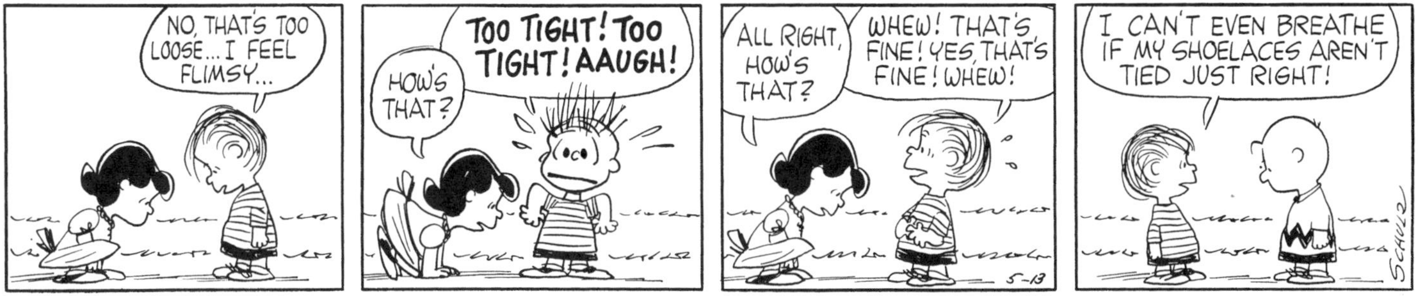
NO, THAT'S TOO LOOSE...I FEEL FLIMSY...
HOW'S THAT?
TOO TIGHT! TOO TIGHT! AAUGH!
ALL RIGHT, HOW'S THAT?
WHEW! THAT'S FINE! YES, THAT'S FINE! WHEW!
5-13
I CAN'T EVEN BREATHE IF MY SHOELACES AREN'T TIED JUST RIGHT!
SCHULZ

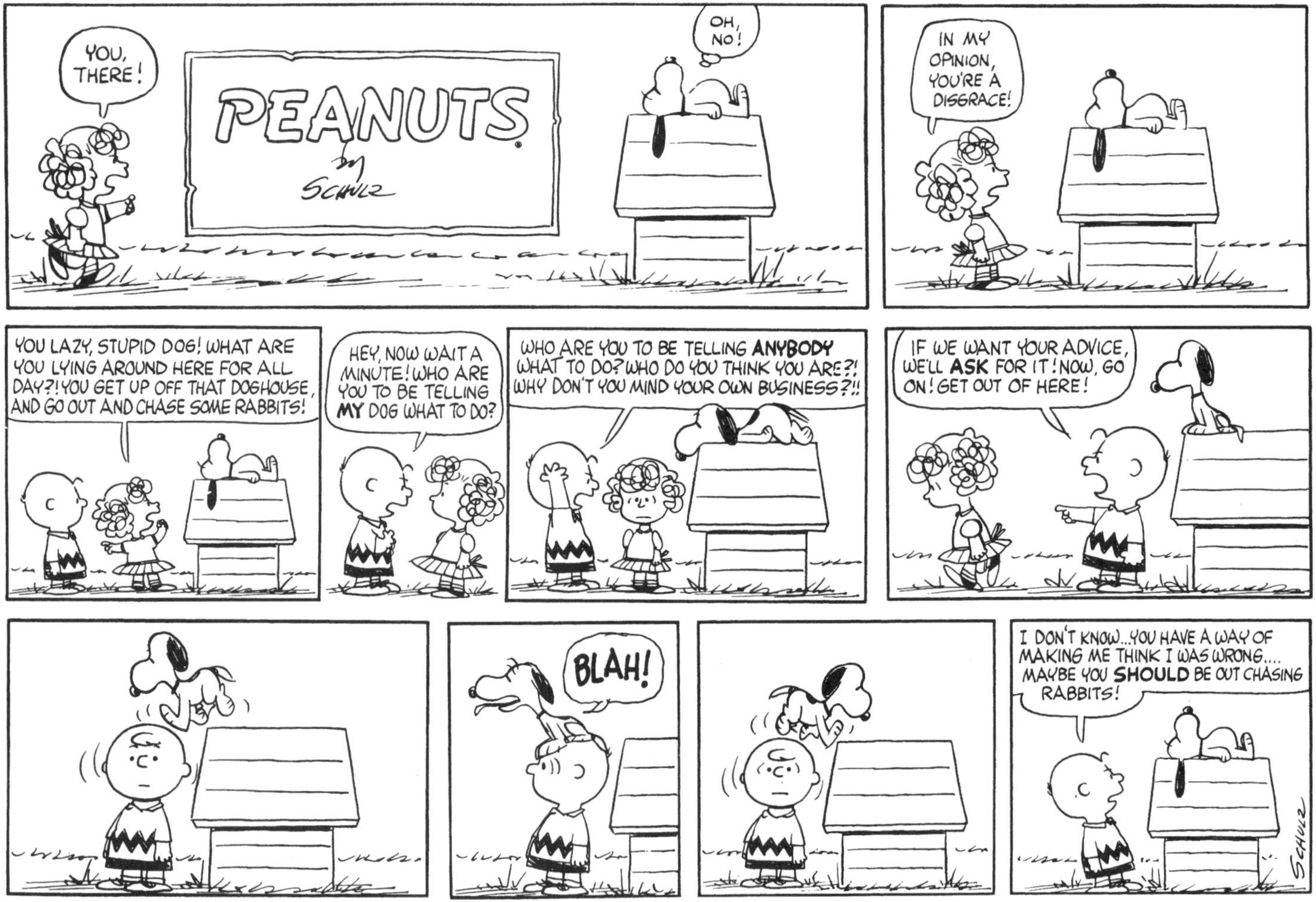
YOU, THERE!
PEANUTS
by SCHULZ
OH, NO!
IN MY OPINION, YOU'RE A DISGRACE!
YOU LAZY, STUPID DOG! WHAT ARE YOU LYING AROUND HERE FOR ALL DAY?! YOU GET UP OFF THAT DOGHOUSE, AND GO OUT AND CHASE SOME RABBITS!
HEY, NOW WAIT A MINUTE! WHO ARE YOU TO BE TELLING **MY** DOG WHAT TO DO?
WHO ARE YOU TO BE TELLING **ANYBODY** WHAT TO DO? WHO DO YOU THINK YOU ARE?! WHY DON'T YOU MIND YOUR OWN BUSINESS?!!
IF WE WANT YOUR ADVICE, WE'LL **ASK** FOR IT! NOW, GO ON! GET OUT OF HERE!
BLAH!
I DON'T KNOW...YOU HAVE A WAY OF MAKING ME THINK I WAS WRONG.... MAYBE YOU **SHOULD** BE OUT CHASING RABBITS!
SCHULZ

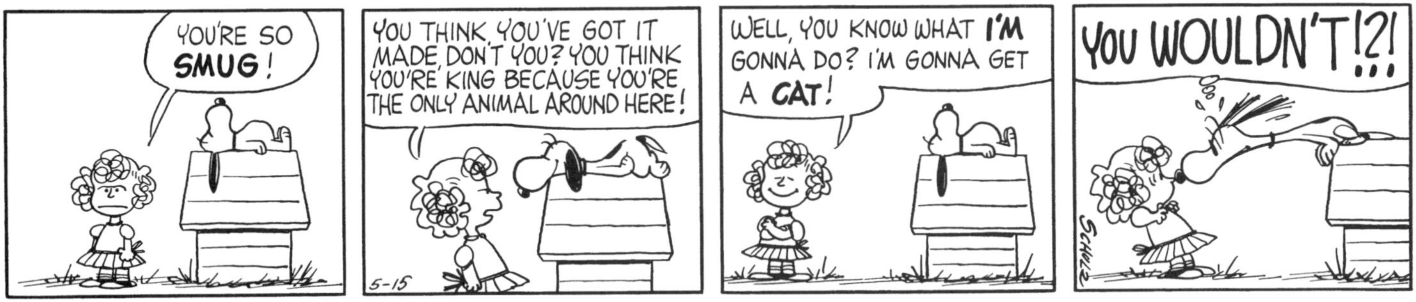
YOU'RE SO SMUG!
YOU THINK YOU'VE GOT IT MADE, DON'T YOU? YOU THINK YOU'RE KING BECAUSE YOU'RE THE ONLY ANIMAL AROUND HERE!
5-15
WELL, YOU KNOW WHAT I'M GONNA DO? I'M GONNA GET A CAT!
YOU WOULDN'T!?!
SCHULZ

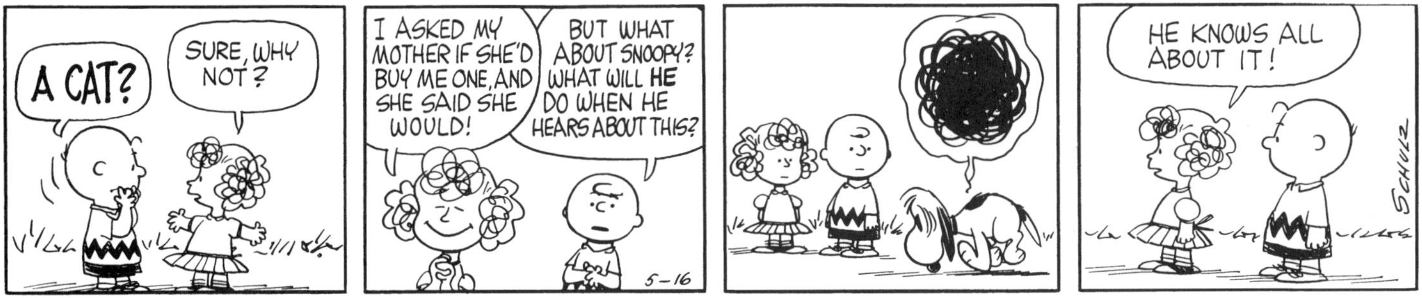
A CAT?
SURE, WHY NOT?
I ASKED MY MOTHER IF SHE'D BUY ME ONE, AND SHE SAID SHE WOULD!
BUT WHAT ABOUT SNOOPY? WHAT WILL HE DO WHEN HE HEARS ABOUT THIS?
5-16
HE KNOWS ALL ABOUT IT!
SCHULZ

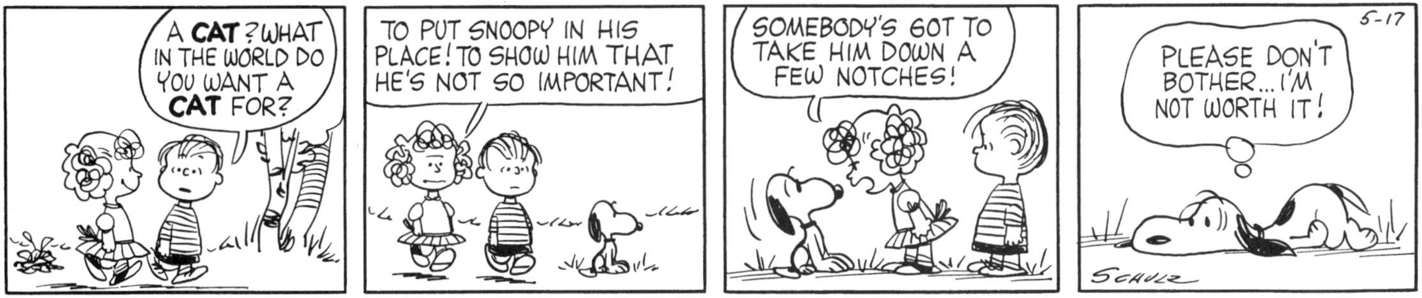
A CAT? WHAT IN THE WORLD DO YOU WANT A CAT FOR?
TO PUT SNOOPY IN HIS PLACE! TO SHOW HIM THAT HE'S NOT SO IMPORTANT!
SOMEBODY'S GOT TO TAKE HIM DOWN A FEW NOTCHES!
5-17
PLEASE DON'T BOTHER... I'M NOT WORTH IT!
SCHULZ

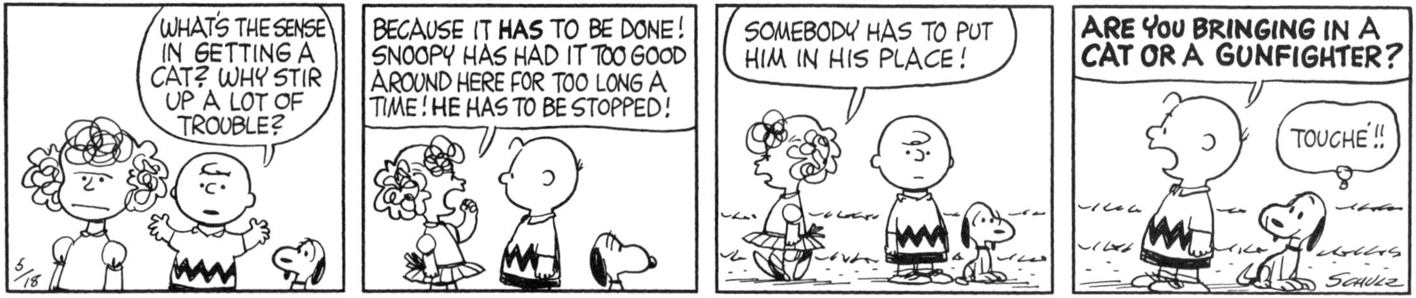
WHAT'S THE SENSE IN GETTING A CAT? WHY STIR UP A LOT OF TROUBLE?
5/18
BECAUSE IT HAS TO BE DONE! SNOOPY HAS HAD IT TOO GOOD AROUND HERE FOR TOO LONG A TIME! HE HAS TO BE STOPPED!
SOMEBODY HAS TO PUT HIM IN HIS PLACE!
ARE YOU BRINGING IN A CAT OR A GUNFIGHTER?
TOUCHÉ!!
SCHULZ

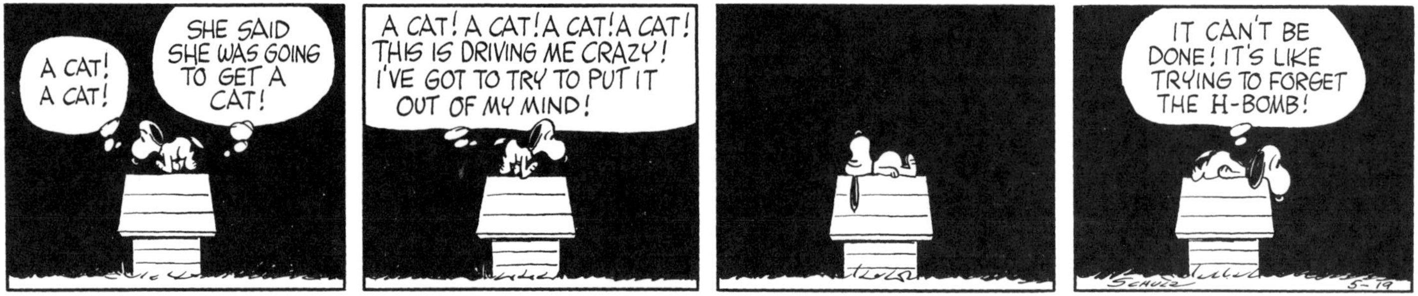
A CAT! A CAT!
SHE SAID SHE WAS GOING TO GET A CAT!
A CAT! A CAT! A CAT! A CAT! THIS IS DRIVING ME CRAZY! I'VE GOT TO TRY TO PUT IT OUT OF MY MIND!
IT CAN'T BE DONE! IT'S LIKE TRYING TO FORGET THE H-BOMB!
SCHULZ
5-19

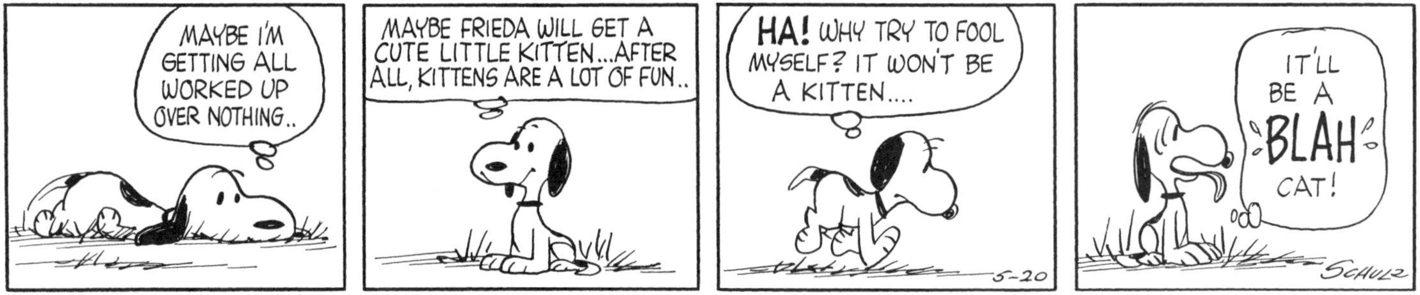
MAYBE I'M GETTING ALL WORKED UP OVER NOTHING..
MAYBE FRIEDA WILL GET A CUTE LITTLE KITTEN...AFTER ALL, KITTENS ARE A LOT OF FUN..
HA! WHY TRY TO FOOL MYSELF? IT WON'T BE A KITTEN....
5-20
IT'LL BE A BLAH CAT!
SCHULZ

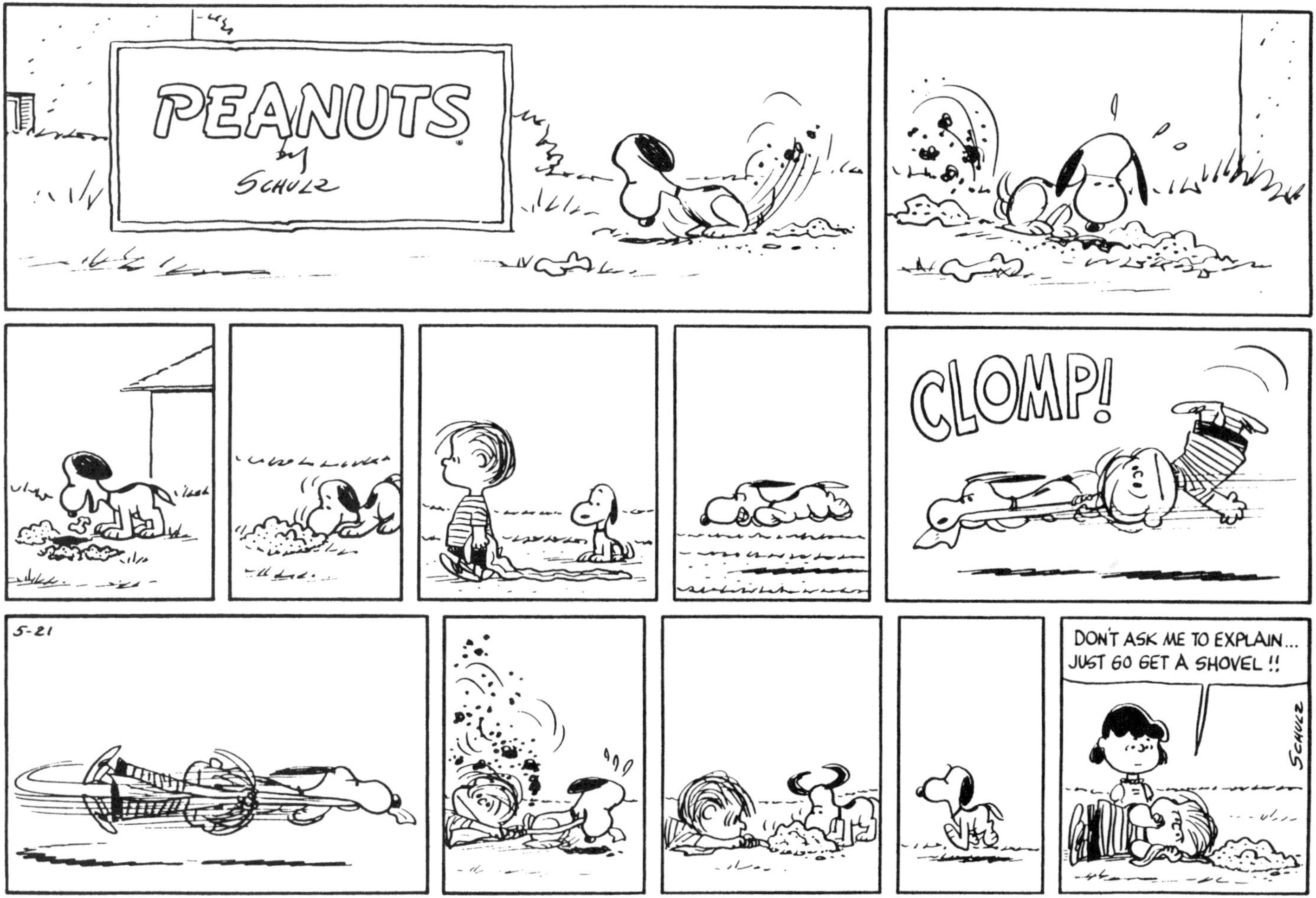
PEANUTS
by
SCHULZ
CLOMP!
5-21
DON'T ASK ME TO EXPLAIN...
JUST GO GET A SHOVEL !!
SCHULZ

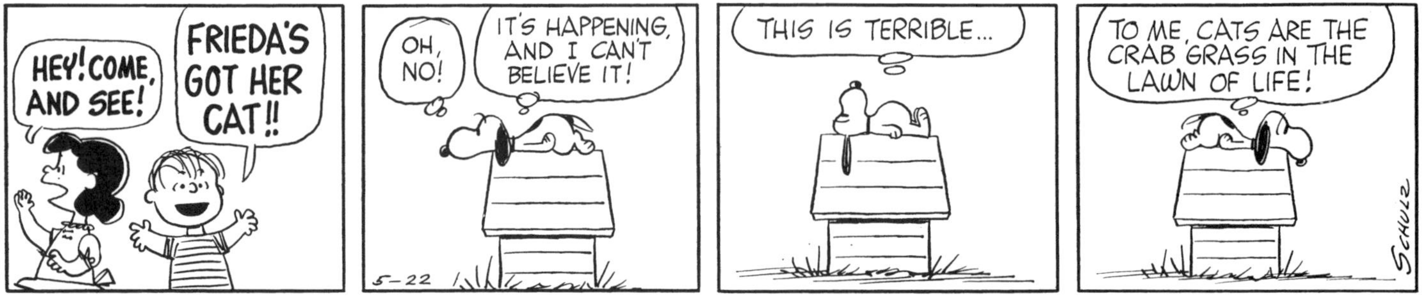
HEY! COME, AND SEE!
FRIEDA'S GOT HER CAT!!
OH, NO!
IT'S HAPPENING, AND I CAN'T BELIEVE IT!
5-22
THIS IS TERRIBLE...
TO ME, CATS ARE THE CRAB GRASS IN THE LAWN OF LIFE!
SCHULZ

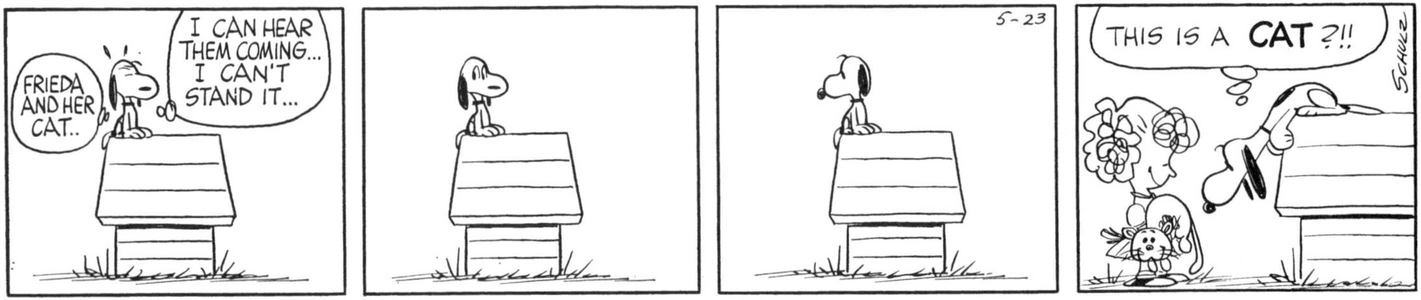
FRIEDA AND HER CAT..
I CAN HEAR THEM COMING... I CAN'T STAND IT...
5-23
THIS IS A CAT?!!
SCHULZ

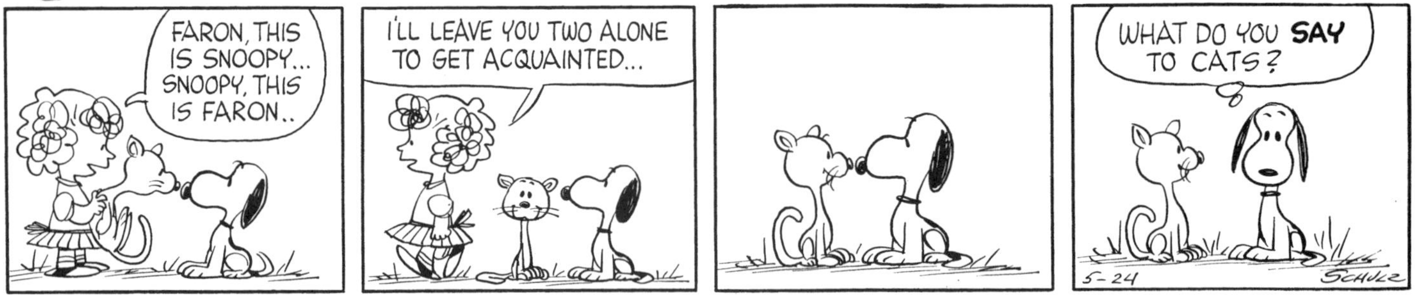
FARON, THIS IS SNOOPY... SNOOPY, THIS IS FARON..
I'LL LEAVE YOU TWO ALONE TO GET ACQUAINTED...
WHAT DO YOU SAY TO CATS?
5-24
SCHULZ

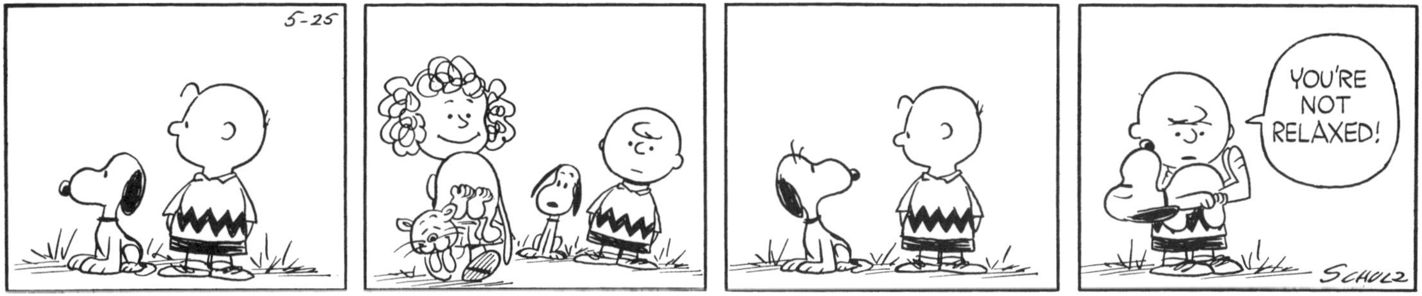
5-25
YOU'RE NOT RELAXED!
SCHULZ

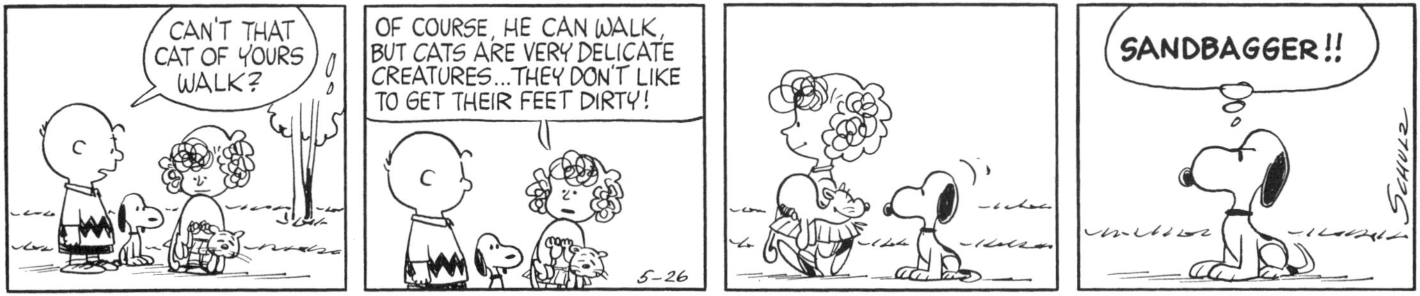
CAN'T THAT CAT OF YOURS WALK?
OF COURSE, HE CAN WALK, BUT CATS ARE VERY DELICATE CREATURES...THEY DON'T LIKE TO GET THEIR FEET DIRTY!
5-26
SANDBAGGER!!
SCHULZ

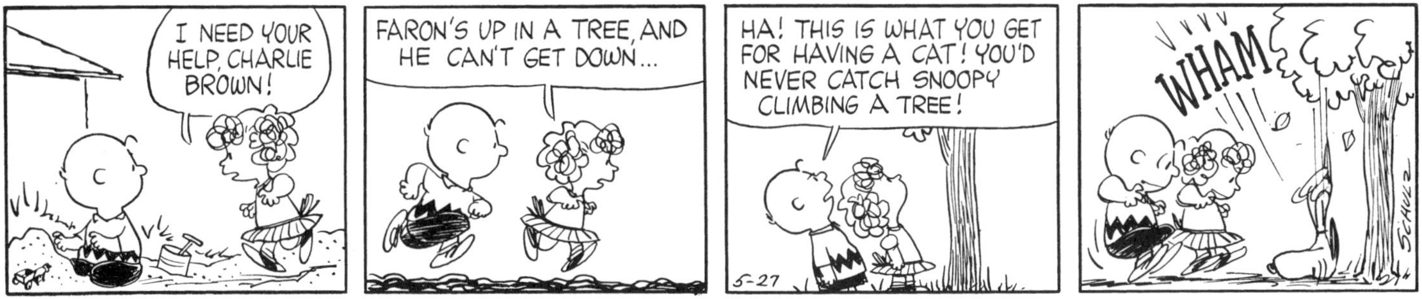
I NEED YOUR HELP, CHARLIE BROWN!
FARON'S UP IN A TREE, AND HE CAN'T GET DOWN...
HA! THIS IS WHAT YOU GET FOR HAVING A CAT! YOU'D NEVER CATCH SNOOPY CLIMBING A TREE!
5-27
WHAM
SCHULZ

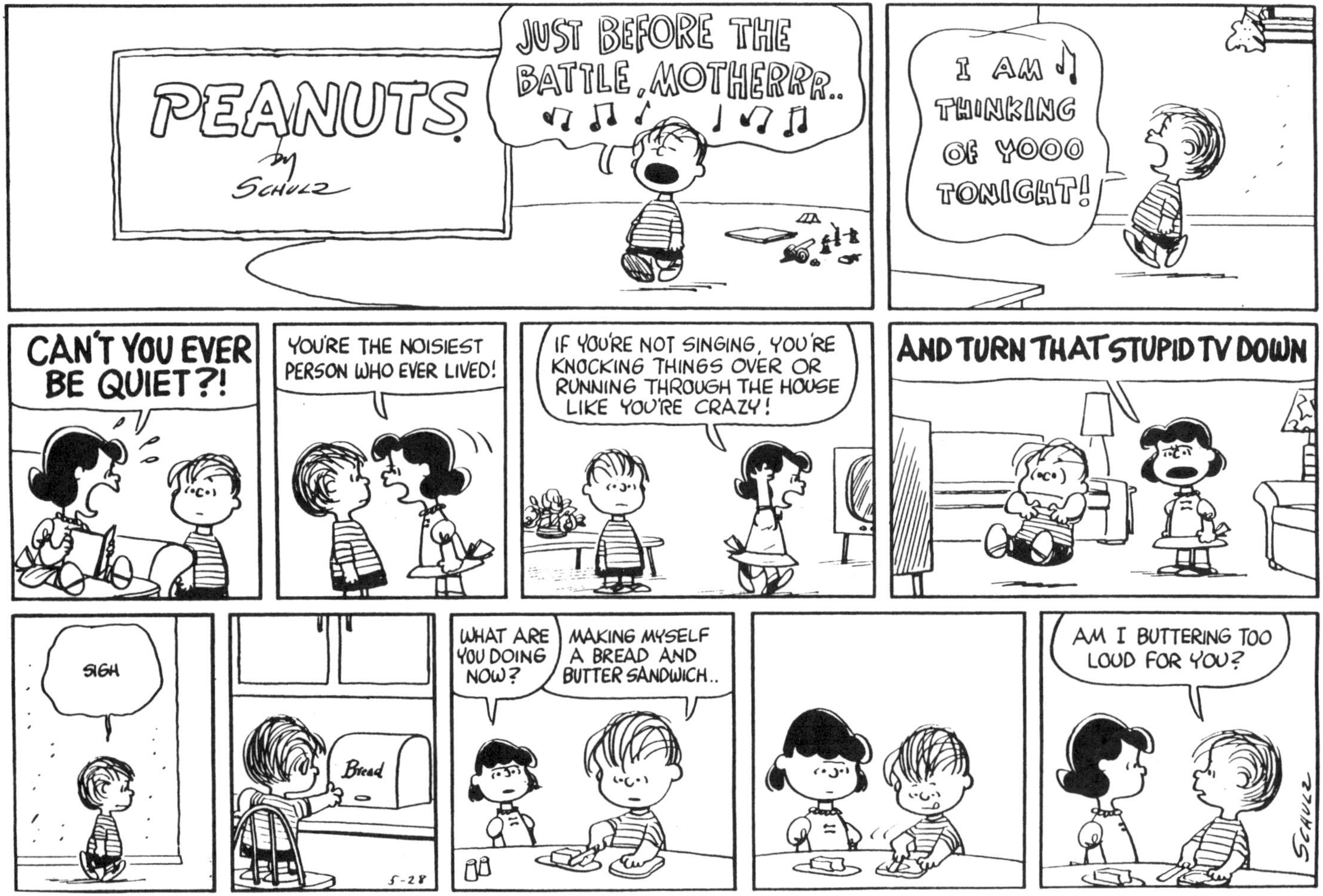
PEANUTS
by Schulz
JUST BEFORE THE BATTLE, MOTHERRRR..
I AM THINKING OF YOOO TONIGHT!
CAN'T YOU EVER BE QUIET?!
YOU'RE THE NOISIEST PERSON WHO EVER LIVED!
IF YOU'RE NOT SINGING, YOU'RE KNOCKING THINGS OVER OR RUNNING THROUGH THE HOUSE LIKE YOU'RE CRAZY!
AND TURN THAT STUPID TV DOWN
SIGH
Bread
5-28
WHAT ARE YOU DOING NOW?
MAKING MYSELF A BREAD AND BUTTER SANDWICH..
AM I BUTTERING TOO LOUD FOR YOU?
SCHULZ

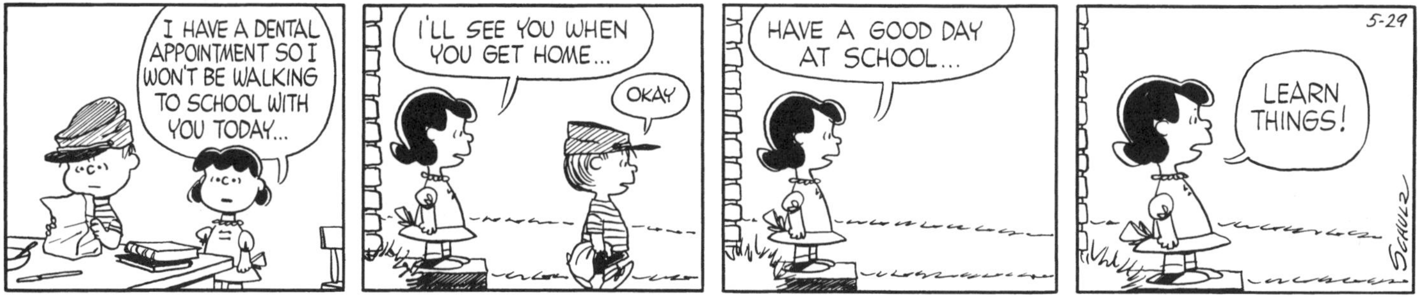
I HAVE A DENTAL APPOINTMENT SO I WON'T BE WALKING TO SCHOOL WITH YOU TODAY...
I'LL SEE YOU WHEN YOU GET HOME...
OKAY
HAVE A GOOD DAY AT SCHOOL...
5-29
LEARN THINGS!
SCHULZ

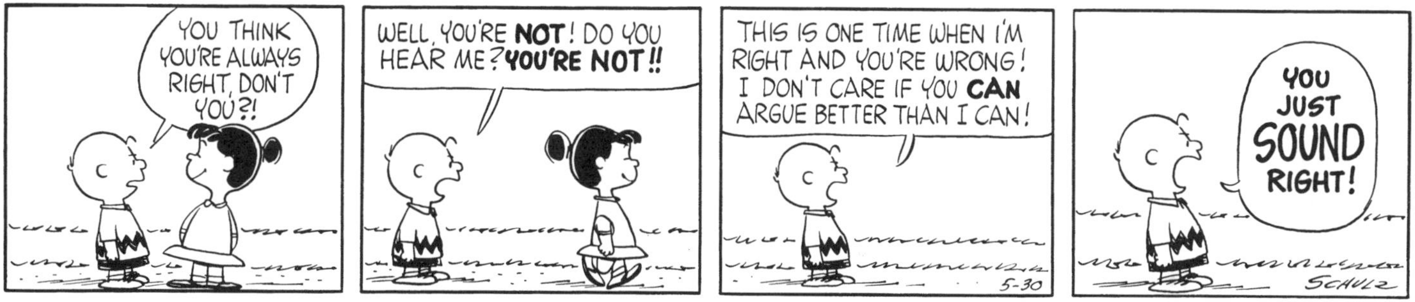
YOU THINK YOU'RE ALWAYS RIGHT, DON'T YOU?!
WELL, YOU'RE **NOT**! DO YOU HEAR ME? **YOU'RE NOT**!!
THIS IS ONE TIME WHEN I'M RIGHT AND YOU'RE WRONG! I DON'T CARE IF YOU **CAN** ARGUE BETTER THAN I CAN!
5-30
YOU JUST SOUND RIGHT!
SCHULZ

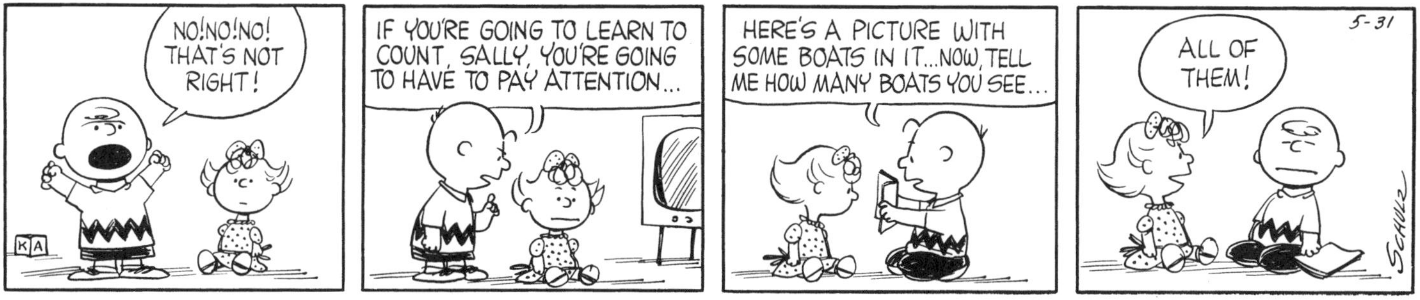
NO!NO!NO! THAT'S NOT RIGHT!
K A
IF YOU'RE GOING TO LEARN TO COUNT, SALLY, YOU'RE GOING TO HAVE TO PAY ATTENTION...
HERE'S A PICTURE WITH SOME BOATS IN IT...NOW, TELL ME HOW MANY BOATS YOU SEE...
5-31
ALL OF THEM!
SCHULZ

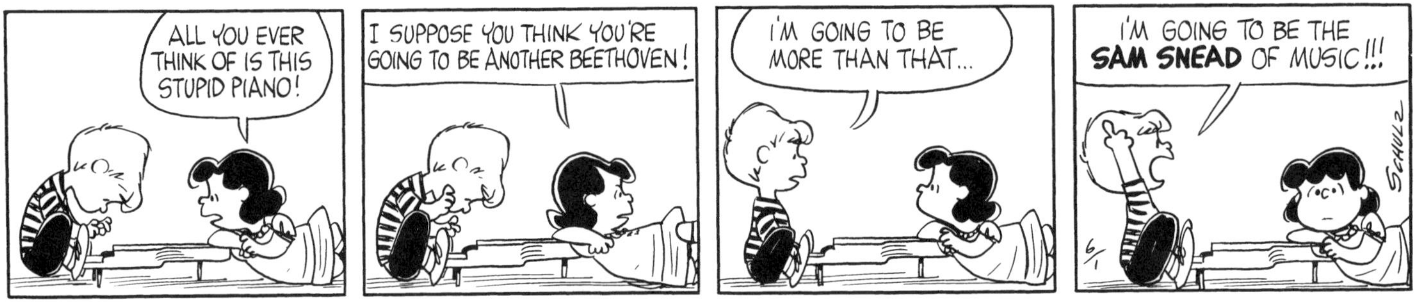
ALL YOU EVER THINK OF IS THIS STUPID PIANO!
I SUPPOSE YOU THINK YOU'RE GOING TO BE ANOTHER BEETHOVEN!
I'M GOING TO BE MORE THAN THAT...
I'M GOING TO BE THE **SAM SNEAD** OF MUSIC!!!
SCHULZ
6/1

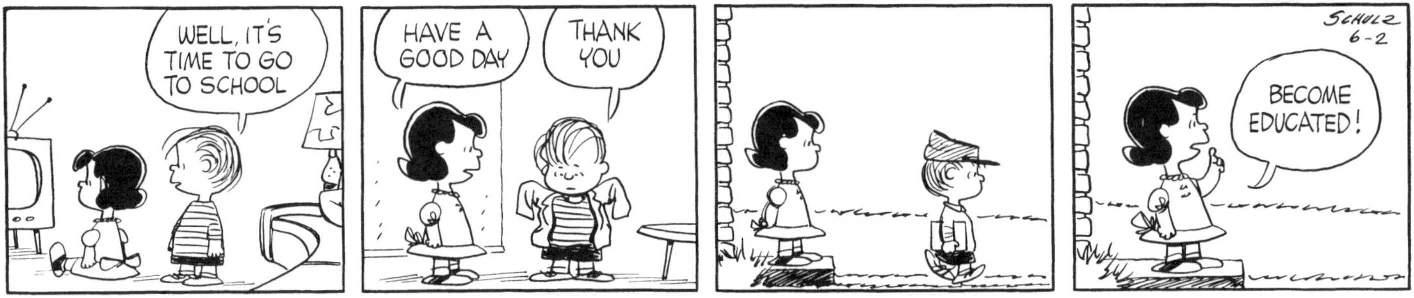
WELL, IT'S TIME TO GO TO SCHOOL
HAVE A GOOD DAY
THANK YOU
SCHULZ
6-2
BECOME EDUCATED!

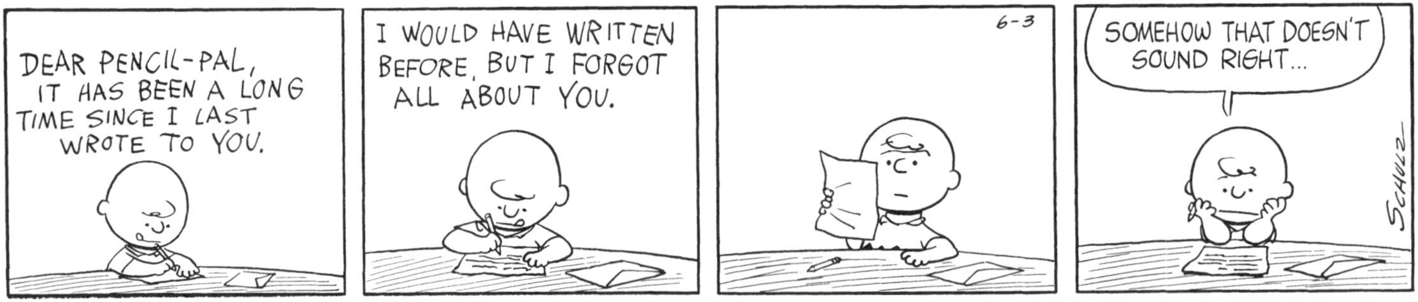
DEAR PENCIL-PAL, IT HAS BEEN A LONG TIME SINCE I LAST WROTE TO YOU.
I WOULD HAVE WRITTEN BEFORE, BUT I FORGOT ALL ABOUT YOU.
6-3
SOMEHOW THAT DOESN'T SOUND RIGHT...
SCHULZ

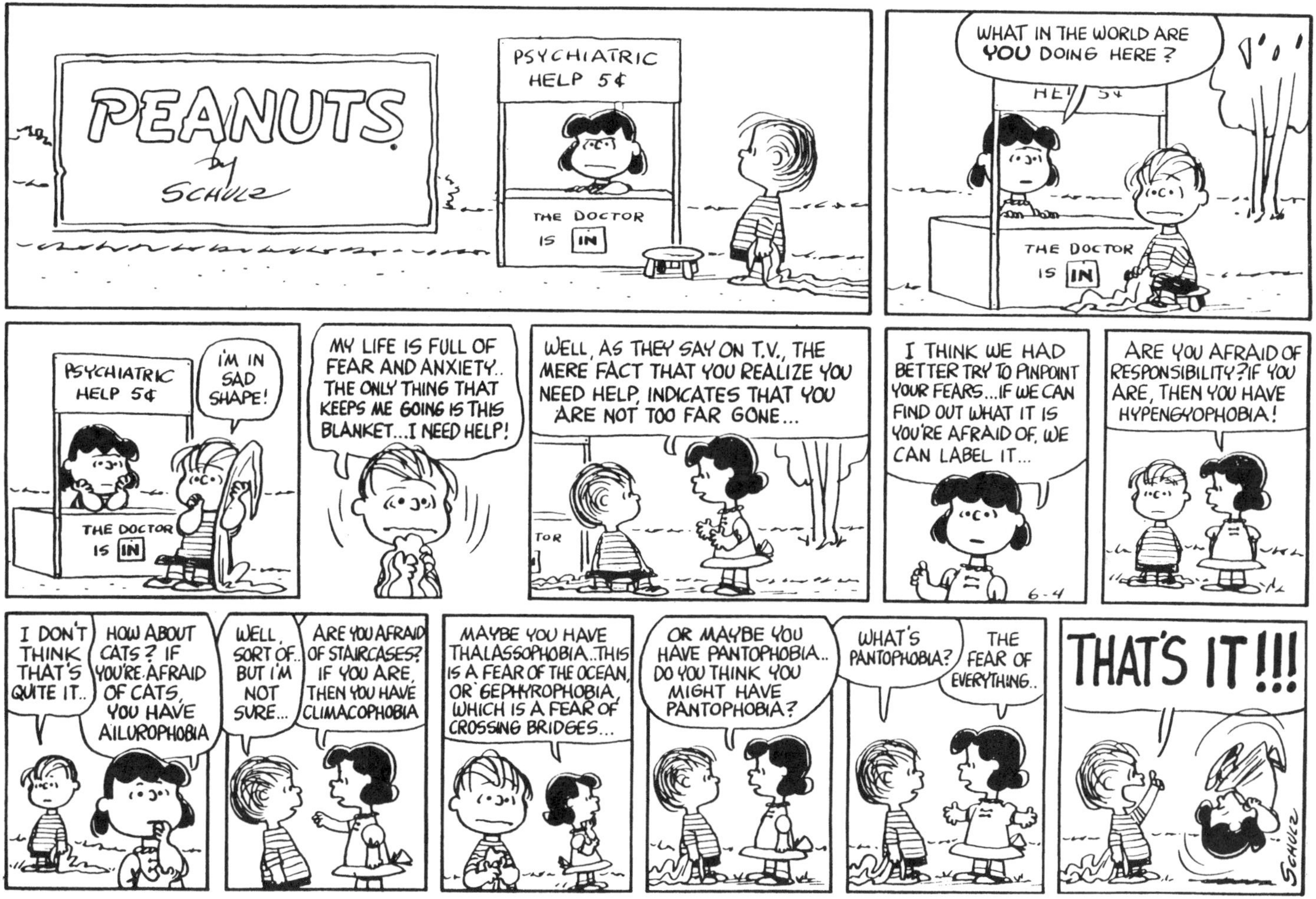
PEANUTS
by SCHULZ
PSYCHIATRIC HELP 5¢
THE DOCTOR IS IN
WHAT IN THE WORLD ARE YOU DOING HERE?
I'M IN SAD SHAPE!
MY LIFE IS FULL OF FEAR AND ANXIETY.. THE ONLY THING THAT KEEPS ME GOING IS THIS BLANKET...I NEED HELP!
WELL, AS THEY SAY ON T.V., THE MERE FACT THAT YOU REALIZE YOU NEED HELP, INDICATES THAT YOU ARE NOT TOO FAR GONE...
I THINK WE HAD BETTER TRY TO PINPOINT YOUR FEARS...IF WE CAN FIND OUT WHAT IT IS YOU'RE AFRAID OF, WE CAN LABEL IT...
6-4
ARE YOU AFRAID OF RESPONSIBILITY? IF YOU ARE, THEN YOU HAVE HYPENGYOPHOBIA!
I DON'T THINK THAT'S QUITE IT..
HOW ABOUT CATS? IF YOU'RE AFRAID OF CATS, YOU HAVE AILUROPHOBIA
WELL, SORT OF.. BUT I'M NOT SURE...
ARE YOU AFRAID OF STAIRCASES? IF YOU ARE, THEN YOU HAVE CLIMACOPHOBIA
MAYBE YOU HAVE THALASSOPHOBIA..THIS IS A FEAR OF THE OCEAN, OR GEPHYROPHOBIA, WHICH IS A FEAR OF CROSSING BRIDGES...
OR MAYBE YOU HAVE PANTOPHOBIA.. DO YOU THINK YOU MIGHT HAVE PANTOPHOBIA?
WHAT'S PANTOPHOBIA?
THE FEAR OF EVERYTHING..
THAT'S IT!!!
SCHULZ

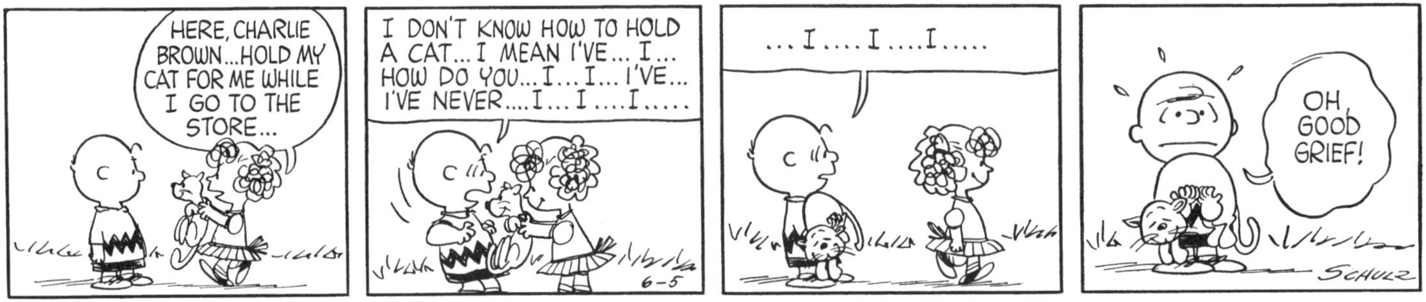
HERE, CHARLIE BROWN...HOLD MY CAT FOR ME WHILE I GO TO THE STORE...
I DON'T KNOW HOW TO HOLD A CAT... I MEAN I'VE... I... HOW DO YOU... I... I... I'VE... I'VE NEVER.... I... I .... I.....
6-5
... I .... I .... I .....
OH, GOOD GRIEF!
SCHULZ

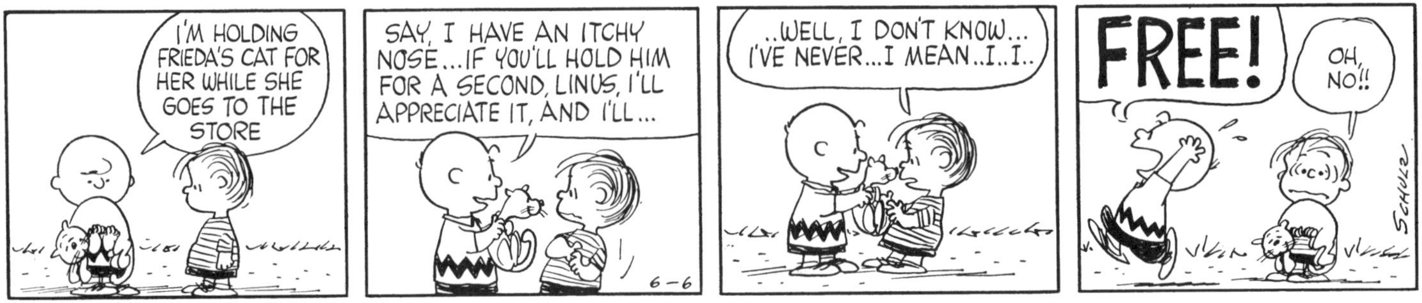
I'M HOLDING FRIEDA'S CAT FOR HER WHILE SHE GOES TO THE STORE
SAY, I HAVE AN ITCHY NOSE...IF YOU'LL HOLD HIM FOR A SECOND, LINUS, I'LL APPRECIATE IT, AND I'LL...
6-6
..WELL, I DON'T KNOW... I'VE NEVER...I MEAN..I..I..
FREE!
OH, NO!!
SCHULZ

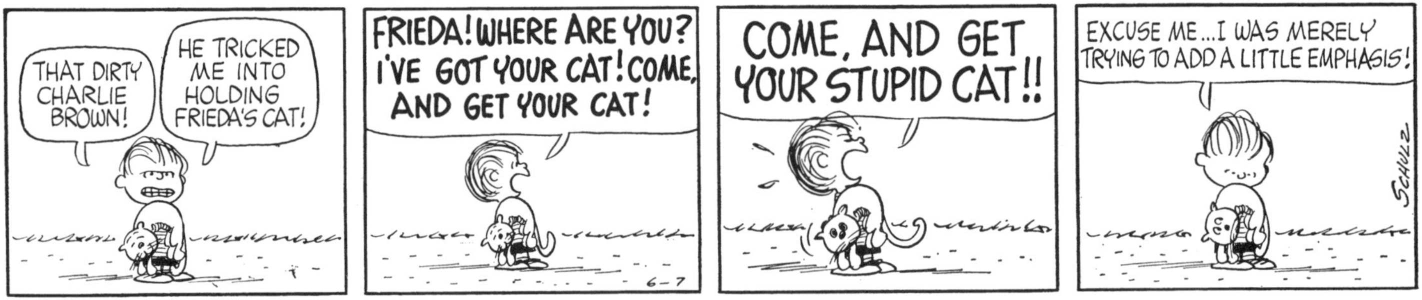
THAT DIRTY CHARLIE BROWN!
HE TRICKED ME INTO HOLDING FRIEDA'S CAT!
FRIEDA! WHERE ARE YOU? I'VE GOT YOUR CAT! COME, AND GET YOUR CAT!
6-7
COME, AND GET YOUR STUPID CAT!!
EXCUSE ME...I WAS MERELY TRYING TO ADD A LITTLE EMPHASIS!
SCHULZ

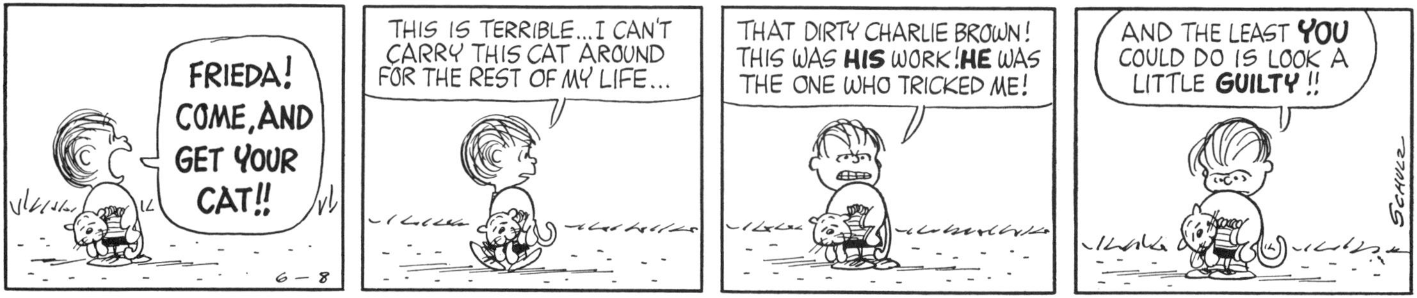
FRIEDA! COME, AND GET YOUR CAT!!
6-8
THIS IS TERRIBLE...I CAN'T CARRY THIS CAT AROUND FOR THE REST OF MY LIFE...
THAT DIRTY CHARLIE BROWN! THIS WAS **HIS** WORK! **HE** WAS THE ONE WHO TRICKED ME!
AND THE LEAST **YOU** COULD DO IS LOOK A LITTLE **GUILTY** !!
SCHULZ

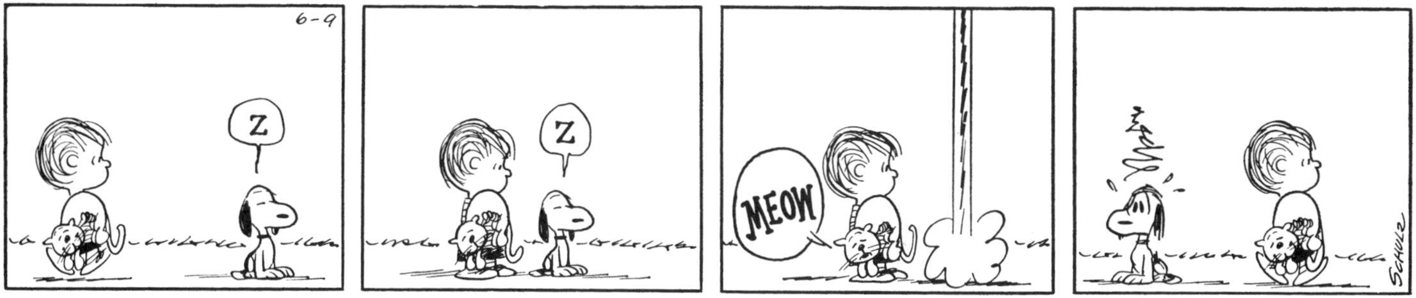
6-9
Z
Z
MEOW
SCHULZ

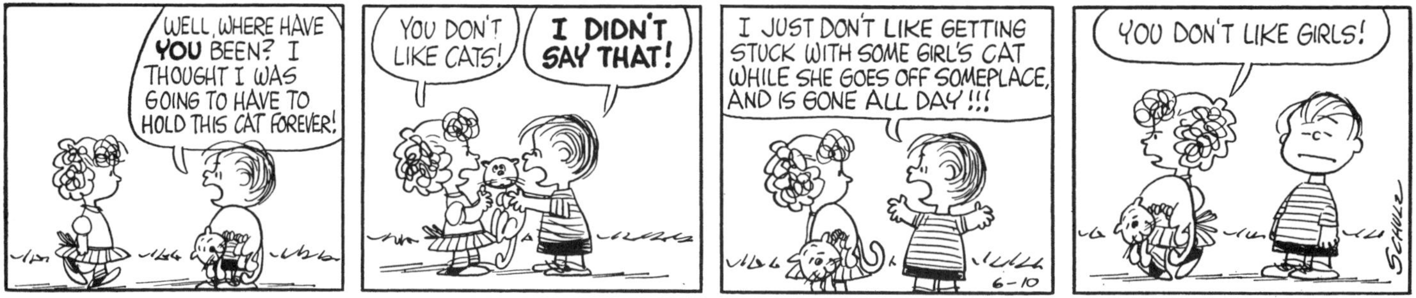
WELL, WHERE HAVE **YOU** BEEN? I THOUGHT I WAS GOING TO HAVE TO HOLD THIS CAT FOREVER!
YOU DON'T LIKE CATS!
I DIDN'T SAY THAT!
I JUST DON'T LIKE GETTING STUCK WITH SOME GIRL'S CAT WHILE SHE GOES OFF SOMEPLACE, AND IS GONE ALL DAY!!!
6-10
YOU DON'T LIKE GIRLS!
SCHULZ

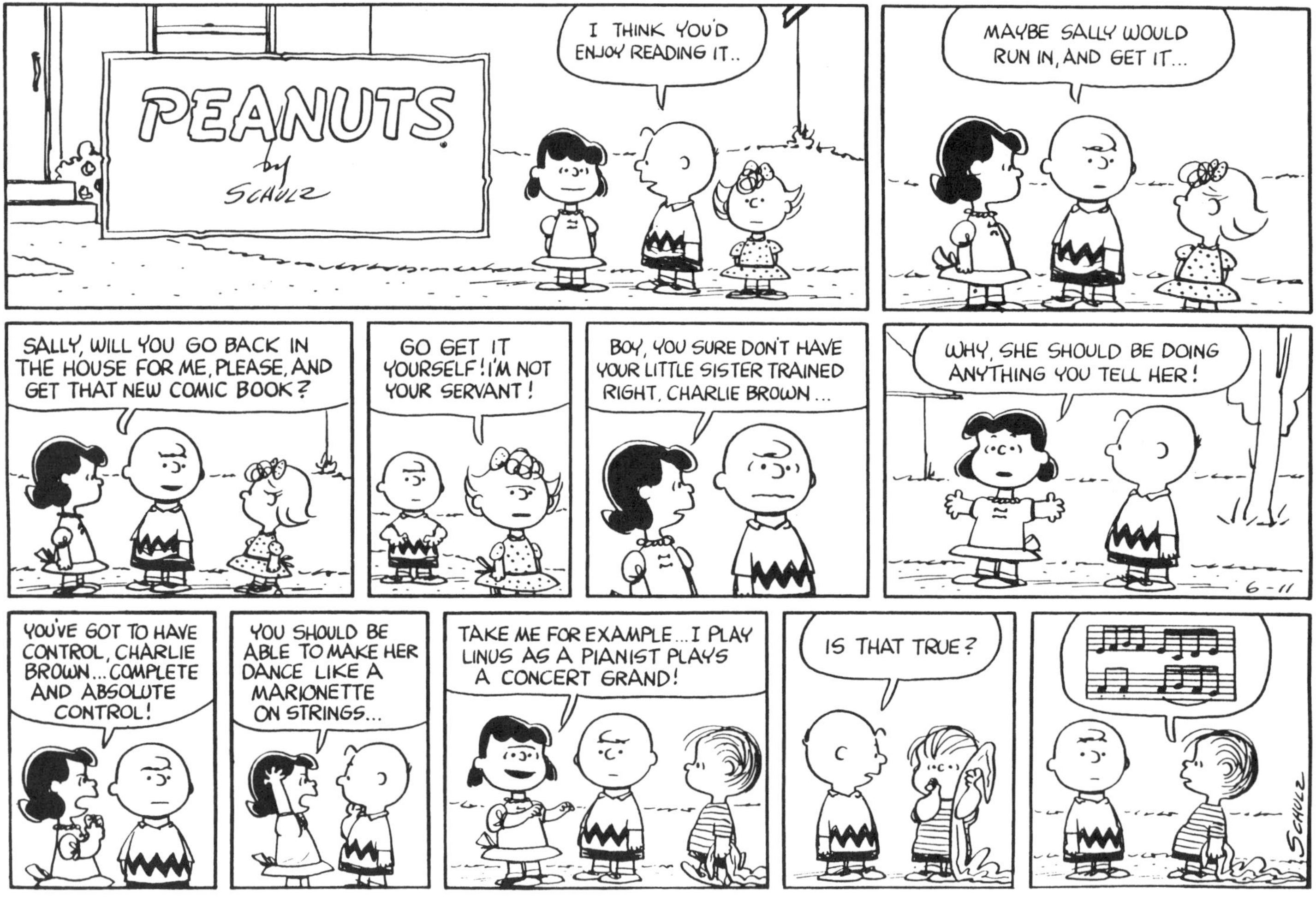
PEANUTS
by SCHULZ
I THINK YOU'D ENJOY READING IT..
MAYBE SALLY WOULD RUN IN, AND GET IT...
SALLY, WILL YOU GO BACK IN THE HOUSE FOR ME, PLEASE, AND GET THAT NEW COMIC BOOK?
GO GET IT YOURSELF! I'M NOT YOUR SERVANT!
BOY, YOU SURE DON'T HAVE YOUR LITTLE SISTER TRAINED RIGHT, CHARLIE BROWN...
WHY, SHE SHOULD BE DOING ANYTHING YOU TELL HER!
6-11
YOU'VE GOT TO HAVE CONTROL, CHARLIE BROWN...COMPLETE AND ABSOLUTE CONTROL!
YOU SHOULD BE ABLE TO MAKE HER DANCE LIKE A MARIONETTE ON STRINGS...
TAKE ME FOR EXAMPLE...I PLAY LINUS AS A PIANIST PLAYS A CONCERT GRAND!
IS THAT TRUE?
SCHULZ

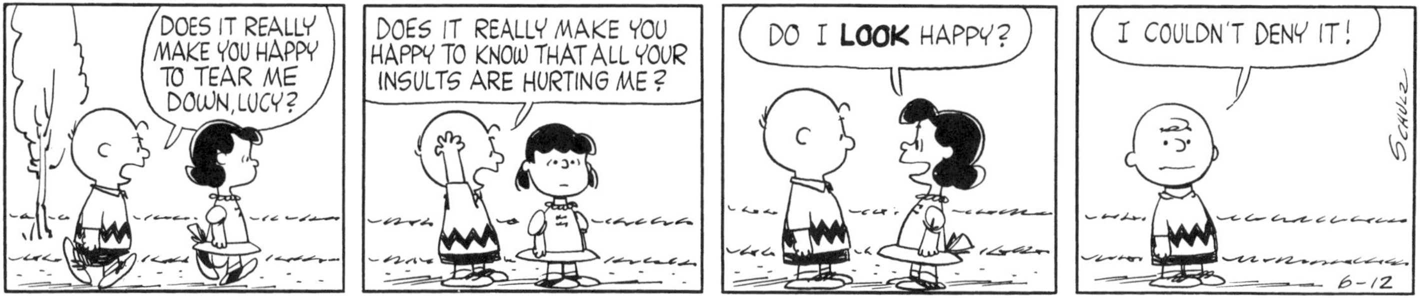
DOES IT REALLY MAKE YOU HAPPY TO TEAR ME DOWN, LUCY?
DOES IT REALLY MAKE YOU HAPPY TO KNOW THAT ALL YOUR INSULTS ARE HURTING ME?
DO I **LOOK** HAPPY?
I COULDN'T DENY IT!
SCHULZ
6-12

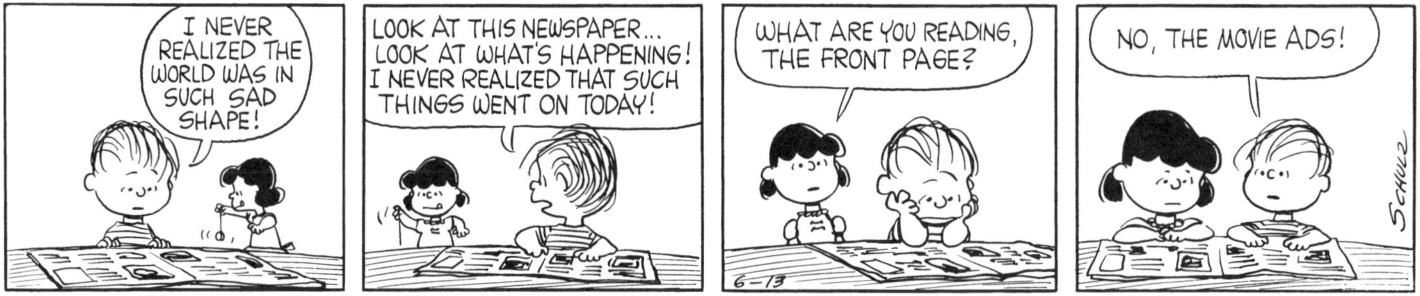
I NEVER REALIZED THE WORLD WAS IN SUCH SAD SHAPE!
LOOK AT THIS NEWSPAPER... LOOK AT WHAT'S HAPPENING! I NEVER REALIZED THAT SUCH THINGS WENT ON TODAY!
WHAT ARE YOU READING, THE FRONT PAGE?
6-13
NO, THE MOVIE ADS!
SCHULZ

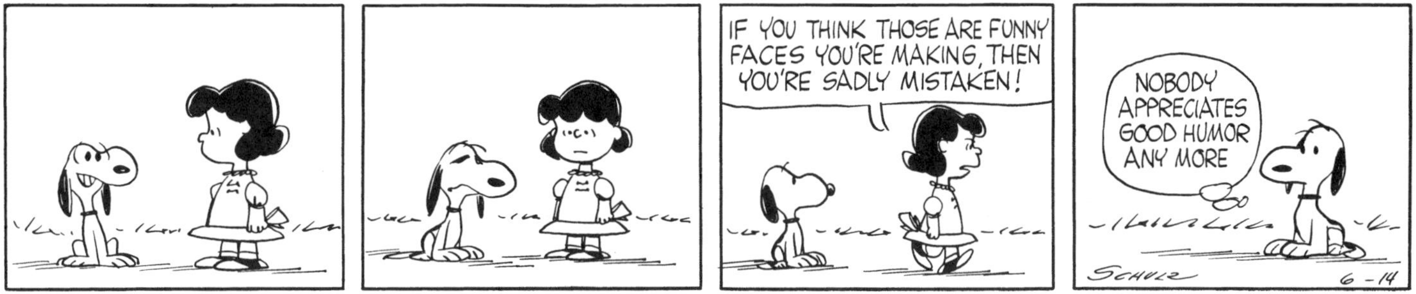
IF YOU THINK THOSE ARE FUNNY FACES YOU'RE MAKING, THEN YOU'RE SADLY MISTAKEN!
NOBODY APPRECIATES GOOD HUMOR ANY MORE
SCHULZ
6-14

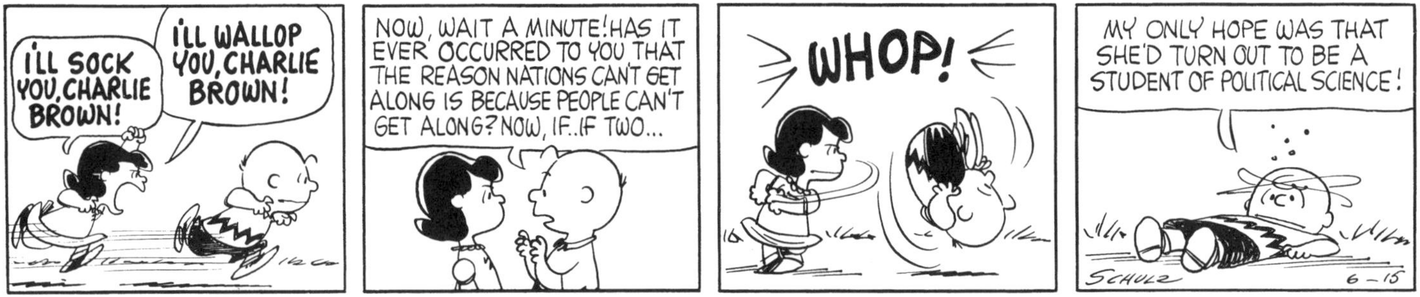
I'LL SOCK YOU, CHARLIE BROWN!
I'LL WALLOP YOU, CHARLIE BROWN!
NOW, WAIT A MINUTE! HAS IT EVER OCCURRED TO YOU THAT THE REASON NATIONS CAN'T GET ALONG IS BECAUSE PEOPLE CAN'T GET ALONG? NOW, IF..IF TWO...
WHOP!
MY ONLY HOPE WAS THAT SHE'D TURN OUT TO BE A STUDENT OF POLITICAL SCIENCE!
SCHULZ
6-15

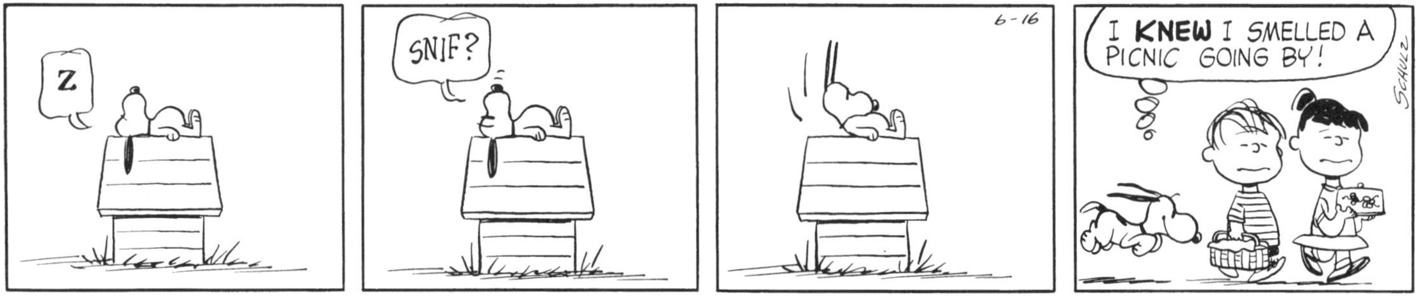
Z
SNIF?
6-16
I **KNEW** I SMELLED A PICNIC GOING BY!
SCHULZ

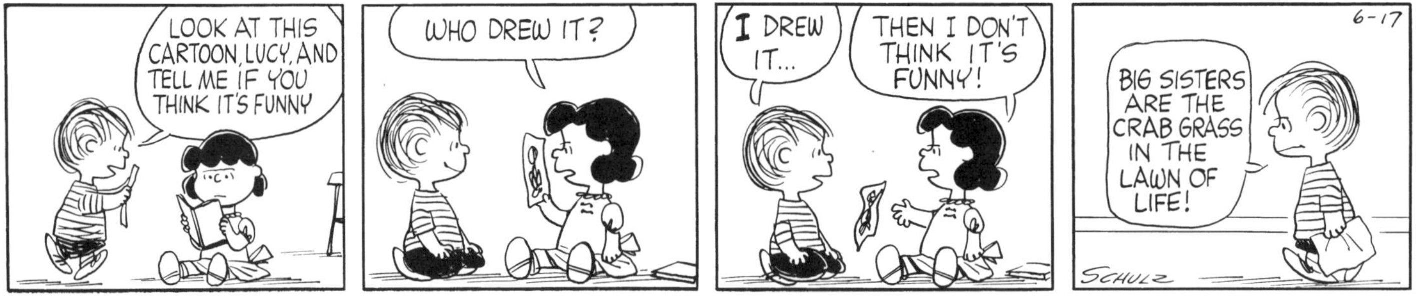
LOOK AT THIS CARTOON, LUCY, AND TELL ME IF YOU THINK IT'S FUNNY
WHO DREW IT?
I DREW IT...
THEN I DON'T THINK IT'S FUNNY!
6-17
BIG SISTERS ARE THE CRAB GRASS IN THE LAWN OF LIFE!
SCHULZ

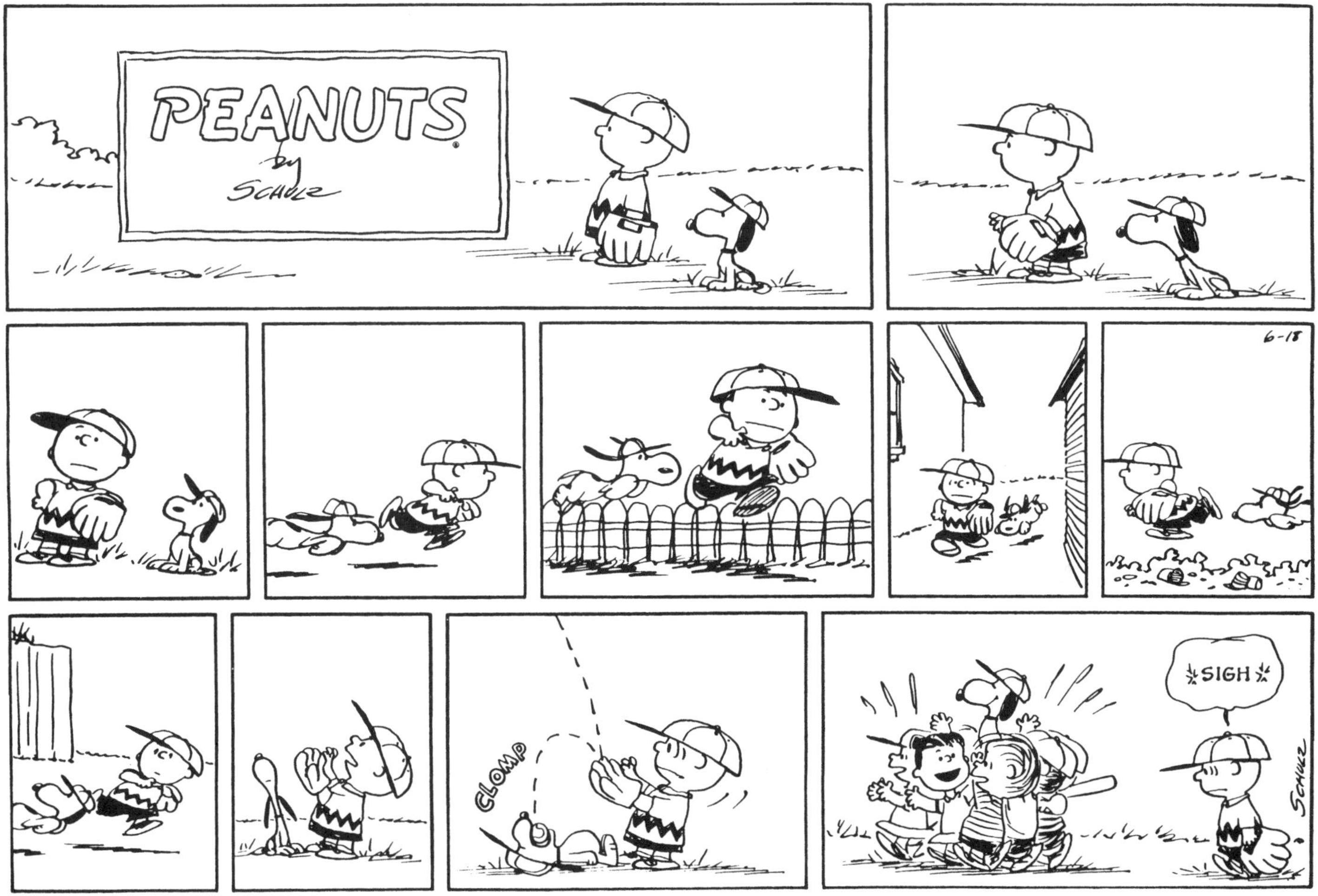
PEANUTS
by
SCHULZ
6-18
CLOMP
SIGH
SCHULZ

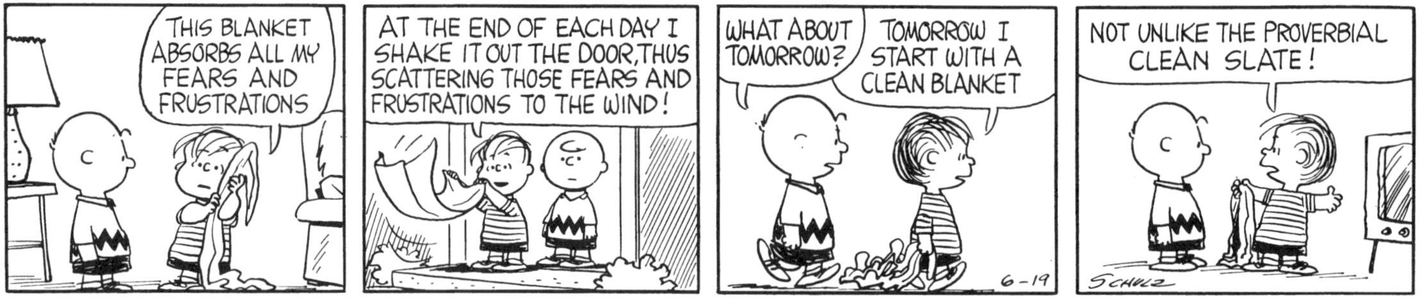
THIS BLANKET ABSORBS ALL MY FEARS AND FRUSTRATIONS
AT THE END OF EACH DAY I SHAKE IT OUT THE DOOR, THUS SCATTERING THOSE FEARS AND FRUSTRATIONS TO THE WIND!
WHAT ABOUT TOMORROW?
TOMORROW I START WITH A CLEAN BLANKET
6-19
NOT UNLIKE THE PROVERBIAL CLEAN SLATE!
SCHULZ

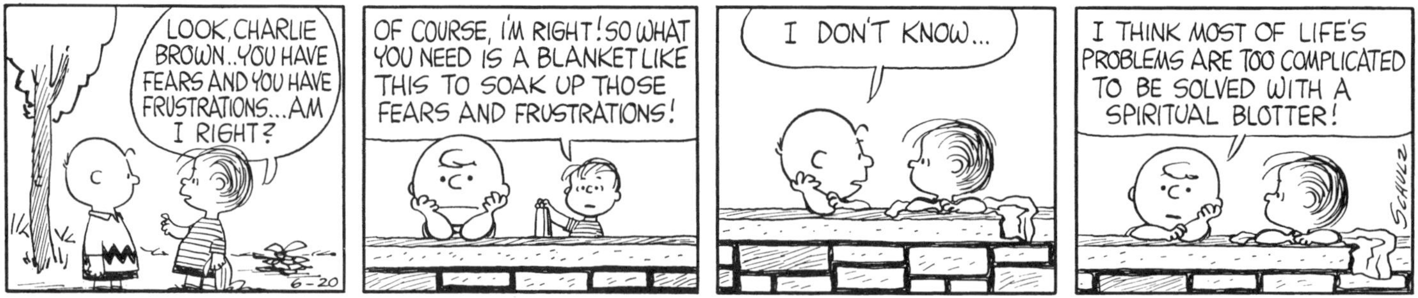
LOOK, CHARLIE BROWN..YOU HAVE FEARS AND YOU HAVE FRUSTRATIONS...AM I RIGHT?
6-20
OF COURSE, I'M RIGHT! SO WHAT YOU NEED IS A BLANKET LIKE THIS TO SOAK UP THOSE FEARS AND FRUSTRATIONS!
I DON'T KNOW...
I THINK MOST OF LIFE'S PROBLEMS ARE TOO COMPLICATED TO BE SOLVED WITH A SPIRITUAL BLOTTER!
SCHULZ

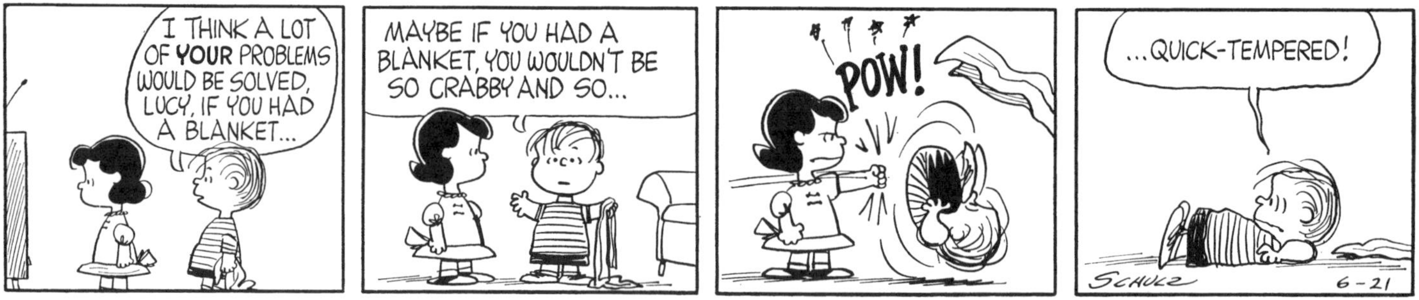
I THINK A LOT OF **YOUR** PROBLEMS WOULD BE SOLVED, LUCY, IF YOU HAD A BLANKET...
MAYBE IF YOU HAD A BLANKET, YOU WOULDN'T BE SO CRABBY AND SO...
POW!
...QUICK-TEMPERED!
SCHULZ
6-21

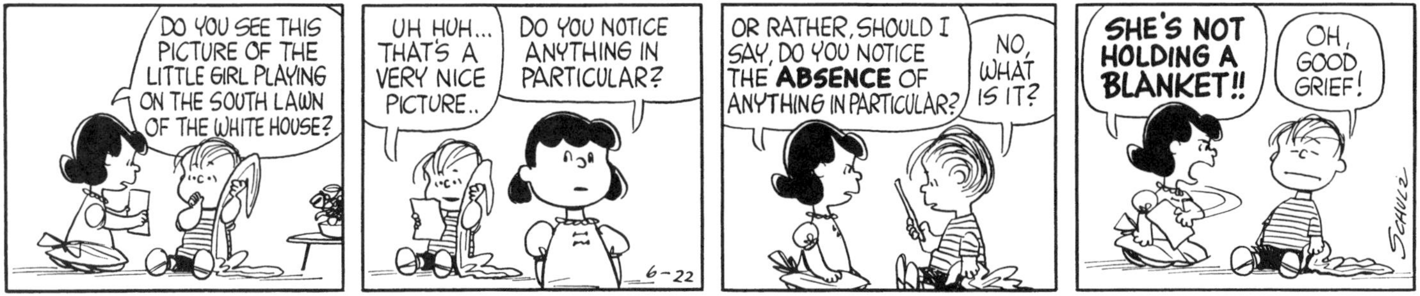
DO YOU SEE THIS PICTURE OF THE LITTLE GIRL PLAYING ON THE SOUTH LAWN OF THE WHITE HOUSE?
UH HUH... THAT'S A VERY NICE PICTURE..
DO YOU NOTICE ANYTHING IN PARTICULAR?
6-22
OR RATHER, SHOULD I SAY, DO YOU NOTICE THE **ABSENCE** OF ANYTHING IN PARTICULAR?
NO, WHAT IS IT?
SHE'S NOT HOLDING A BLANKET!!
OH, GOOD GRIEF!
SCHULZ

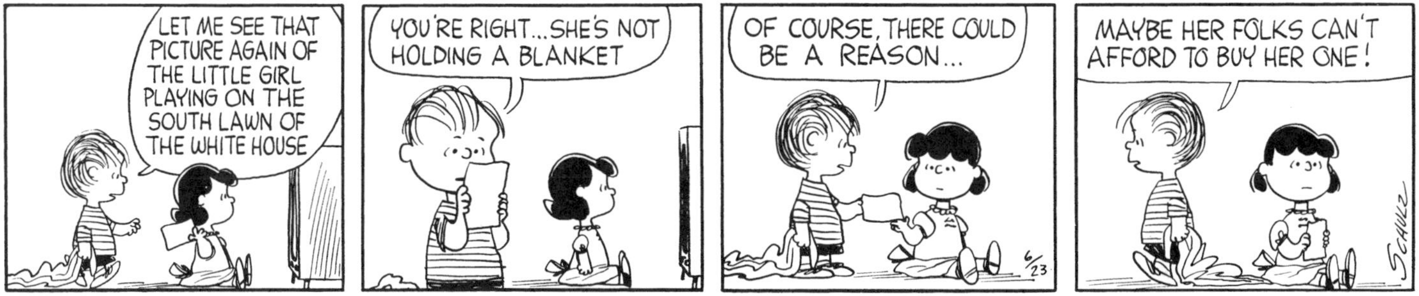
LET ME SEE THAT PICTURE AGAIN OF THE LITTLE GIRL PLAYING ON THE SOUTH LAWN OF THE WHITE HOUSE
YOU'RE RIGHT...SHE'S NOT HOLDING A BLANKET
OF COURSE, THERE COULD BE A REASON...
6/23
MAYBE HER FOLKS CAN'T AFFORD TO BUY HER ONE!
SCHULZ

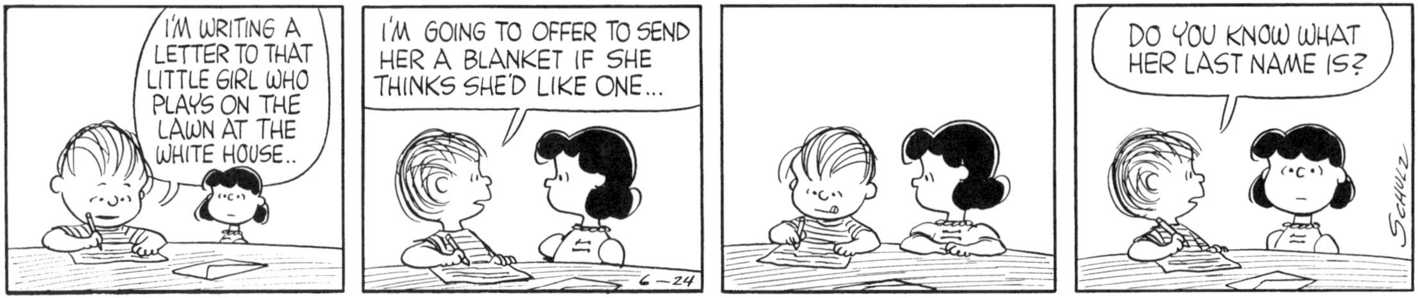
I'M WRITING A LETTER TO THAT LITTLE GIRL WHO PLAYS ON THE LAWN AT THE WHITE HOUSE..
I'M GOING TO OFFER TO SEND HER A BLANKET IF SHE THINKS SHE'D LIKE ONE...
6-24
DO YOU KNOW WHAT HER LAST NAME IS?
SCHULZ

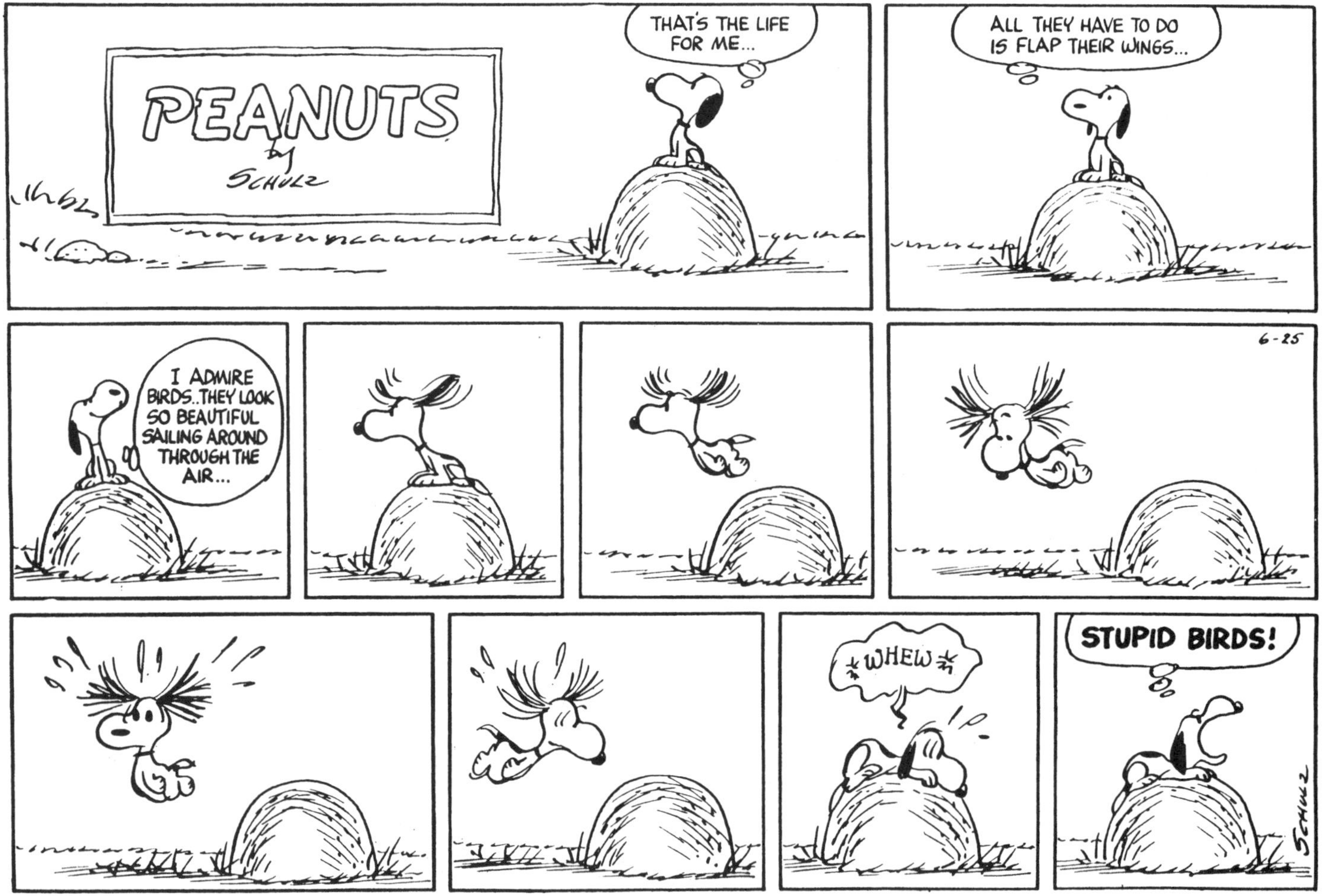
PEANUTS
by
SCHULZ
THAT'S THE LIFE FOR ME...
ALL THEY HAVE TO DO IS FLAP THEIR WINGS...
I ADMIRE BIRDS..THEY LOOK SO BEAUTIFUL SAILING AROUND THROUGH THE AIR...
6-25
WHEW
STUPID BIRDS!
SCHULZ

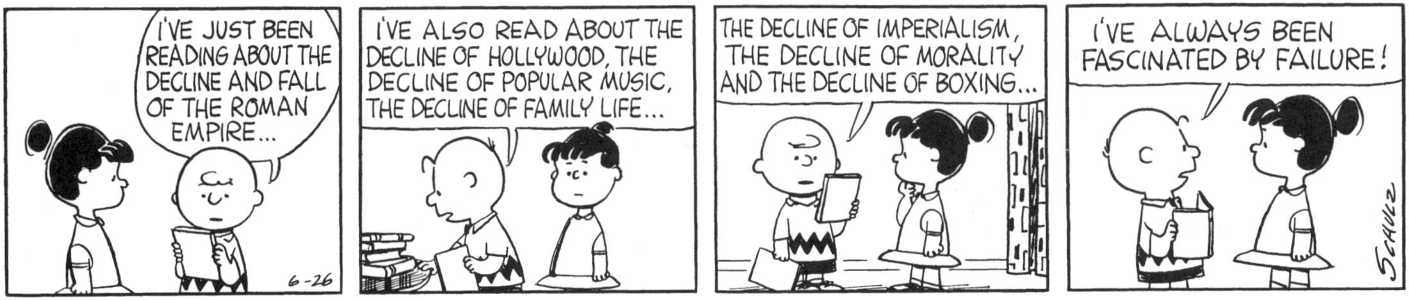
I'VE JUST BEEN READING ABOUT THE DECLINE AND FALL OF THE ROMAN EMPIRE...
6-26
I'VE ALSO READ ABOUT THE DECLINE OF HOLLYWOOD, THE DECLINE OF POPULAR MUSIC, THE DECLINE OF FAMILY LIFE...
THE DECLINE OF IMPERIALISM, THE DECLINE OF MORALITY AND THE DECLINE OF BOXING...
I'VE ALWAYS BEEN FASCINATED BY FAILURE!
SCHULZ

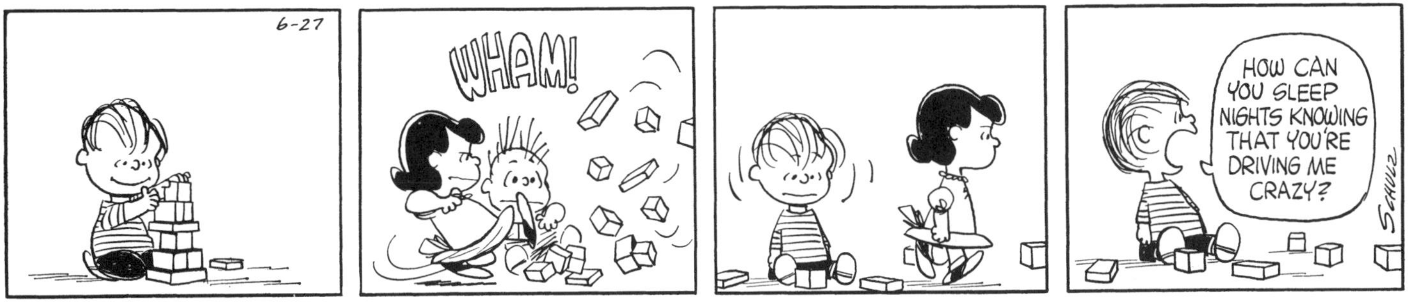
6-27
WHAM!
HOW CAN YOU SLEEP NIGHTS KNOWING THAT YOU'RE DRIVING ME CRAZY?
SCHULZ

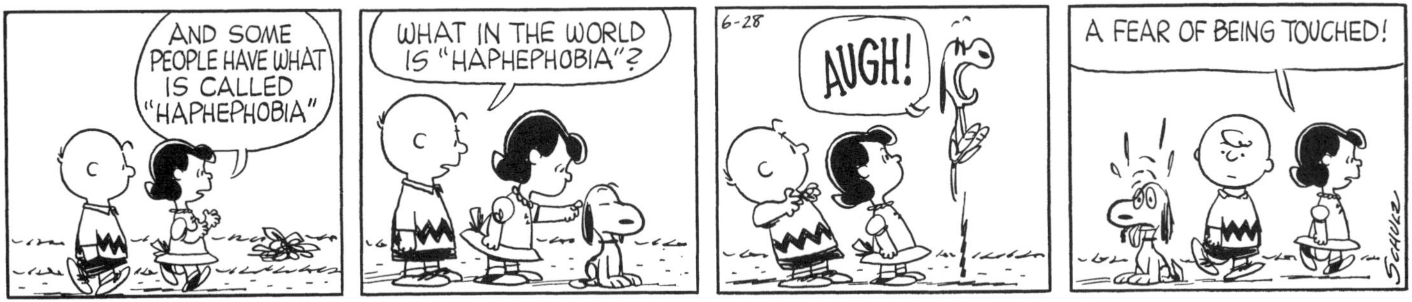
AND SOME PEOPLE HAVE WHAT IS CALLED "HAPHEPHOBIA"
WHAT IN THE WORLD IS "HAPHEPHOBIA"?
6-28
AUGH!
A FEAR OF BEING TOUCHED!
SCHULZ

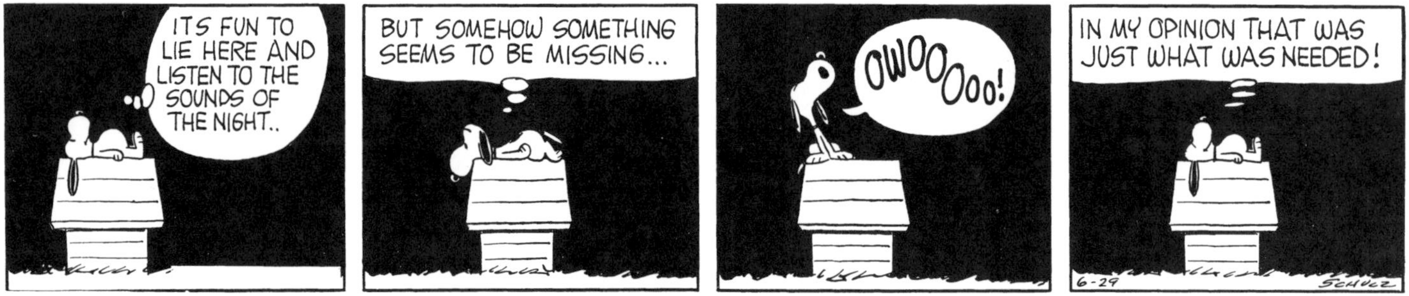
ITS FUN TO LIE HERE AND LISTEN TO THE SOUNDS OF THE NIGHT..
BUT SOMEHOW SOMETHING SEEMS TO BE MISSING...
OWOOOOoo!
IN MY OPINION THAT WAS JUST WHAT WAS NEEDED!
6-29
SCHULZ

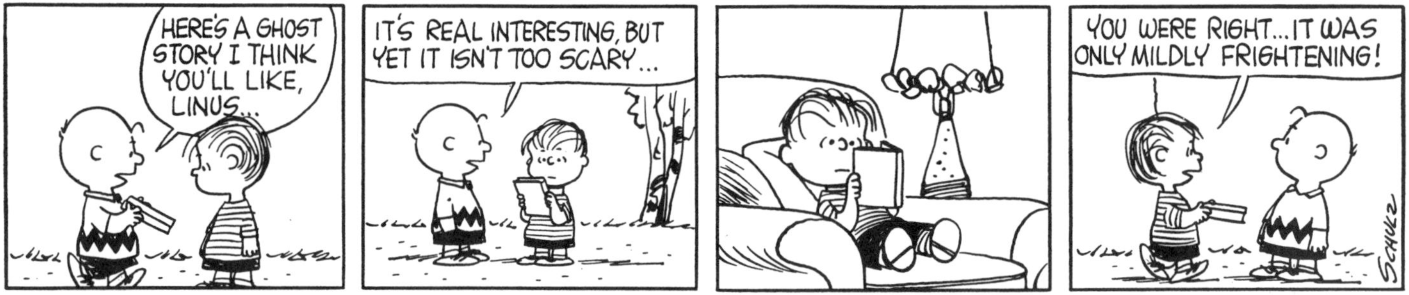
HERE'S A GHOST STORY I THINK YOU'LL LIKE, LINUS...
IT'S REAL INTERESTING, BUT YET IT ISN'T TOO SCARY...
YOU WERE RIGHT...IT WAS ONLY MILDLY FRIGHTENING!
SCHULZ

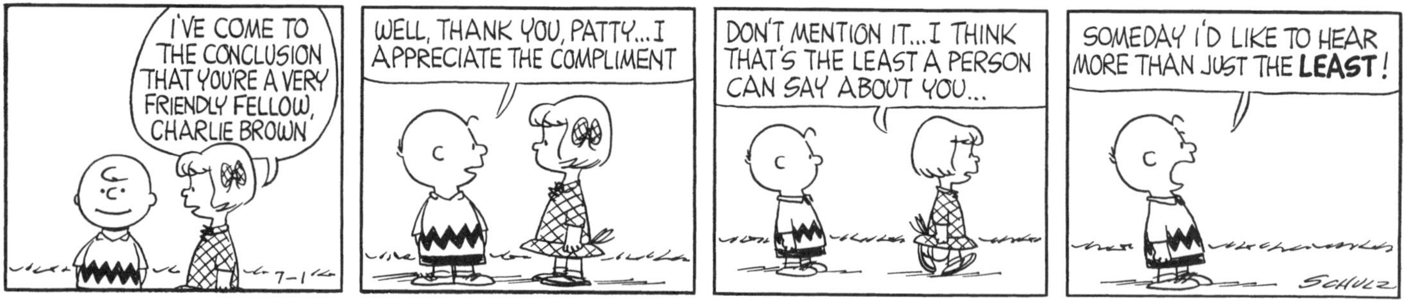
I'VE COME TO THE CONCLUSION THAT YOU'RE A VERY FRIENDLY FELLOW, CHARLIE BROWN
7-1
WELL, THANK YOU, PATTY...I APPRECIATE THE COMPLIMENT
DON'T MENTION IT...I THINK THAT'S THE LEAST A PERSON CAN SAY ABOUT YOU...
SOMEDAY I'D LIKE TO HEAR MORE THAN JUST THE **LEAST**!
SCHULZ

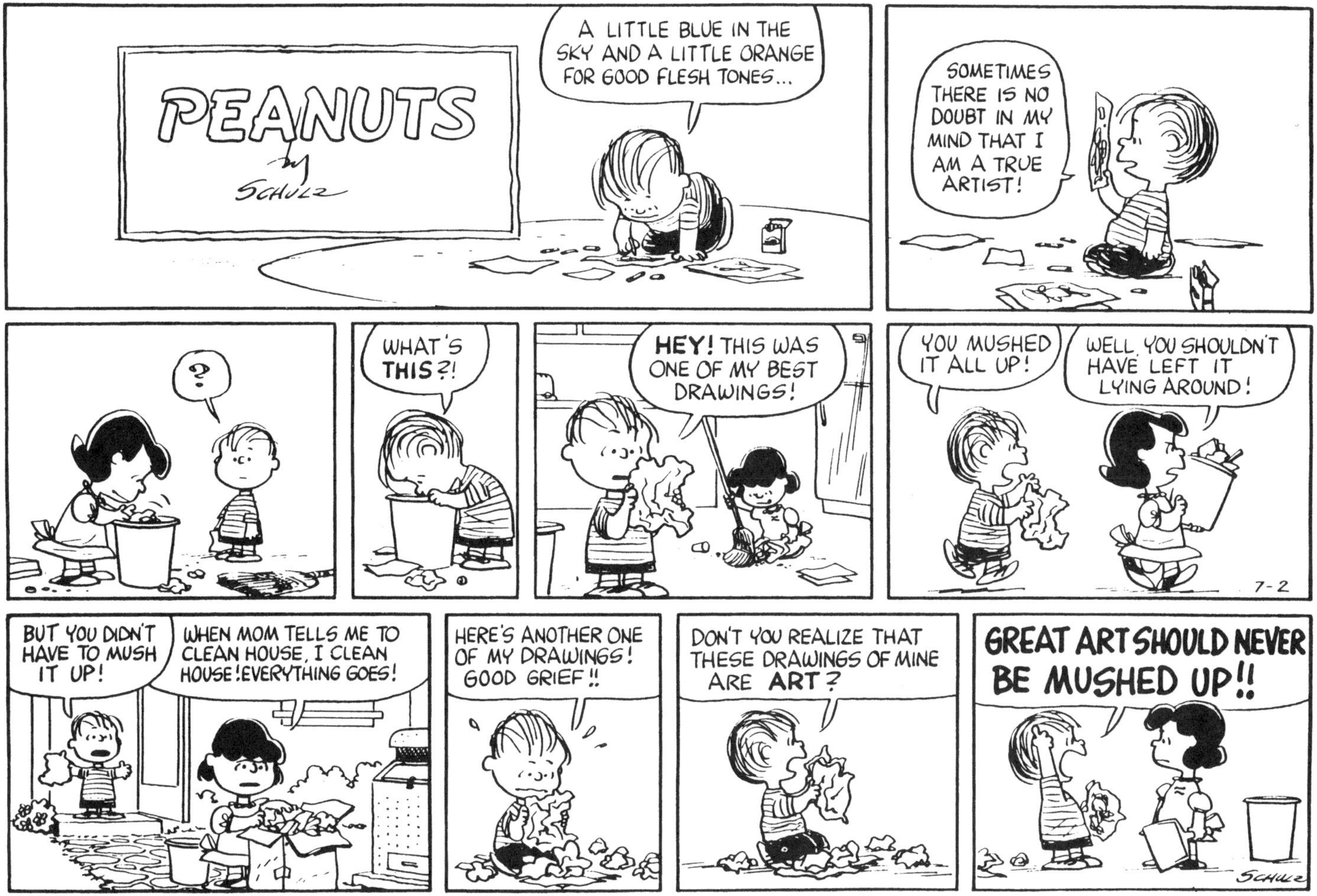
PEANUTS
by
SCHULZ
A LITTLE BLUE IN THE SKY AND A LITTLE ORANGE FOR GOOD FLESH TONES...
SOMETIMES THERE IS NO DOUBT IN MY MIND THAT I AM A TRUE ARTIST!
?
WHAT'S **THIS**?!
HEY! THIS WAS ONE OF MY BEST DRAWINGS!
YOU MUSHED IT ALL UP!
WELL, YOU SHOULDN'T HAVE LEFT IT LYING AROUND!
7-2
BUT YOU DIDN'T HAVE TO MUSH IT UP!
WHEN MOM TELLS ME TO CLEAN HOUSE, I CLEAN HOUSE! EVERYTHING GOES!
HERE'S ANOTHER ONE OF MY DRAWINGS! GOOD GRIEF!!
DON'T YOU REALIZE THAT THESE DRAWINGS OF MINE ARE **ART**?
GREAT ART SHOULD NEVER BE MUSHED UP!!
SCHULZ

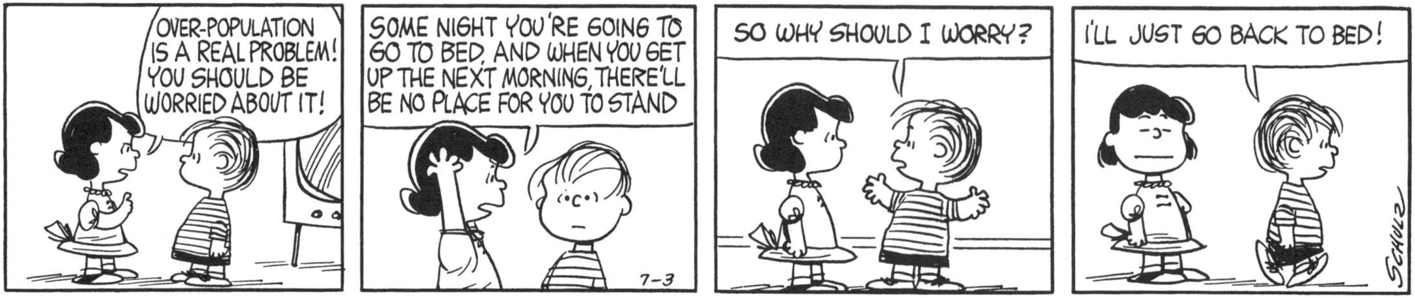
OVER-POPULATION IS A REAL PROBLEM! YOU SHOULD BE WORRIED ABOUT IT!
SOME NIGHT YOU'RE GOING TO GO TO BED, AND WHEN YOU GET UP THE NEXT MORNING, THERE'LL BE NO PLACE FOR YOU TO STAND
7-3
SO WHY SHOULD I WORRY?
I'LL JUST GO BACK TO BED!
SCHULZ

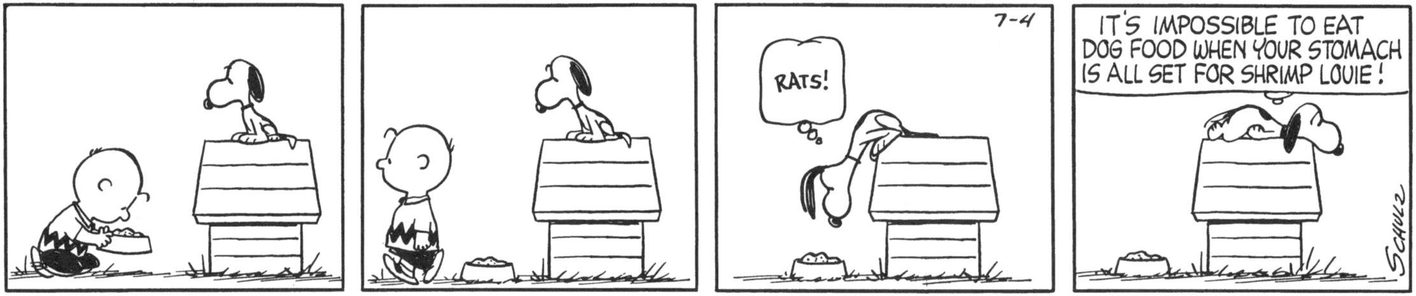
7-4
RATS!
IT'S IMPOSSIBLE TO EAT DOG FOOD WHEN YOUR STOMACH IS ALL SET FOR SHRIMP LOUIE!
SCHULZ

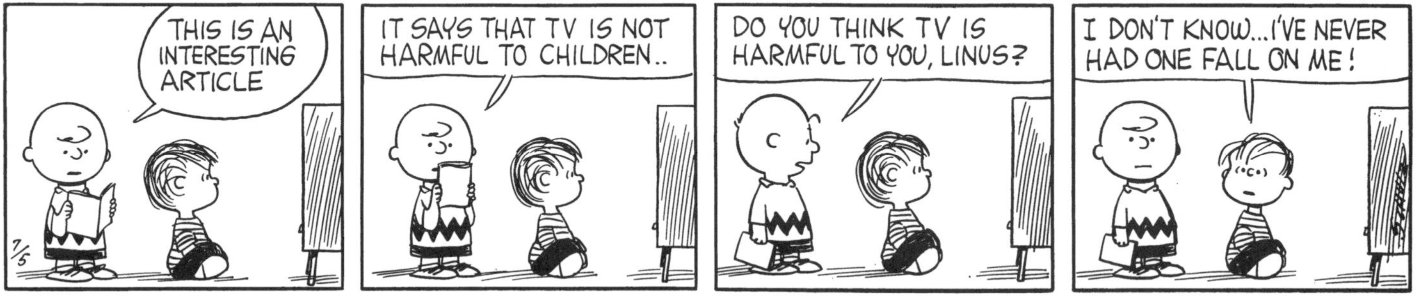
THIS IS AN INTERESTING ARTICLE
7/5
IT SAYS THAT TV IS NOT HARMFUL TO CHILDREN..
DO YOU THINK TV IS HARMFUL TO YOU, LINUS?
I DON'T KNOW...I'VE NEVER HAD ONE FALL ON ME!

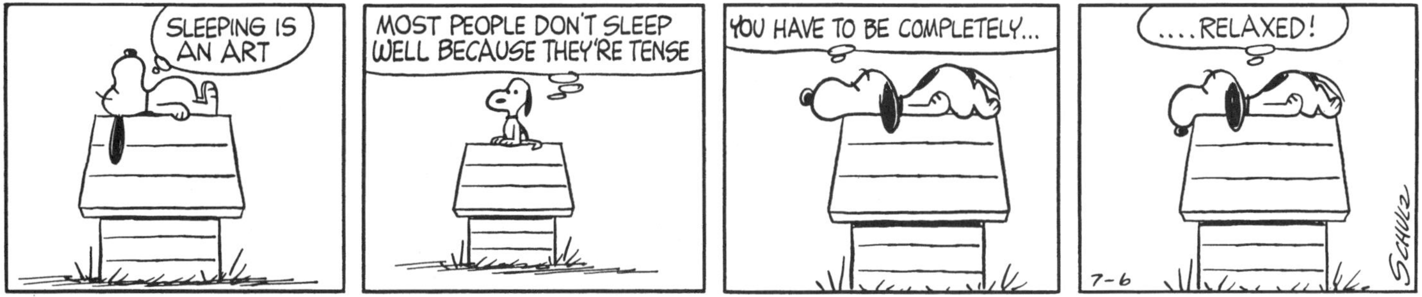
SLEEPING IS AN ART
MOST PEOPLE DON'T SLEEP WELL BECAUSE THEY'RE TENSE
YOU HAVE TO BE COMPLETELY...
....RELAXED!

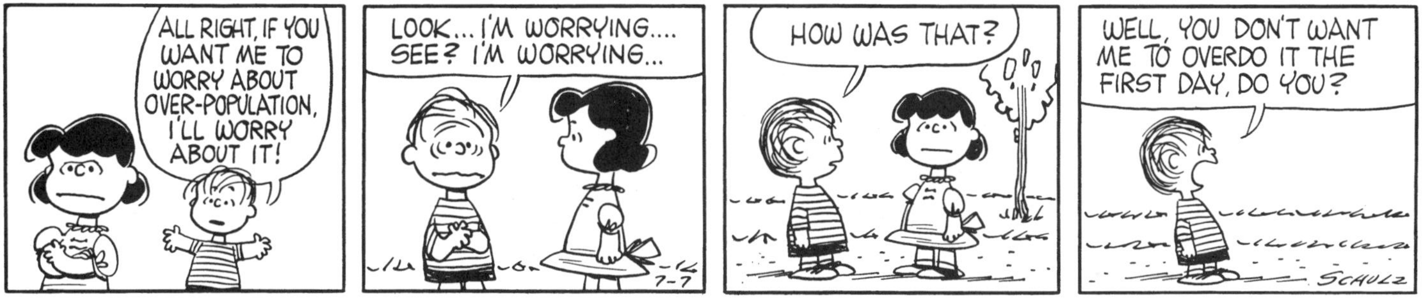
ALL RIGHT, IF YOU WANT ME TO WORRY ABOUT OVER-POPULATION, I'LL WORRY ABOUT IT!
LOOK... I'M WORRYING.... SEE? I'M WORRYING...
HOW WAS THAT?
WELL, YOU DON'T WANT ME TO OVERDO IT THE FIRST DAY, DO YOU?

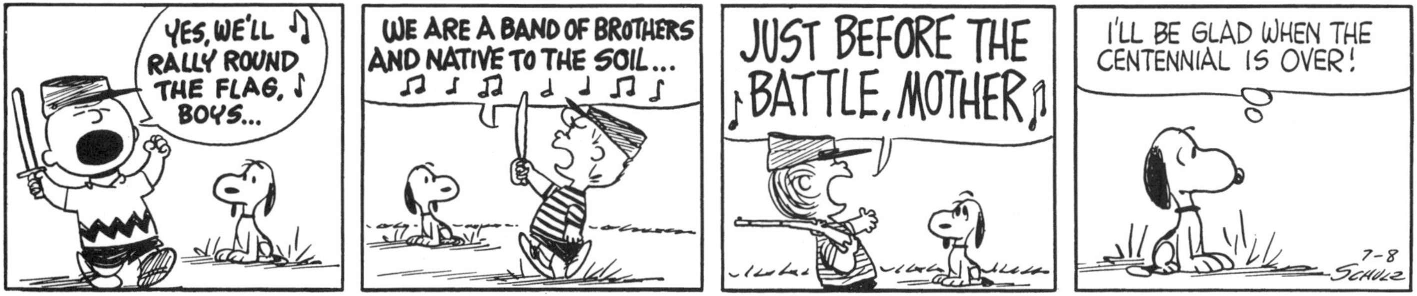
YES, WE'LL RALLY ROUND THE FLAG, BOYS...
WE ARE A BAND OF BROTHERS AND NATIVE TO THE SOIL...
JUST BEFORE THE BATTLE, MOTHER
I'LL BE GLAD WHEN THE CENTENNIAL IS OVER!

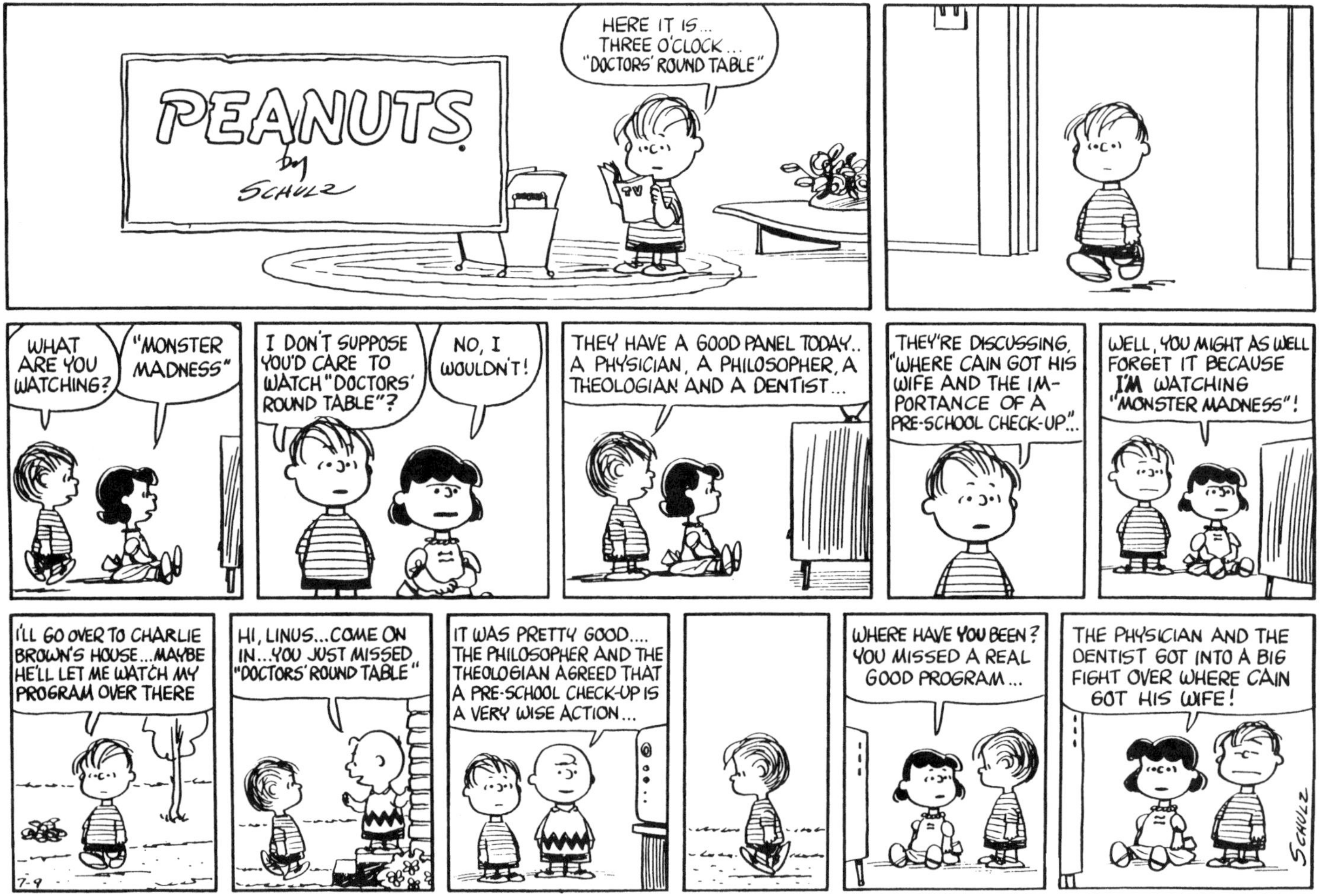
PEANUTS
by SCHULZ
HERE IT IS... THREE O'CLOCK... "DOCTORS' ROUND TABLE"
TV
WHAT ARE YOU WATCHING?
"MONSTER MADNESS"
I DON'T SUPPOSE YOU'D CARE TO WATCH "DOCTORS' ROUND TABLE"?
NO, I WOULDN'T!
THEY HAVE A GOOD PANEL TODAY.. A PHYSICIAN, A PHILOSOPHER, A THEOLOGIAN AND A DENTIST...
THEY'RE DISCUSSING, "WHERE CAIN GOT HIS WIFE AND THE IMPORTANCE OF A PRE-SCHOOL CHECK-UP"...
WELL, YOU MIGHT AS WELL FORGET IT BECAUSE I'M WATCHING "MONSTER MADNESS"!
I'LL GO OVER TO CHARLIE BROWN'S HOUSE...MAYBE HE'LL LET ME WATCH MY PROGRAM OVER THERE
7-9
HI, LINUS...COME ON IN...YOU JUST MISSED "DOCTORS' ROUND TABLE"
IT WAS PRETTY GOOD.... THE PHILOSOPHER AND THE THEOLOGIAN AGREED THAT A PRE-SCHOOL CHECK-UP IS A VERY WISE ACTION...
WHERE HAVE YOU BEEN? YOU MISSED A REAL GOOD PROGRAM...
THE PHYSICIAN AND THE DENTIST GOT INTO A BIG FIGHT OVER WHERE CAIN GOT HIS WIFE!
SCHULZ

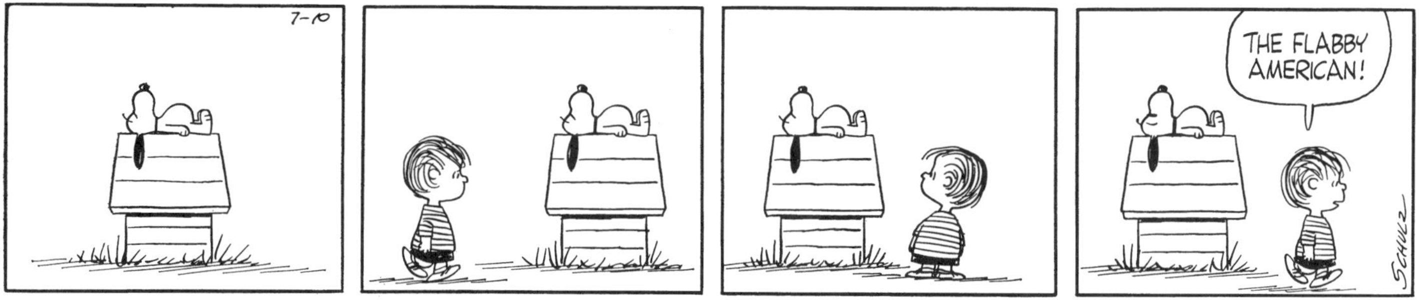
7-10
THE FLABBY AMERICAN!
SCHULZ

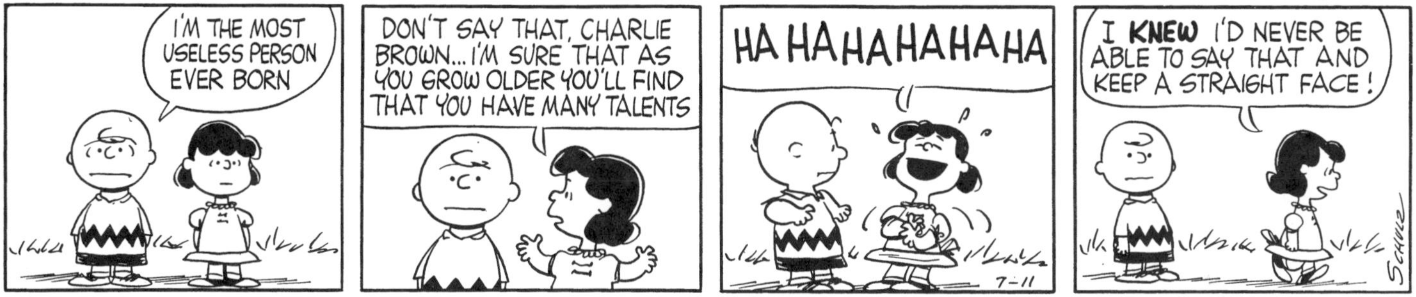
I'M THE MOST USELESS PERSON EVER BORN
DON'T SAY THAT, CHARLIE BROWN... I'M SURE THAT AS YOU GROW OLDER YOU'LL FIND THAT YOU HAVE MANY TALENTS
HA HA HA HA HA HA HA HA
7-11
I **KNEW** I'D NEVER BE ABLE TO SAY THAT AND KEEP A STRAIGHT FACE!
SCHULZ

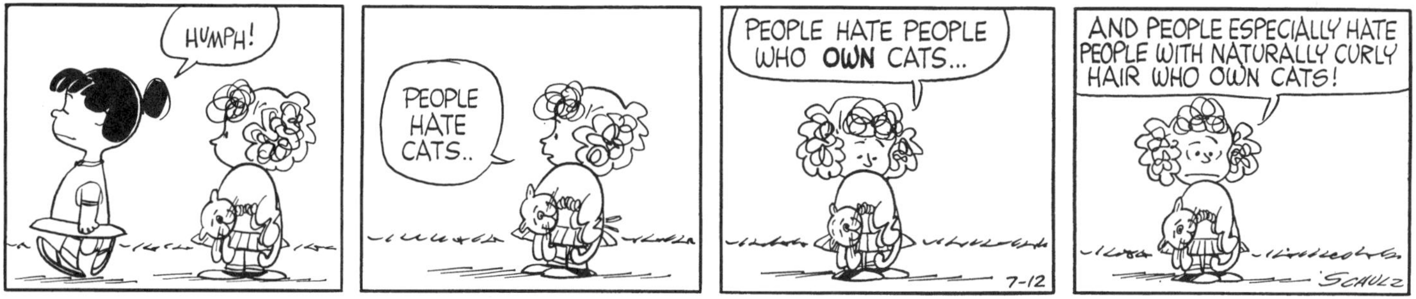
HUMPH!
PEOPLE HATE CATS..
PEOPLE HATE PEOPLE WHO **OWN** CATS...
7-12
AND PEOPLE ESPECIALLY HATE PEOPLE WITH NATURALLY CURLY HAIR WHO OWN CATS!
SCHULZ

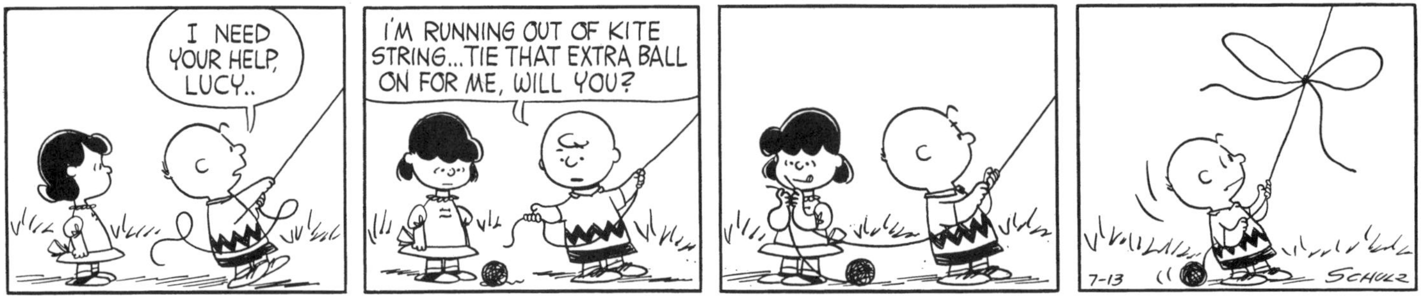
I NEED YOUR HELP, LUCY..
I'M RUNNING OUT OF KITE STRING...TIE THAT EXTRA BALL ON FOR ME, WILL YOU?
7-13
SCHULZ

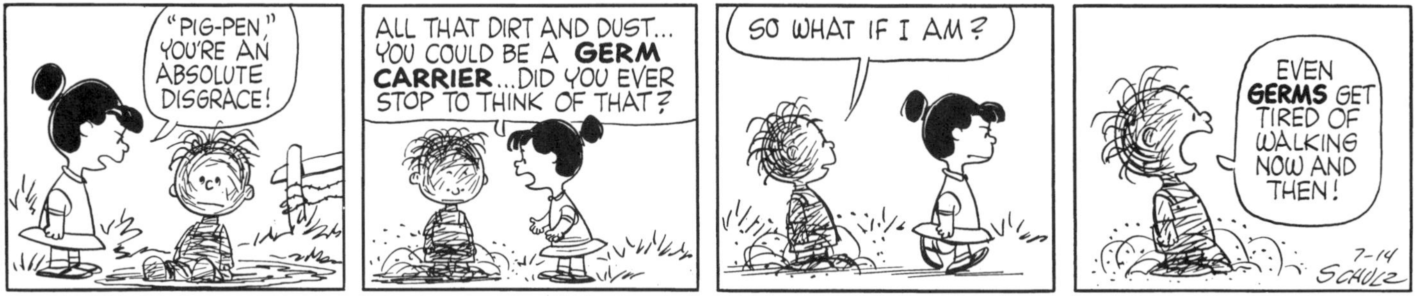
"PIG-PEN," YOU'RE AN ABSOLUTE DISGRACE!
ALL THAT DIRT AND DUST... YOU COULD BE A **GERM CARRIER**...DID YOU EVER STOP TO THINK OF THAT?
SO WHAT IF I AM?
EVEN **GERMS** GET TIRED OF WALKING NOW AND THEN!
7-14
SCHULZ

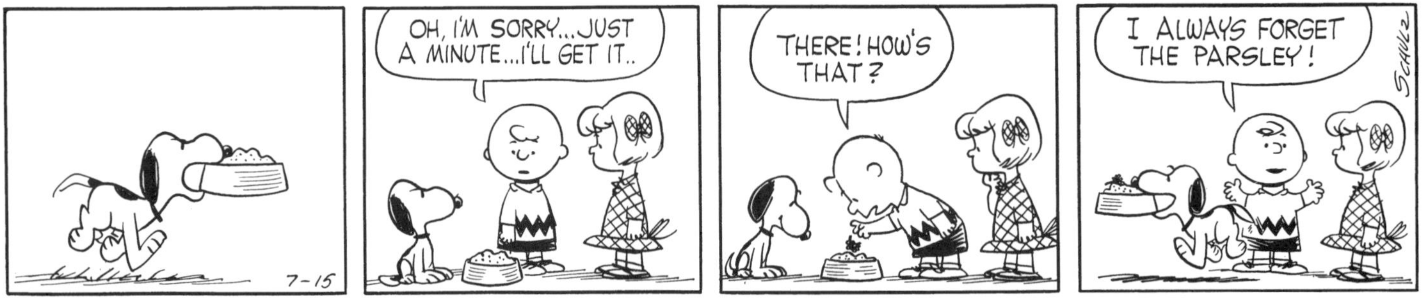
7-15
OH, I'M SORRY...JUST A MINUTE...I'LL GET IT..
THERE! HOW'S THAT?
I ALWAYS FORGET THE PARSLEY!
SCHULZ

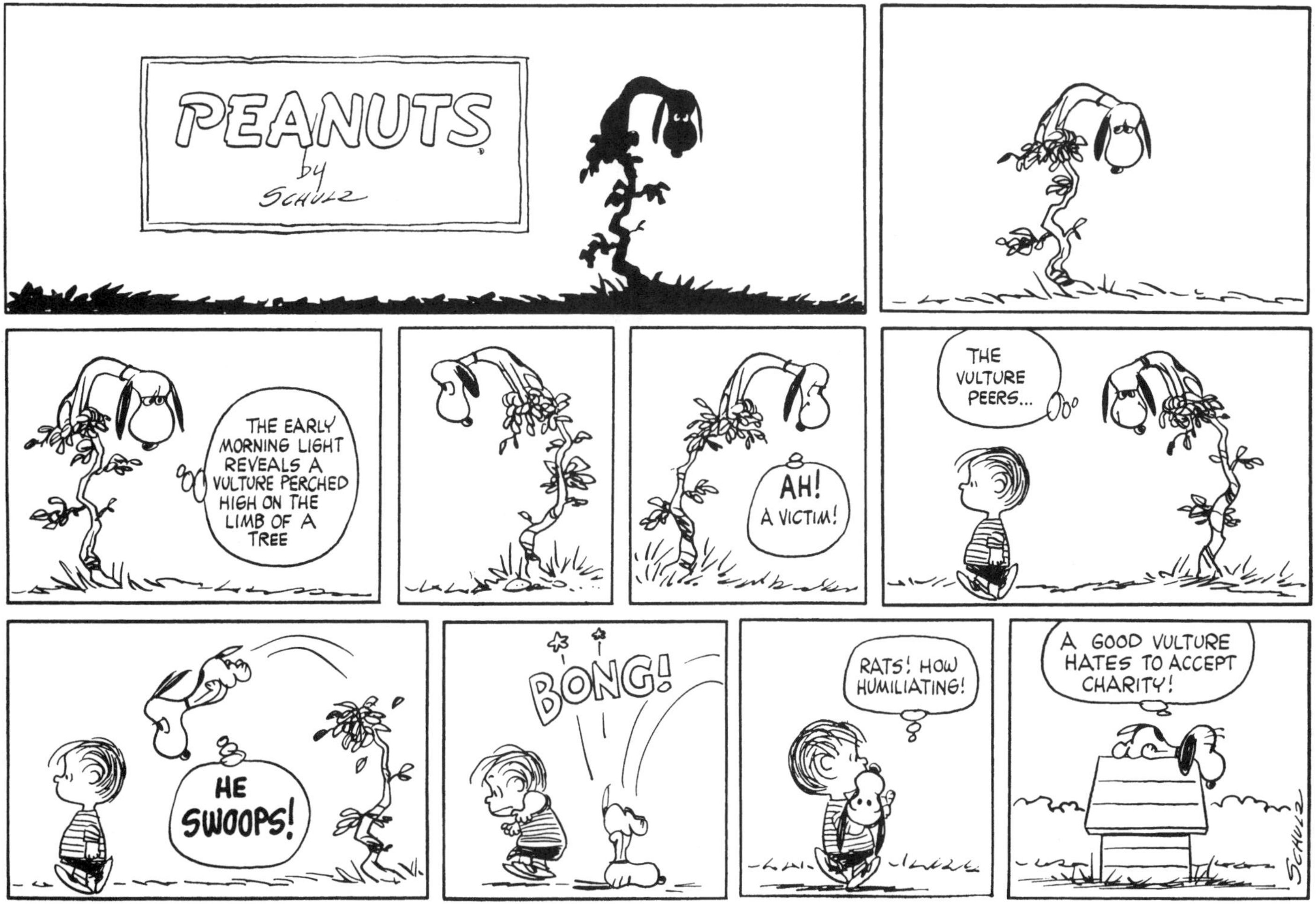
PEANUTS
by
SCHULZ
THE EARLY MORNING LIGHT REVEALS A VULTURE PERCHED HIGH ON THE LIMB OF A TREE
AH! A VICTIM!
THE VULTURE PEERS...
HE SWOOPS!
BONG!
RATS! HOW HUMILIATING!
A GOOD VULTURE HATES TO ACCEPT CHARITY!
SCHULZ

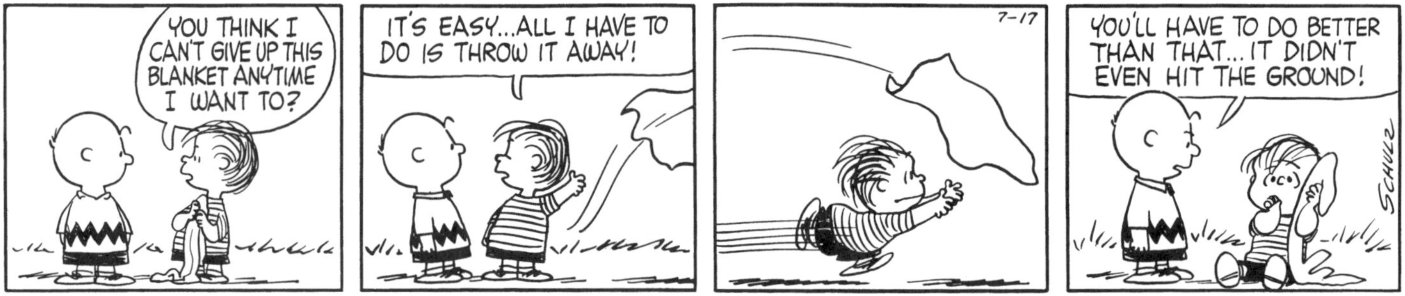
YOU THINK I CAN'T GIVE UP THIS BLANKET ANYTIME I WANT TO?
IT'S EASY...ALL I HAVE TO DO IS THROW IT AWAY!
7-17
YOU'LL HAVE TO DO BETTER THAN THAT... IT DIDN'T EVEN HIT THE GROUND!
SCHULZ

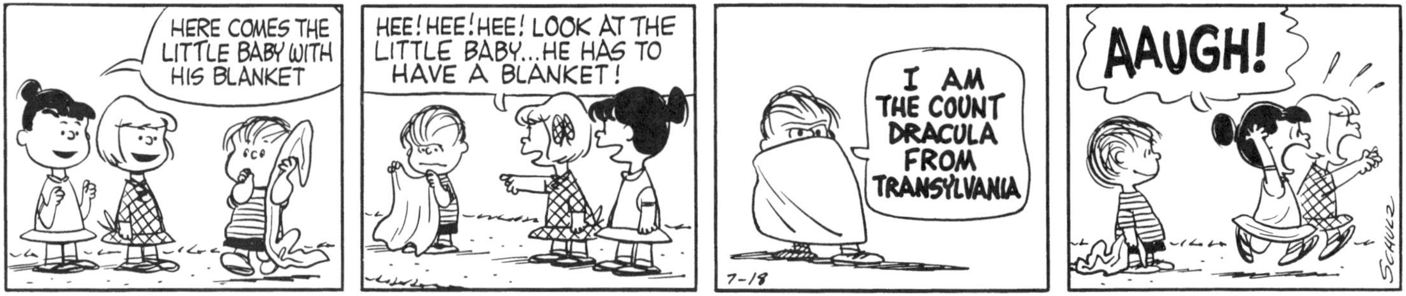
HERE COMES THE LITTLE BABY WITH HIS BLANKET
HEE! HEE! HEE! LOOK AT THE LITTLE BABY...HE HAS TO HAVE A BLANKET!
I AM THE COUNT DRACULA FROM TRANSYLVANIA
7-18
AAUGH!
SCHULZ

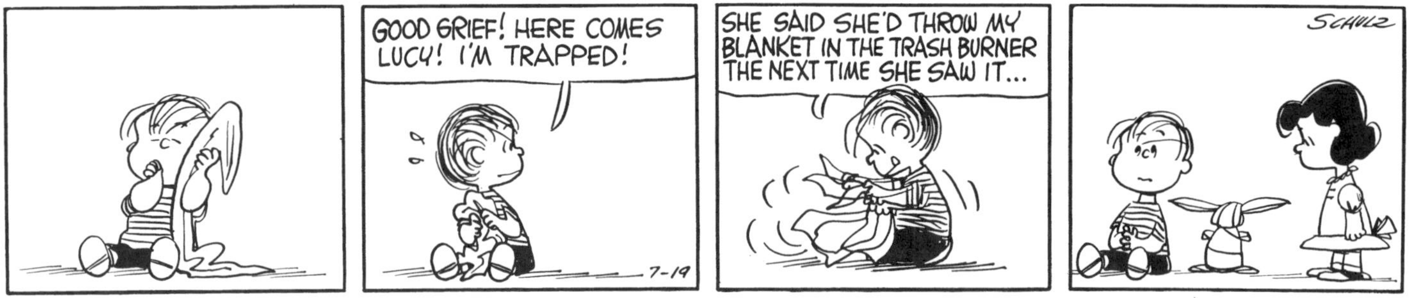
GOOD GRIEF! HERE COMES LUCY! I'M TRAPPED!
7-19
SHE SAID SHE'D THROW MY BLANKET IN THE TRASH BURNER THE NEXT TIME SHE SAW IT...
SCHULZ

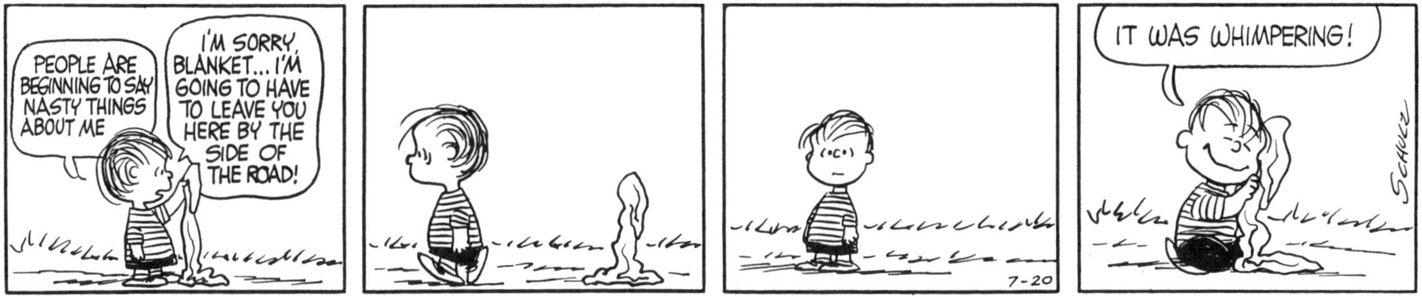
PEOPLE ARE BEGINNING TO SAY NASTY THINGS ABOUT ME
I'M SORRY, BLANKET... I'M GOING TO HAVE TO LEAVE YOU HERE BY THE SIDE OF THE ROAD!
7-20
IT WAS WHIMPERING!
SCHULZ

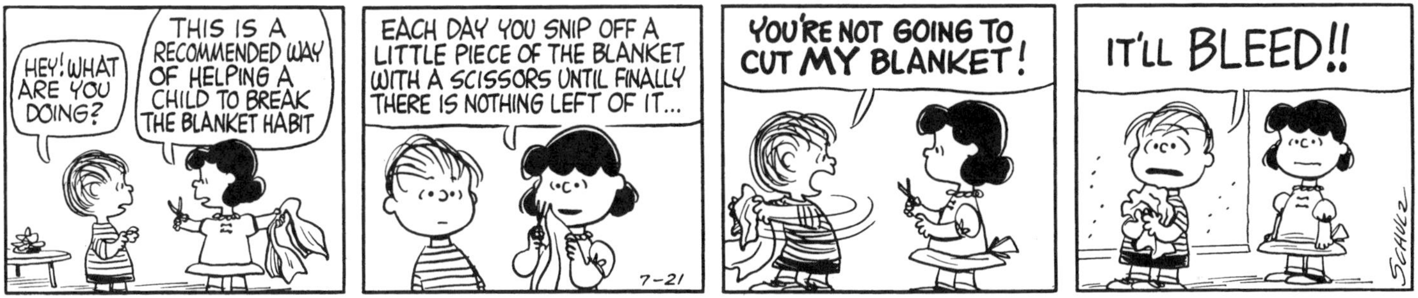
HEY! WHAT ARE YOU DOING?
THIS IS A RECOMMENDED WAY OF HELPING A CHILD TO BREAK THE BLANKET HABIT
EACH DAY YOU SNIP OFF A LITTLE PIECE OF THE BLANKET WITH A SCISSORS UNTIL FINALLY THERE IS NOTHING LEFT OF IT...
7-21
YOU'RE NOT GOING TO CUT MY BLANKET!
IT'LL BLEED!!
SCHULZ

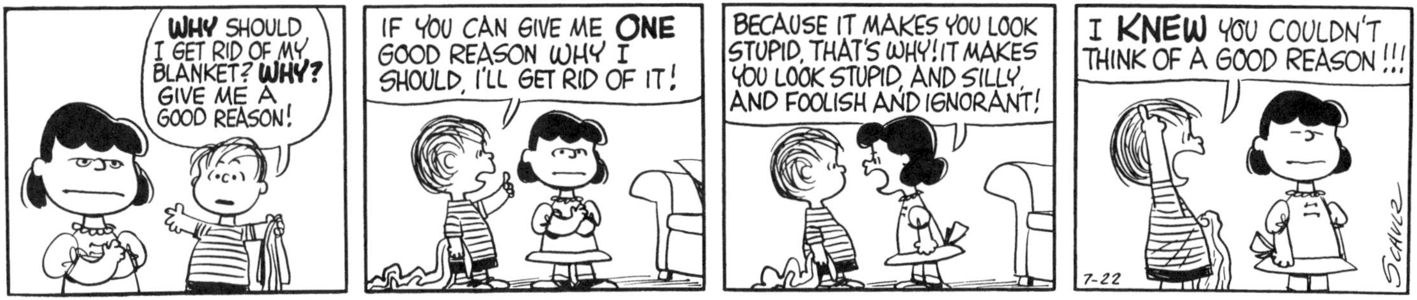
WHY SHOULD I GET RID OF MY BLANKET? WHY? GIVE ME A GOOD REASON!
IF YOU CAN GIVE ME ONE GOOD REASON WHY I SHOULD, I'LL GET RID OF IT!
BECAUSE IT MAKES YOU LOOK STUPID, THAT'S WHY! IT MAKES YOU LOOK STUPID, AND SILLY, AND FOOLISH AND IGNORANT!
I KNEW YOU COULDN'T THINK OF A GOOD REASON!!!
7-22
SCHULZ

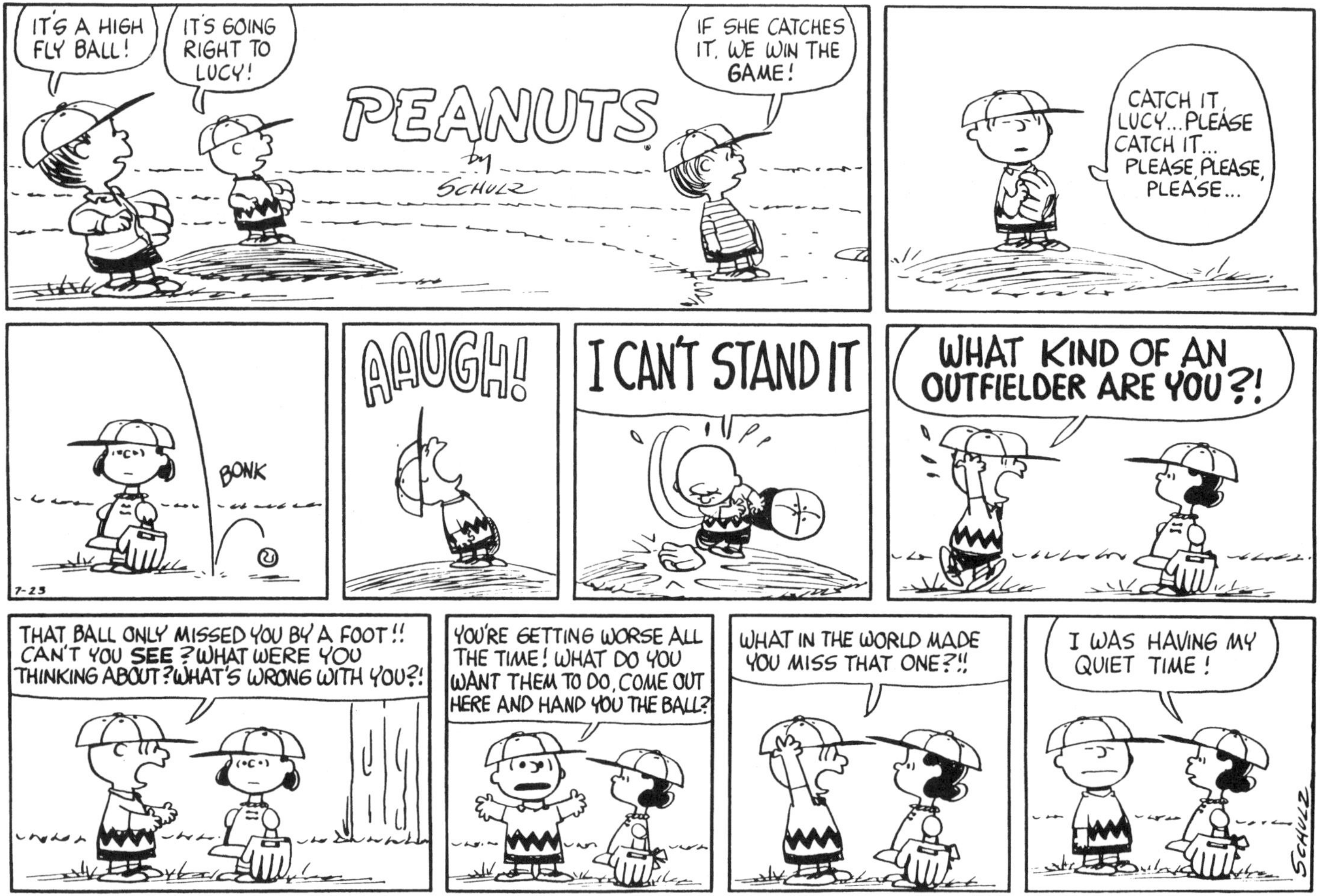
IT'S A HIGH FLY BALL!
IT'S GOING RIGHT TO LUCY!
PEANUTS
by SCHULZ
IF SHE CATCHES IT, WE WIN THE GAME!
CATCH IT, LUCY...PLEASE CATCH IT... PLEASE, PLEASE, PLEASE...
BONK
7-23
AAUGH!
I CAN'T STAND IT
WHAT KIND OF AN OUTFIELDER ARE YOU?!
THAT BALL ONLY MISSED YOU BY A FOOT!! CAN'T YOU SEE? WHAT WERE YOU THINKING ABOUT? WHAT'S WRONG WITH YOU?!
YOU'RE GETTING WORSE ALL THE TIME! WHAT DO YOU WANT THEM TO DO, COME OUT HERE AND HAND YOU THE BALL?
WHAT IN THE WORLD MADE YOU MISS THAT ONE?!!
I WAS HAVING MY QUIET TIME!
SCHULZ

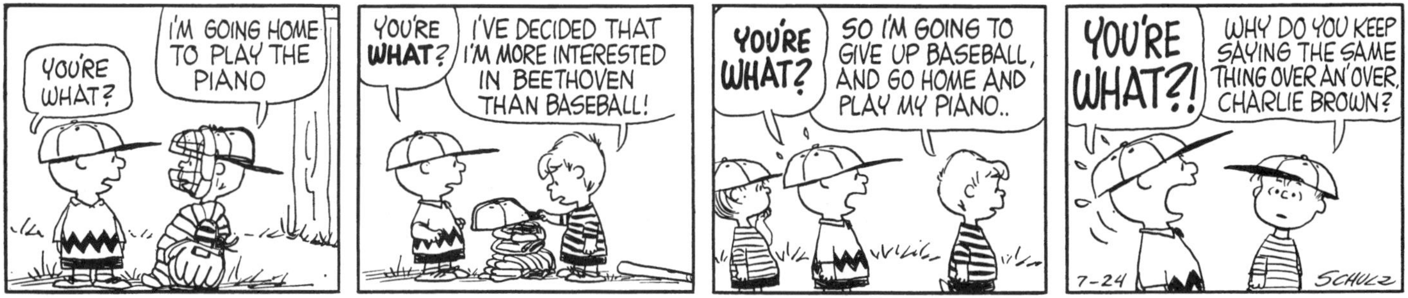
I'M GOING HOME TO PLAY THE PIANO
YOU'RE WHAT?
YOU'RE WHAT?
I'VE DECIDED THAT I'M MORE INTERESTED IN BEETHOVEN THAN BASEBALL!
YOU'RE WHAT?
SO I'M GOING TO GIVE UP BASEBALL, AND GO HOME AND PLAY MY PIANO..
YOU'RE WHAT?!
WHY DO YOU KEEP SAYING THE SAME THING OVER AN' OVER, CHARLIE BROWN?
7-24
SCHULZ

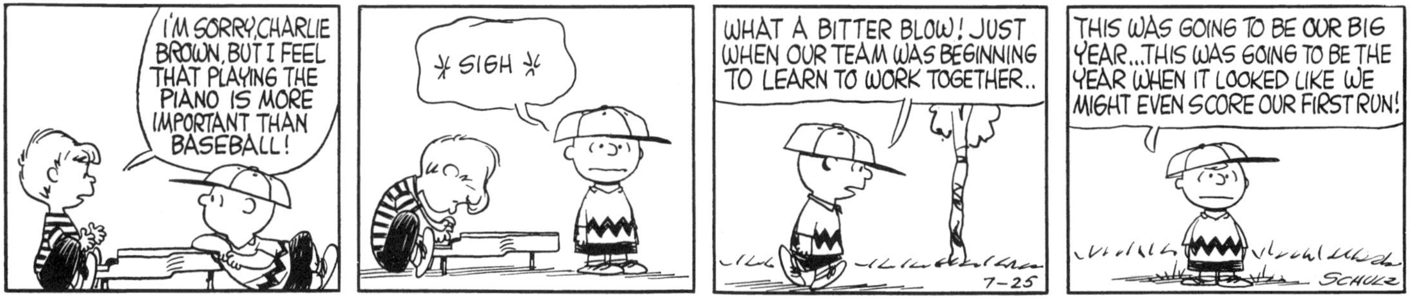
I'M SORRY, CHARLIE BROWN, BUT I FEEL THAT PLAYING THE PIANO IS MORE IMPORTANT THAN BASEBALL!
* SIGH *
WHAT A BITTER BLOW! JUST WHEN OUR TEAM WAS BEGINNING TO LEARN TO WORK TOGETHER..
7-25
THIS WAS GOING TO BE OUR BIG YEAR...THIS WAS GOING TO BE THE YEAR WHEN IT LOOKED LIKE WE MIGHT EVEN SCORE OUR FIRST RUN!
SCHULZ

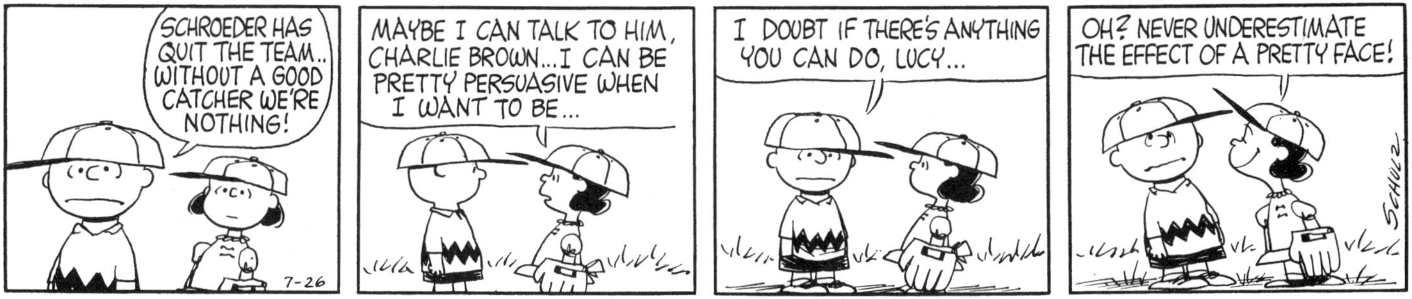
SCHROEDER HAS QUIT THE TEAM.. WITHOUT A GOOD CATCHER WE'RE NOTHING!
7-26
MAYBE I CAN TALK TO HIM, CHARLIE BROWN...I CAN BE PRETTY PERSUASIVE WHEN I WANT TO BE...
I DOUBT IF THERE'S ANYTHING YOU CAN DO, LUCY...
OH? NEVER UNDERESTIMATE THE EFFECT OF A PRETTY FACE!
SCHULZ

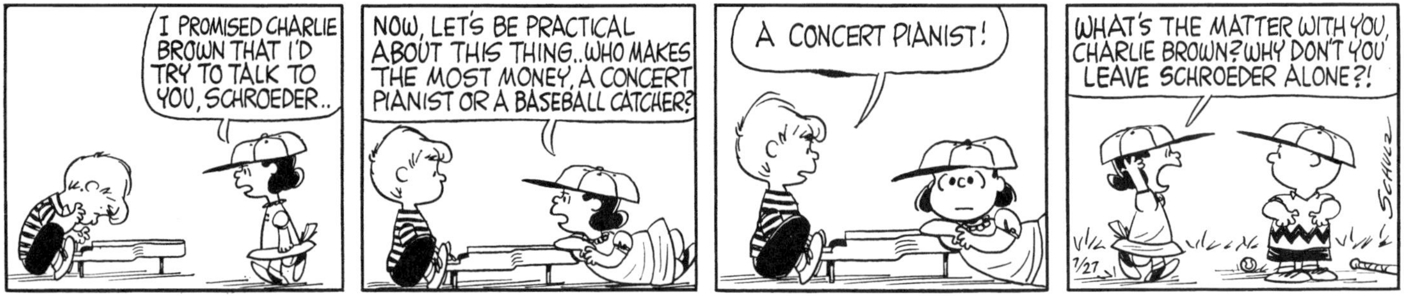
I PROMISED CHARLIE BROWN THAT I'D TRY TO TALK TO YOU, SCHROEDER..
NOW, LET'S BE PRACTICAL ABOUT THIS THING..WHO MAKES THE MOST MONEY, A CONCERT PIANIST OR A BASEBALL CATCHER?
A CONCERT PIANIST!
WHAT'S THE MATTER WITH YOU, CHARLIE BROWN? WHY DON'T YOU LEAVE SCHROEDER ALONE?!
SCHULZ
7/27

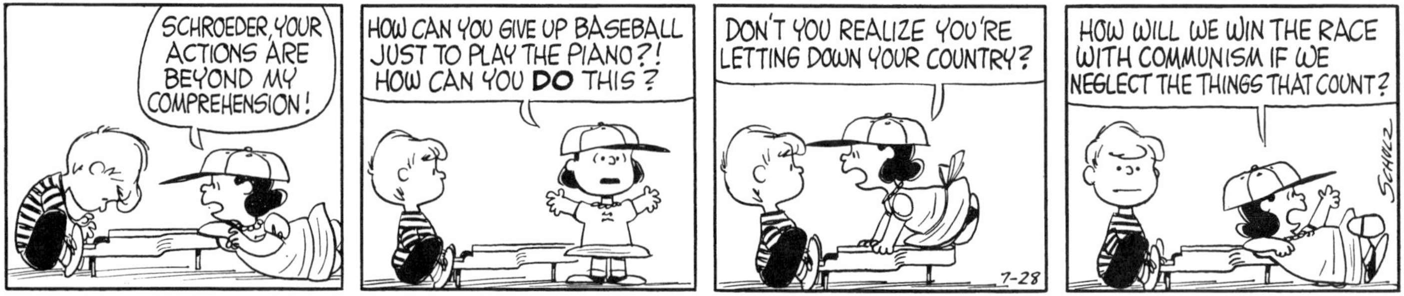
SCHROEDER, YOUR ACTIONS ARE BEYOND MY COMPREHENSION!
HOW CAN YOU GIVE UP BASEBALL JUST TO PLAY THE PIANO?! HOW CAN YOU **DO** THIS?
DON'T YOU REALIZE YOU'RE LETTING DOWN YOUR COUNTRY?
7-28
HOW WILL WE WIN THE RACE WITH COMMUNISM IF WE NEGLECT THE THINGS THAT COUNT?
SCHULZ

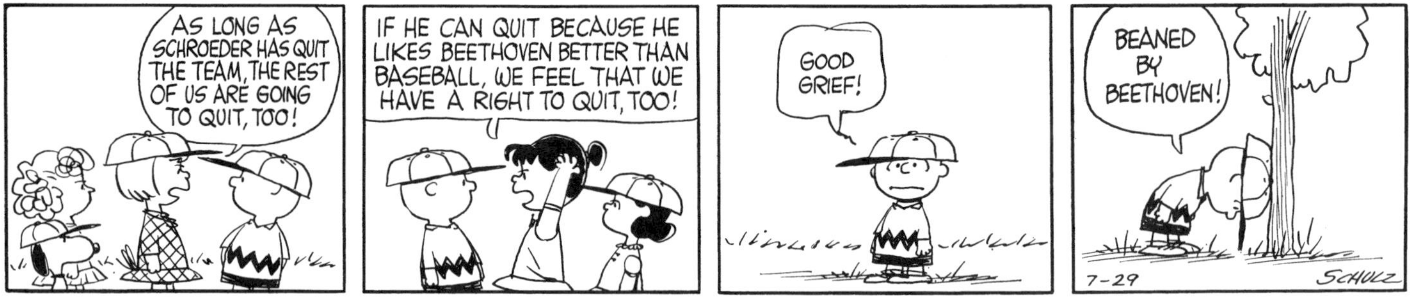
AS LONG AS SCHROEDER HAS QUIT THE TEAM, THE REST OF US ARE GOING TO QUIT, TOO!
IF HE CAN QUIT BECAUSE HE LIKES BEETHOVEN BETTER THAN BASEBALL, WE FEEL THAT WE HAVE A RIGHT TO QUIT, TOO!
GOOD GRIEF!
BEANED BY BEETHOVEN!
7-29
SCHULZ

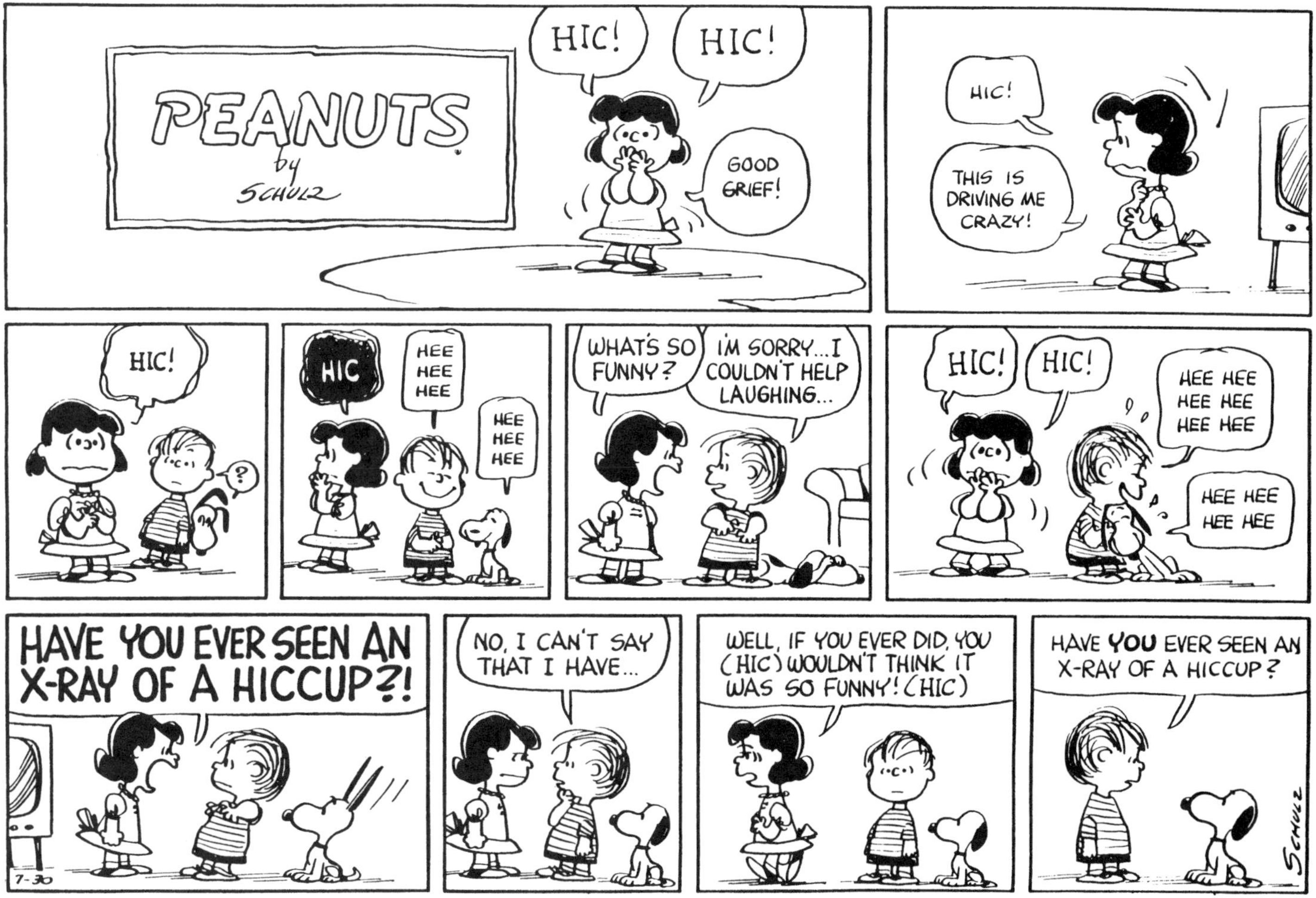
PEANUTS
by SCHULZ
HIC!
HIC!
GOOD GRIEF!
HIC!
THIS IS DRIVING ME CRAZY!
HIC!
?
HIC
HEE HEE HEE
HEE HEE HEE
WHAT'S SO FUNNY?
I'M SORRY...I COULDN'T HELP LAUGHING...
HIC!
HIC!
HEE HEE HEE HEE HEE HEE
HEE HEE HEE HEE
HAVE YOU EVER SEEN AN X-RAY OF A HICCUP?!
7-30
NO, I CAN'T SAY THAT I HAVE...
WELL, IF YOU EVER DID, YOU (HIC) WOULDN'T THINK IT WAS SO FUNNY! (HIC)
HAVE **YOU** EVER SEEN AN X-RAY OF A HICCUP?
SCHULZ

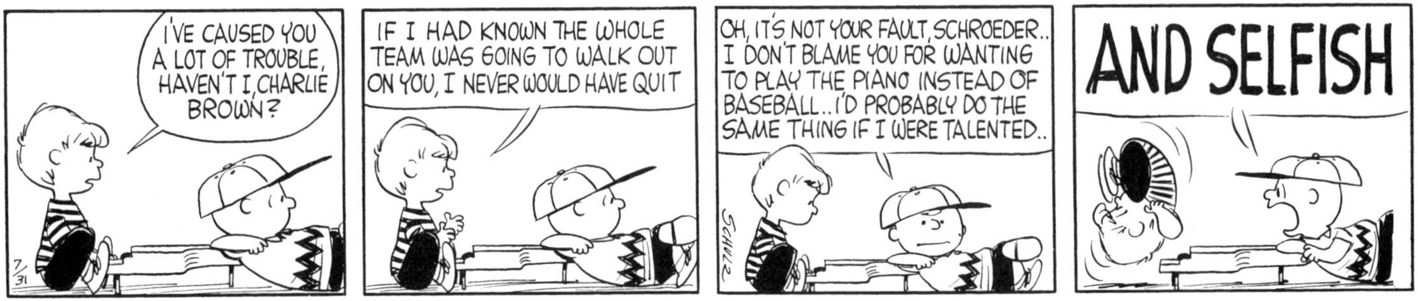
I'VE CAUSED YOU A LOT OF TROUBLE, HAVEN'T I, CHARLIE BROWN?
IF I HAD KNOWN THE WHOLE TEAM WAS GOING TO WALK OUT ON YOU, I NEVER WOULD HAVE QUIT
OH, IT'S NOT YOUR FAULT, SCHROEDER.. I DON'T BLAME YOU FOR WANTING TO PLAY THE PIANO INSTEAD OF BASEBALL..I'D PROBABLY DO THE SAME THING IF I WERE TALENTED..
AND SELFISH

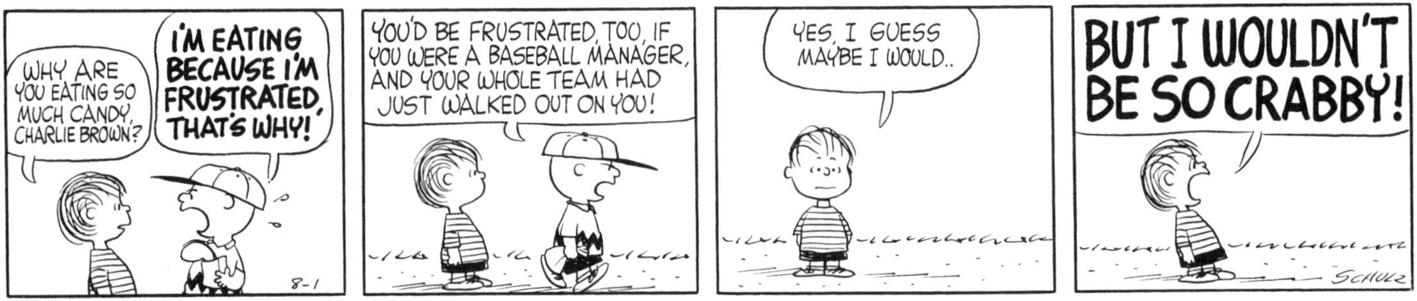
WHY ARE YOU EATING SO MUCH CANDY, CHARLIE BROWN?
I'M EATING BECAUSE I'M FRUSTRATED, THAT'S WHY!
YOU'D BE FRUSTRATED, TOO, IF YOU WERE A BASEBALL MANAGER, AND YOUR WHOLE TEAM HAD JUST WALKED OUT ON YOU!
YES, I GUESS MAYBE I WOULD..
BUT I WOULDN'T BE SO CRABBY!

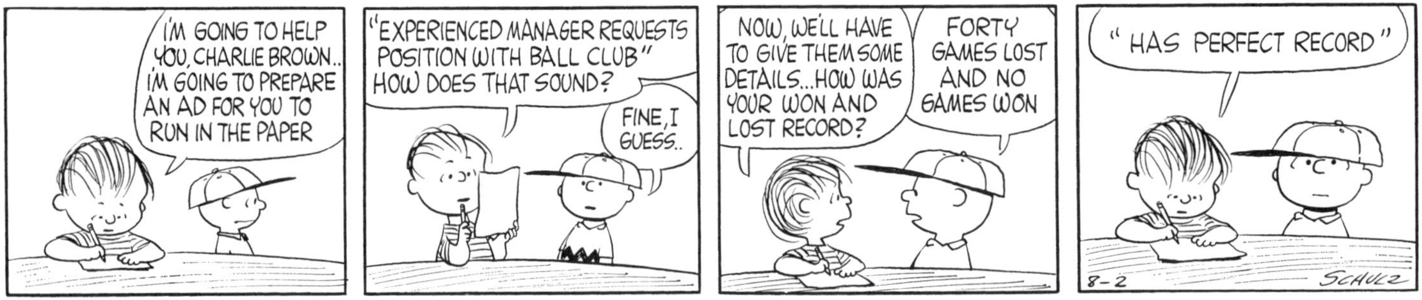
I'M GOING TO HELP YOU, CHARLIE BROWN.. I'M GOING TO PREPARE AN AD FOR YOU TO RUN IN THE PAPER
"EXPERIENCED MANAGER REQUESTS POSITION WITH BALL CLUB" HOW DOES THAT SOUND?
FINE, I GUESS..
NOW, WE'LL HAVE TO GIVE THEM SOME DETAILS...HOW WAS YOUR WON AND LOST RECORD?
FORTY GAMES LOST AND NO GAMES WON
" HAS PERFECT RECORD "

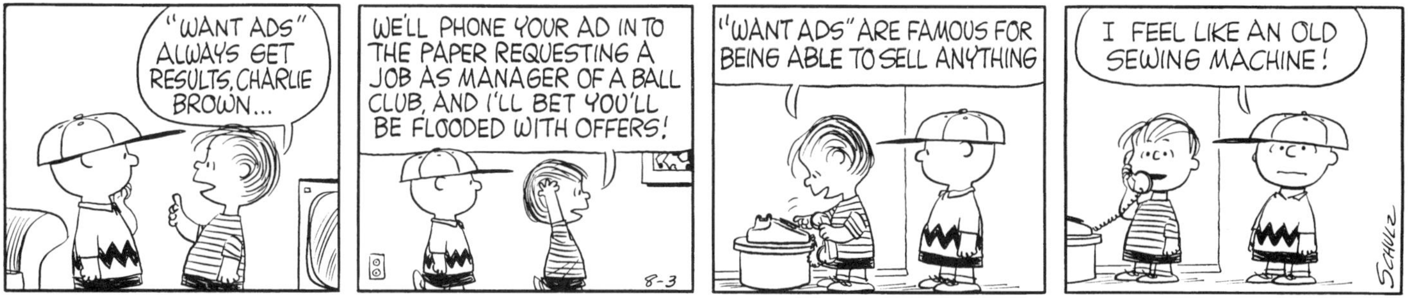
"WANT ADS" ALWAYS GET RESULTS, CHARLIE BROWN...
WE'LL PHONE YOUR AD IN TO THE PAPER REQUESTING A JOB AS MANAGER OF A BALL CLUB, AND I'LL BET YOU'LL BE FLOODED WITH OFFERS!
8-3
"WANT ADS" ARE FAMOUS FOR BEING ABLE TO SELL ANYTHING
I FEEL LIKE AN OLD SEWING MACHINE!
SCHULZ

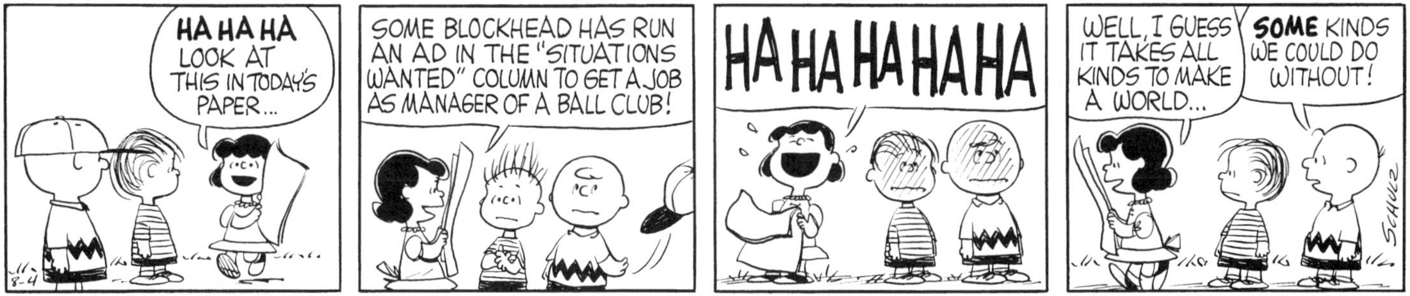
HA HA HA LOOK AT THIS IN TODAY'S PAPER...
8-4
SOME BLOCKHEAD HAS RUN AN AD IN THE "SITUATIONS WANTED" COLUMN TO GET A JOB AS MANAGER OF A BALL CLUB!
HA HA HA HA HA HA
WELL, I GUESS IT TAKES ALL KINDS TO MAKE A WORLD...
SOME KINDS WE COULD DO WITHOUT!
SCHULZ

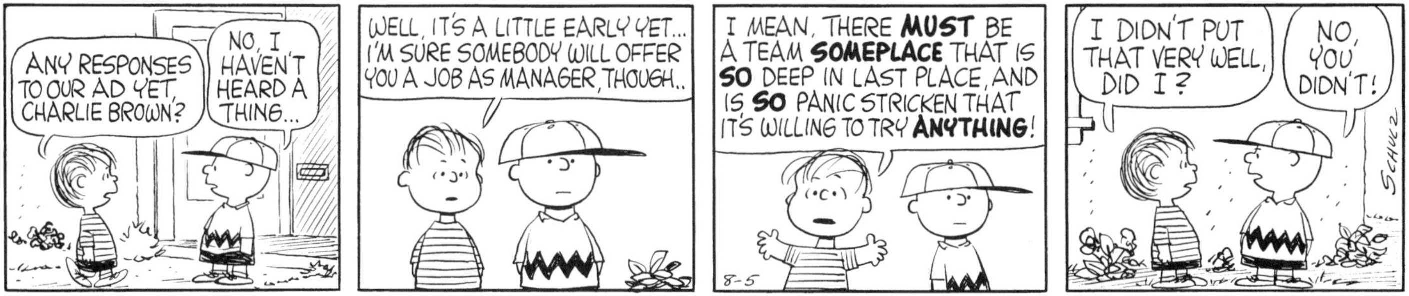
ANY RESPONSES TO OUR AD YET, CHARLIE BROWN?
NO, I HAVEN'T HEARD A THING...
WELL, IT'S A LITTLE EARLY YET... I'M SURE SOMEBODY WILL OFFER YOU A JOB AS MANAGER, THOUGH..
I MEAN, THERE MUST BE A TEAM SOMEPLACE THAT IS SO DEEP IN LAST PLACE, AND IS SO PANIC STRICKEN THAT IT'S WILLING TO TRY ANYTHING!
8-5
I DIDN'T PUT THAT VERY WELL, DID I?
NO, YOU DIDN'T!
SCHULZ

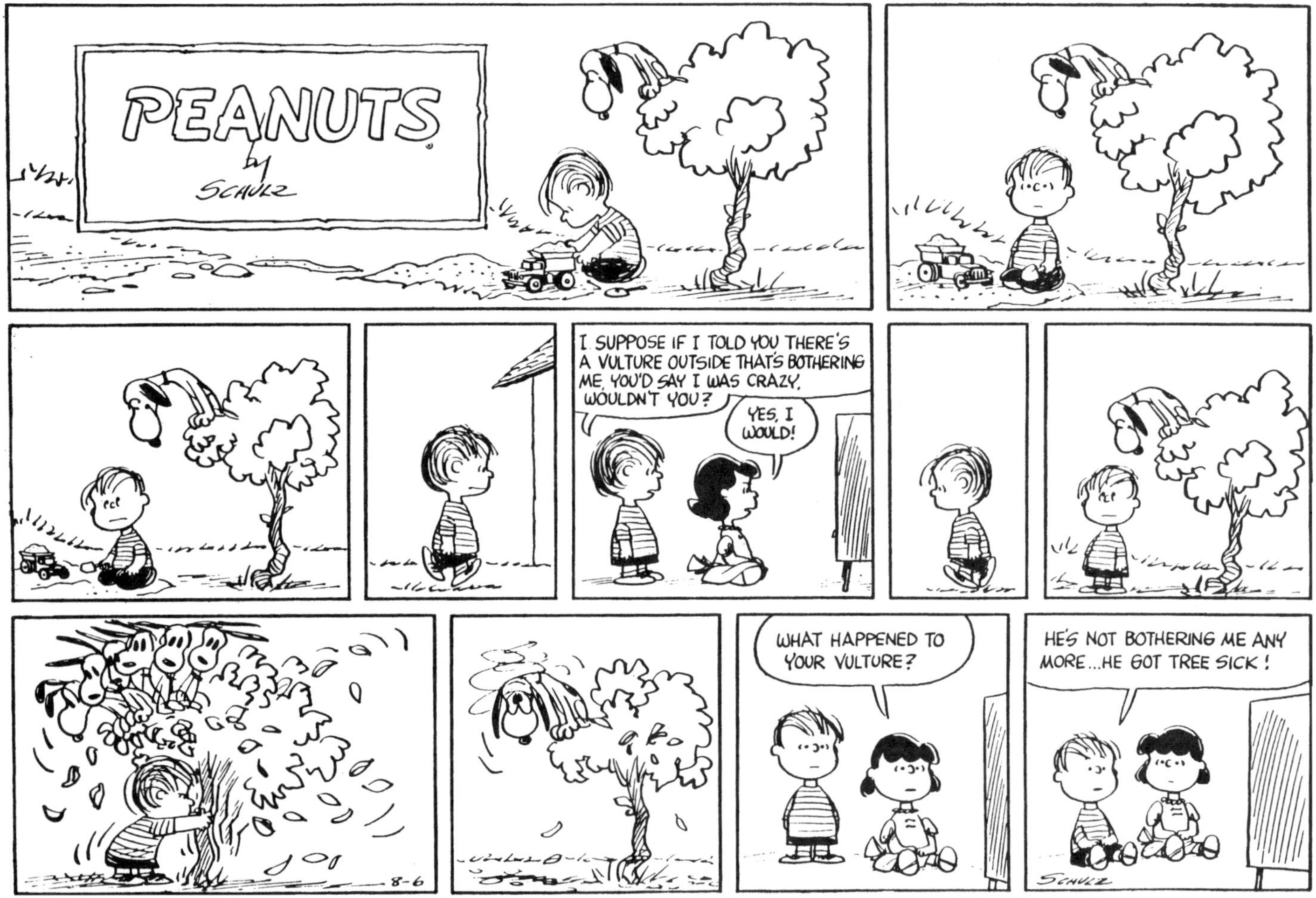
PEANUTS
by SCHULZ
I SUPPOSE IF I TOLD YOU THERE'S A VULTURE OUTSIDE THAT'S BOTHERING ME, YOU'D SAY I WAS CRAZY, WOULDN'T YOU?
YES, I WOULD!
8-6
WHAT HAPPENED TO YOUR VULTURE?
HE'S NOT BOTHERING ME ANY MORE...HE GOT TREE SICK!
SCHULZ

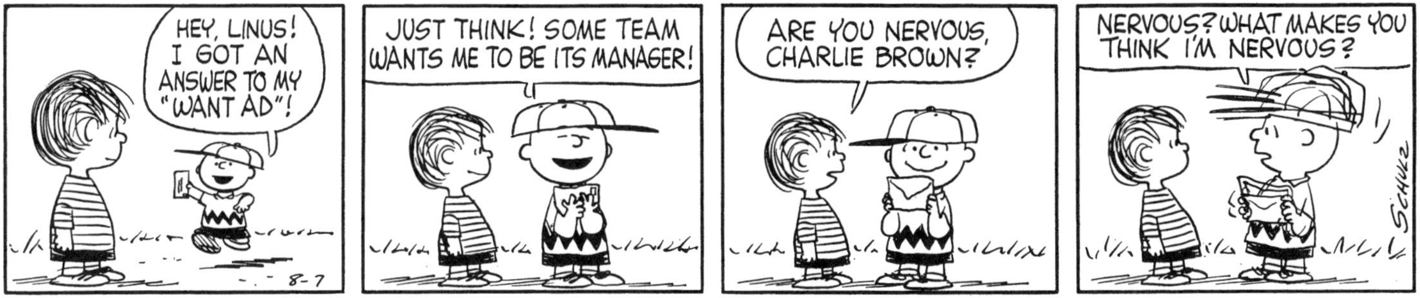
HEY, LINUS! I GOT AN ANSWER TO MY "WANT AD"!
8-7
JUST THINK! SOME TEAM WANTS ME TO BE ITS MANAGER!
ARE YOU NERVOUS, CHARLIE BROWN?
NERVOUS? WHAT MAKES YOU THINK I'M NERVOUS?
SCHULZ

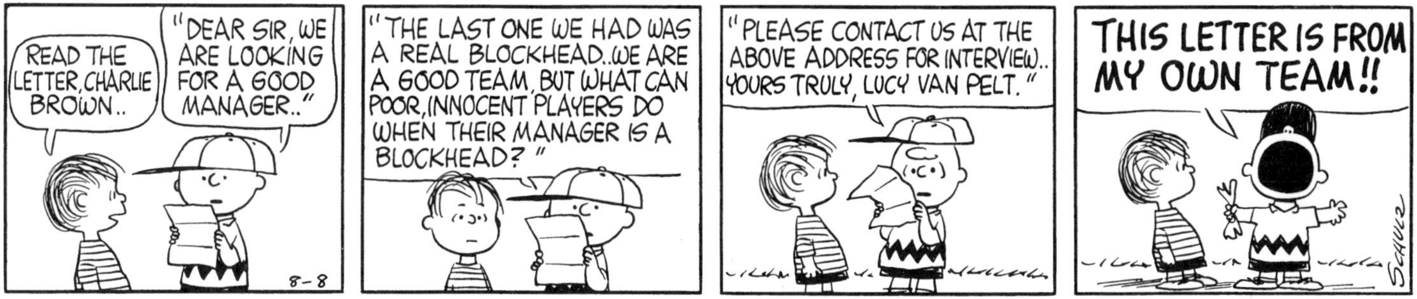
READ THE LETTER, CHARLIE BROWN..
"DEAR SIR, WE ARE LOOKING FOR A GOOD MANAGER.."
8-8
"THE LAST ONE WE HAD WAS A REAL BLOCKHEAD..WE ARE A GOOD TEAM, BUT WHAT CAN POOR, INNOCENT PLAYERS DO WHEN THEIR MANAGER IS A BLOCKHEAD?"
"PLEASE CONTACT US AT THE ABOVE ADDRESS FOR INTERVIEW.. YOURS TRULY, LUCY VAN PELT."
THIS LETTER IS FROM MY OWN TEAM!!
SCHULZ

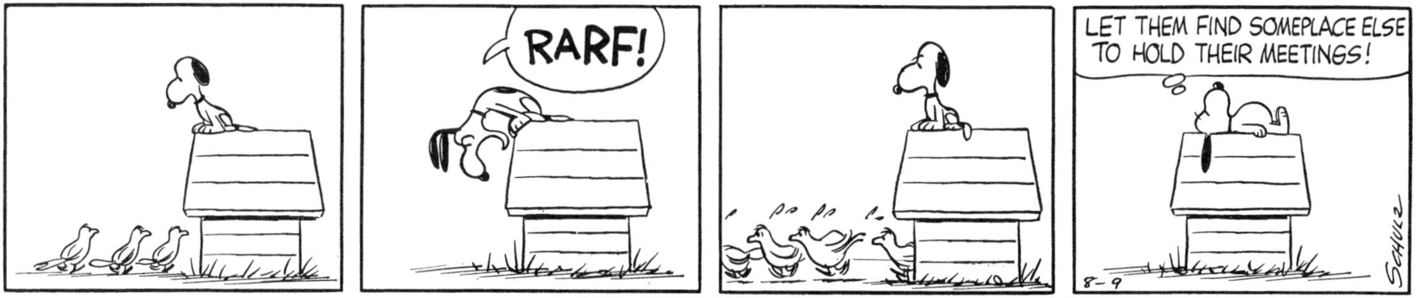
RARF!
LET THEM FIND SOMEPLACE ELSE TO HOLD THEIR MEETINGS!
8-9
SCHULZ

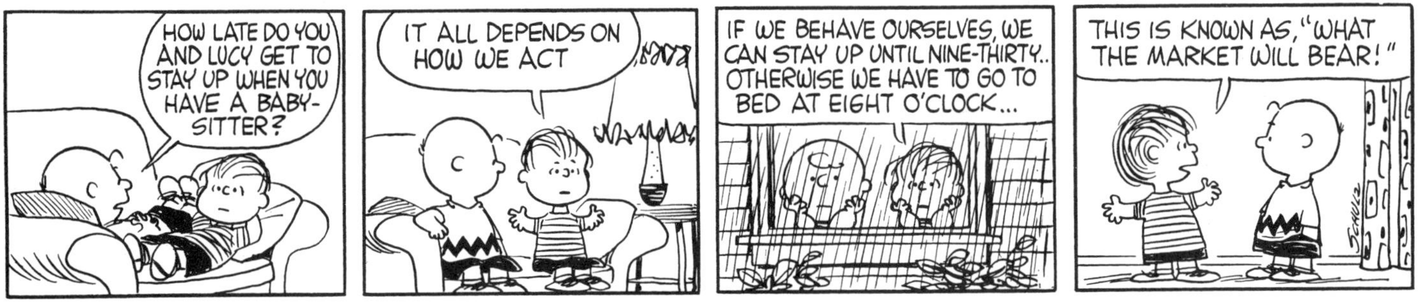
HOW LATE DO YOU AND LUCY GET TO STAY UP WHEN YOU HAVE A BABY-SITTER?
IT ALL DEPENDS ON HOW WE ACT
IF WE BEHAVE OURSELVES, WE CAN STAY UP UNTIL NINE-THIRTY.. OTHERWISE WE HAVE TO GO TO BED AT EIGHT O'CLOCK...
THIS IS KNOWN AS, "WHAT THE MARKET WILL BEAR!"
SCHULZ

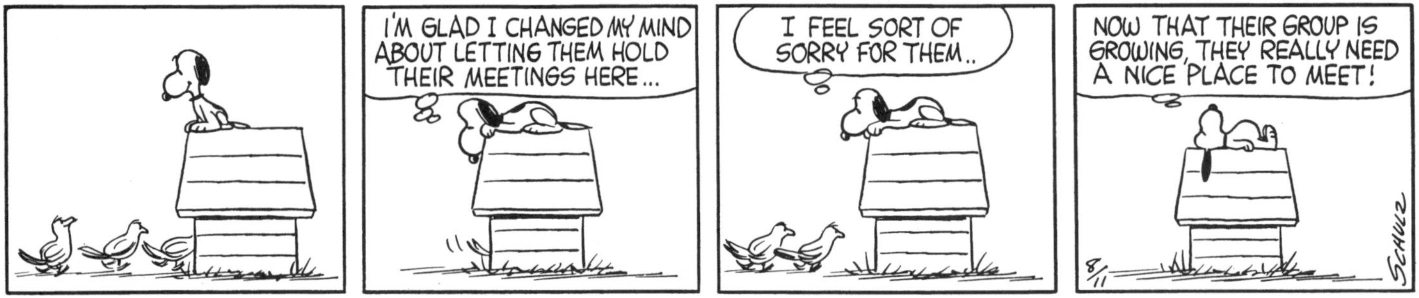
I'M GLAD I CHANGED MY MIND ABOUT LETTING THEM HOLD THEIR MEETINGS HERE...
I FEEL SORT OF SORRY FOR THEM..
NOW THAT THEIR GROUP IS GROWING, THEY REALLY NEED A NICE PLACE TO MEET!
8/11
SCHULZ

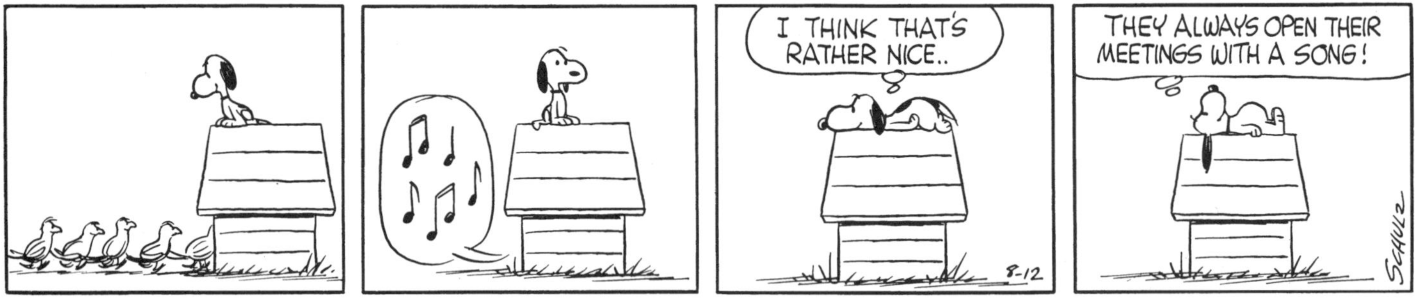
I THINK THAT'S RATHER NICE..
8-12
THEY ALWAYS OPEN THEIR MEETINGS WITH A SONG!
SCHULZ

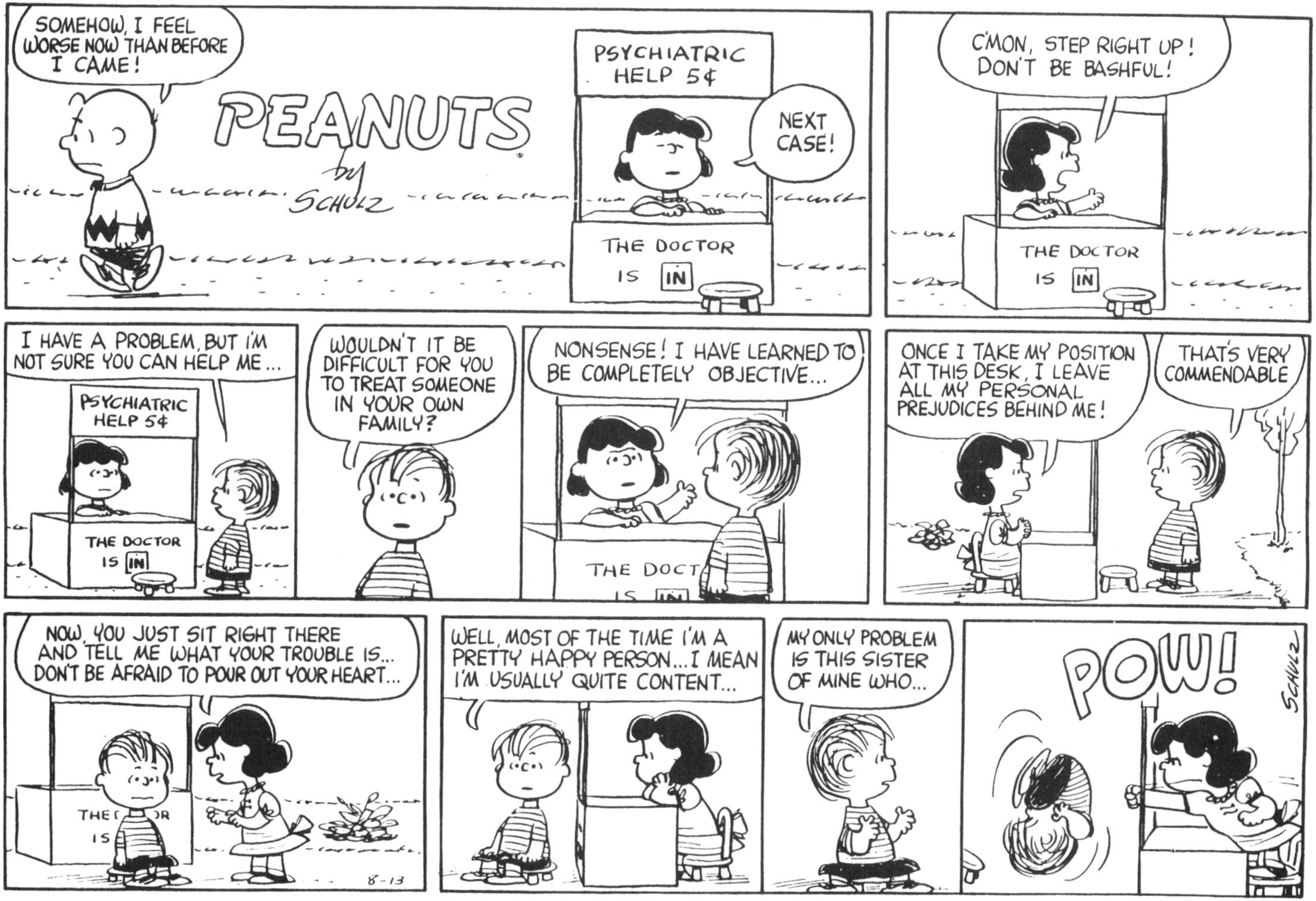
SOMEHOW, I FEEL WORSE NOW THAN BEFORE I CAME!
PEANUTS
by SCHULZ
PSYCHIATRIC HELP 5¢
NEXT CASE!
THE DOCTOR IS IN
C'MON, STEP RIGHT UP! DON'T BE BASHFUL!
THE DOCTOR IS IN
I HAVE A PROBLEM, BUT I'M NOT SURE YOU CAN HELP ME...
PSYCHIATRIC HELP 5¢
THE DOCTOR IS IN
WOULDN'T IT BE DIFFICULT FOR YOU TO TREAT SOMEONE IN YOUR OWN FAMILY?
NONSENSE! I HAVE LEARNED TO BE COMPLETELY OBJECTIVE...
ONCE I TAKE MY POSITION AT THIS DESK, I LEAVE ALL MY PERSONAL PREJUDICES BEHIND ME!
THAT'S VERY COMMENDABLE
NOW, YOU JUST SIT RIGHT THERE AND TELL ME WHAT YOUR TROUBLE IS... DON'T BE AFRAID TO POUR OUT YOUR HEART...
8-13
WELL, MOST OF THE TIME I'M A PRETTY HAPPY PERSON... I MEAN I'M USUALLY QUITE CONTENT...
MY ONLY PROBLEM IS THIS SISTER OF MINE WHO...
POW!
SCHULZ

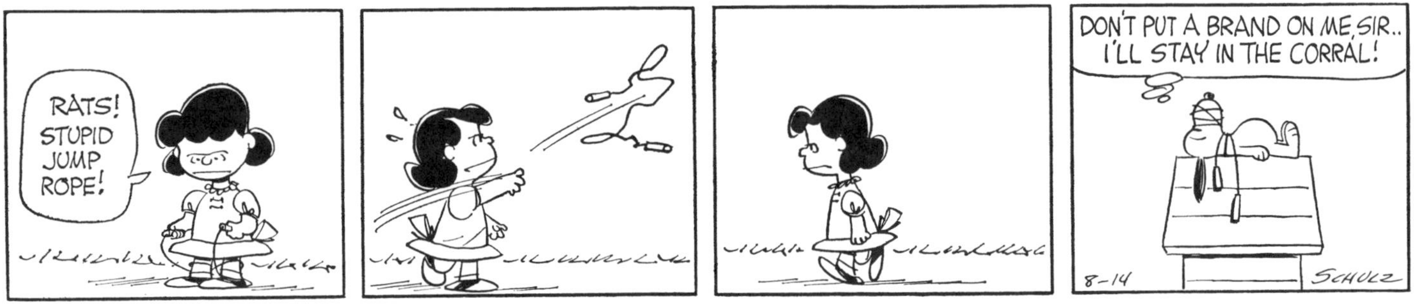
RATS! STUPID JUMP ROPE!
DON'T PUT A BRAND ON ME, SIR.. I'LL STAY IN THE CORRAL!
8-14
SCHULZ

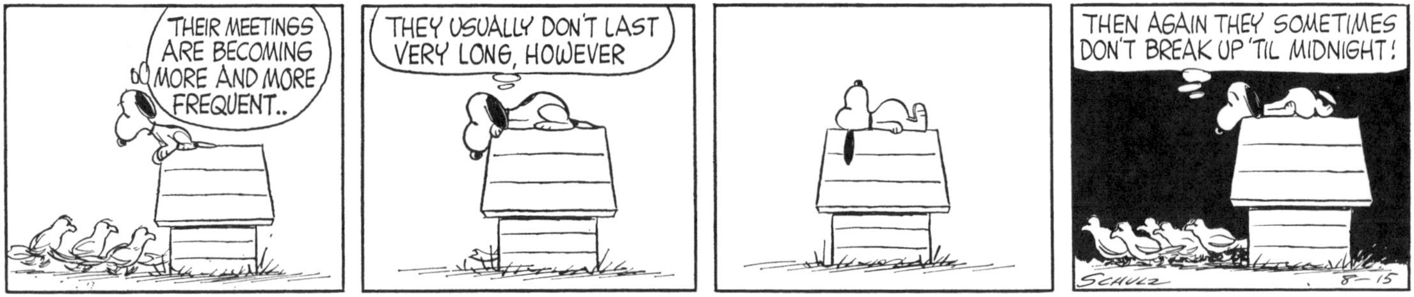
THEIR MEETINGS ARE BECOMING MORE AND MORE FREQUENT..
THEY USUALLY DON'T LAST VERY LONG, HOWEVER
THEN AGAIN THEY SOMETIMES DON'T BREAK UP 'TIL MIDNIGHT!
SCHULZ
8-15

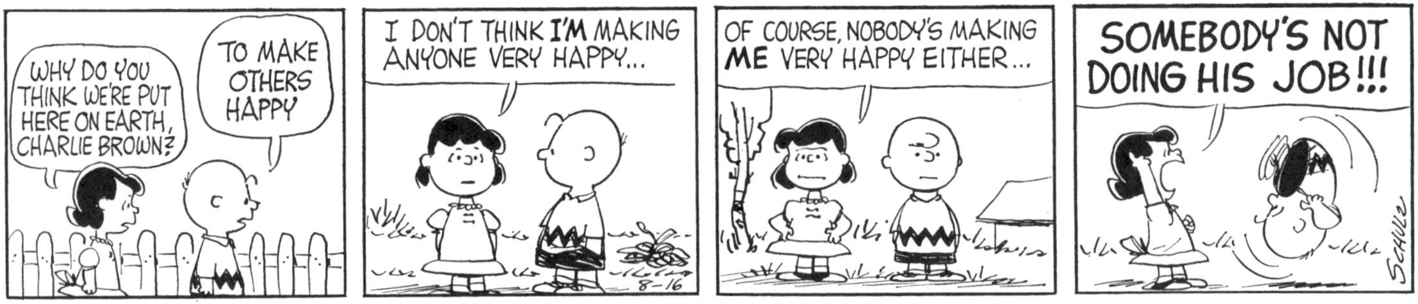
WHY DO YOU THINK WE'RE PUT HERE ON EARTH, CHARLIE BROWN?
TO MAKE OTHERS HAPPY
I DON'T THINK I'M MAKING ANYONE VERY HAPPY...
8-16
OF COURSE, NOBODY'S MAKING ME VERY HAPPY EITHER...
SOMEBODY'S NOT DOING HIS JOB!!!
SCHULZ

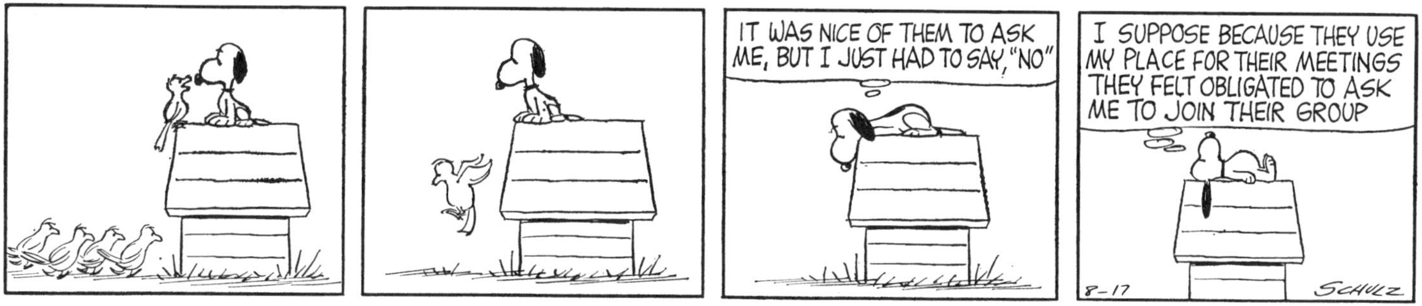
IT WAS NICE OF THEM TO ASK ME, BUT I JUST HAD TO SAY, "NO"
I SUPPOSE BECAUSE THEY USE MY PLACE FOR THEIR MEETINGS THEY FELT OBLIGATED TO ASK ME TO JOIN THEIR GROUP
8-17
SCHULZ

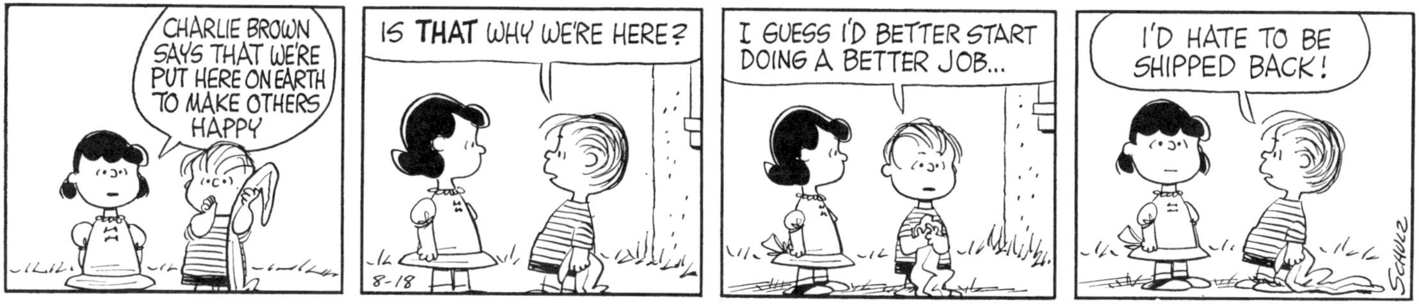
CHARLIE BROWN SAYS THAT WE'RE PUT HERE ON EARTH TO MAKE OTHERS HAPPY
IS **THAT** WHY WE'RE HERE?
8-18
I GUESS I'D BETTER START DOING A BETTER JOB...
I'D HATE TO BE SHIPPED BACK!
SCHULZ

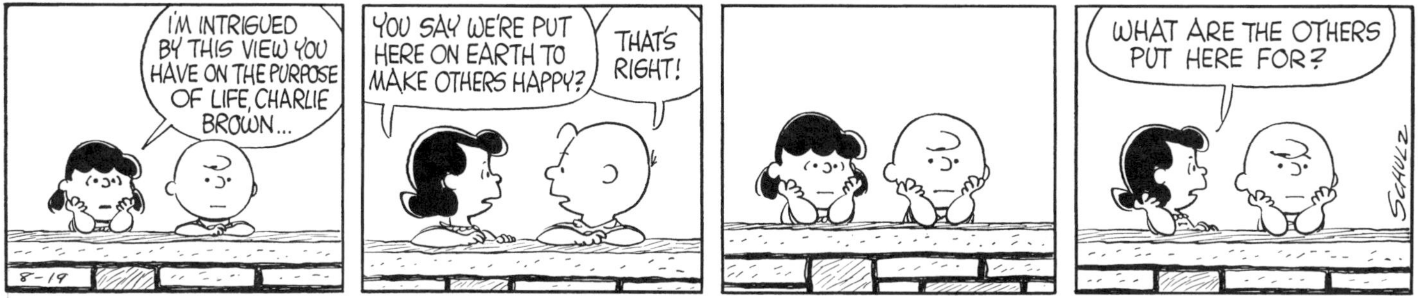
I'M INTRIGUED BY THIS VIEW YOU HAVE ON THE PURPOSE OF LIFE, CHARLIE BROWN...
8-19
YOU SAY WE'RE PUT HERE ON EARTH TO MAKE OTHERS HAPPY?
THAT'S RIGHT!
WHAT ARE THE OTHERS PUT HERE FOR?
SCHULZ

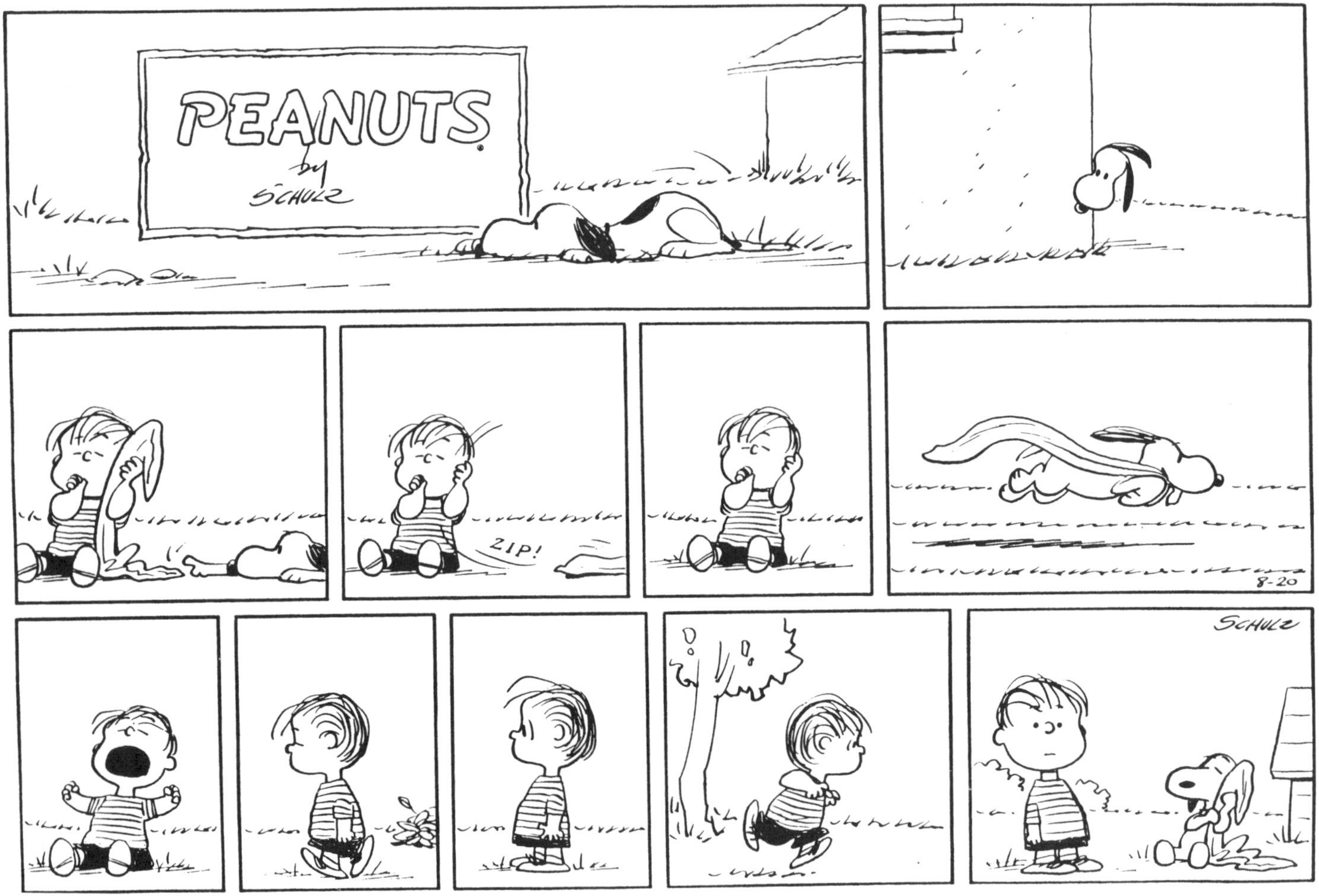
PEANUTS
by
SCHULZ
ZIP!
8-20
SCHULZ

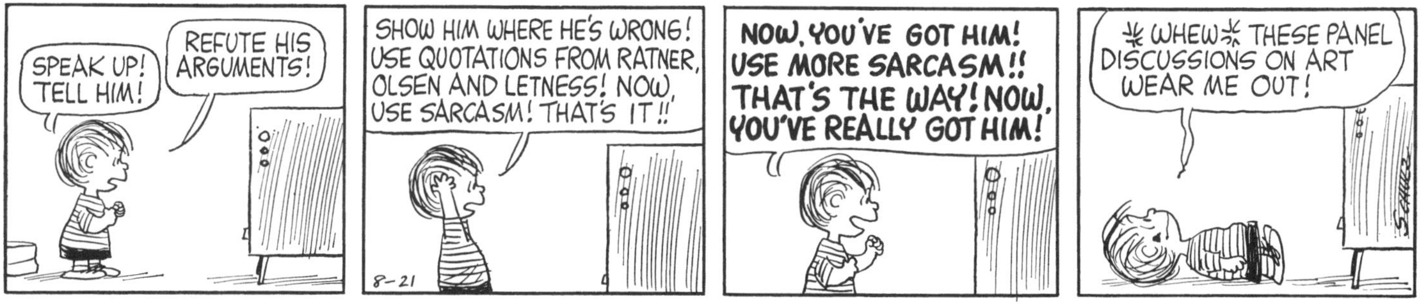
SPEAK UP! TELL HIM!
REFUTE HIS ARGUMENTS!
SHOW HIM WHERE HE'S WRONG! USE QUOTATIONS FROM RATNER, OLSEN AND LETNESS! NOW, USE SARCASM! THAT'S IT!!
8-21
NOW, YOU'VE GOT HIM! USE MORE SARCASM!! THAT'S THE WAY! NOW, YOU'VE REALLY GOT HIM!
WHEW THESE PANEL DISCUSSIONS ON ART WEAR ME OUT!
SCHULZ

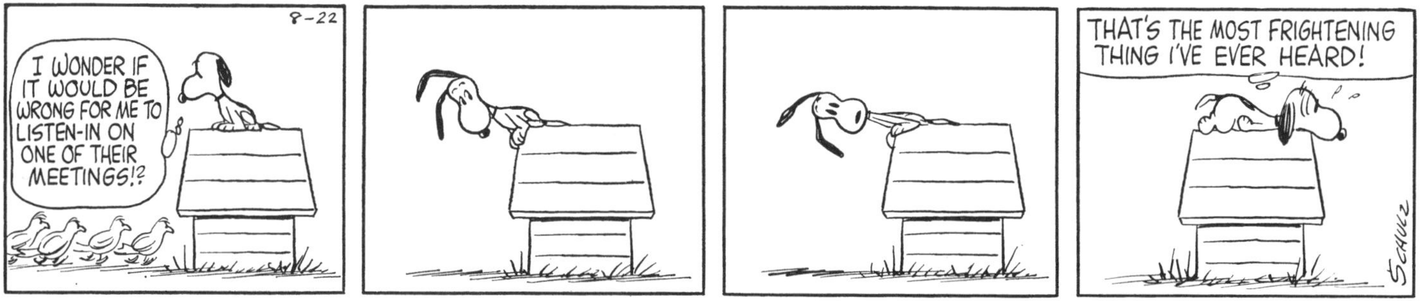
8-22
I WONDER IF IT WOULD BE WRONG FOR ME TO LISTEN-IN ON ONE OF THEIR MEETINGS!?
THAT'S THE MOST FRIGHTENING THING I'VE EVER HEARD!
SCHULZ

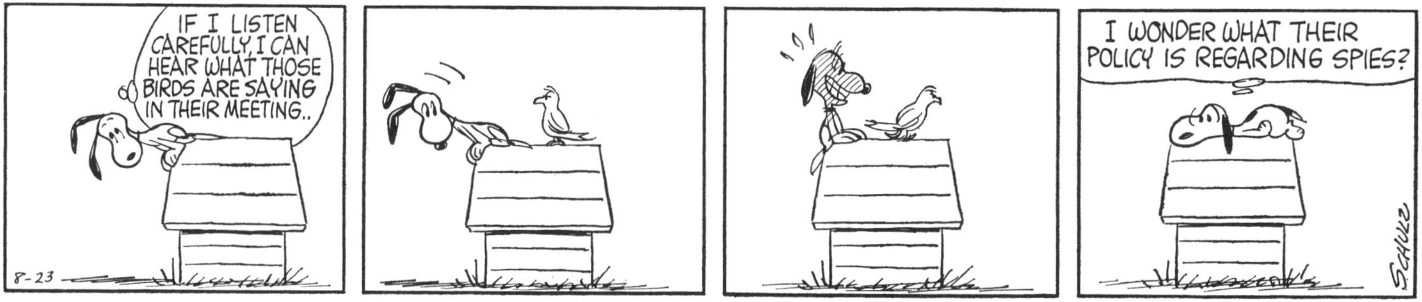
IF I LISTEN CAREFULLY, I CAN HEAR WHAT THOSE BIRDS ARE SAYING IN THEIR MEETING..
8-23
I WONDER WHAT THEIR POLICY IS REGARDING SPIES?
SCHULZ

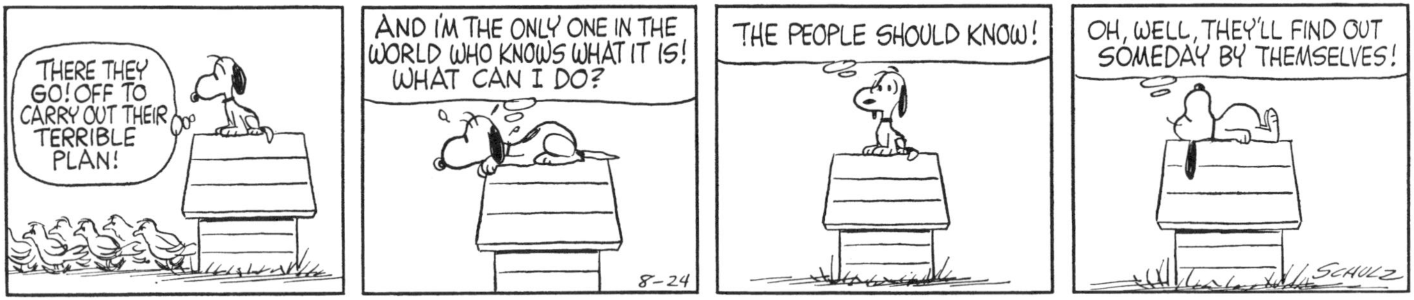
THERE THEY GO! OFF TO CARRY OUT THEIR TERRIBLE PLAN!
AND I'M THE ONLY ONE IN THE WORLD WHO KNOWS WHAT IT IS! WHAT CAN I DO?
8-24
THE PEOPLE SHOULD KNOW!
OH, WELL, THEY'LL FIND OUT SOMEDAY BY THEMSELVES!
SCHULZ

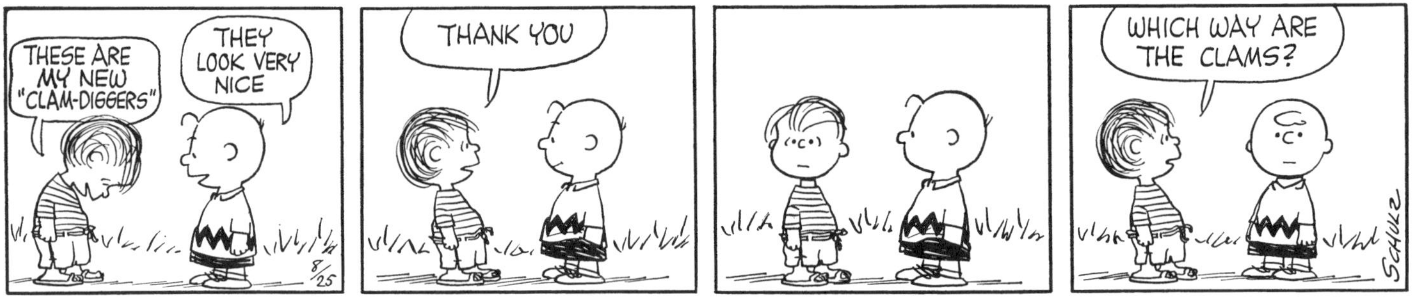
THESE ARE MY NEW "CLAM-DIGGERS"
THEY LOOK VERY NICE
8/25
THANK YOU
WHICH WAY ARE THE CLAMS?
SCHULZ

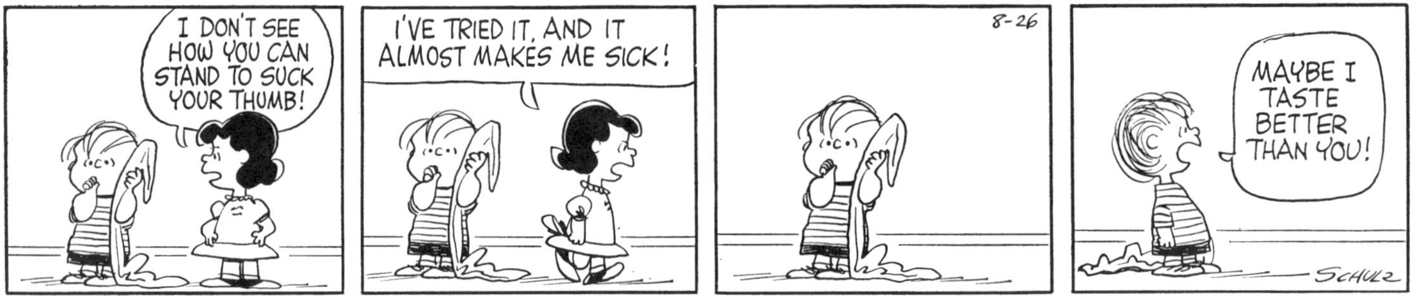
I DON'T SEE HOW YOU CAN STAND TO SUCK YOUR THUMB!
I'VE TRIED IT, AND IT ALMOST MAKES ME SICK!
8-26
MAYBE I TASTE BETTER THAN YOU!
SCHULZ

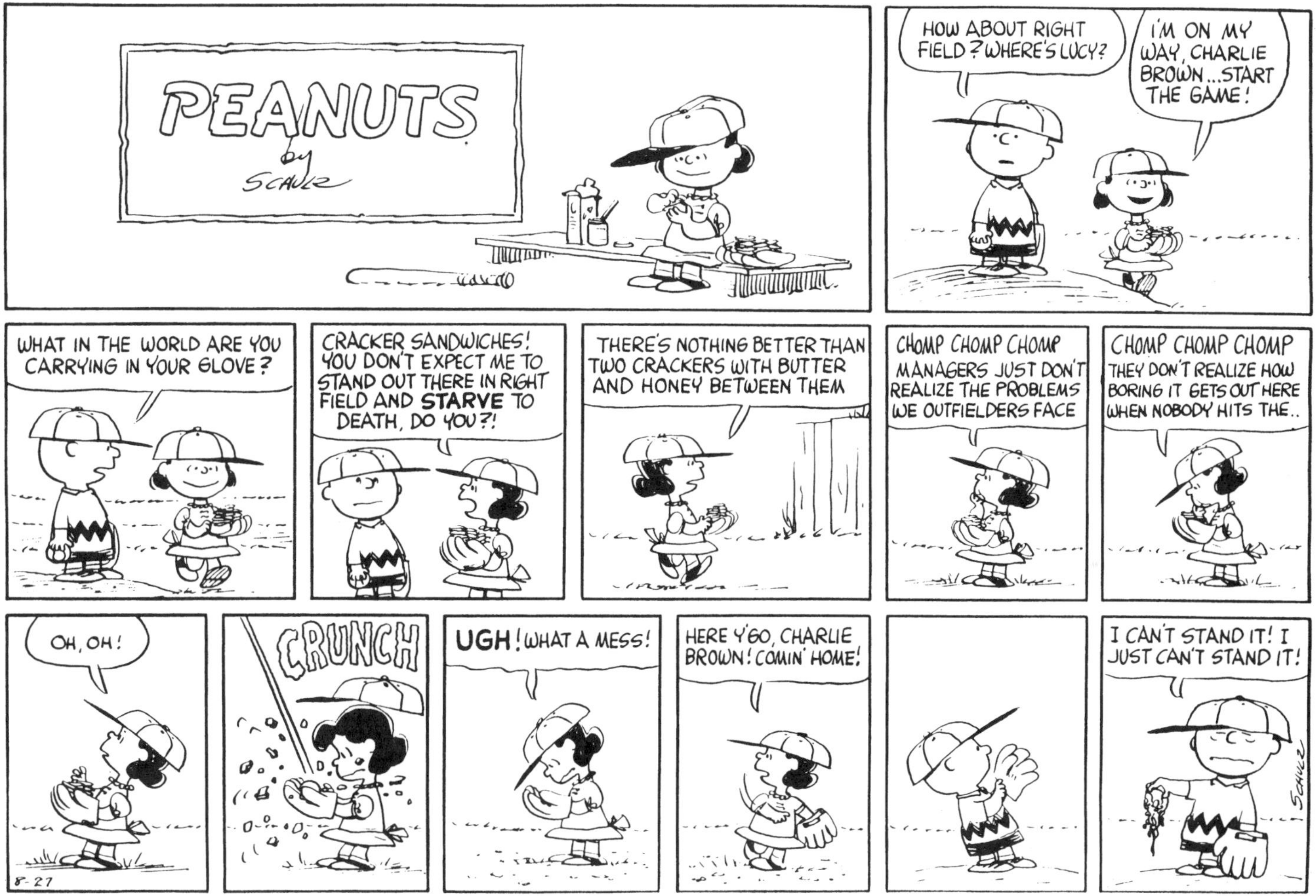
PEANUTS
by
SCHULZ
HOW ABOUT RIGHT FIELD? WHERE'S LUCY?
I'M ON MY WAY, CHARLIE BROWN...START THE GAME!
WHAT IN THE WORLD ARE YOU CARRYING IN YOUR GLOVE?
CRACKER SANDWICHES! YOU DON'T EXPECT ME TO STAND OUT THERE IN RIGHT FIELD AND STARVE TO DEATH, DO YOU?!
THERE'S NOTHING BETTER THAN TWO CRACKERS WITH BUTTER AND HONEY BETWEEN THEM
CHOMP CHOMP CHOMP
MANAGERS JUST DON'T REALIZE THE PROBLEMS WE OUTFIELDERS FACE
CHOMP CHOMP CHOMP
THEY DON'T REALIZE HOW BORING IT GETS OUT HERE WHEN NOBODY HITS THE..
OH, OH!
8-27
CRUNCH
UGH! WHAT A MESS!
HERE Y'GO, CHARLIE BROWN! COMIN' HOME!
SCHULZ
I CAN'T STAND IT! I JUST CAN'T STAND IT!

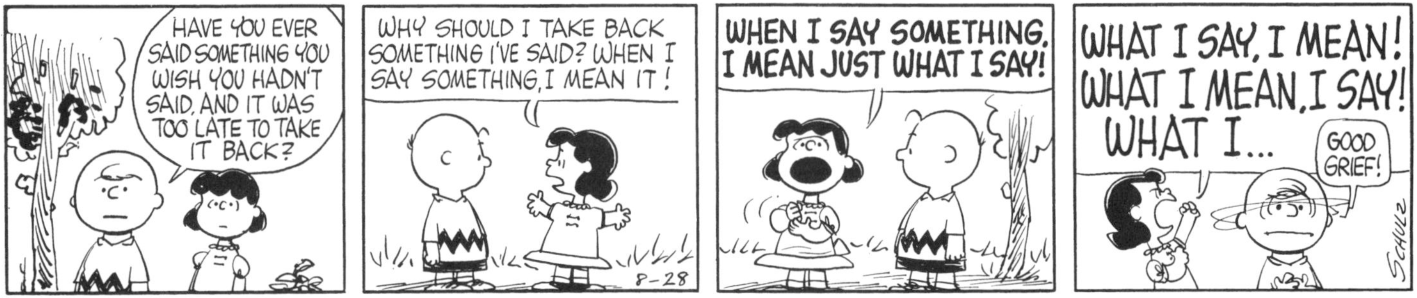
HAVE YOU EVER SAID SOMETHING YOU WISH YOU HADN'T SAID, AND IT WAS TOO LATE TO TAKE IT BACK?
WHY SHOULD I TAKE BACK SOMETHING I'VE SAID? WHEN I SAY SOMETHING, I MEAN IT!
8-28
WHEN I SAY SOMETHING, I MEAN JUST WHAT I SAY!
WHAT I SAY, I MEAN! WHAT I MEAN, I SAY! WHAT I...
GOOD GRIEF!
SCHULZ

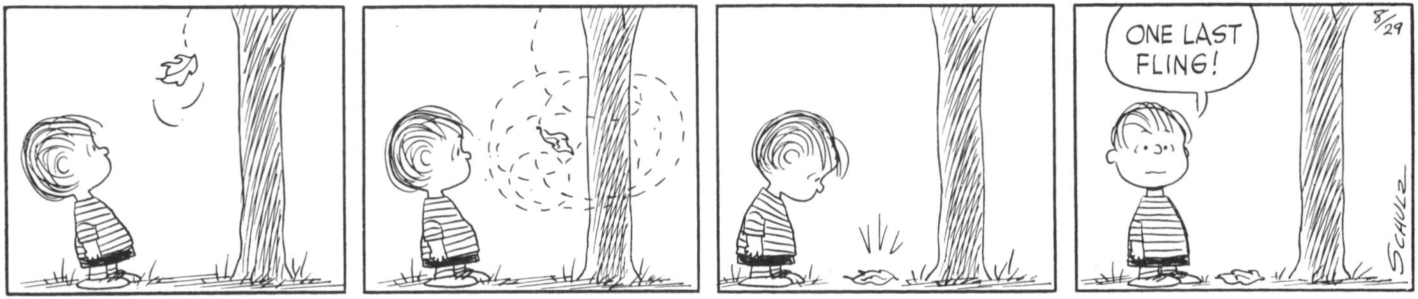
ONE LAST FLING!
8/29
SCHULZ

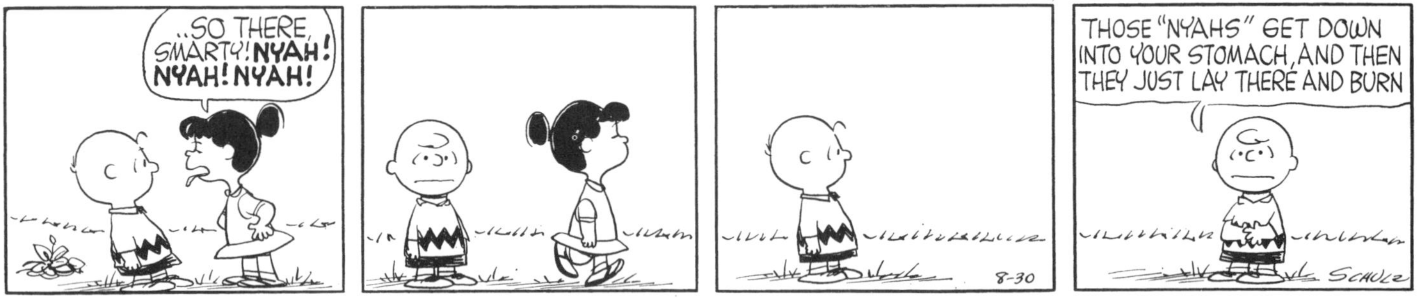
..SO THERE, SMARTY! NYAH! NYAH! NYAH!
8-30
THOSE "NYAHS" GET DOWN INTO YOUR STOMACH, AND THEN THEY JUST LAY THERE AND BURN
SCHULZ

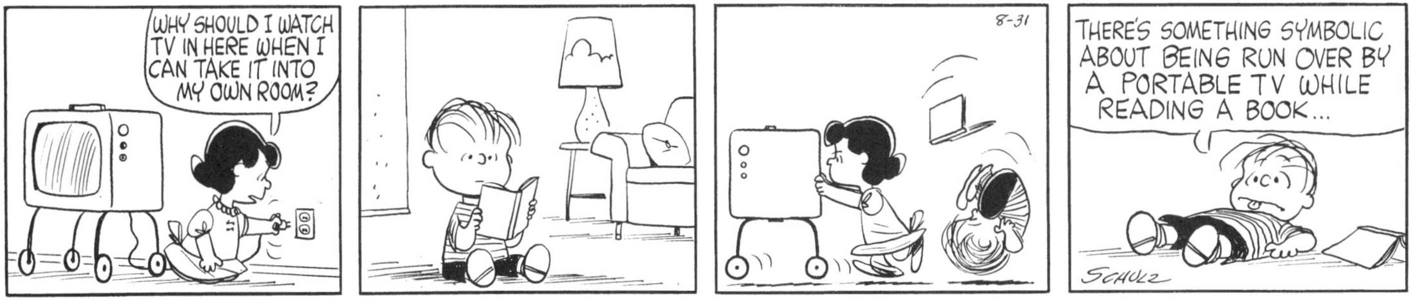
WHY SHOULD I WATCH TV IN HERE WHEN I CAN TAKE IT INTO MY OWN ROOM?
8-31
THERE'S SOMETHING SYMBOLIC ABOUT BEING RUN OVER BY A PORTABLE TV WHILE READING A BOOK...
SCHULZ

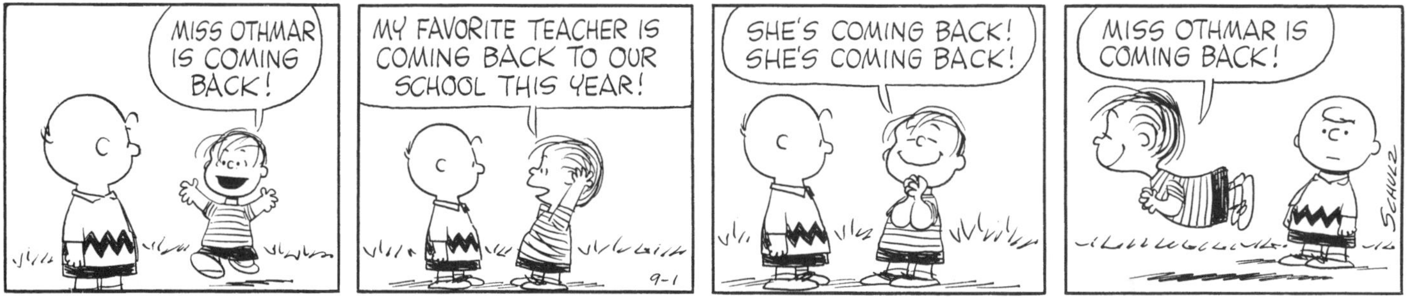
MISS OTHMAR IS COMING BACK!
MY FAVORITE TEACHER IS COMING BACK TO OUR SCHOOL THIS YEAR!
9-1
SHE'S COMING BACK! SHE'S COMING BACK!
MISS OTHMAR IS COMING BACK!
SCHULZ

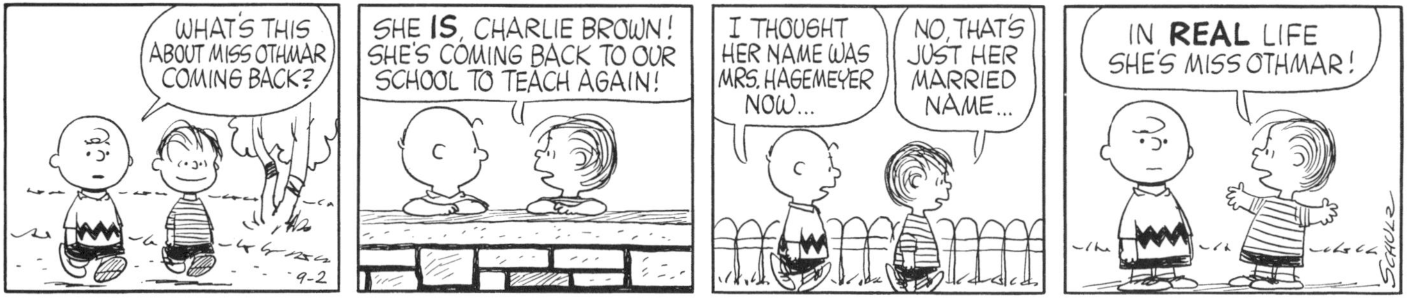
WHAT'S THIS ABOUT MISS OTHMAR COMING BACK?
9-2
SHE **IS**, CHARLIE BROWN! SHE'S COMING BACK TO OUR SCHOOL TO TEACH AGAIN!
I THOUGHT HER NAME WAS MRS. HAGEMEYER NOW...
NO, THAT'S JUST HER MARRIED NAME...
IN **REAL** LIFE SHE'S MISS OTHMAR!
SCHULZ

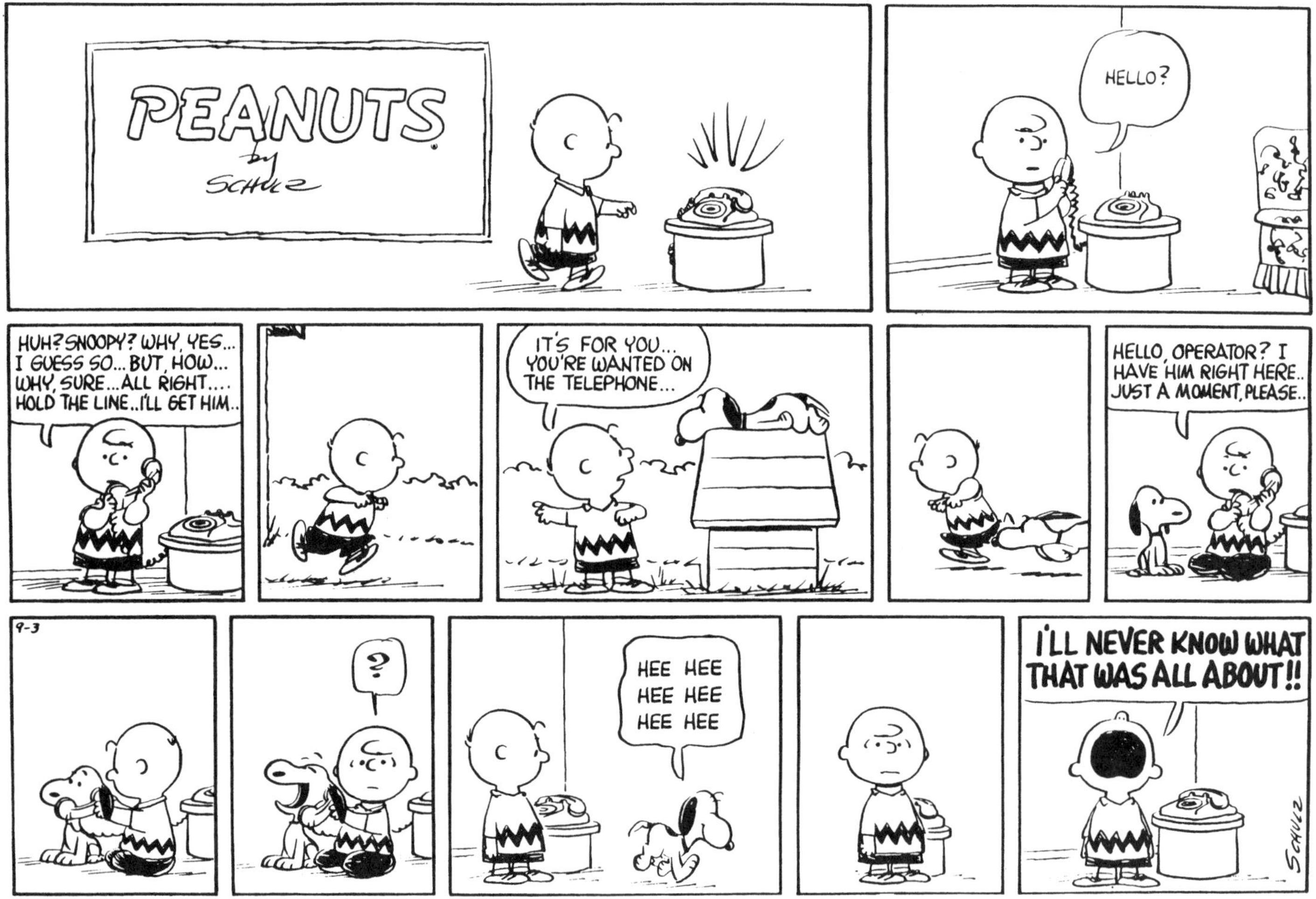
PEANUTS
by SCHULZ
HELLO?
HUH? SNOOPY? WHY, YES... I GUESS SO... BUT, HOW... WHY, SURE... ALL RIGHT.... HOLD THE LINE.. I'LL GET HIM..
IT'S FOR YOU... YOU'RE WANTED ON THE TELEPHONE...
HELLO, OPERATOR? I HAVE HIM RIGHT HERE.. JUST A MOMENT, PLEASE..
9-3
?
HEE HEE HEE HEE HEE HEE
I'LL NEVER KNOW WHAT THAT WAS ALL ABOUT!!
SCHULZ

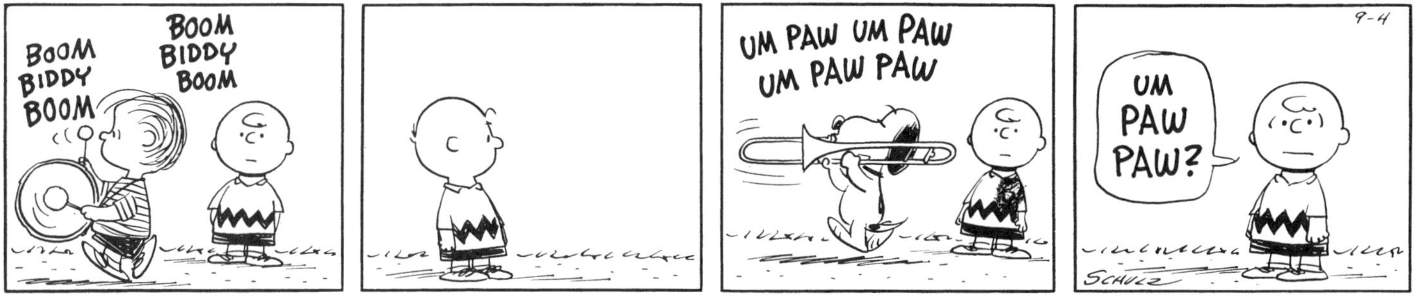
BOOM BIDDY BOOM
BOOM BIDDY BOOM
UM PAW UM PAW UM PAW PAW
9-4
UM PAW PAW?
SCHULZ

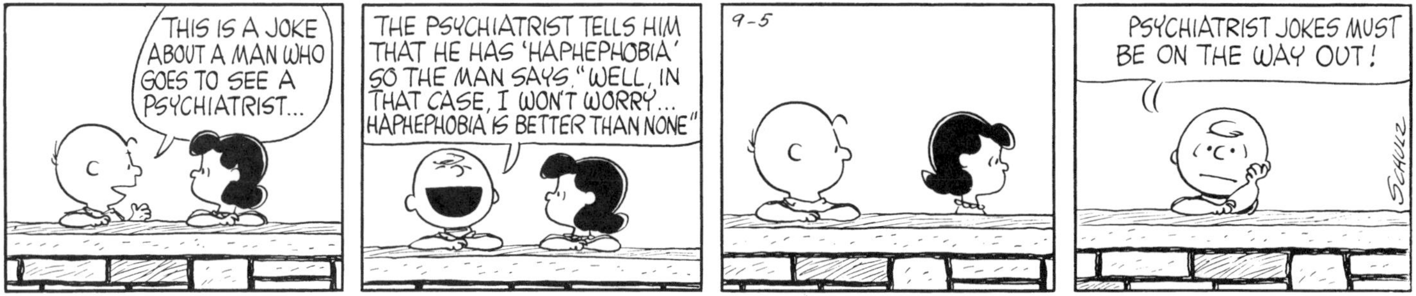
THIS IS A JOKE ABOUT A MAN WHO GOES TO SEE A PSYCHIATRIST...
THE PSYCHIATRIST TELLS HIM THAT HE HAS 'HAPHEPHOBIA' SO THE MAN SAYS, "WELL, IN THAT CASE, I WON'T WORRY... HAPHEPHOBIA IS BETTER THAN NONE"
9-5
PSYCHIATRIST JOKES MUST BE ON THE WAY OUT!
SCHULZ

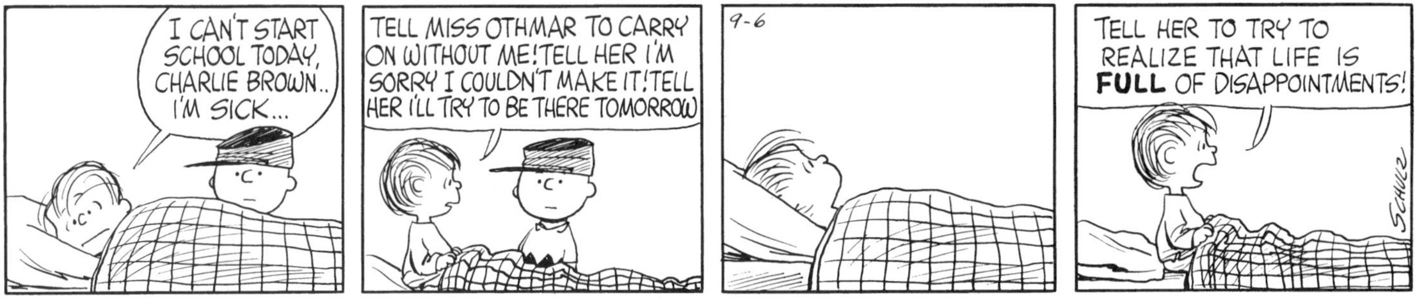
I CAN'T START SCHOOL TODAY, CHARLIE BROWN.. I'M SICK...
TELL MISS OTHMAR TO CARRY ON WITHOUT ME! TELL HER I'M SORRY I COULDN'T MAKE IT! TELL HER I'LL TRY TO BE THERE TOMORROW
9-6
TELL HER TO TRY TO REALIZE THAT LIFE IS FULL OF DISAPPOINTMENTS!
SCHULZ

Panel 1: IT WAS GOOD TO BE BACK IN SCHOOL AGAIN...

Panel 2: IT WAS GOOD JUST TO SIT THERE AND WATCH MISS OTHMAR IN ACTION...

Panel 3: OF COURSE, I ADMIRE **ALL** TEACHERS, BUT MISS OTHMAR IS A GEM AMONG GEMS...

Panel 4: ONE WONDERS WHAT THE NATIONAL EDUCATION ASSOCIATION DID TO DESERVE SUCH A BREAK

Panel 5: I CAN'T HIT YOU NOW BECAUSE YOU'RE BIGGER THAN I AM...

Panel 6: BUT YOU JUST WAIT... IN A FEW MORE YEARS I'LL BE BIGGER THAN YOU ARE!

Panel 7: BY THEN I'LL BE A LADY, AND YOU CAN'T HIT A LADY, SO NYAH, NYAH, NYAH!

Panel 8: I'M LIVING IN A STACKED DECK!

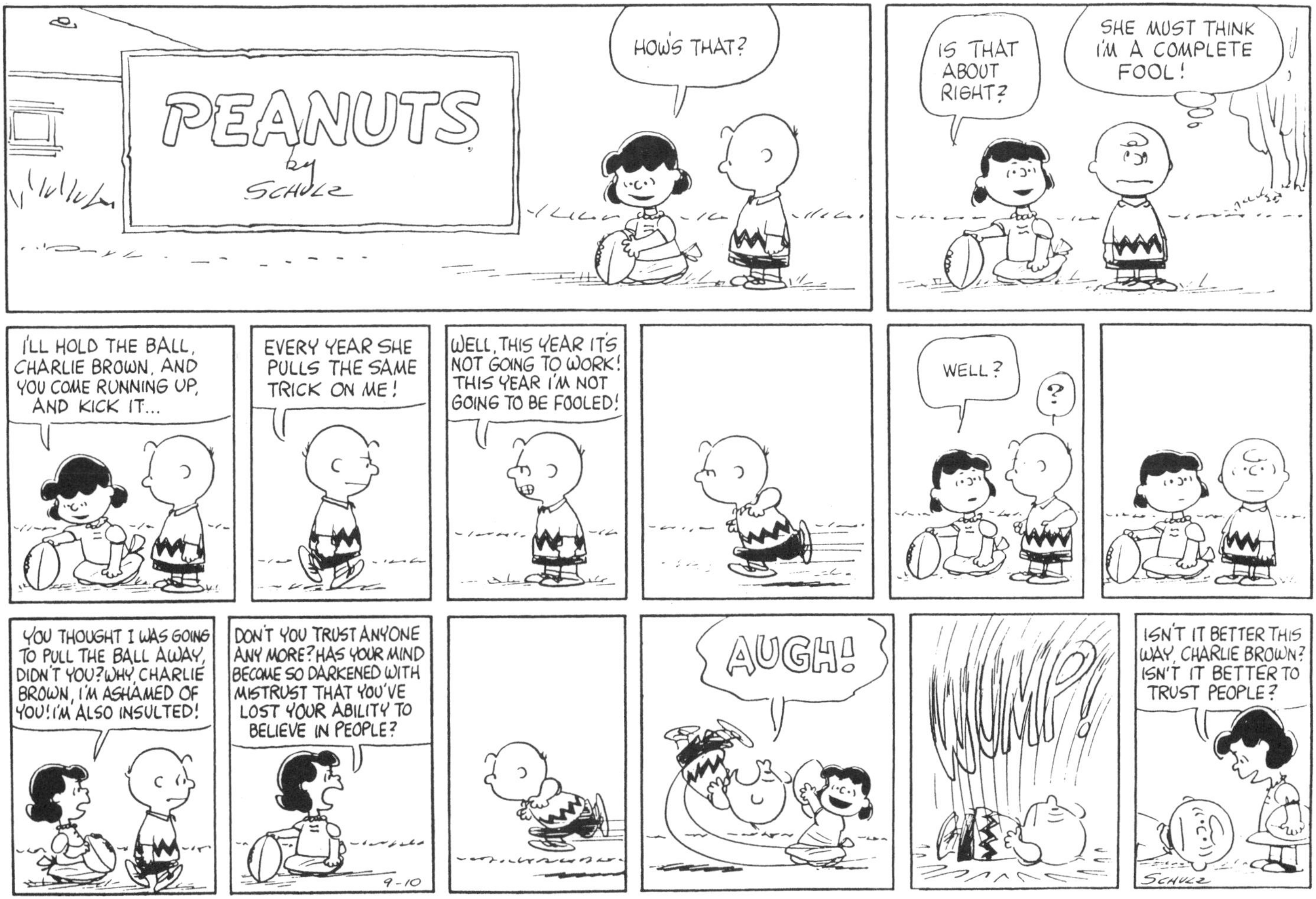
PEANUTS
by SCHULZ
HOW'S THAT?
IS THAT ABOUT RIGHT?
SHE MUST THINK I'M A COMPLETE FOOL!
I'LL HOLD THE BALL, CHARLIE BROWN, AND YOU COME RUNNING UP, AND KICK IT...
EVERY YEAR SHE PULLS THE SAME TRICK ON ME!
WELL, THIS YEAR IT'S NOT GOING TO WORK! THIS YEAR I'M NOT GOING TO BE FOOLED!
WELL?
?
YOU THOUGHT I WAS GOING TO PULL THE BALL AWAY, DIDN'T YOU? WHY, CHARLIE BROWN, I'M ASHAMED OF YOU! I'M ALSO INSULTED!
DON'T YOU TRUST ANYONE ANY MORE? HAS YOUR MIND BECOME SO DARKENED WITH MISTRUST THAT YOU'VE LOST YOUR ABILITY TO BELIEVE IN PEOPLE?
9-10
AUGH!
WUMP!
ISN'T IT BETTER THIS WAY, CHARLIE BROWN? ISN'T IT BETTER TO TRUST PEOPLE?
SCHULZ

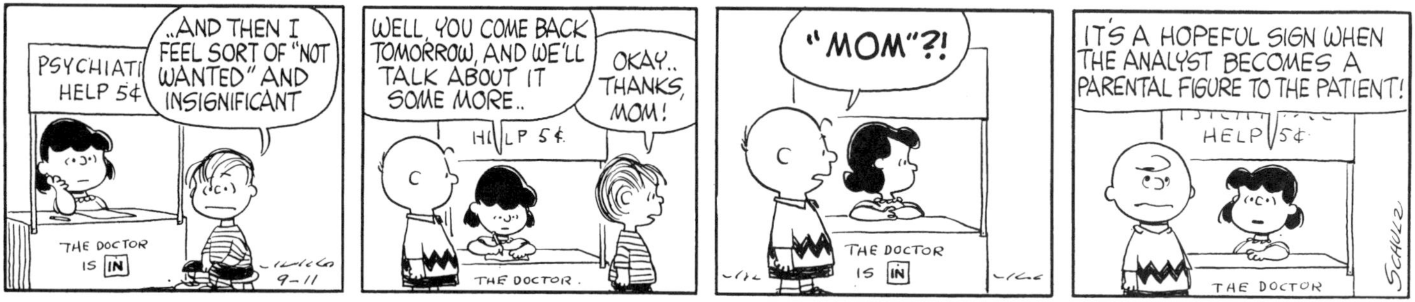
PSYCHIATI
HELP 5¢
..AND THEN I FEEL SORT OF "NOT WANTED" AND INSIGNIFICANT
THE DOCTOR IS IN
9-11
WELL, YOU COME BACK TOMORROW, AND WE'LL TALK ABOUT IT SOME MORE..
OKAY.. THANKS, MOM!
"MOM"?!
THE DOCTOR IS IN
IT'S A HOPEFUL SIGN WHEN THE ANALYST BECOMES A PARENTAL FIGURE TO THE PATIENT!
HELP 5¢
THE DOCTOR
SCHULZ

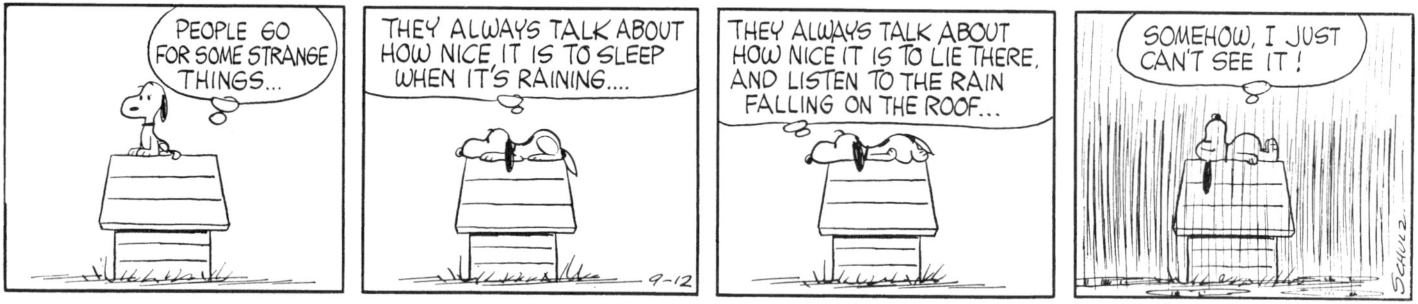
PEOPLE GO FOR SOME STRANGE THINGS...
THEY ALWAYS TALK ABOUT HOW NICE IT IS TO SLEEP WHEN IT'S RAINING....
9-12
THEY ALWAYS TALK ABOUT HOW NICE IT IS TO LIE THERE, AND LISTEN TO THE RAIN FALLING ON THE ROOF...
SOMEHOW, I JUST CAN'T SEE IT!
SCHULZ

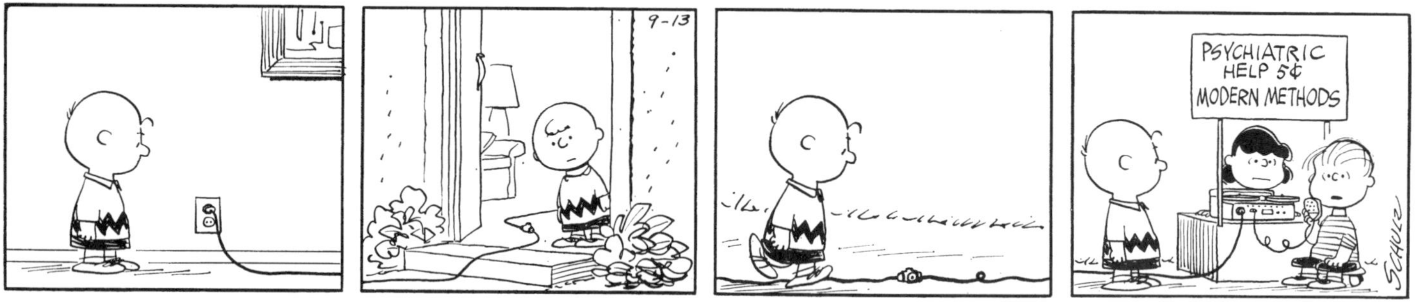
9-13
PSYCHIATRIC
HELP 5¢
MODERN METHODS
SCHULZ

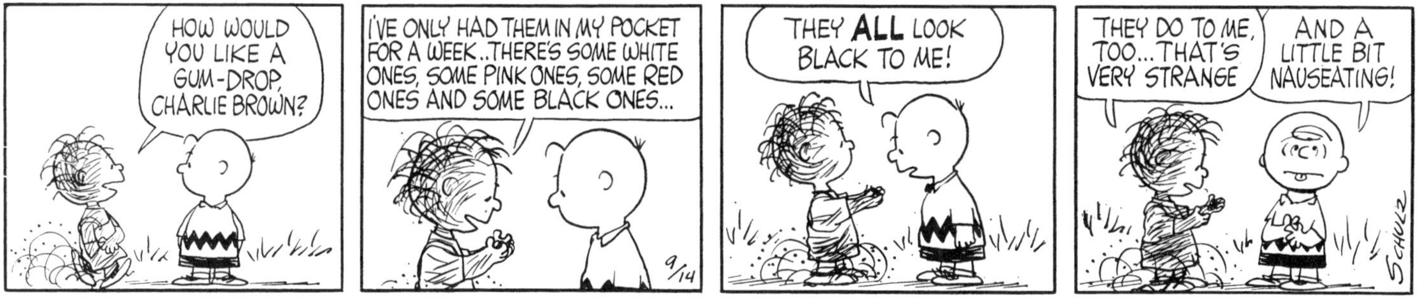
HOW WOULD YOU LIKE A GUM-DROP, CHARLIE BROWN?
I'VE ONLY HAD THEM IN MY POCKET FOR A WEEK..THERE'S SOME WHITE ONES, SOME PINK ONES, SOME RED ONES AND SOME BLACK ONES...
9/14
THEY ALL LOOK BLACK TO ME!
THEY DO TO ME, TOO...THAT'S VERY STRANGE
AND A LITTLE BIT NAUSEATING!
SCHULZ

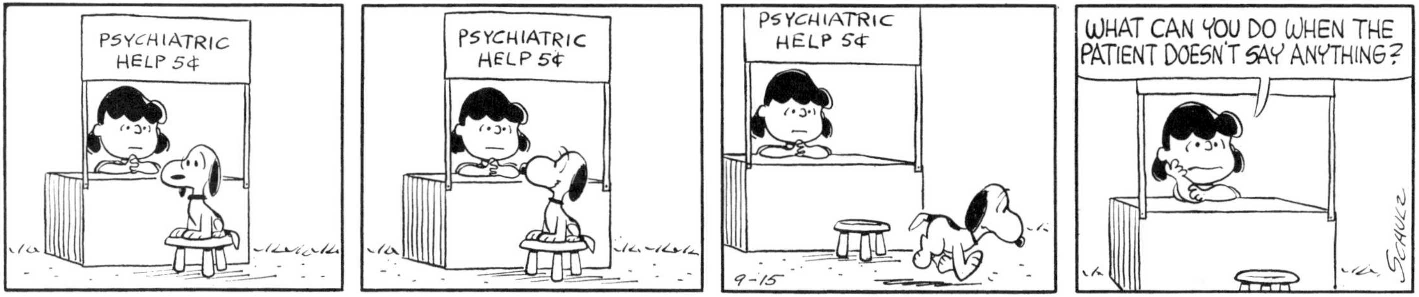
PSYCHIATRIC HELP 5¢
PSYCHIATRIC HELP 5¢
PSYCHIATRIC HELP 5¢
9-15
WHAT CAN YOU DO WHEN THE PATIENT DOESN'T SAY ANYTHING?
SCHULZ

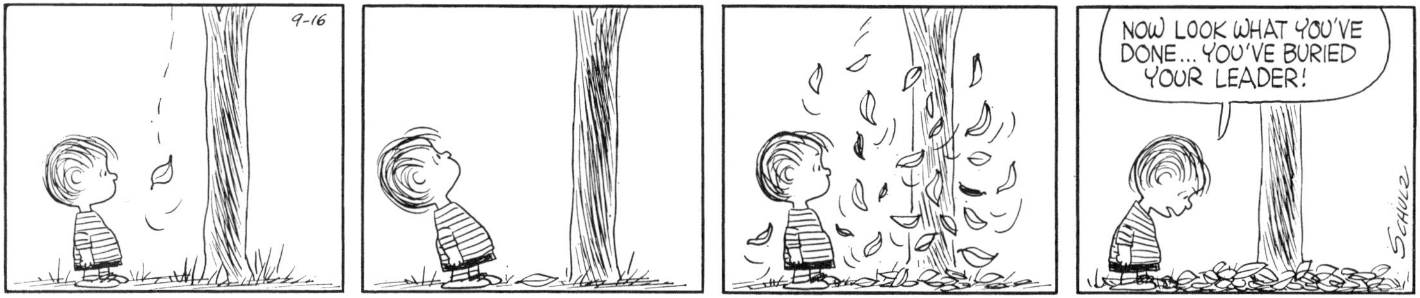
9-16
NOW LOOK WHAT YOU'VE DONE... YOU'VE BURIED YOUR LEADER!
SCHULZ

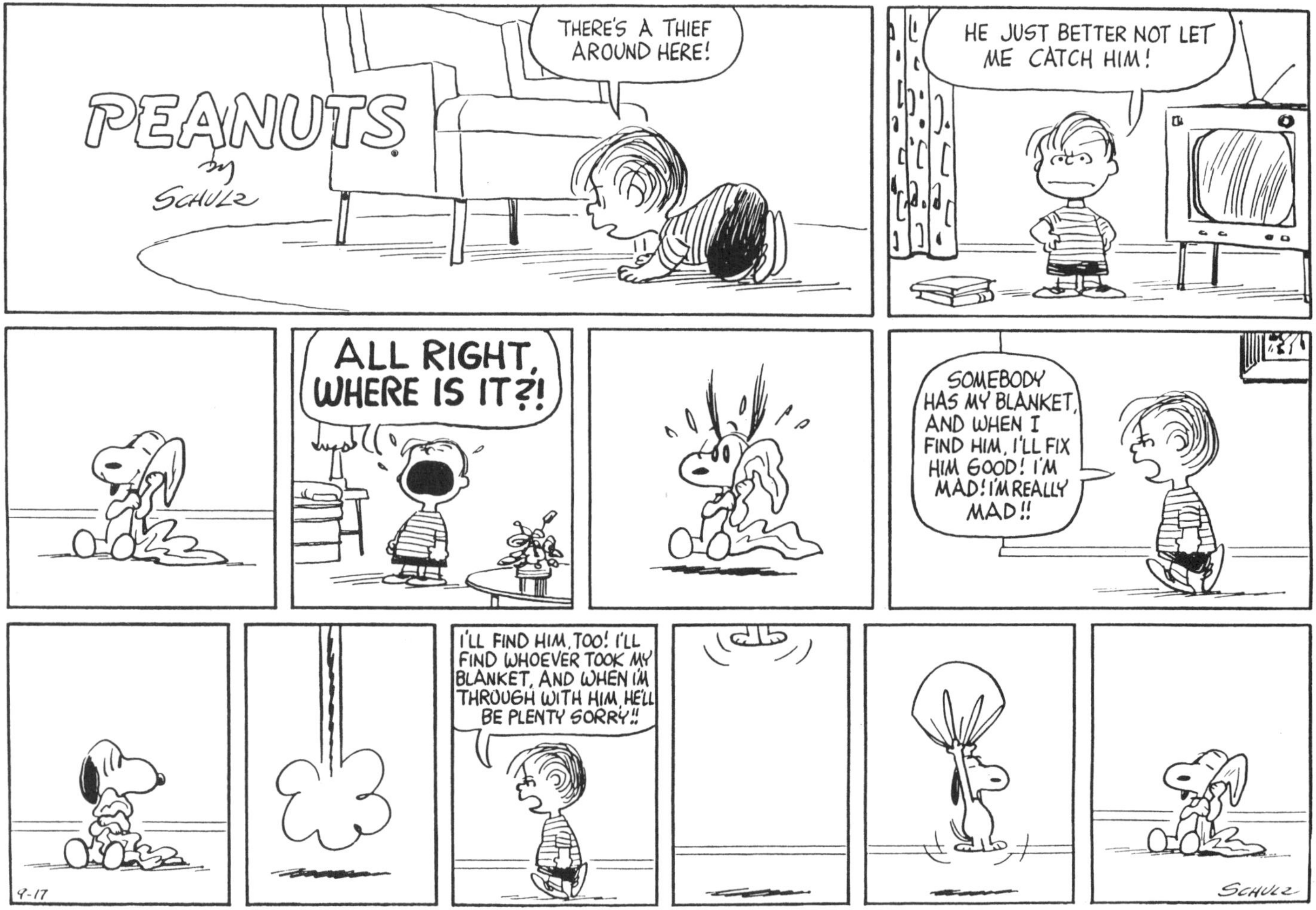
PEANUTS
by SCHULZ
THERE'S A THIEF AROUND HERE!
HE JUST BETTER NOT LET ME CATCH HIM!
ALL RIGHT, WHERE IS IT?!
SOMEBODY HAS MY BLANKET, AND WHEN I FIND HIM, I'LL FIX HIM GOOD! I'M MAD! I'M REALLY MAD!!
9-17
I'LL FIND HIM, TOO! I'LL FIND WHOEVER TOOK MY BLANKET, AND WHEN I'M THROUGH WITH HIM, HE'LL BE PLENTY SORRY!!
SCHULZ

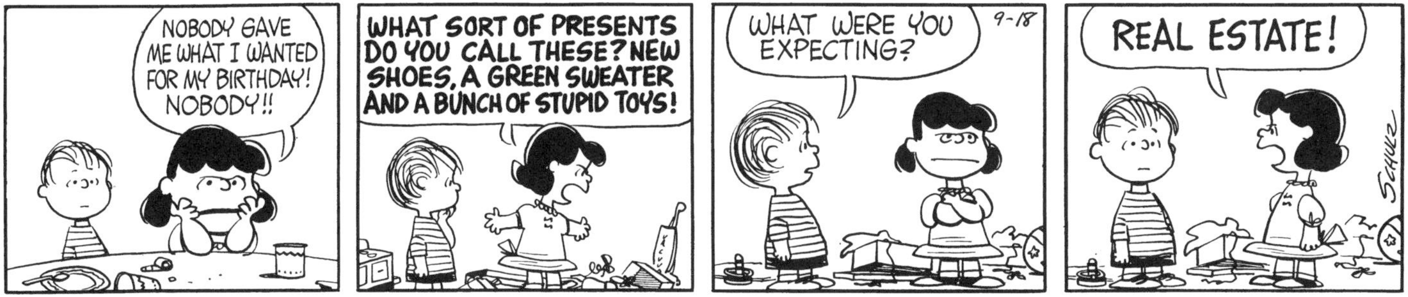
NOBODY GAVE ME WHAT I WANTED FOR MY BIRTHDAY! NOBODY!!
WHAT SORT OF PRESENTS DO YOU CALL THESE? NEW SHOES, A GREEN SWEATER AND A BUNCH OF STUPID TOYS!
WHAT WERE YOU EXPECTING?
9-18
REAL ESTATE!
SCHULZ

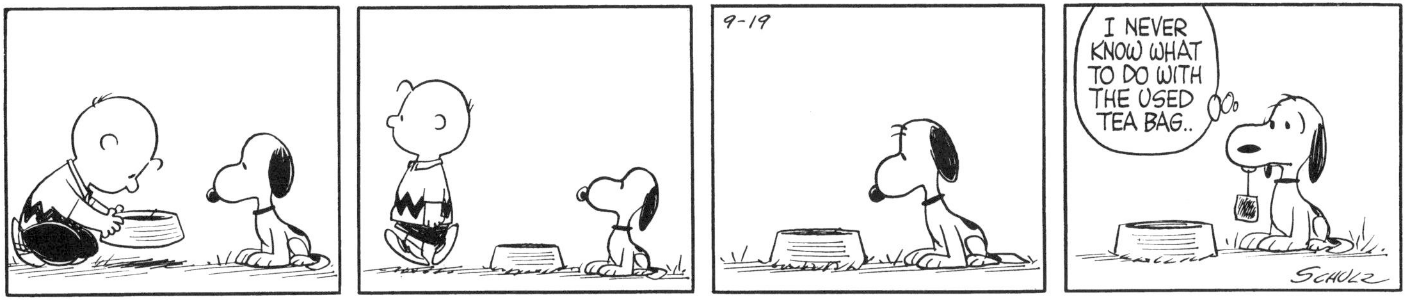
9-19
I NEVER KNOW WHAT TO DO WITH THE USED TEA BAG..
SCHULZ

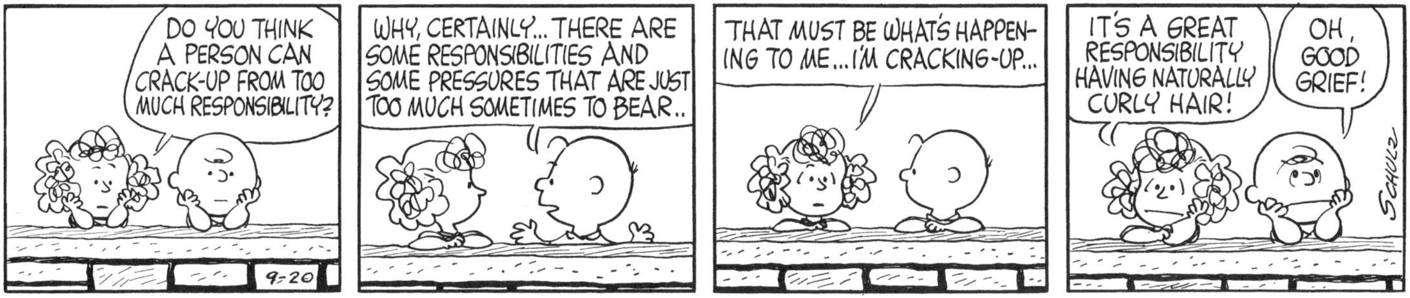
DO YOU THINK A PERSON CAN CRACK-UP FROM TOO MUCH RESPONSIBILITY?
9-20
WHY, CERTAINLY... THERE ARE SOME RESPONSIBILITIES AND SOME PRESSURES THAT ARE JUST TOO MUCH SOMETIMES TO BEAR..
THAT MUST BE WHAT'S HAPPENING TO ME... I'M CRACKING-UP...
IT'S A GREAT RESPONSIBILITY HAVING NATURALLY CURLY HAIR!
OH, GOOD GRIEF!
SCHULZ

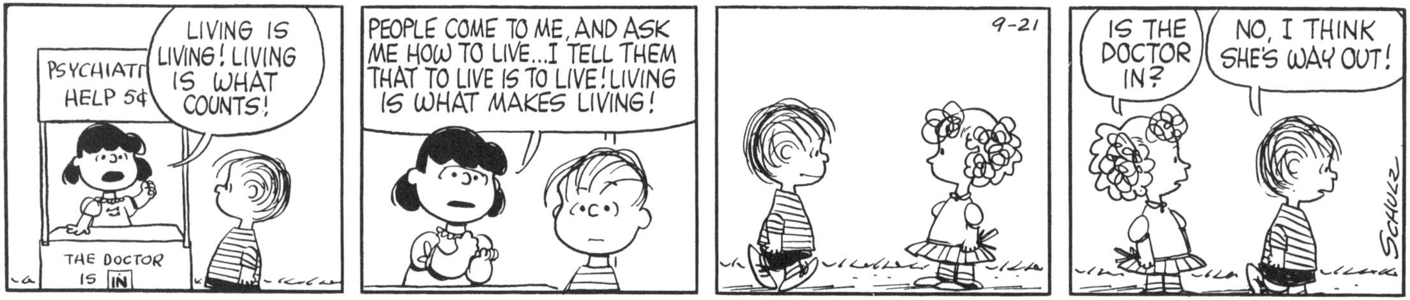
PSYCHIAT
HELP 5¢
LIVING IS LIVING! LIVING IS WHAT COUNTS!
THE DOCTOR IS IN
PEOPLE COME TO ME, AND ASK ME HOW TO LIVE...I TELL THEM THAT TO LIVE IS TO LIVE! LIVING IS WHAT MAKES LIVING!
9-21
IS THE DOCTOR IN?
NO, I THINK SHE'S WAY OUT!
SCHULZ

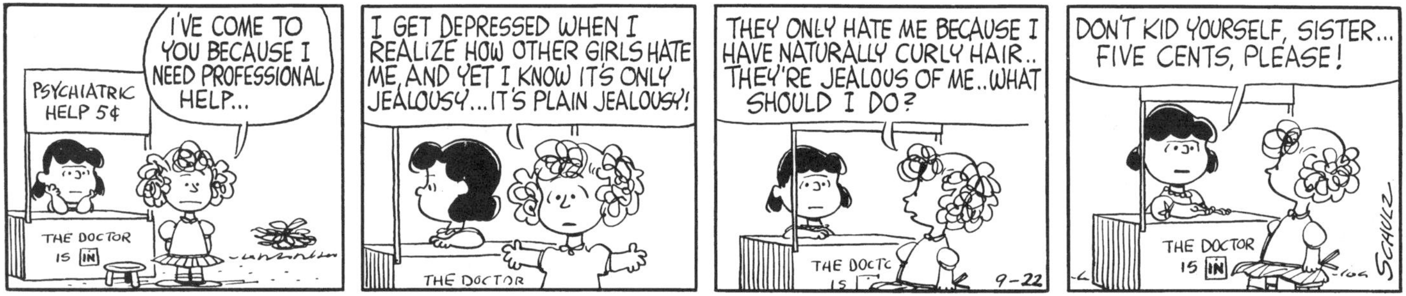
PSYCHIATRIC HELP 5¢
I'VE COME TO YOU BECAUSE I NEED PROFESSIONAL HELP...
THE DOCTOR IS IN
I GET DEPRESSED WHEN I REALIZE HOW OTHER GIRLS HATE ME, AND YET I KNOW IT'S ONLY JEALOUSY...IT'S PLAIN JEALOUSY!
THE DOCTOR
THEY ONLY HATE ME BECAUSE I HAVE NATURALLY CURLY HAIR.. THEY'RE JEALOUS OF ME..WHAT SHOULD I DO?
9-22
DON'T KID YOURSELF, SISTER... FIVE CENTS, PLEASE!
THE DOCTOR IS IN
SCHULZ

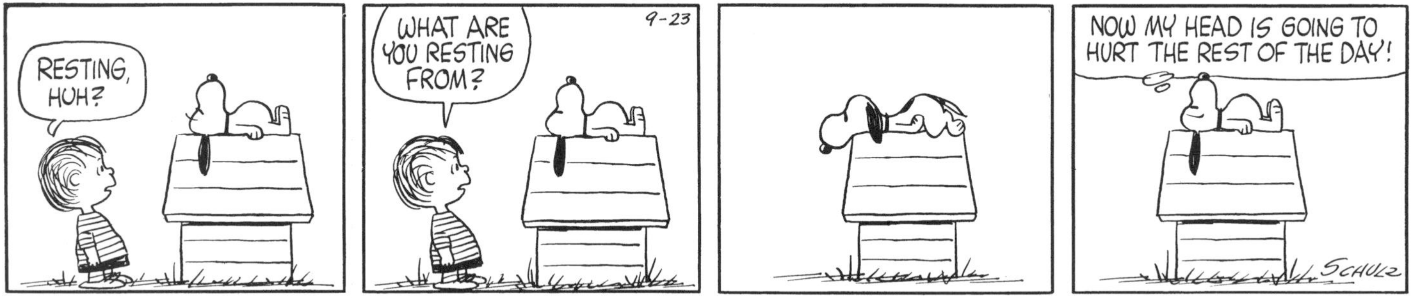
RESTING, HUH?
9-23
WHAT ARE YOU RESTING FROM?
NOW MY HEAD IS GOING TO HURT THE REST OF THE DAY!
SCHULZ

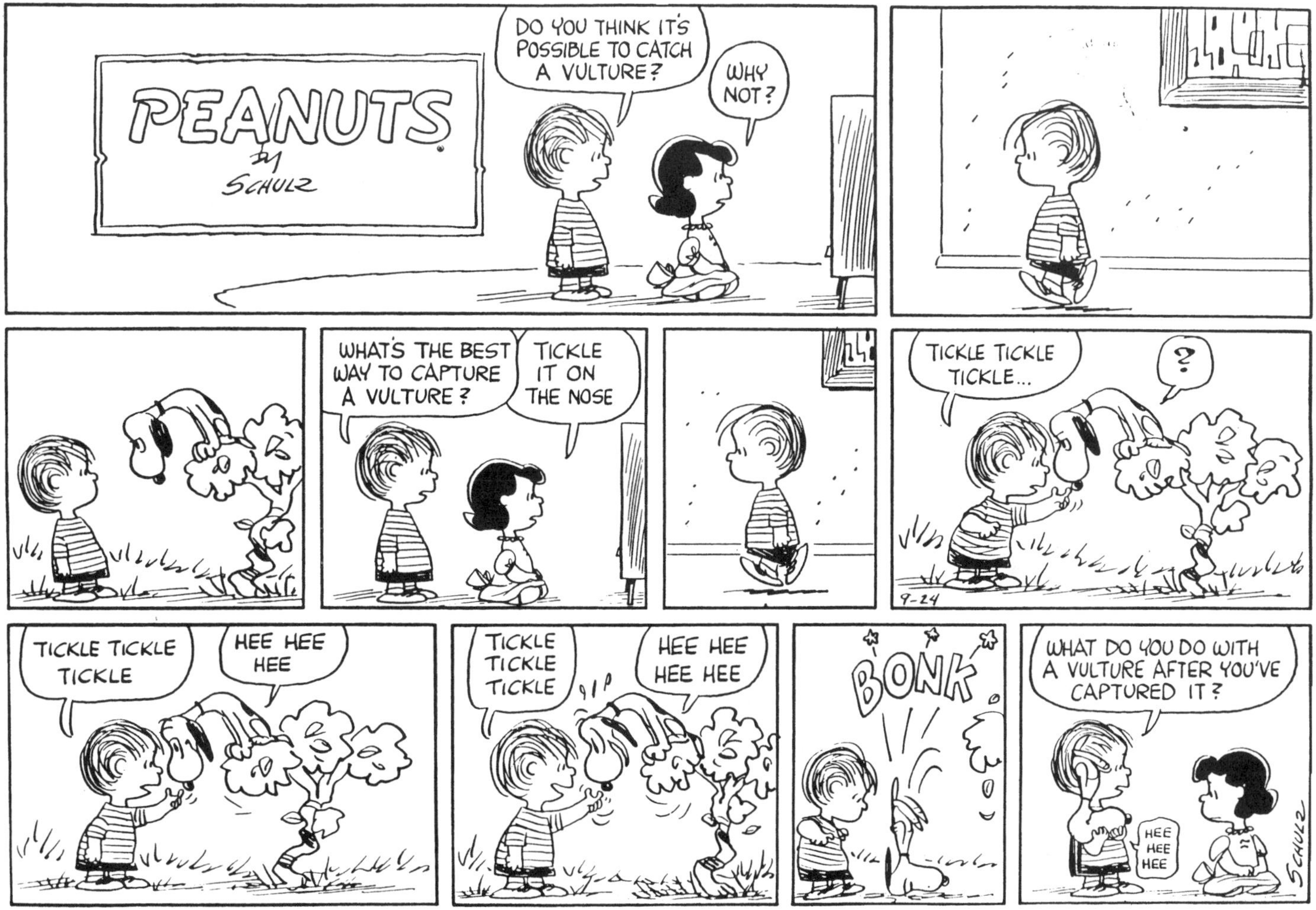
PEANUTS
by SCHULZ
DO YOU THINK IT'S POSSIBLE TO CATCH A VULTURE?
WHY NOT?
WHAT'S THE BEST WAY TO CAPTURE A VULTURE?
TICKLE IT ON THE NOSE
TICKLE TICKLE TICKLE...
?
9-24
TICKLE TICKLE TICKLE
HEE HEE HEE
TICKLE TICKLE TICKLE
HEE HEE HEE HEE
BONK
WHAT DO YOU DO WITH A VULTURE AFTER YOU'VE CAPTURED IT?
HEE HEE HEE
SCHULZ

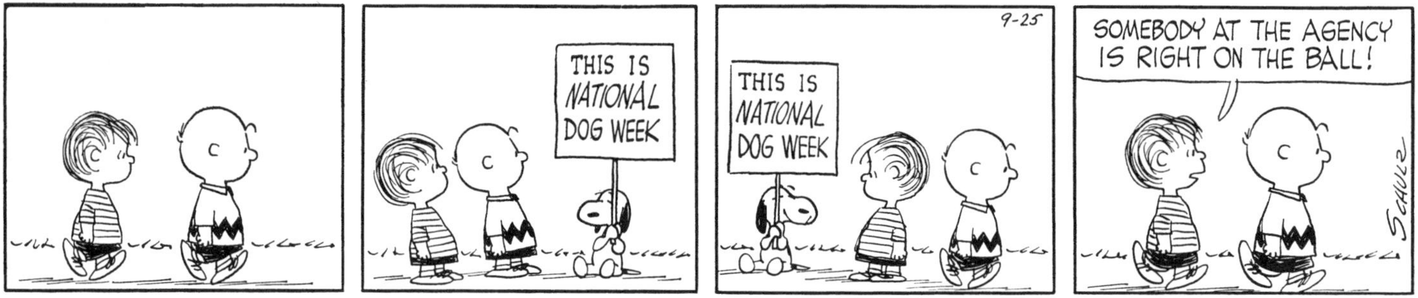
THIS IS NATIONAL DOG WEEK
9-25
THIS IS NATIONAL DOG WEEK
SOMEBODY AT THE AGENCY IS RIGHT ON THE BALL!
SCHULZ

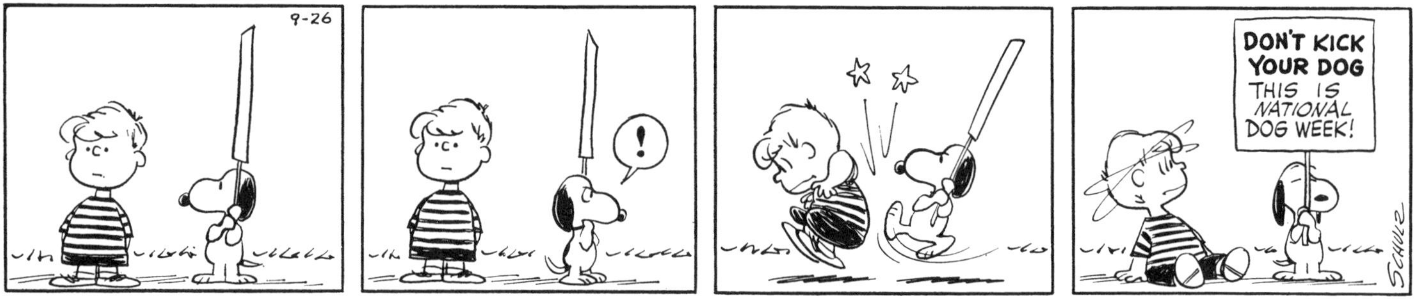
9-26
!
DON'T KICK YOUR DOG THIS IS NATIONAL DOG WEEK!
SCHULZ

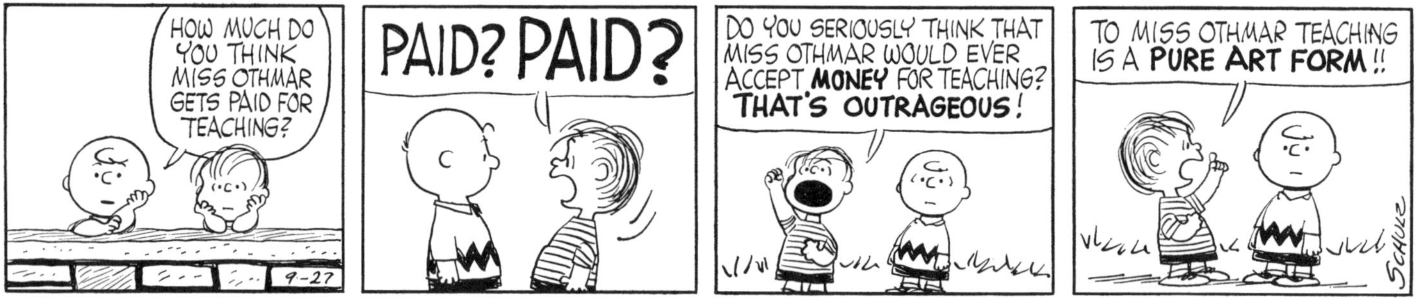
HOW MUCH DO YOU THINK MISS OTHMAR GETS PAID FOR TEACHING?
9-27
PAID? PAID?
DO YOU SERIOUSLY THINK THAT MISS OTHMAR WOULD EVER ACCEPT MONEY FOR TEACHING? THAT'S OUTRAGEOUS!
TO MISS OTHMAR TEACHING IS A PURE ART FORM!!
SCHULZ

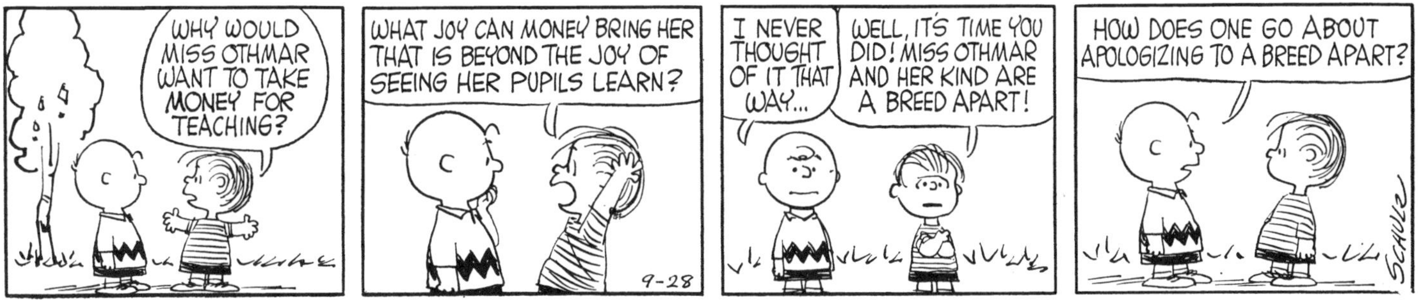
WHY WOULD MISS OTHMAR WANT TO TAKE MONEY FOR TEACHING?
WHAT JOY CAN MONEY BRING HER THAT IS BEYOND THE JOY OF SEEING HER PUPILS LEARN?
9-28
I NEVER THOUGHT OF IT THAT WAY...
WELL, IT'S TIME YOU DID! MISS OTHMAR AND HER KIND ARE A BREED APART!
HOW DOES ONE GO ABOUT APOLOGIZING TO A BREED APART?
SCHULZ

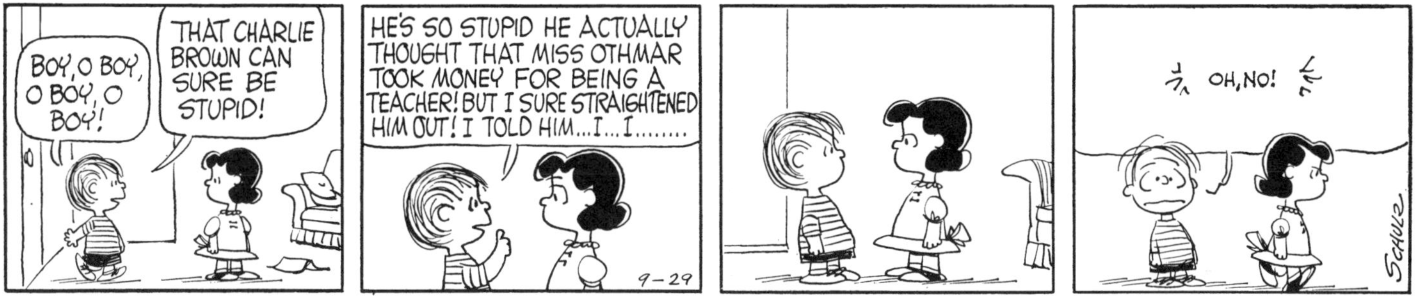
BOY, O BOY, O BOY, O BOY!
THAT CHARLIE BROWN CAN SURE BE STUPID!
HE'S SO STUPID HE ACTUALLY THOUGHT THAT MISS OTHMAR TOOK MONEY FOR BEING A TEACHER! BUT I SURE STRAIGHTENED HIM OUT! I TOLD HIM...I...I........
9-29
OH, NO!
SCHULZ

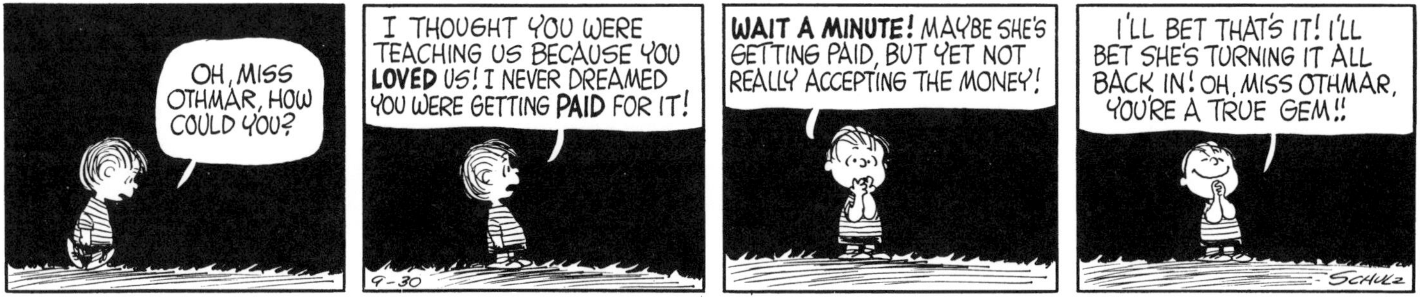
OH, MISS OTHMAR, HOW COULD YOU?
I THOUGHT YOU WERE TEACHING US BECAUSE YOU LOVED US! I NEVER DREAMED YOU WERE GETTING PAID FOR IT!
9-30
WAIT A MINUTE! MAYBE SHE'S GETTING PAID, BUT YET NOT REALLY ACCEPTING THE MONEY!
I'LL BET THAT'S IT! I'LL BET SHE'S TURNING IT ALL BACK IN! OH, MISS OTHMAR, YOU'RE A TRUE GEM!!
SCHULZ

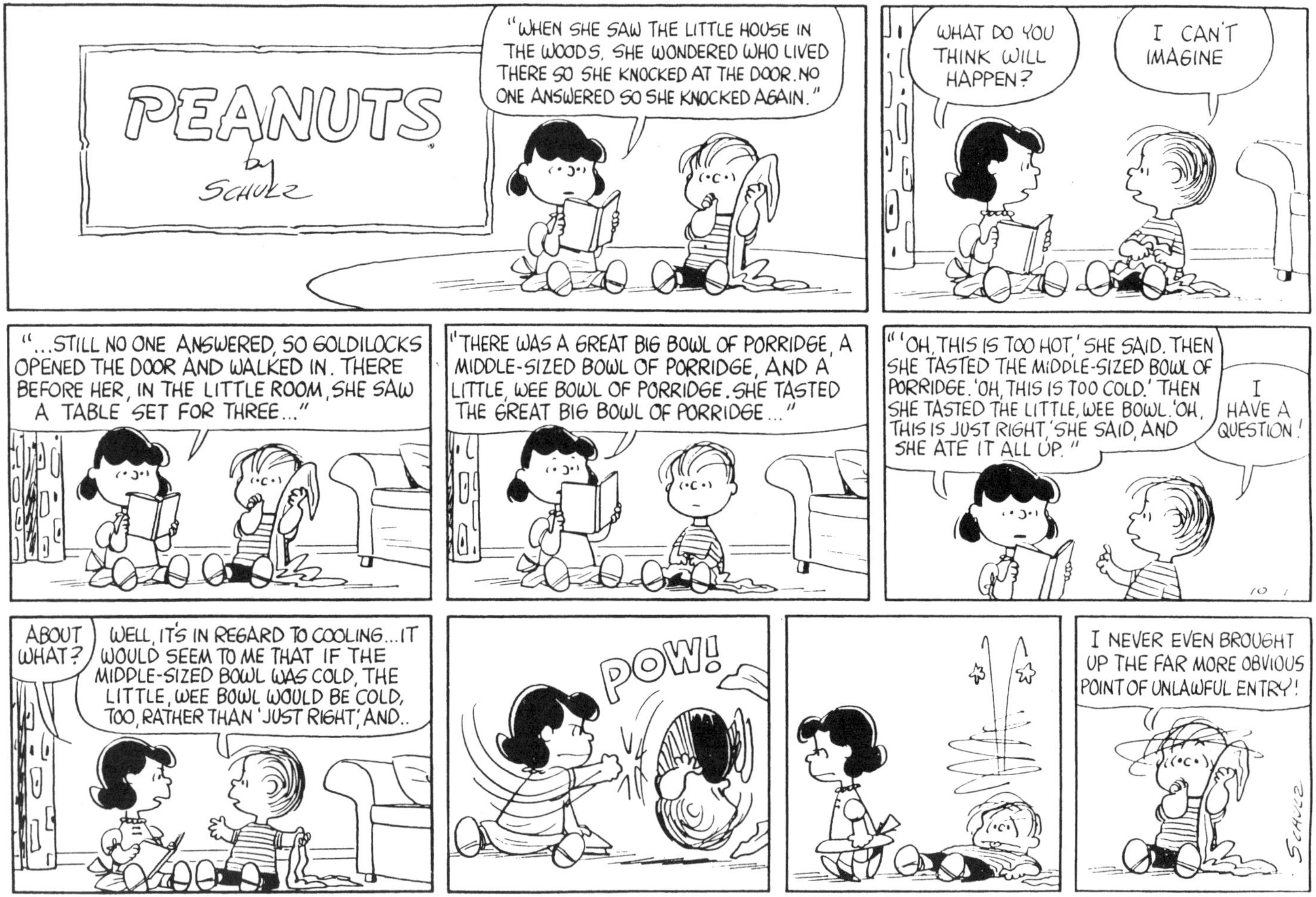
PEANUTS
by SCHULZ
"WHEN SHE SAW THE LITTLE HOUSE IN THE WOODS, SHE WONDERED WHO LIVED THERE SO SHE KNOCKED AT THE DOOR. NO ONE ANSWERED SO SHE KNOCKED AGAIN."
WHAT DO YOU THINK WILL HAPPEN?
I CAN'T IMAGINE
"...STILL NO ONE ANSWERED, SO GOLDILOCKS OPENED THE DOOR AND WALKED IN. THERE BEFORE HER, IN THE LITTLE ROOM, SHE SAW A TABLE SET FOR THREE..."
"THERE WAS A GREAT BIG BOWL OF PORRIDGE, A MIDDLE-SIZED BOWL OF PORRIDGE, AND A LITTLE, WEE BOWL OF PORRIDGE. SHE TASTED THE GREAT BIG BOWL OF PORRIDGE..."
"'OH, THIS IS TOO HOT,' SHE SAID. THEN SHE TASTED THE MIDDLE-SIZED BOWL OF PORRIDGE. 'OH, THIS IS TOO COLD.' THEN SHE TASTED THE LITTLE, WEE BOWL. 'OH, THIS IS JUST RIGHT,' SHE SAID, AND SHE ATE IT ALL UP."
I HAVE A QUESTION!
ABOUT WHAT?
WELL, IT'S IN REGARD TO COOLING...IT WOULD SEEM TO ME THAT IF THE MIDDLE-SIZED BOWL WAS COLD, THE LITTLE, WEE BOWL WOULD BE COLD, TOO, RATHER THAN 'JUST RIGHT,' AND..
POW!
I NEVER EVEN BROUGHT UP THE FAR MORE OBVIOUS POINT OF UNLAWFUL ENTRY!
SCHULZ

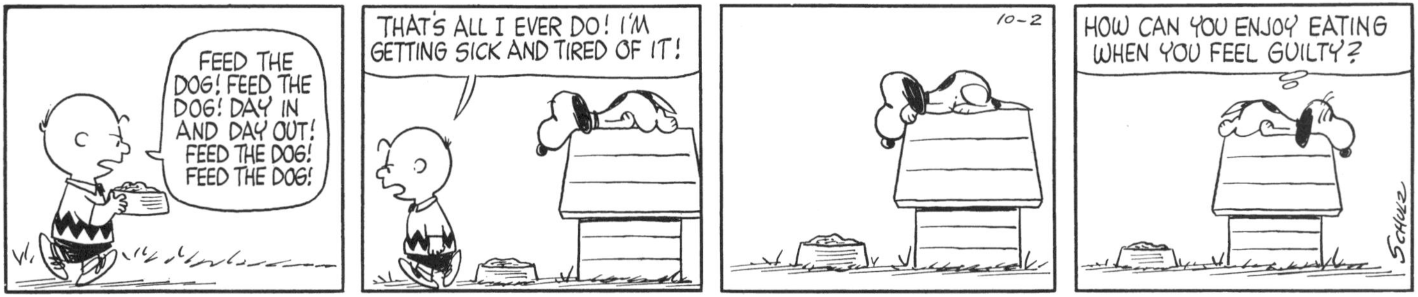
FEED THE DOG! FEED THE DOG! DAY IN AND DAY OUT! FEED THE DOG! FEED THE DOG!
THAT'S ALL I EVER DO! I'M GETTING SICK AND TIRED OF IT!
10-2
HOW CAN YOU ENJOY EATING WHEN YOU FEEL GUILTY?
SCHULZ

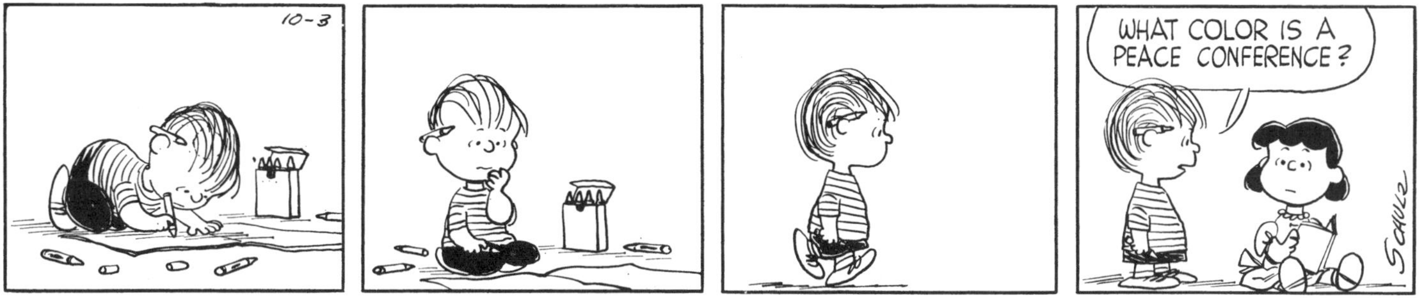
10-3
WHAT COLOR IS A PEACE CONFERENCE?
SCHULZ

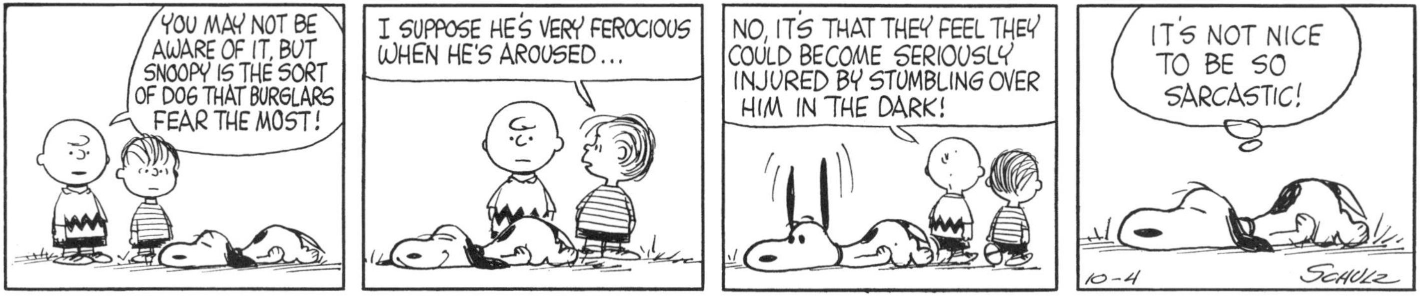
YOU MAY NOT BE AWARE OF IT, BUT SNOOPY IS THE SORT OF DOG THAT BURGLARS FEAR THE MOST!
I SUPPOSE HE'S VERY FEROCIOUS WHEN HE'S AROUSED...
NO, IT'S THAT THEY FEEL THEY COULD BECOME SERIOUSLY INJURED BY STUMBLING OVER HIM IN THE DARK!
IT'S NOT NICE TO BE SO SARCASTIC!
10-4
SCHULZ

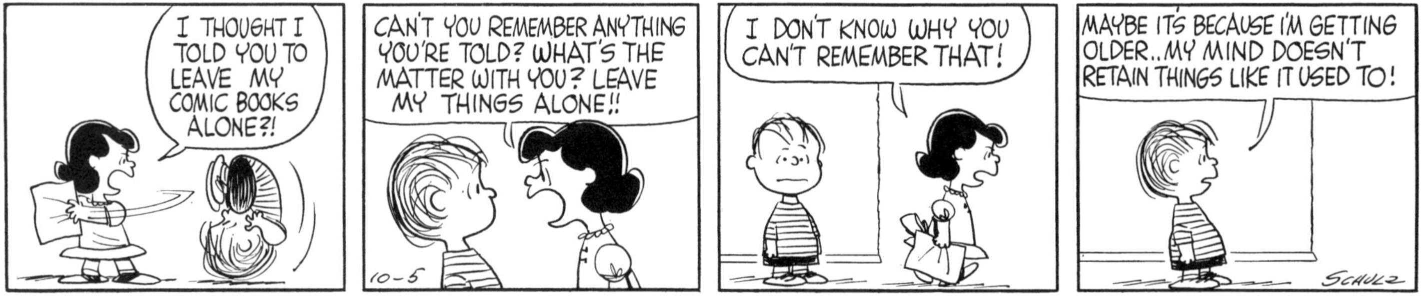
I THOUGHT I TOLD YOU TO LEAVE MY COMIC BOOKS ALONE?!
CAN'T YOU REMEMBER ANYTHING YOU'RE TOLD? WHAT'S THE MATTER WITH YOU? LEAVE MY THINGS ALONE!!
I DON'T KNOW WHY YOU CAN'T REMEMBER THAT!
MAYBE IT'S BECAUSE I'M GETTING OLDER..MY MIND DOESN'T RETAIN THINGS LIKE IT USED TO!

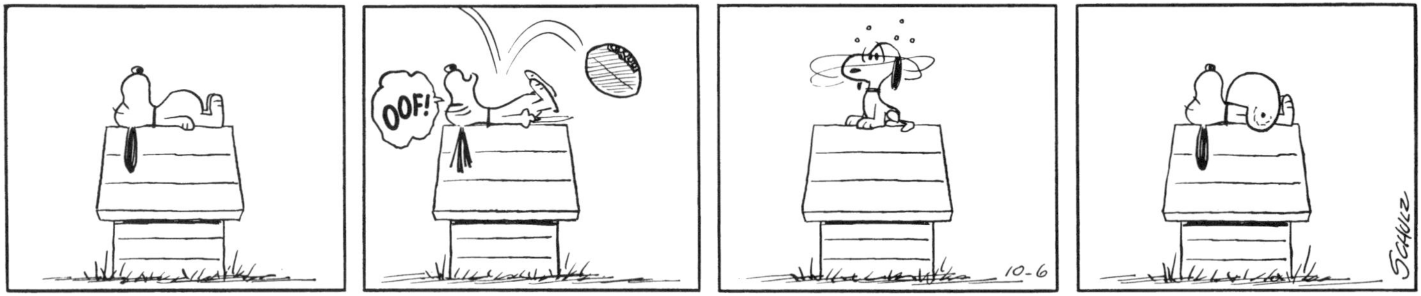
OOF!

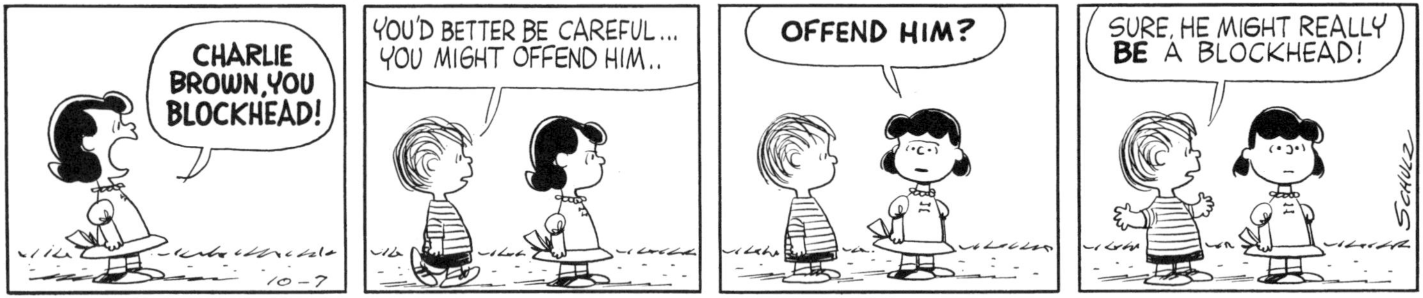
CHARLIE BROWN, YOU BLOCKHEAD!
YOU'D BETTER BE CAREFUL... YOU MIGHT OFFEND HIM..
OFFEND HIM?
SURE, HE MIGHT REALLY BE A BLOCKHEAD!

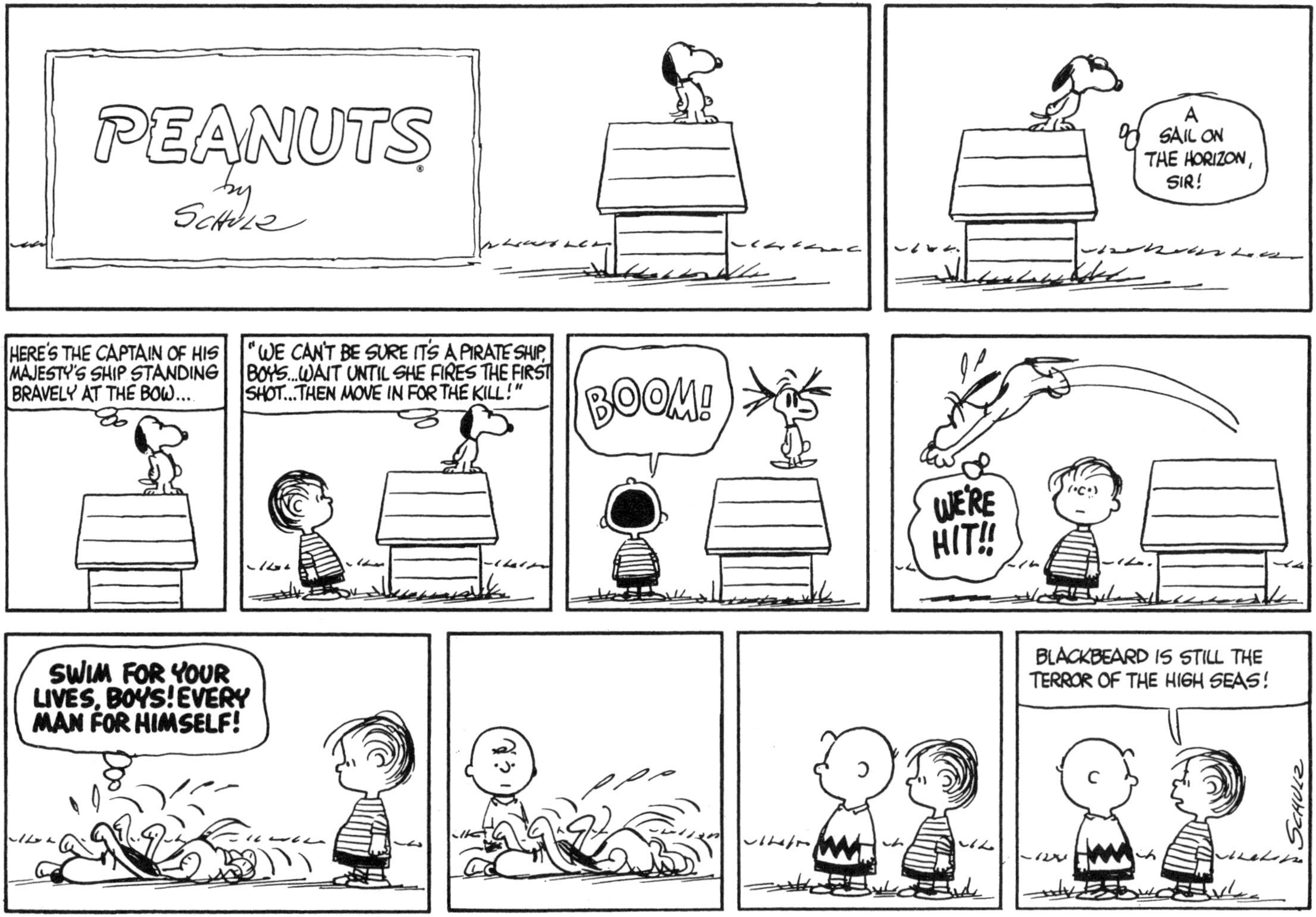
PEANUTS
by SCHULZ
A SAIL ON THE HORIZON, SIR!
HERE'S THE CAPTAIN OF HIS MAJESTY'S SHIP STANDING BRAVELY AT THE BOW...
"WE CAN'T BE SURE IT'S A PIRATE SHIP, BOYS...WAIT UNTIL SHE FIRES THE FIRST SHOT...THEN MOVE IN FOR THE KILL!"
BOOM!
WE'RE HIT!!
SWIM FOR YOUR LIVES, BOYS! EVERY MAN FOR HIMSELF!
BLACKBEARD IS STILL THE TERROR OF THE HIGH SEAS!
SCHULZ

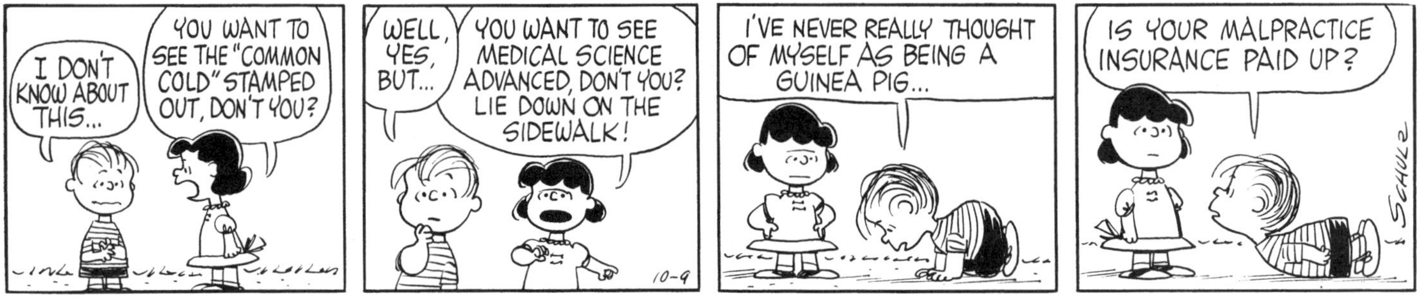
I DON'T KNOW ABOUT THIS...
YOU WANT TO SEE THE "COMMON COLD" STAMPED OUT, DON'T YOU?
WELL, YES, BUT...
YOU WANT TO SEE MEDICAL SCIENCE ADVANCED, DON'T YOU? LIE DOWN ON THE SIDEWALK!
10-9
I'VE NEVER REALLY THOUGHT OF MYSELF AS BEING A GUINEA PIG...
IS YOUR MALPRACTICE INSURANCE PAID UP?
SCHULZ

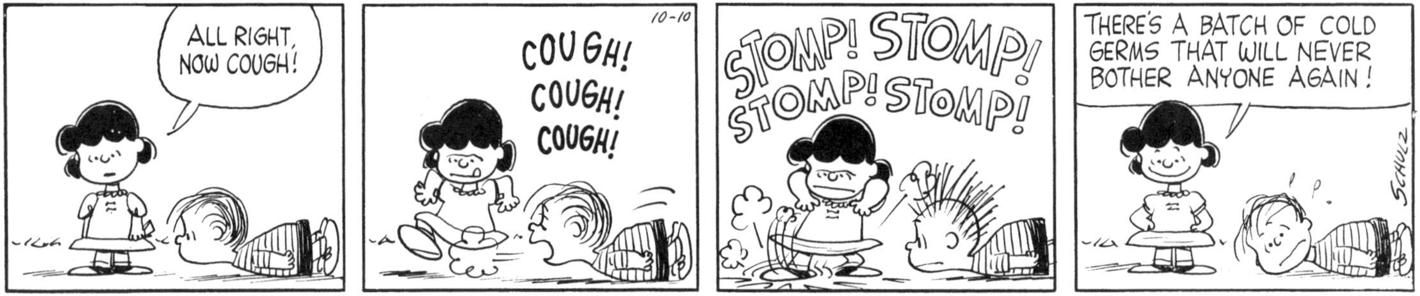
ALL RIGHT, NOW COUGH!
10-10
COUGH! COUGH! COUGH!
STOMP! STOMP! STOMP! STOMP!
THERE'S A BATCH OF COLD GERMS THAT WILL NEVER BOTHER ANYONE AGAIN!
SCHULZ

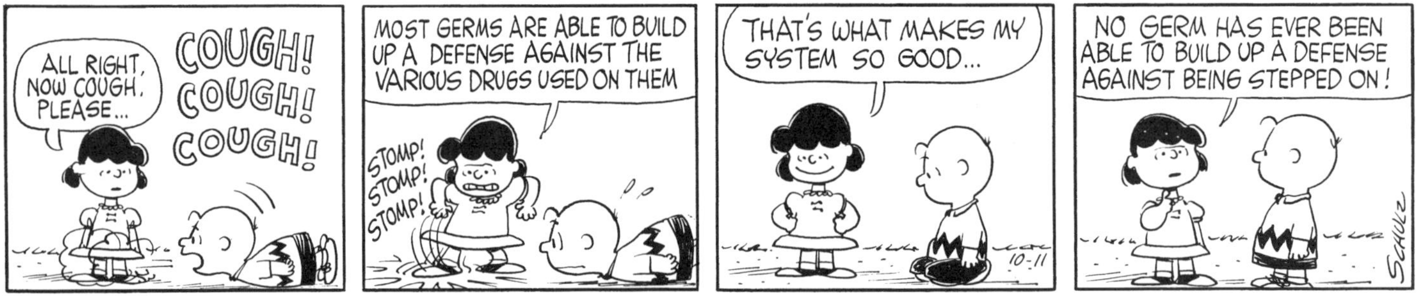
ALL RIGHT, NOW COUGH, PLEASE...
COUGH! COUGH! COUGH!
MOST GERMS ARE ABLE TO BUILD UP A DEFENSE AGAINST THE VARIOUS DRUGS USED ON THEM
STOMP! STOMP! STOMP!
THAT'S WHAT MAKES MY SYSTEM SO GOOD...
10-11
NO GERM HAS EVER BEEN ABLE TO BUILD UP A DEFENSE AGAINST BEING STEPPED ON!
SCHULZ

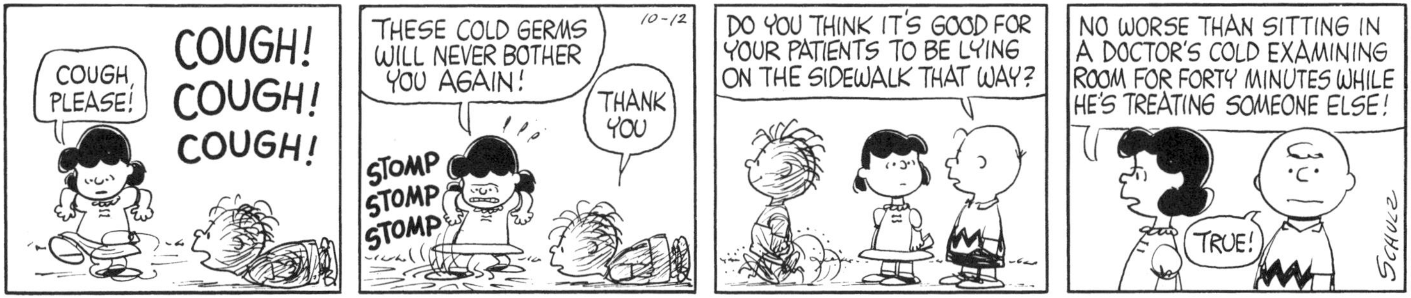
COUGH, PLEASE!
COUGH! COUGH! COUGH!
10-12
THESE COLD GERMS WILL NEVER BOTHER YOU AGAIN!
STOMP STOMP STOMP
THANK YOU
DO YOU THINK IT'S GOOD FOR YOUR PATIENTS TO BE LYING ON THE SIDEWALK THAT WAY?
NO WORSE THAN SITTING IN A DOCTOR'S COLD EXAMINING ROOM FOR FORTY MINUTES WHILE HE'S TREATING SOMEONE ELSE!
TRUE!
SCHULZ

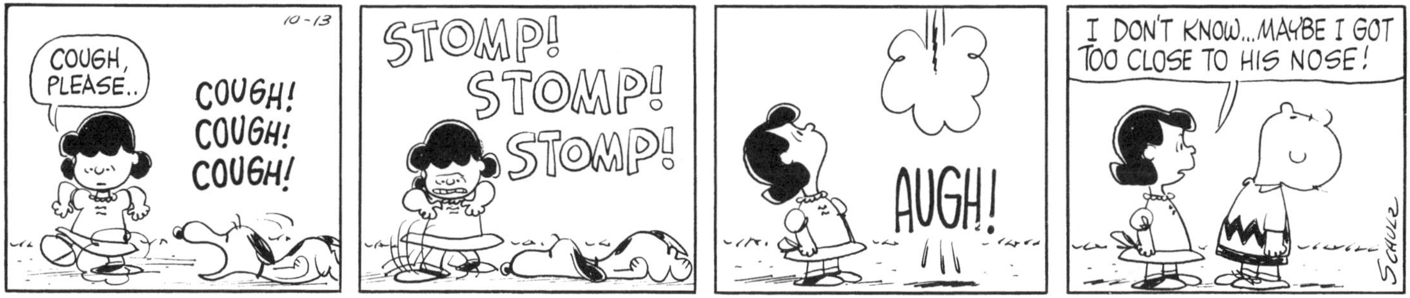
10-13
COUGH, PLEASE..
COUGH! COUGH! COUGH!
STOMP! STOMP! STOMP!
AUGH!
I DON'T KNOW...MAYBE I GOT TOO CLOSE TO HIS NOSE!
SCHULZ

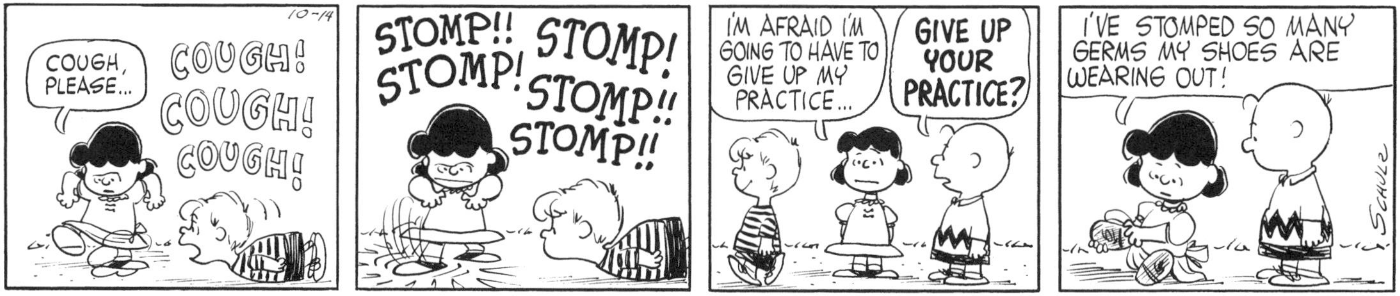
10-14
COUGH, PLEASE...
COUGH! COUGH! COUGH!
STOMP!! STOMP!
STOMP! STOMP!! STOMP!!
I'M AFRAID I'M GOING TO HAVE TO GIVE UP MY PRACTICE...
GIVE UP YOUR PRACTICE?
I'VE STOMPED SO MANY GERMS MY SHOES ARE WEARING OUT!
SCHULZ

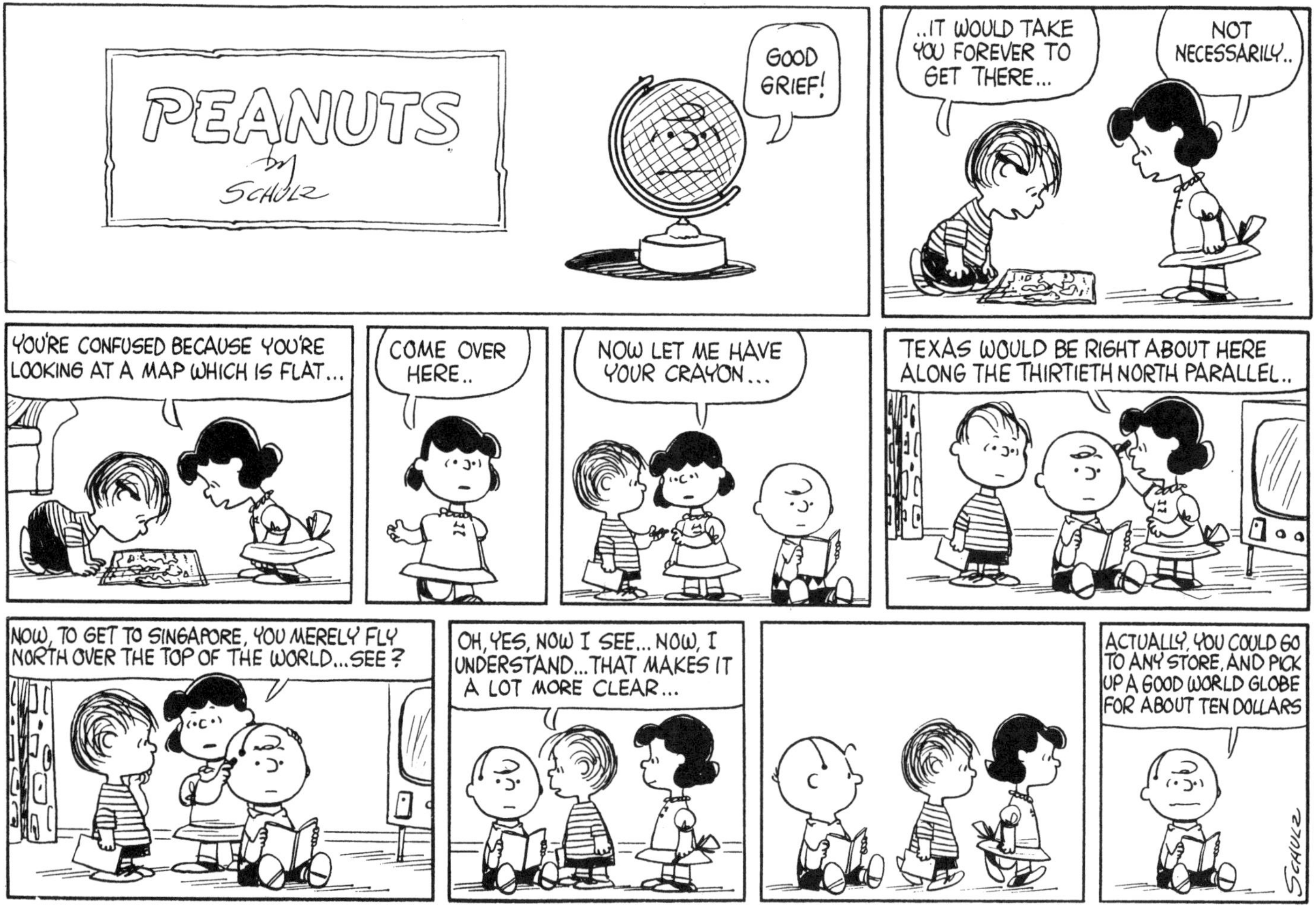
PEANUTS
by SCHULZ
GOOD GRIEF!
..IT WOULD TAKE YOU FOREVER TO GET THERE...
NOT NECESSARILY..
YOU'RE CONFUSED BECAUSE YOU'RE LOOKING AT A MAP WHICH IS FLAT...
COME OVER HERE..
NOW LET ME HAVE YOUR CRAYON...
TEXAS WOULD BE RIGHT ABOUT HERE ALONG THE THIRTIETH NORTH PARALLEL..
NOW, TO GET TO SINGAPORE, YOU MERELY FLY NORTH OVER THE TOP OF THE WORLD...SEE?
OH, YES, NOW I SEE... NOW, I UNDERSTAND...THAT MAKES IT A LOT MORE CLEAR...
ACTUALLY, YOU COULD GO TO ANY STORE, AND PICK UP A GOOD WORLD GLOBE FOR ABOUT TEN DOLLARS
SCHULZ

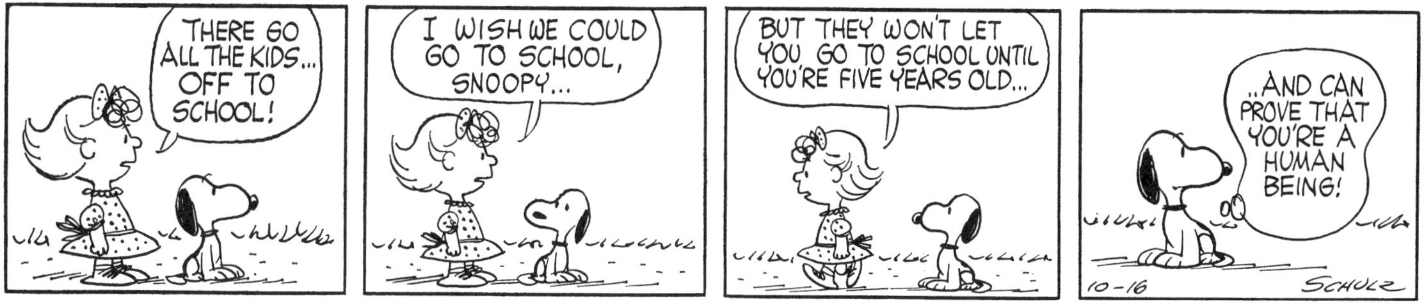
THERE GO ALL THE KIDS... OFF TO SCHOOL!
I WISH WE COULD GO TO SCHOOL, SNOOPY...
BUT THEY WON'T LET YOU GO TO SCHOOL UNTIL YOU'RE FIVE YEARS OLD...
..AND CAN PROVE THAT YOU'RE A HUMAN BEING!
10-16
SCHULZ

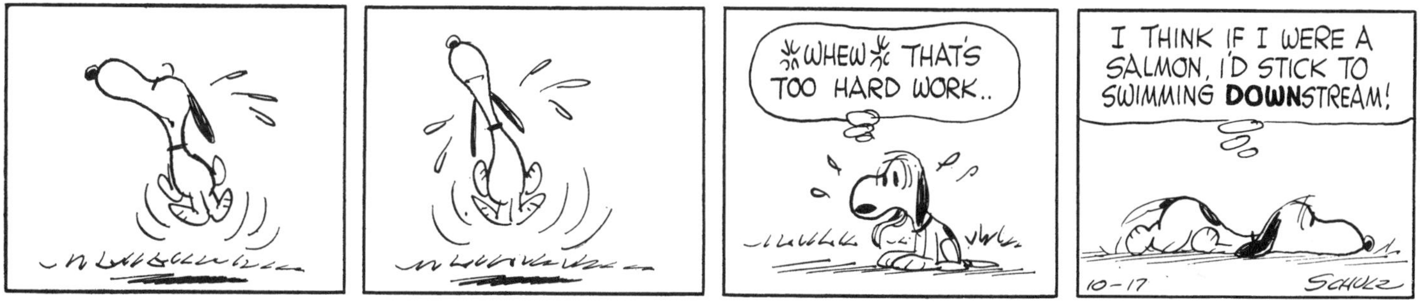
WHEW THAT'S TOO HARD WORK..
I THINK IF I WERE A SALMON, I'D STICK TO SWIMMING **DOWN**STREAM!
10-17
SCHULZ

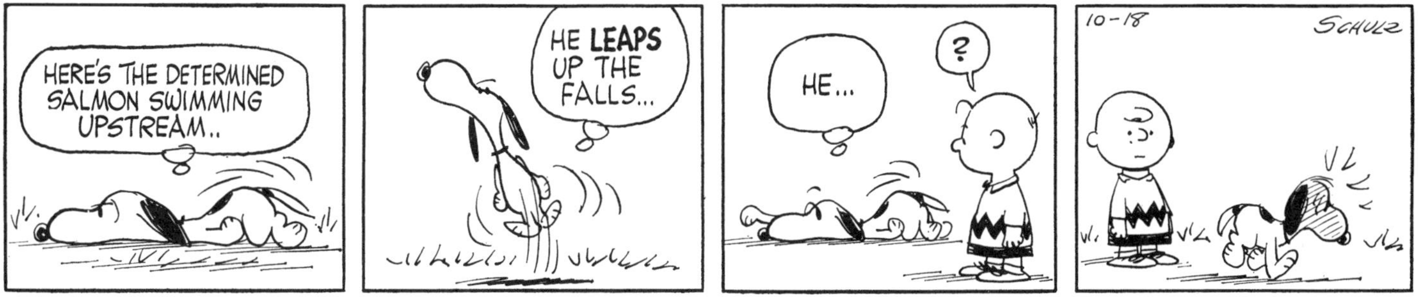
HERE'S THE DETERMINED SALMON SWIMMING UPSTREAM..
HE **LEAPS** UP THE FALLS...
HE...
?
10-18
SCHULZ

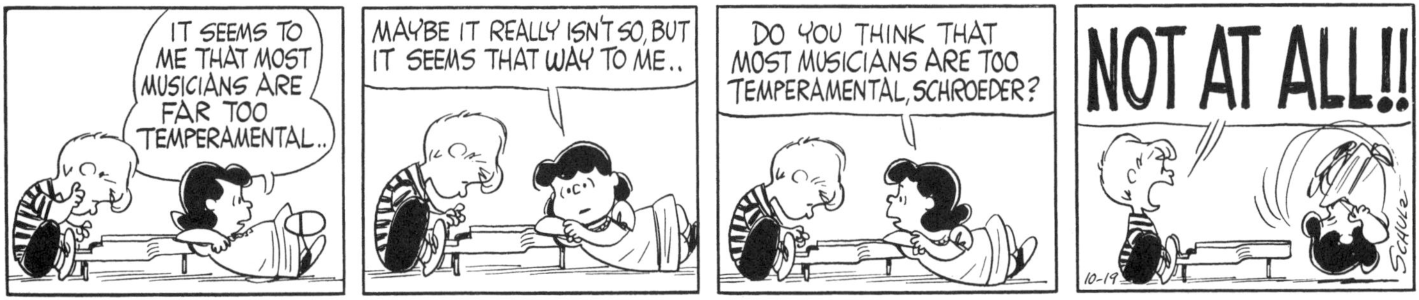
IT SEEMS TO ME THAT MOST MUSICIANS ARE FAR TOO TEMPERAMENTAL..
MAYBE IT REALLY ISN'T SO, BUT IT SEEMS THAT WAY TO ME..
DO YOU THINK THAT MOST MUSICIANS ARE TOO TEMPERAMENTAL, SCHROEDER?
NOT AT ALL!!

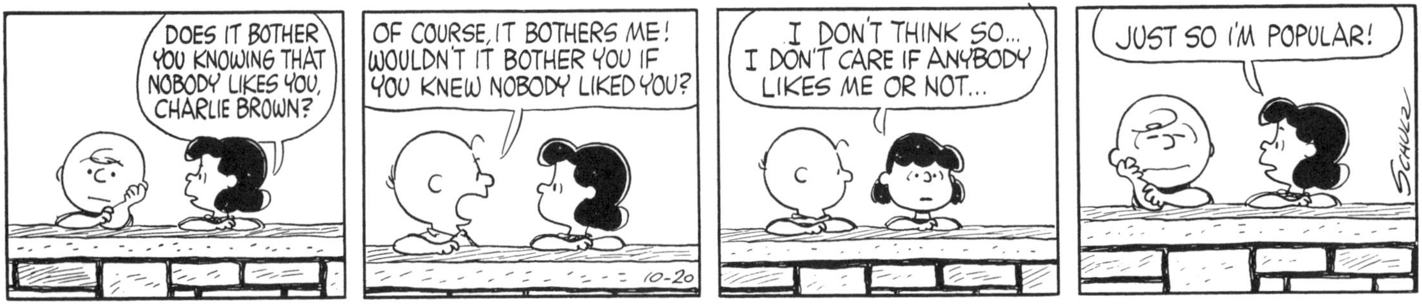
DOES IT BOTHER YOU KNOWING THAT NOBODY LIKES YOU, CHARLIE BROWN?
OF COURSE, IT BOTHERS ME! WOULDN'T IT BOTHER YOU IF YOU KNEW NOBODY LIKED YOU?
I DON'T THINK SO... I DON'T CARE IF ANYBODY LIKES ME OR NOT...
JUST SO I'M POPULAR!

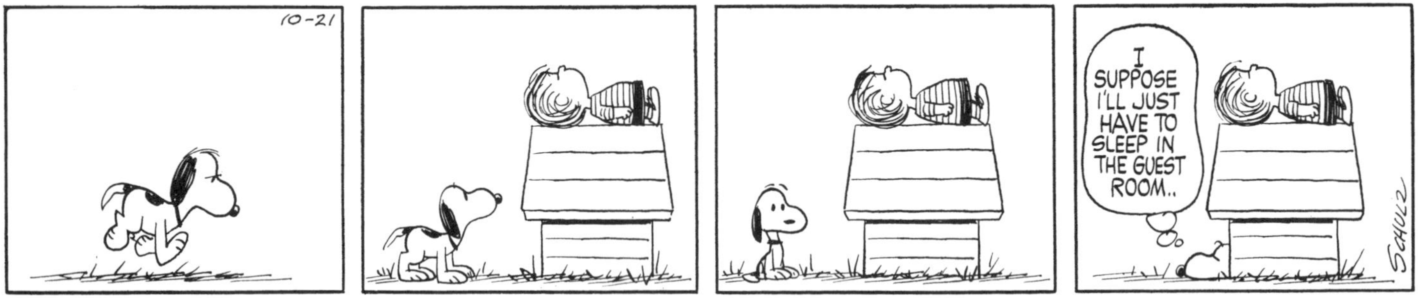
I SUPPOSE I'LL JUST HAVE TO SLEEP IN THE GUEST ROOM..

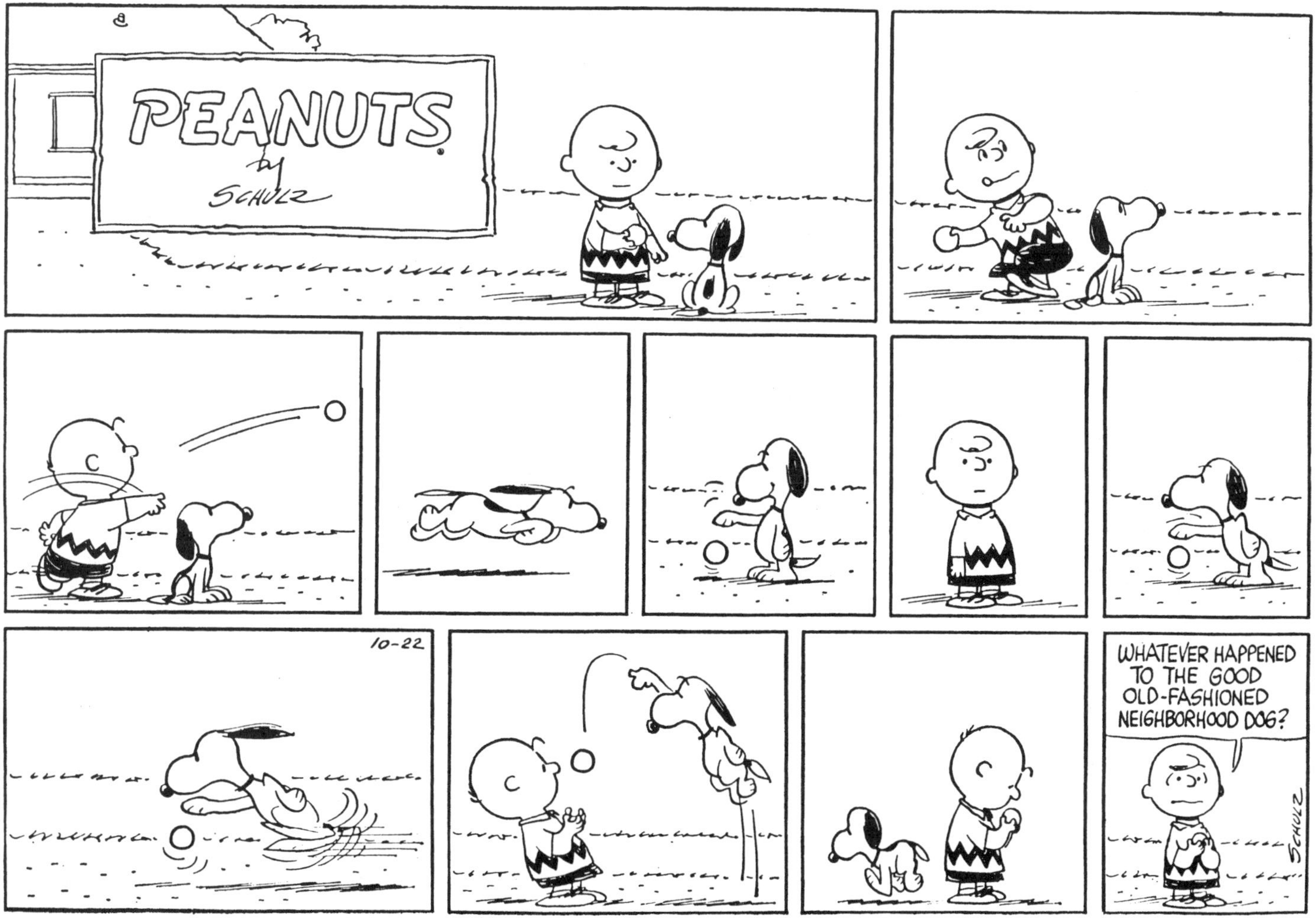
PEANUTS
by
SCHULZ
10-22
WHATEVER HAPPENED TO THE GOOD OLD-FASHIONED NEIGHBORHOOD DOG?
SCHULZ

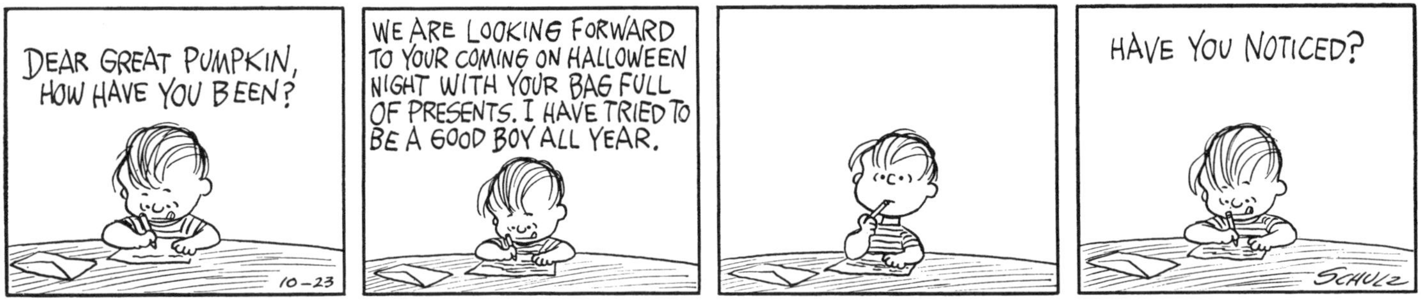
DEAR GREAT PUMPKIN, HOW HAVE YOU BEEN?
WE ARE LOOKING FORWARD TO YOUR COMING ON HALLOWEEN NIGHT WITH YOUR BAG FULL OF PRESENTS. I HAVE TRIED TO BE A GOOD BOY ALL YEAR.
HAVE YOU NOTICED?

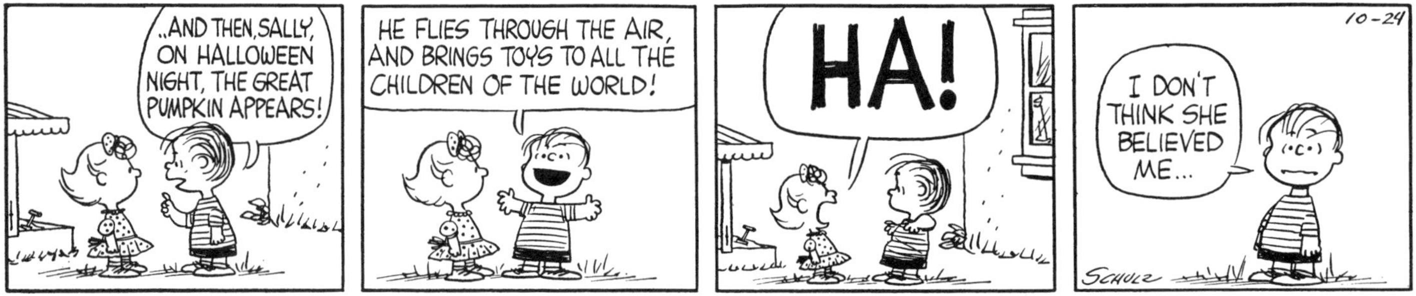
..AND THEN, SALLY, ON HALLOWEEN NIGHT, THE GREAT PUMPKIN APPEARS!
HE FLIES THROUGH THE AIR, AND BRINGS TOYS TO ALL THE CHILDREN OF THE WORLD!
HA!
I DON'T THINK SHE BELIEVED ME...

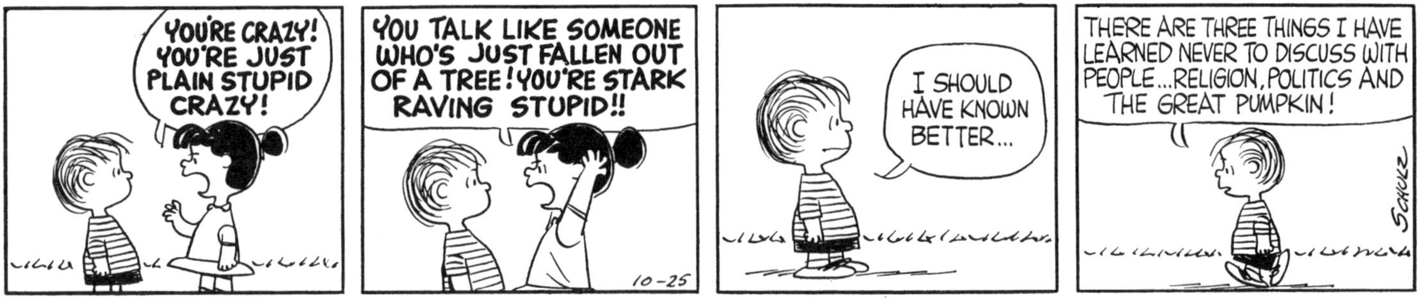
YOU'RE CRAZY! YOU'RE JUST PLAIN STUPID CRAZY!
YOU TALK LIKE SOMEONE WHO'S JUST FALLEN OUT OF A TREE! YOU'RE STARK RAVING STUPID!!
I SHOULD HAVE KNOWN BETTER...
THERE ARE THREE THINGS I HAVE LEARNED NEVER TO DISCUSS WITH PEOPLE...RELIGION, POLITICS AND THE GREAT PUMPKIN!

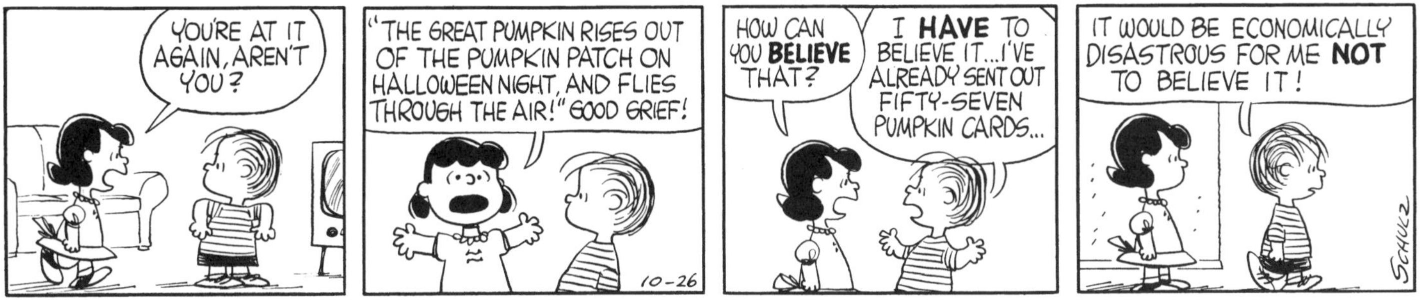
YOU'RE AT IT AGAIN, AREN'T YOU?
"THE GREAT PUMPKIN RISES OUT OF THE PUMPKIN PATCH ON HALLOWEEN NIGHT, AND FLIES THROUGH THE AIR!" GOOD GRIEF!
10-26
HOW CAN YOU **BELIEVE** THAT?
I **HAVE** TO BELIEVE IT...I'VE ALREADY SENT OUT FIFTY-SEVEN PUMPKIN CARDS...
IT WOULD BE ECONOMICALLY DISASTROUS FOR ME **NOT** TO BELIEVE IT!
SCHULZ

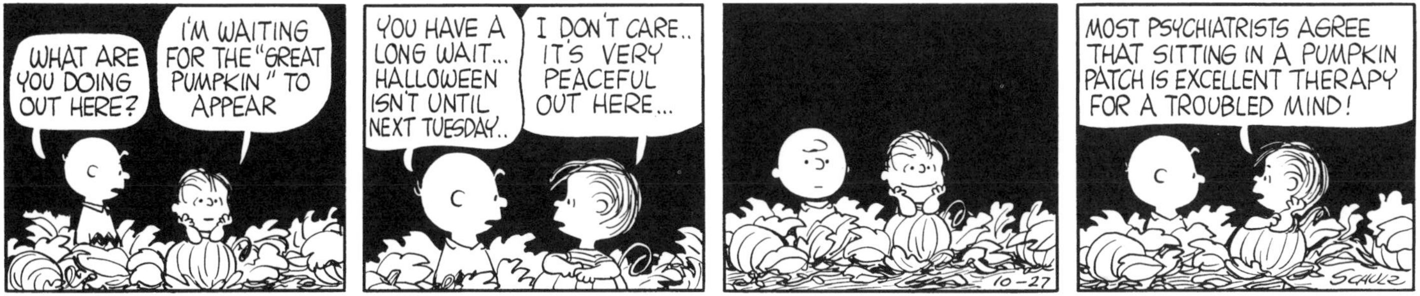
WHAT ARE YOU DOING OUT HERE?
I'M WAITING FOR THE "GREAT PUMPKIN" TO APPEAR
YOU HAVE A LONG WAIT... HALLOWEEN ISN'T UNTIL NEXT TUESDAY..
I DON'T CARE.. IT'S VERY PEACEFUL OUT HERE...
10-27
MOST PSYCHIATRISTS AGREE THAT SITTING IN A PUMPKIN PATCH IS EXCELLENT THERAPY FOR A TROUBLED MIND!
SCHULZ

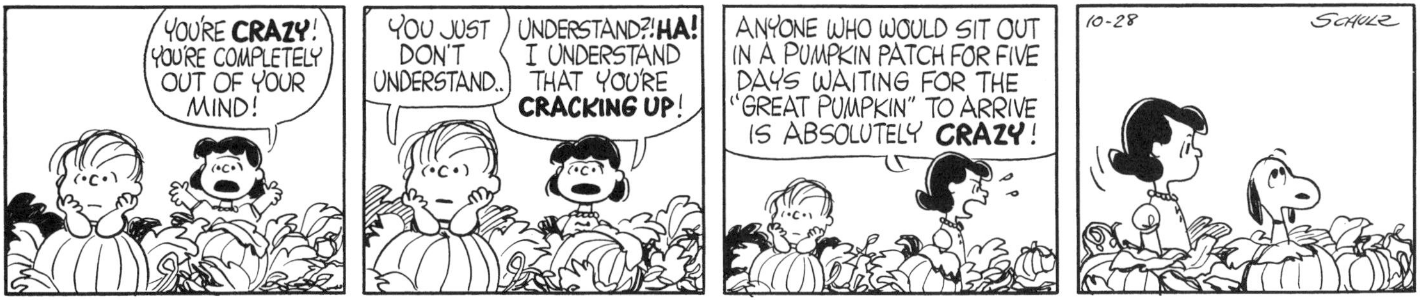
YOU'RE **CRAZY**! YOU'RE COMPLETELY OUT OF YOUR MIND!
YOU JUST DON'T UNDERSTAND..
UNDERSTAND?! **HA!** I UNDERSTAND THAT YOU'RE **CRACKING UP**!
ANYONE WHO WOULD SIT OUT IN A PUMPKIN PATCH FOR FIVE DAYS WAITING FOR THE "GREAT PUMPKIN" TO ARRIVE IS ABSOLUTELY **CRAZY**!
10-28
SCHULZ

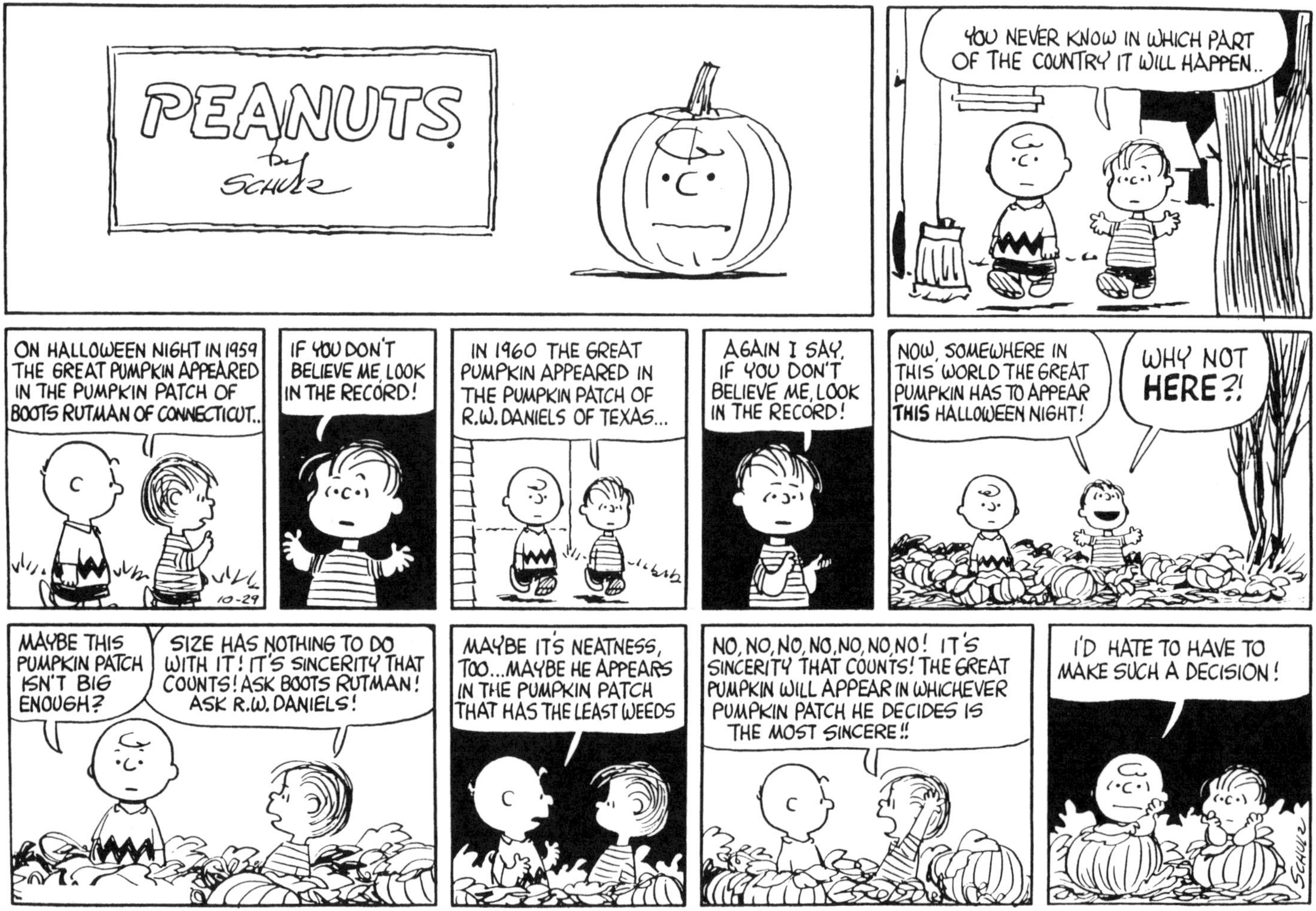
PEANUTS
by SCHULZ
YOU NEVER KNOW IN WHICH PART OF THE COUNTRY IT WILL HAPPEN..
ON HALLOWEEN NIGHT IN 1959 THE GREAT PUMPKIN APPEARED IN THE PUMPKIN PATCH OF BOOTS RUTMAN OF CONNECTICUT..
10-29
IF YOU DON'T BELIEVE ME, LOOK IN THE RECORD!
IN 1960 THE GREAT PUMPKIN APPEARED IN THE PUMPKIN PATCH OF R.W. DANIELS OF TEXAS...
AGAIN I SAY, IF YOU DON'T BELIEVE ME, LOOK IN THE RECORD!
NOW, SOMEWHERE IN THIS WORLD THE GREAT PUMPKIN HAS TO APPEAR THIS HALLOWEEN NIGHT!
WHY NOT HERE?!
MAYBE THIS PUMPKIN PATCH ISN'T BIG ENOUGH?
SIZE HAS NOTHING TO DO WITH IT! IT'S SINCERITY THAT COUNTS! ASK BOOTS RUTMAN! ASK R.W. DANIELS!
MAYBE IT'S NEATNESS, TOO...MAYBE HE APPEARS IN THE PUMPKIN PATCH THAT HAS THE LEAST WEEDS
NO, NO, NO, NO, NO, NO, NO! IT'S SINCERITY THAT COUNTS! THE GREAT PUMPKIN WILL APPEAR IN WHICHEVER PUMPKIN PATCH HE DECIDES IS THE MOST SINCERE!!
I'D HATE TO HAVE TO MAKE SUCH A DECISION!
SCHULZ

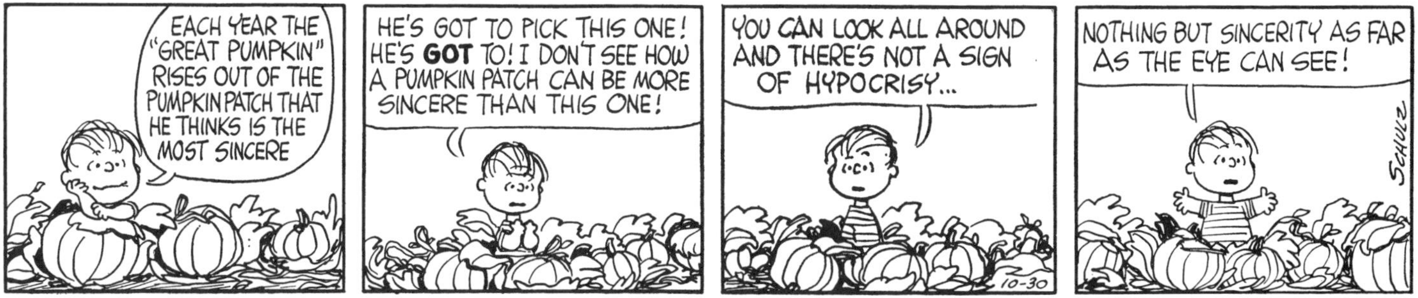
EACH YEAR THE "GREAT PUMPKIN" RISES OUT OF THE PUMPKIN PATCH THAT HE THINKS IS THE MOST SINCERE
HE'S GOT TO PICK THIS ONE! HE'S **GOT** TO! I DON'T SEE HOW A PUMPKIN PATCH CAN BE MORE SINCERE THAN THIS ONE!
YOU CAN LOOK ALL AROUND AND THERE'S NOT A SIGN OF HYPOCRISY...
10-30
NOTHING BUT SINCERITY AS FAR AS THE EYE CAN SEE!
SCHULZ

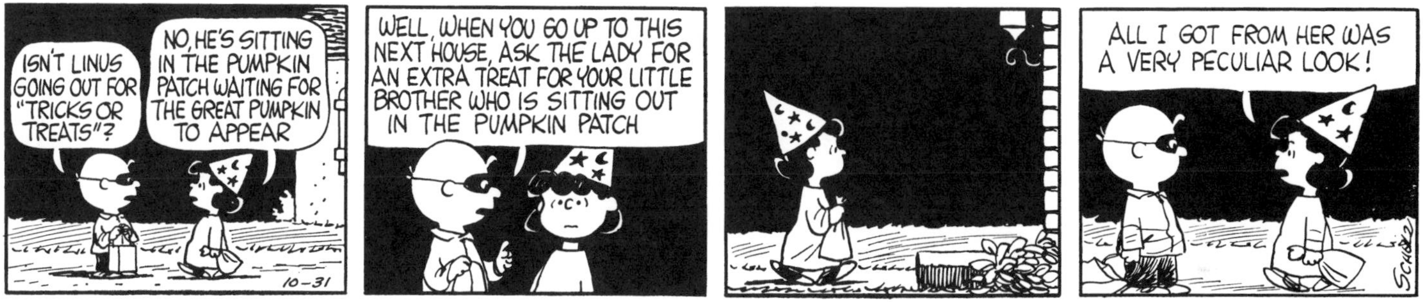
ISN'T LINUS GOING OUT FOR "TRICKS OR TREATS"?
NO, HE'S SITTING IN THE PUMPKIN PATCH WAITING FOR THE GREAT PUMPKIN TO APPEAR
10-31
WELL, WHEN YOU GO UP TO THIS NEXT HOUSE, ASK THE LADY FOR AN EXTRA TREAT FOR YOUR LITTLE BROTHER WHO IS SITTING OUT IN THE PUMPKIN PATCH
ALL I GOT FROM HER WAS A VERY PECULIAR LOOK!
SCHULZ

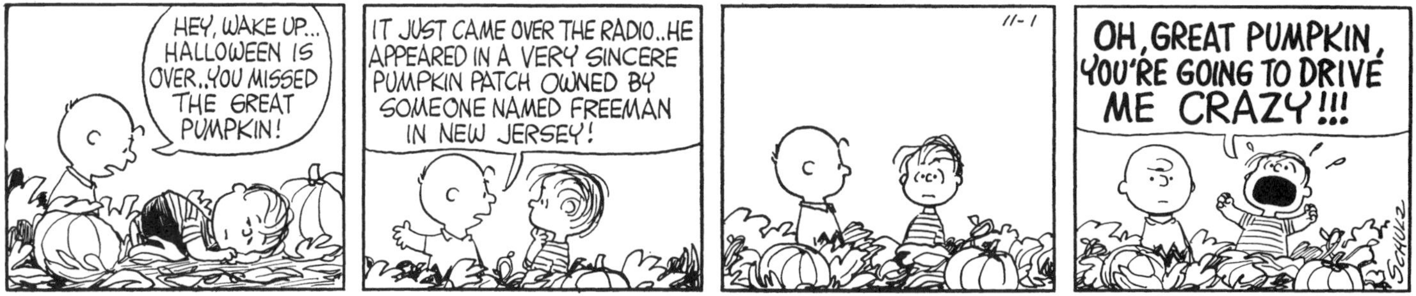
HEY, WAKE UP... HALLOWEEN IS OVER..YOU MISSED THE GREAT PUMPKIN!
IT JUST CAME OVER THE RADIO..HE APPEARED IN A VERY SINCERE PUMPKIN PATCH OWNED BY SOMEONE NAMED FREEMAN IN NEW JERSEY!
11-1
OH, GREAT PUMPKIN, YOU'RE GOING TO DRIVE ME CRAZY!!!
SCHULZ

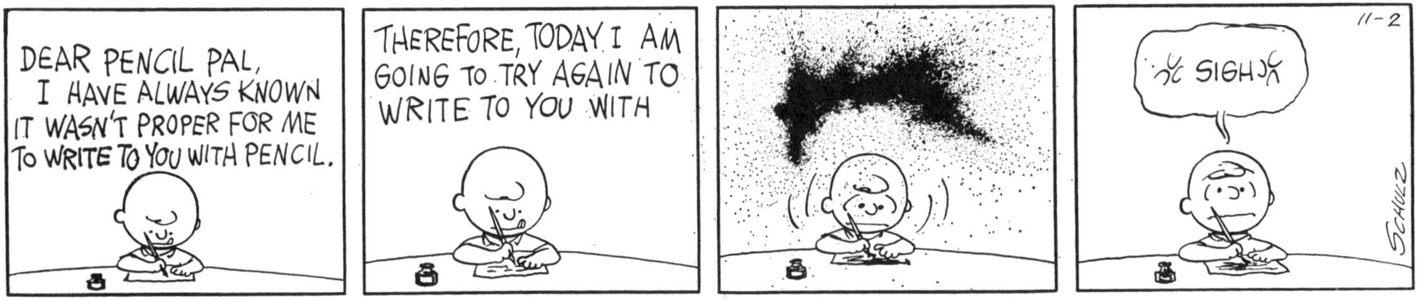
DEAR PENCIL PAL,
I HAVE ALWAYS KNOWN IT WASN'T PROPER FOR ME TO WRITE TO YOU WITH PENCIL.
THEREFORE, TODAY I AM GOING TO TRY AGAIN TO WRITE TO YOU WITH
SIGH
11-2
SCHULZ

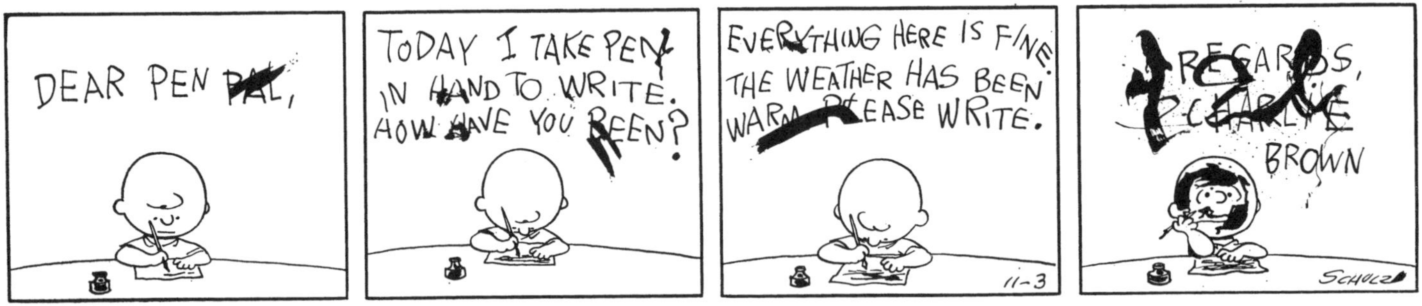
DEAR PEN PAL,
TODAY I TAKE PEN IN HAND TO WRITE. HOW HAVE YOU BEEN?
EVERYTHING HERE IS FINE. THE WEATHER HAS BEEN WARM PLEASE WRITE.
11-3
REGARDS, CHARLIE BROWN
SCHULZ

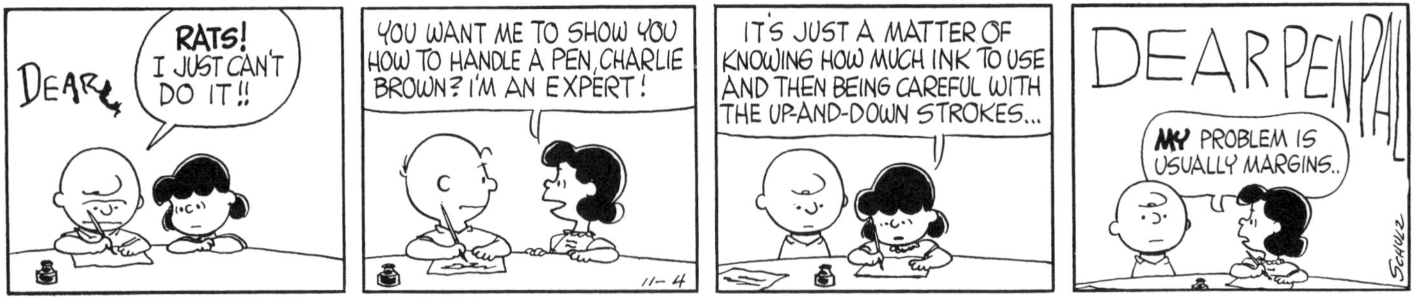
DEAR
RATS! I JUST CAN'T DO IT!!
YOU WANT ME TO SHOW YOU HOW TO HANDLE A PEN, CHARLIE BROWN? I'M AN EXPERT!
11-4
IT'S JUST A MATTER OF KNOWING HOW MUCH INK TO USE AND THEN BEING CAREFUL WITH THE UP-AND-DOWN STROKES...
DEAR PEN PAL
MY PROBLEM IS USUALLY MARGINS..
SCHULZ

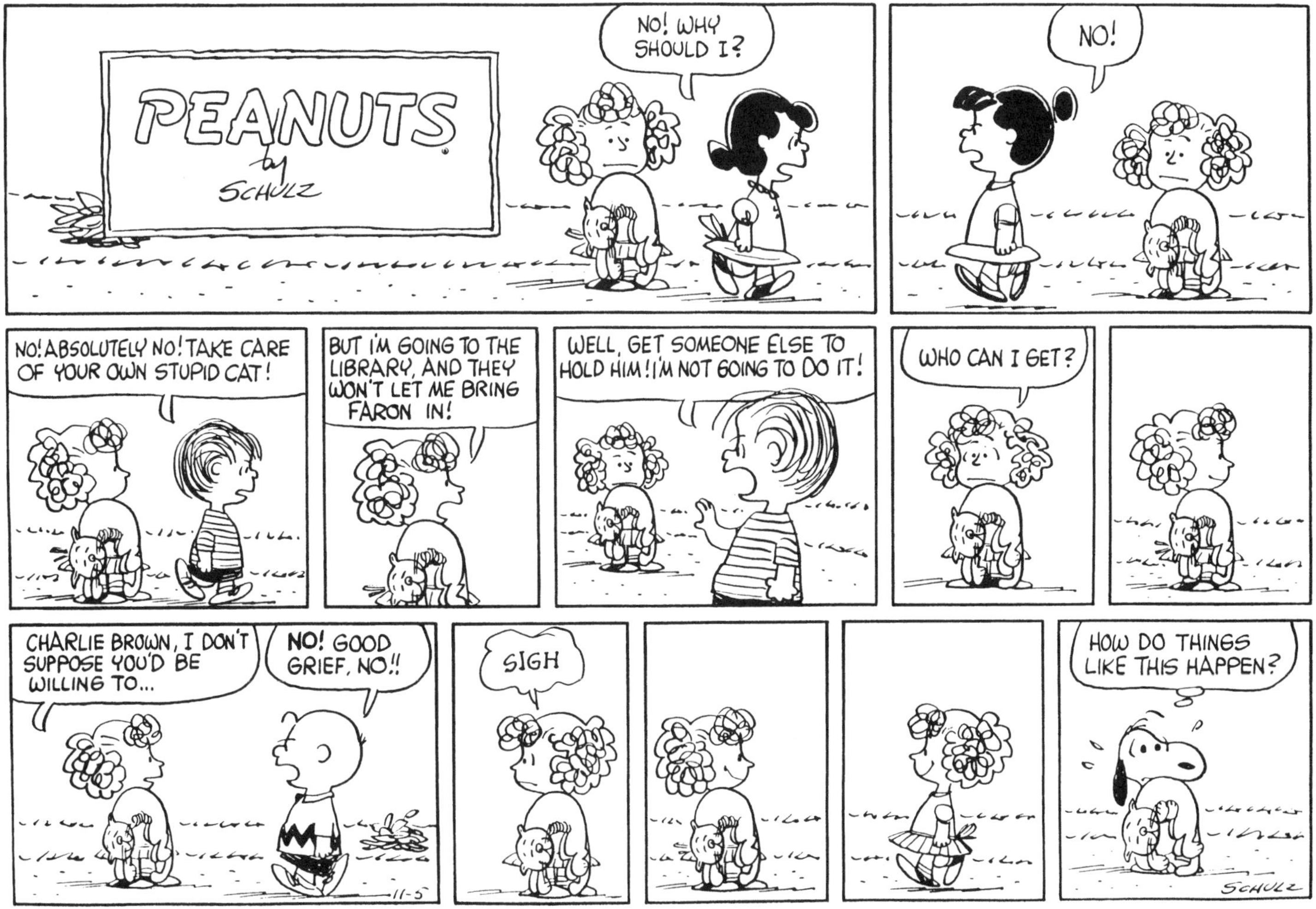
PEANUTS
by SCHULZ
NO! WHY SHOULD I?
NO!
NO! ABSOLUTELY NO! TAKE CARE OF YOUR OWN STUPID CAT!
BUT I'M GOING TO THE LIBRARY, AND THEY WON'T LET ME BRING FARON IN!
WELL, GET SOMEONE ELSE TO HOLD HIM! I'M NOT GOING TO DO IT!
WHO CAN I GET?
CHARLIE BROWN, I DON'T SUPPOSE YOU'D BE WILLING TO...
NO! GOOD GRIEF, NO!!
11-5
SIGH
HOW DO THINGS LIKE THIS HAPPEN?
SCHULZ

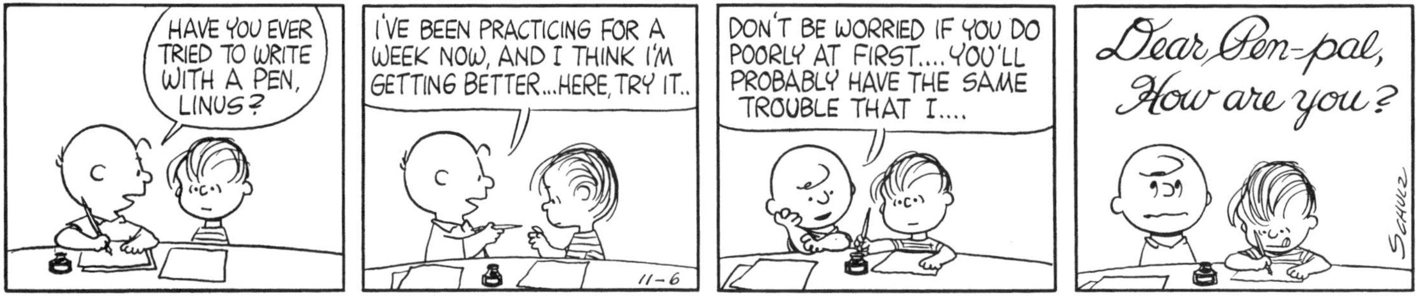
HAVE YOU EVER TRIED TO WRITE WITH A PEN, LINUS?
I'VE BEEN PRACTICING FOR A WEEK NOW, AND I THINK I'M GETTING BETTER...HERE, TRY IT..
11-6
DON'T BE WORRIED IF YOU DO POORLY AT FIRST....YOU'LL PROBABLY HAVE THE SAME TROUBLE THAT I....
Dear Pen-pal, How are you?
SCHULZ

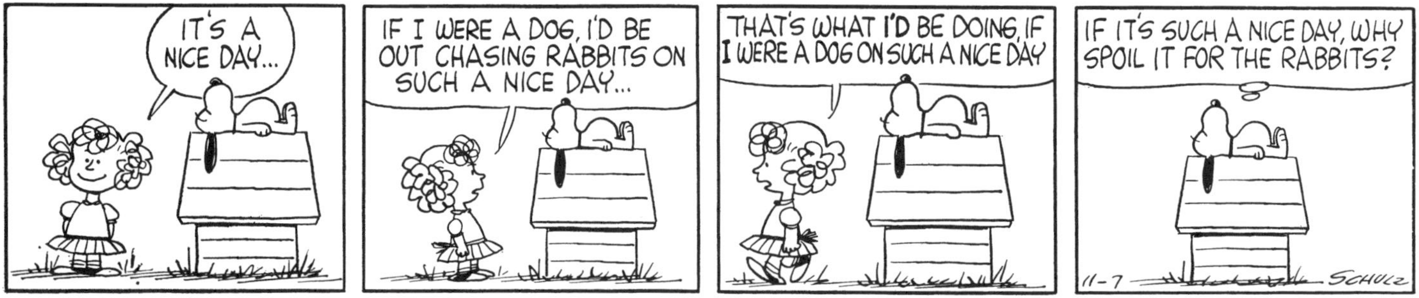
IT'S A NICE DAY...
IF I WERE A DOG, I'D BE OUT CHASING RABBITS ON SUCH A NICE DAY...
THAT'S WHAT I'D BE DOING, IF I WERE A DOG ON SUCH A NICE DAY
IF IT'S SUCH A NICE DAY, WHY SPOIL IT FOR THE RABBITS?
11-7
SCHULZ

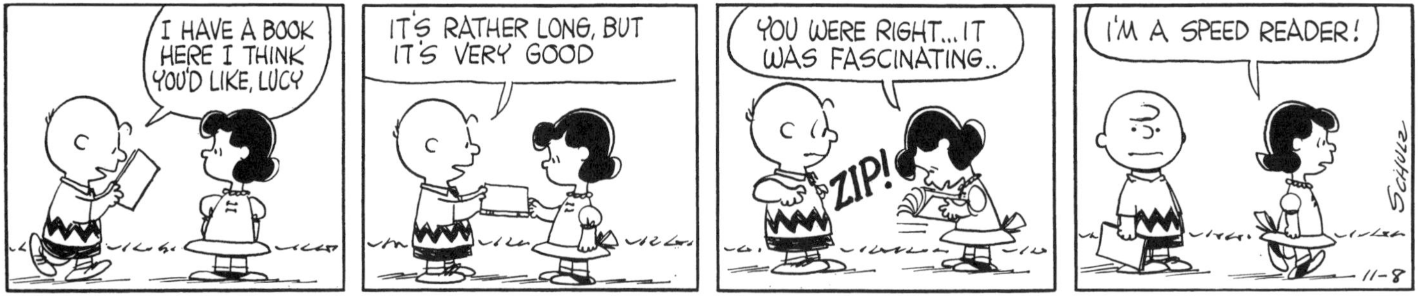
I HAVE A BOOK HERE I THINK YOU'D LIKE, LUCY
IT'S RATHER LONG, BUT IT'S VERY GOOD
YOU WERE RIGHT...IT WAS FASCINATING..
ZIP!
I'M A SPEED READER!
SCHULZ
11-8

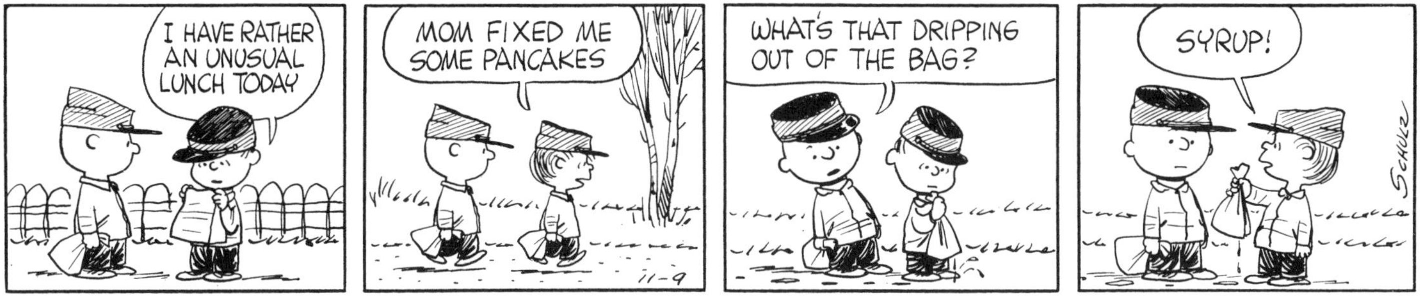
I HAVE RATHER AN UNUSUAL LUNCH TODAY
MOM FIXED ME SOME PANCAKES
11-9
WHAT'S THAT DRIPPING OUT OF THE BAG?
SYRUP!
SCHULZ

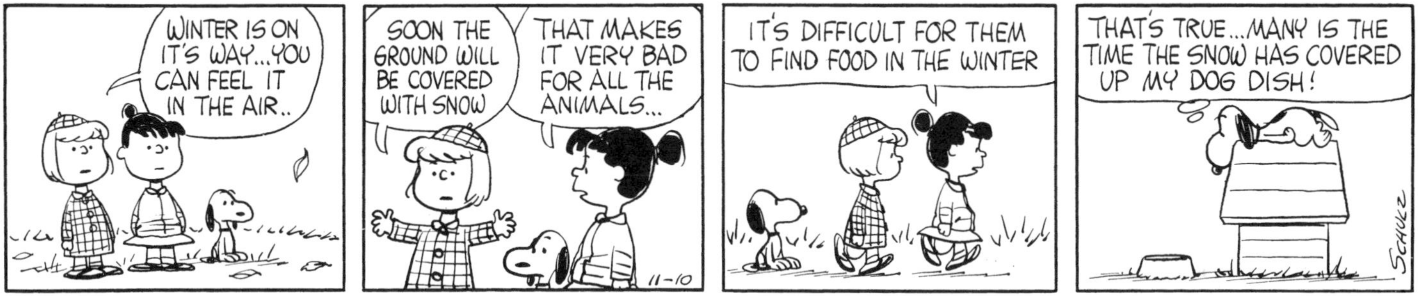
WINTER IS ON IT'S WAY...YOU CAN FEEL IT IN THE AIR..
SOON THE GROUND WILL BE COVERED WITH SNOW
THAT MAKES IT VERY BAD FOR ALL THE ANIMALS...
11-10
IT'S DIFFICULT FOR THEM TO FIND FOOD IN THE WINTER
THAT'S TRUE...MANY IS THE TIME THE SNOW HAS COVERED UP MY DOG DISH!
SCHULZ

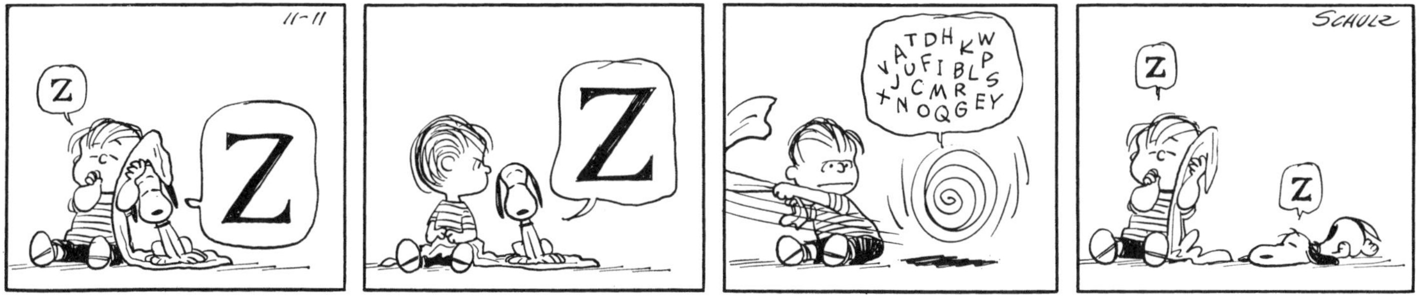
11-11
Z
Z
Z
V ATDH KW
JUFI BL P S
X J C M R
N O Q G E Y
SCHULZ
Z
Z

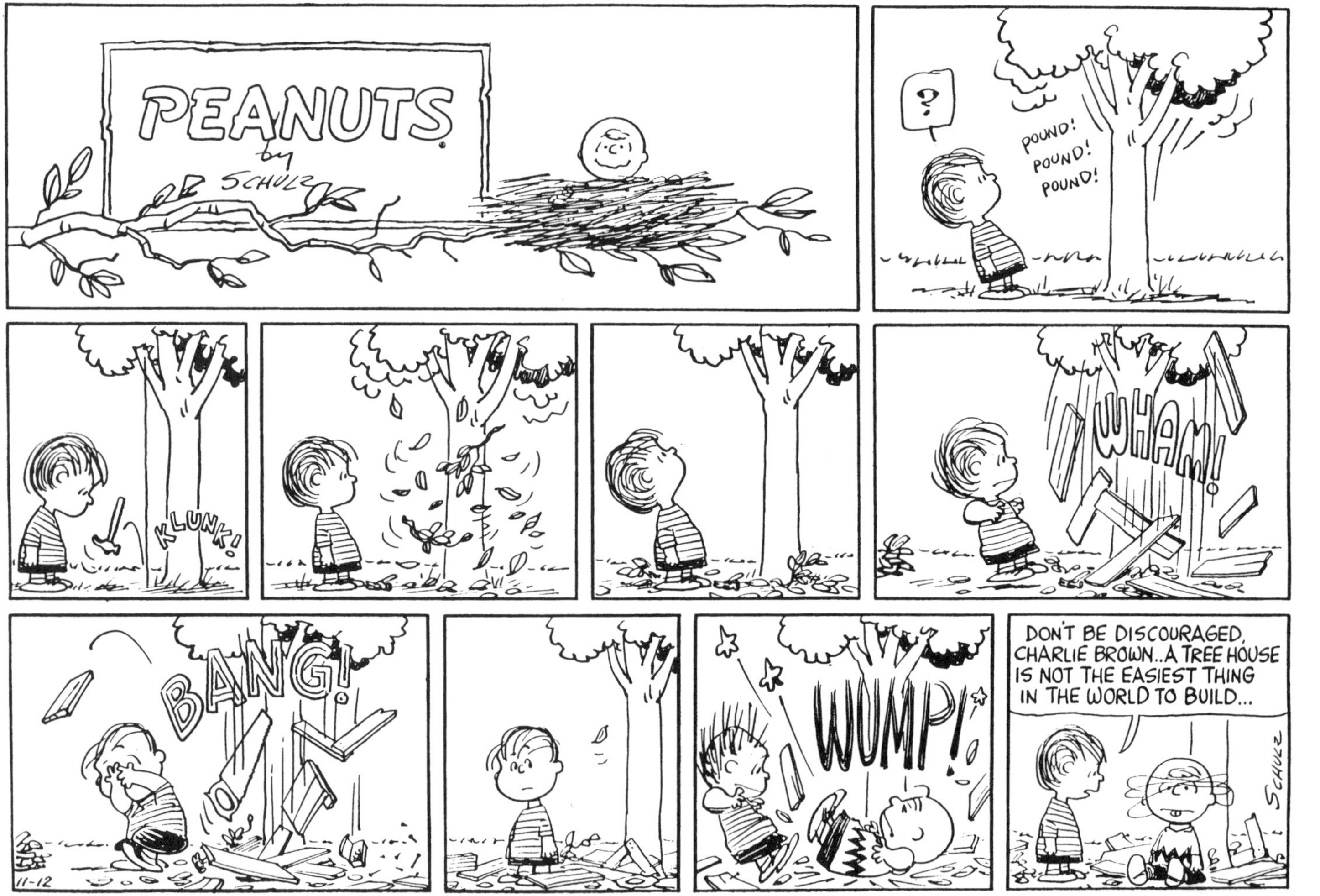
PEANUTS
by
SCHULZ
?
POUND! POUND! POUND!
KLUNK!
WHAM!
BANG!
WUMP!
DON'T BE DISCOURAGED, CHARLIE BROWN..A TREE HOUSE IS NOT THE EASIEST THING IN THE WORLD TO BUILD...
SCHULZ
11-12

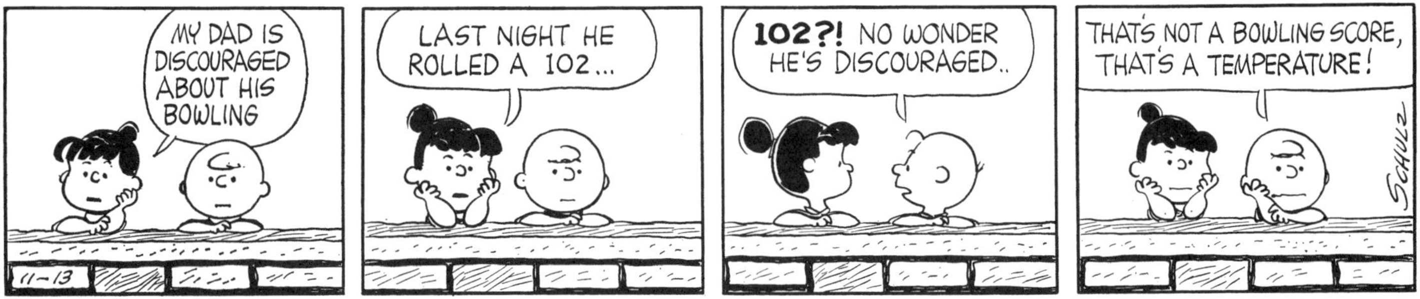
MY DAD IS DISCOURAGED ABOUT HIS BOWLING
LAST NIGHT HE ROLLED A 102...
102?! NO WONDER HE'S DISCOURAGED..
THAT'S NOT A BOWLING SCORE, THAT'S A TEMPERATURE!
11-13
SCHULZ

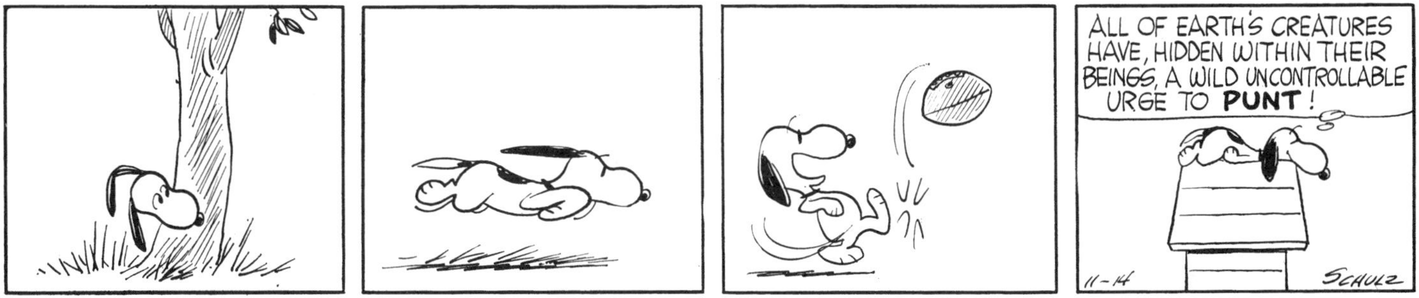
ALL OF EARTH'S CREATURES HAVE, HIDDEN WITHIN THEIR BEINGS, A WILD UNCONTROLLABLE URGE TO **PUNT**!
11-14
SCHULZ

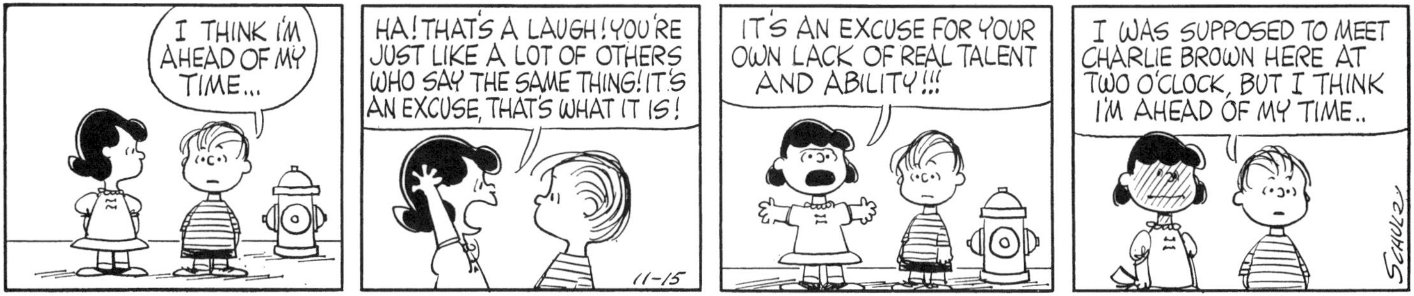
I THINK I'M AHEAD OF MY TIME...
HA! THAT'S A LAUGH! YOU'RE JUST LIKE A LOT OF OTHERS WHO SAY THE SAME THING! IT'S AN EXCUSE, THAT'S WHAT IT IS!
11-15
IT'S AN EXCUSE FOR YOUR OWN LACK OF REAL TALENT AND ABILITY!!!
I WAS SUPPOSED TO MEET CHARLIE BROWN HERE AT TWO O'CLOCK, BUT I THINK I'M AHEAD OF MY TIME..
SCHULZ

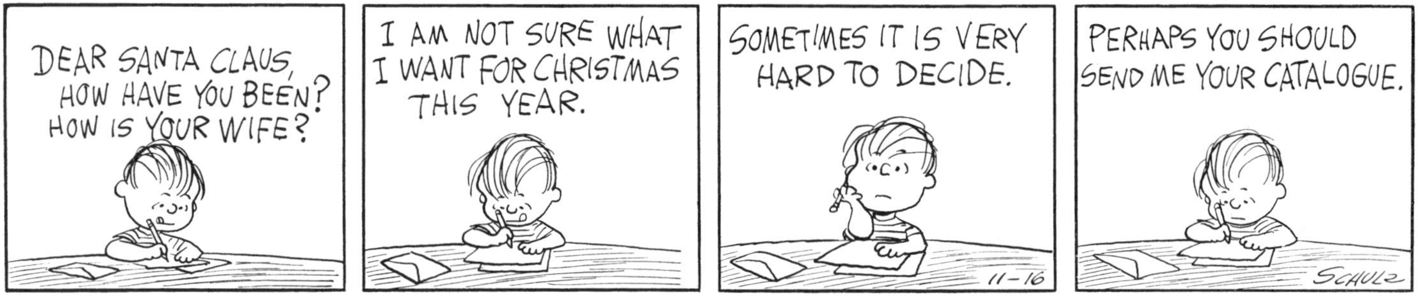
DEAR SANTA CLAUS, HOW HAVE YOU BEEN? HOW IS YOUR WIFE?
I AM NOT SURE WHAT I WANT FOR CHRISTMAS THIS YEAR.
SOMETIMES IT IS VERY HARD TO DECIDE.
11-16
PERHAPS YOU SHOULD SEND ME YOUR CATALOGUE.
SCHULZ

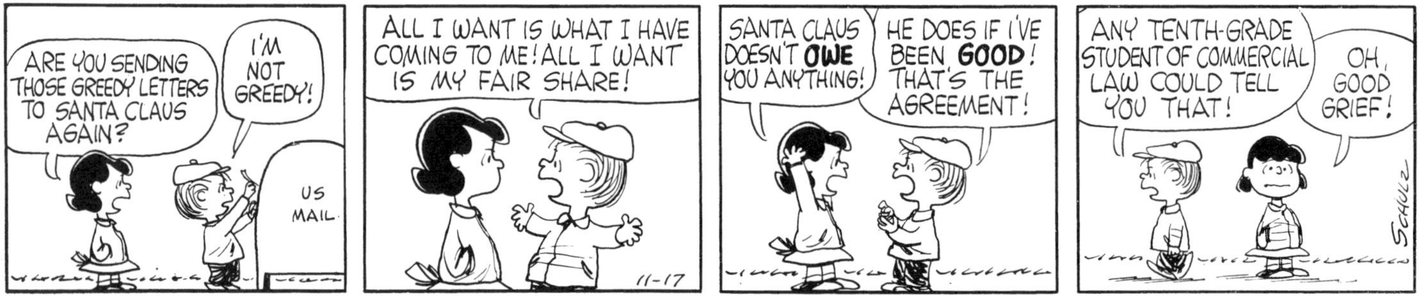
ARE YOU SENDING THOSE GREEDY LETTERS TO SANTA CLAUS AGAIN?
I'M NOT GREEDY!
US MAIL
ALL I WANT IS WHAT I HAVE COMING TO ME! ALL I WANT IS MY FAIR SHARE!
11-17
SANTA CLAUS DOESN'T OWE YOU ANYTHING!
HE DOES IF I'VE BEEN GOOD! THAT'S THE AGREEMENT!
ANY TENTH-GRADE STUDENT OF COMMERCIAL LAW COULD TELL YOU THAT!
OH, GOOD GRIEF!
SCHULZ

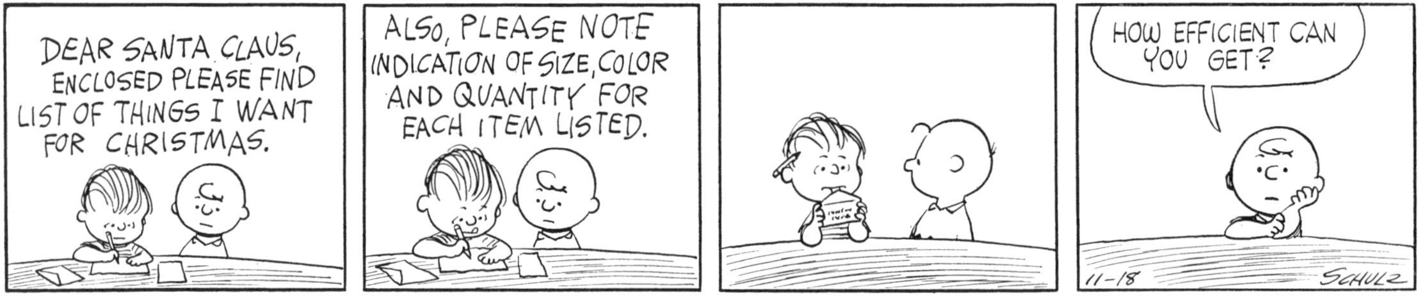
DEAR SANTA CLAUS, ENCLOSED PLEASE FIND LIST OF THINGS I WANT FOR CHRISTMAS.
ALSO, PLEASE NOTE INDICATION OF SIZE, COLOR AND QUANTITY FOR EACH ITEM LISTED.
HOW EFFICIENT CAN YOU GET?
11-18
SCHULZ

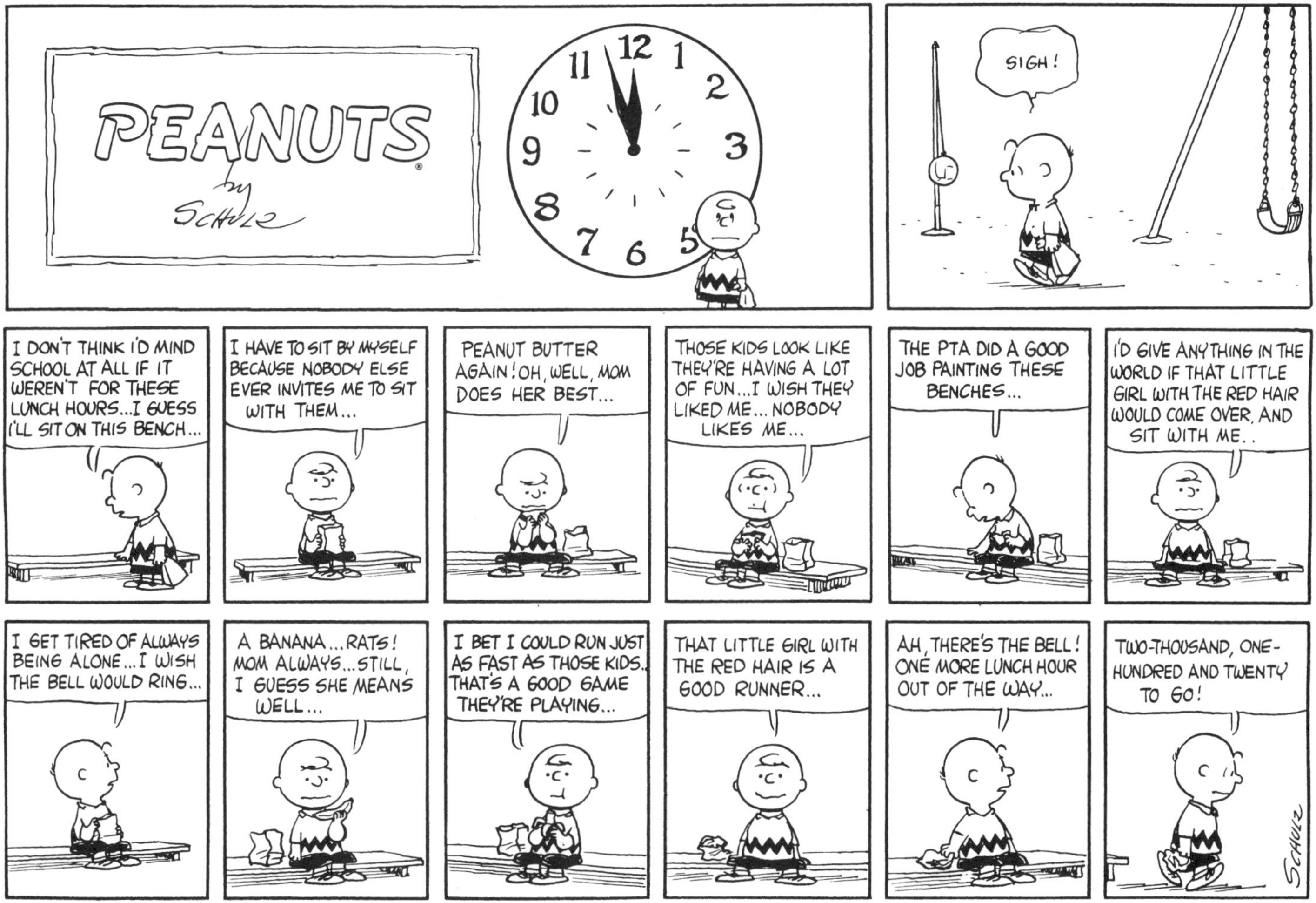
PEANUTS
by SCHULZ
SIGH!
I DON'T THINK I'D MIND SCHOOL AT ALL IF IT WEREN'T FOR THESE LUNCH HOURS...I GUESS I'LL SIT ON THIS BENCH...
I HAVE TO SIT BY MYSELF BECAUSE NOBODY ELSE EVER INVITES ME TO SIT WITH THEM...
PEANUT BUTTER AGAIN! OH, WELL, MOM DOES HER BEST...
THOSE KIDS LOOK LIKE THEY'RE HAVING A LOT OF FUN...I WISH THEY LIKED ME... NOBODY LIKES ME...
THE PTA DID A GOOD JOB PAINTING THESE BENCHES...
I'D GIVE ANYTHING IN THE WORLD IF THAT LITTLE GIRL WITH THE RED HAIR WOULD COME OVER AND SIT WITH ME..
I GET TIRED OF ALWAYS BEING ALONE...I WISH THE BELL WOULD RING...
A BANANA...RATS! MOM ALWAYS...STILL, I GUESS SHE MEANS WELL...
I BET I COULD RUN JUST AS FAST AS THOSE KIDS.. THAT'S A GOOD GAME THEY'RE PLAYING...
THAT LITTLE GIRL WITH THE RED HAIR IS A GOOD RUNNER...
AH, THERE'S THE BELL! ONE MORE LUNCH HOUR OUT OF THE WAY...
TWO-THOUSAND, ONE-HUNDRED AND TWENTY TO GO!
SCHULZ

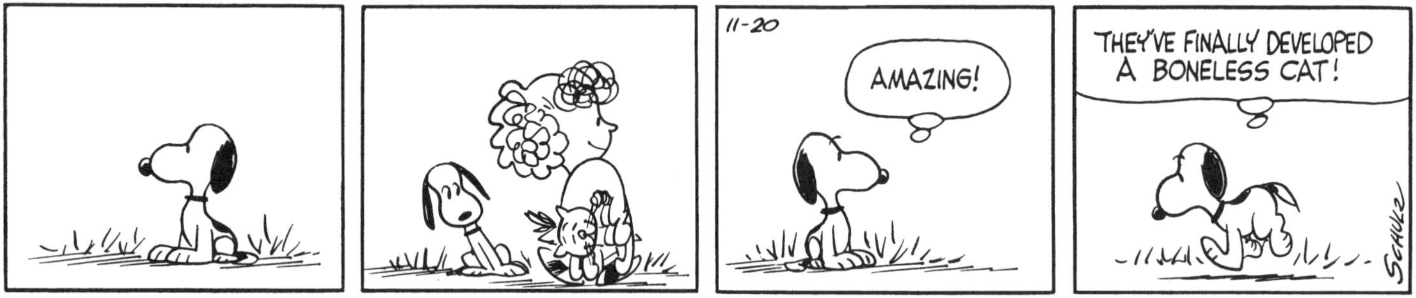
AMAZING!
THEY'VE FINALLY DEVELOPED A BONELESS CAT!

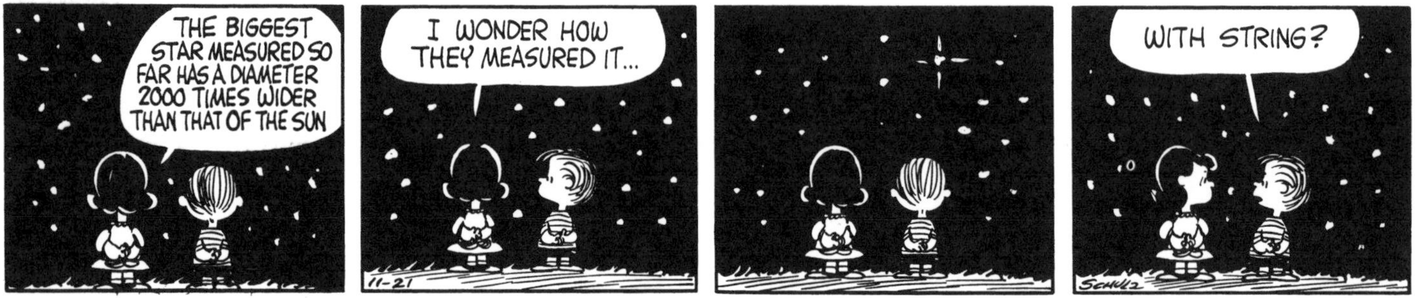
THE BIGGEST STAR MEASURED SO FAR HAS A DIAMETER 2000 TIMES WIDER THAN THAT OF THE SUN
I WONDER HOW THEY MEASURED IT...
WITH STRING?

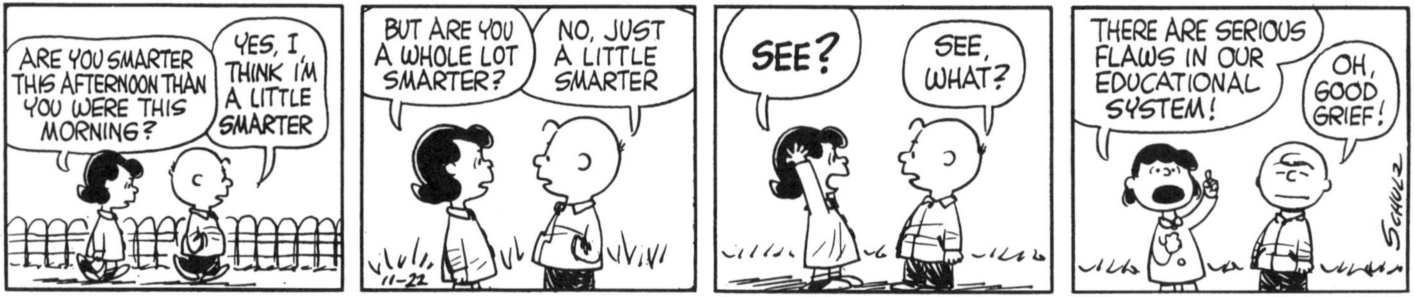
ARE YOU SMARTER THIS AFTERNOON THAN YOU WERE THIS MORNING?
YES, I THINK I'M A LITTLE SMARTER
BUT ARE YOU A WHOLE LOT SMARTER?
NO, JUST A LITTLE SMARTER
SEE?
SEE, WHAT?
THERE ARE SERIOUS FLAWS IN OUR EDUCATIONAL SYSTEM!
OH, GOOD GRIEF!

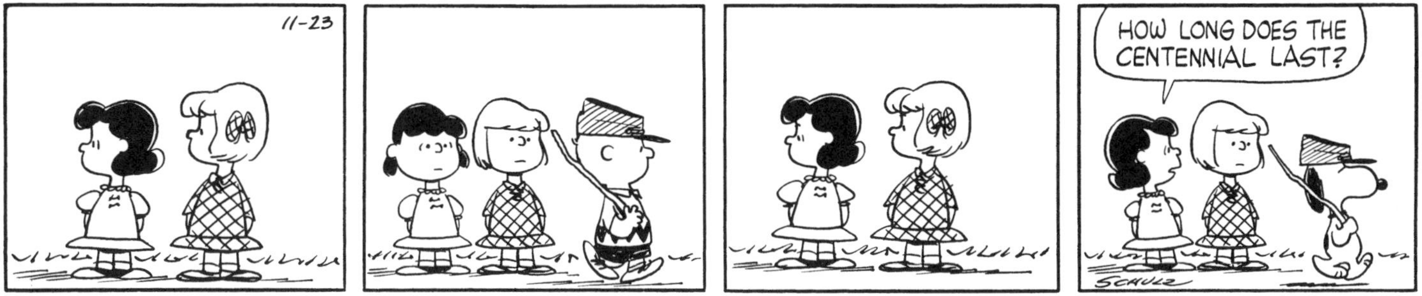
11-23
HOW LONG DOES THE CENTENNIAL LAST?
SCHULZ

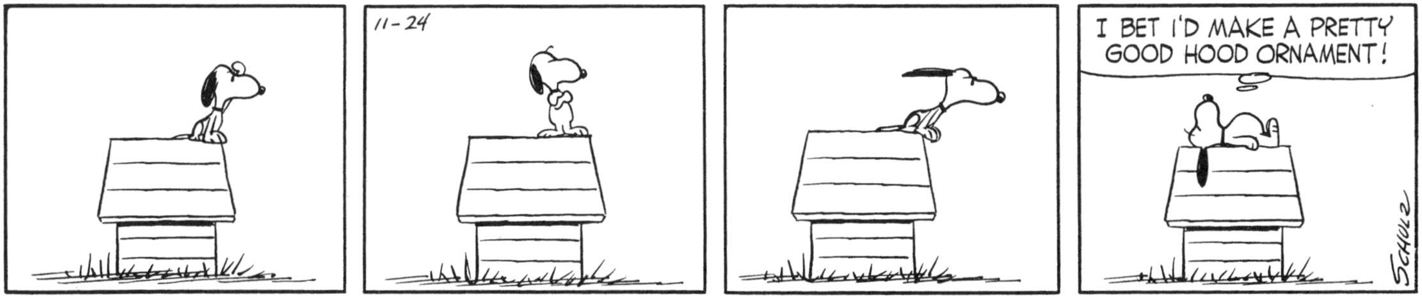
11-24
I BET I'D MAKE A PRETTY GOOD HOOD ORNAMENT!
SCHULZ

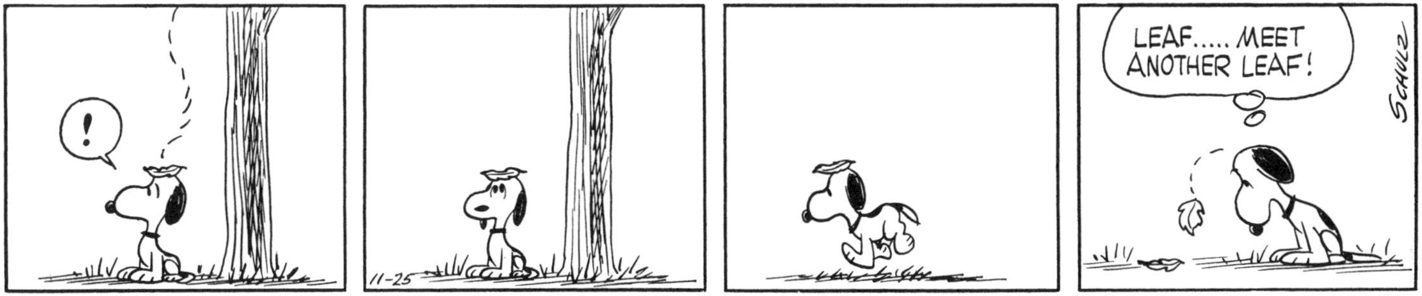
!
11-25
LEAF..... MEET ANOTHER LEAF!
SCHULZ

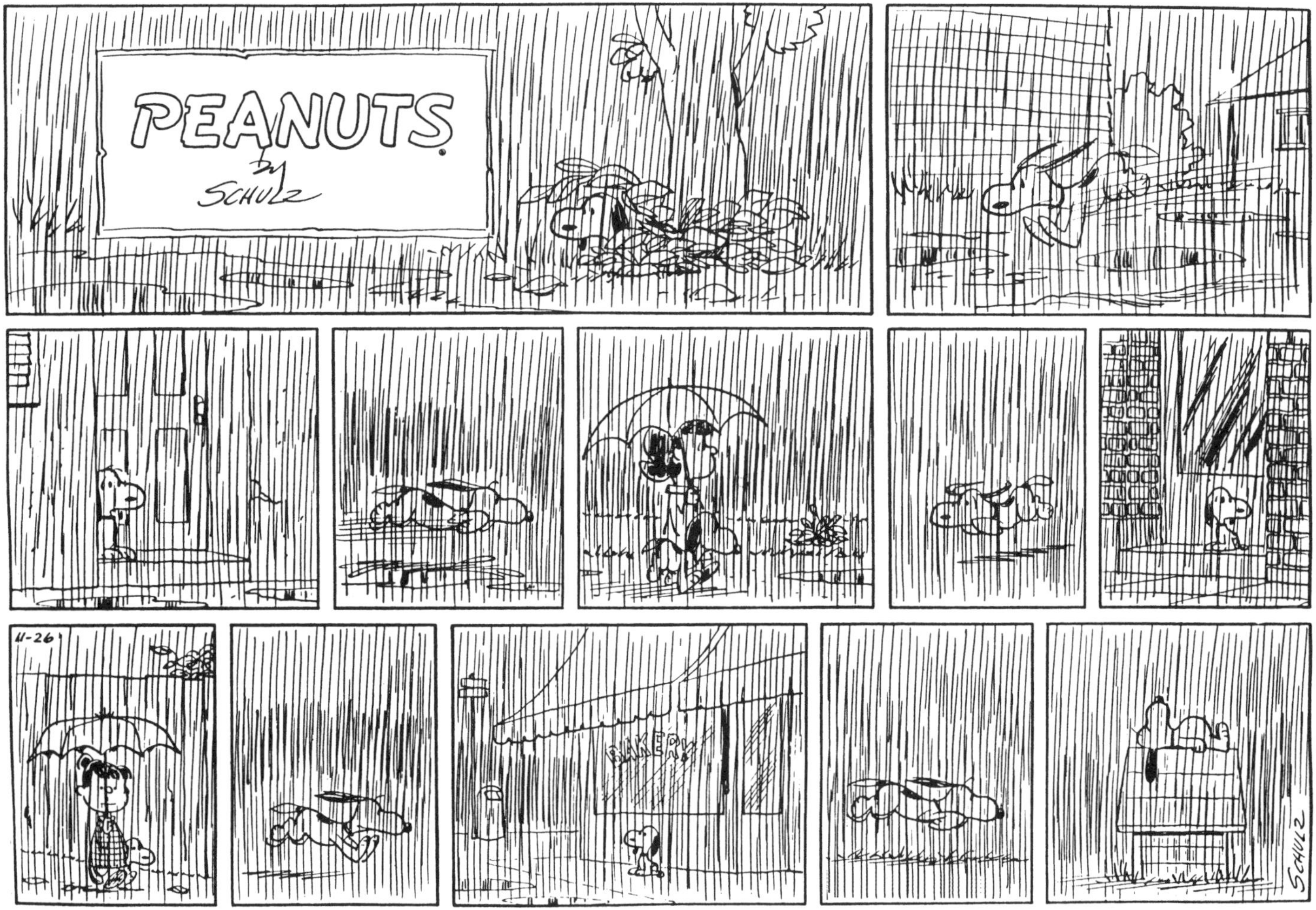
PEANUTS
by
SCHULZ
11-26
BAKERY
SCHULZ

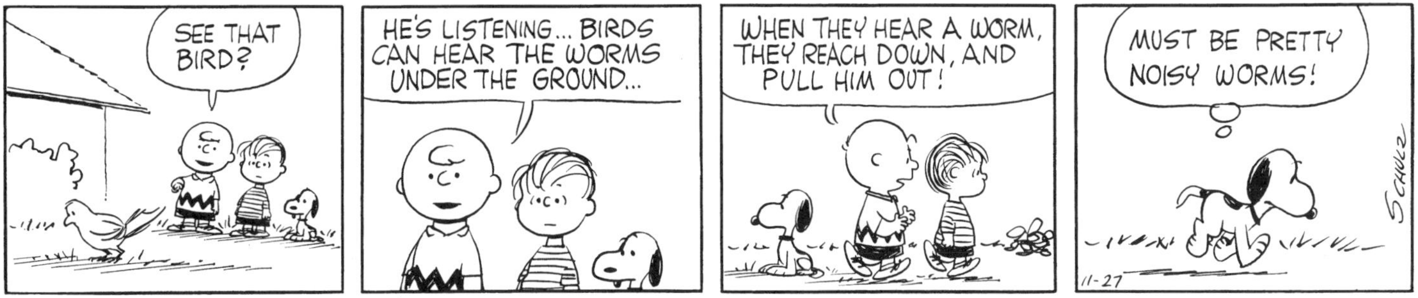
SEE THAT BIRD?
HE'S LISTENING... BIRDS CAN HEAR THE WORMS UNDER THE GROUND...
WHEN THEY HEAR A WORM, THEY REACH DOWN, AND PULL HIM OUT!
MUST BE PRETTY NOISY WORMS!
11-27
SCHULZ

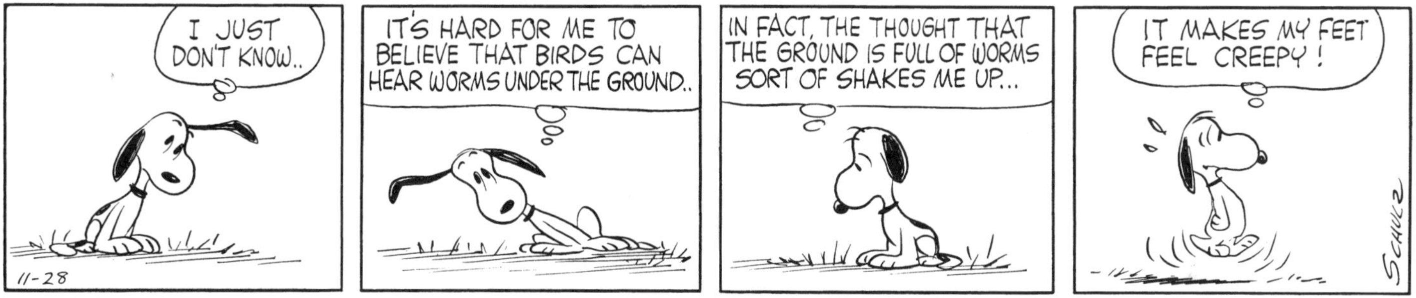
I JUST DON'T KNOW..
11-28
IT'S HARD FOR ME TO BELIEVE THAT BIRDS CAN HEAR WORMS UNDER THE GROUND..
IN FACT, THE THOUGHT THAT THE GROUND IS FULL OF WORMS SORT OF SHAKES ME UP...
IT MAKES MY FEET FEEL CREEPY!
SCHULZ

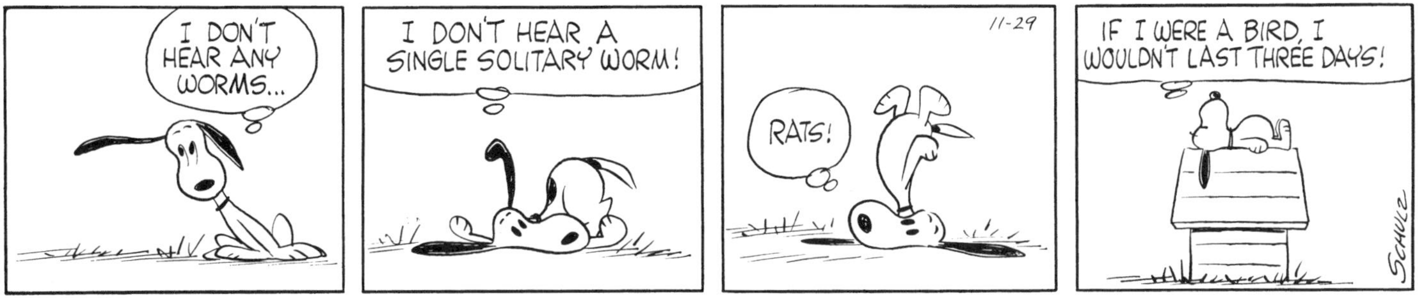
I DON'T HEAR ANY WORMS...
I DON'T HEAR A SINGLE SOLITARY WORM!
11-29
RATS!
IF I WERE A BIRD, I WOULDN'T LAST THREE DAYS!
SCHULZ

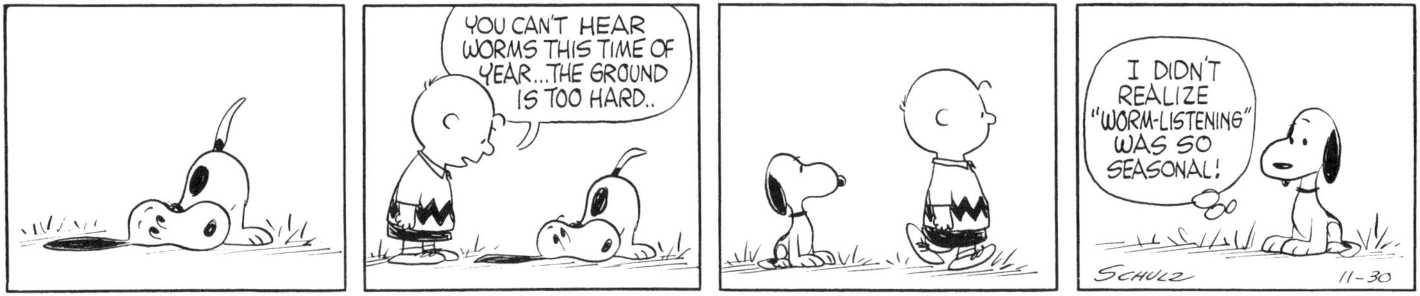
YOU CAN'T HEAR WORMS THIS TIME OF YEAR...THE GROUND IS TOO HARD..
I DIDN'T REALIZE "WORM-LISTENING" WAS SO SEASONAL!
SCHULZ
11-30

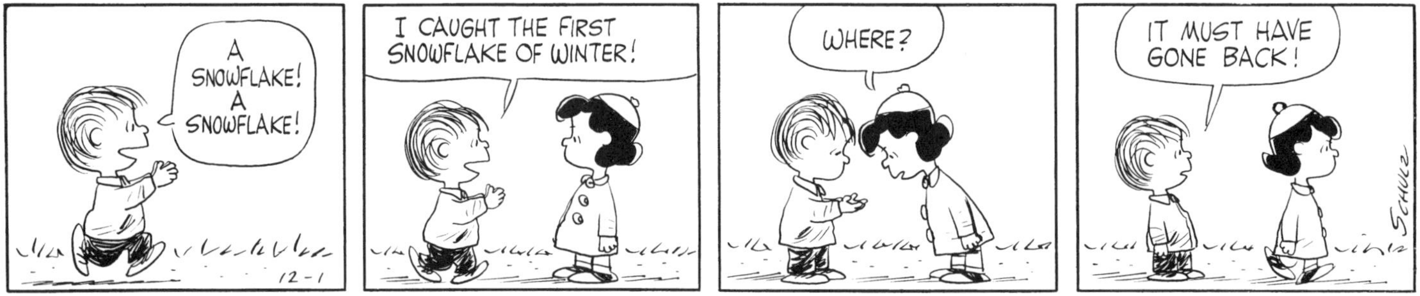
A SNOWFLAKE! A SNOWFLAKE!
12-1
I CAUGHT THE FIRST SNOWFLAKE OF WINTER!
WHERE?
IT MUST HAVE GONE BACK!
SCHULZ

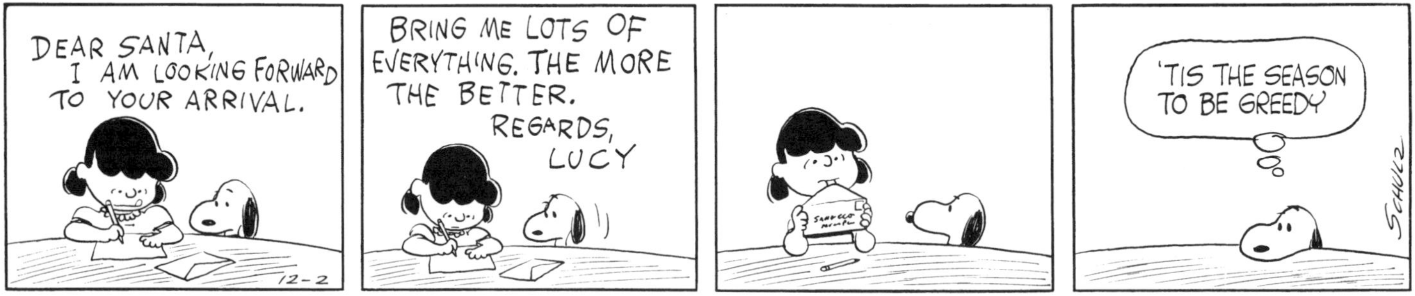
DEAR SANTA, I AM LOOKING FORWARD TO YOUR ARRIVAL.
12-2
BRING ME LOTS OF EVERYTHING. THE MORE THE BETTER.
REGARDS, LUCY
'TIS THE SEASON TO BE GREEDY
SCHULZ

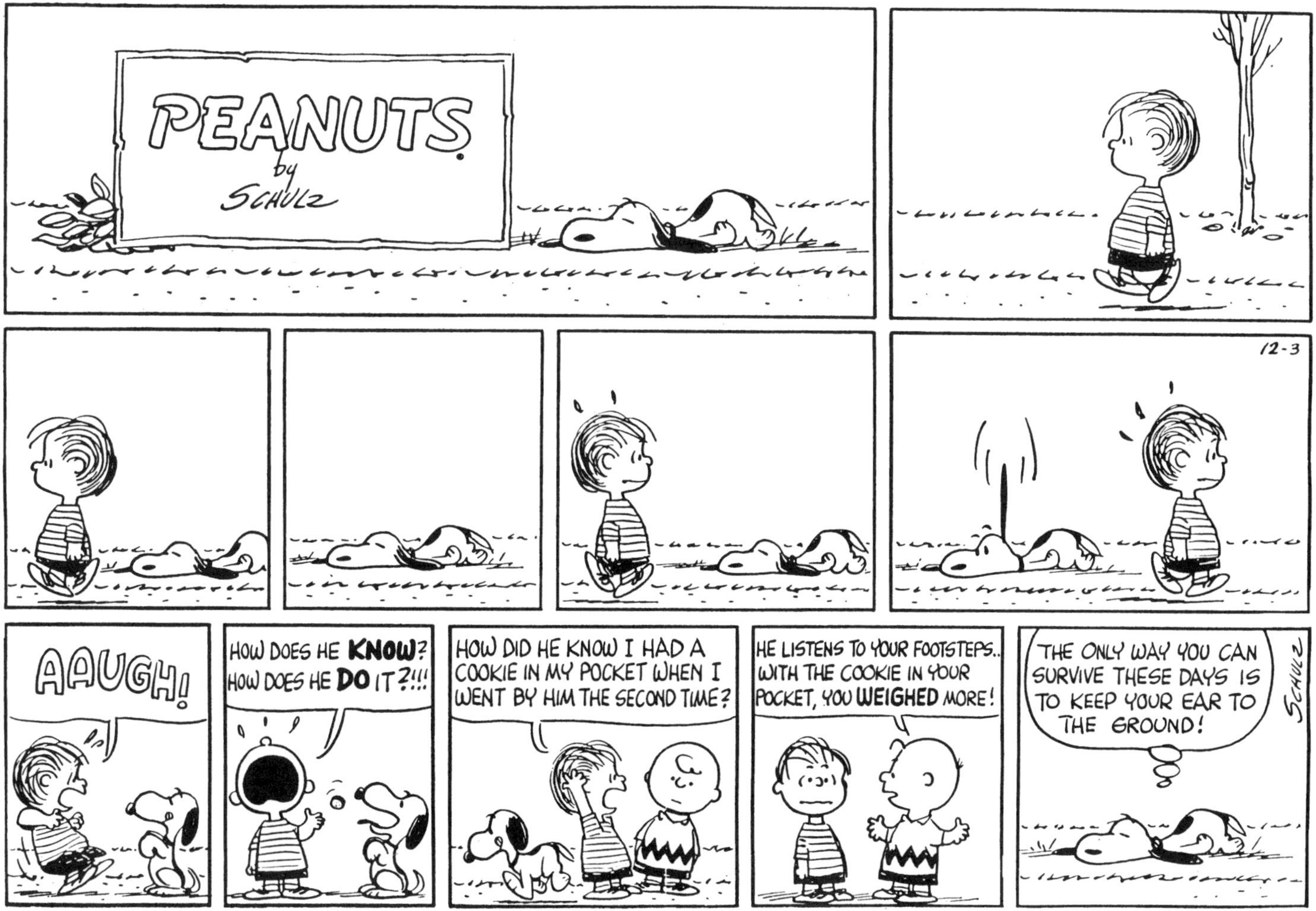
PEANUTS
by
SCHULZ
12-3
AAUGH!
HOW DOES HE KNOW? HOW DOES HE DO IT?!!!
HOW DID HE KNOW I HAD A COOKIE IN MY POCKET WHEN I WENT BY HIM THE SECOND TIME?
HE LISTENS TO YOUR FOOTSTEPS.. WITH THE COOKIE IN YOUR POCKET, YOU WEIGHED MORE!
THE ONLY WAY YOU CAN SURVIVE THESE DAYS IS TO KEEP YOUR EAR TO THE GROUND!
SCHULZ

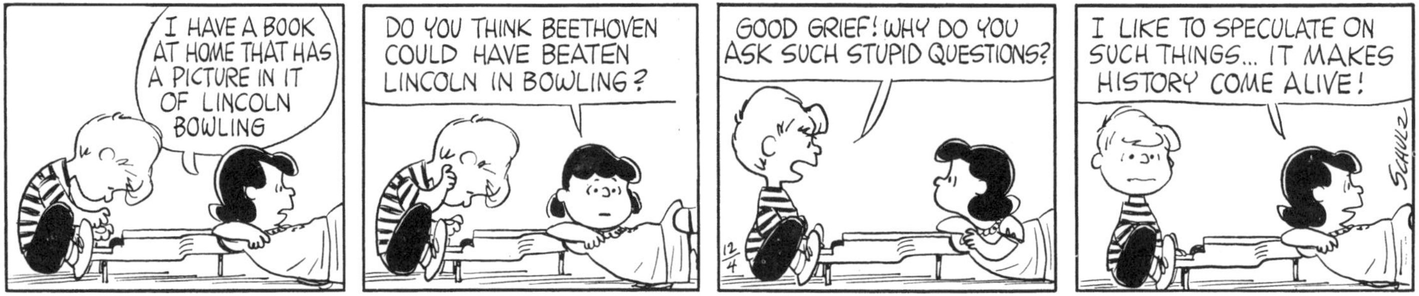
I HAVE A BOOK AT HOME THAT HAS A PICTURE IN IT OF LINCOLN BOWLING
DO YOU THINK BEETHOVEN COULD HAVE BEATEN LINCOLN IN BOWLING?
GOOD GRIEF! WHY DO YOU ASK SUCH STUPID QUESTIONS?
12/4
I LIKE TO SPECULATE ON SUCH THINGS... IT MAKES HISTORY COME ALIVE!
SCHULZ

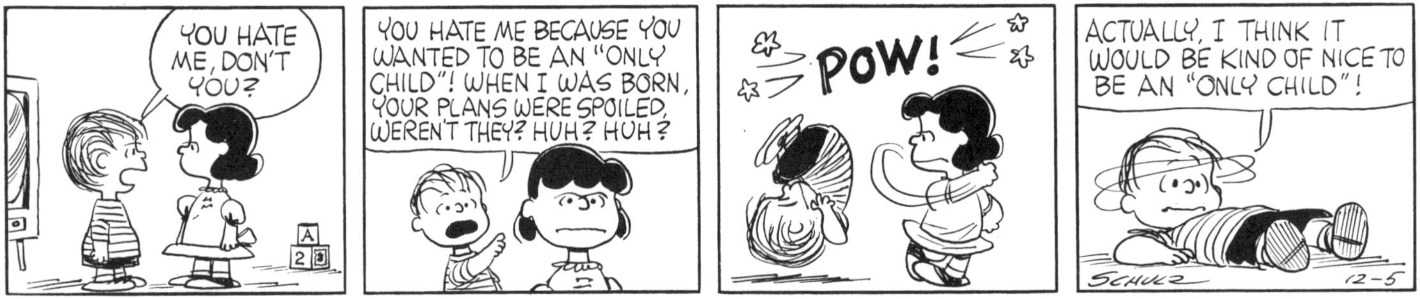
YOU HATE ME, DON'T YOU?
A
2
YOU HATE ME BECAUSE YOU WANTED TO BE AN "ONLY CHILD"! WHEN I WAS BORN, YOUR PLANS WERE SPOILED, WEREN'T THEY? HUH? HUH?
POW!
ACTUALLY, I THINK IT WOULD BE KIND OF NICE TO BE AN "ONLY CHILD"!
SCHULZ
12-5

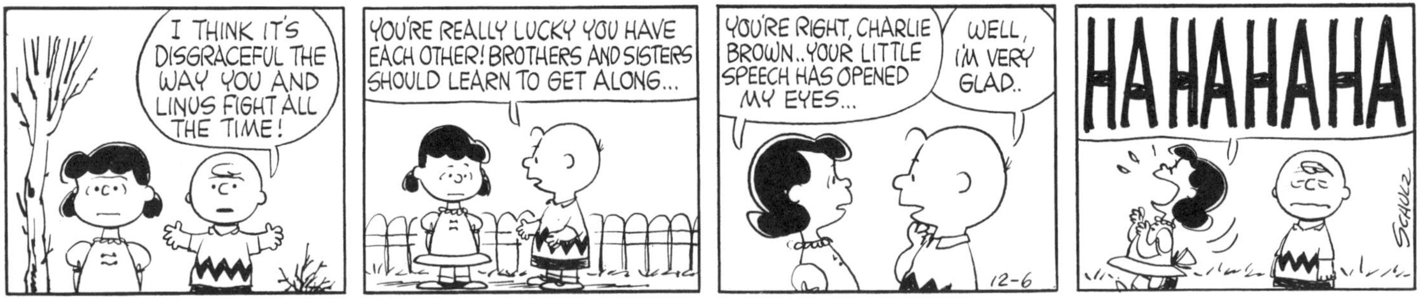
I THINK IT'S DISGRACEFUL THE WAY YOU AND LINUS FIGHT ALL THE TIME!
YOU'RE REALLY LUCKY YOU HAVE EACH OTHER! BROTHERS AND SISTERS SHOULD LEARN TO GET ALONG...
YOU'RE RIGHT, CHARLIE BROWN.. YOUR LITTLE SPEECH HAS OPENED MY EYES...
WELL, I'M VERY GLAD..
12-6
HAHAHAHA
SCHULZ

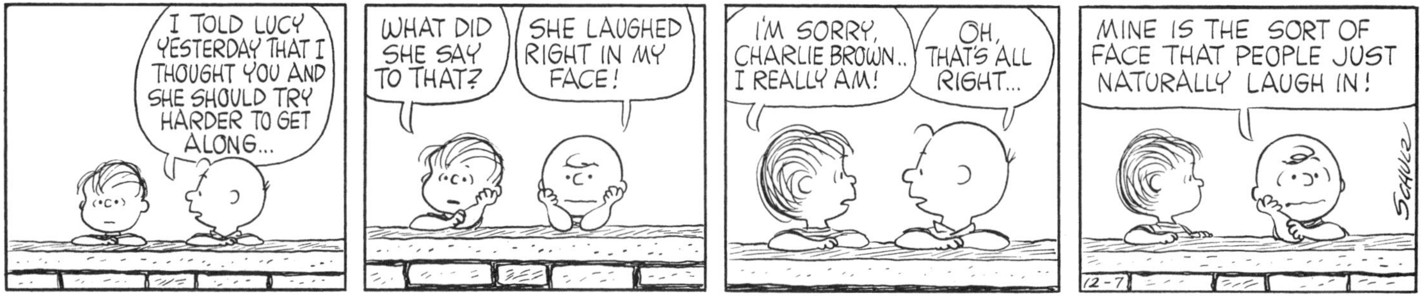
I TOLD LUCY YESTERDAY THAT I THOUGHT YOU AND SHE SHOULD TRY HARDER TO GET ALONG...
WHAT DID SHE SAY TO THAT?
SHE LAUGHED RIGHT IN MY FACE!
I'M SORRY, CHARLIE BROWN.. I REALLY AM!
OH, THAT'S ALL RIGHT...
MINE IS THE SORT OF FACE THAT PEOPLE JUST NATURALLY LAUGH IN!
SCHULZ
12-7

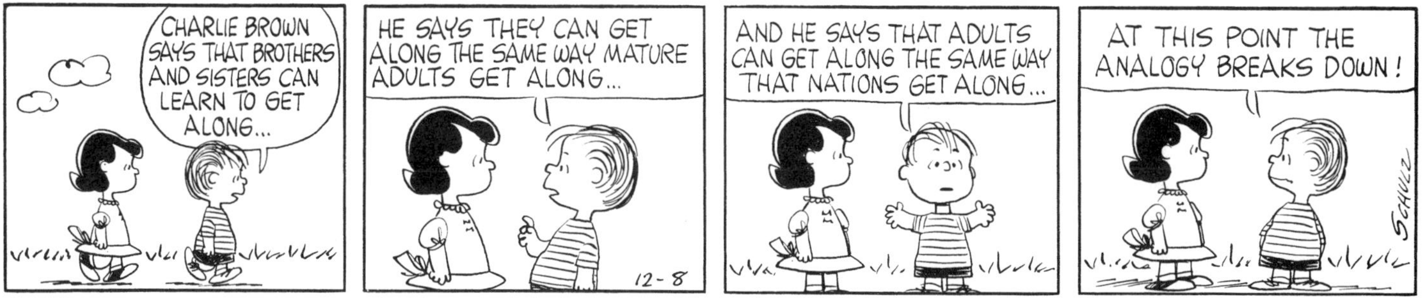
CHARLIE BROWN SAYS THAT BROTHERS AND SISTERS CAN LEARN TO GET ALONG...
HE SAYS THEY CAN GET ALONG THE SAME WAY MATURE ADULTS GET ALONG...
12-8
AND HE SAYS THAT ADULTS CAN GET ALONG THE SAME WAY THAT NATIONS GET ALONG...
AT THIS POINT THE ANALOGY BREAKS DOWN!
SCHULZ

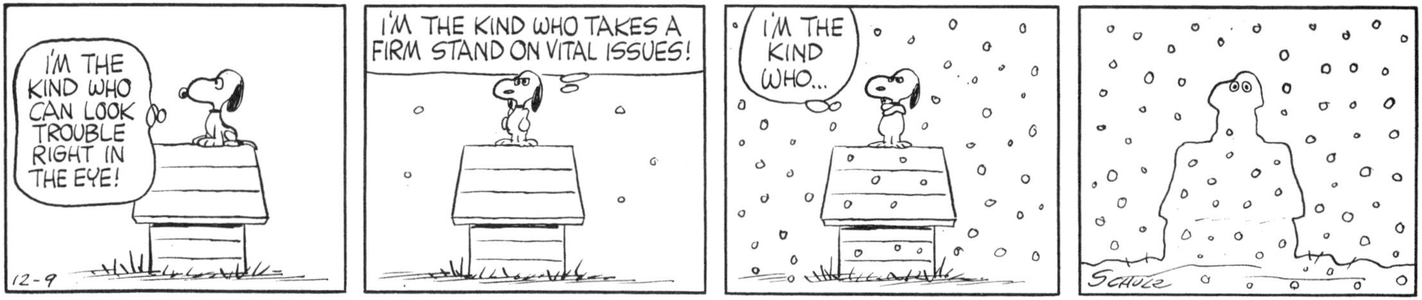
I'M THE KIND WHO CAN LOOK TROUBLE RIGHT IN THE EYE!
12-9
I'M THE KIND WHO TAKES A FIRM STAND ON VITAL ISSUES!
I'M THE KIND WHO...
SCHULZ

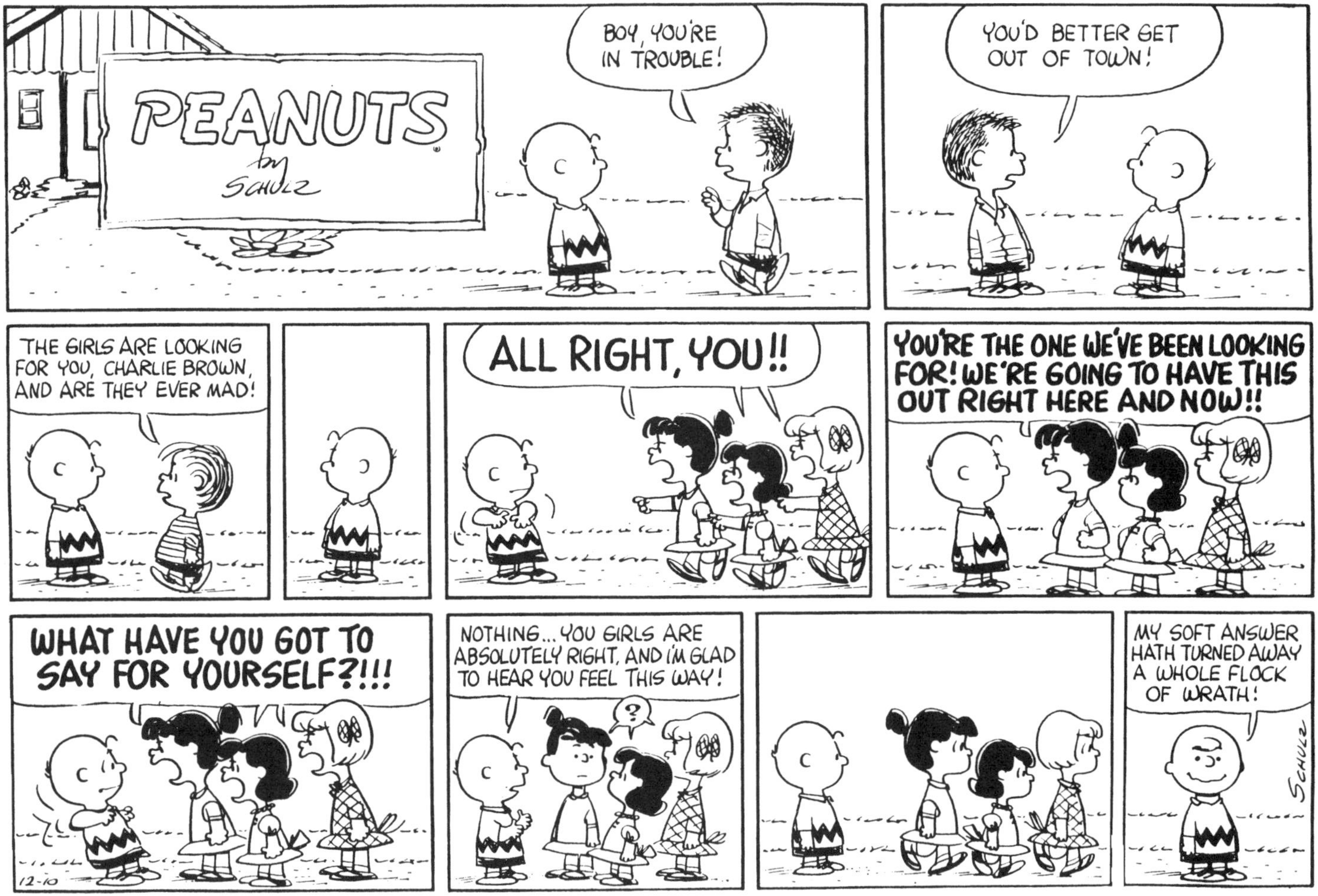
PEANUTS
by SCHULZ
BOY, YOU'RE IN TROUBLE!
YOU'D BETTER GET OUT OF TOWN!
THE GIRLS ARE LOOKING FOR YOU, CHARLIE BROWN, AND ARE THEY EVER MAD!
ALL RIGHT, YOU!!
YOU'RE THE ONE WE'VE BEEN LOOKING FOR! WE'RE GOING TO HAVE THIS OUT RIGHT HERE AND NOW!!
WHAT HAVE YOU GOT TO SAY FOR YOURSELF?!!!
12-10
NOTHING... YOU GIRLS ARE ABSOLUTELY RIGHT, AND I'M GLAD TO HEAR YOU FEEL THIS WAY!
?
MY SOFT ANSWER HATH TURNED AWAY A WHOLE FLOCK OF WRATH!
SCHULZ

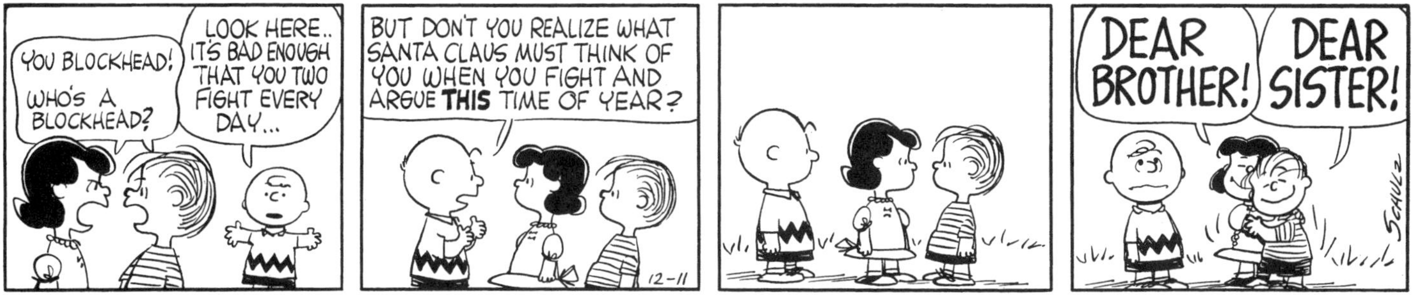
YOU BLOCKHEAD!
WHO'S A BLOCKHEAD?
LOOK HERE.. IT'S BAD ENOUGH THAT YOU TWO FIGHT EVERY DAY...
BUT DON'T YOU REALIZE WHAT SANTA CLAUS MUST THINK OF YOU WHEN YOU FIGHT AND ARGUE THIS TIME OF YEAR?
12-11
DEAR BROTHER!
DEAR SISTER!
SCHULZ

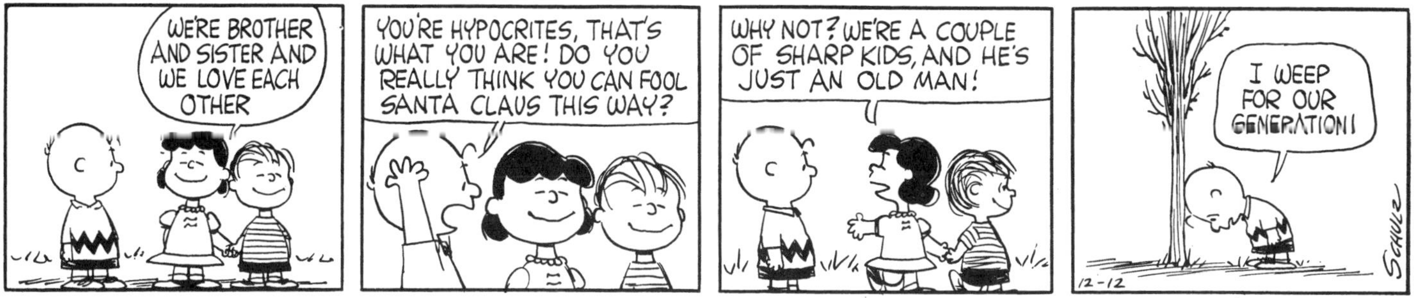
WE'RE BROTHER AND SISTER AND WE LOVE EACH OTHER
YOU'RE HYPOCRITES, THAT'S WHAT YOU ARE! DO YOU REALLY THINK YOU CAN FOOL SANTA CLAUS THIS WAY?
WHY NOT? WE'RE A COUPLE OF SHARP KIDS, AND HE'S JUST AN OLD MAN!
I WEEP FOR OUR GENERATION!
SCHULZ
12-12

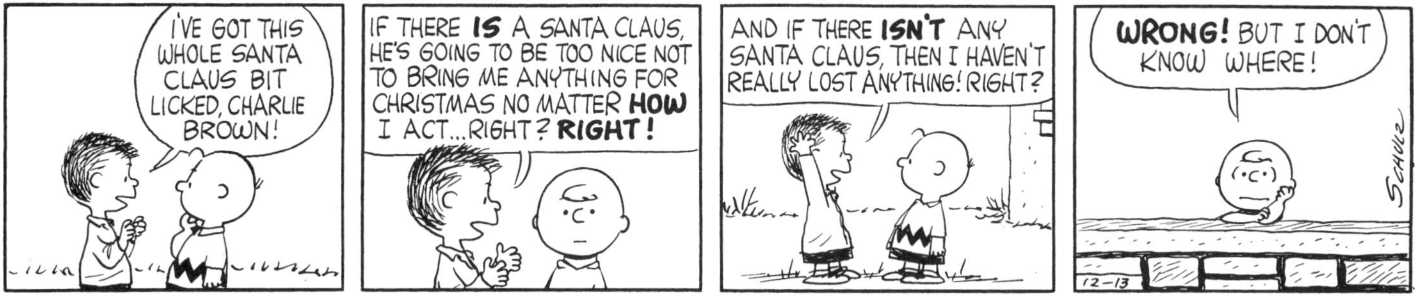
I'VE GOT THIS WHOLE SANTA CLAUS BIT LICKED, CHARLIE BROWN!
IF THERE IS A SANTA CLAUS, HE'S GOING TO BE TOO NICE NOT TO BRING ME ANYTHING FOR CHRISTMAS NO MATTER HOW I ACT...RIGHT? RIGHT!
AND IF THERE ISN'T ANY SANTA CLAUS, THEN I HAVEN'T REALLY LOST ANYTHING! RIGHT?
WRONG! BUT I DON'T KNOW WHERE!
SCHULZ
12-13

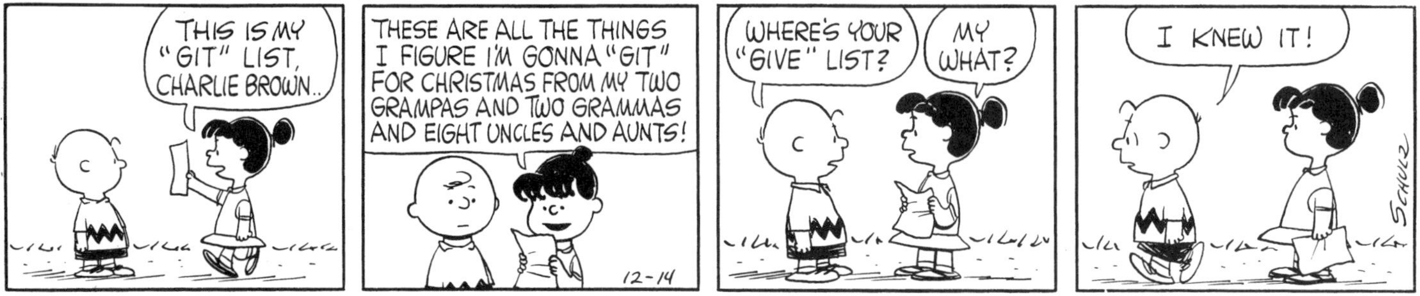
THIS IS MY "GIT" LIST, CHARLIE BROWN..
THESE ARE ALL THE THINGS I FIGURE I'M GONNA "GIT" FOR CHRISTMAS FROM MY TWO GRAMPAS AND TWO GRAMMAS AND EIGHT UNCLES AND AUNTS!
12-14
WHERE'S YOUR "GIVE" LIST?
MY WHAT?
I KNEW IT!
SCHULZ

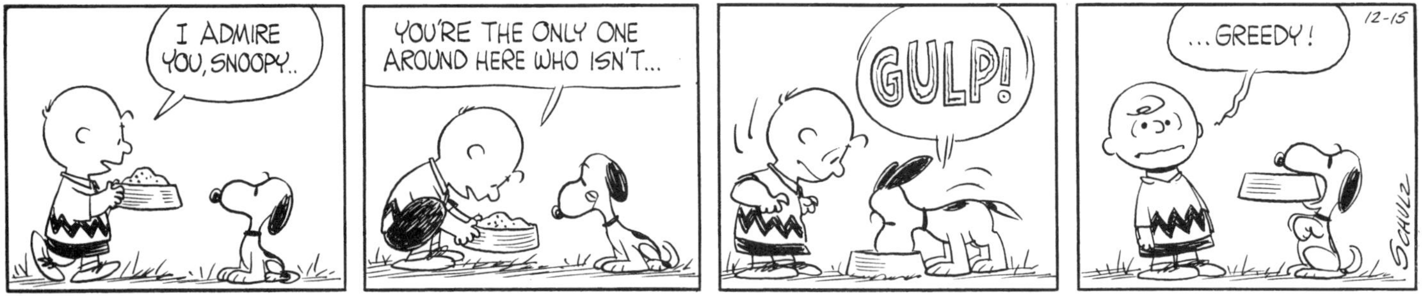
I ADMIRE YOU, SNOOPY..
YOU'RE THE ONLY ONE AROUND HERE WHO ISN'T...
GULP!
12-15
...GREEDY!
SCHULZ

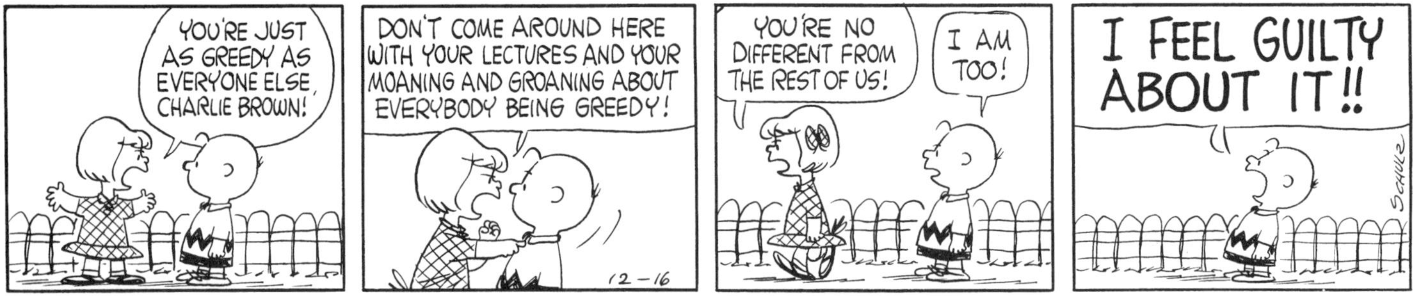
YOU'RE JUST AS GREEDY AS EVERYONE ELSE, CHARLIE BROWN!
DON'T COME AROUND HERE WITH YOUR LECTURES AND YOUR MOANING AND GROANING ABOUT EVERYBODY BEING GREEDY!
12-16
YOU'RE NO DIFFERENT FROM THE REST OF US!
I AM TOO!
I FEEL GUILTY ABOUT IT!!
SCHULZ

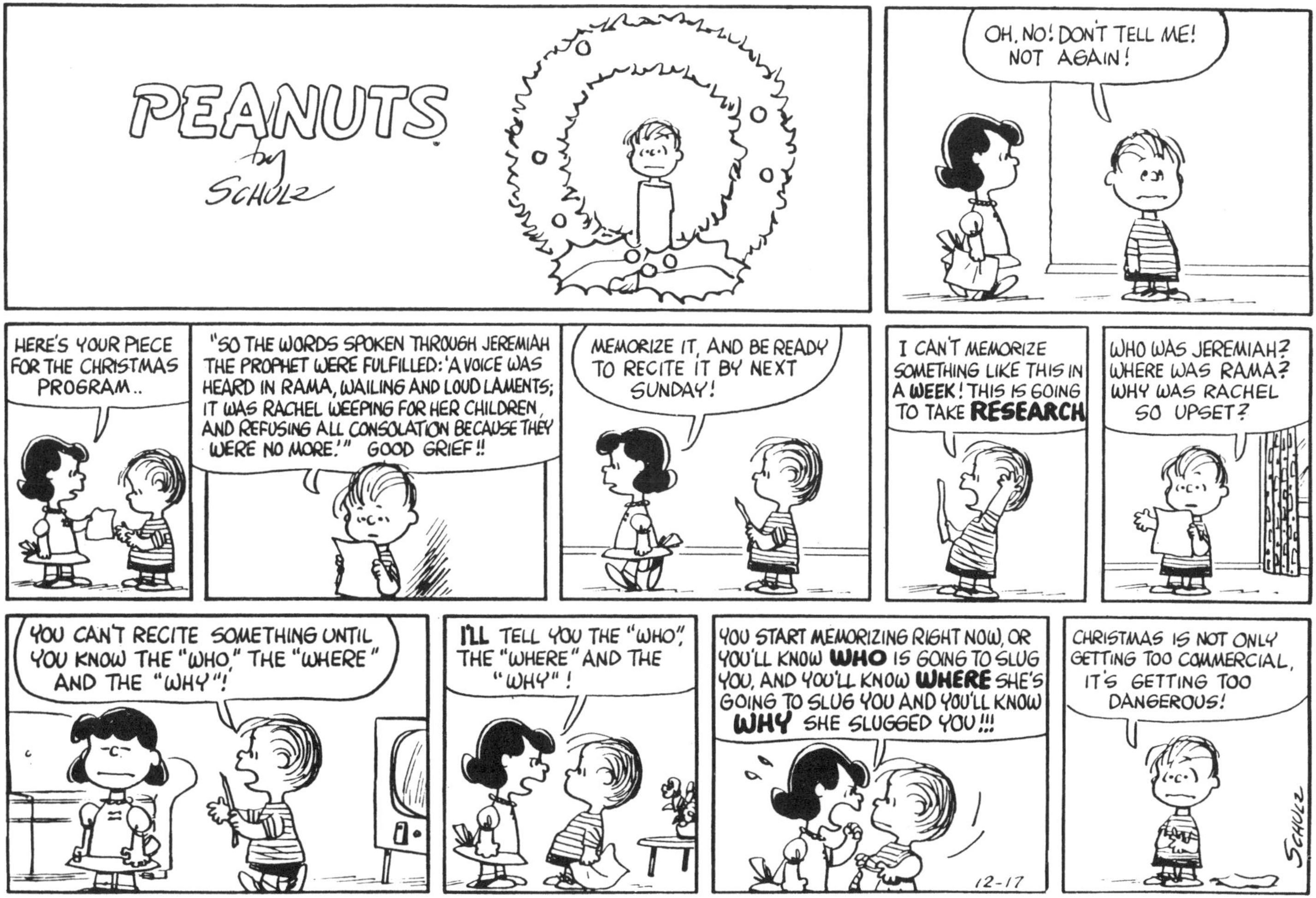
PEANUTS
by SCHULZ
OH, NO! DON'T TELL ME! NOT AGAIN!
HERE'S YOUR PIECE FOR THE CHRISTMAS PROGRAM..
"SO THE WORDS SPOKEN THROUGH JEREMIAH THE PROPHET WERE FULFILLED: 'A VOICE WAS HEARD IN RAMA, WAILING AND LOUD LAMENTS; IT WAS RACHEL WEEPING FOR HER CHILDREN, AND REFUSING ALL CONSOLATION BECAUSE THEY WERE NO MORE.'" GOOD GRIEF!!
MEMORIZE IT, AND BE READY TO RECITE IT BY NEXT SUNDAY!
I CAN'T MEMORIZE SOMETHING LIKE THIS IN A WEEK! THIS IS GOING TO TAKE RESEARCH
WHO WAS JEREMIAH? WHERE WAS RAMA? WHY WAS RACHEL SO UPSET?
YOU CAN'T RECITE SOMETHING UNTIL YOU KNOW THE "WHO," THE "WHERE" AND THE "WHY"!
I'LL TELL YOU THE "WHO", THE "WHERE" AND THE "WHY"!
YOU START MEMORIZING RIGHT NOW, OR YOU'LL KNOW WHO IS GOING TO SLUG YOU, AND YOU'LL KNOW WHERE SHE'S GOING TO SLUG YOU AND YOU'LL KNOW WHY SHE SLUGGED YOU!!!
12-17
CHRISTMAS IS NOT ONLY GETTING TOO COMMERCIAL, IT'S GETTING TOO DANGEROUS!
SCHULZ

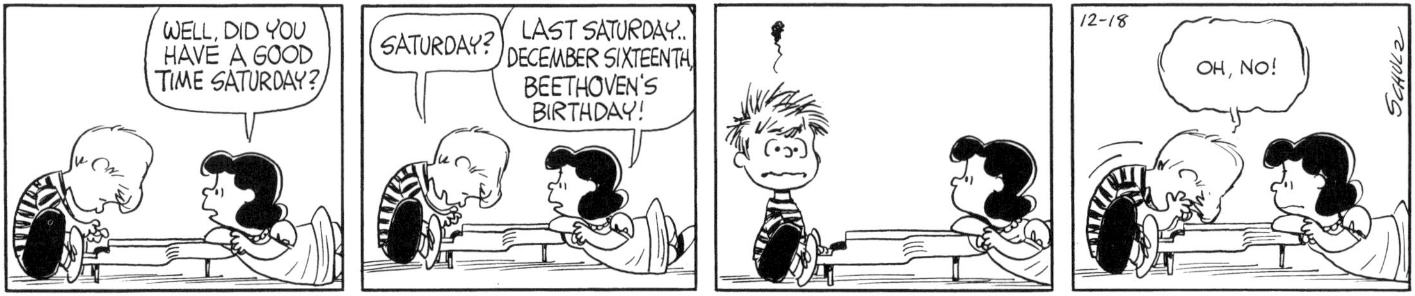
WELL, DID YOU HAVE A GOOD TIME SATURDAY?
SATURDAY?
LAST SATURDAY.. DECEMBER SIXTEENTH, BEETHOVEN'S BIRTHDAY!
12-18
OH, NO!
SCHULZ

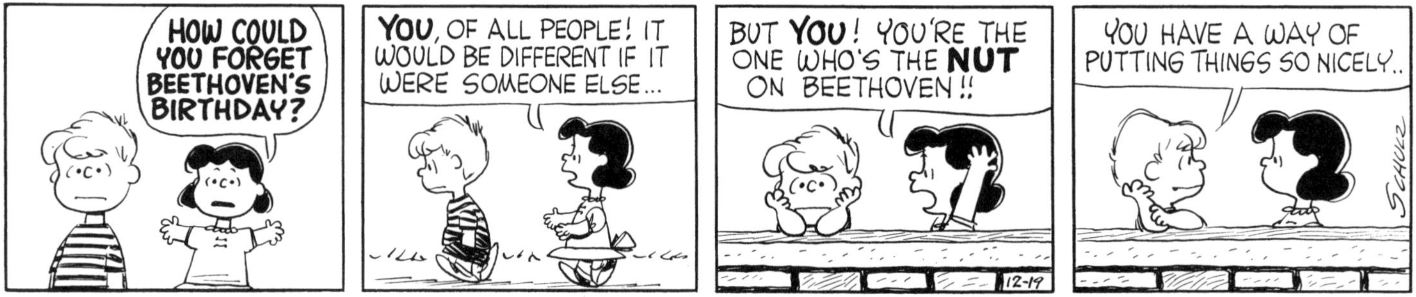
HOW COULD YOU FORGET BEETHOVEN'S BIRTHDAY?
YOU, OF ALL PEOPLE! IT WOULD BE DIFFERENT IF IT WERE SOMEONE ELSE...
BUT YOU! YOU'RE THE ONE WHO'S THE NUT ON BEETHOVEN!!
12-19
YOU HAVE A WAY OF PUTTING THINGS SO NICELY..
SCHULZ

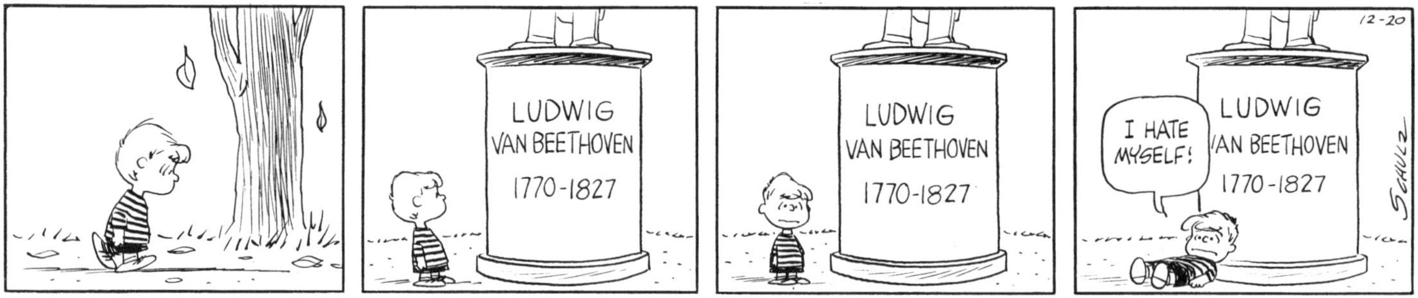
LUDWIG VAN BEETHOVEN 1770-1827
LUDWIG VAN BEETHOVEN 1770-1827
12-20
I HATE MYSELF!
LUDWIG VAN BEETHOVEN 1770-1827
SCHULZ

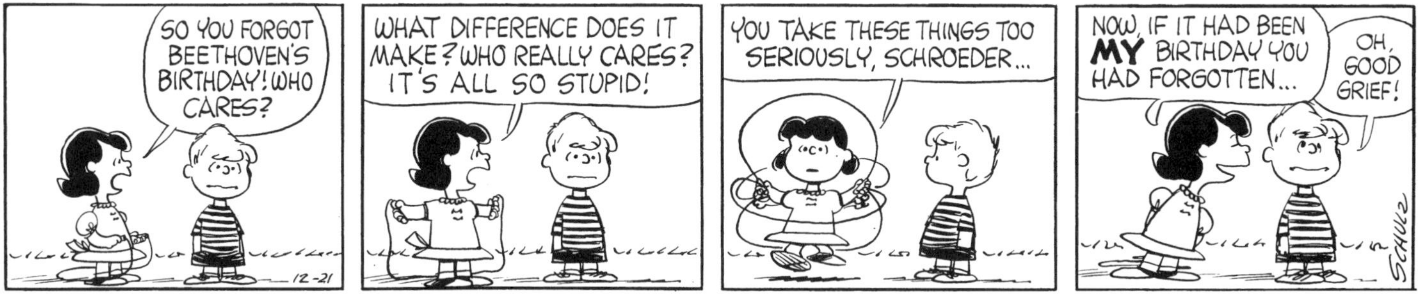
SO YOU FORGOT BEETHOVEN'S BIRTHDAY! WHO CARES?
12-21
WHAT DIFFERENCE DOES IT MAKE? WHO REALLY CARES? IT'S ALL SO STUPID!
YOU TAKE THESE THINGS TOO SERIOUSLY, SCHROEDER...
NOW, IF IT HAD BEEN MY BIRTHDAY YOU HAD FORGOTTEN...
OH, GOOD GRIEF!
SCHULZ

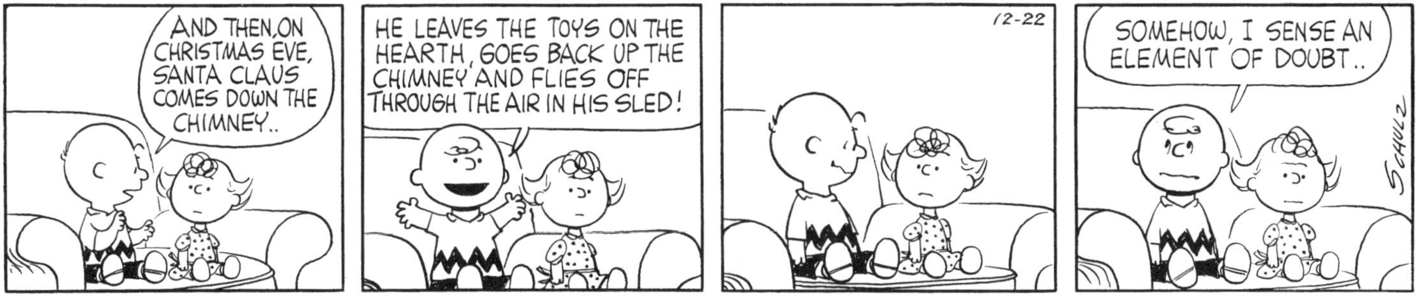
AND THEN, ON CHRISTMAS EVE, SANTA CLAUS COMES DOWN THE CHIMNEY..
HE LEAVES THE TOYS ON THE HEARTH, GOES BACK UP THE CHIMNEY AND FLIES OFF THROUGH THE AIR IN HIS SLED!
12-22
SOMEHOW, I SENSE AN ELEMENT OF DOUBT..
SCHULZ

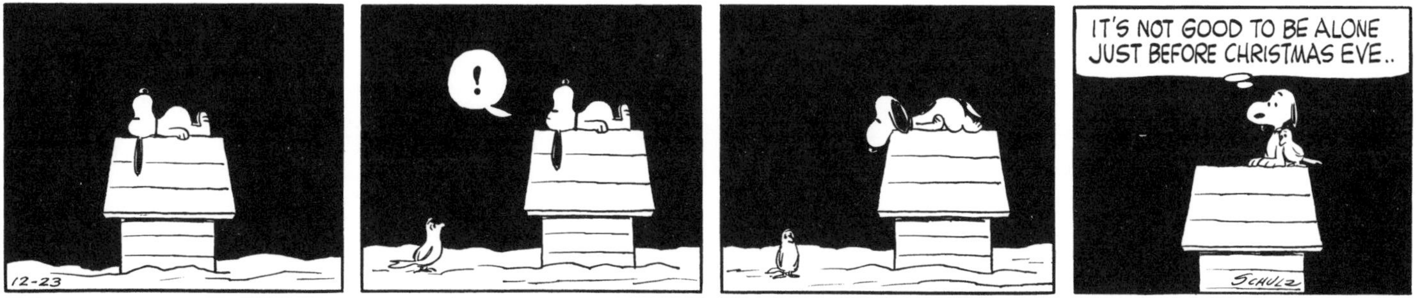
12-23
!
IT'S NOT GOOD TO BE ALONE JUST BEFORE CHRISTMAS EVE..
SCHULZ

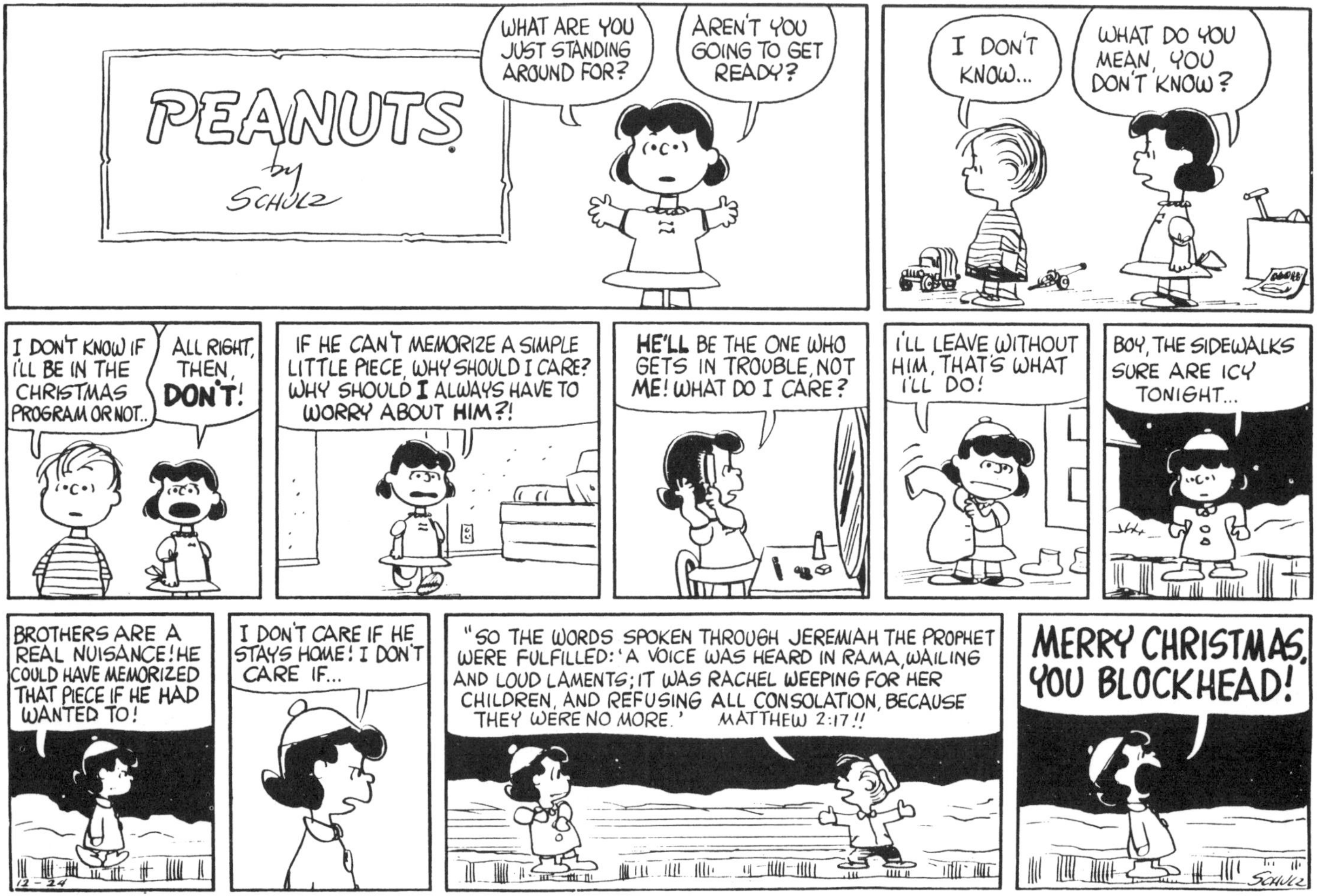
PEANUTS
by SCHULZ
WHAT ARE YOU JUST STANDING AROUND FOR?
AREN'T YOU GOING TO GET READY?
I DON'T KNOW...
WHAT DO YOU MEAN, YOU DON'T KNOW?
I DON'T KNOW IF I'LL BE IN THE CHRISTMAS PROGRAM OR NOT..
ALL RIGHT, THEN, DON'T!
IF HE CAN'T MEMORIZE A SIMPLE LITTLE PIECE, WHY SHOULD I CARE? WHY SHOULD I ALWAYS HAVE TO WORRY ABOUT HIM?!
HE'LL BE THE ONE WHO GETS IN TROUBLE, NOT ME! WHAT DO I CARE?
I'LL LEAVE WITHOUT HIM, THAT'S WHAT I'LL DO!
BOY, THE SIDEWALKS SURE ARE ICY TONIGHT...
BROTHERS ARE A REAL NUISANCE! HE COULD HAVE MEMORIZED THAT PIECE IF HE HAD WANTED TO!
12-24
I DON'T CARE IF HE STAYS HOME! I DON'T CARE IF...
"SO THE WORDS SPOKEN THROUGH JEREMIAH THE PROPHET WERE FULFILLED: 'A VOICE WAS HEARD IN RAMA, WAILING AND LOUD LAMENTS; IT WAS RACHEL WEEPING FOR HER CHILDREN, AND REFUSING ALL CONSOLATION, BECAUSE THEY WERE NO MORE.' MATTHEW 2:17!!
MERRY CHRISTMAS, YOU BLOCKHEAD!
SCHULZ

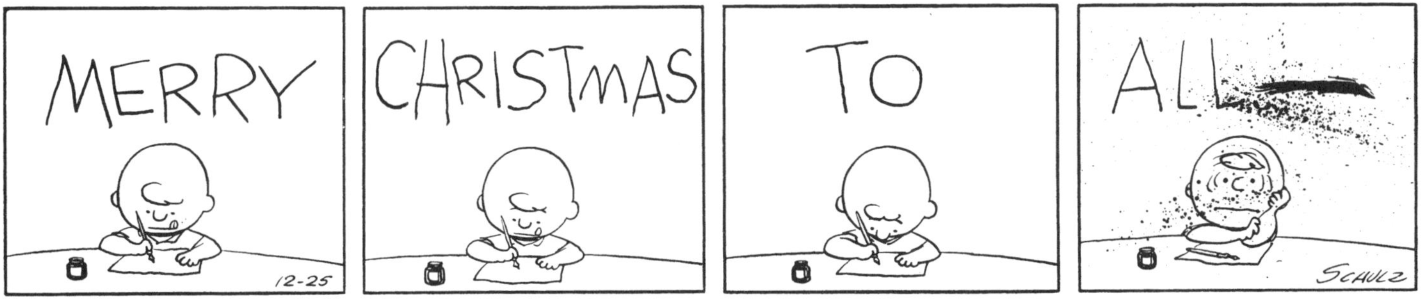
MERRY
CHRISTMAS
TO
ALL
12-25
SCHULZ

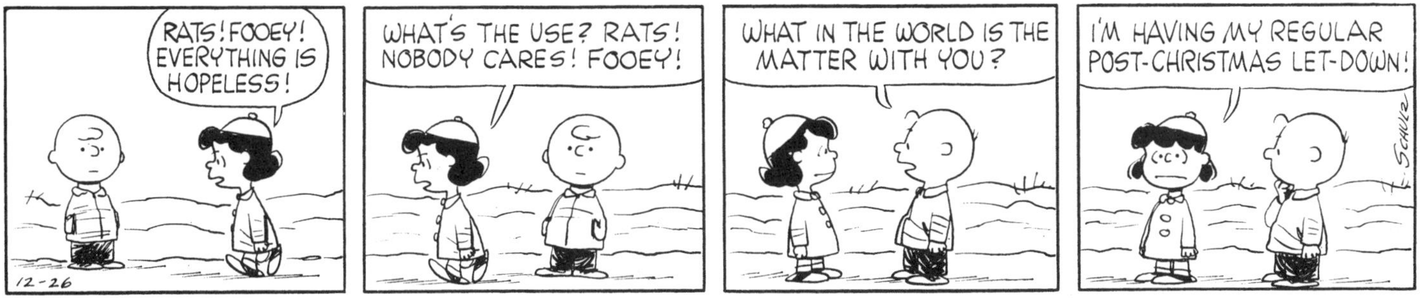
RATS! FOOEY! EVERYTHING IS HOPELESS!
12-26
WHAT'S THE USE? RATS! NOBODY CARES! FOOEY!
WHAT IN THE WORLD IS THE MATTER WITH YOU?
I'M HAVING MY REGULAR POST-CHRISTMAS LET-DOWN!
SCHULZ

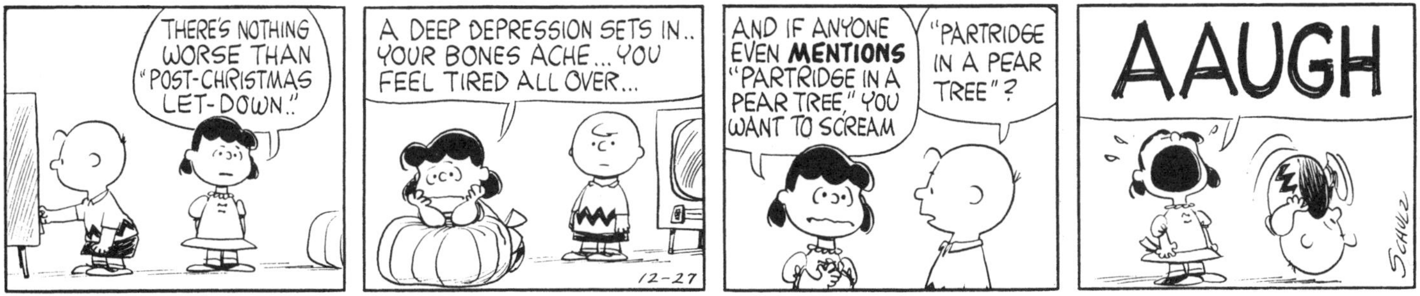
THERE'S NOTHING WORSE THAN "POST-CHRISTMAS LET-DOWN."
A DEEP DEPRESSION SETS IN.. YOUR BONES ACHE... YOU FEEL TIRED ALL OVER...
12-27
AND IF ANYONE EVEN **MENTIONS** "PARTRIDGE IN A PEAR TREE," YOU WANT TO SCREAM
"PARTRIDGE IN A PEAR TREE"?
AAUGH
SCHULZ

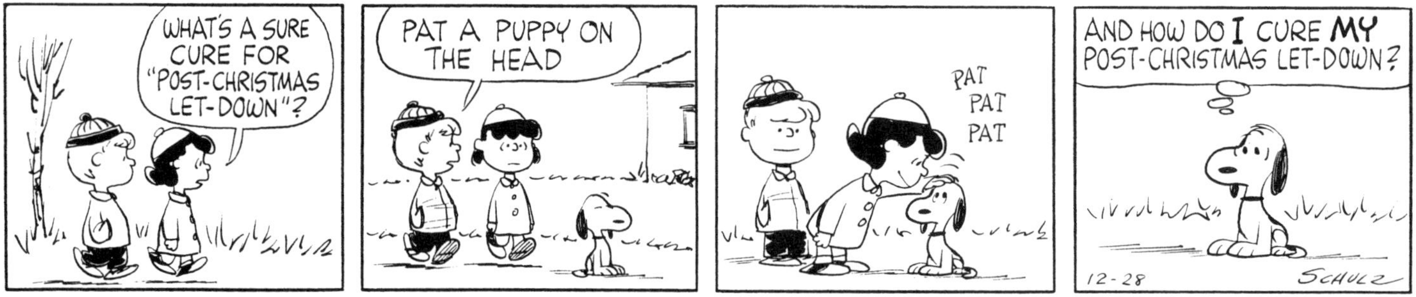
WHAT'S A SURE CURE FOR "POST-CHRISTMAS LET-DOWN"?
PAT A PUPPY ON THE HEAD
PAT PAT PAT
AND HOW DO I CURE MY POST-CHRISTMAS LET-DOWN?
12-28
SCHULZ

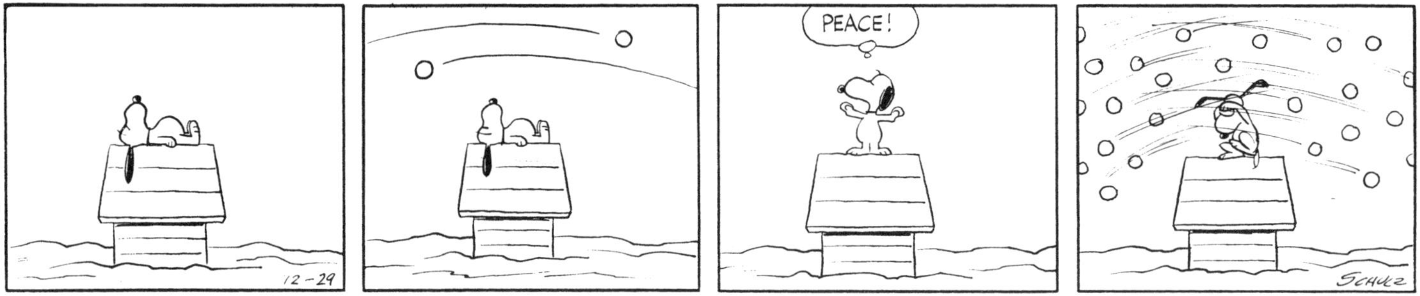
12-29
PEACE!
SCHULZ

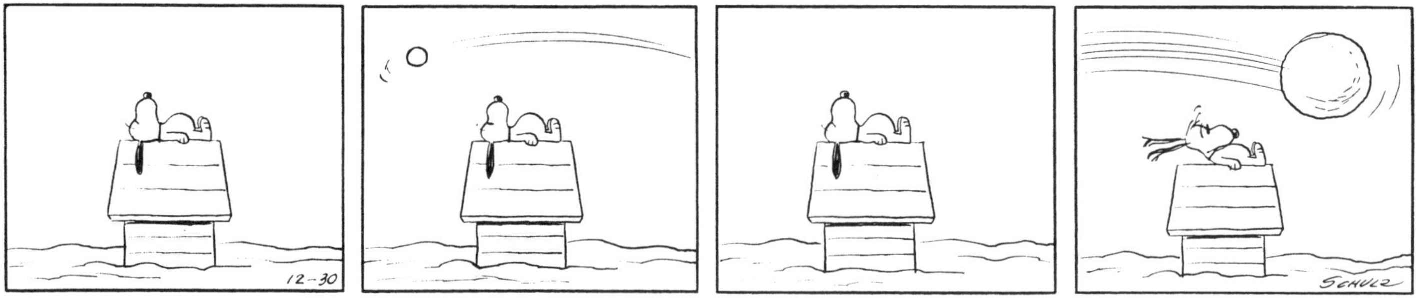
12-30
SCHULZ

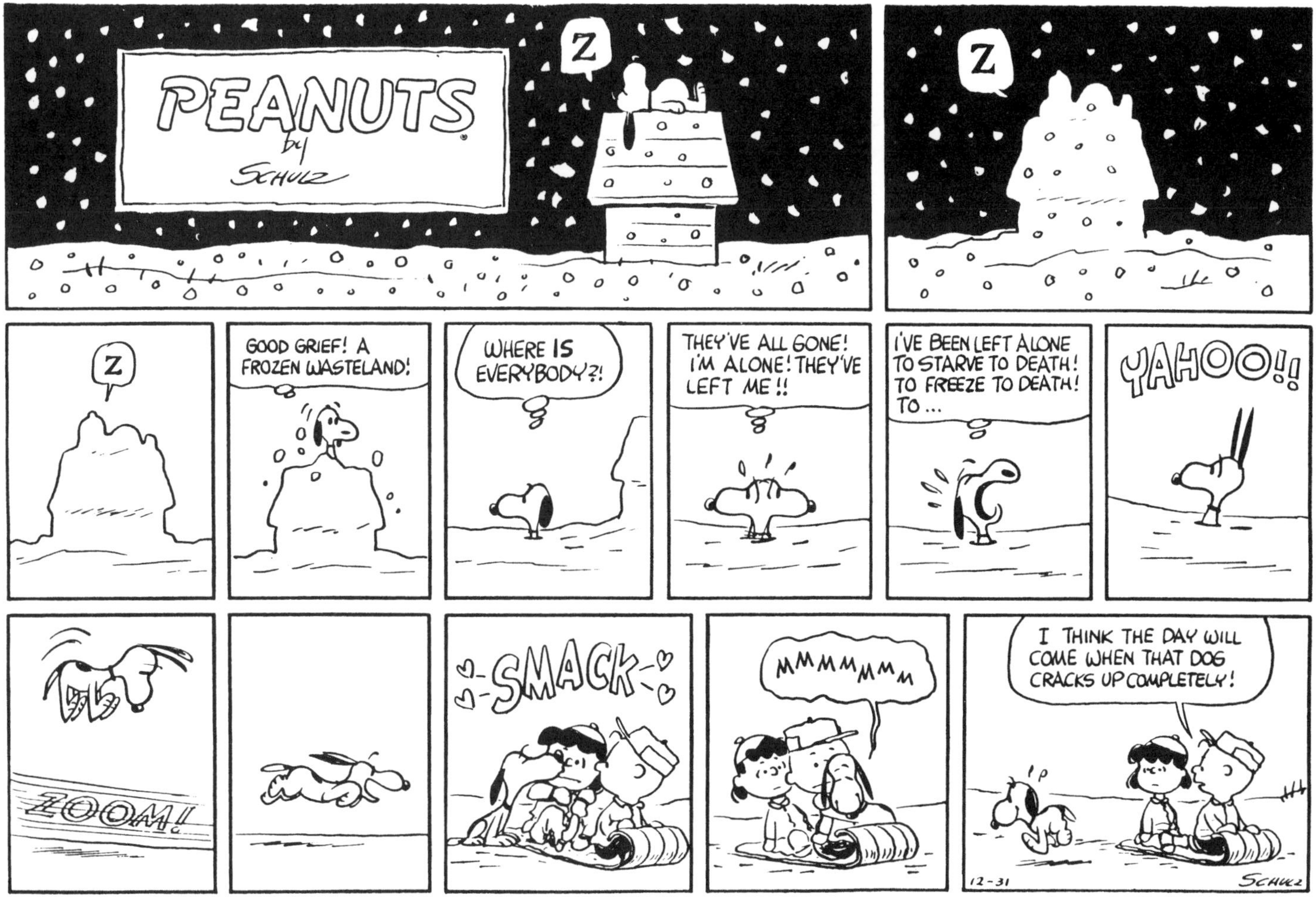
PEANUTS
by
SCHULZ
Z
Z
Z
GOOD GRIEF! A FROZEN WASTELAND!
WHERE IS EVERYBODY?!
THEY'VE ALL GONE! I'M ALONE! THEY'VE LEFT ME!!
I'VE BEEN LEFT ALONE TO STARVE TO DEATH! TO FREEZE TO DEATH! TO...
YAHOO!!
ZOOM!
SMACK
MMMMMMM
I THINK THE DAY WILL COME WHEN THAT DOG CRACKS UP COMPLETELY!
12-31
SCHULZ

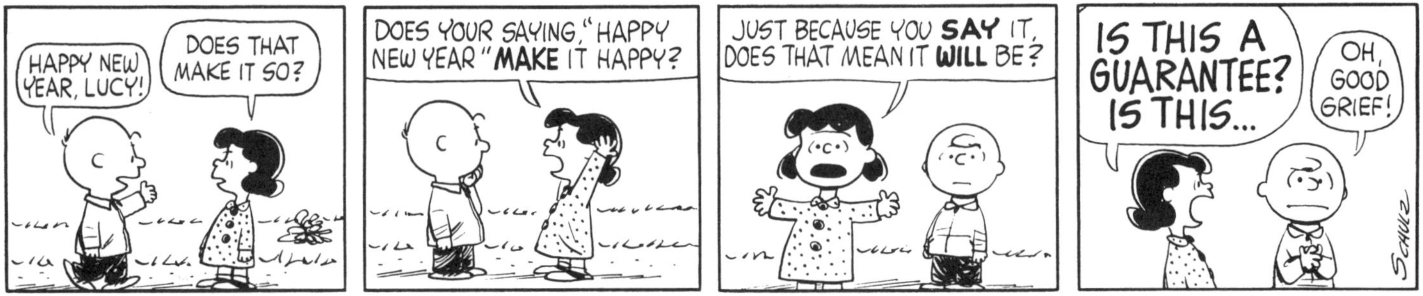
HAPPY NEW YEAR, LUCY!
DOES THAT MAKE IT SO?
DOES YOUR SAYING, "HAPPY NEW YEAR" **MAKE** IT HAPPY?
JUST BECAUSE YOU **SAY** IT, DOES THAT MEAN IT **WILL** BE?
IS THIS A GUARANTEE? IS THIS...
OH, GOOD GRIEF!
SCHULZ

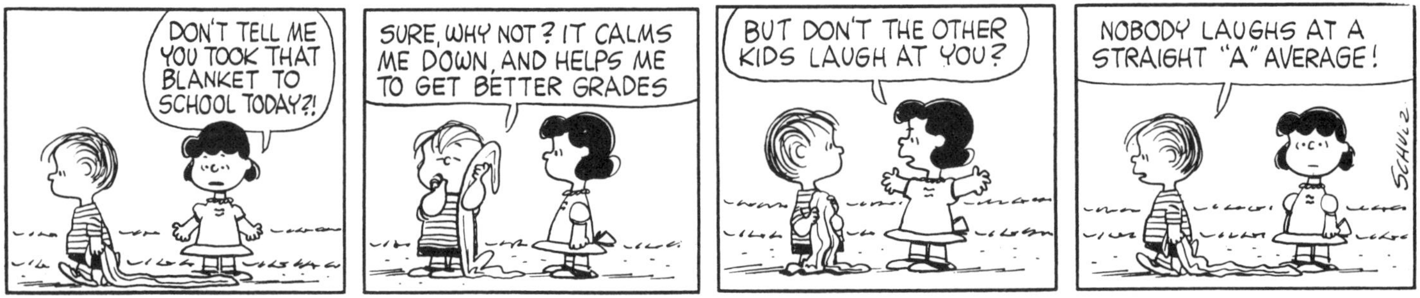
DON'T TELL ME YOU TOOK THAT BLANKET TO SCHOOL TODAY?!
SURE, WHY NOT? IT CALMS ME DOWN, AND HELPS ME TO GET BETTER GRADES
BUT DON'T THE OTHER KIDS LAUGH AT YOU?
NOBODY LAUGHS AT A STRAIGHT "A" AVERAGE!
SCHULZ

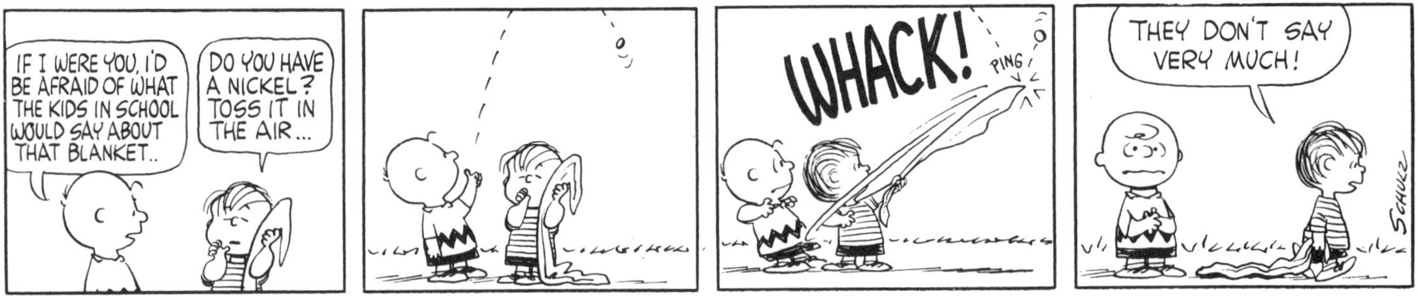
IF I WERE YOU, I'D BE AFRAID OF WHAT THE KIDS IN SCHOOL WOULD SAY ABOUT THAT BLANKET..
DO YOU HAVE A NICKEL? TOSS IT IN THE AIR...
WHACK!
PING
THEY DON'T SAY VERY MUCH!
SCHULZ

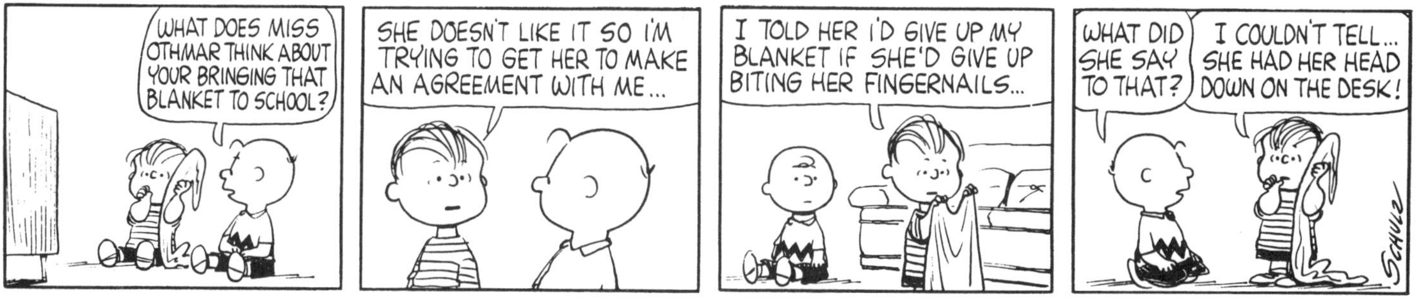
WHAT DOES MISS OTHMAR THINK ABOUT YOUR BRINGING THAT BLANKET TO SCHOOL?
SHE DOESN'T LIKE IT SO I'M TRYING TO GET HER TO MAKE AN AGREEMENT WITH ME...
I TOLD HER I'D GIVE UP MY BLANKET IF SHE'D GIVE UP BITING HER FINGERNAILS...
WHAT DID SHE SAY TO THAT?
I COULDN'T TELL... SHE HAD HER HEAD DOWN ON THE DESK!
SCHULZ

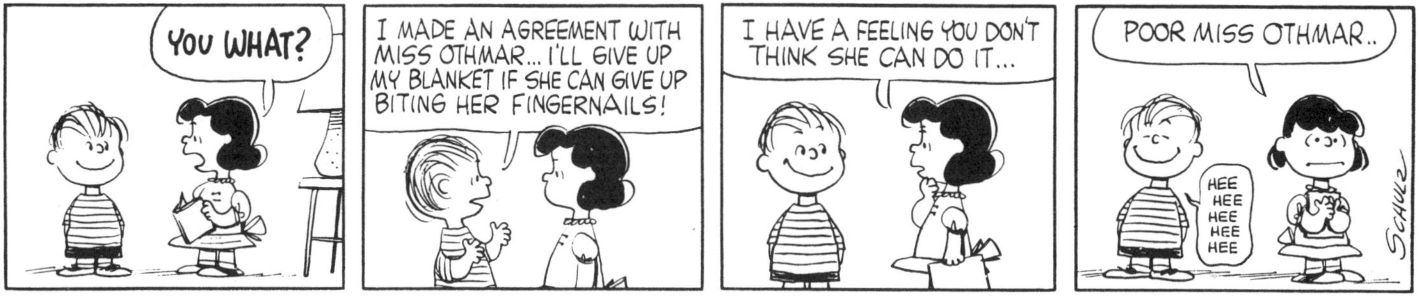
YOU WHAT?
I MADE AN AGREEMENT WITH MISS OTHMAR... I'LL GIVE UP MY BLANKET IF SHE CAN GIVE UP BITING HER FINGERNAILS!
I HAVE A FEELING YOU DON'T THINK SHE CAN DO IT...
POOR MISS OTHMAR..
HEE HEE HEE HEE HEE
SCHULZ

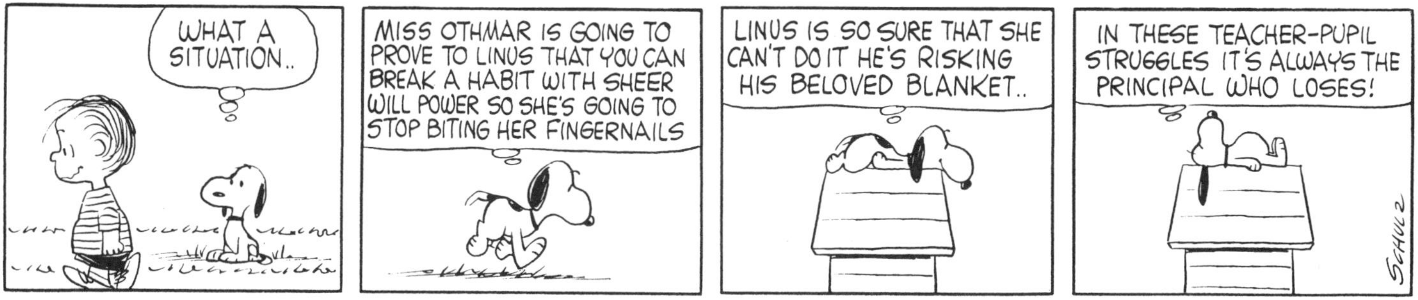
WHAT A SITUATION..
MISS OTHMAR IS GOING TO PROVE TO LINUS THAT YOU CAN BREAK A HABIT WITH SHEER WILL POWER SO SHE'S GOING TO STOP BITING HER FINGERNAILS
LINUS IS SO SURE THAT SHE CAN'T DO IT HE'S RISKING HIS BELOVED BLANKET..
IN THESE TEACHER-PUPIL STRUGGLES IT'S ALWAYS THE PRINCIPAL WHO LOSES!
SCHULZ

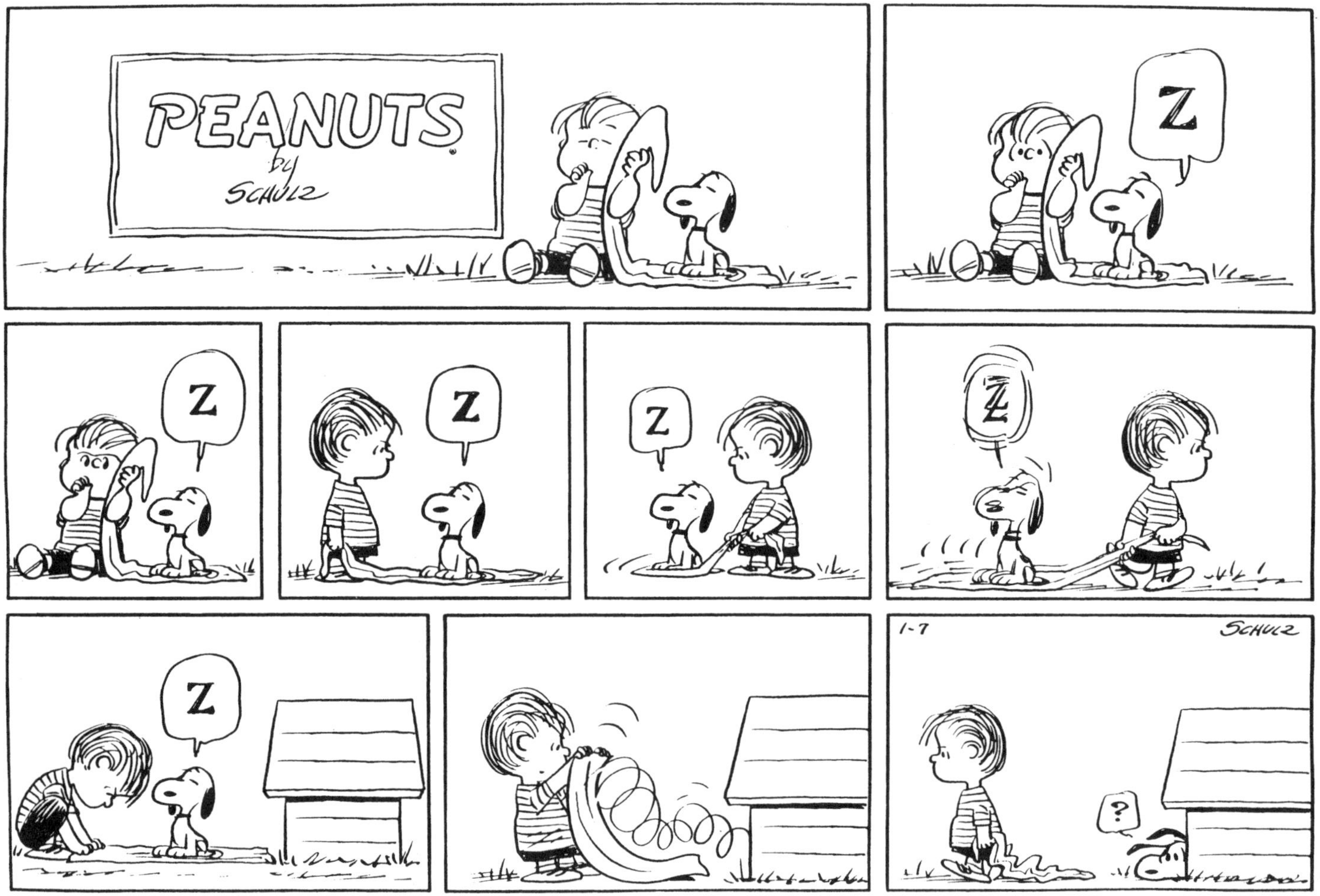
PEANUTS
by
SCHULZ
Z
Z
Z
Z
Z
Z
1-7
SCHULZ
?

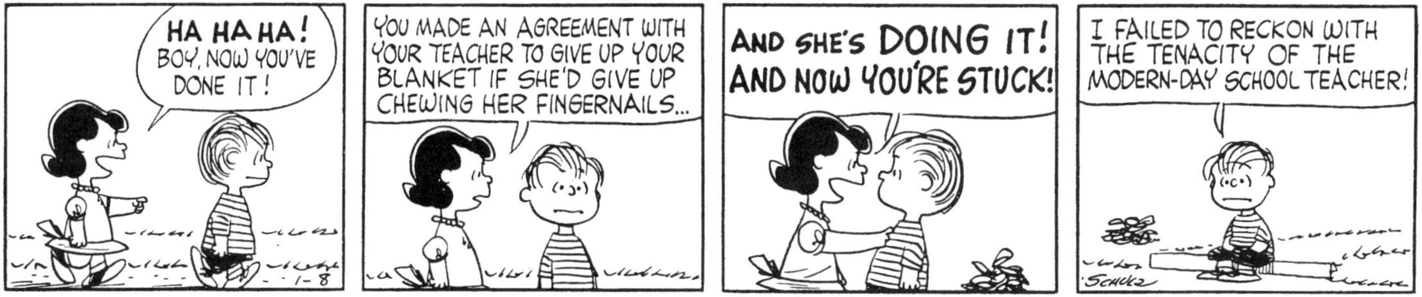
HA HA HA! BOY, NOW YOU'VE DONE IT!
YOU MADE AN AGREEMENT WITH YOUR TEACHER TO GIVE UP YOUR BLANKET IF SHE'D GIVE UP CHEWING HER FINGERNAILS...
AND SHE'S DOING IT! AND NOW YOU'RE STUCK!
I FAILED TO RECKON WITH THE TENACITY OF THE MODERN-DAY SCHOOL TEACHER!
1-8
SCHULZ

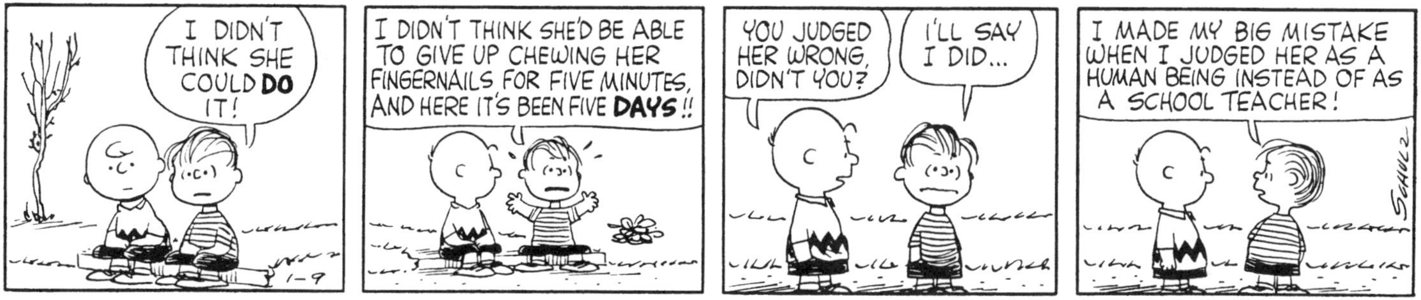
I DIDN'T THINK SHE COULD DO IT!
1-9
I DIDN'T THINK SHE'D BE ABLE TO GIVE UP CHEWING HER FINGERNAILS FOR FIVE MINUTES, AND HERE IT'S BEEN FIVE DAYS!!
YOU JUDGED HER WRONG, DIDN'T YOU?
I'LL SAY I DID...
I MADE MY BIG MISTAKE WHEN I JUDGED HER AS A HUMAN BEING INSTEAD OF AS A SCHOOL TEACHER!
SCHULZ

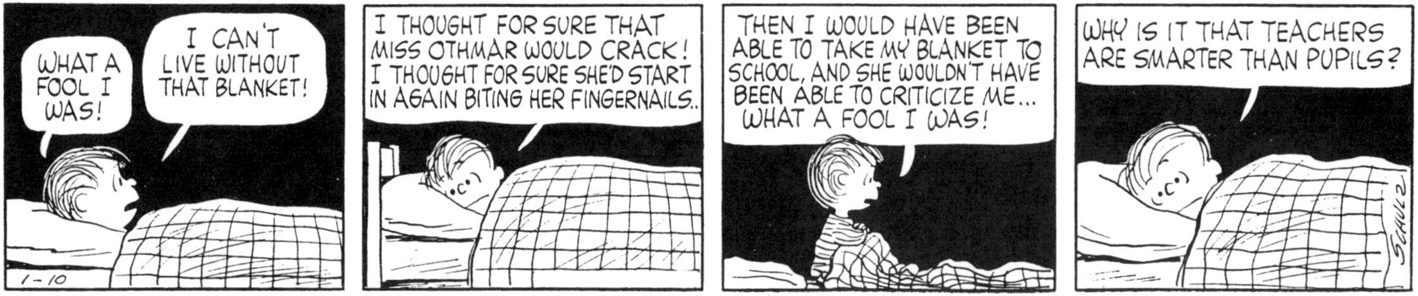
WHAT A FOOL I WAS!
I CAN'T LIVE WITHOUT THAT BLANKET!
1-10
I THOUGHT FOR SURE THAT MISS OTHMAR WOULD CRACK! I THOUGHT FOR SURE SHE'D START IN AGAIN BITING HER FINGERNAILS..
THEN I WOULD HAVE BEEN ABLE TO TAKE MY BLANKET TO SCHOOL, AND SHE WOULDN'T HAVE BEEN ABLE TO CRITICIZE ME... WHAT A FOOL I WAS!
SCHULZ
WHY IS IT THAT TEACHERS ARE SMARTER THAN PUPILS?

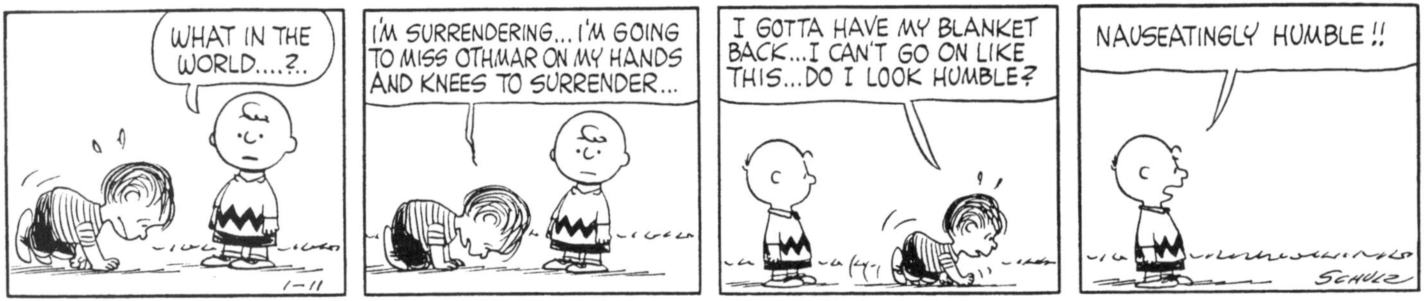
WHAT IN THE WORLD....?..
1-11
I'M SURRENDERING... I'M GOING TO MISS OTHMAR ON MY HANDS AND KNEES TO SURRENDER...
I GOTTA HAVE MY BLANKET BACK...I CAN'T GO ON LIKE THIS...DO I LOOK HUMBLE?
NAUSEATINGLY HUMBLE!!
SCHULZ

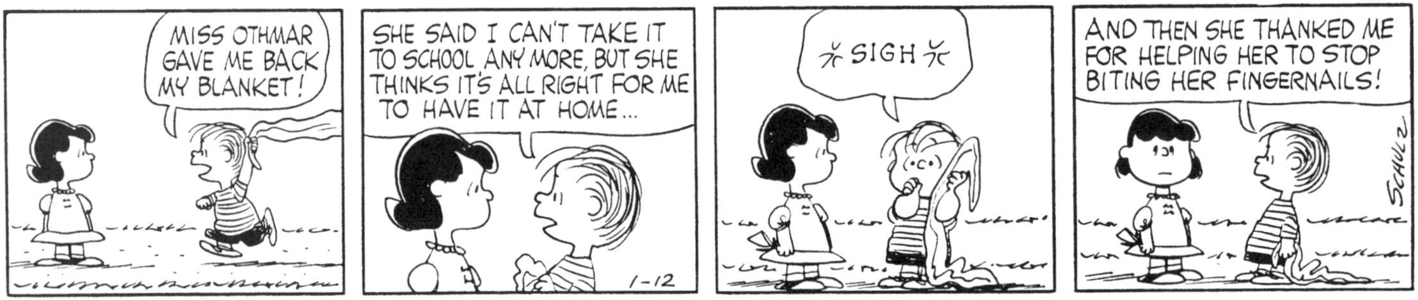
MISS OTHMAR GAVE ME BACK MY BLANKET!
SHE SAID I CAN'T TAKE IT TO SCHOOL ANY MORE, BUT SHE THINKS IT'S ALL RIGHT FOR ME TO HAVE IT AT HOME...
1-12
SIGH
AND THEN SHE THANKED ME FOR HELPING HER TO STOP BITING HER FINGERNAILS!
SCHULZ

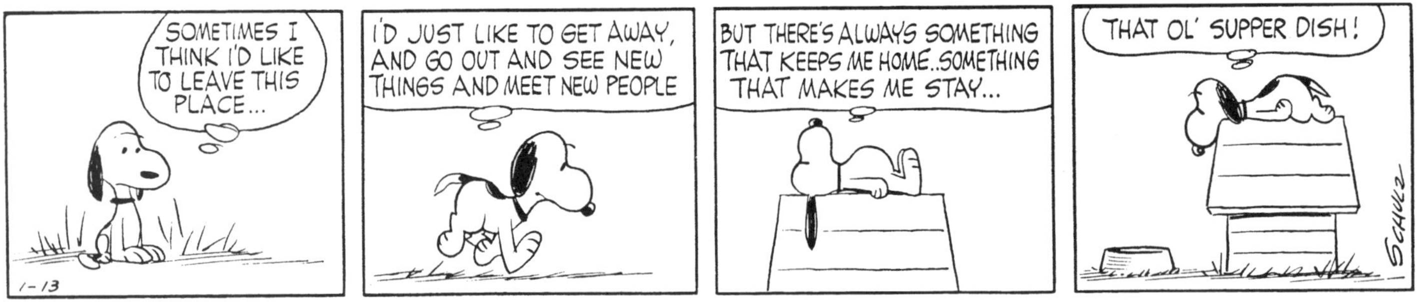
SOMETIMES I THINK I'D LIKE TO LEAVE THIS PLACE...
1-13
I'D JUST LIKE TO GET AWAY, AND GO OUT AND SEE NEW THINGS AND MEET NEW PEOPLE
BUT THERE'S ALWAYS SOMETHING THAT KEEPS ME HOME..SOMETHING THAT MAKES ME STAY...
THAT OL' SUPPER DISH!
SCHULZ

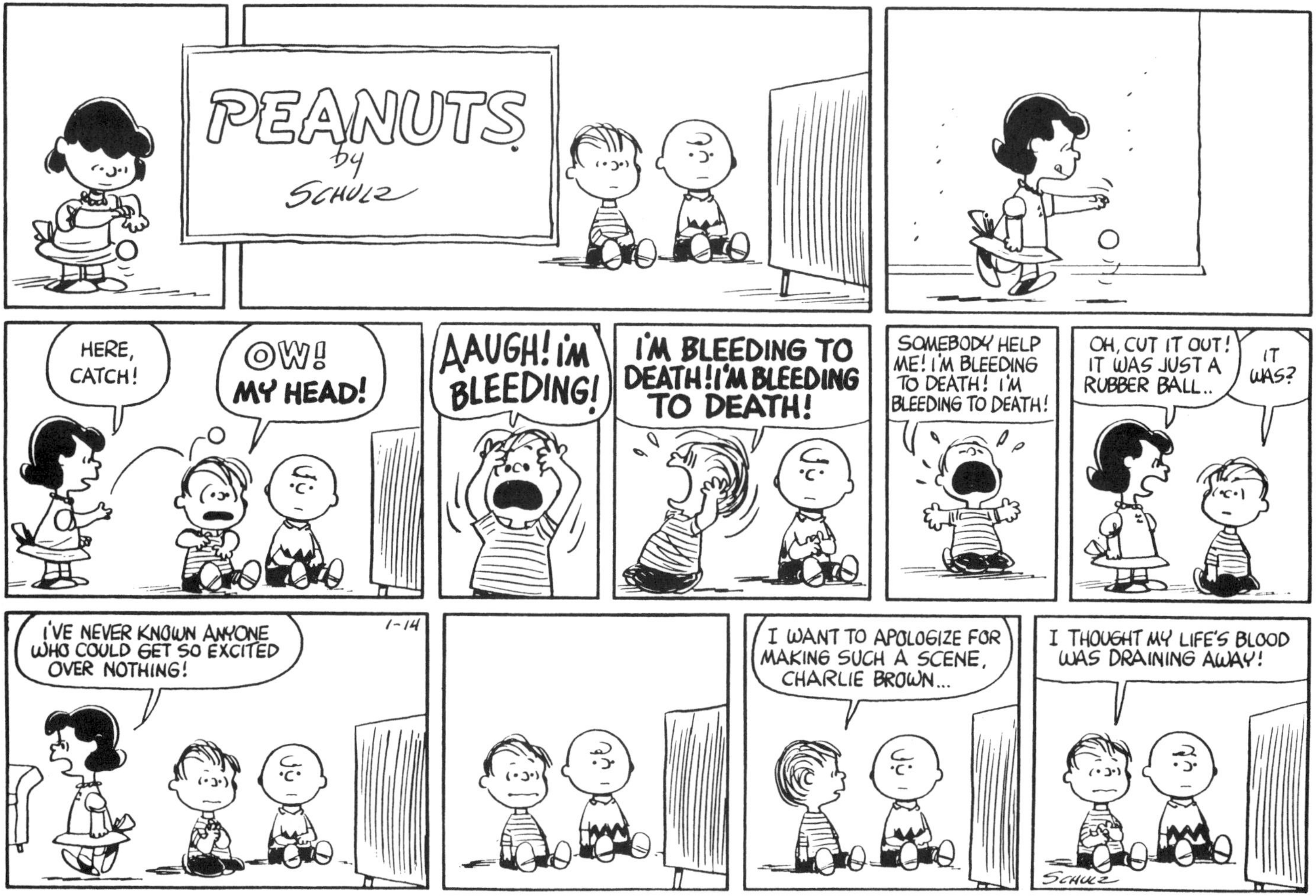
PEANUTS
by
SCHULZ
HERE, CATCH!
OW! MY HEAD!
AAUGH! I'M BLEEDING!
I'M BLEEDING TO DEATH! I'M BLEEDING TO DEATH!
SOMEBODY HELP ME! I'M BLEEDING TO DEATH! I'M BLEEDING TO DEATH!
OH, CUT IT OUT! IT WAS JUST A RUBBER BALL..
IT WAS?
I'VE NEVER KNOWN ANYONE WHO COULD GET SO EXCITED OVER NOTHING!
1-14
I WANT TO APOLOGIZE FOR MAKING SUCH A SCENE, CHARLIE BROWN...
I THOUGHT MY LIFE'S BLOOD WAS DRAINING AWAY!
SCHULZ

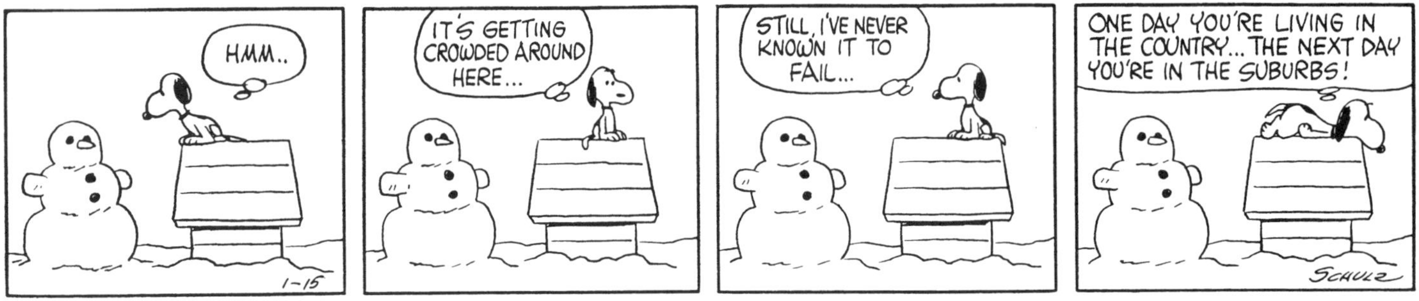
HMM..
1-15
IT'S GETTING CROWDED AROUND HERE...
STILL, I'VE NEVER KNOWN IT TO FAIL...
ONE DAY YOU'RE LIVING IN THE COUNTRY... THE NEXT DAY YOU'RE IN THE SUBURBS!
SCHULZ

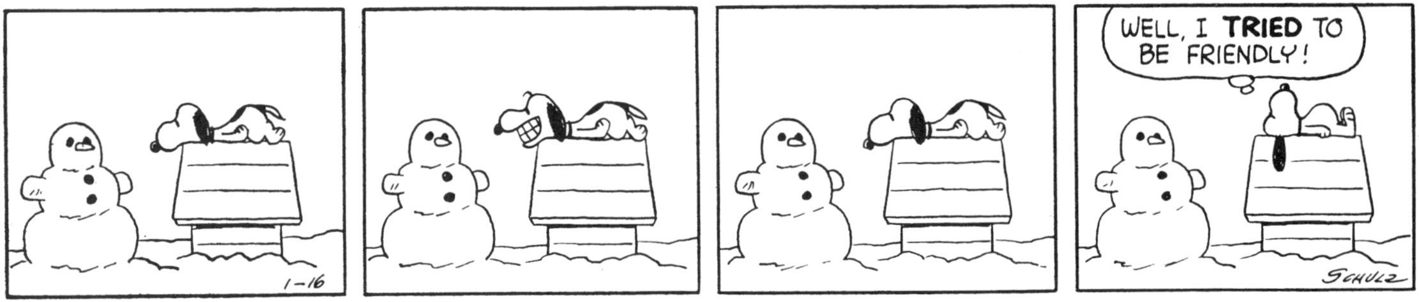
1-16
WELL, I **TRIED** TO BE FRIENDLY!
SCHULZ

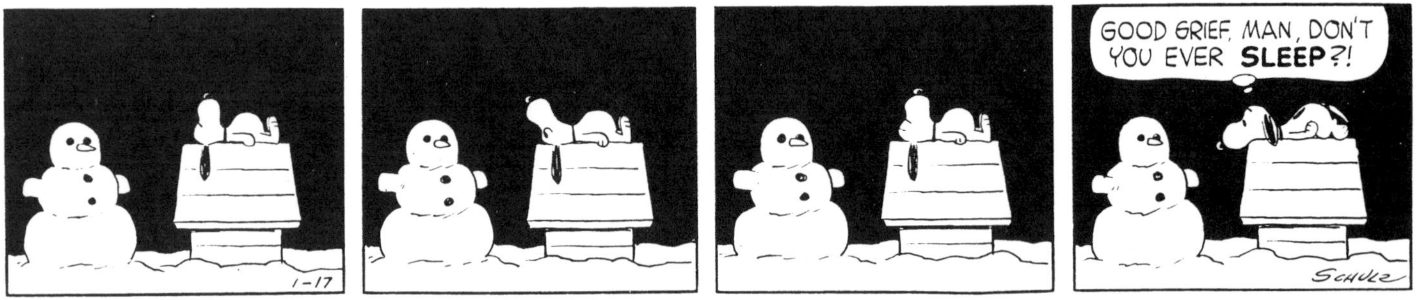
1-17
GOOD GRIEF, MAN, DON'T YOU EVER **SLEEP**?!
SCHULZ

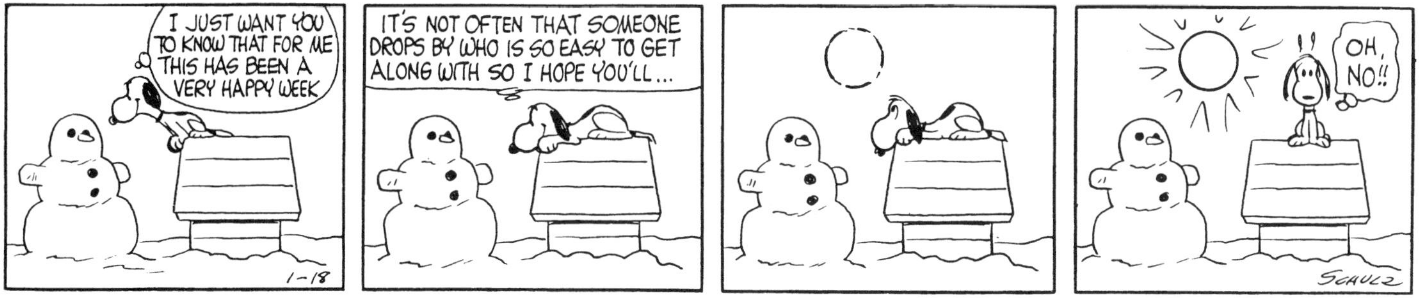
I JUST WANT YOU TO KNOW THAT FOR ME THIS HAS BEEN A VERY HAPPY WEEK
1-18
IT'S NOT OFTEN THAT SOMEONE DROPS BY WHO IS SO EASY TO GET ALONG WITH SO I HOPE YOU'LL...
OH, NO!!
SCHULZ

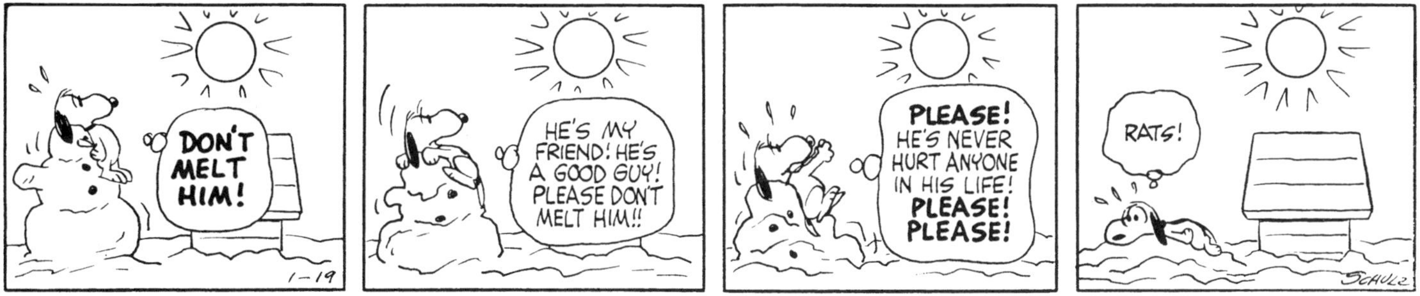
DON'T MELT HIM!
1-19
HE'S MY FRIEND! HE'S A GOOD GUY! PLEASE DON'T MELT HIM!!
PLEASE! HE'S NEVER HURT ANYONE IN HIS LIFE! PLEASE! PLEASE!
RATS!
SCHULZ

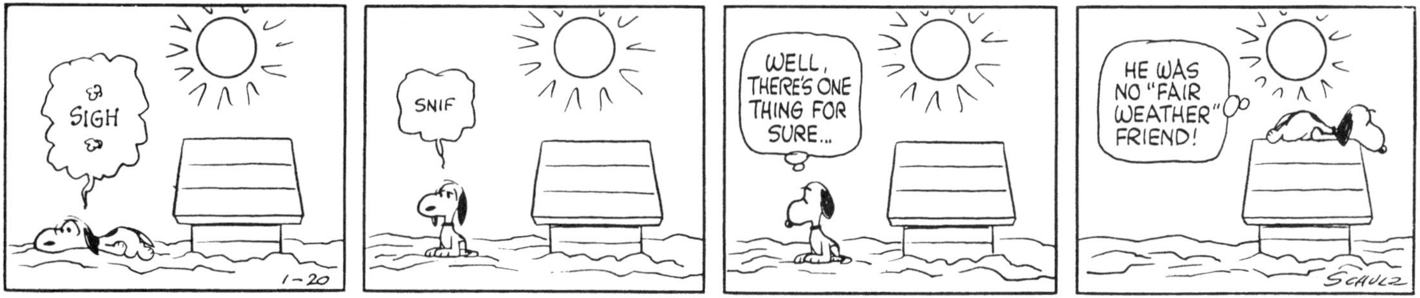
SIGH
1-20
SNIF
WELL, THERE'S ONE THING FOR SURE...
HE WAS NO "FAIR WEATHER" FRIEND!
SCHULZ

PEANUTS BY SCHULZ

ZIP!

I GOT IT!

YOU GIMME BACK MY BLANKET!

NO! I'VE GOT IT, AND I'M GOING TO KEEP IT! THIS IS THE START YOU NEED TO BREAK THE HABIT!

APPARENTLY YOU HAVEN'T READ THE LATEST SCIENTIFIC REPORTS..

A BLANKET IS AS IMPORTANT TO A CHILD AS A HOBBY IS TO AN ADULT..

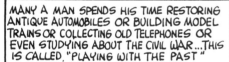

MANY A MAN SPENDS HIS TIME RESTORING ANTIQUE AUTOMOBILES OR BUILDING MODEL TRAINS OR COLLECTING OLD TELEPHONES OR EVEN STUDYING ABOUT THE CIVIL WAR...THIS IS CALLED "PLAYING WITH THE PAST"

1-21

REALLY?

CERTAINLY!!! AND THIS IS GOOD FOR IT HELPS THESE MEN TO COPE WITH THEIR EVERYDAY PROBLEMS...

NOW I FEEL THAT IT IS ABSOLUTELY NECESSARY FOR ME TO GET MY BLANKET BACK SO I'M JUST GOING TO GIVE IT A GOOD...

..YANK!

IT'S SURPRISING WHAT YOU CAN ACCOMPLISH WITH A LITTLE SMOOTH TALKING AND SOME FAST ACTION!

SCHULZ

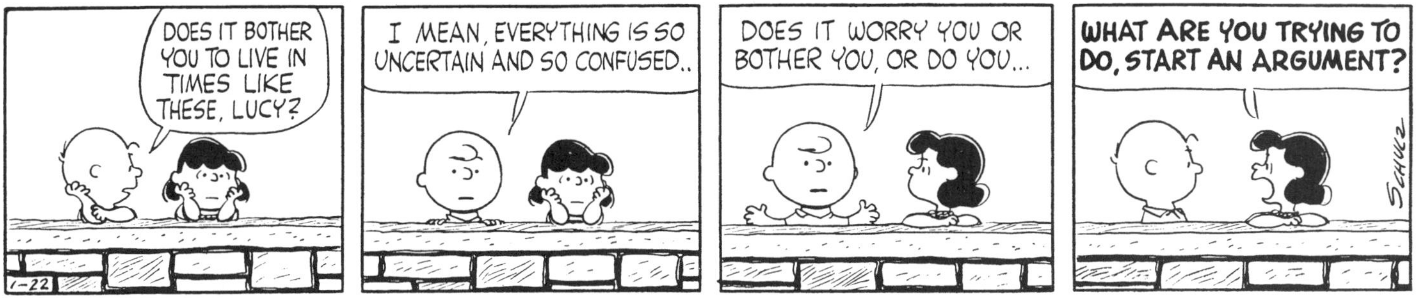

1-22
DOES IT BOTHER YOU TO LIVE IN TIMES LIKE THESE, LUCY?
I MEAN, EVERYTHING IS SO UNCERTAIN AND SO CONFUSED..
DOES IT WORRY YOU OR BOTHER YOU, OR DO YOU...
WHAT ARE YOU TRYING TO DO, START AN ARGUMENT?
SCHULZ

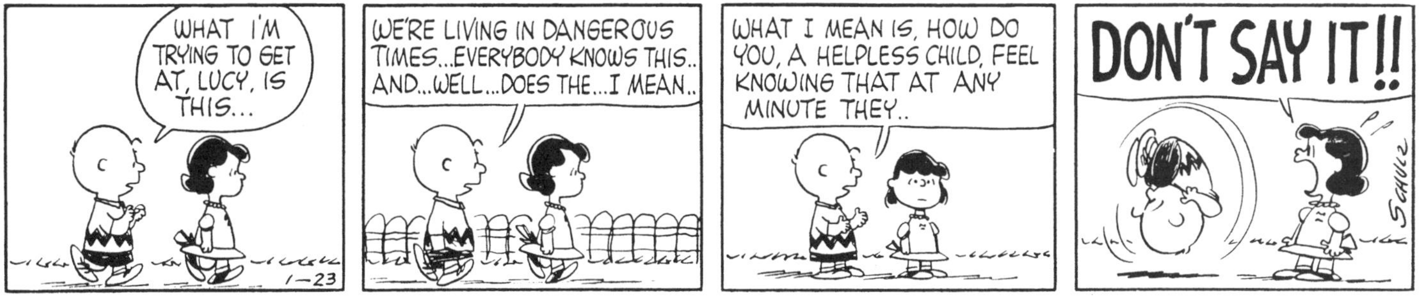

WHAT I'M TRYING TO GET AT, LUCY, IS THIS...
1-23
WE'RE LIVING IN DANGEROUS TIMES...EVERYBODY KNOWS THIS.. AND...WELL...DOES THE...I MEAN..
WHAT I MEAN IS, HOW DO YOU, A HELPLESS CHILD, FEEL KNOWING THAT AT ANY MINUTE THEY..
DON'T SAY IT!!
SCHULZ

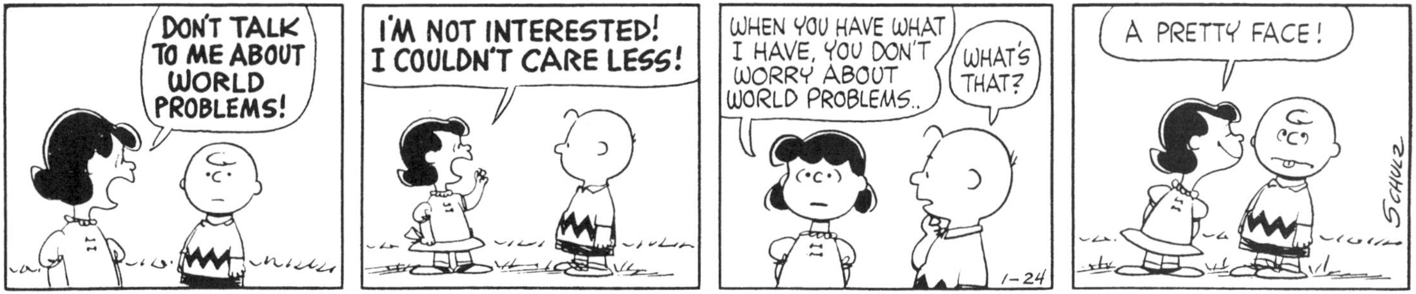

DON'T TALK TO ME ABOUT WORLD PROBLEMS!
I'M NOT INTERESTED! I COULDN'T CARE LESS!
WHEN YOU HAVE WHAT I HAVE, YOU DON'T WORRY ABOUT WORLD PROBLEMS..
WHAT'S THAT?
1-24
A PRETTY FACE!
SCHULZ

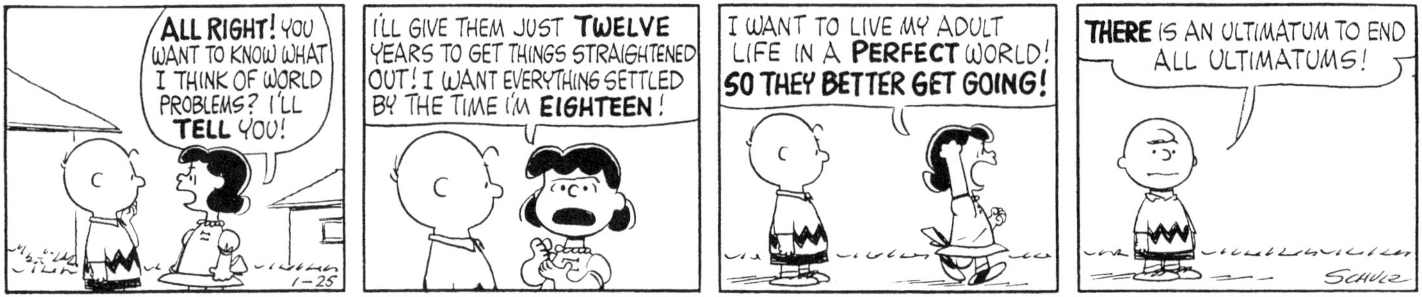
ALL RIGHT! YOU WANT TO KNOW WHAT I THINK OF WORLD PROBLEMS? I'LL TELL YOU!
1-25
I'LL GIVE THEM JUST TWELVE YEARS TO GET THINGS STRAIGHTENED OUT! I WANT EVERYTHING SETTLED BY THE TIME I'M EIGHTEEN!
I WANT TO LIVE MY ADULT LIFE IN A PERFECT WORLD! SO THEY BETTER GET GOING!
THERE IS AN ULTIMATUM TO END ALL ULTIMATUMS!
SCHULZ

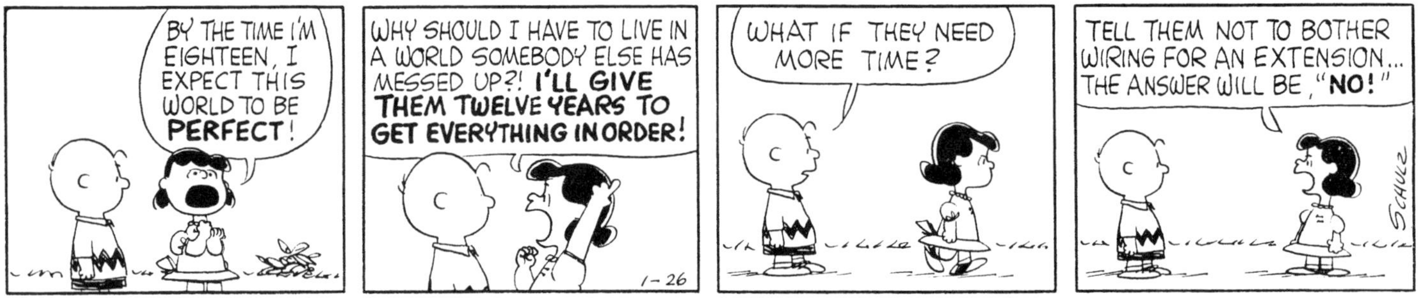
BY THE TIME I'M EIGHTEEN, I EXPECT THIS WORLD TO BE PERFECT!
WHY SHOULD I HAVE TO LIVE IN A WORLD SOMEBODY ELSE HAS MESSED UP?! I'LL GIVE THEM TWELVE YEARS TO GET EVERYTHING IN ORDER!
1-26
WHAT IF THEY NEED MORE TIME?
TELL THEM NOT TO BOTHER WIRING FOR AN EXTENSION... THE ANSWER WILL BE, "NO!"
SCHULZ

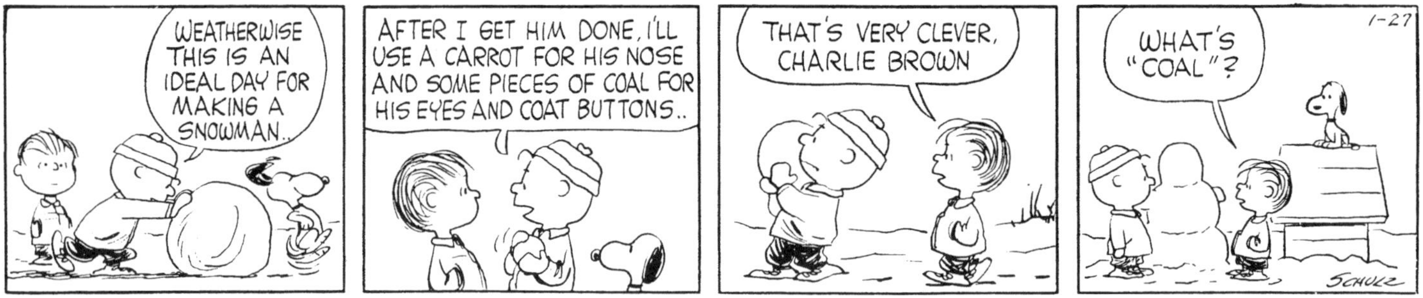
WEATHERWISE THIS IS AN IDEAL DAY FOR MAKING A SNOWMAN..
AFTER I GET HIM DONE, I'LL USE A CARROT FOR HIS NOSE AND SOME PIECES OF COAL FOR HIS EYES AND COAT BUTTONS..
THAT'S VERY CLEVER, CHARLIE BROWN
1-27
WHAT'S "COAL"?
SCHULZ

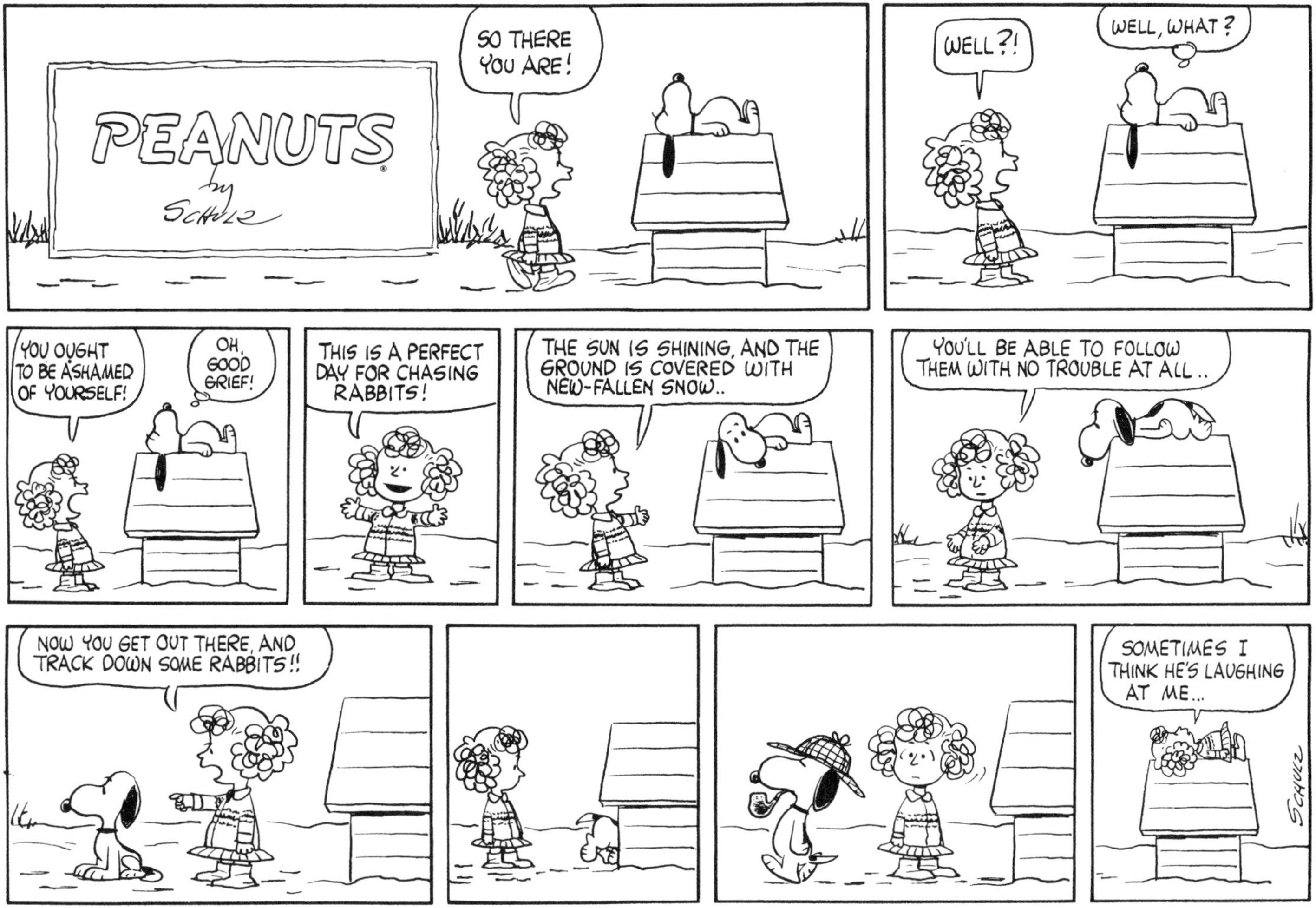
PEANUTS
by SCHULZ
SO THERE YOU ARE!
WELL?!
WELL, WHAT?
YOU OUGHT TO BE ASHAMED OF YOURSELF!
OH, GOOD GRIEF!
THIS IS A PERFECT DAY FOR CHASING RABBITS!
THE SUN IS SHINING, AND THE GROUND IS COVERED WITH NEW-FALLEN SNOW..
YOU'LL BE ABLE TO FOLLOW THEM WITH NO TROUBLE AT ALL..
NOW YOU GET OUT THERE, AND TRACK DOWN SOME RABBITS!!
SOMETIMES I THINK HE'S LAUGHING AT ME...
SCHULZ

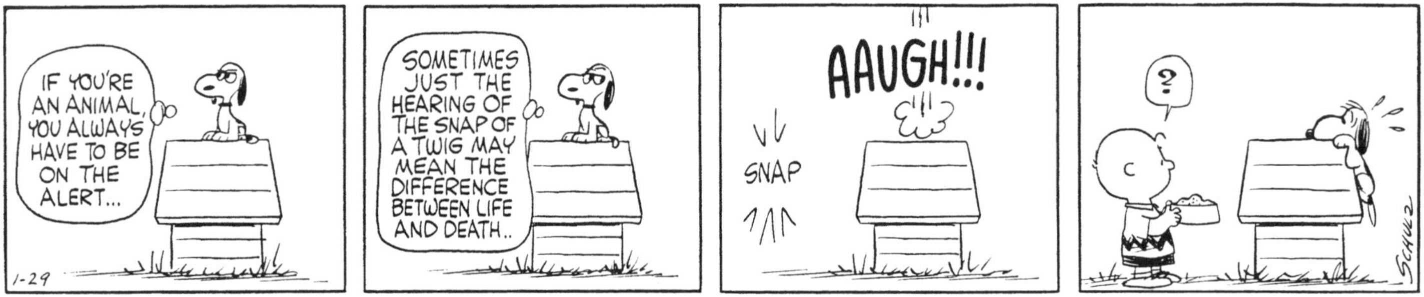
IF YOU'RE AN ANIMAL, YOU ALWAYS HAVE TO BE ON THE ALERT...
SOMETIMES JUST THE HEARING OF THE SNAP OF A TWIG MAY MEAN THE DIFFERENCE BETWEEN LIFE AND DEATH..
SNAP
AAUGH!!!
?
SCHULZ

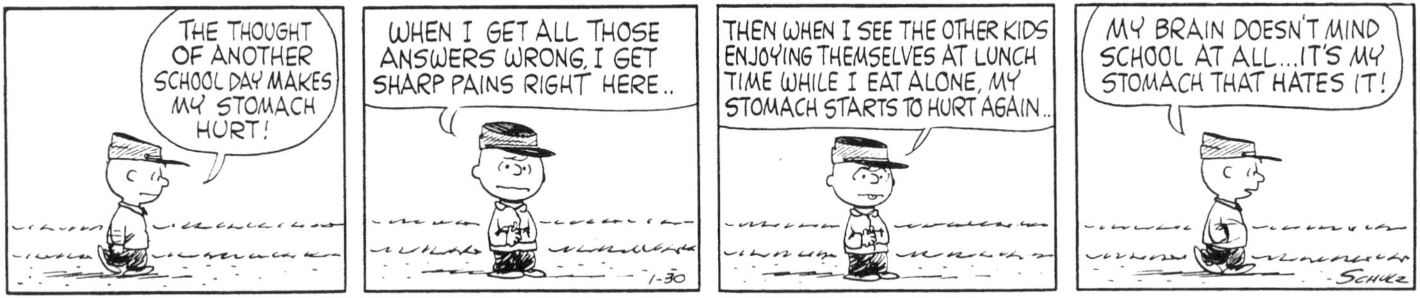
THE THOUGHT OF ANOTHER SCHOOL DAY MAKES MY STOMACH HURT!
WHEN I GET ALL THOSE ANSWERS WRONG, I GET SHARP PAINS RIGHT HERE..
THEN WHEN I SEE THE OTHER KIDS ENJOYING THEMSELVES AT LUNCH TIME WHILE I EAT ALONE, MY STOMACH STARTS TO HURT AGAIN..
MY BRAIN DOESN'T MIND SCHOOL AT ALL...IT'S MY STOMACH THAT HATES IT!
SCHULZ

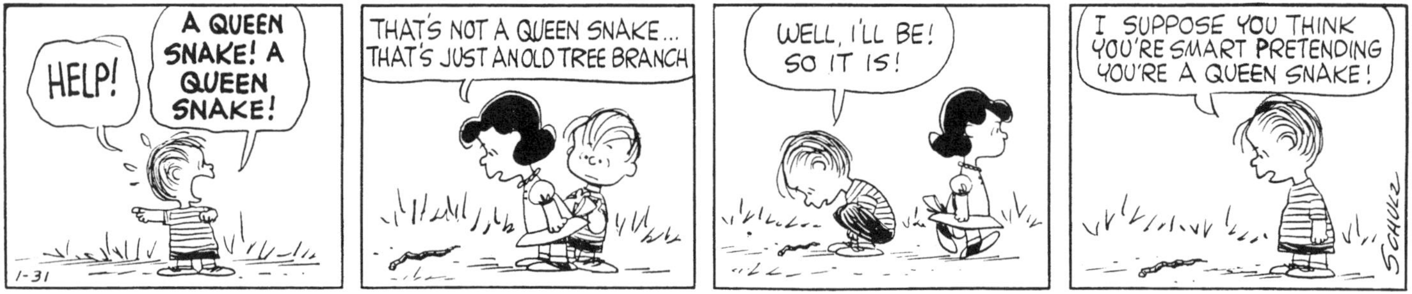
HELP!
A QUEEN SNAKE! A QUEEN SNAKE!
THAT'S NOT A QUEEN SNAKE... THAT'S JUST AN OLD TREE BRANCH
WELL, I'LL BE! SO IT IS!
I SUPPOSE YOU THINK YOU'RE SMART PRETENDING YOU'RE A QUEEN SNAKE!
SCHULZ

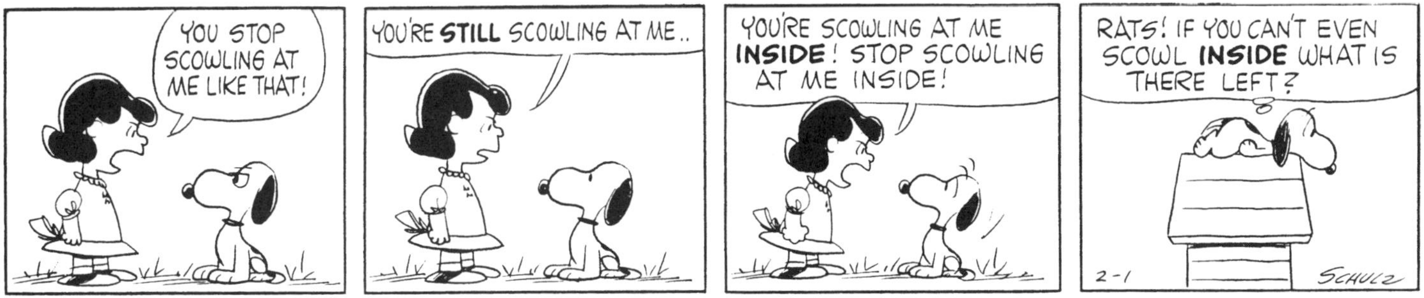
YOU STOP SCOWLING AT ME LIKE THAT!
YOU'RE **STILL** SCOWLING AT ME..
YOU'RE SCOWLING AT ME **INSIDE**! STOP SCOWLING AT ME INSIDE!
RATS! IF YOU CAN'T EVEN SCOWL **INSIDE** WHAT IS THERE LEFT?
2-1
SCHULZ

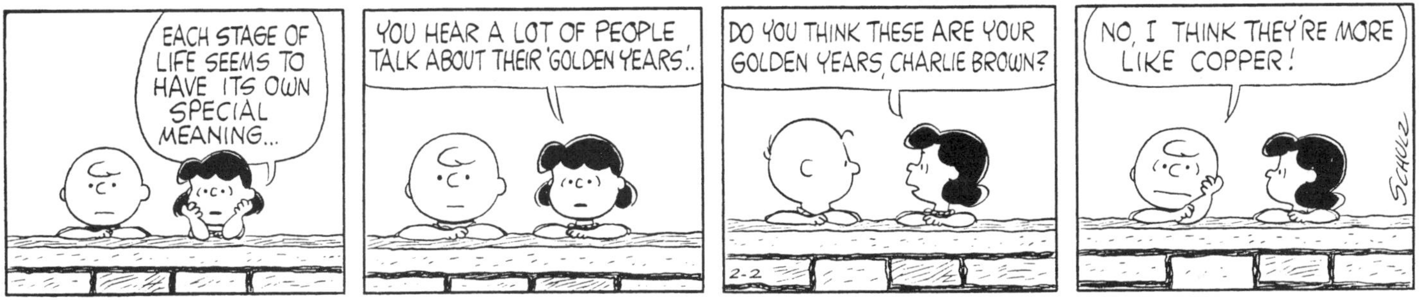
EACH STAGE OF LIFE SEEMS TO HAVE ITS OWN SPECIAL MEANING...
YOU HEAR A LOT OF PEOPLE TALK ABOUT THEIR 'GOLDEN YEARS'..
DO YOU THINK THESE ARE YOUR GOLDEN YEARS, CHARLIE BROWN?
2-2
NO, I THINK THEY'RE MORE LIKE COPPER!
SCHULZ

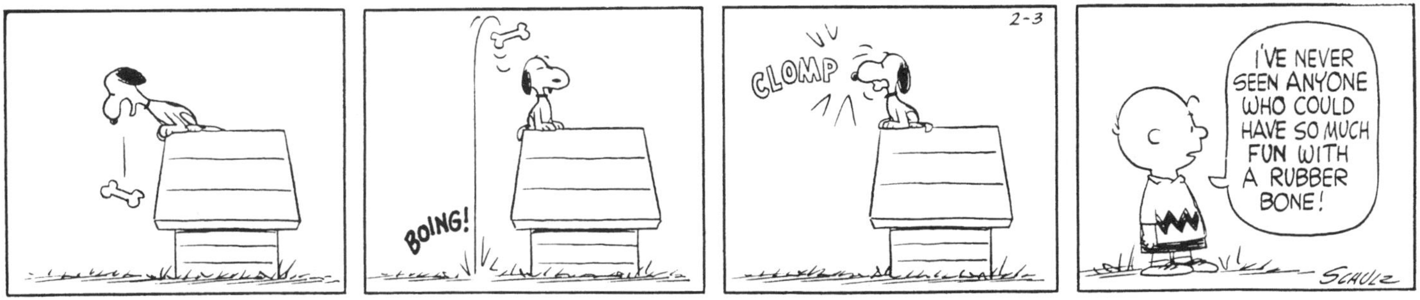
BOING!
2-3
CLOMP
I'VE NEVER SEEN ANYONE WHO COULD HAVE SO MUCH FUN WITH A RUBBER BONE!
SCHULZ

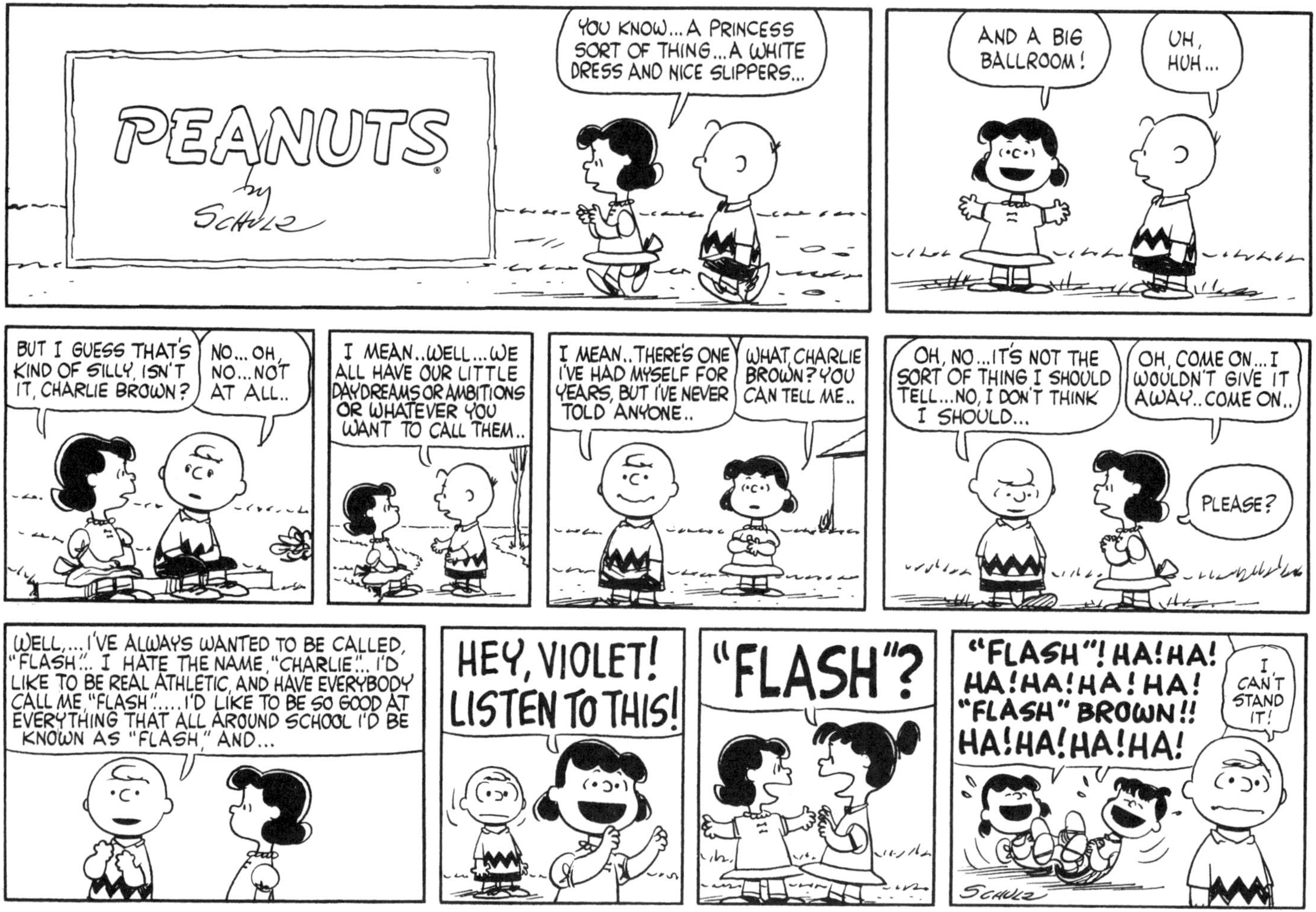
PEANUTS
by SCHULZ
YOU KNOW...A PRINCESS SORT OF THING...A WHITE DRESS AND NICE SLIPPERS...
AND A BIG BALLROOM!
UH, HUH...
BUT I GUESS THAT'S KIND OF SILLY, ISN'T IT, CHARLIE BROWN?
NO...OH, NO...NOT AT ALL..
I MEAN..WELL...WE ALL HAVE OUR LITTLE DAYDREAMS OR AMBITIONS OR WHATEVER YOU WANT TO CALL THEM..
I MEAN..THERE'S ONE I'VE HAD MYSELF FOR YEARS, BUT I'VE NEVER TOLD ANYONE..
WHAT, CHARLIE BROWN? YOU CAN TELL ME..
OH, NO...IT'S NOT THE SORT OF THING I SHOULD TELL...NO, I DON'T THINK I SHOULD...
OH, COME ON...I WOULDN'T GIVE IT AWAY..COME ON..
PLEASE?
WELL,...I'VE ALWAYS WANTED TO BE CALLED, "FLASH"... I HATE THE NAME, "CHARLIE"... I'D LIKE TO BE REAL ATHLETIC, AND HAVE EVERYBODY CALL ME, "FLASH".....I'D LIKE TO BE SO GOOD AT EVERYTHING THAT ALL AROUND SCHOOL I'D BE KNOWN AS "FLASH," AND...
HEY, VIOLET! LISTEN TO THIS!
"FLASH"?
"FLASH"! HA! HA! HA! HA! HA! HA! "FLASH" BROWN!! HA! HA! HA! HA!
I CAN'T STAND IT!
SCHULZ

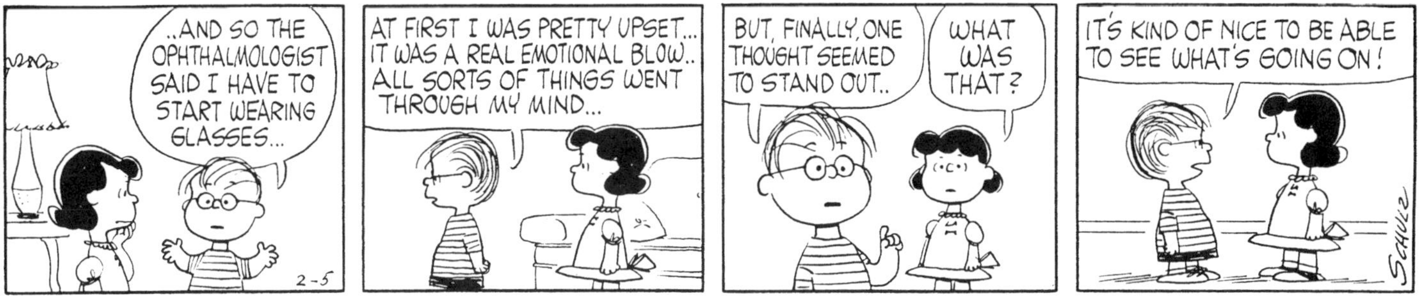
..AND SO THE OPHTHALMOLOGIST SAID I HAVE TO START WEARING GLASSES...
2-5
AT FIRST I WAS PRETTY UPSET... IT WAS A REAL EMOTIONAL BLOW.. ALL SORTS OF THINGS WENT THROUGH MY MIND...
BUT, FINALLY, ONE THOUGHT SEEMED TO STAND OUT..
WHAT WAS THAT?
IT'S KIND OF NICE TO BE ABLE TO SEE WHAT'S GOING ON!
SCHULZ

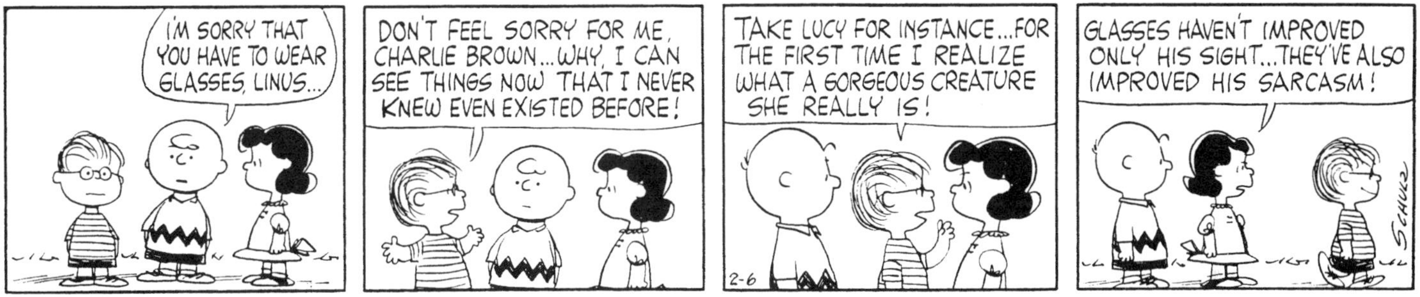
I'M SORRY THAT YOU HAVE TO WEAR GLASSES, LINUS...
DON'T FEEL SORRY FOR ME, CHARLIE BROWN...WHY, I CAN SEE THINGS NOW THAT I NEVER KNEW EVEN EXISTED BEFORE!
TAKE LUCY FOR INSTANCE...FOR THE FIRST TIME I REALIZE WHAT A GORGEOUS CREATURE SHE REALLY IS!
2-6
GLASSES HAVEN'T IMPROVED ONLY HIS SIGHT...THEY'VE ALSO IMPROVED HIS SARCASM!
SCHULZ

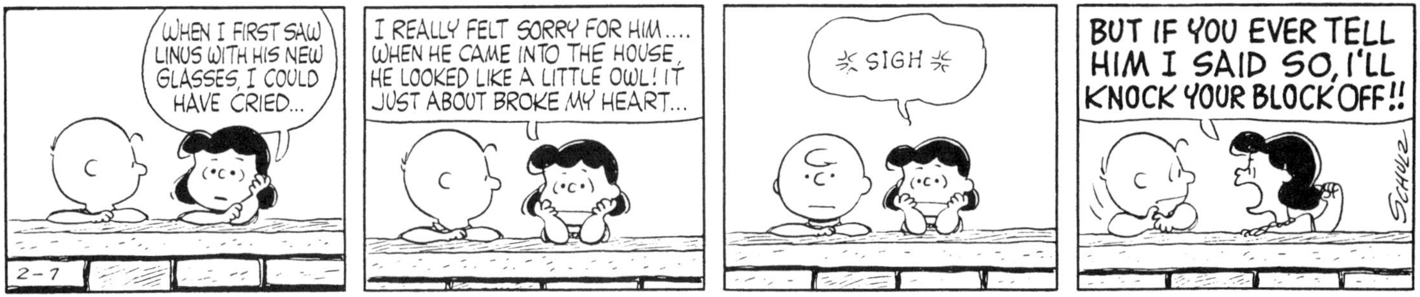
WHEN I FIRST SAW LINUS WITH HIS NEW GLASSES, I COULD HAVE CRIED...
2-7
I REALLY FELT SORRY FOR HIM.... WHEN HE CAME INTO THE HOUSE, HE LOOKED LIKE A LITTLE OWL! IT JUST ABOUT BROKE MY HEART...
SIGH
BUT IF YOU EVER TELL HIM I SAID SO, I'LL KNOCK YOUR BLOCK OFF!!
SCHULZ

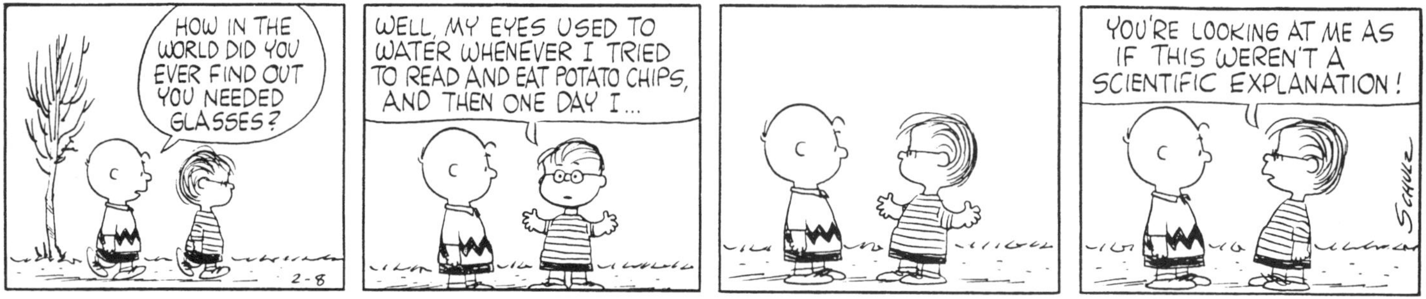
HOW IN THE WORLD DID YOU EVER FIND OUT YOU NEEDED GLASSES?
2-8
WELL, MY EYES USED TO WATER WHENEVER I TRIED TO READ AND EAT POTATO CHIPS, AND THEN ONE DAY I...
YOU'RE LOOKING AT ME AS IF THIS WEREN'T A SCIENTIFIC EXPLANATION!
SCHULZ

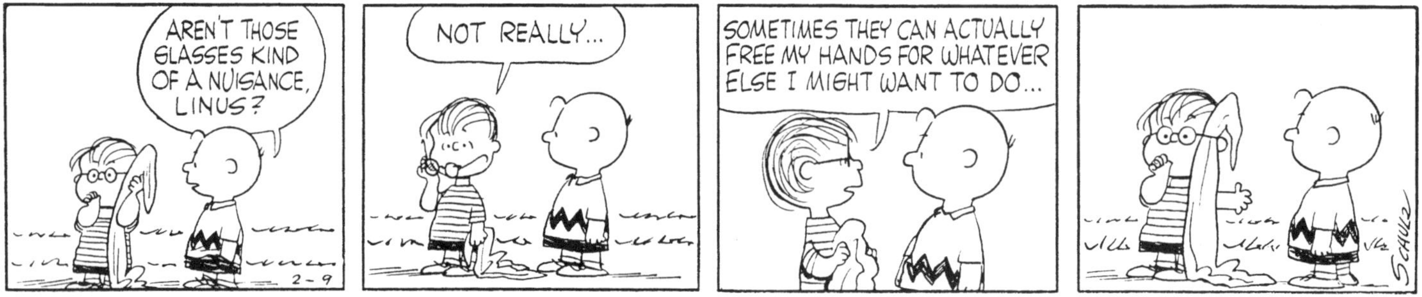
AREN'T THOSE GLASSES KIND OF A NUISANCE, LINUS?
2-9
NOT REALLY...
SOMETIMES THEY CAN ACTUALLY FREE MY HANDS FOR WHATEVER ELSE I MIGHT WANT TO DO...
SCHULZ

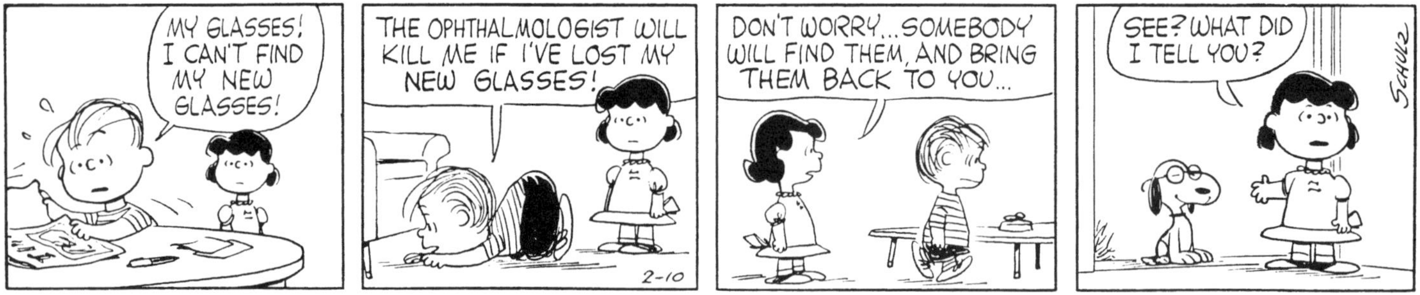
MY GLASSES! I CAN'T FIND MY NEW GLASSES!
THE OPHTHALMOLOGIST WILL KILL ME IF I'VE LOST MY NEW GLASSES!
2-10
DON'T WORRY...SOMEBODY WILL FIND THEM, AND BRING THEM BACK TO YOU...
SEE? WHAT DID I TELL YOU?
SCHULZ

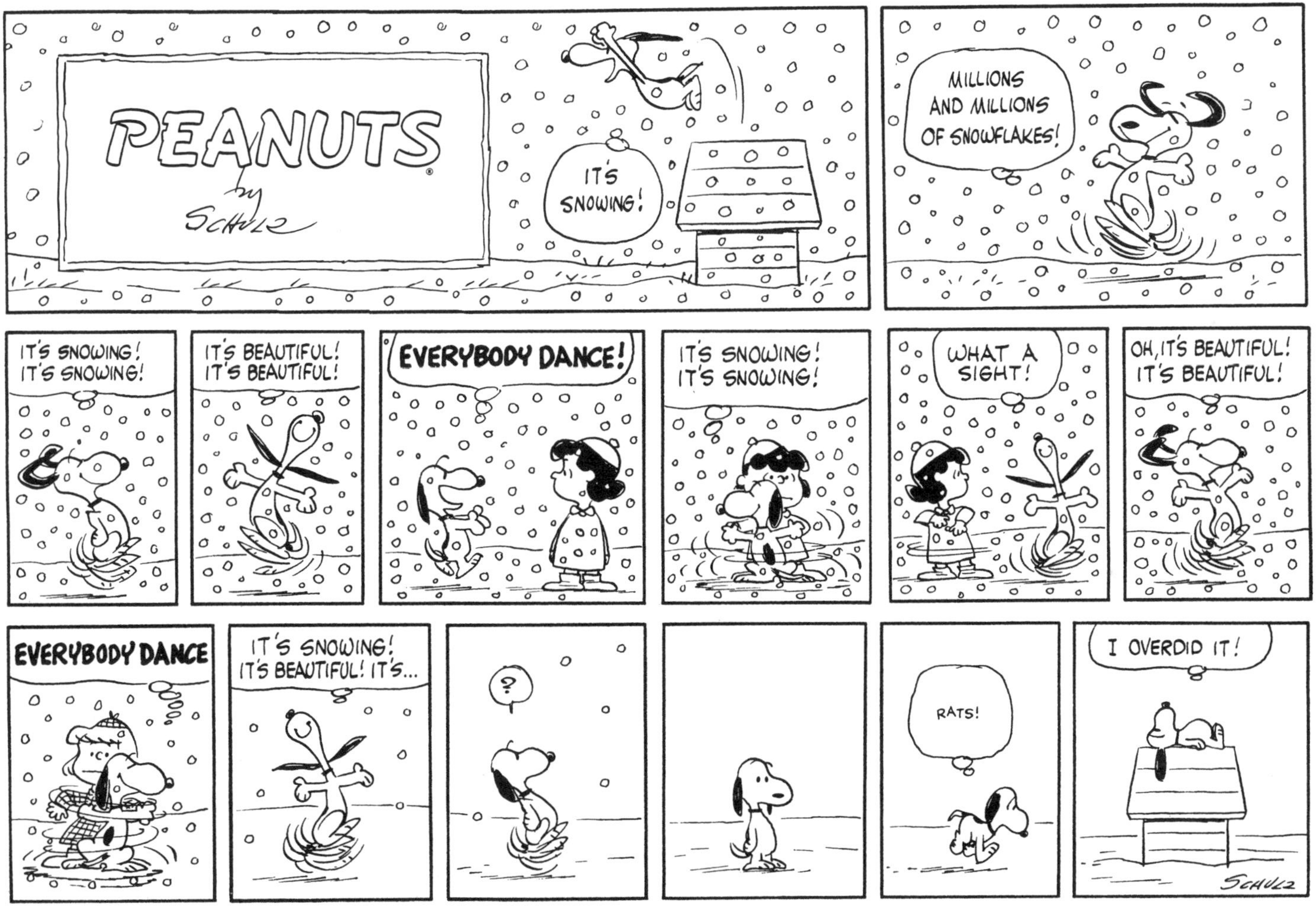
PEANUTS
by SCHULZ
IT'S SNOWING!
MILLIONS AND MILLIONS OF SNOWFLAKES!
IT'S SNOWING! IT'S SNOWING!
IT'S BEAUTIFUL! IT'S BEAUTIFUL!
EVERYBODY DANCE!
IT'S SNOWING! IT'S SNOWING!
WHAT A SIGHT!
OH, IT'S BEAUTIFUL! IT'S BEAUTIFUL!
EVERYBODY DANCE
IT'S SNOWING! IT'S BEAUTIFUL! IT'S...
?
RATS!
I OVERDID IT!
SCHULZ

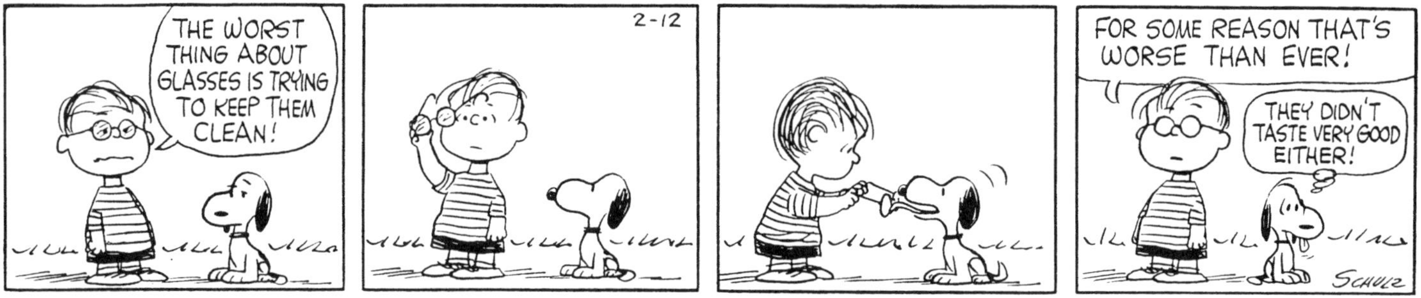
THE WORST THING ABOUT GLASSES IS TRYING TO KEEP THEM CLEAN!
2-12
FOR SOME REASON THAT'S WORSE THAN EVER!
THEY DIDN'T TASTE VERY GOOD EITHER!
SCHULZ

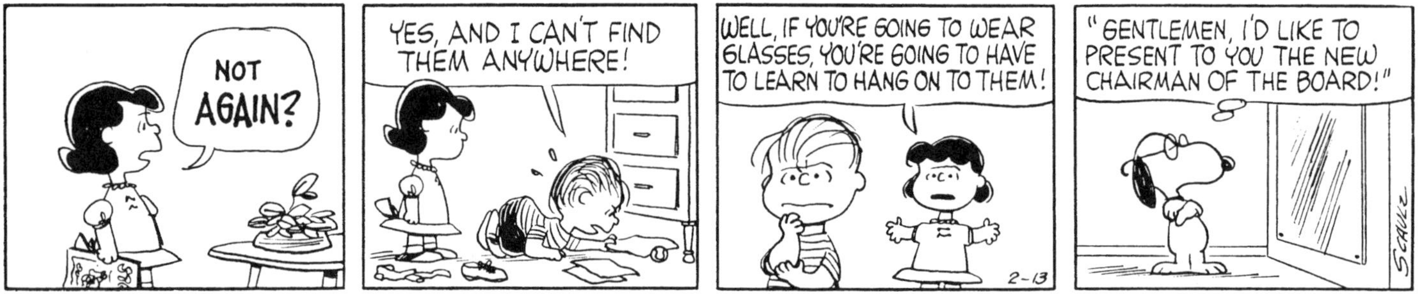
NOT AGAIN?
YES, AND I CAN'T FIND THEM ANYWHERE!
WELL, IF YOU'RE GOING TO WEAR GLASSES, YOU'RE GOING TO HAVE TO LEARN TO HANG ON TO THEM!
2-13
"GENTLEMEN, I'D LIKE TO PRESENT TO YOU THE NEW CHAIRMAN OF THE BOARD!"
SCHULZ

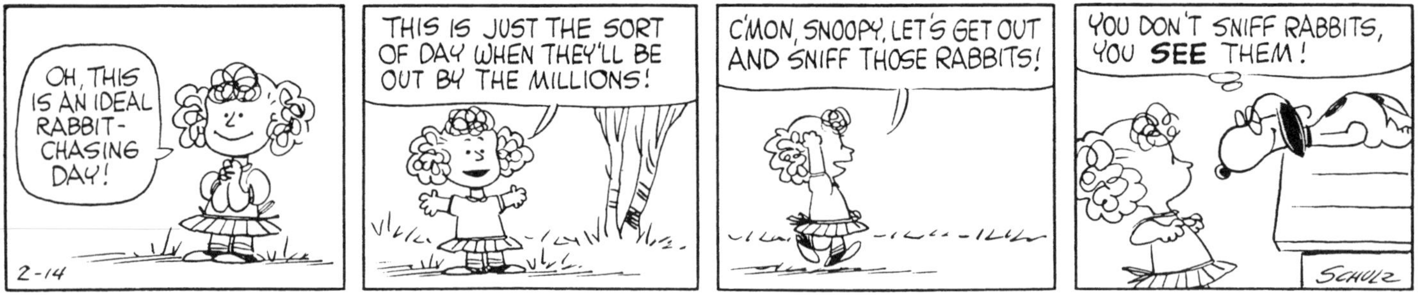
OH, THIS IS AN IDEAL RABBIT-CHASING DAY!
2-14
THIS IS JUST THE SORT OF DAY WHEN THEY'LL BE OUT BY THE MILLIONS!
C'MON, SNOOPY, LET'S GET OUT AND SNIFF THOSE RABBITS!
YOU DON'T SNIFF RABBITS, YOU SEE THEM!
SCHULZ

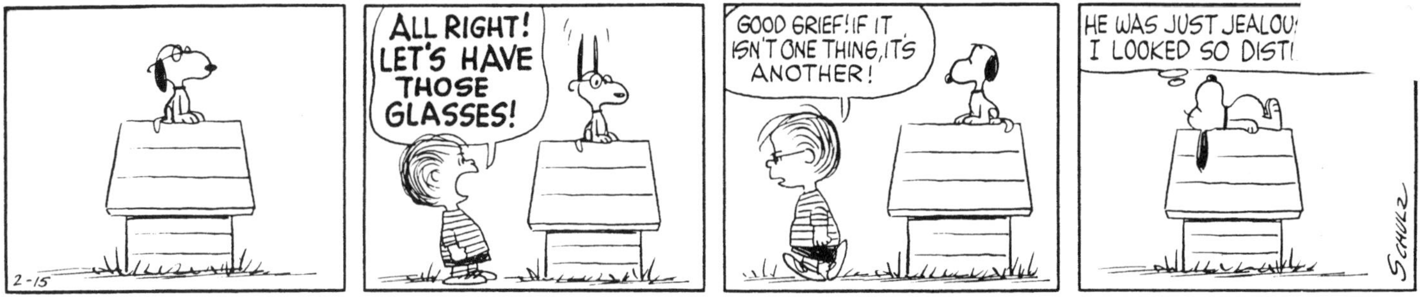
2-15
ALL RIGHT! LET'S HAVE THOSE GLASSES!
GOOD GRIEF! IF IT ISN'T ONE THING, IT'S ANOTHER!
HE WAS JUST JEALOU
I LOOKED SO DISTI
SCHULZ

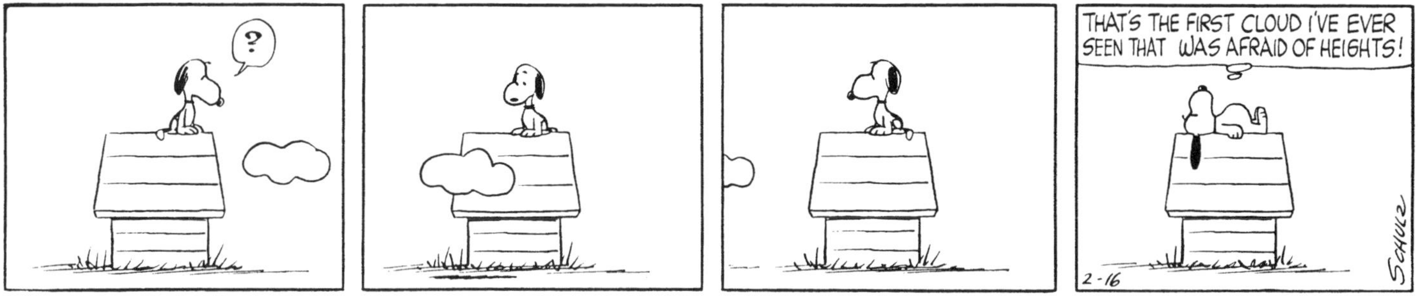
?
THAT'S THE FIRST CLOUD I'VE EVER SEEN THAT WAS AFRAID OF HEIGHTS!
2-16
SCHULZ

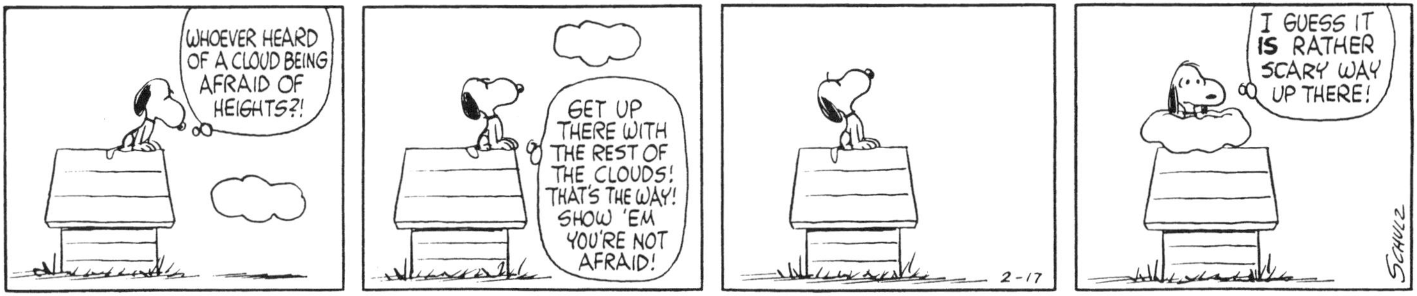
WHOEVER HEARD OF A CLOUD BEING AFRAID OF HEIGHTS?!
GET UP THERE WITH THE REST OF THE CLOUDS! THAT'S THE WAY! SHOW 'EM YOU'RE NOT AFRAID!
2-17
I GUESS IT **IS** RATHER SCARY WAY UP THERE!
SCHULZ

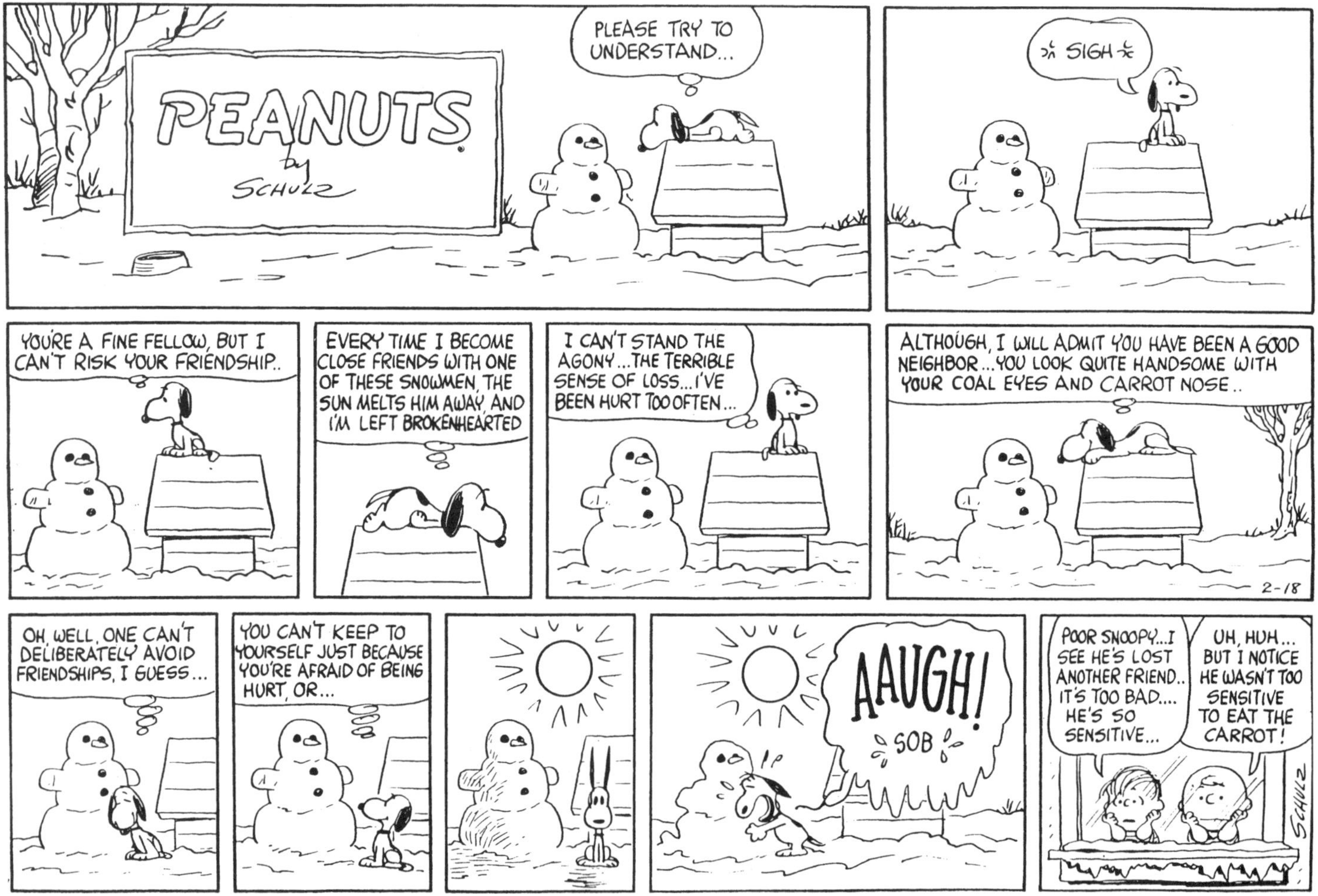
PEANUTS
by SCHULZ
PLEASE TRY TO UNDERSTAND...
SIGH
YOU'RE A FINE FELLOW, BUT I CAN'T RISK YOUR FRIENDSHIP..
EVERY TIME I BECOME CLOSE FRIENDS WITH ONE OF THESE SNOWMEN, THE SUN MELTS HIM AWAY, AND I'M LEFT BROKENHEARTED
I CAN'T STAND THE AGONY...THE TERRIBLE SENSE OF LOSS...I'VE BEEN HURT TOO OFTEN...
ALTHOUGH, I WILL ADMIT YOU HAVE BEEN A GOOD NEIGHBOR...YOU LOOK QUITE HANDSOME WITH YOUR COAL EYES AND CARROT NOSE..
2-18
OH, WELL, ONE CAN'T DELIBERATELY AVOID FRIENDSHIPS, I GUESS...
YOU CAN'T KEEP TO YOURSELF JUST BECAUSE YOU'RE AFRAID OF BEING HURT, OR...
AAUGH!
SOB
POOR SNOOPY...I SEE HE'S LOST ANOTHER FRIEND.. IT'S TOO BAD.... HE'S SO SENSITIVE...
UH, HUH... BUT I NOTICE HE WASN'T TOO SENSITIVE TO EAT THE CARROT!
SCHULZ

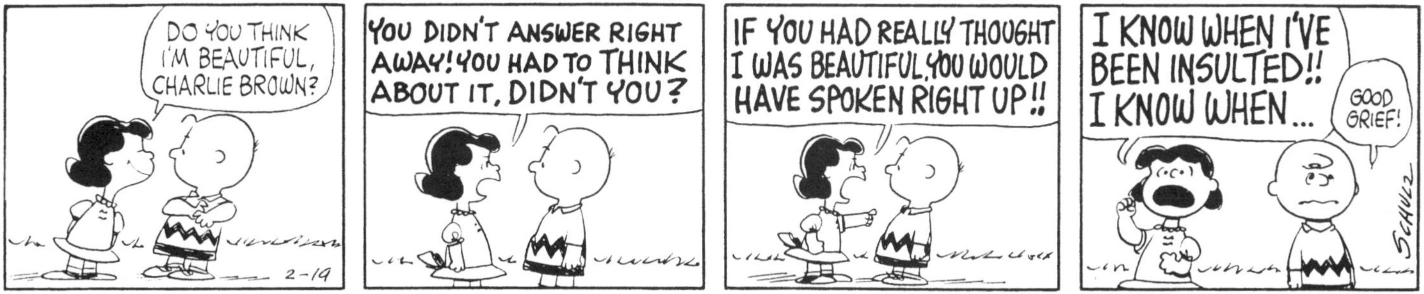
DO YOU THINK I'M BEAUTIFUL, CHARLIE BROWN?
2-19
YOU DIDN'T ANSWER RIGHT AWAY! YOU HAD TO THINK ABOUT IT, DIDN'T YOU?
IF YOU HAD REALLY THOUGHT I WAS BEAUTIFUL, YOU WOULD HAVE SPOKEN RIGHT UP!!
I KNOW WHEN I'VE BEEN INSULTED!! I KNOW WHEN...
GOOD GRIEF!
SCHULZ

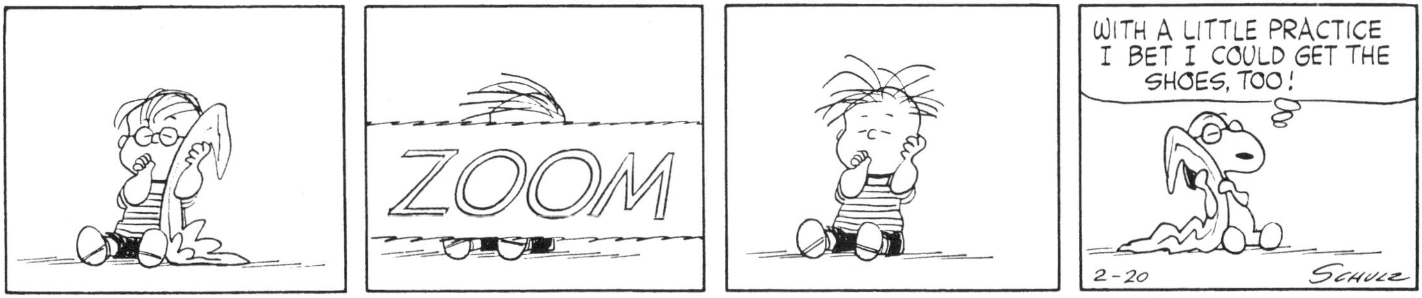
ZOOM
WITH A LITTLE PRACTICE I BET I COULD GET THE SHOES, TOO!
2-20
SCHULZ

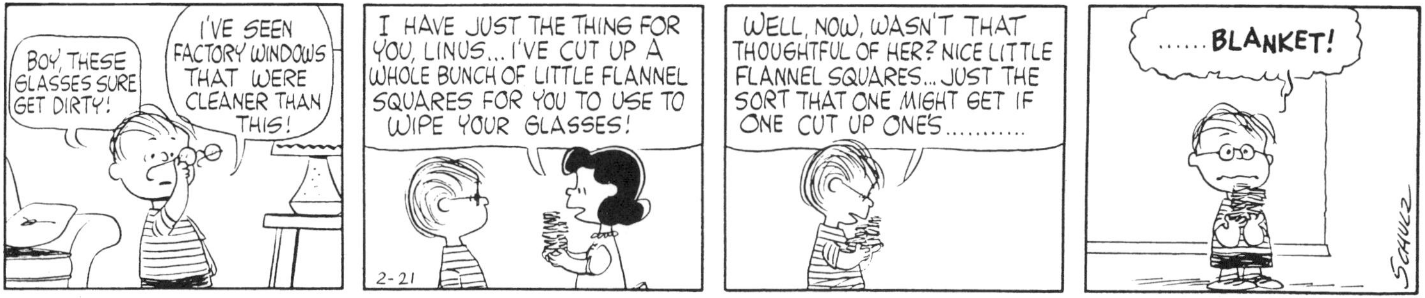
BOY, THESE GLASSES SURE GET DIRTY!
I'VE SEEN FACTORY WINDOWS THAT WERE CLEANER THAN THIS!
I HAVE JUST THE THING FOR YOU, LINUS... I'VE CUT UP A WHOLE BUNCH OF LITTLE FLANNEL SQUARES FOR YOU TO USE TO WIPE YOUR GLASSES!
2-21
WELL, NOW, WASN'T THAT THOUGHTFUL OF HER? NICE LITTLE FLANNEL SQUARES... JUST THE SORT THAT ONE MIGHT GET IF ONE CUT UP ONE'S..........
......BLANKET!
SCHULZ

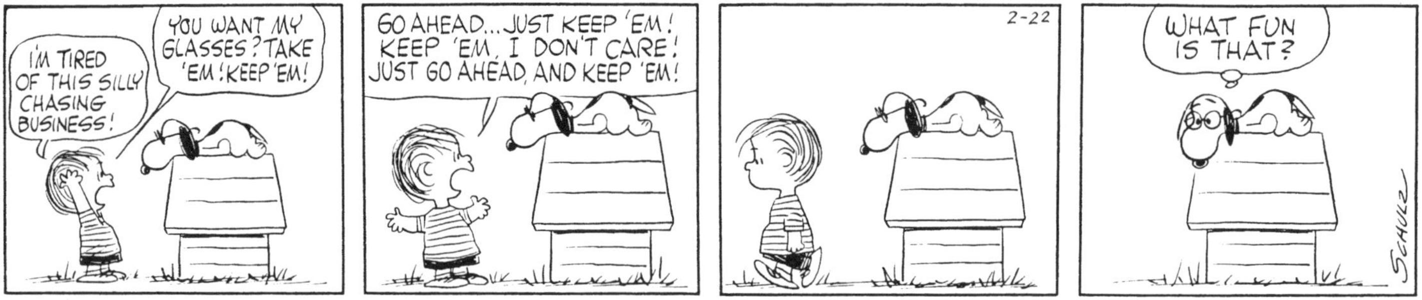
I'M TIRED OF THIS SILLY CHASING BUSINESS!
YOU WANT MY GLASSES? TAKE 'EM! KEEP 'EM!
GO AHEAD...JUST KEEP 'EM! KEEP 'EM, I DON'T CARE! JUST GO AHEAD, AND KEEP 'EM!
2-22
WHAT FUN IS THAT?
SCHULZ

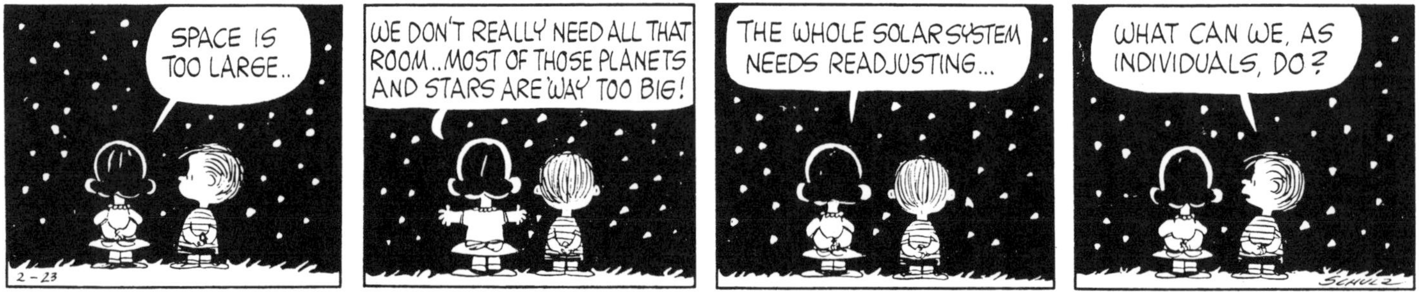
SPACE IS TOO LARGE..
2-23
WE DON'T REALLY NEED ALL THAT ROOM..MOST OF THOSE PLANETS AND STARS ARE 'WAY TOO BIG!
THE WHOLE SOLAR SYSTEM NEEDS READJUSTING...
WHAT CAN WE, AS INDIVIDUALS, DO?
SCHULZ

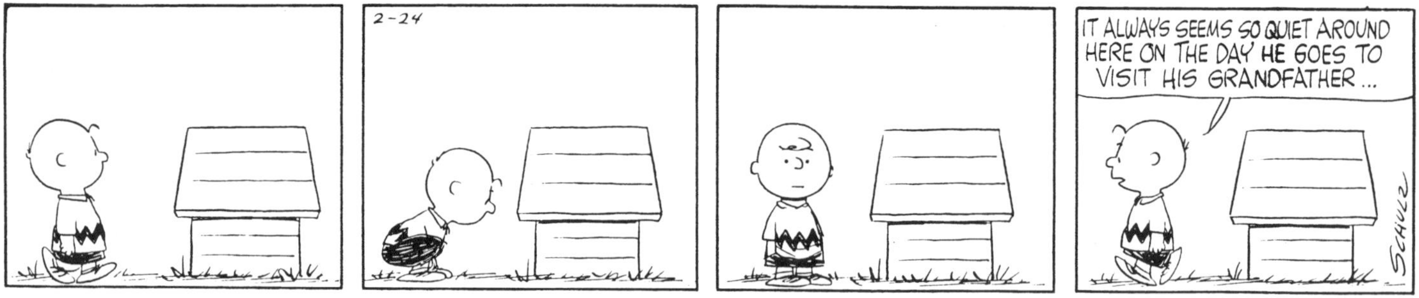
2-24
IT ALWAYS SEEMS SO QUIET AROUND HERE ON THE DAY HE GOES TO VISIT HIS GRANDFATHER...
SCHULZ

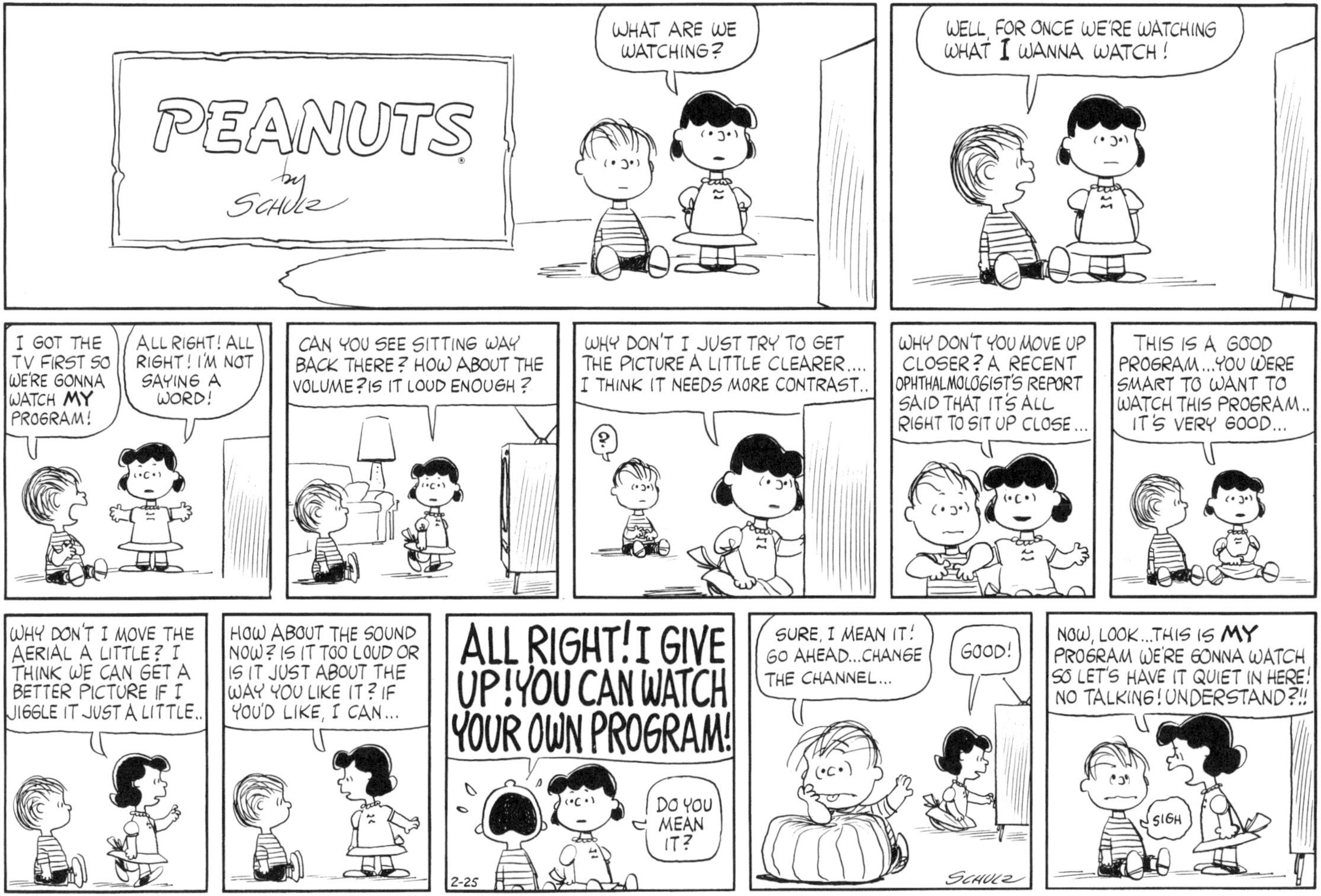

PEANUTS
by SCHULZ
WHAT ARE WE WATCHING?
WELL, FOR ONCE WE'RE WATCHING WHAT I WANNA WATCH!
I GOT THE TV FIRST SO WE'RE GONNA WATCH MY PROGRAM!
ALL RIGHT! ALL RIGHT! I'M NOT SAYING A WORD!
CAN YOU SEE SITTING WAY BACK THERE? HOW ABOUT THE VOLUME? IS IT LOUD ENOUGH?
WHY DON'T I JUST TRY TO GET THE PICTURE A LITTLE CLEARER.... I THINK IT NEEDS MORE CONTRAST..
?
WHY DON'T YOU MOVE UP CLOSER? A RECENT OPHTHALMOLOGIST'S REPORT SAID THAT IT'S ALL RIGHT TO SIT UP CLOSE...
THIS IS A GOOD PROGRAM...YOU WERE SMART TO WANT TO WATCH THIS PROGRAM.. IT'S VERY GOOD...
WHY DON'T I MOVE THE AERIAL A LITTLE? I THINK WE CAN GET A BETTER PICTURE IF I JIGGLE IT JUST A LITTLE..
HOW ABOUT THE SOUND NOW? IS IT TOO LOUD OR IS IT JUST ABOUT THE WAY YOU LIKE IT? IF YOU'D LIKE, I CAN...
ALL RIGHT! I GIVE UP! YOU CAN WATCH YOUR OWN PROGRAM!
DO YOU MEAN IT?
2-25
SURE, I MEAN IT! GO AHEAD...CHANGE THE CHANNEL...
GOOD!
SCHULZ
NOW, LOOK...THIS IS MY PROGRAM WE'RE GONNA WATCH SO LET'S HAVE IT QUIET IN HERE! NO TALKING! UNDERSTAND?!!
SIGH

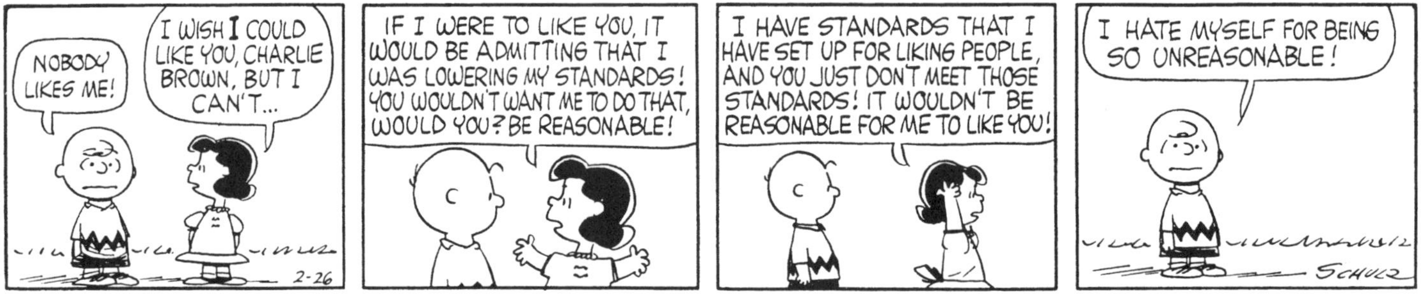
NOBODY LIKES ME!
I WISH I COULD LIKE YOU, CHARLIE BROWN, BUT I CAN'T...
2-26
IF I WERE TO LIKE YOU, IT WOULD BE ADMITTING THAT I WAS LOWERING MY STANDARDS! YOU WOULDN'T WANT ME TO DO THAT, WOULD YOU? BE REASONABLE!
I HAVE STANDARDS THAT I HAVE SET UP FOR LIKING PEOPLE, AND YOU JUST DON'T MEET THOSE STANDARDS! IT WOULDN'T BE REASONABLE FOR ME TO LIKE YOU!
I HATE MYSELF FOR BEING SO UNREASONABLE!
SCHULZ

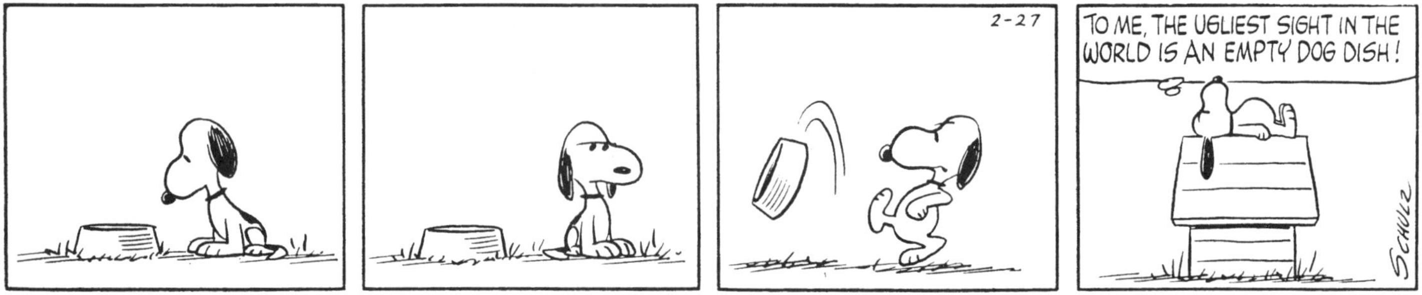
2-27
TO ME, THE UGLIEST SIGHT IN THE WORLD IS AN EMPTY DOG DISH!
SCHULZ

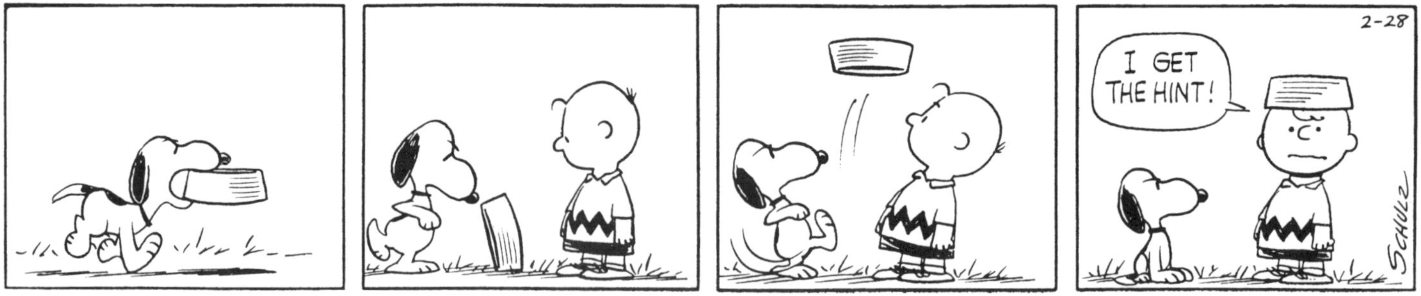
2-28
I GET THE HINT!
SCHULZ

Panel 1: YOU HAD YOUR SUPPER! DON'T COME AROUND HERE BEGGING FOR MORE!

Panel 2: IF YOU HAD YOUR WAY, YOU'D BE EATING ALL DAY LONG!

Panel 3: I EAT BECAUSE I'M FRUSTRATED... 3-1

Panel 4: AND I'M FRUSTRATED BECAUSE I DON'T GET TO EAT ENOUGH!

Panel 5: HMM...MAYBE I'VE BEEN WRONG...

Panel 6: IT SAYS HERE IN THE PAPER THAT IT IS ALL RIGHT TO GIVE YOUR DOG LITTLE SNACKS BETWEEN MEALS...

Panel 7: 3-2

Panel 8: YOU CAN ACCOMPLISH A LOT ONCE YOU GET THE SYMPATHY OF THE PRESS!

Panel 9: I CAN'T GET THIS KITE UP IN THE AIR! I JUST CAN'T!!

Panel 10: WHY NOT LEAVE IT ON THE GROUND? ACTUALLY, IT LOOKS KIND OF NICE LYING THERE...THE RED COLOR MAKES A NICE CONTRAST WITH ALL THIS GREEN GRASS... 3-3

Panel 11: IT PROBABLY WOULDN'T LOOK HALF AS GOOD UP THERE AGAINST THAT PALE BLUE SKY... NO, I ACTUALLY THINK THAT THIS SHADE OF RED GOES BEST WITH...

Panel 12: GET OUT OF HERE!

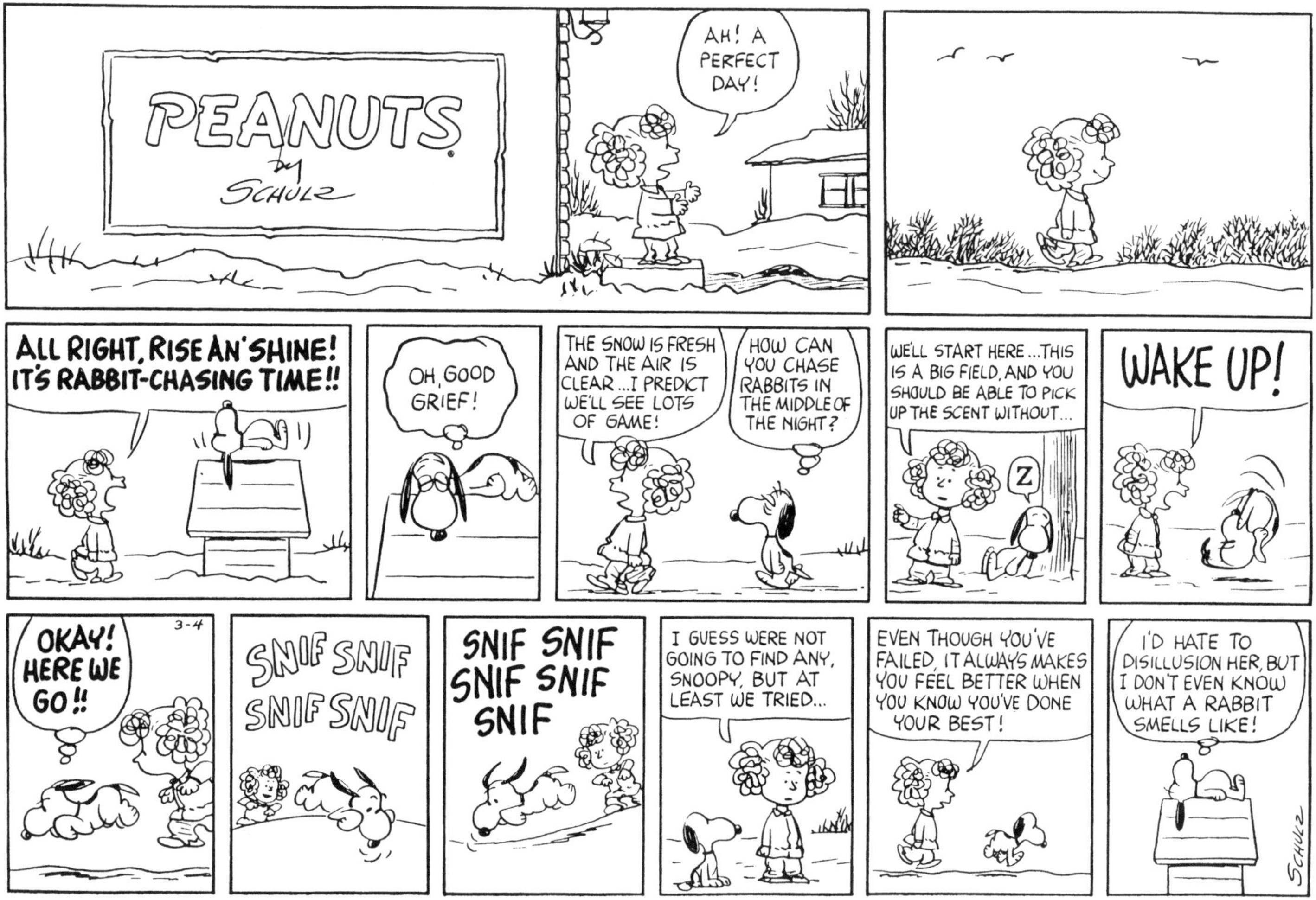
PEANUTS
by SCHULZ
AH! A PERFECT DAY!
ALL RIGHT, RISE AN' SHINE! IT'S RABBIT-CHASING TIME!!
OH, GOOD GRIEF!
THE SNOW IS FRESH AND THE AIR IS CLEAR...I PREDICT WE'LL SEE LOTS OF GAME!
HOW CAN YOU CHASE RABBITS IN THE MIDDLE OF THE NIGHT?
WE'LL START HERE...THIS IS A BIG FIELD, AND YOU SHOULD BE ABLE TO PICK UP THE SCENT WITHOUT...
Z
WAKE UP!
OKAY! HERE WE GO!!
3-4
SNIF SNIF SNIF SNIF
SNIF SNIF SNIF SNIF SNIF
I GUESS WERE NOT GOING TO FIND ANY, SNOOPY, BUT AT LEAST WE TRIED...
EVEN THOUGH YOU'VE FAILED, IT ALWAYS MAKES YOU FEEL BETTER WHEN YOU KNOW YOU'VE DONE YOUR BEST!
I'D HATE TO DISILLUSION HER, BUT I DON'T EVEN KNOW WHAT A RABBIT SMELLS LIKE!
SCHULZ

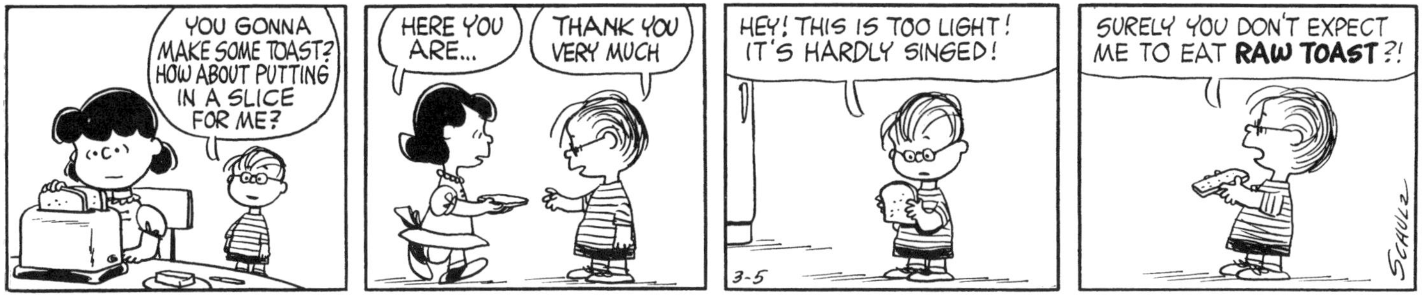
YOU GONNA MAKE SOME TOAST? HOW ABOUT PUTTING IN A SLICE FOR ME?
HERE YOU ARE...
THANK YOU VERY MUCH
HEY! THIS IS TOO LIGHT! IT'S HARDLY SINGED!
SURELY YOU DON'T EXPECT ME TO EAT **RAW TOAST**?!
3-5
SCHULZ

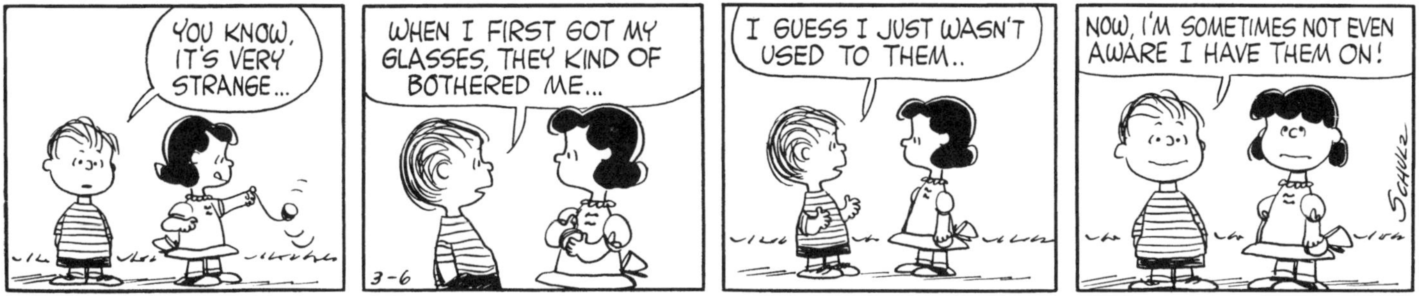
YOU KNOW, IT'S VERY STRANGE...
WHEN I FIRST GOT MY GLASSES, THEY KIND OF BOTHERED ME...
I GUESS I JUST WASN'T USED TO THEM..
NOW, I'M SOMETIMES NOT EVEN AWARE I HAVE THEM ON!
3-6
SCHULZ

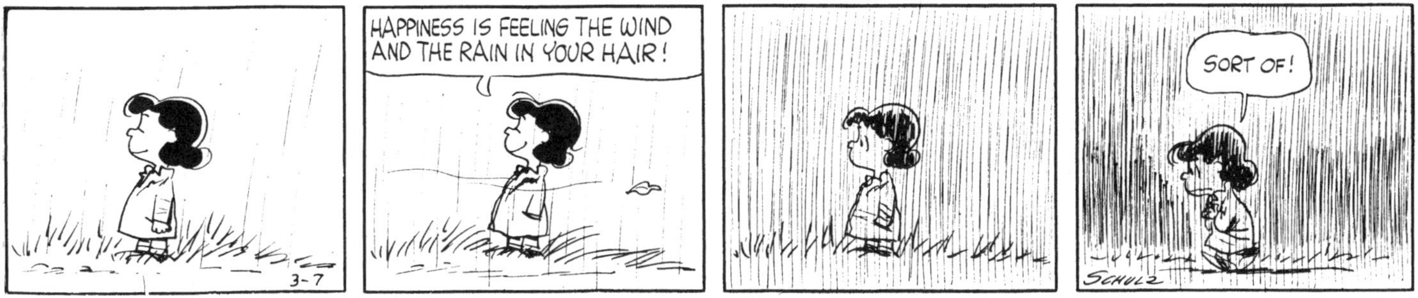
3-7
HAPPINESS IS FEELING THE WIND AND THE RAIN IN YOUR HAIR!
SORT OF!
SCHULZ

Panel 1: OF COURSE, I REALIZE THAT THERE WILL ALWAYS BE CRITICISM..

Panel 2: ALL MEDIUMS OF ENTERTAINMENT GO THROUGH THIS..EVEN OUR HIGHER ART FORMS HAVE THEIR DETRACTORS...THE THEATRE SEEMS ESPECIALLY VULNERABLE..

Panel 3: AND GOODNESS KNOWS HOW MUCH CRITICISM IS LEVELED AT OUR TELEVISION PROGRAMMING..ONE SOMETIMES WONDERS IF IT IS POSSIBLE EVER TO PLEASE THE VAST MAJORITY OF PEOPLE...

Panel 4: THE MOST RECENT CRITICISM IS THAT THERE IS TOO LITTLE ACTION AND FAR TOO MUCH TALKING IN THE MODERN-DAY COMIC STRIP... WHAT DO YOU THINK ABOUT THIS?

RIDICULOUS!

3-8 / SCHULZ

Panel 5: SAY, DID YOU KNOW THAT THIS IS "CHILDREN'S ART MONTH"?

Panel 6: WHY **THIS** MONTH? WHY NOT **LAST** MONTH? WHY NOT **NEXT** MONTH? WHY **THIS** MONTH?

Panel 7: HOW CAN YOU NARROW DOWN ART TO ONE PARTICULAR TIME OF THE YEAR? **ART MUST BE UNCONFINED! ART MUST HAVE FREEDOM!**

Panel 8: YOU CAN'T SAY, "TODAY WE WILL PRODUCE A WORK OF ART!" YOU CAN'T SAY...

OH, GOOD GRIEF!

3-9 / SCHULZ

Panel 9: MY LIFE HAS BECOME A BORE!

Panel 10: EVERYTHING I SEE I'VE SEEN BEFORE..

Panel 11: I NEED TO SET MY FACE TOWARD NEW HORIZONS..

3-10 / SCHULZ

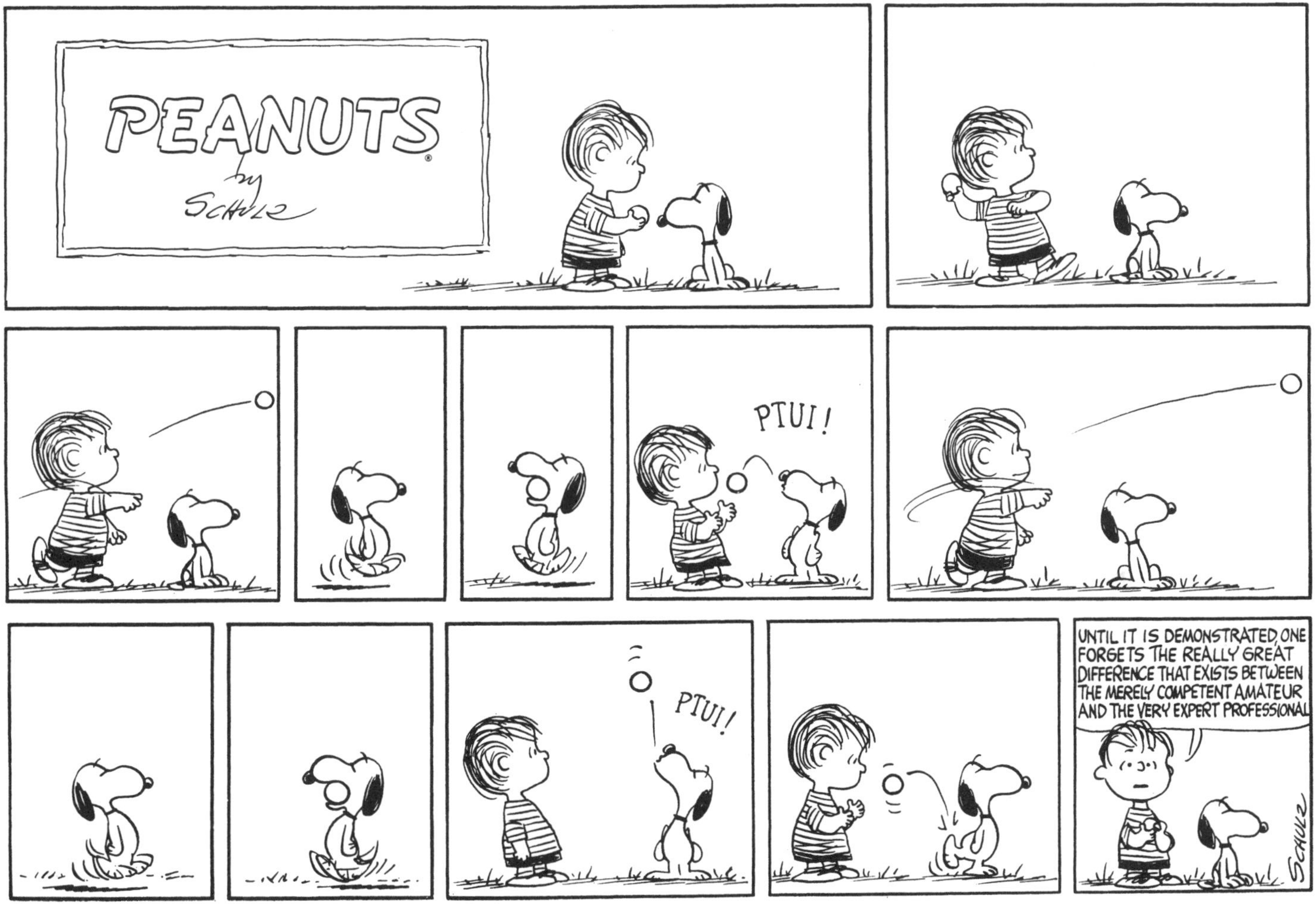
PEANUTS
by SCHULZ
PTUI!
PTUI!
UNTIL IT IS DEMONSTRATED, ONE FORGETS THE REALLY GREAT DIFFERENCE THAT EXISTS BETWEEN THE MERELY COMPETENT AMATEUR AND THE VERY EXPERT PROFESSIONAL
SCHULZ

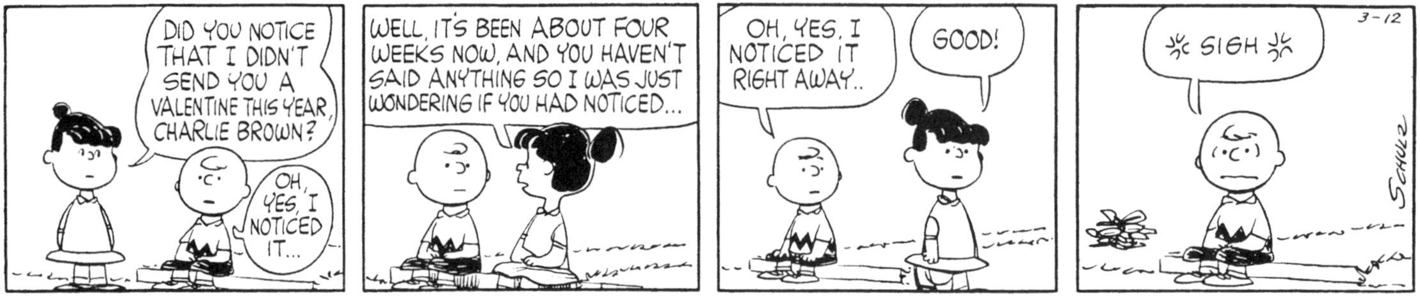
DID YOU NOTICE THAT I DIDN'T SEND YOU A VALENTINE THIS YEAR, CHARLIE BROWN?
OH, YES, I NOTICED IT...
WELL, IT'S BEEN ABOUT FOUR WEEKS NOW, AND YOU HAVEN'T SAID ANYTHING SO I WAS JUST WONDERING IF YOU HAD NOTICED...
OH, YES, I NOTICED IT RIGHT AWAY..
GOOD!
SIGH
3-12
SCHULZ

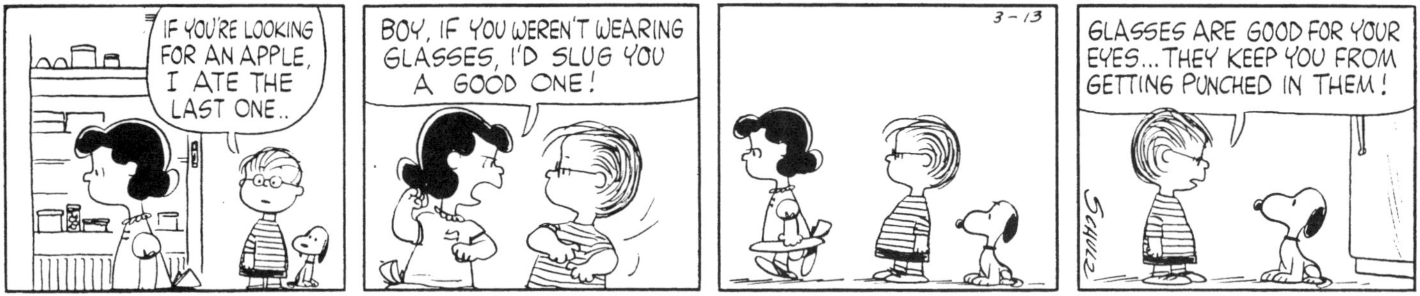
IF YOU'RE LOOKING FOR AN APPLE, I ATE THE LAST ONE..
BOY, IF YOU WEREN'T WEARING GLASSES, I'D SLUG YOU A GOOD ONE!
3-13
GLASSES ARE GOOD FOR YOUR EYES...THEY KEEP YOU FROM GETTING PUNCHED IN THEM!
SCHULZ

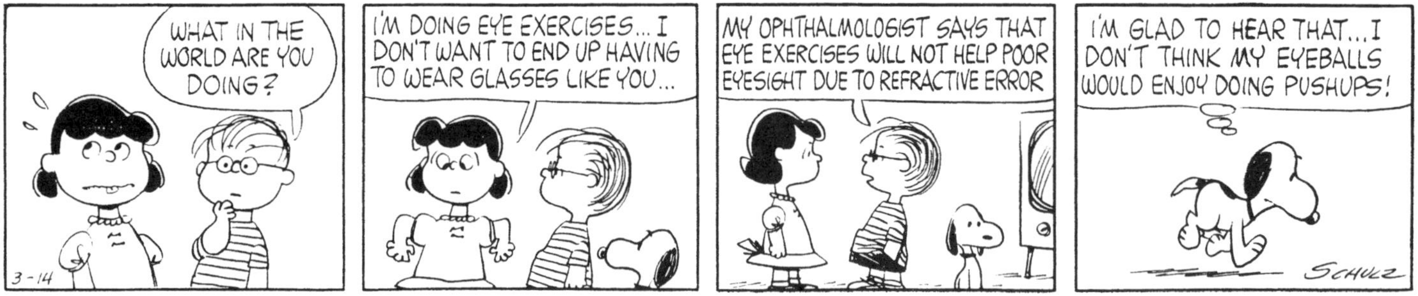
WHAT IN THE WORLD ARE YOU DOING?
3-14
I'M DOING EYE EXERCISES... I DON'T WANT TO END UP HAVING TO WEAR GLASSES LIKE YOU...
MY OPHTHALMOLOGIST SAYS THAT EYE EXERCISES WILL NOT HELP POOR EYESIGHT DUE TO REFRACTIVE ERROR
I'M GLAD TO HEAR THAT...I DON'T THINK MY EYEBALLS WOULD ENJOY DOING PUSHUPS!
SCHULZ

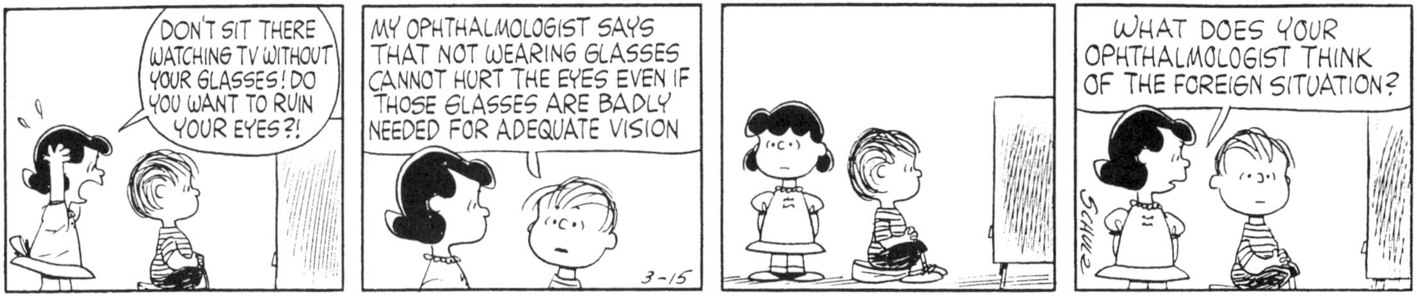
DON'T SIT THERE WATCHING TV WITHOUT YOUR GLASSES! DO YOU WANT TO RUIN YOUR EYES?!
MY OPHTHALMOLOGIST SAYS THAT NOT WEARING GLASSES CANNOT HURT THE EYES EVEN IF THOSE GLASSES ARE BADLY NEEDED FOR ADEQUATE VISION
3-15
WHAT DOES YOUR OPHTHALMOLOGIST THINK OF THE FOREIGN SITUATION?
SCHULZ

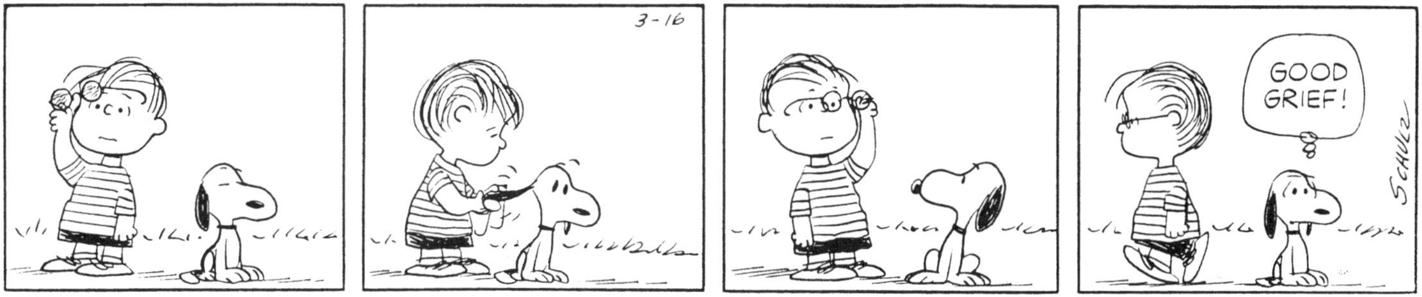
3-16
GOOD GRIEF!
SCHULZ

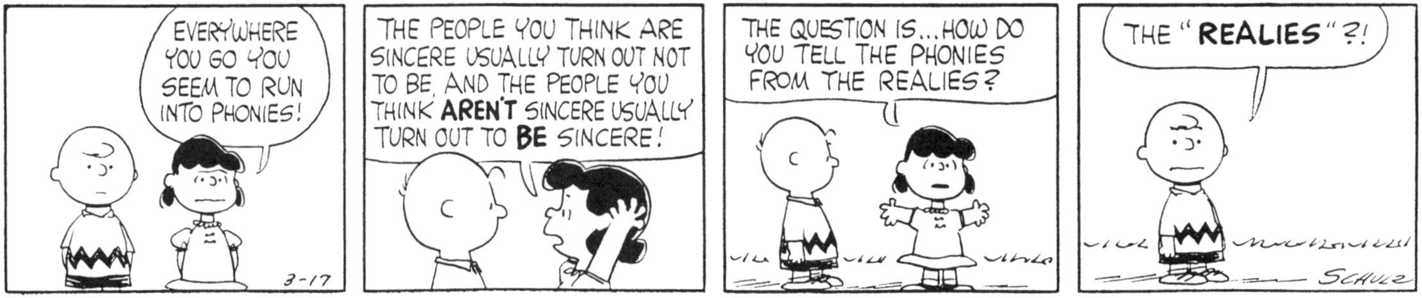
EVERYWHERE YOU GO YOU SEEM TO RUN INTO PHONIES!
3-17
THE PEOPLE YOU THINK ARE SINCERE USUALLY TURN OUT NOT TO BE, AND THE PEOPLE YOU THINK **AREN'T** SINCERE USUALLY TURN OUT TO **BE** SINCERE!
THE QUESTION IS...HOW DO YOU TELL THE PHONIES FROM THE REALIES?
THE "**REALIES**"?!
SCHULZ

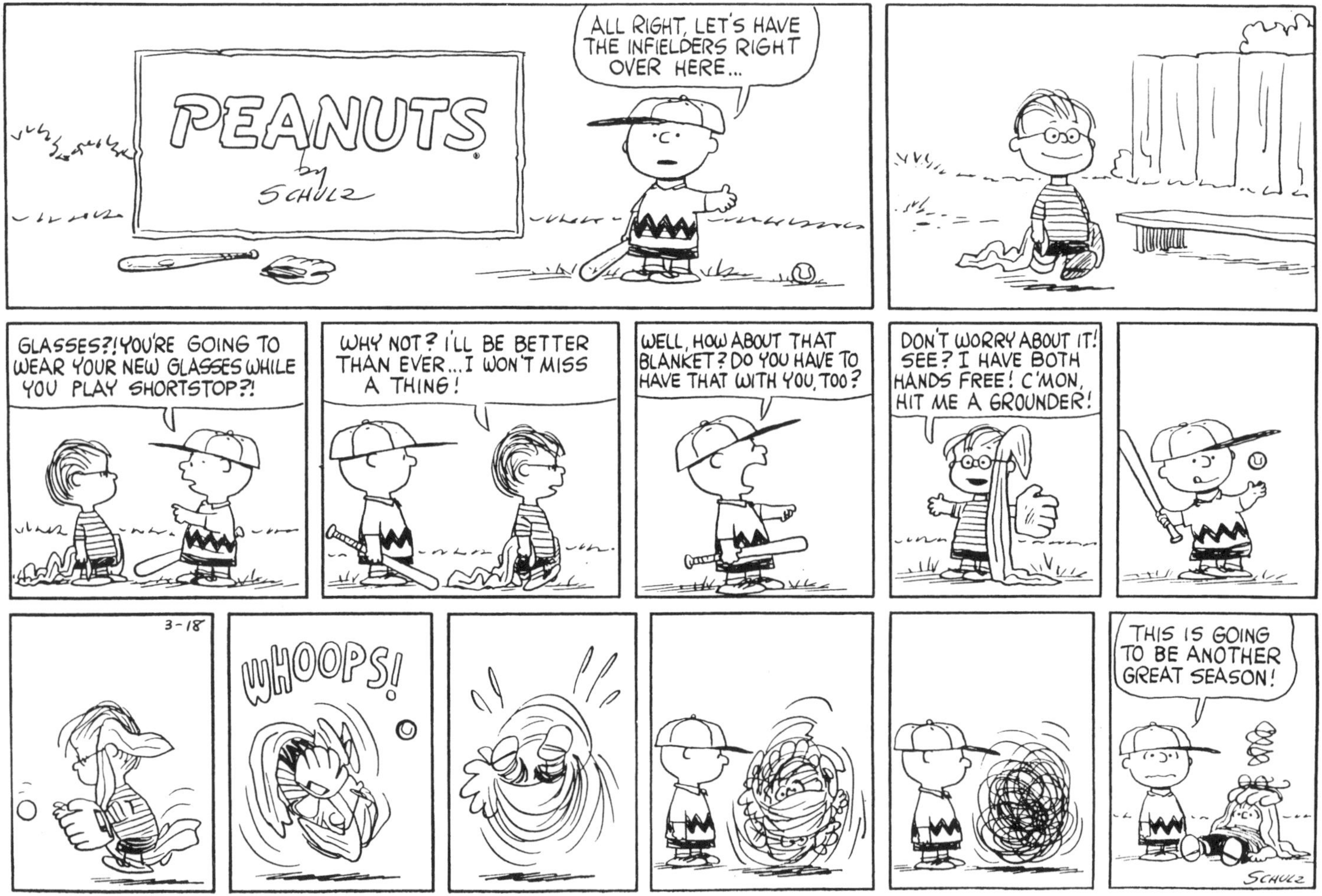
PEANUTS
by SCHULZ
ALL RIGHT, LET'S HAVE THE INFIELDERS RIGHT OVER HERE...
GLASSES?! YOU'RE GOING TO WEAR YOUR NEW GLASSES WHILE YOU PLAY SHORTSTOP?!
WHY NOT? I'LL BE BETTER THAN EVER... I WON'T MISS A THING!
WELL, HOW ABOUT THAT BLANKET? DO YOU HAVE TO HAVE THAT WITH YOU, TOO?
DON'T WORRY ABOUT IT! SEE? I HAVE BOTH HANDS FREE! C'MON, HIT ME A GROUNDER!
3-18
WHOOPS!
THIS IS GOING TO BE ANOTHER GREAT SEASON!
SCHULZ

Panel 1: I'VE DECIDED WE NEED A BASEBALL SCOUT!

Panel 2: WE NEED SOMEONE TO GO OVER, AND MINGLE WITH THE OTHER TEAM, AND FIND OUT THEIR STRENGTH AND WEAKNESSES..

Panel 3: IT CAN BE A VERY DANGEROUS JOB, OF COURSE, BUT IT'S A JOB THAT NEEDS TO BE DONE, AND...

Panel 4: I'VE FOUND YOU A VOLUNTEER!

3-19

Panel 5: YOU WANT ME TO BE A SPY?

NOT A SPY.. A SCOUT! A BASEBALL SCOUT!

Panel 6: I'LL ADMIT IT'S A DANGEROUS JOB, BUT IT HAS TO BE DONE!

Panel 7: NOW, I SUPPOSE THE FIRST QUESTION THAT COMES TO YOUR MIND IS, "**WHY** DOES THIS JOB HAVE TO BE DONE?"

3-20

Panel 8: NO, THE FIRST QUESTION THAT COMES TO MY MIND IS, "**WHY ME?**"

Panel 9: ALL RIGHT, SO I'M A BASEBALL SCOUT...WHAT DO I DO?

YOU GO, AND FIND OUT ALL YOU CAN ABOUT THEIR PITCHERS AND HITTERS..

Panel 10: WRITE EVERYTHING YOU FIND OUT ON THIS SQUARE OF BUBBLE GUM..IF THEY SUSPECT THAT YOU'RE SCOUTING THEM, YOU CAN JUST CHEW UP THE EVIDENCE...

Panel 11: WELL, GOOD LUCK, OL' BUDDY...

THANK YOU, CHARLIE BROWN..

3-21

Panel 12: SOMEHOW I HAVE THE FEELING OF IMPENDING DOOM!

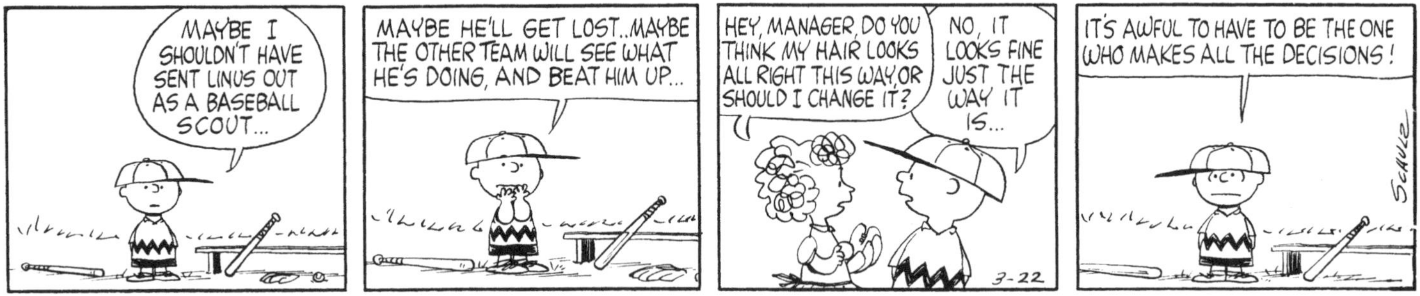
MAYBE I SHOULDN'T HAVE SENT LINUS OUT AS A BASEBALL SCOUT...
MAYBE HE'LL GET LOST..MAYBE THE OTHER TEAM WILL SEE WHAT HE'S DOING, AND BEAT HIM UP...
HEY, MANAGER, DO YOU THINK MY HAIR LOOKS ALL RIGHT THIS WAY, OR SHOULD I CHANGE IT?
NO, IT LOOKS FINE JUST THE WAY IT IS...
3-22
IT'S AWFUL TO HAVE TO BE THE ONE WHO MAKES ALL THE DECISIONS!
SCHULZ

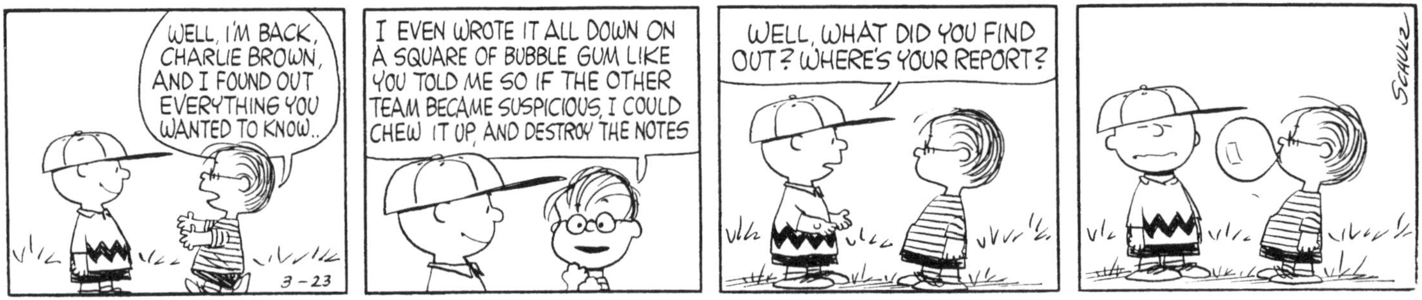
WELL, I'M BACK, CHARLIE BROWN, AND I FOUND OUT EVERYTHING YOU WANTED TO KNOW..
3-23
I EVEN WROTE IT ALL DOWN ON A SQUARE OF BUBBLE GUM LIKE YOU TOLD ME SO IF THE OTHER TEAM BECAME SUSPICIOUS, I COULD CHEW IT UP, AND DESTROY THE NOTES
WELL, WHAT DID YOU FIND OUT? WHERE'S YOUR REPORT?
SCHULZ

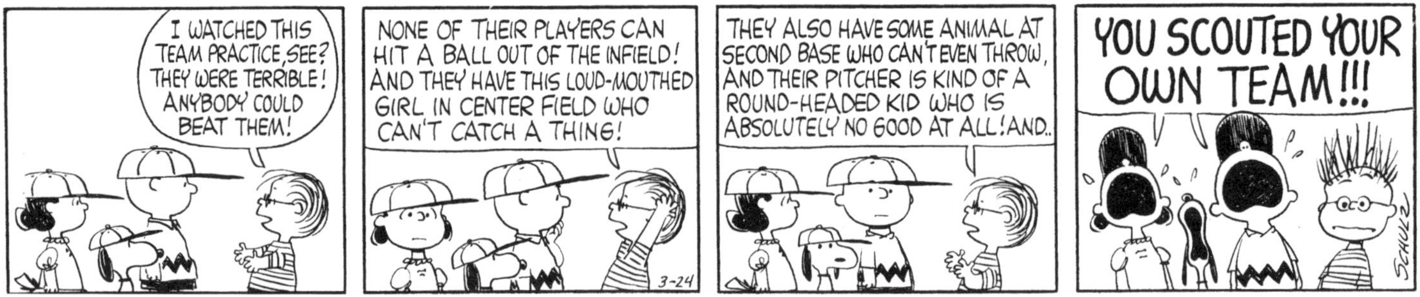
I WATCHED THIS TEAM PRACTICE, SEE? THEY WERE TERRIBLE! ANYBODY COULD BEAT THEM!
NONE OF THEIR PLAYERS CAN HIT A BALL OUT OF THE INFIELD! AND THEY HAVE THIS LOUD-MOUTHED GIRL IN CENTER FIELD WHO CAN'T CATCH A THING!
3-24
THEY ALSO HAVE SOME ANIMAL AT SECOND BASE WHO CAN'T EVEN THROW, AND THEIR PITCHER IS KIND OF A ROUND-HEADED KID WHO IS ABSOLUTELY NO GOOD AT ALL! AND..
YOU SCOUTED YOUR OWN TEAM!!!
SCHULZ

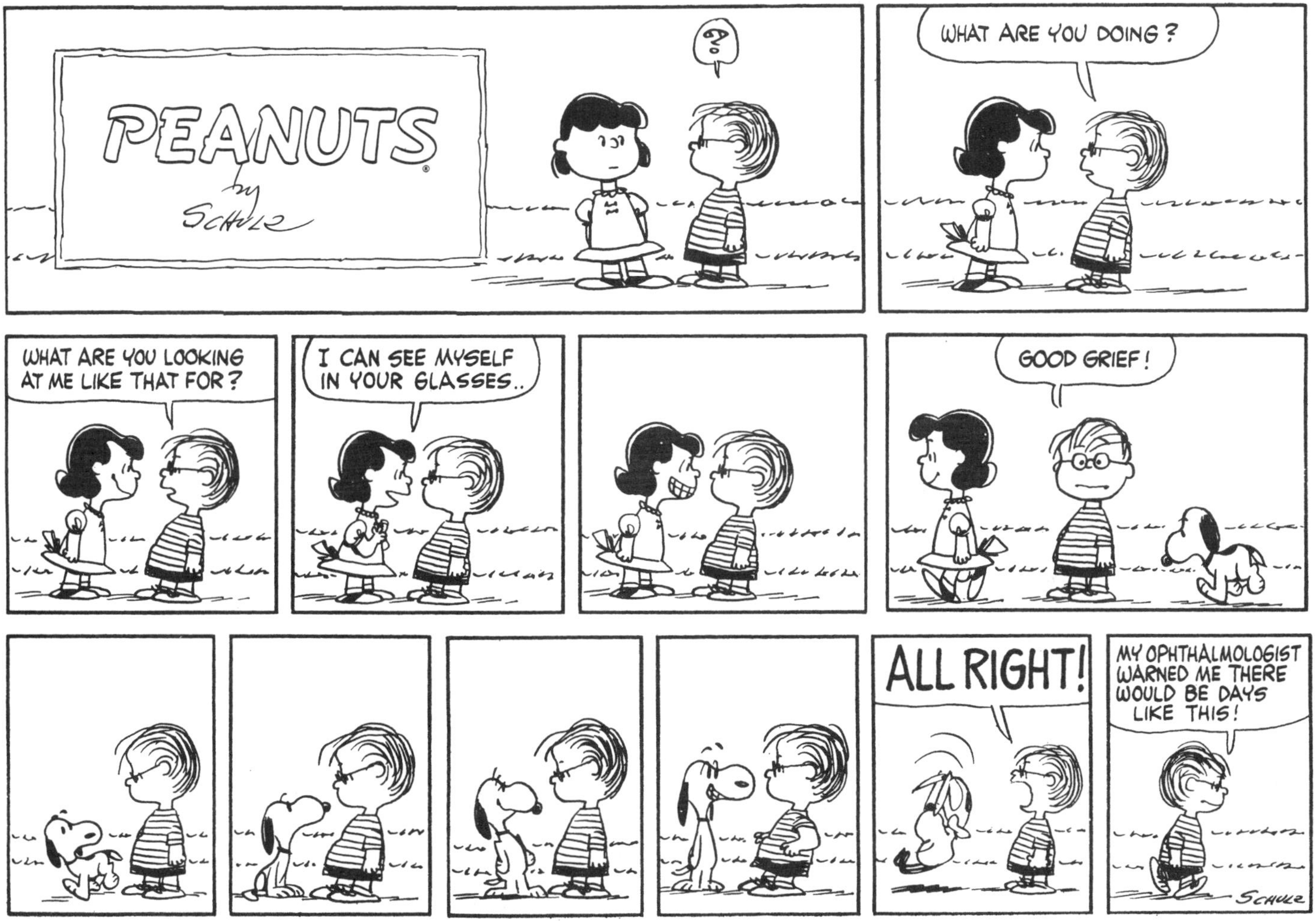
PEANUTS
by
SCHULZ
?
WHAT ARE YOU DOING?
WHAT ARE YOU LOOKING AT ME LIKE THAT FOR?
I CAN SEE MYSELF IN YOUR GLASSES..
GOOD GRIEF!
ALL RIGHT!
MY OPHTHALMOLOGIST WARNED ME THERE WOULD BE DAYS LIKE THIS!
SCHULZ

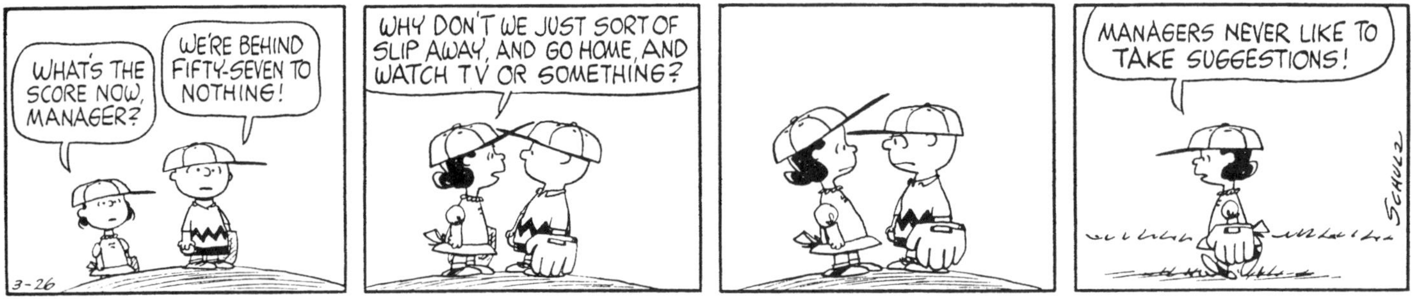
WHAT'S THE SCORE NOW, MANAGER?
WE'RE BEHIND FIFTY-SEVEN TO NOTHING!
3-26
WHY DON'T WE JUST SORT OF SLIP AWAY, AND GO HOME, AND WATCH TV OR SOMETHING?
MANAGERS NEVER LIKE TO TAKE SUGGESTIONS!
SCHULZ

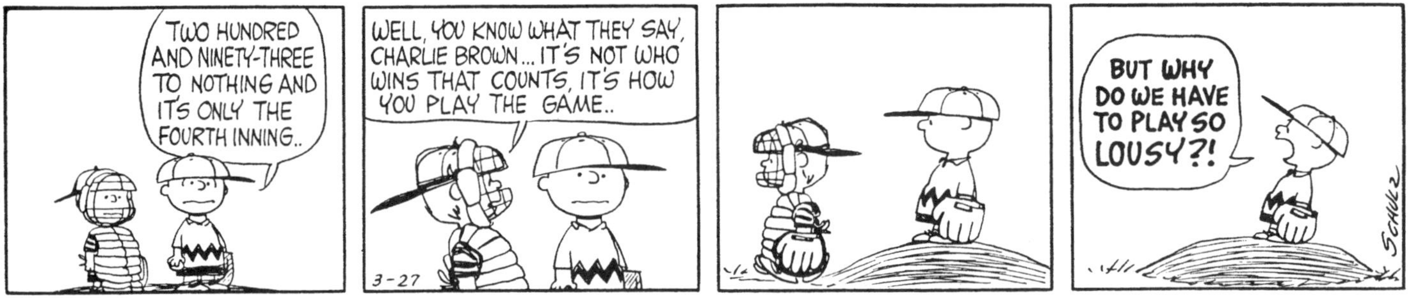
TWO HUNDRED AND NINETY-THREE TO NOTHING AND IT'S ONLY THE FOURTH INNING..
WELL, YOU KNOW WHAT THEY SAY, CHARLIE BROWN... IT'S NOT WHO WINS THAT COUNTS, IT'S HOW YOU PLAY THE GAME..
3-27
BUT WHY DO WE HAVE TO PLAY SO LOUSY?!
SCHULZ

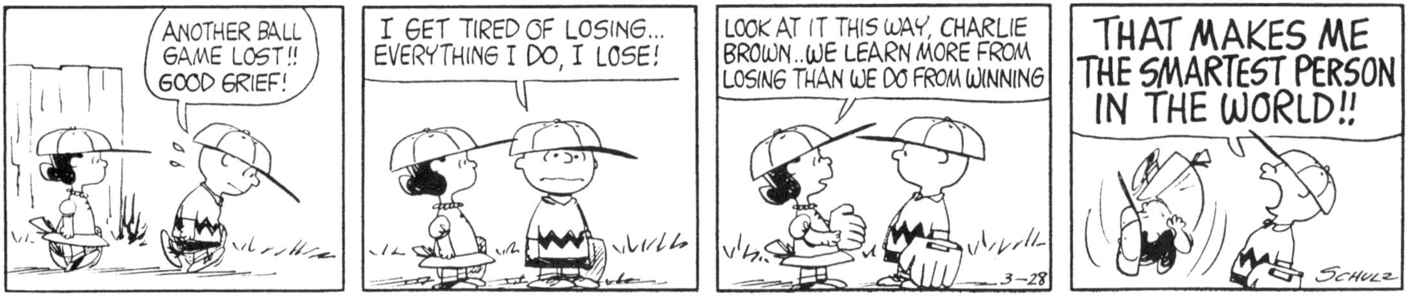
ANOTHER BALL GAME LOST!! GOOD GRIEF!
I GET TIRED OF LOSING... EVERYTHING I DO, I LOSE!
LOOK AT IT THIS WAY, CHARLIE BROWN..WE LEARN MORE FROM LOSING THAN WE DO FROM WINNING
3-28
THAT MAKES ME THE SMARTEST PERSON IN THE WORLD!!
SCHULZ

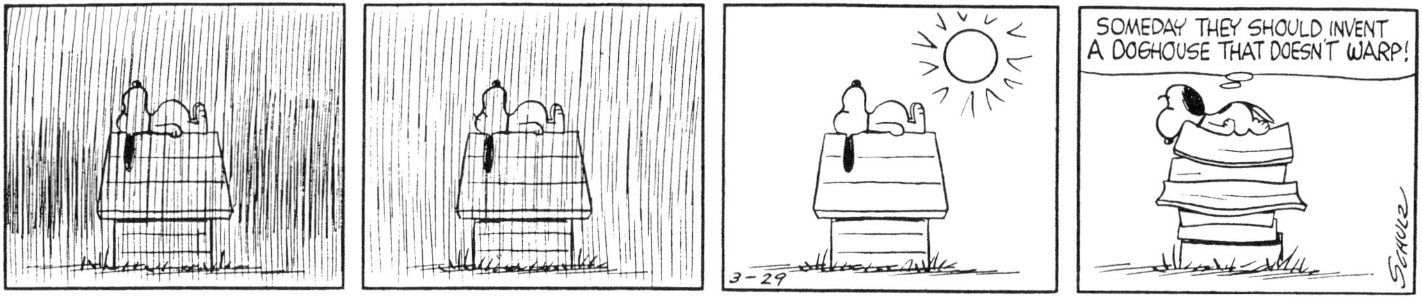
3-29
SOMEDAY THEY SHOULD INVENT A DOGHOUSE THAT DOESN'T WARP!
SCHULZ

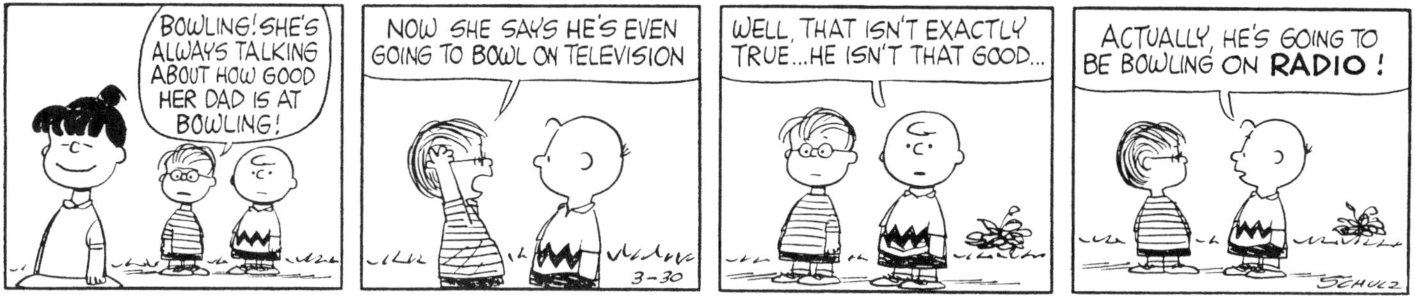
BOWLING! SHE'S ALWAYS TALKING ABOUT HOW GOOD HER DAD IS AT BOWLING!
NOW SHE SAYS HE'S EVEN GOING TO BOWL ON TELEVISION
3-30
WELL, THAT ISN'T EXACTLY TRUE...HE ISN'T THAT GOOD...
ACTUALLY, HE'S GOING TO BE BOWLING ON **RADIO** !
SCHULZ

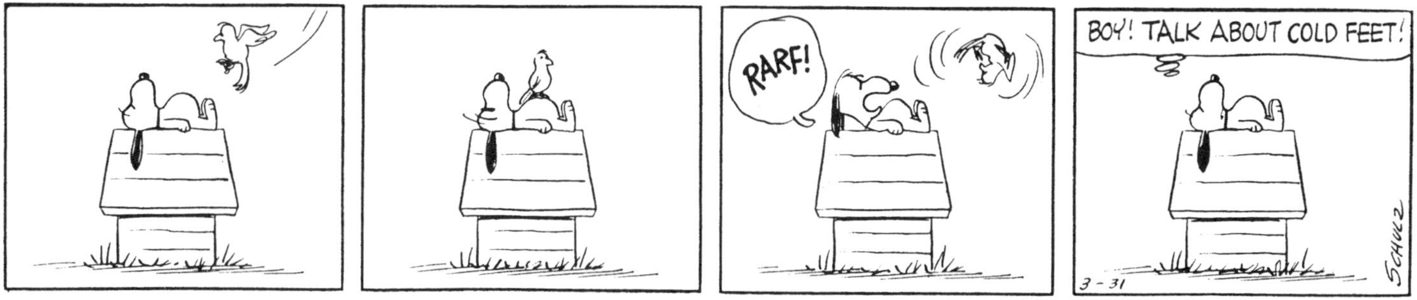
RARF!
BOY! TALK ABOUT COLD FEET!
3-31
SCHULZ

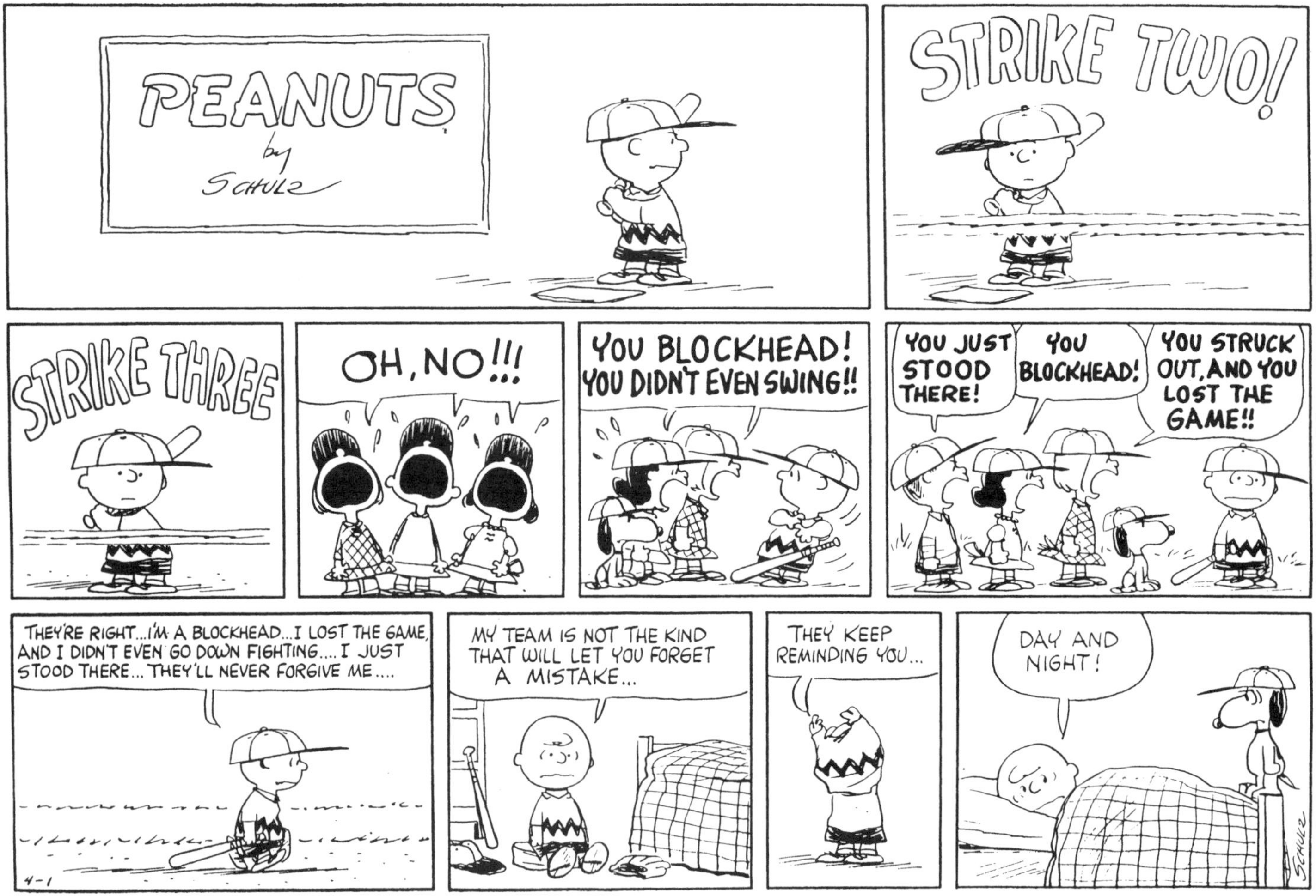
PEANUTS
by
SCHULZ
STRIKE TWO!
STRIKE THREE
OH, NO!!!
YOU BLOCKHEAD! YOU DIDN'T EVEN SWING!!
YOU JUST STOOD THERE!
YOU BLOCKHEAD!
YOU STRUCK OUT, AND YOU LOST THE GAME!!
THEY'RE RIGHT...I'M A BLOCKHEAD...I LOST THE GAME, AND I DIDN'T EVEN GO DOWN FIGHTING.... I JUST STOOD THERE... THEY'LL NEVER FORGIVE ME....
4-1
MY TEAM IS NOT THE KIND THAT WILL LET YOU FORGET A MISTAKE...
THEY KEEP REMINDING YOU...
DAY AND NIGHT!
SCHULZ

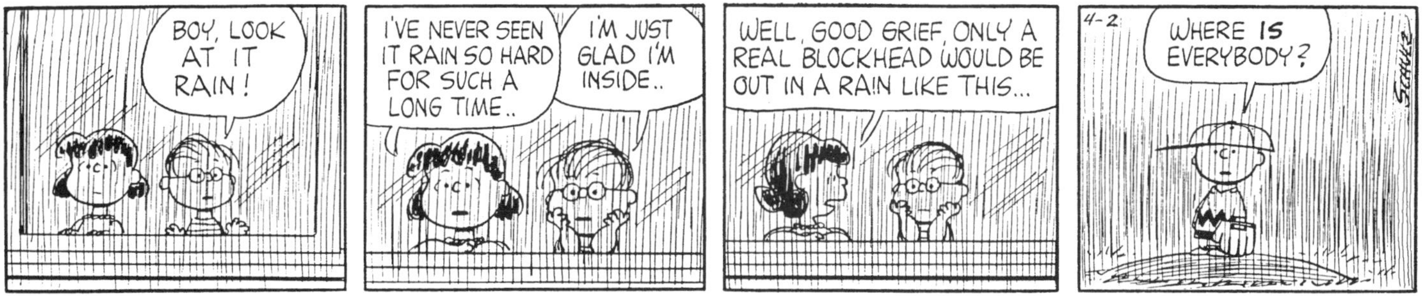
BOY, LOOK AT IT RAIN!
I'VE NEVER SEEN IT RAIN SO HARD FOR SUCH A LONG TIME..
I'M JUST GLAD I'M INSIDE..
WELL, GOOD GRIEF, ONLY A REAL BLOCKHEAD WOULD BE OUT IN A RAIN LIKE THIS...
4-2
WHERE **IS** EVERYBODY?
SCHULZ

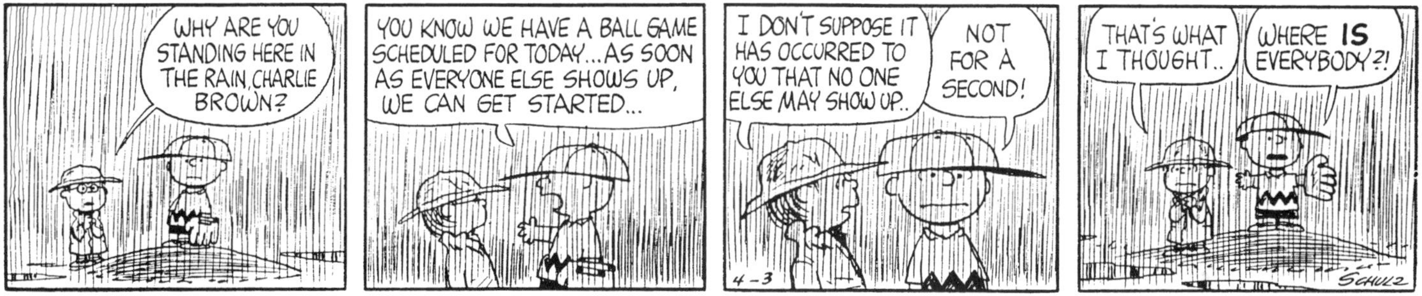
WHY ARE YOU STANDING HERE IN THE RAIN, CHARLIE BROWN?
YOU KNOW WE HAVE A BALL GAME SCHEDULED FOR TODAY...AS SOON AS EVERYONE ELSE SHOWS UP, WE CAN GET STARTED...
I DON'T SUPPOSE IT HAS OCCURRED TO YOU THAT NO ONE ELSE MAY SHOW UP..
NOT FOR A SECOND!
4-3
THAT'S WHAT I THOUGHT..
WHERE **IS** EVERYBODY?!
SCHULZ

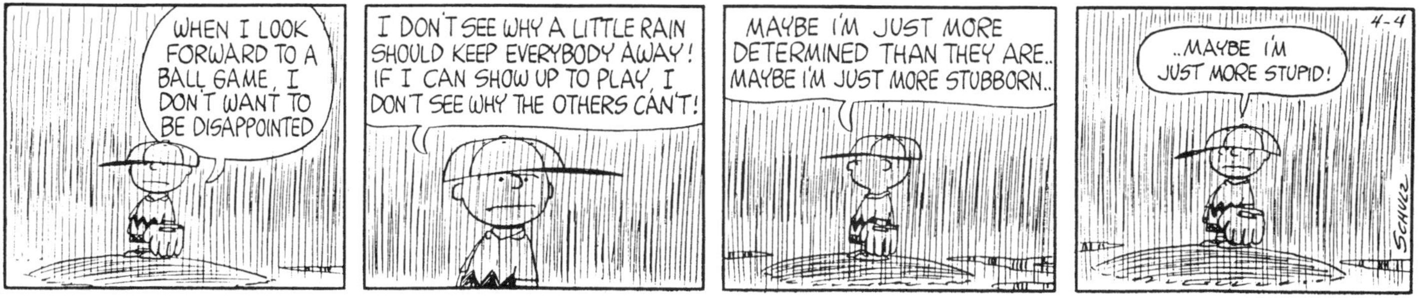
WHEN I LOOK FORWARD TO A BALL GAME, I DON'T WANT TO BE DISAPPOINTED
I DON'T SEE WHY A LITTLE RAIN SHOULD KEEP EVERYBODY AWAY! IF I CAN SHOW UP TO PLAY, I DON'T SEE WHY THE OTHERS CAN'T!
MAYBE I'M JUST MORE DETERMINED THAN THEY ARE.. MAYBE I'M JUST MORE STUBBORN..
4-4
..MAYBE I'M JUST MORE STUPID!
SCHULZ

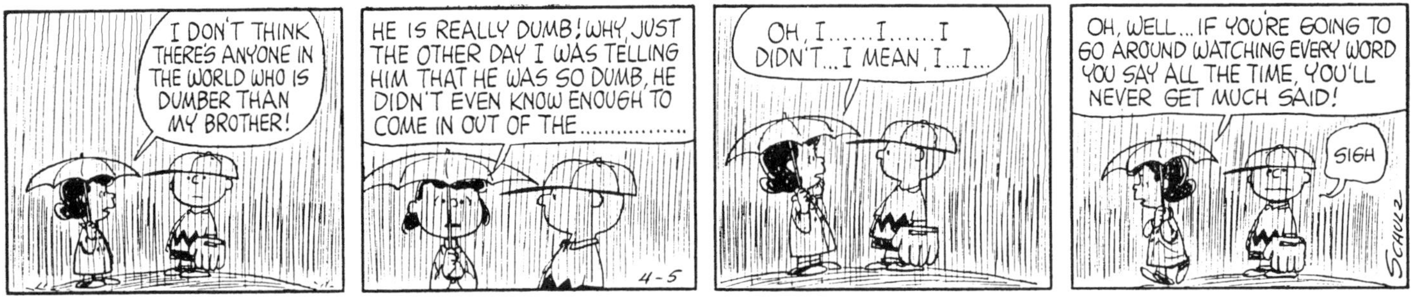
I DON'T THINK THERE'S ANYONE IN THE WORLD WHO IS DUMBER THAN MY BROTHER!
HE IS REALLY DUMB! WHY, JUST THE OTHER DAY I WAS TELLING HIM THAT HE WAS SO DUMB, HE DIDN'T EVEN KNOW ENOUGH TO COME IN OUT OF THE...............
4-5
OH, I......I......I DIDN'T...I MEAN, I...I...
OH, WELL...IF YOU'RE GOING TO GO AROUND WATCHING EVERY WORD YOU SAY ALL THE TIME, YOU'LL NEVER GET MUCH SAID!
SIGH
SCHULZ

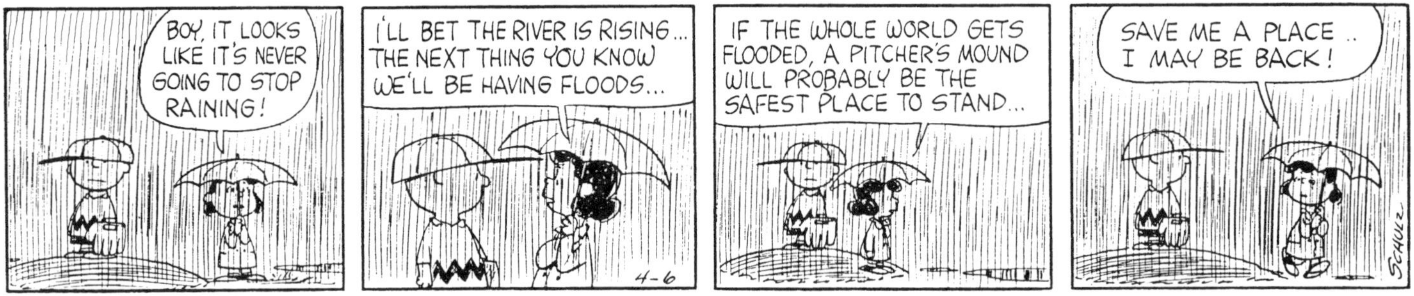
BOY, IT LOOKS LIKE IT'S NEVER GOING TO STOP RAINING!
I'LL BET THE RIVER IS RISING... THE NEXT THING YOU KNOW WE'LL BE HAVING FLOODS...
4-6
IF THE WHOLE WORLD GETS FLOODED, A PITCHER'S MOUND WILL PROBABLY BE THE SAFEST PLACE TO STAND...
SAVE ME A PLACE .. I MAY BE BACK!
SCHULZ

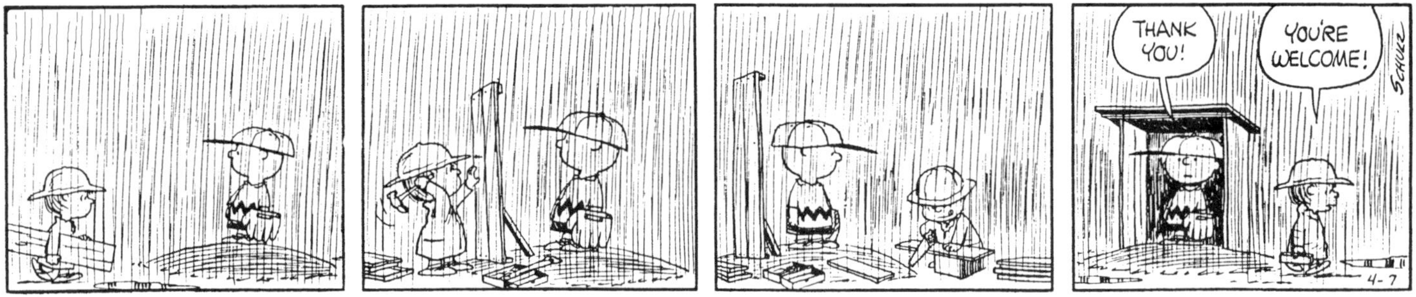
THANK YOU!
YOU'RE WELCOME!
SCHULZ
4-7

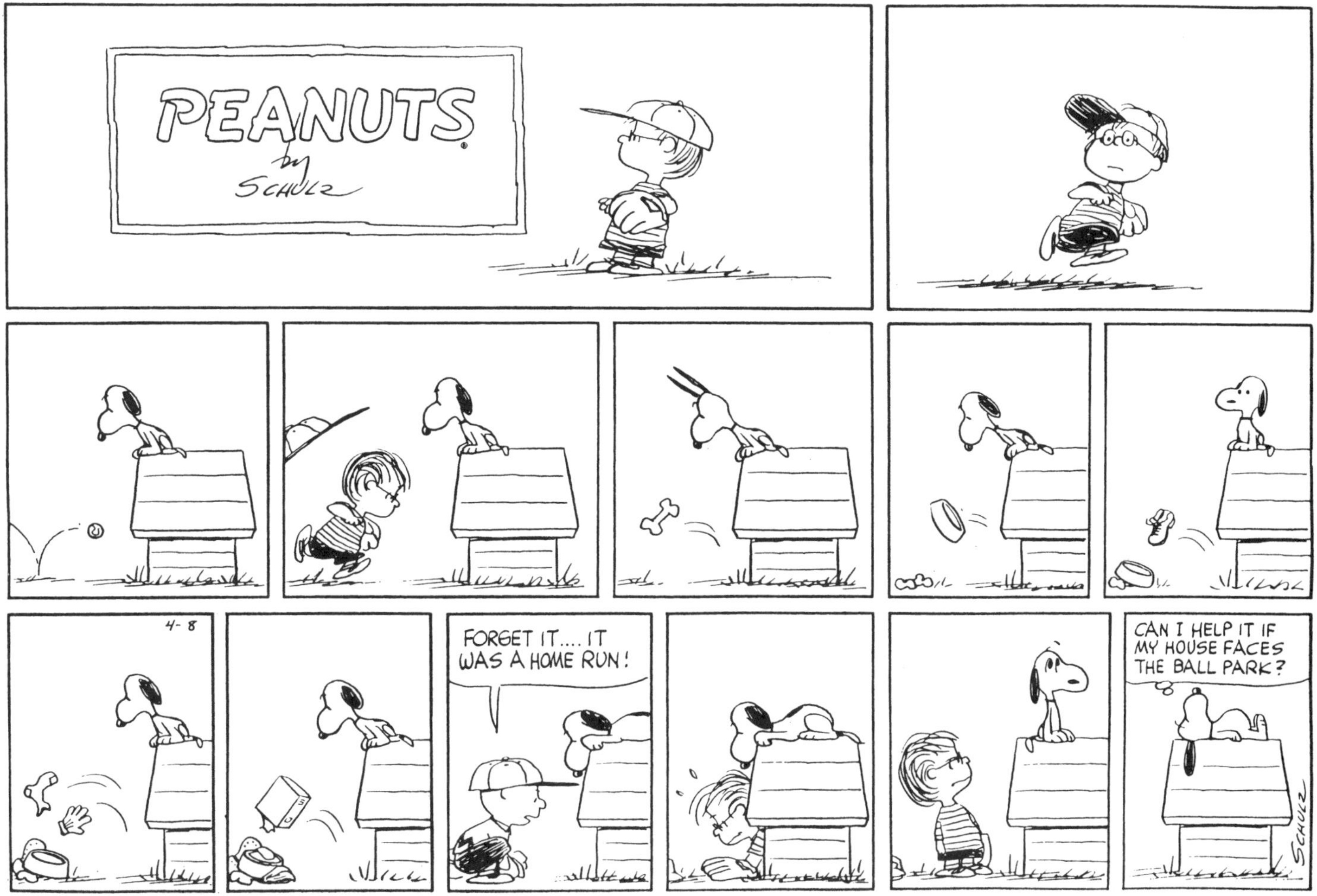
PEANUTS
by SCHULZ
4-8
FORGET IT.... IT WAS A HOME RUN!
CAN I HELP IT IF MY HOUSE FACES THE BALL PARK?
SCHULZ

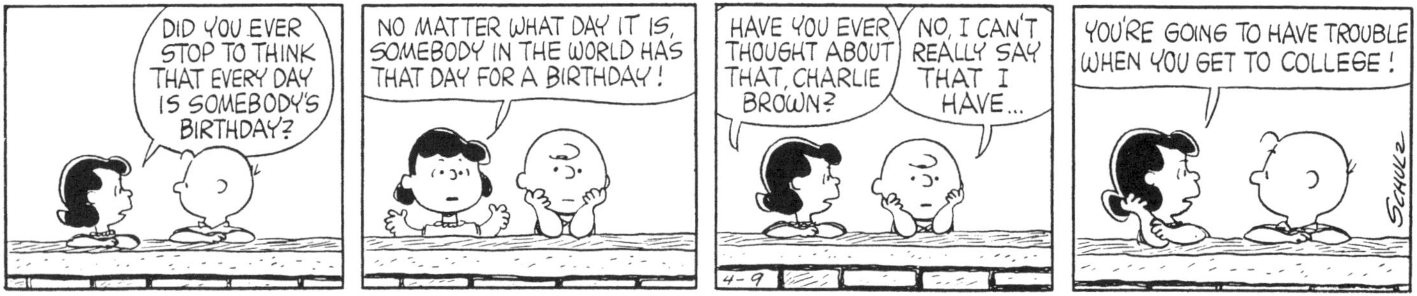
DID YOU EVER STOP TO THINK THAT EVERY DAY IS SOMEBODY'S BIRTHDAY?
NO MATTER WHAT DAY IT IS, SOMEBODY IN THE WORLD HAS THAT DAY FOR A BIRTHDAY!
HAVE YOU EVER THOUGHT ABOUT THAT, CHARLIE BROWN?
NO, I CAN'T REALLY SAY THAT I HAVE...
YOU'RE GOING TO HAVE TROUBLE WHEN YOU GET TO COLLEGE!
SCHULZ
4-9

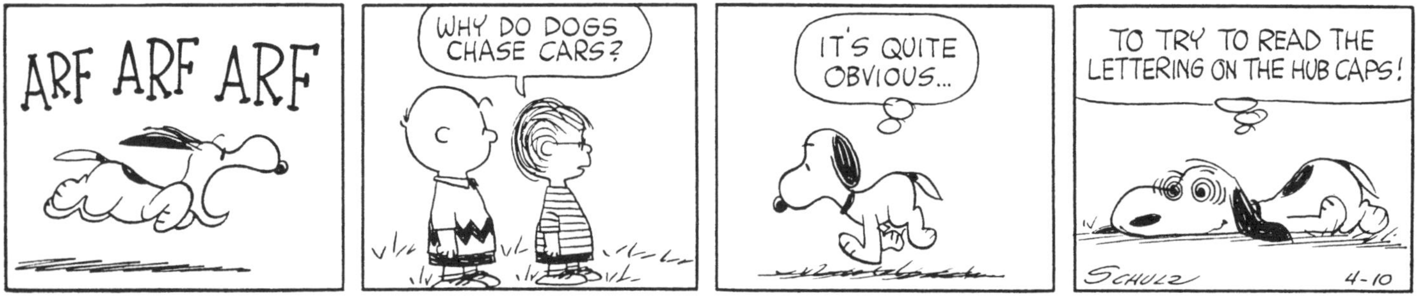
ARF ARF ARF
WHY DO DOGS CHASE CARS?
IT'S QUITE OBVIOUS...
TO TRY TO READ THE LETTERING ON THE HUB CAPS!
SCHULZ
4-10

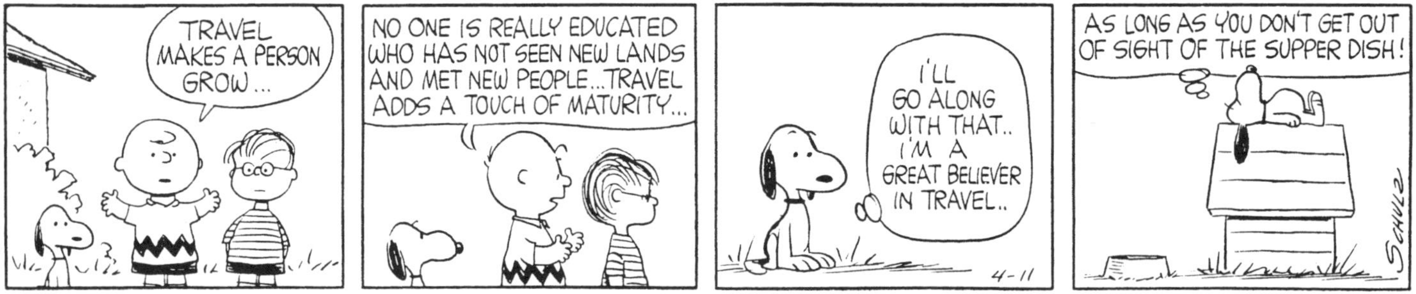
TRAVEL MAKES A PERSON GROW...
NO ONE IS REALLY EDUCATED WHO HAS NOT SEEN NEW LANDS AND MET NEW PEOPLE...TRAVEL ADDS A TOUCH OF MATURITY...
I'LL GO ALONG WITH THAT.. I'M A GREAT BELIEVER IN TRAVEL..
AS LONG AS YOU DON'T GET OUT OF SIGHT OF THE SUPPER DISH!
SCHULZ
4-11

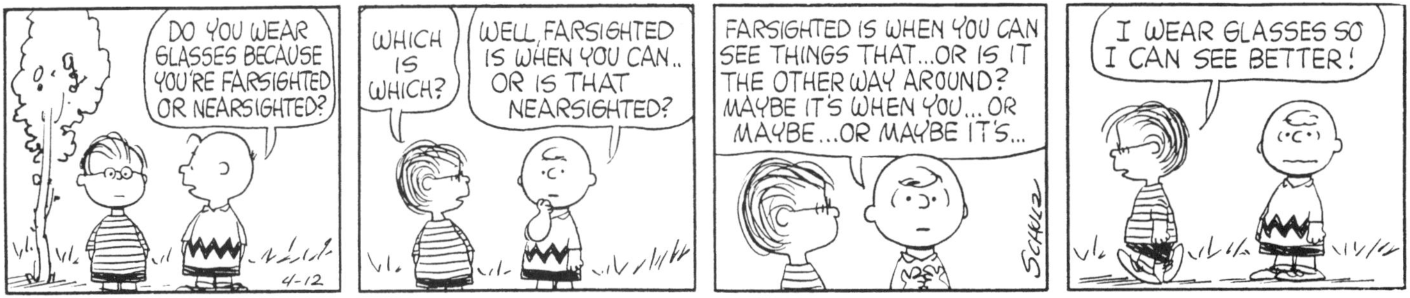
DO YOU WEAR GLASSES BECAUSE YOU'RE FARSIGHTED OR NEARSIGHTED?
WHICH IS WHICH?
WELL, FARSIGHTED IS WHEN YOU CAN.. OR IS THAT NEARSIGHTED?
FARSIGHTED IS WHEN YOU CAN SEE THINGS THAT...OR IS IT THE OTHER WAY AROUND? MAYBE IT'S WHEN YOU...OR MAYBE...OR MAYBE IT'S...
I WEAR GLASSES SO I CAN SEE BETTER!

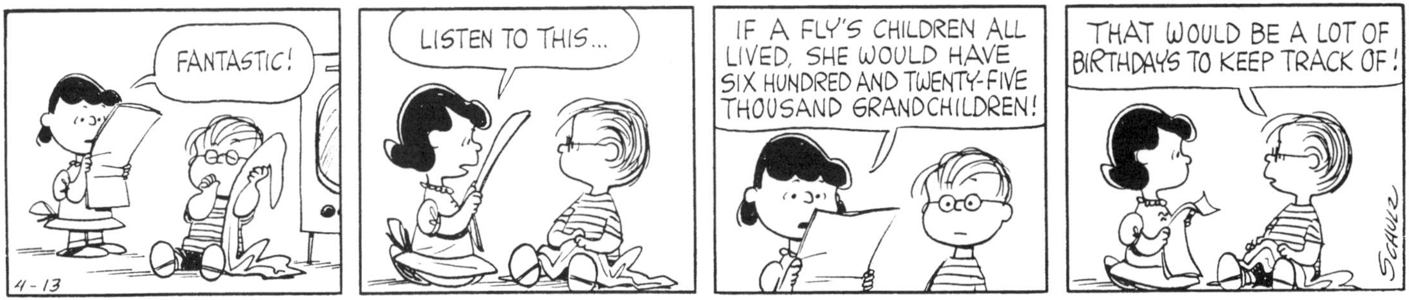
FANTASTIC!
LISTEN TO THIS...
IF A FLY'S CHILDREN ALL LIVED, SHE WOULD HAVE SIX HUNDRED AND TWENTY-FIVE THOUSAND GRANDCHILDREN!
THAT WOULD BE A LOT OF BIRTHDAYS TO KEEP TRACK OF!

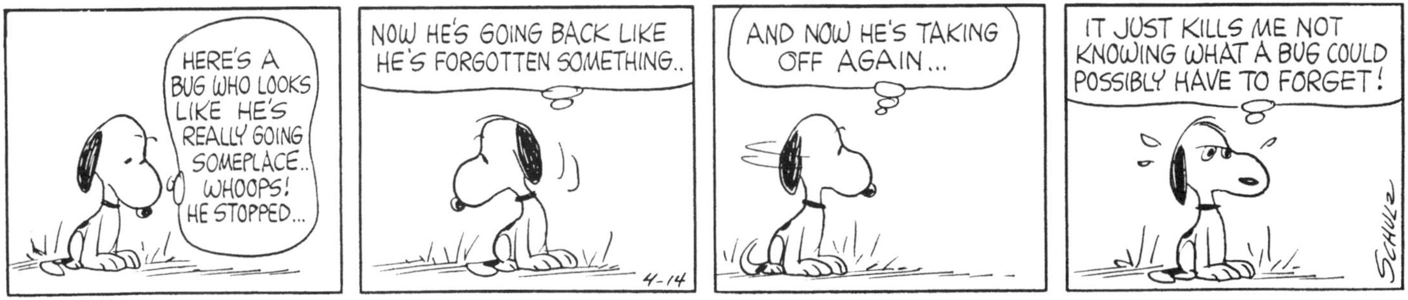
HERE'S A BUG WHO LOOKS LIKE HE'S REALLY GOING SOMEPLACE.. WHOOPS! HE STOPPED...
NOW HE'S GOING BACK LIKE HE'S FORGOTTEN SOMETHING..
AND NOW HE'S TAKING OFF AGAIN...
IT JUST KILLS ME NOT KNOWING WHAT A BUG COULD POSSIBLY HAVE TO FORGET!

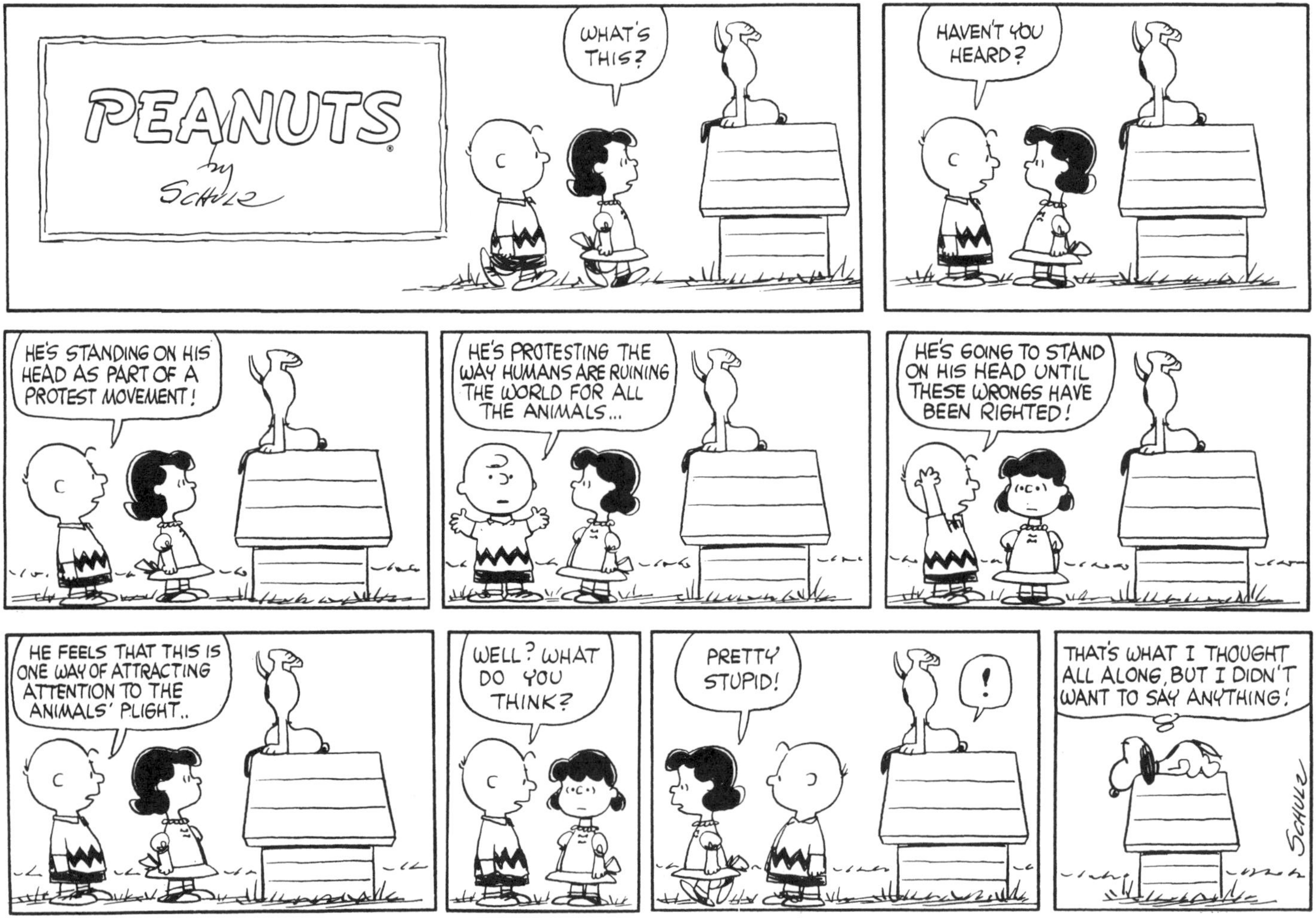
PEANUTS®
by SCHULZ
WHAT'S THIS?
HAVEN'T YOU HEARD?
HE'S STANDING ON HIS HEAD AS PART OF A PROTEST MOVEMENT!
HE'S PROTESTING THE WAY HUMANS ARE RUINING THE WORLD FOR ALL THE ANIMALS...
HE'S GOING TO STAND ON HIS HEAD UNTIL THESE WRONGS HAVE BEEN RIGHTED!
HE FEELS THAT THIS IS ONE WAY OF ATTRACTING ATTENTION TO THE ANIMALS' PLIGHT..
WELL? WHAT DO YOU THINK?
PRETTY STUPID!
!
THAT'S WHAT I THOUGHT ALL ALONG, BUT I DIDN'T WANT TO SAY ANYTHING!
SCHULZ

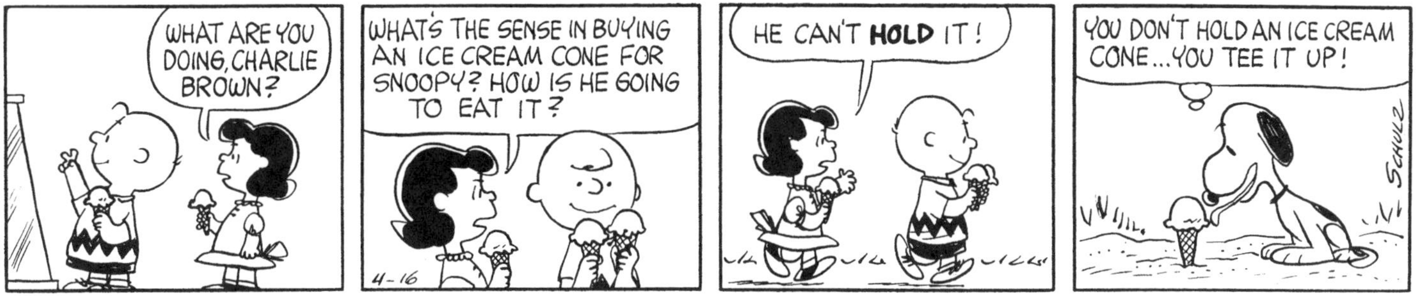
WHAT ARE YOU DOING, CHARLIE BROWN?
WHAT'S THE SENSE IN BUYING AN ICE CREAM CONE FOR SNOOPY? HOW IS HE GOING TO EAT IT?
4-16
HE CAN'T **HOLD** IT!
YOU DON'T HOLD AN ICE CREAM CONE...YOU TEE IT UP!
SCHULZ

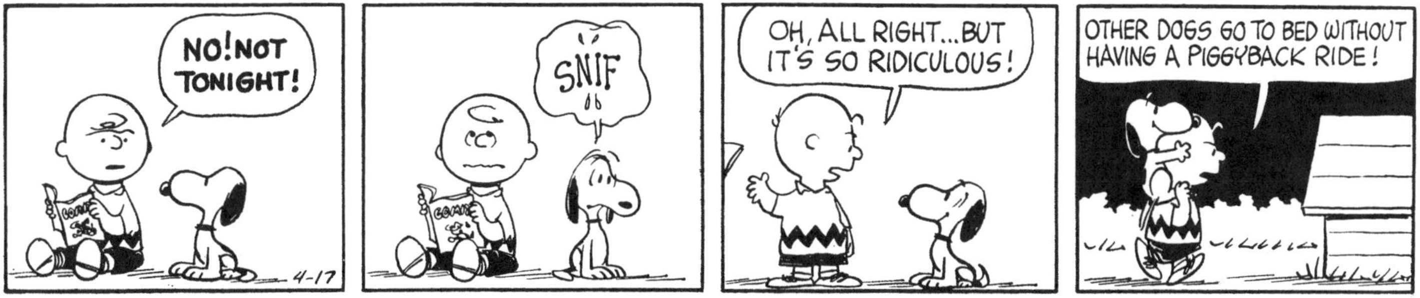
NO! NOT TONIGHT!
4-17
SNIF
OH, ALL RIGHT...BUT IT'S SO RIDICULOUS!
OTHER DOGS GO TO BED WITHOUT HAVING A PIGGYBACK RIDE!

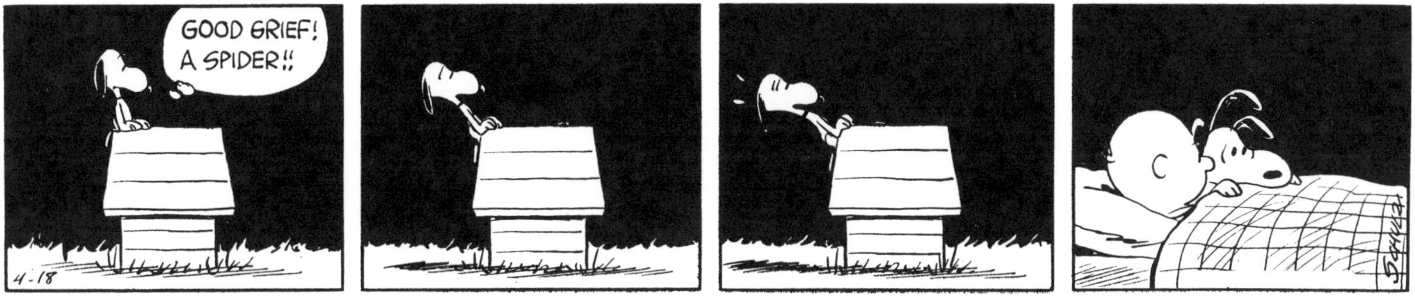
GOOD GRIEF! A SPIDER!!
4-18
SCHULZ

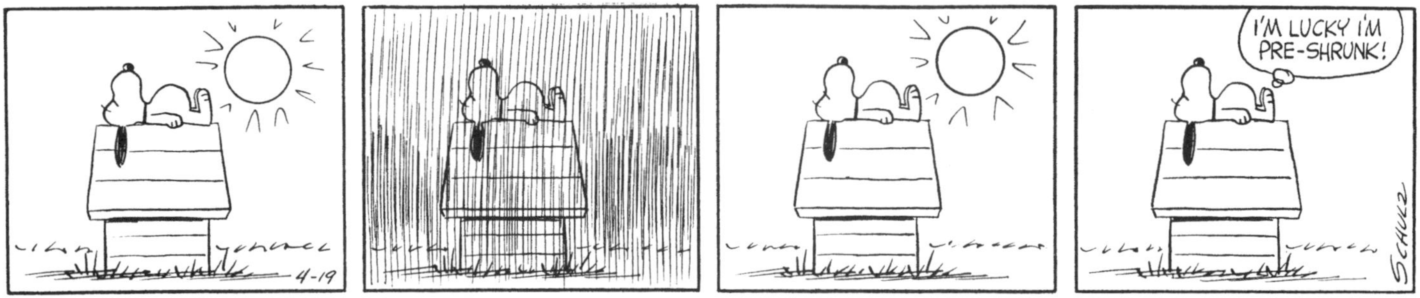
I'M LUCKY I'M PRE-SHRUNK!

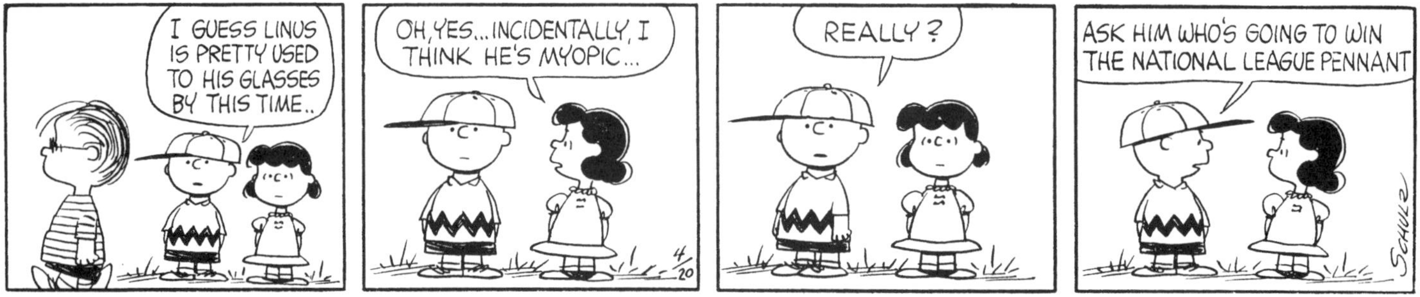
I GUESS LINUS IS PRETTY USED TO HIS GLASSES BY THIS TIME..
OH, YES... INCIDENTALLY, I THINK HE'S MYOPIC...
REALLY?
ASK HIM WHO'S GOING TO WIN THE NATIONAL LEAGUE PENNANT

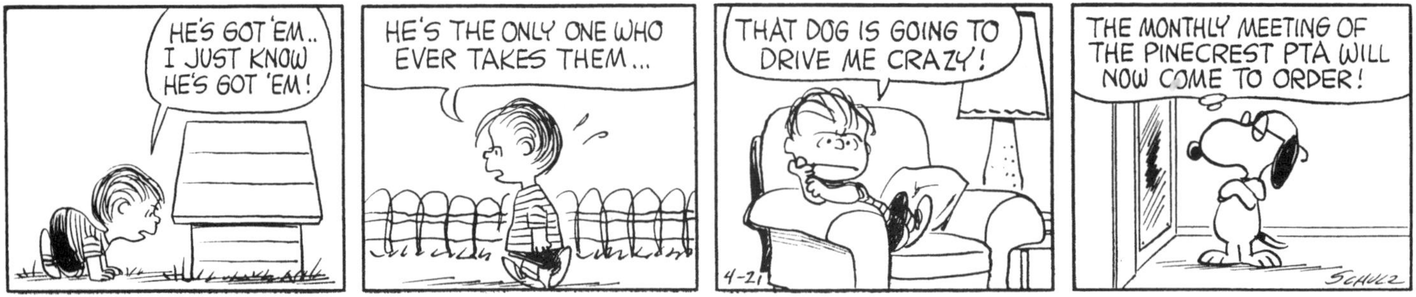
HE'S GOT 'EM.. I JUST KNOW HE'S GOT 'EM!
HE'S THE ONLY ONE WHO EVER TAKES THEM...
THAT DOG IS GOING TO DRIVE ME CRAZY!
THE MONTHLY MEETING OF THE PINECREST PTA WILL NOW COME TO ORDER!

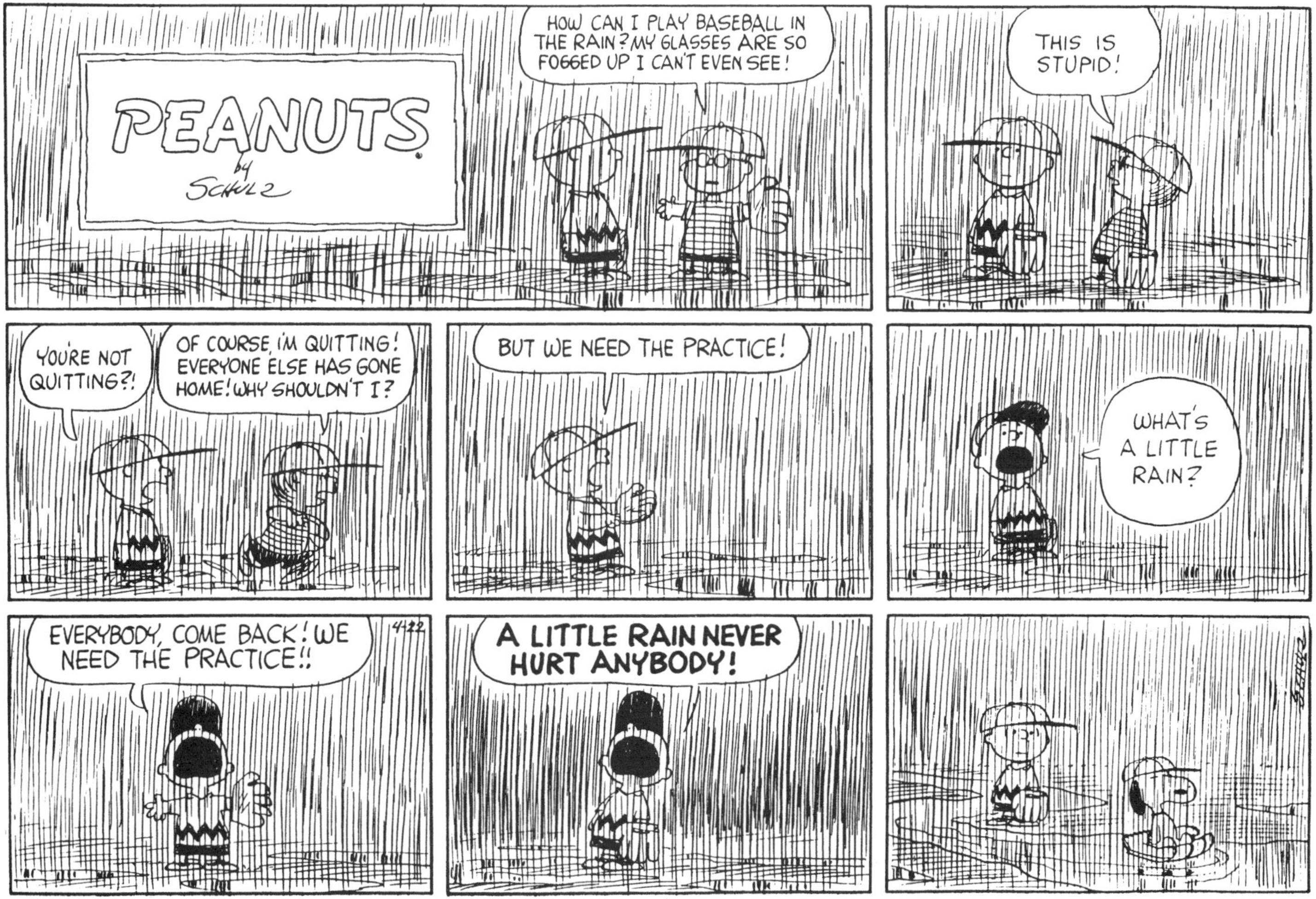
PEANUTS
by
SCHULZ
HOW CAN I PLAY BASEBALL IN THE RAIN? MY GLASSES ARE SO FOGGED UP I CAN'T EVEN SEE!
THIS IS STUPID!
YOU'RE NOT QUITTING?!
OF COURSE, I'M QUITTING! EVERYONE ELSE HAS GONE HOME! WHY SHOULDN'T I?
BUT WE NEED THE PRACTICE!
WHAT'S A LITTLE RAIN?
4-22
EVERYBODY, COME BACK! WE NEED THE PRACTICE!!
A LITTLE RAIN NEVER HURT ANYBODY!
SCHULZ

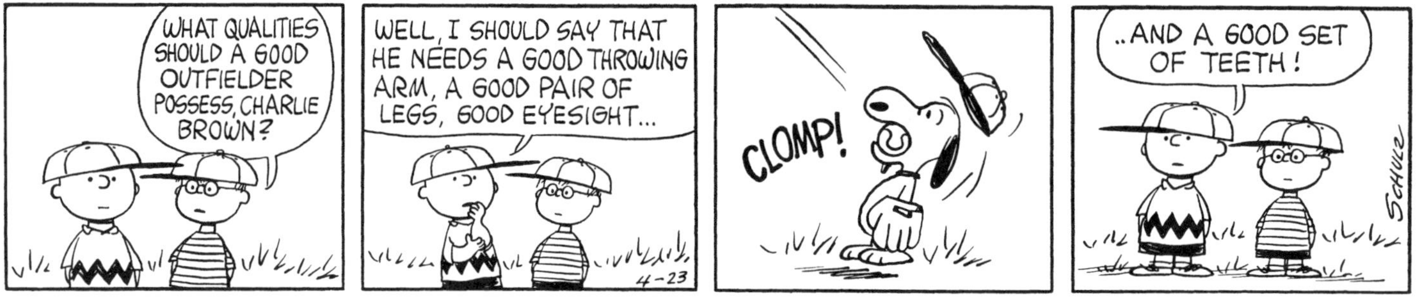
WHAT QUALITIES SHOULD A GOOD OUTFIELDER POSSESS, CHARLIE BROWN?
WELL, I SHOULD SAY THAT HE NEEDS A GOOD THROWING ARM, A GOOD PAIR OF LEGS, GOOD EYESIGHT...
CLOMP!
..AND A GOOD SET OF TEETH!

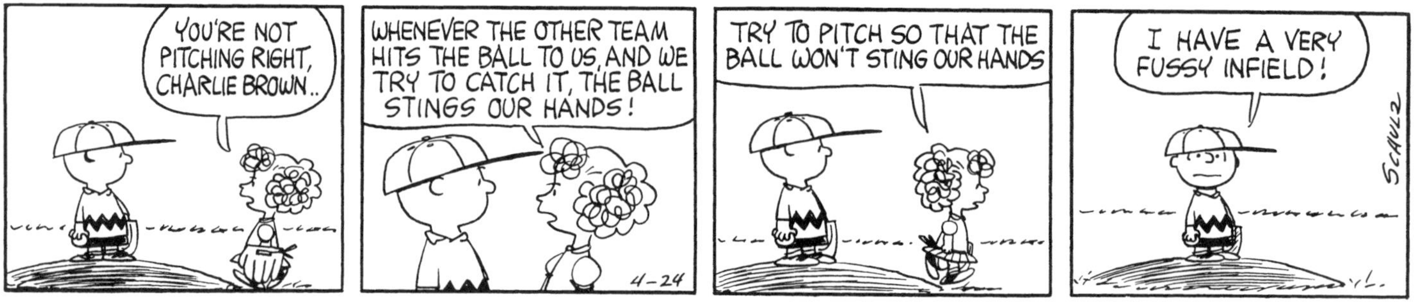
YOU'RE NOT PITCHING RIGHT, CHARLIE BROWN..
WHENEVER THE OTHER TEAM HITS THE BALL TO US, AND WE TRY TO CATCH IT, THE BALL STINGS OUR HANDS!
TRY TO PITCH SO THAT THE BALL WON'T STING OUR HANDS
I HAVE A VERY FUSSY INFIELD!

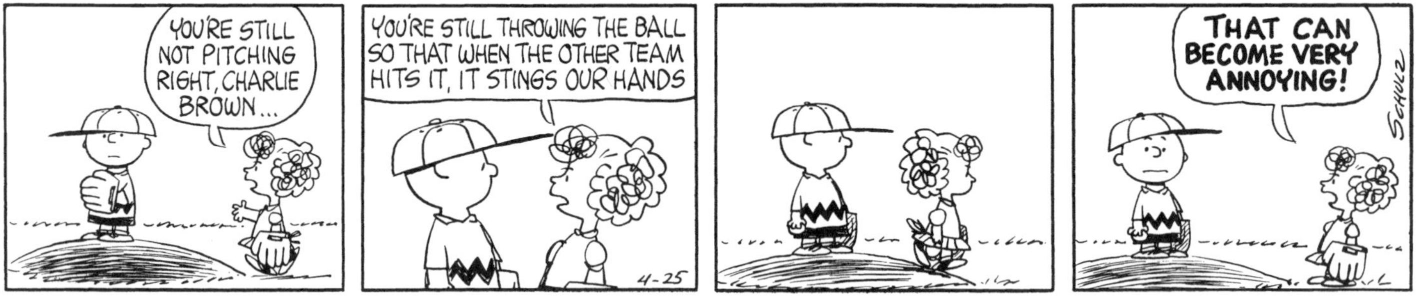
YOU'RE STILL NOT PITCHING RIGHT, CHARLIE BROWN...
YOU'RE STILL THROWING THE BALL SO THAT WHEN THE OTHER TEAM HITS IT, IT STINGS OUR HANDS
THAT CAN BECOME VERY ANNOYING!

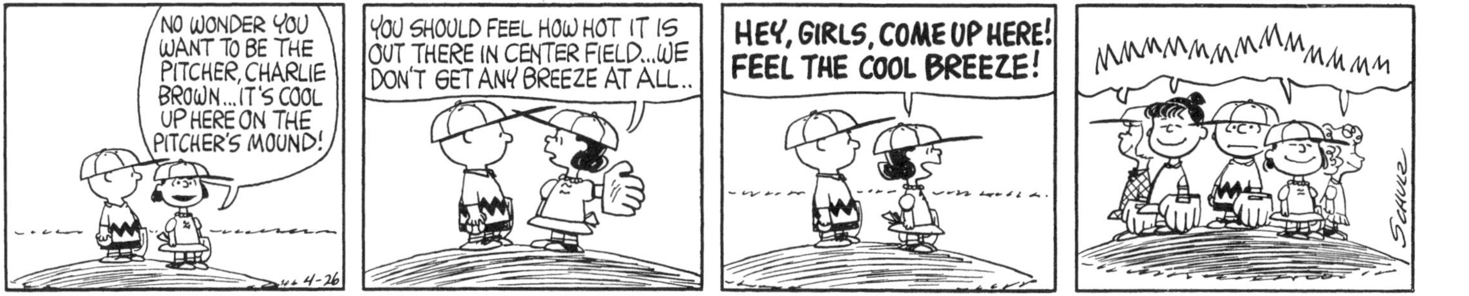
NO WONDER YOU WANT TO BE THE PITCHER, CHARLIE BROWN...IT'S COOL UP HERE ON THE PITCHER'S MOUND!
4-26
YOU SHOULD FEEL HOW HOT IT IS OUT THERE IN CENTER FIELD...WE DON'T GET ANY BREEZE AT ALL..
HEY, GIRLS, COME UP HERE! FEEL THE COOL BREEZE!
MMMMMMMMMMMMMMMMMM
SCHULZ

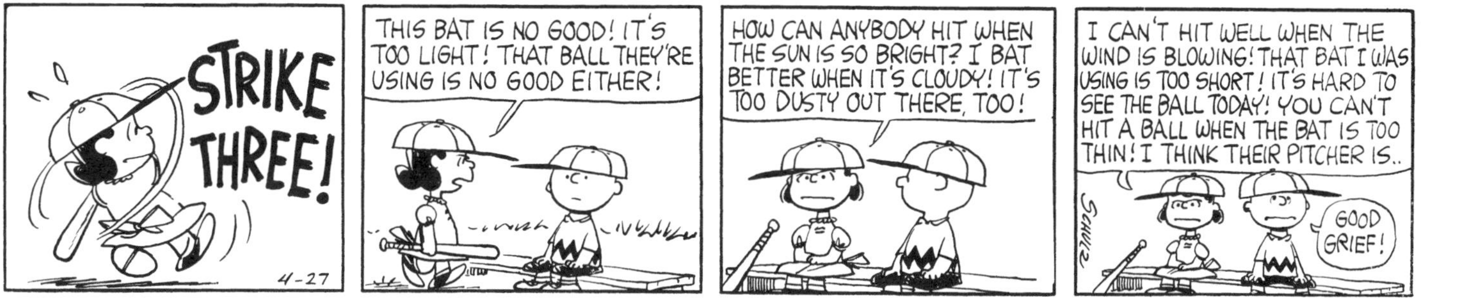
STRIKE THREE!
4-27
THIS BAT IS NO GOOD! IT'S TOO LIGHT! THAT BALL THEY'RE USING IS NO GOOD EITHER!
HOW CAN ANYBODY HIT WHEN THE SUN IS SO BRIGHT? I BAT BETTER WHEN IT'S CLOUDY! IT'S TOO DUSTY OUT THERE, TOO!
I CAN'T HIT WELL WHEN THE WIND IS BLOWING! THAT BAT I WAS USING IS TOO SHORT! IT'S HARD TO SEE THE BALL TODAY! YOU CAN'T HIT A BALL WHEN THE BAT IS TOO THIN! I THINK THEIR PITCHER IS..
GOOD GRIEF!
SCHULZ

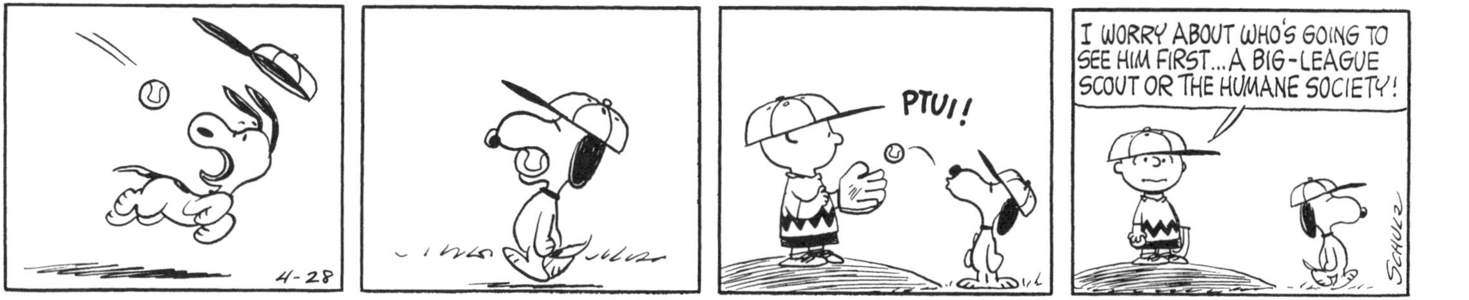
4-28
PTUI!
I WORRY ABOUT WHO'S GOING TO SEE HIM FIRST...A BIG-LEAGUE SCOUT OR THE HUMANE SOCIETY!
SCHULZ

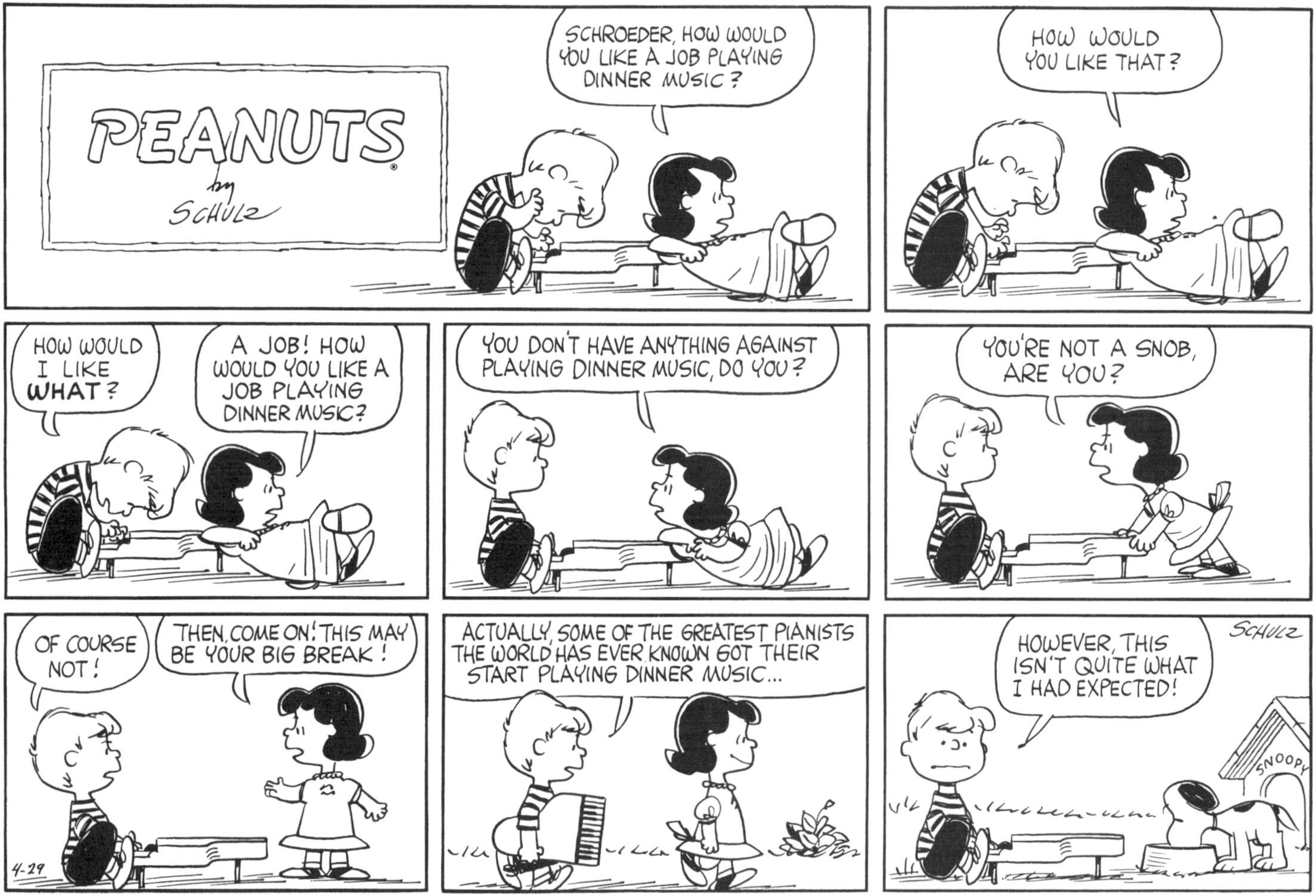
PEANUTS
by SCHULZ
SCHROEDER, HOW WOULD YOU LIKE A JOB PLAYING DINNER MUSIC?
HOW WOULD YOU LIKE THAT?
HOW WOULD I LIKE WHAT?
A JOB! HOW WOULD YOU LIKE A JOB PLAYING DINNER MUSIC?
YOU DON'T HAVE ANYTHING AGAINST PLAYING DINNER MUSIC, DO YOU?
YOU'RE NOT A SNOB, ARE YOU?
OF COURSE NOT!
THEN, COME ON! THIS MAY BE YOUR BIG BREAK!
4-29
ACTUALLY, SOME OF THE GREATEST PIANISTS THE WORLD HAS EVER KNOWN GOT THEIR START PLAYING DINNER MUSIC...
SCHULZ
HOWEVER, THIS ISN'T QUITE WHAT I HAD EXPECTED!
SNOOPY

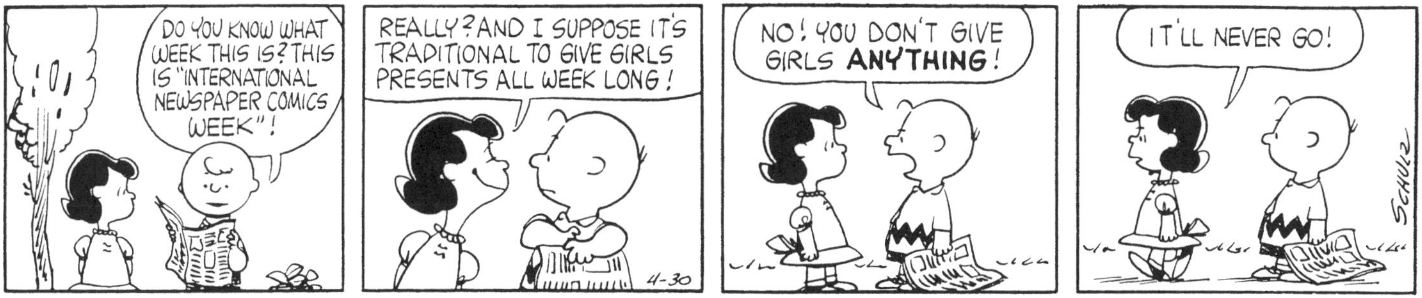
DO YOU KNOW WHAT WEEK THIS IS? THIS IS "INTERNATIONAL NEWSPAPER COMICS WEEK"!
REALLY? AND I SUPPOSE IT'S TRADITIONAL TO GIVE GIRLS PRESENTS ALL WEEK LONG!
4-30
NO! YOU DON'T GIVE GIRLS **ANYTHING**!
IT'LL NEVER GO!
SCHULZ

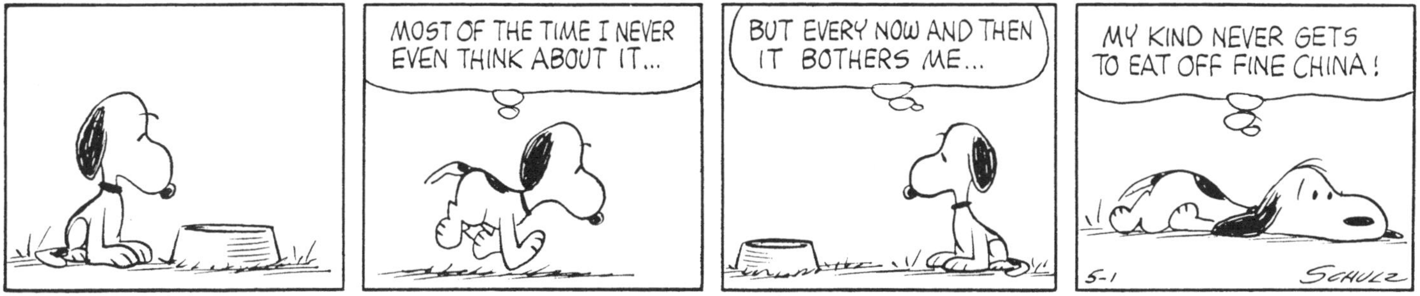
MOST OF THE TIME I NEVER EVEN THINK ABOUT IT...
BUT EVERY NOW AND THEN IT BOTHERS ME...
MY KIND NEVER GETS TO EAT OFF FINE CHINA!
5-1
SCHULZ

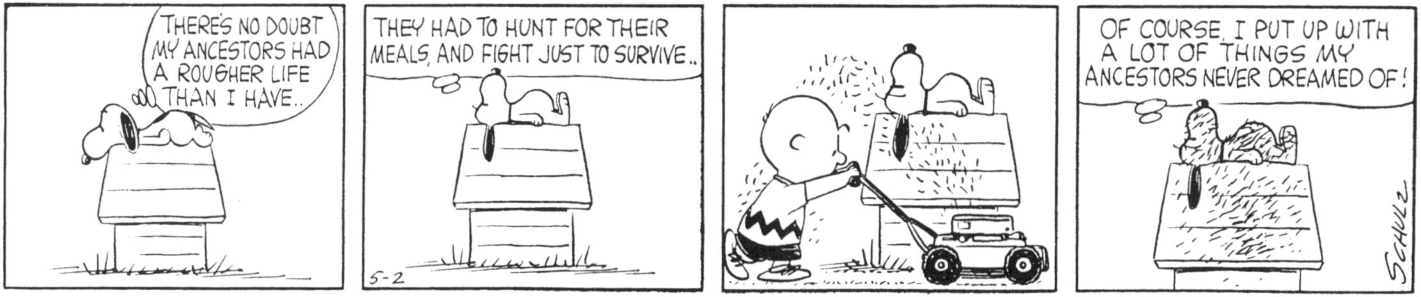
THERE'S NO DOUBT MY ANCESTORS HAD A ROUGHER LIFE THAN I HAVE..
THEY HAD TO HUNT FOR THEIR MEALS, AND FIGHT JUST TO SURVIVE..
5-2
OF COURSE, I PUT UP WITH A LOT OF THINGS MY ANCESTORS NEVER DREAMED OF!
SCHULZ

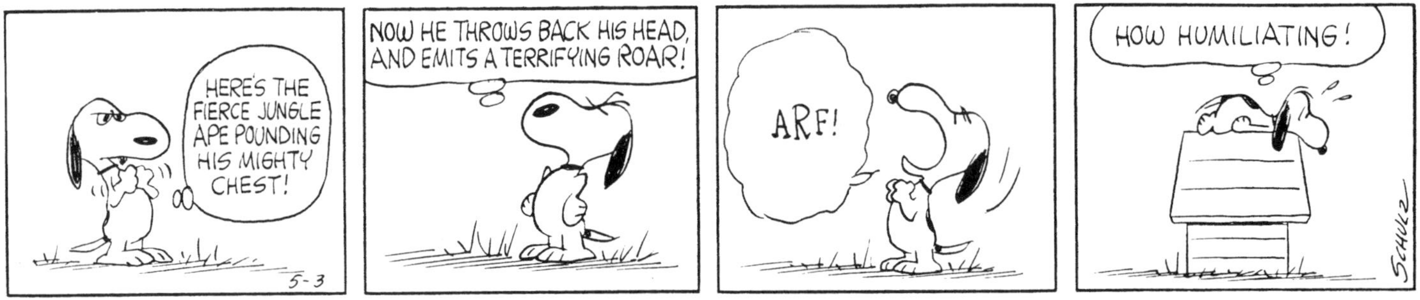
HERE'S THE FIERCE JUNGLE APE POUNDING HIS MIGHTY CHEST!
5-3
NOW HE THROWS BACK HIS HEAD, AND EMITS A TERRIFYING ROAR!
ARF!
HOW HUMILIATING!
SCHULZ

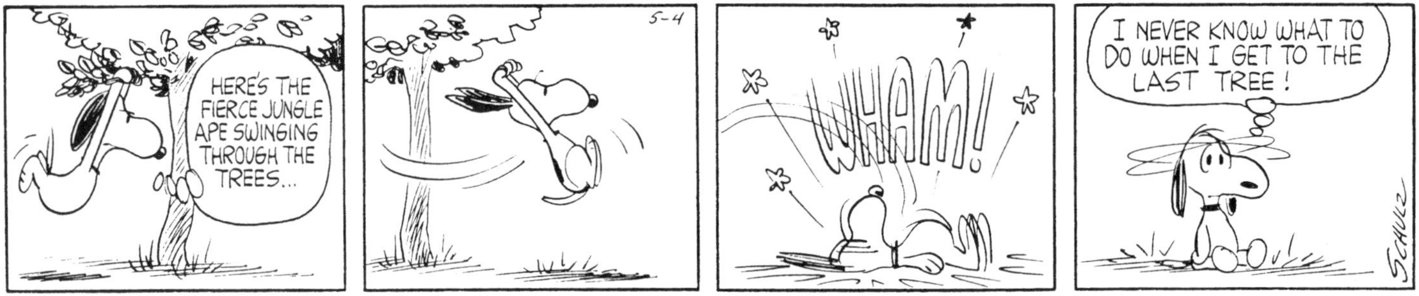
HERE'S THE FIERCE JUNGLE APE SWINGING THROUGH THE TREES...
5-4
WHAM!
I NEVER KNOW WHAT TO DO WHEN I GET TO THE LAST TREE!
SCHULZ

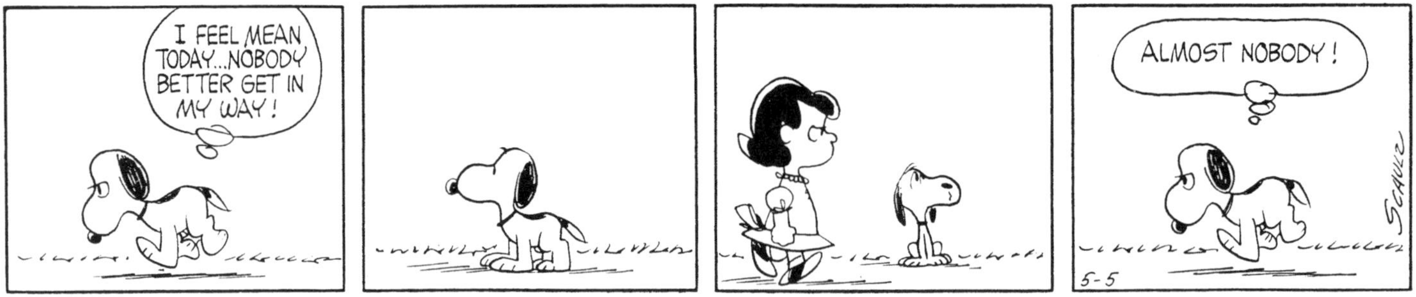
I FEEL MEAN TODAY...NOBODY BETTER GET IN MY WAY!
ALMOST NOBODY!
5-5
SCHULZ

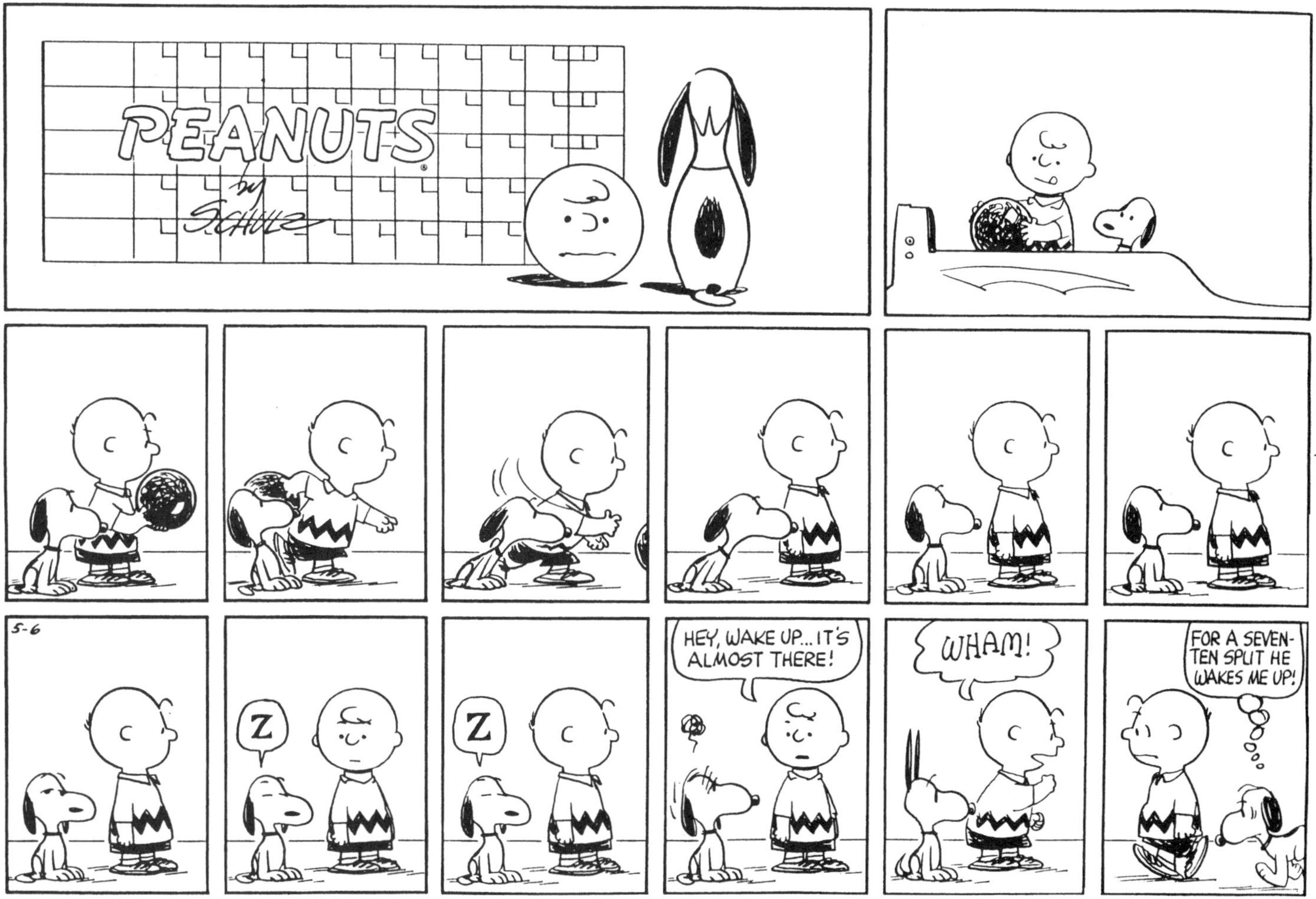
PEANUTS
by SCHULZ
5-6
Z
Z
HEY, WAKE UP... IT'S ALMOST THERE!
WHAM!
FOR A SEVEN-TEN SPLIT HE WAKES ME UP!

Panel 1: THIS IS A REPORT ON WHAT SORT OF MEN MAKE THE BEST HUSBANDS

Panel 2: DENTISTS, DRAFTSMEN, HOCKEY PLAYERS, WELL-DIGGERS AND LUMBER SALESMEN RATE THE HIGHEST... PIANO PLAYERS RATE SHOCKINGLY LOW!

Panel 3: WHERE DID YOU GET A REPORT LIKE THAT?

Panel 4: I JUST MADE IT UP!

Panel 5: SCHROEDER, DO YOU THINK A PRETTY GIRL IS LIKE A MELODY?

Panel 6: I CAN'T SAY... I'VE NEVER KNOWN ANY PRETTY GIRLS!

Panel 8: MAY YOUR STUPID PIANO BE DEVOURED BY TERMITES!

Panel 9: I HAVE A FRIEND WHO PLAYS THE ACCORDION..

Panel 10: HE CAN PLAY POLKAS, WALTZES, SCHOTTISHES...ALL SORTS OF THINGS...YOU KNOW, THE KIND OF TUNES THAT PEOPLE LIKE TO HEAR

Panel 11: AAUGH!

Panel 12: I KNEW THAT WOULD GET HIM!

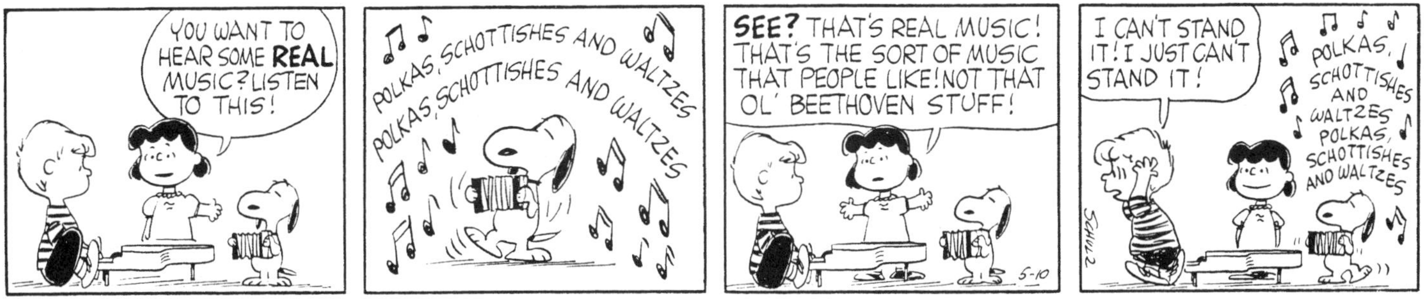
YOU WANT TO HEAR SOME **REAL** MUSIC? LISTEN TO THIS!
POLKAS, SCHOTTISHES AND WALTZES
POLKAS, SCHOTTISHES AND WALTZES
SEE? THAT'S REAL MUSIC! THAT'S THE SORT OF MUSIC THAT PEOPLE LIKE! NOT THAT OL' BEETHOVEN STUFF!
5-10
I CAN'T STAND IT! I JUST CAN'T STAND IT!
POLKAS, SCHOTTISHES AND WALTZES
POLKAS, SCHOTTISHES AND WALTZES
SCHULZ

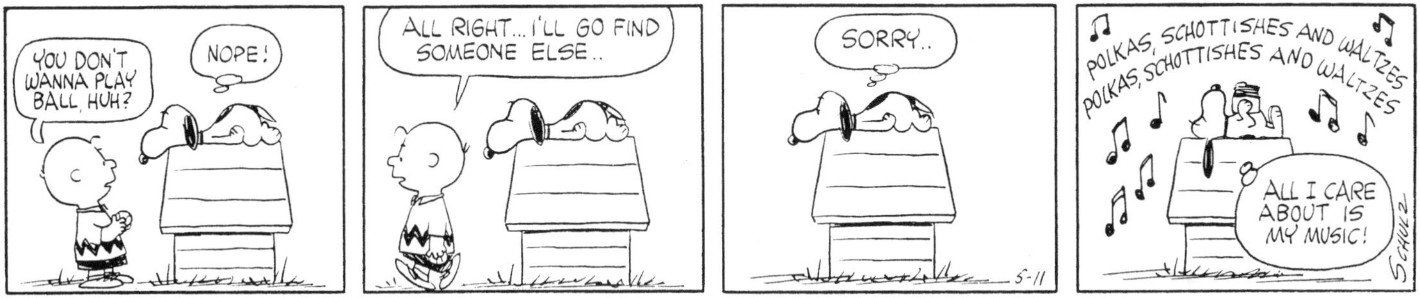
YOU DON'T WANNA PLAY BALL, HUH?
NOPE!
ALL RIGHT... I'LL GO FIND SOMEONE ELSE..
SORRY..
5-11
POLKAS, SCHOTTISHES AND WALTZES
POLKAS, SCHOTTISHES AND WALTZES
ALL I CARE ABOUT IS MY MUSIC!
SCHULZ

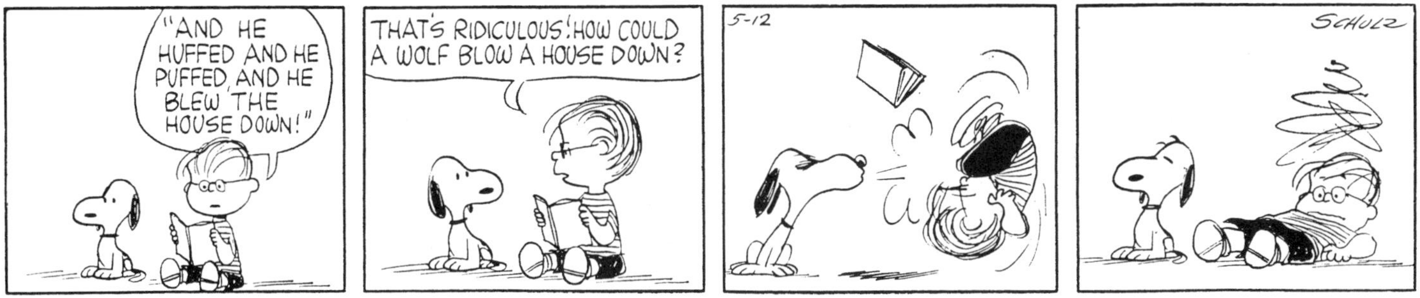
"AND HE HUFFED AND HE PUFFED, AND HE BLEW THE HOUSE DOWN!"
THAT'S RIDICULOUS! HOW COULD A WOLF BLOW A HOUSE DOWN?
5-12
SCHULZ

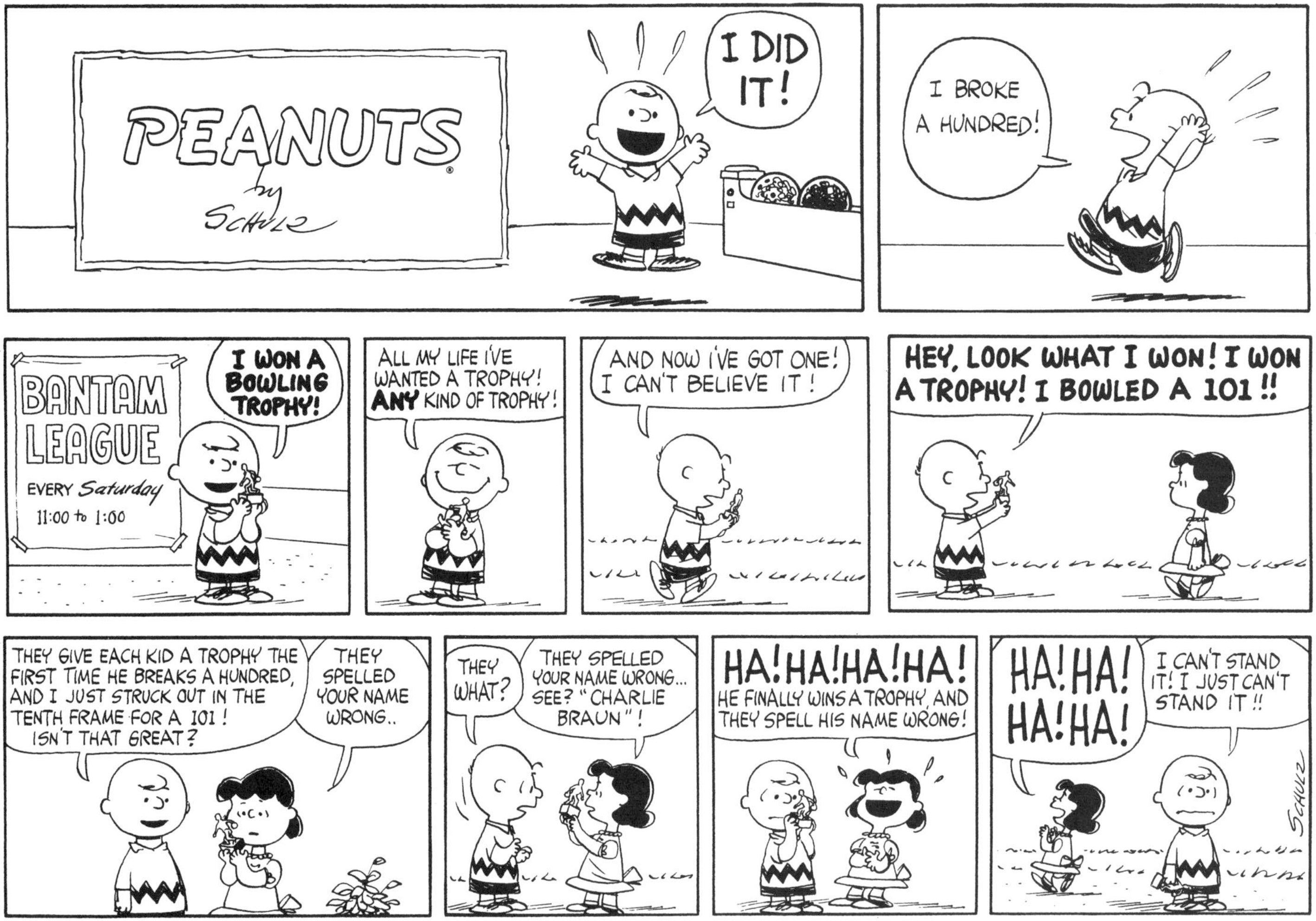
PEANUTS
by Schulz
I DID IT!
I BROKE A HUNDRED!
BANTAM LEAGUE
EVERY Saturday
11:00 to 1:00
I WON A BOWLING TROPHY!
ALL MY LIFE I'VE WANTED A TROPHY! ANY KIND OF TROPHY!
AND NOW I'VE GOT ONE! I CAN'T BELIEVE IT!
HEY, LOOK WHAT I WON! I WON A TROPHY! I BOWLED A 101!!
THEY GIVE EACH KID A TROPHY THE FIRST TIME HE BREAKS A HUNDRED, AND I JUST STRUCK OUT IN THE TENTH FRAME FOR A 101! ISN'T THAT GREAT?
THEY SPELLED YOUR NAME WRONG..
THEY WHAT?
THEY SPELLED YOUR NAME WRONG... SEE? "CHARLIE BRAUN"!
HA! HA! HA! HA!
HE FINALLY WINS A TROPHY, AND THEY SPELL HIS NAME WRONG!
HA! HA! HA! HA!
I CAN'T STAND IT! I JUST CAN'T STAND IT!!
SCHULZ

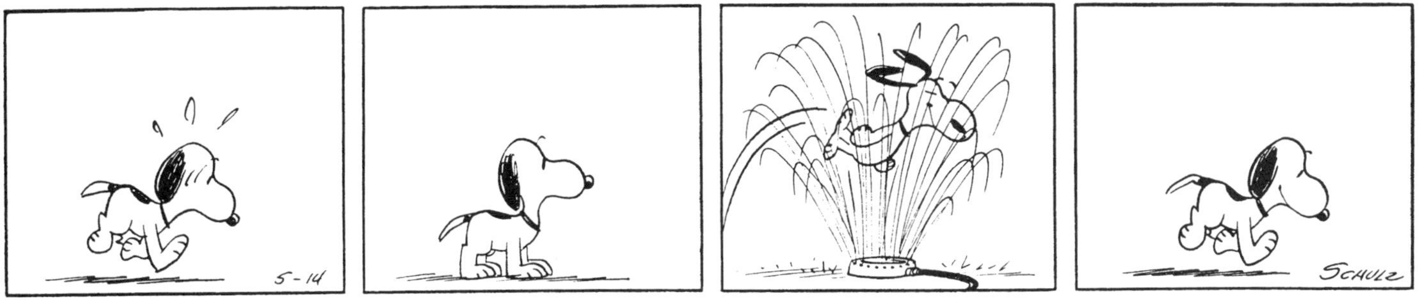

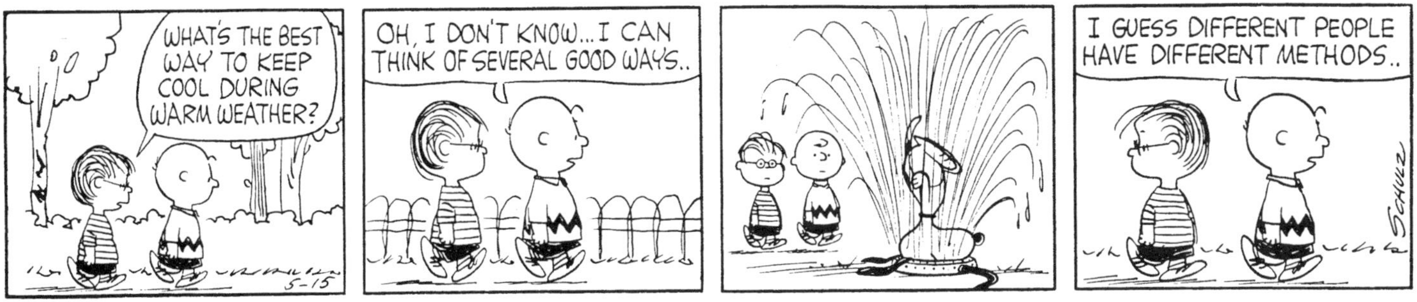
WHAT'S THE BEST WAY TO KEEP COOL DURING WARM WEATHER?
OH, I DON'T KNOW... I CAN THINK OF SEVERAL GOOD WAYS..
I GUESS DIFFERENT PEOPLE HAVE DIFFERENT METHODS..

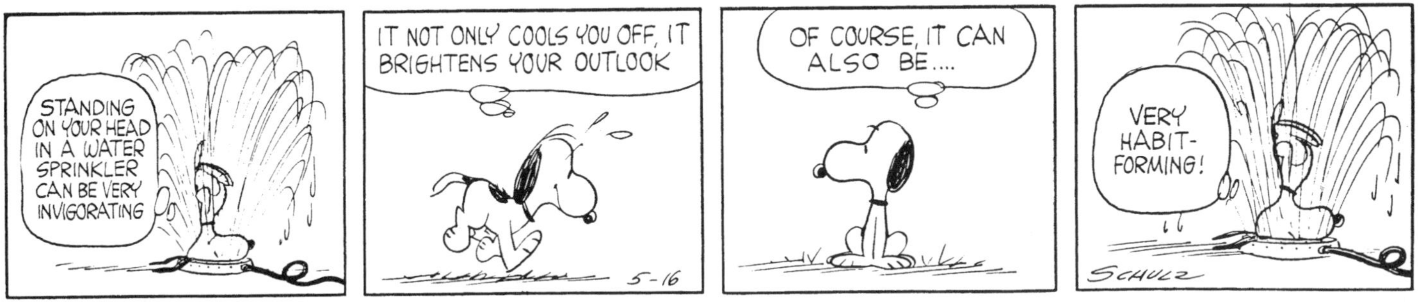
STANDING ON YOUR HEAD IN A WATER SPRINKLER CAN BE VERY INVIGORATING
IT NOT ONLY COOLS YOU OFF, IT BRIGHTENS YOUR OUTLOOK
OF COURSE, IT CAN ALSO BE....
VERY HABIT-FORMING!

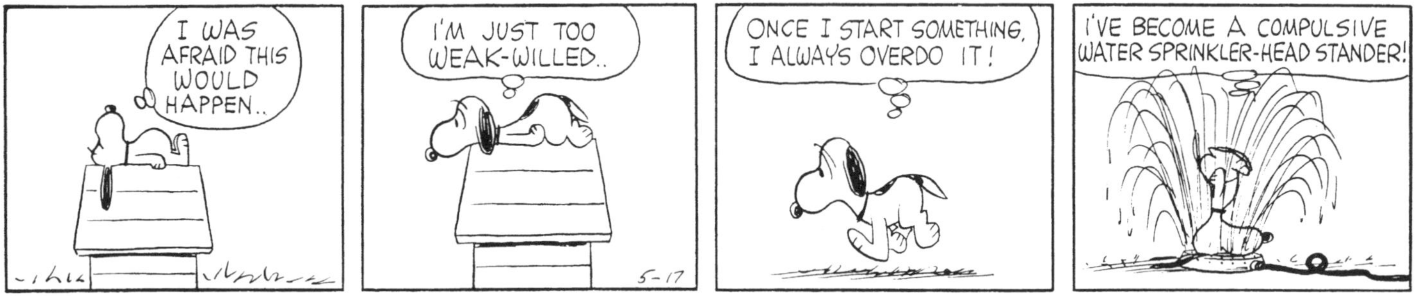
I WAS AFRAID THIS WOULD HAPPEN..
I'M JUST TOO WEAK-WILLED..
5-17
ONCE I START SOMETHING, I ALWAYS OVERDO IT!
I'VE BECOME A COMPULSIVE WATER SPRINKLER-HEAD STANDER!

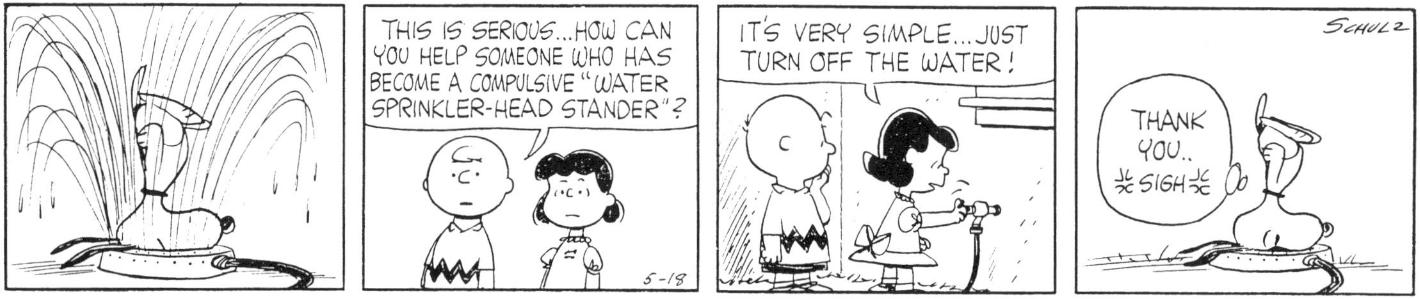
THIS IS SERIOUS...HOW CAN YOU HELP SOMEONE WHO HAS BECOME A COMPULSIVE "WATER SPRINKLER-HEAD STANDER"?
5-18
IT'S VERY SIMPLE...JUST TURN OFF THE WATER!
SCHULZ
THANK YOU.. SIGH

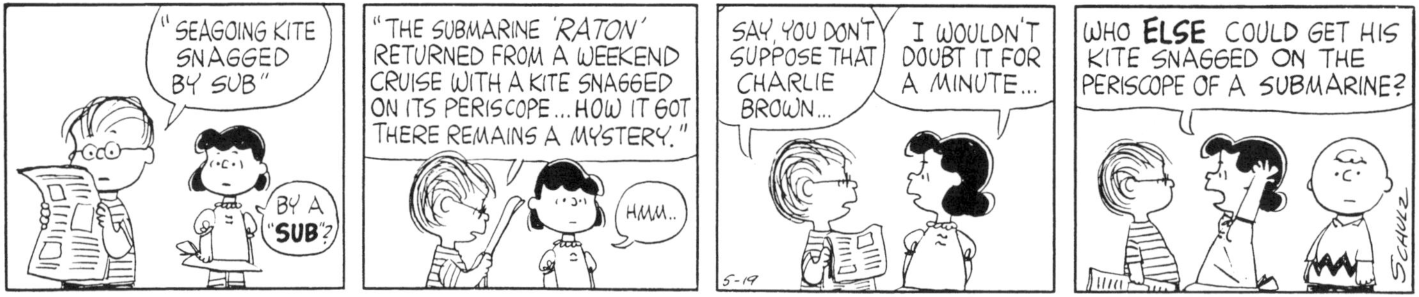
"SEAGOING KITE SNAGGED BY SUB"
BY A "SUB"?
"THE SUBMARINE 'RATON' RETURNED FROM A WEEKEND CRUISE WITH A KITE SNAGGED ON ITS PERISCOPE...HOW IT GOT THERE REMAINS A MYSTERY."
HMM..
SAY, YOU DON'T SUPPOSE THAT CHARLIE BROWN...
I WOULDN'T DOUBT IT FOR A MINUTE...
5-19
WHO ELSE COULD GET HIS KITE SNAGGED ON THE PERISCOPE OF A SUBMARINE?
SCHULZ

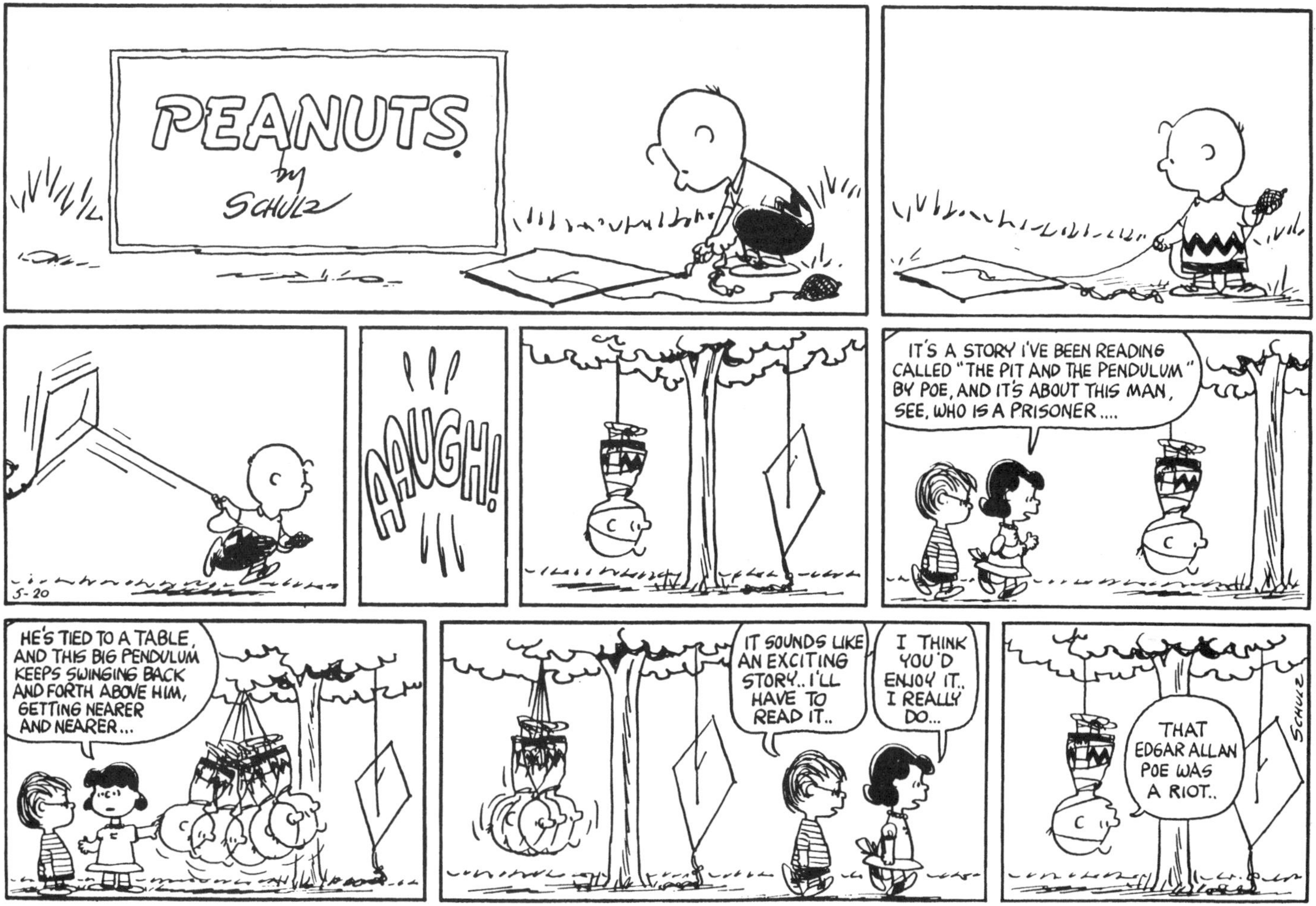
PEANUTS
by SCHULZ
5-20
AAUGH!
IT'S A STORY I'VE BEEN READING CALLED "THE PIT AND THE PENDULUM" BY POE, AND IT'S ABOUT THIS MAN, SEE, WHO IS A PRISONER....
HE'S TIED TO A TABLE, AND THIS BIG PENDULUM KEEPS SWINGING BACK AND FORTH ABOVE HIM, GETTING NEARER AND NEARER...
IT SOUNDS LIKE AN EXCITING STORY.. I'LL HAVE TO READ IT..
I THINK YOU'D ENJOY IT.. I REALLY DO...
THAT EDGAR ALLAN POE WAS A RIOT..
SCHULZ

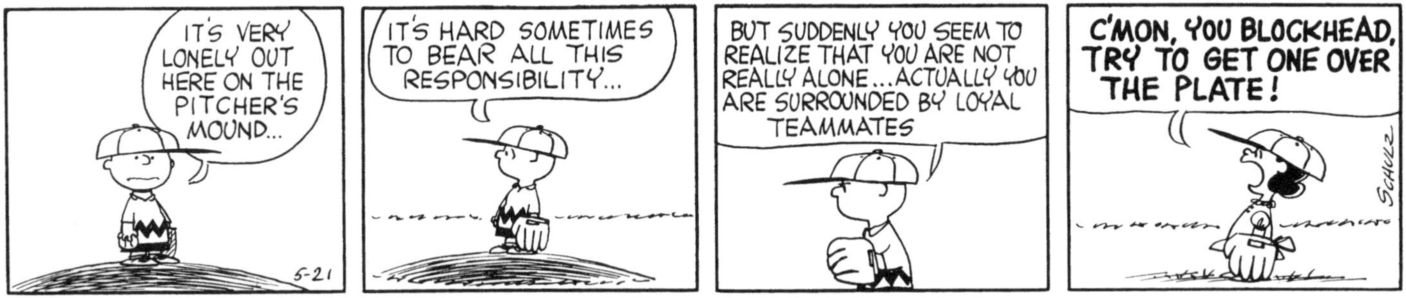
IT'S VERY LONELY OUT HERE ON THE PITCHER'S MOUND...
5-21
IT'S HARD SOMETIMES TO BEAR ALL THIS RESPONSIBILITY...
BUT SUDDENLY YOU SEEM TO REALIZE THAT YOU ARE NOT REALLY ALONE...ACTUALLY YOU ARE SURROUNDED BY LOYAL TEAMMATES
C'MON, YOU BLOCKHEAD, TRY TO GET ONE OVER THE PLATE!
SCHULZ

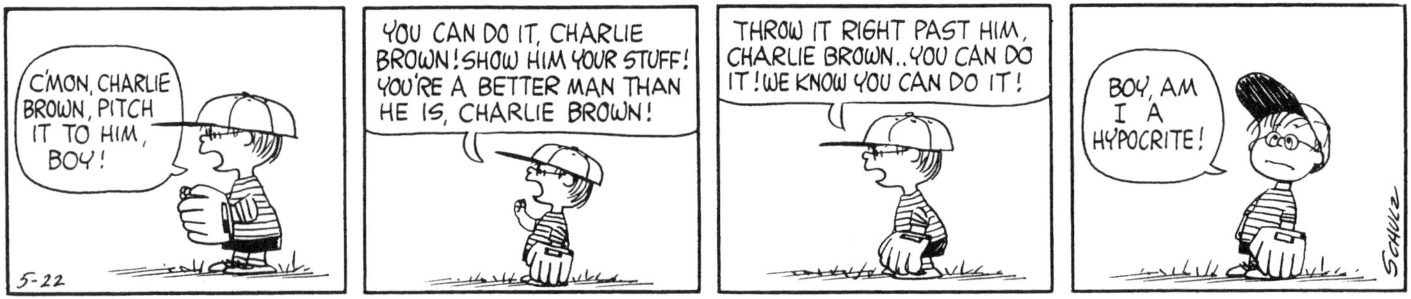
C'MON, CHARLIE BROWN, PITCH IT TO HIM, BOY!
5-22
YOU CAN DO IT, CHARLIE BROWN! SHOW HIM YOUR STUFF! YOU'RE A BETTER MAN THAN HE IS, CHARLIE BROWN!
THROW IT RIGHT PAST HIM, CHARLIE BROWN..YOU CAN DO IT! WE KNOW YOU CAN DO IT!
BOY, AM I A HYPOCRITE!
SCHULZ

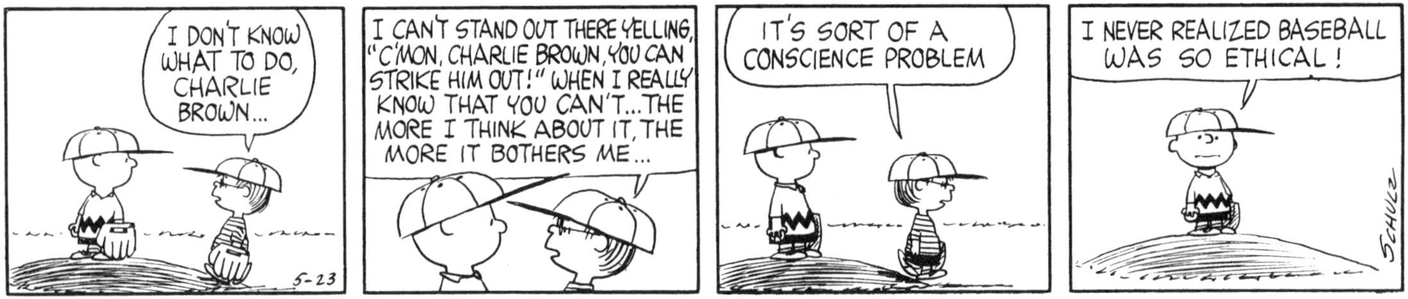
I DON'T KNOW WHAT TO DO, CHARLIE BROWN...
5-23
I CAN'T STAND OUT THERE YELLING, "C'MON, CHARLIE BROWN, YOU CAN STRIKE HIM OUT!" WHEN I REALLY KNOW THAT YOU CAN'T...THE MORE I THINK ABOUT IT, THE MORE IT BOTHERS ME...
IT'S SORT OF A CONSCIENCE PROBLEM
I NEVER REALIZED BASEBALL WAS SO ETHICAL!
SCHULZ

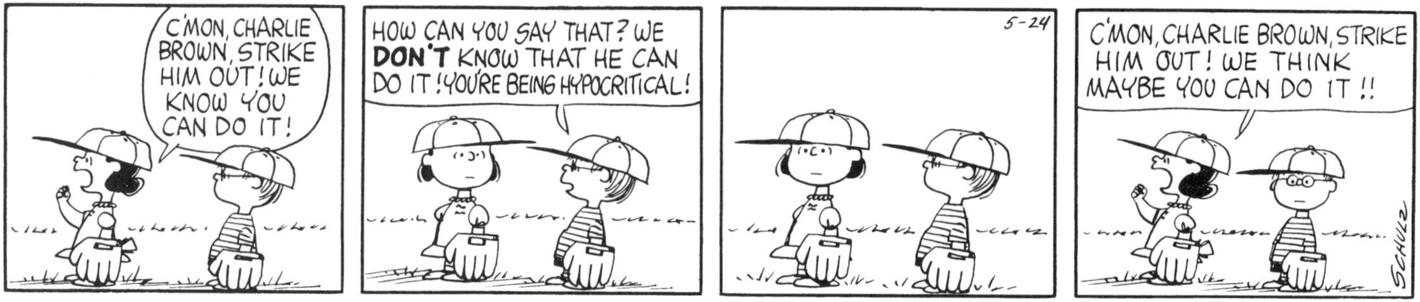
C'MON, CHARLIE BROWN, STRIKE HIM OUT! WE KNOW YOU CAN DO IT!
HOW CAN YOU SAY THAT? WE **DON'T** KNOW THAT HE CAN DO IT! YOU'RE BEING HYPOCRITICAL!
5-24
C'MON, CHARLIE BROWN, STRIKE HIM OUT! WE THINK MAYBE YOU CAN DO IT!!
SCHULZ

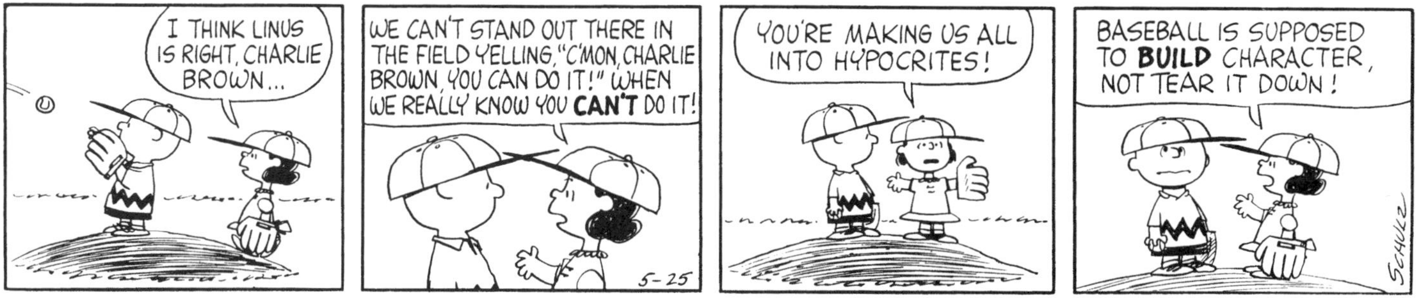
I THINK LINUS IS RIGHT, CHARLIE BROWN...
WE CAN'T STAND OUT THERE IN THE FIELD YELLING, "C'MON, CHARLIE BROWN, YOU CAN DO IT!" WHEN WE REALLY KNOW YOU **CAN'T** DO IT!
5-25
YOU'RE MAKING US ALL INTO HYPOCRITES!
BASEBALL IS SUPPOSED TO **BUILD** CHARACTER, NOT TEAR IT DOWN!
SCHULZ

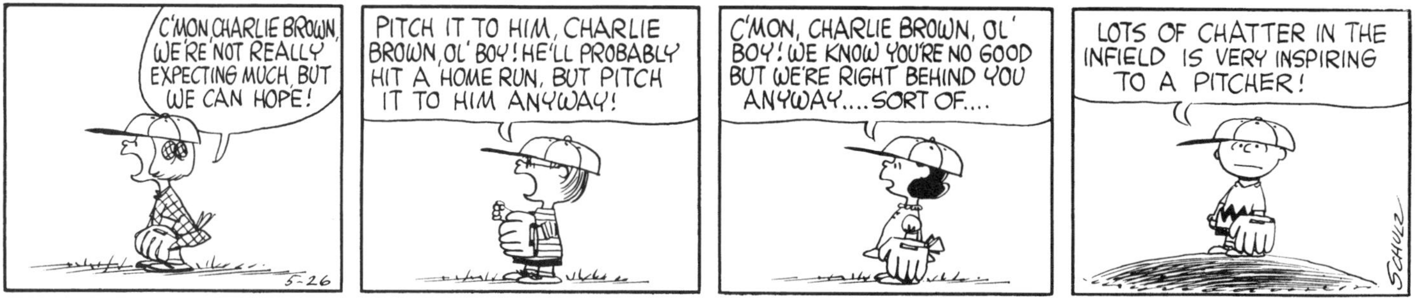
C'MON, CHARLIE BROWN, WE'RE NOT REALLY EXPECTING MUCH, BUT WE CAN HOPE!
5-26
PITCH IT TO HIM, CHARLIE BROWN, OL' BOY! HE'LL PROBABLY HIT A HOME RUN, BUT PITCH IT TO HIM ANYWAY!
C'MON, CHARLIE BROWN, OL' BOY! WE KNOW YOU'RE NO GOOD BUT WE'RE RIGHT BEHIND YOU ANYWAY.... SORT OF....
LOTS OF CHATTER IN THE INFIELD IS VERY INSPIRING TO A PITCHER!
SCHULZ

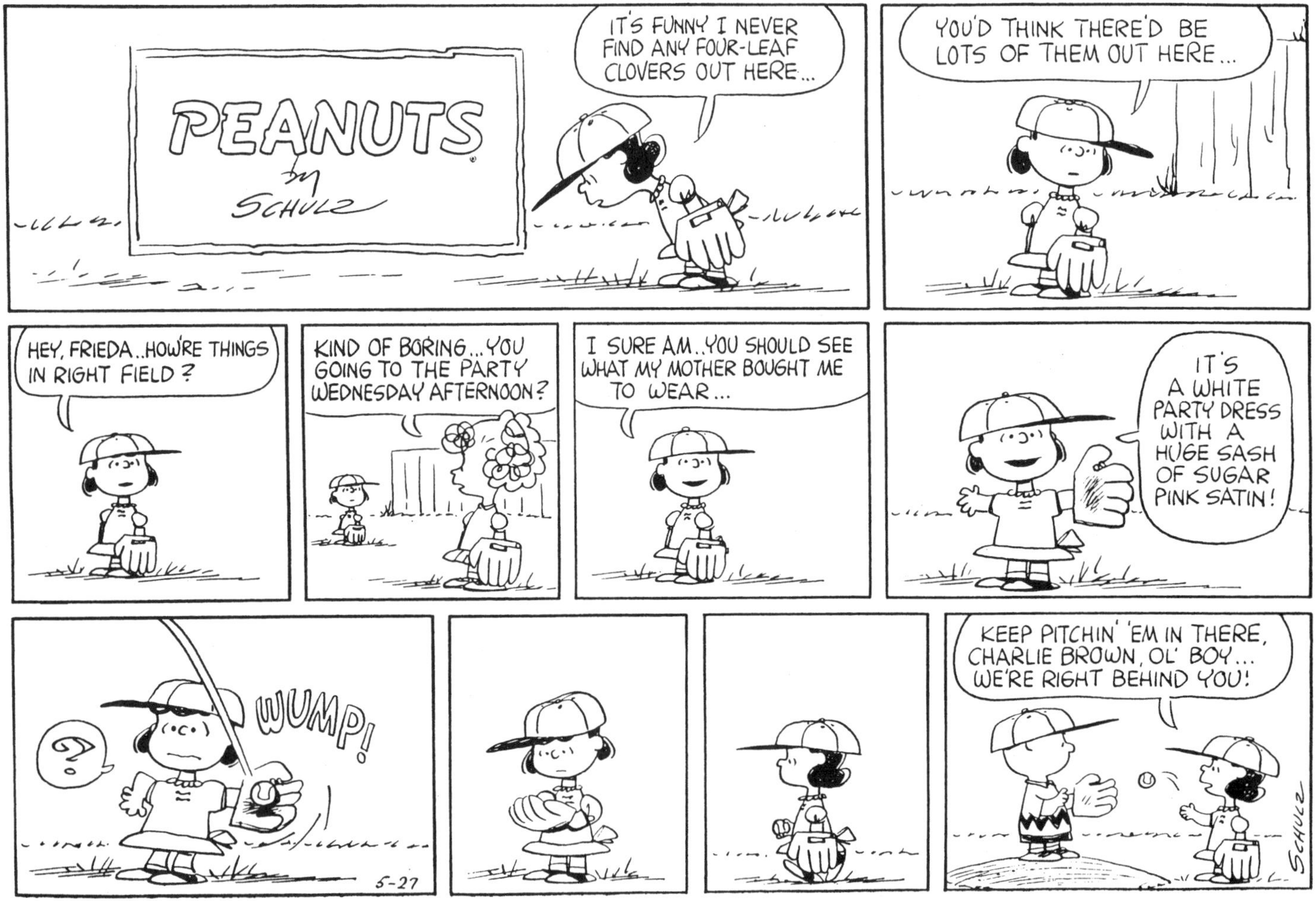
PEANUTS
by SCHULZ
IT'S FUNNY I NEVER FIND ANY FOUR-LEAF CLOVERS OUT HERE...
YOU'D THINK THERE'D BE LOTS OF THEM OUT HERE...
HEY, FRIEDA..HOW'RE THINGS IN RIGHT FIELD?
KIND OF BORING...YOU GOING TO THE PARTY WEDNESDAY AFTERNOON?
I SURE AM..YOU SHOULD SEE WHAT MY MOTHER BOUGHT ME TO WEAR...
IT'S A WHITE PARTY DRESS WITH A HUGE SASH OF SUGAR PINK SATIN!
?
WUMP!
5-27
KEEP PITCHIN' 'EM IN THERE, CHARLIE BROWN, OL' BOY... WE'RE RIGHT BEHIND YOU!
SCHULZ

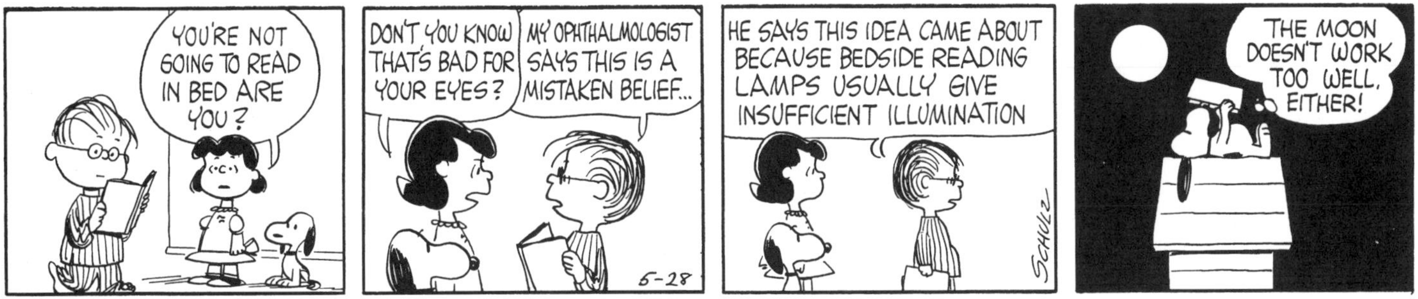
YOU'RE NOT GOING TO READ IN BED ARE YOU?
DON'T YOU KNOW THAT'S BAD FOR YOUR EYES?
MY OPHTHALMOLOGIST SAYS THIS IS A MISTAKEN BELIEF...
5-28
HE SAYS THIS IDEA CAME ABOUT BECAUSE BEDSIDE READING LAMPS USUALLY GIVE INSUFFICIENT ILLUMINATION
SCHULZ
THE MOON DOESN'T WORK TOO WELL, EITHER!

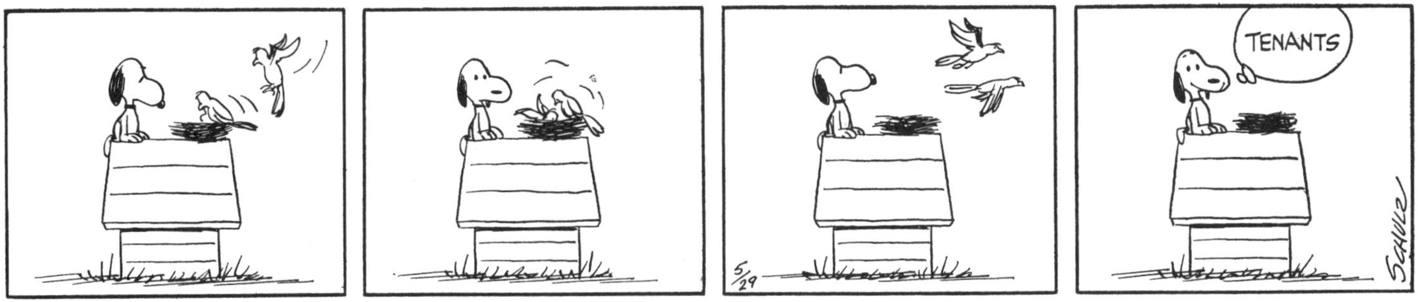
5/29
TENANTS
SCHULZ

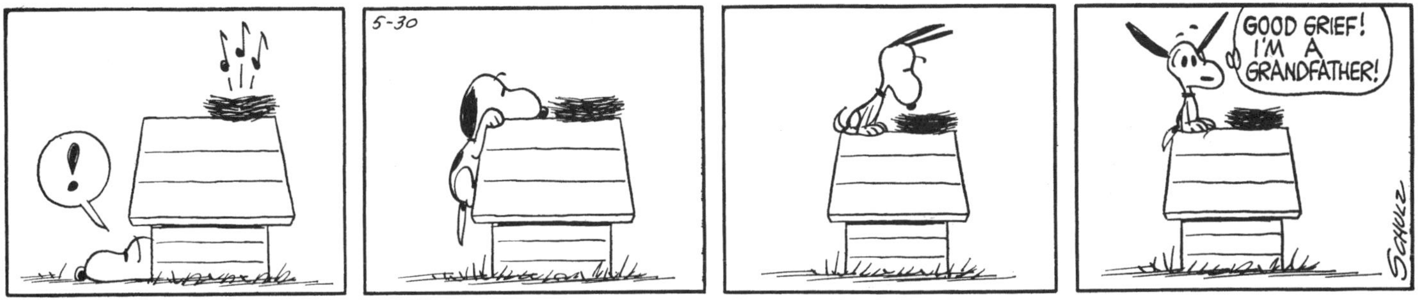
!
5-30
GOOD GRIEF! I'M A GRANDFATHER!
SCHULZ

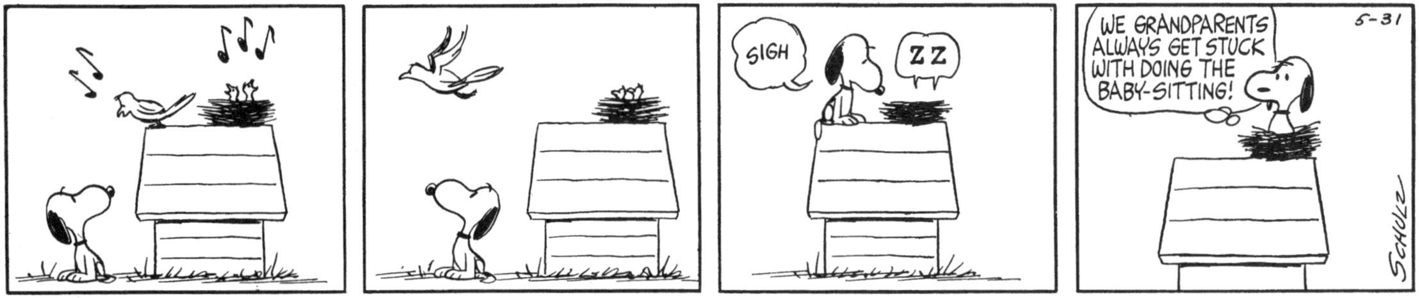
SIGH
Z Z
5-31
WE GRANDPARENTS ALWAYS GET STUCK WITH DOING THE BABY-SITTING!
SCHULZ

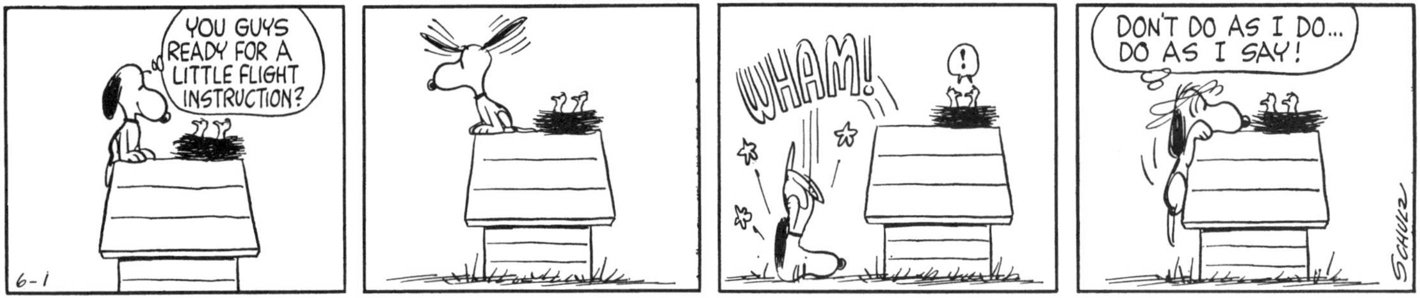
YOU GUYS READY FOR A LITTLE FLIGHT INSTRUCTION?
6-1
WHAM!
!
DON'T DO AS I DO... DO AS I SAY!
SCHULZ

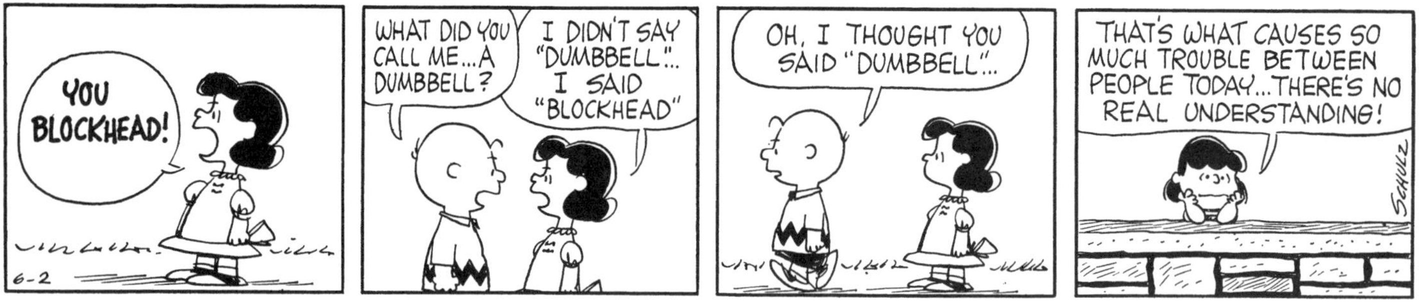
YOU BLOCKHEAD!
6-2
WHAT DID YOU CALL ME...A DUMBBELL?
I DIDN'T SAY "DUMBBELL"... I SAID "BLOCKHEAD"
OH, I THOUGHT YOU SAID "DUMBBELL"...
THAT'S WHAT CAUSES SO MUCH TROUBLE BETWEEN PEOPLE TODAY...THERE'S NO REAL UNDERSTANDING!
SCHULZ

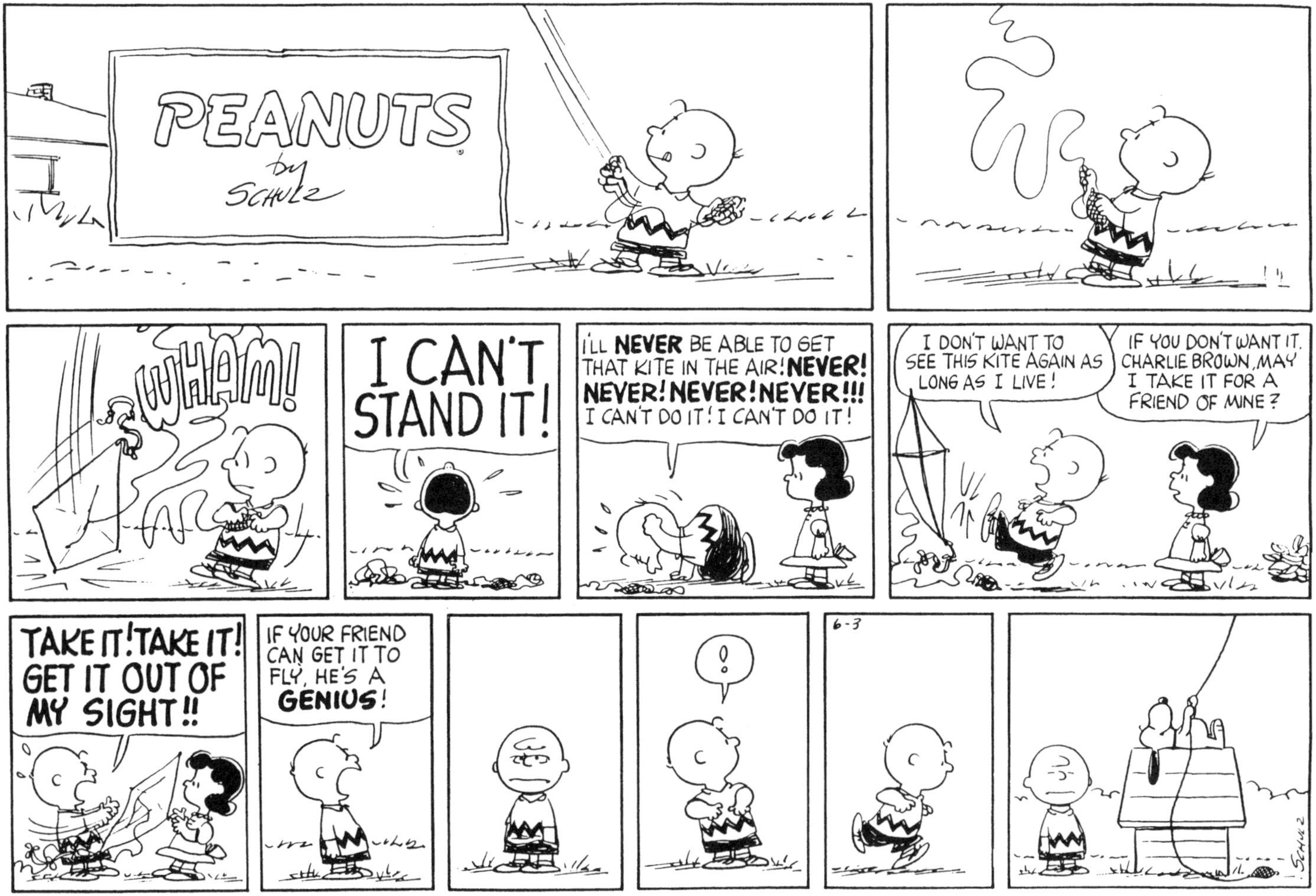
PEANUTS
by SCHULZ
WHAM!
I CAN'T STAND IT!
I'LL NEVER BE ABLE TO GET THAT KITE IN THE AIR! NEVER! NEVER! NEVER! NEVER!!! I CAN'T DO IT! I CAN'T DO IT!
I DON'T WANT TO SEE THIS KITE AGAIN AS LONG AS I LIVE!
IF YOU DON'T WANT IT, CHARLIE BROWN, MAY I TAKE IT FOR A FRIEND OF MINE?
TAKE IT! TAKE IT! GET IT OUT OF MY SIGHT!!
IF YOUR FRIEND CAN GET IT TO FLY, HE'S A GENIUS!
!
6-3
SCHULZ

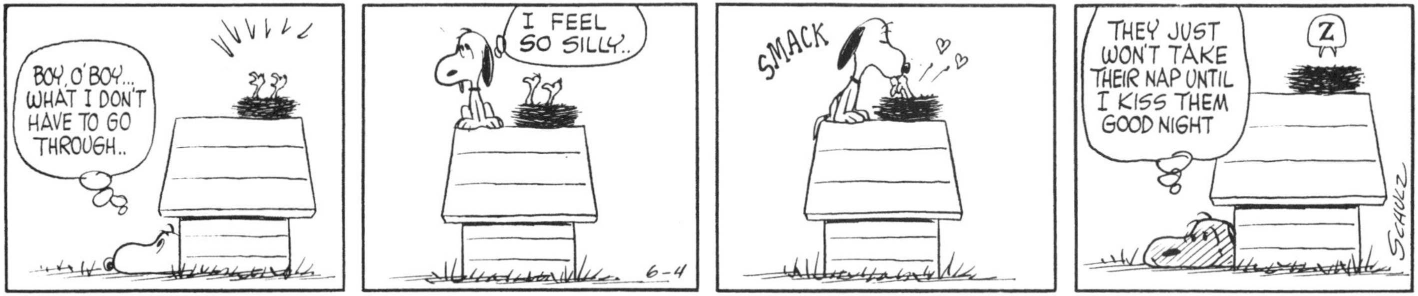
BOY, O' BOY... WHAT I DON'T HAVE TO GO THROUGH..
I FEEL SO SILLY..
6-4
SMACK
THEY JUST WON'T TAKE THEIR NAP UNTIL I KISS THEM GOOD NIGHT
Z
SCHULZ

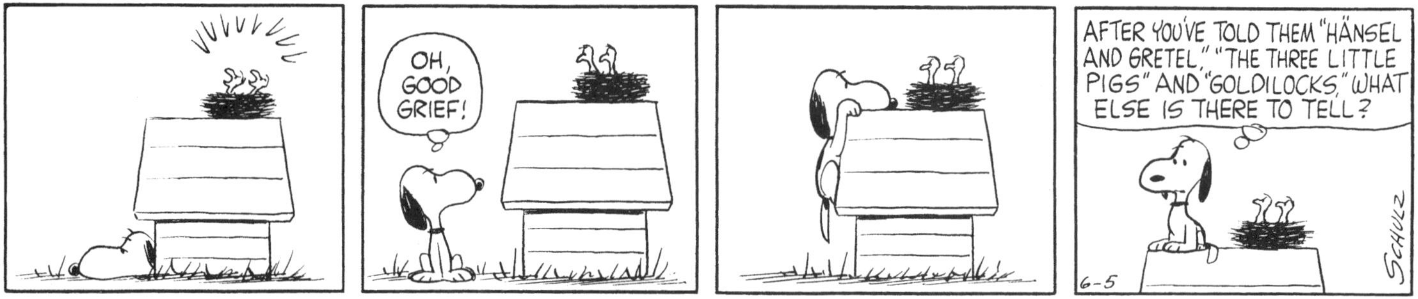
OH, GOOD GRIEF!
AFTER YOU'VE TOLD THEM "HÄNSEL AND GRETEL," "THE THREE LITTLE PIGS" AND "GOLDILOCKS," WHAT ELSE IS THERE TO TELL?
SCHULZ
6-5

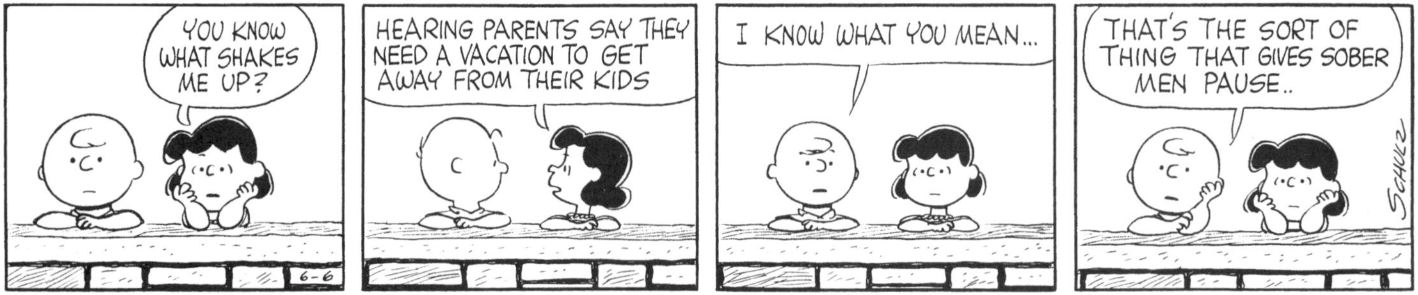
YOU KNOW WHAT SHAKES ME UP?
6-6
HEARING PARENTS SAY THEY NEED A VACATION TO GET AWAY FROM THEIR KIDS
I KNOW WHAT YOU MEAN...
THAT'S THE SORT OF THING THAT GIVES SOBER MEN PAUSE..
SCHULZ

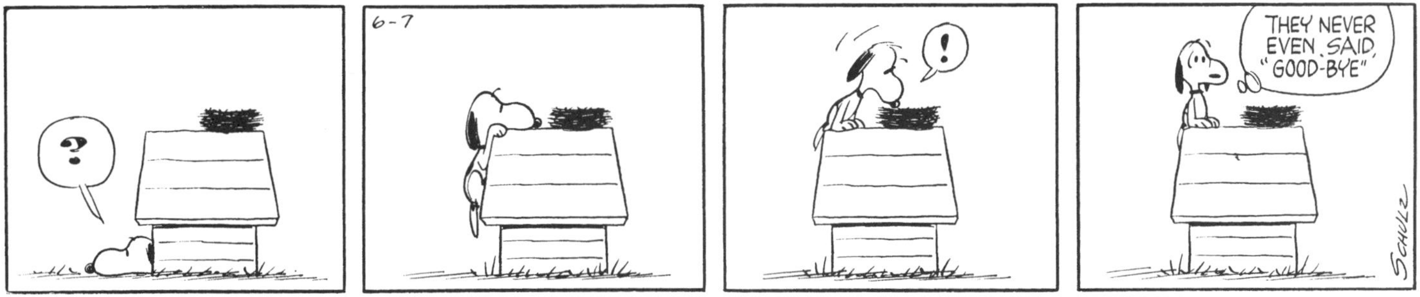
?
6-7
!
THEY NEVER EVEN SAID "GOOD-BYE"
SCHULZ

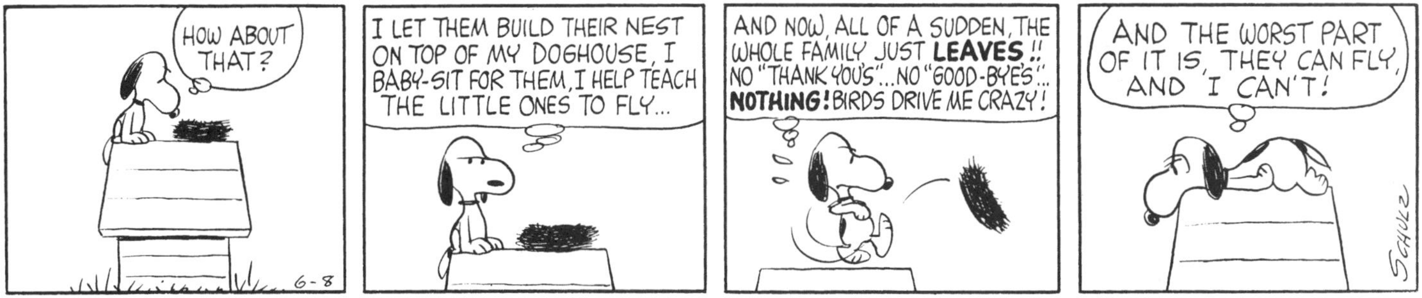
HOW ABOUT THAT?
6-8
I LET THEM BUILD THEIR NEST ON TOP OF MY DOGHOUSE, I BABY-SIT FOR THEM, I HELP TEACH THE LITTLE ONES TO FLY...
AND NOW, ALL OF A SUDDEN, THE WHOLE FAMILY JUST **LEAVES**!! NO "THANK YOU'S"... NO "GOOD-BYE'S"... **NOTHING!** BIRDS DRIVE ME CRAZY!
AND THE WORST PART OF IT IS, THEY CAN FLY, AND I CAN'T!
SCHULZ

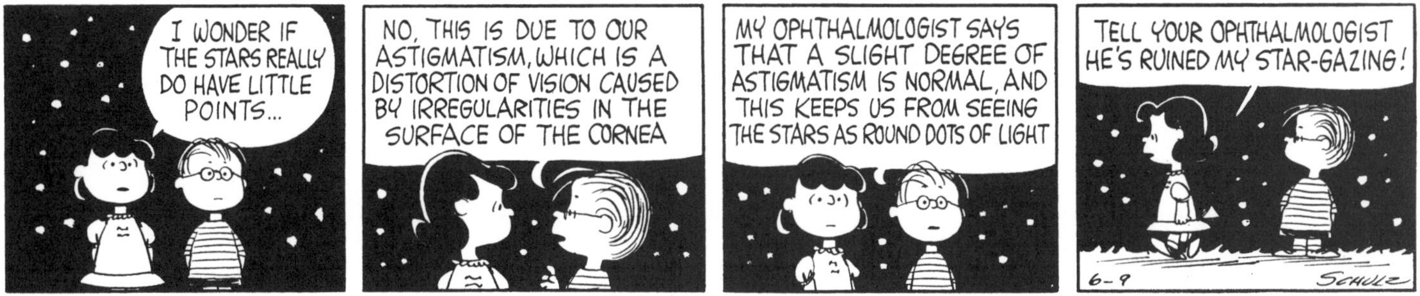
I WONDER IF THE STARS REALLY DO HAVE LITTLE POINTS...
NO, THIS IS DUE TO OUR ASTIGMATISM, WHICH IS A DISTORTION OF VISION CAUSED BY IRREGULARITIES IN THE SURFACE OF THE CORNEA
MY OPHTHALMOLOGIST SAYS THAT A SLIGHT DEGREE OF ASTIGMATISM IS NORMAL, AND THIS KEEPS US FROM SEEING THE STARS AS ROUND DOTS OF LIGHT
TELL YOUR OPHTHALMOLOGIST HE'S RUINED MY STAR-GAZING!
6-9
SCHULZ

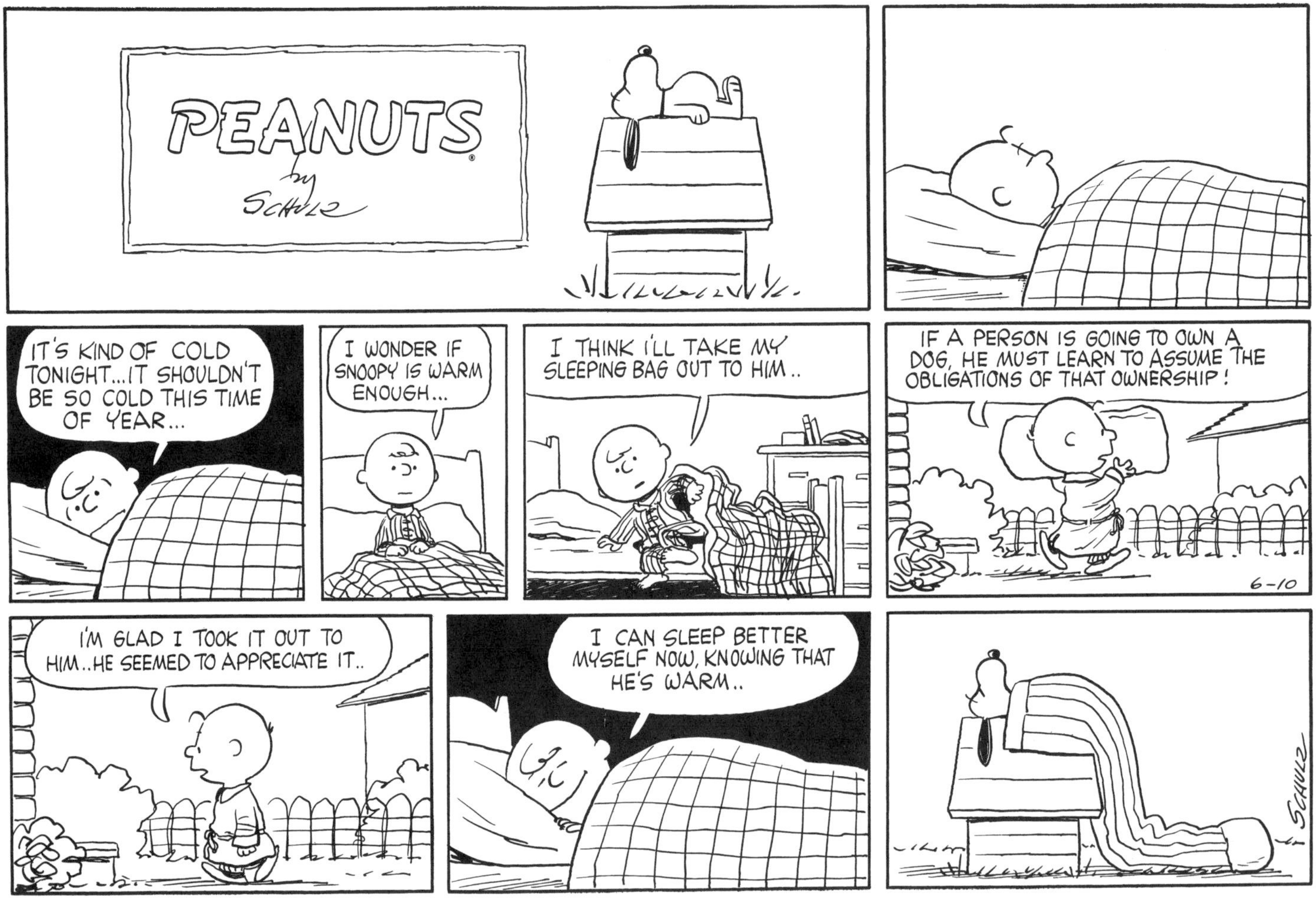
PEANUTS
by SCHULZ
IT'S KIND OF COLD TONIGHT...IT SHOULDN'T BE SO COLD THIS TIME OF YEAR...
I WONDER IF SNOOPY IS WARM ENOUGH...
I THINK I'LL TAKE MY SLEEPING BAG OUT TO HIM..
IF A PERSON IS GOING TO OWN A DOG, HE MUST LEARN TO ASSUME THE OBLIGATIONS OF THAT OWNERSHIP!
6-10
I'M GLAD I TOOK IT OUT TO HIM..HE SEEMED TO APPRECIATE IT..
I CAN SLEEP BETTER MYSELF NOW, KNOWING THAT HE'S WARM..
SCHULZ

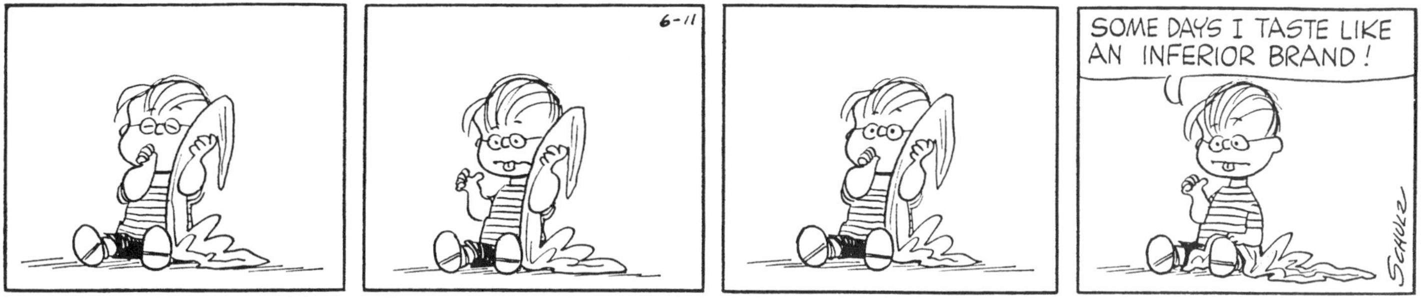
6-11
SOME DAYS I TASTE LIKE AN INFERIOR BRAND!
SCHULZ

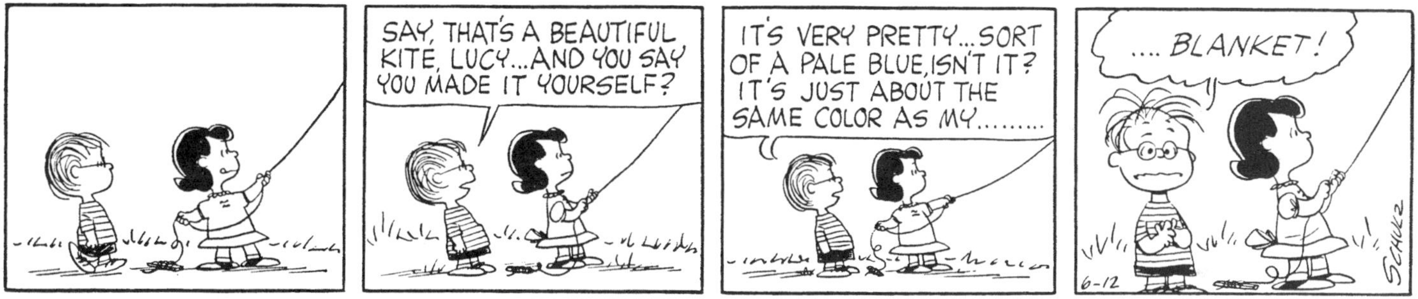
SAY, THAT'S A BEAUTIFUL KITE, LUCY...AND YOU SAY YOU MADE IT YOURSELF?
IT'S VERY PRETTY...SORT OF A PALE BLUE, ISN'T IT? IT'S JUST ABOUT THE SAME COLOR AS MY........
....BLANKET!
SCHULZ
6-12

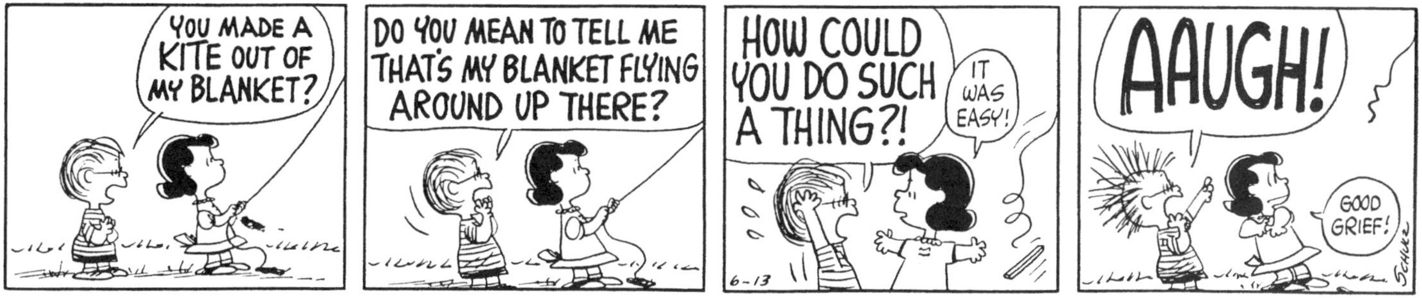
YOU MADE A KITE OUT OF MY BLANKET?
DO YOU MEAN TO TELL ME THAT'S MY BLANKET FLYING AROUND UP THERE?
HOW COULD YOU DO SUCH A THING?!
IT WAS EASY!
6-13
AAUGH!
GOOD GRIEF!
SCHULZ

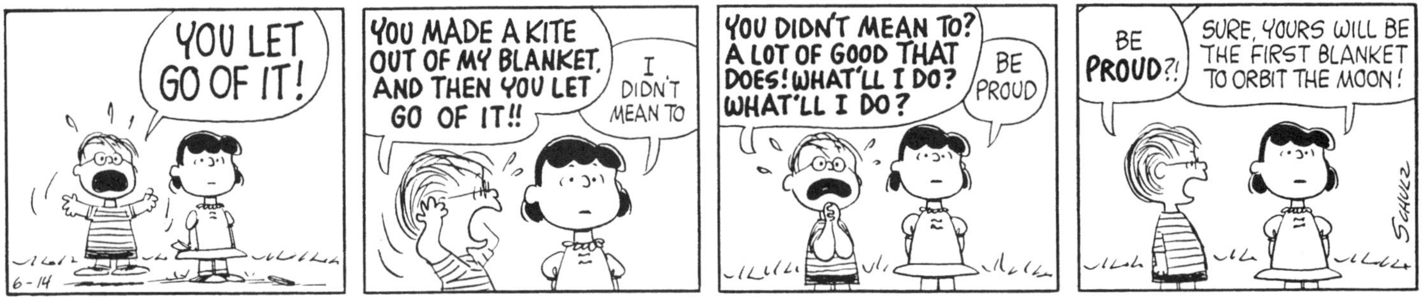
YOU LET GO OF IT!
6-14
YOU MADE A KITE OUT OF MY BLANKET, AND THEN YOU LET GO OF IT!!
I DIDN'T MEAN TO
YOU DIDN'T MEAN TO? A LOT OF GOOD THAT DOES! WHAT'LL I DO? WHAT'LL I DO?
BE PROUD
BE PROUD?!
SURE, YOURS WILL BE THE FIRST BLANKET TO ORBIT THE MOON!
SCHULZ

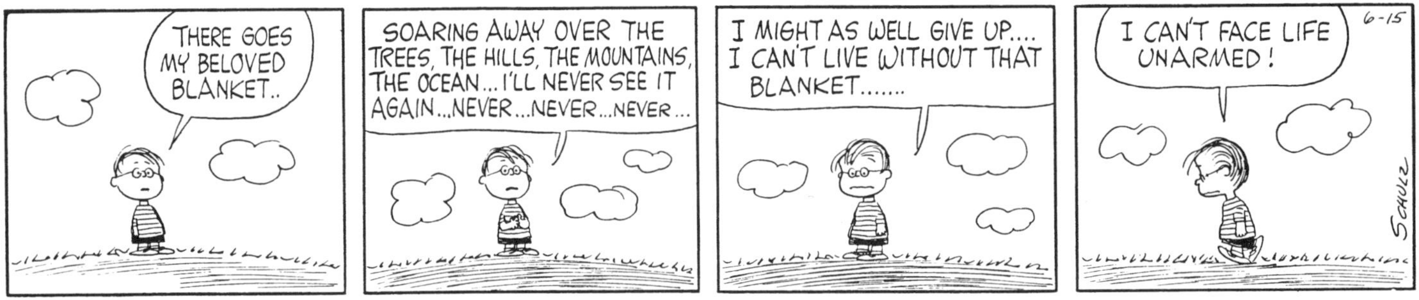
THERE GOES MY BELOVED BLANKET..
SOARING AWAY OVER THE TREES, THE HILLS, THE MOUNTAINS, THE OCEAN... I'LL NEVER SEE IT AGAIN...NEVER...NEVER...NEVER...
I MIGHT AS WELL GIVE UP.... I CAN'T LIVE WITHOUT THAT BLANKET.......
6-15
I CAN'T FACE LIFE UNARMED!
SCHULZ

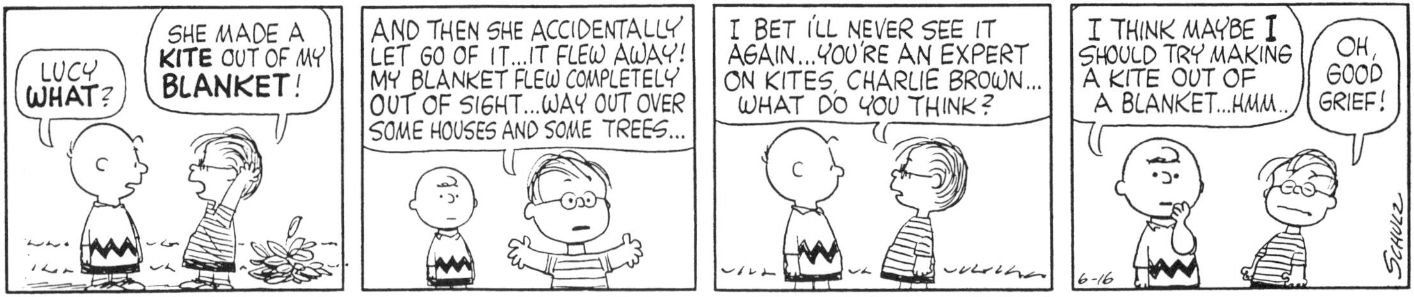
SHE MADE A KITE OUT OF MY BLANKET!
LUCY WHAT?
AND THEN SHE ACCIDENTALLY LET GO OF IT...IT FLEW AWAY! MY BLANKET FLEW COMPLETELY OUT OF SIGHT...WAY OUT OVER SOME HOUSES AND SOME TREES...
I BET I'LL NEVER SEE IT AGAIN...YOU'RE AN EXPERT ON KITES, CHARLIE BROWN... WHAT DO YOU THINK?
I THINK MAYBE I SHOULD TRY MAKING A KITE OUT OF A BLANKET...HMM..
OH, GOOD GRIEF!
6-16
SCHULZ

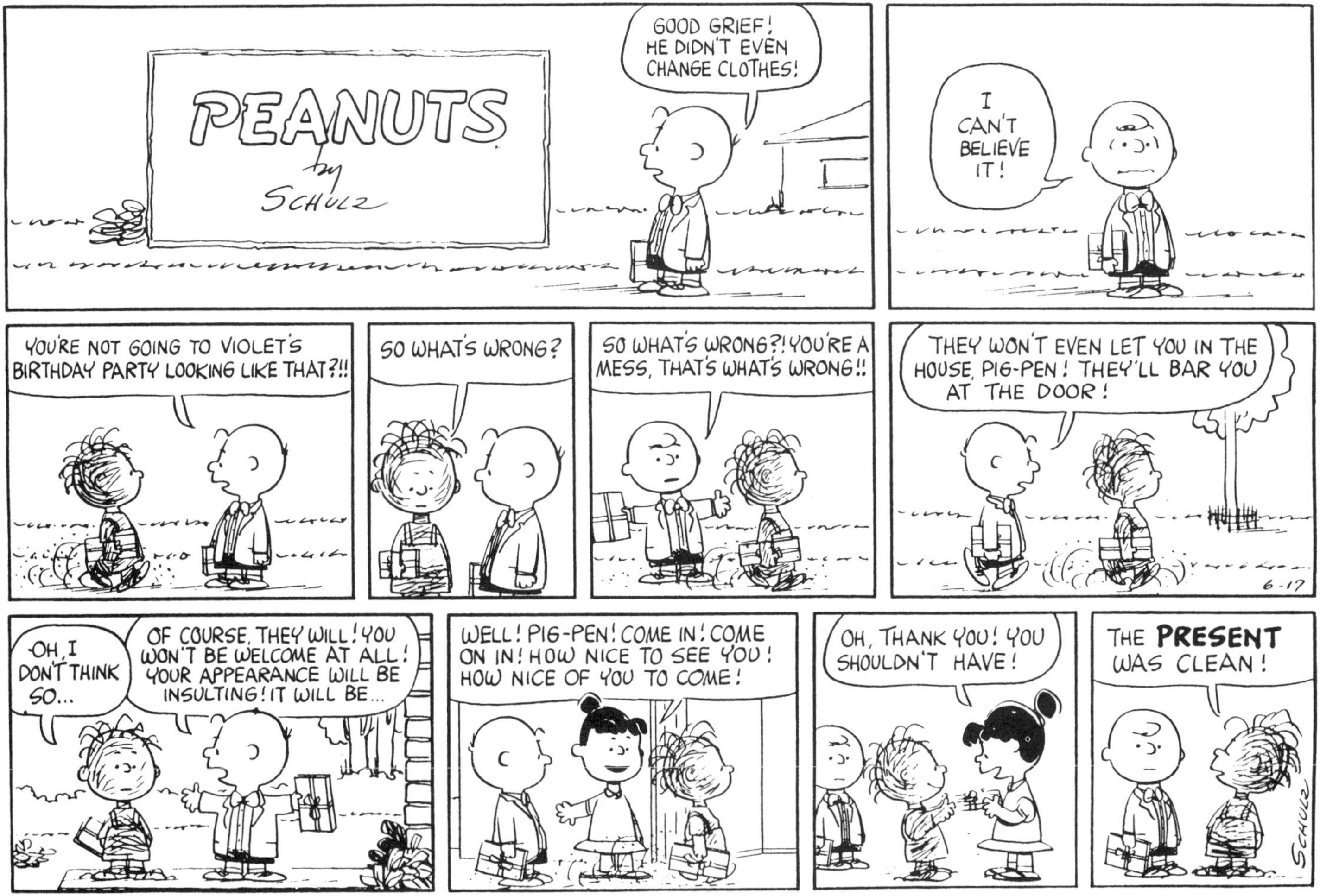
PEANUTS
by SCHULZ
GOOD GRIEF! HE DIDN'T EVEN CHANGE CLOTHES!
I CAN'T BELIEVE IT!
YOU'RE NOT GOING TO VIOLET'S BIRTHDAY PARTY LOOKING LIKE THAT?!!
SO WHAT'S WRONG?
SO WHAT'S WRONG?! YOU'RE A MESS, THAT'S WHAT'S WRONG!!
THEY WON'T EVEN LET YOU IN THE HOUSE, PIG-PEN! THEY'LL BAR YOU AT THE DOOR!
6-17
OH, I DON'T THINK SO...
OF COURSE, THEY WILL! YOU WON'T BE WELCOME AT ALL! YOUR APPEARANCE WILL BE INSULTING! IT WILL BE...
WELL! PIG-PEN! COME IN! COME ON IN! HOW NICE TO SEE YOU! HOW NICE OF YOU TO COME!
OH, THANK YOU! YOU SHOULDN'T HAVE!
THE **PRESENT** WAS CLEAN!
SCHULZ

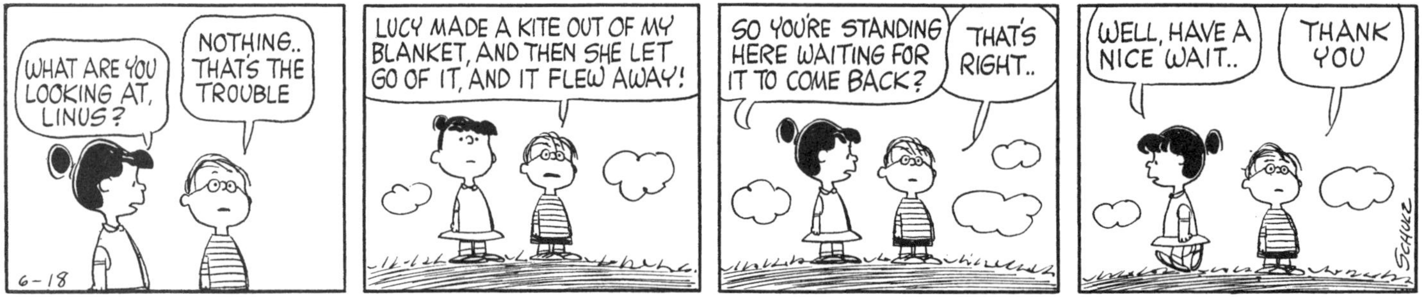
WHAT ARE YOU LOOKING AT, LINUS?
NOTHING.. THAT'S THE TROUBLE
6-18
LUCY MADE A KITE OUT OF MY BLANKET, AND THEN SHE LET GO OF IT, AND IT FLEW AWAY!
SO YOU'RE STANDING HERE WAITING FOR IT TO COME BACK?
THAT'S RIGHT..
WELL, HAVE A NICE WAIT..
THANK YOU
SCHULZ

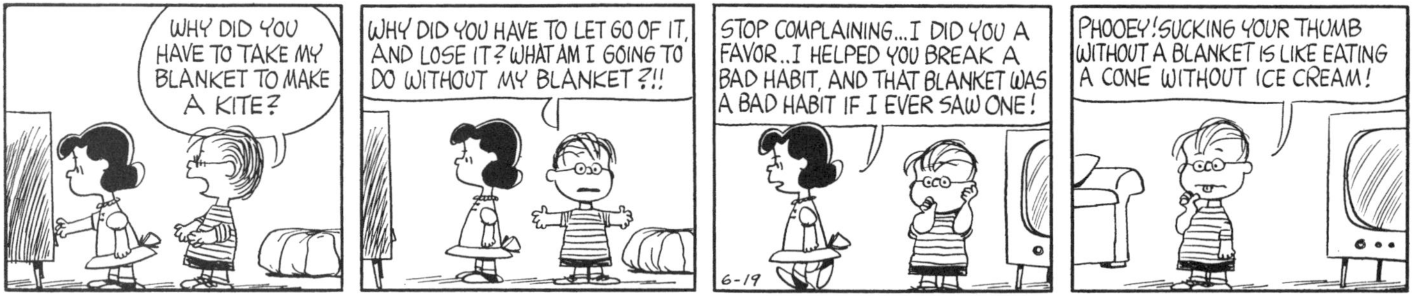
WHY DID YOU HAVE TO TAKE MY BLANKET TO MAKE A KITE?
WHY DID YOU HAVE TO LET GO OF IT, AND LOSE IT? WHAT AM I GOING TO DO WITHOUT MY BLANKET?!!
STOP COMPLAINING...I DID YOU A FAVOR..I HELPED YOU BREAK A BAD HABIT, AND THAT BLANKET WAS A BAD HABIT IF I EVER SAW ONE!
6-19
PHOOEY! SUCKING YOUR THUMB WITHOUT A BLANKET IS LIKE EATING A CONE WITHOUT ICE CREAM!

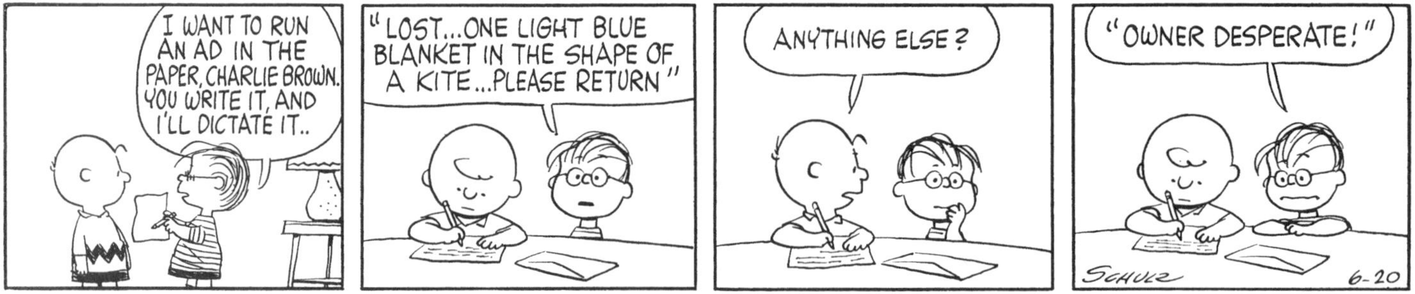
I WANT TO RUN AN AD IN THE PAPER, CHARLIE BROWN. YOU WRITE IT, AND I'LL DICTATE IT..
"LOST...ONE LIGHT BLUE BLANKET IN THE SHAPE OF A KITE...PLEASE RETURN"
ANYTHING ELSE?
"OWNER DESPERATE!"
SCHULZ
6-20

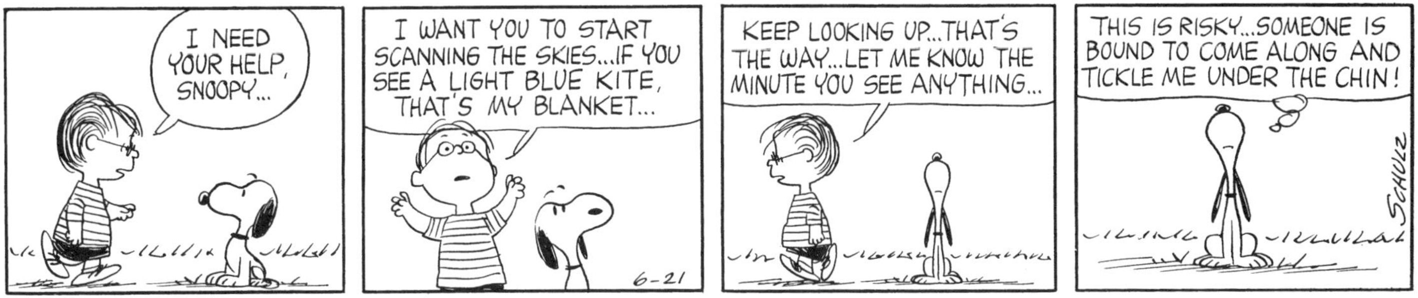
I NEED YOUR HELP, SNOOPY...
I WANT YOU TO START SCANNING THE SKIES...IF YOU SEE A LIGHT BLUE KITE, THAT'S MY BLANKET...
6-21
KEEP LOOKING UP...THAT'S THE WAY...LET ME KNOW THE MINUTE YOU SEE ANYTHING...
THIS IS RISKY...SOMEONE IS BOUND TO COME ALONG AND TICKLE ME UNDER THE CHIN!
SCHULZ

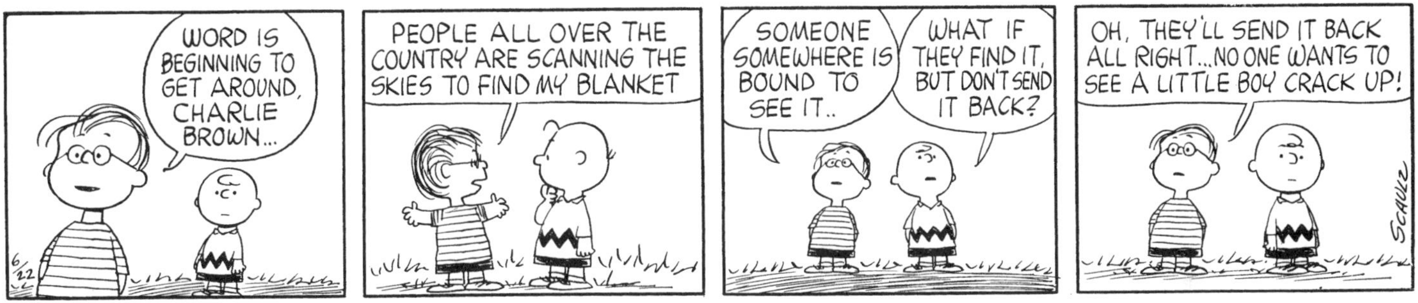
WORD IS BEGINNING TO GET AROUND, CHARLIE BROWN...
6/22
PEOPLE ALL OVER THE COUNTRY ARE SCANNING THE SKIES TO FIND MY BLANKET
SOMEONE SOMEWHERE IS BOUND TO SEE IT..
WHAT IF THEY FIND IT, BUT DON'T SEND IT BACK?
OH, THEY'LL SEND IT BACK ALL RIGHT...NO ONE WANTS TO SEE A LITTLE BOY CRACK UP!
SCHULZ

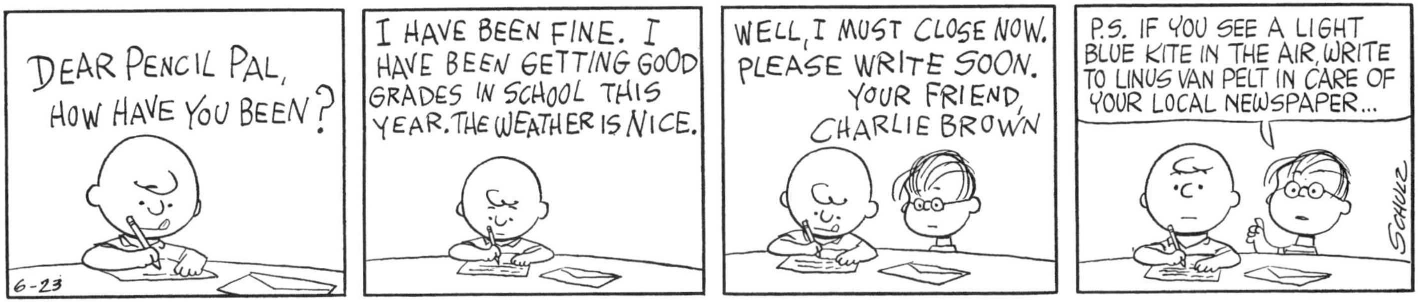
DEAR PENCIL PAL, HOW HAVE YOU BEEN?
6-23
I HAVE BEEN FINE. I HAVE BEEN GETTING GOOD GRADES IN SCHOOL THIS YEAR. THE WEATHER IS NICE.
WELL, I MUST CLOSE NOW. PLEASE WRITE SOON. YOUR FRIEND, CHARLIE BROWN
P.S. IF YOU SEE A LIGHT BLUE KITE IN THE AIR, WRITE TO LINUS VAN PELT IN CARE OF YOUR LOCAL NEWSPAPER...
SCHULZ

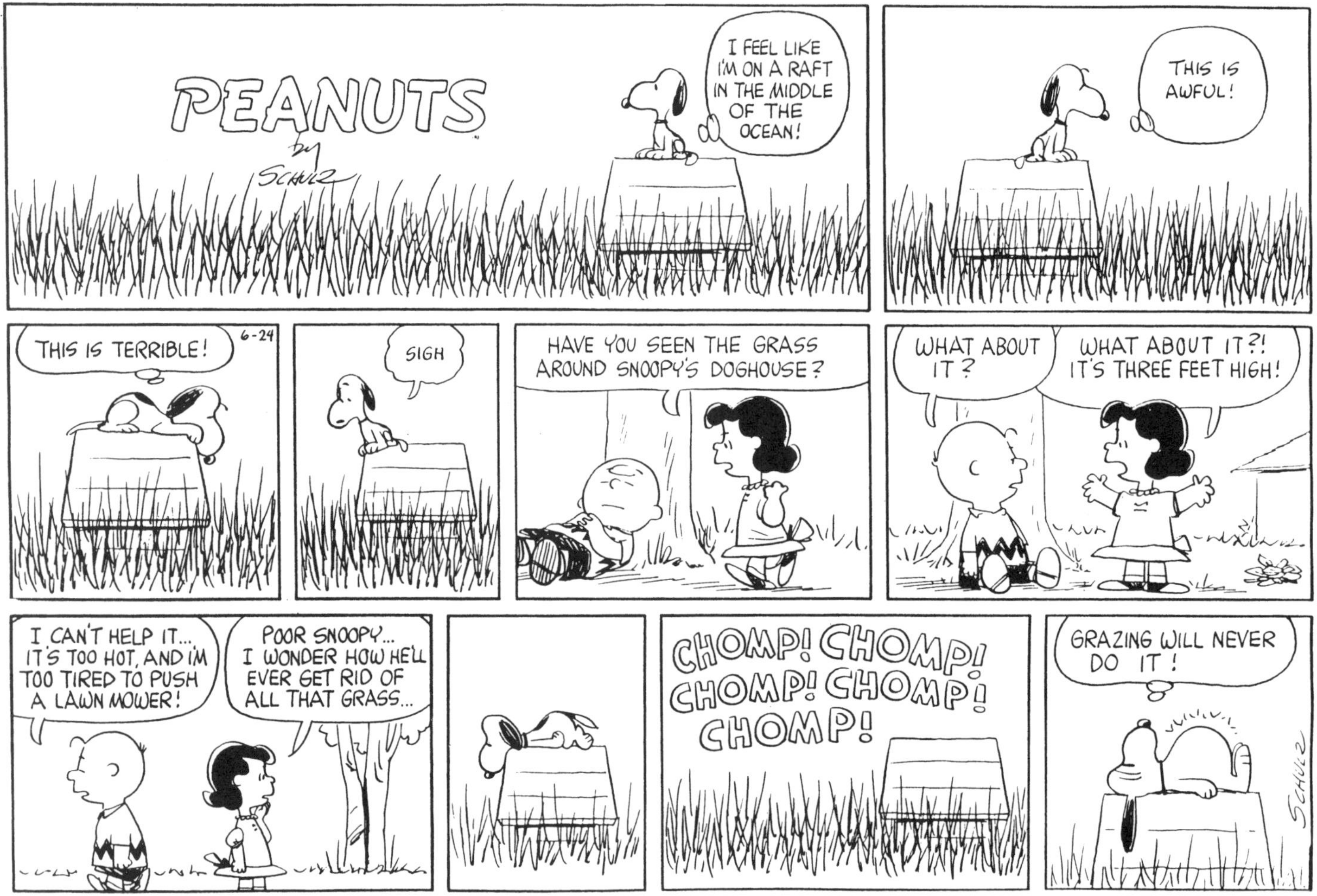
PEANUTS
by SCHULZ
I FEEL LIKE I'M ON A RAFT IN THE MIDDLE OF THE OCEAN!
THIS IS AWFUL!
THIS IS TERRIBLE!
6-24
SIGH
HAVE YOU SEEN THE GRASS AROUND SNOOPY'S DOGHOUSE?
WHAT ABOUT IT?
WHAT ABOUT IT?! IT'S THREE FEET HIGH!
I CAN'T HELP IT... IT'S TOO HOT, AND I'M TOO TIRED TO PUSH A LAWN MOWER!
POOR SNOOPY... I WONDER HOW HE'LL EVER GET RID OF ALL THAT GRASS...
CHOMP! CHOMP! CHOMP! CHOMP! CHOMP!
GRAZING WILL NEVER DO IT!
SCHULZ

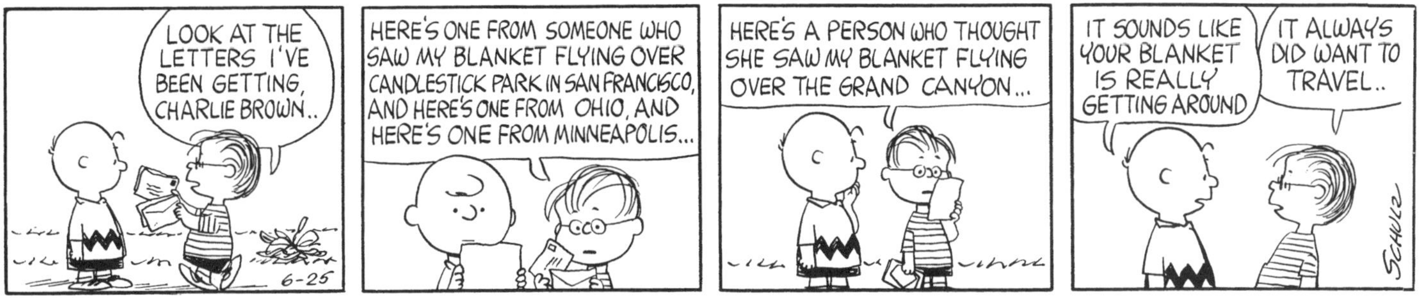
LOOK AT THE LETTERS I'VE BEEN GETTING, CHARLIE BROWN..
6-25
HERE'S ONE FROM SOMEONE WHO SAW MY BLANKET FLYING OVER CANDLESTICK PARK IN SAN FRANCISCO, AND HERE'S ONE FROM OHIO, AND HERE'S ONE FROM MINNEAPOLIS...
HERE'S A PERSON WHO THOUGHT SHE SAW MY BLANKET FLYING OVER THE GRAND CANYON...
IT SOUNDS LIKE YOUR BLANKET IS REALLY GETTING AROUND
IT ALWAYS DID WANT TO TRAVEL..
SCHULZ

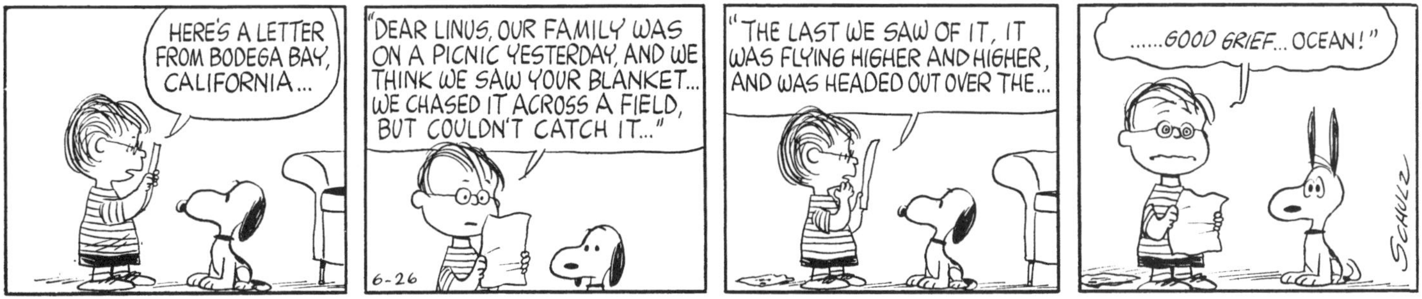
HERE'S A LETTER FROM BODEGA BAY, CALIFORNIA...
"DEAR LINUS, OUR FAMILY WAS ON A PICNIC YESTERDAY, AND WE THINK WE SAW YOUR BLANKET... WE CHASED IT ACROSS A FIELD, BUT COULDN'T CATCH IT..."
6-26
"THE LAST WE SAW OF IT, IT WAS FLYING HIGHER AND HIGHER, AND WAS HEADED OUT OVER THE...
......GOOD GRIEF... OCEAN!"
SCHULZ

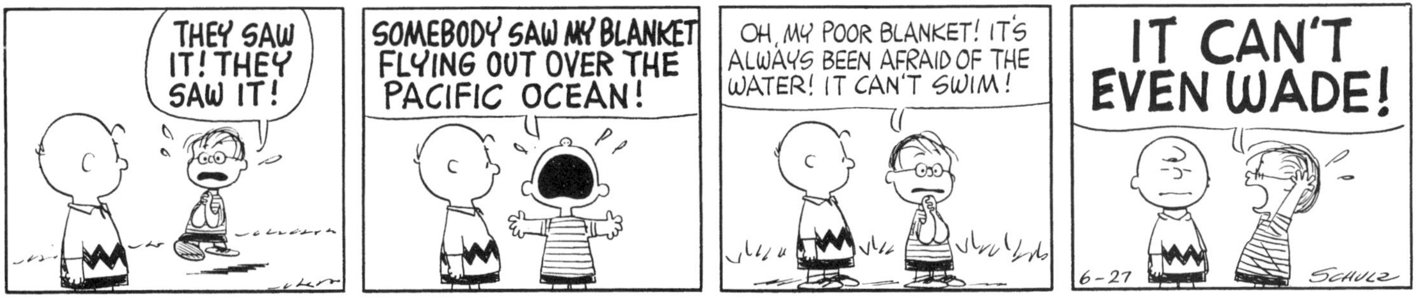
THEY SAW IT! THEY SAW IT!
SOMEBODY SAW MY BLANKET FLYING OUT OVER THE PACIFIC OCEAN!
OH, MY POOR BLANKET! IT'S ALWAYS BEEN AFRAID OF THE WATER! IT CAN'T SWIM!
IT CAN'T EVEN WADE!
6-27
SCHULZ

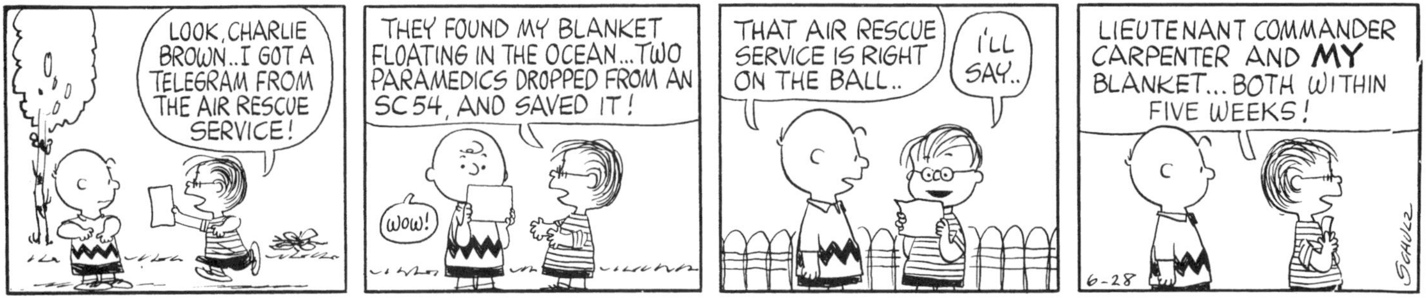
LOOK, CHARLIE BROWN..I GOT A TELEGRAM FROM THE AIR RESCUE SERVICE!
THEY FOUND MY BLANKET FLOATING IN THE OCEAN...TWO PARAMEDICS DROPPED FROM AN SC54, AND SAVED IT!
WOW!
THAT AIR RESCUE SERVICE IS RIGHT ON THE BALL..
I'LL SAY..
LIEUTENANT COMMANDER CARPENTER AND **MY** BLANKET...BOTH WITHIN FIVE WEEKS!
6-28
SCHULZ

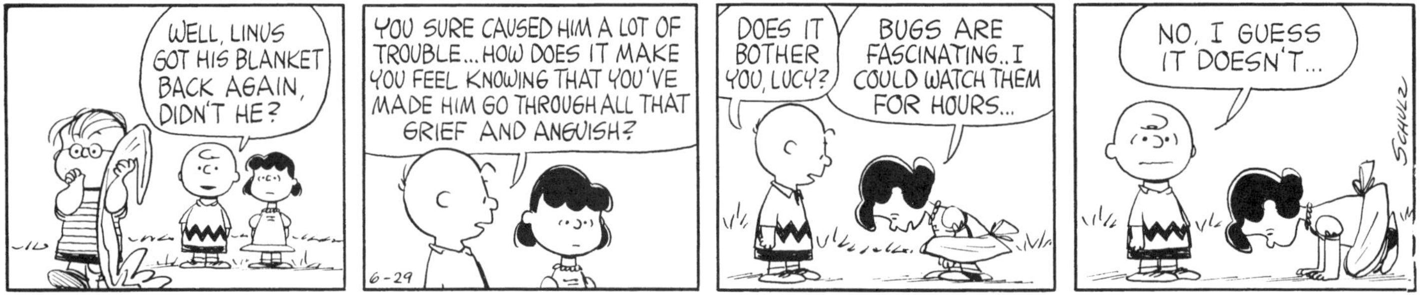
WELL, LINUS GOT HIS BLANKET BACK AGAIN, DIDN'T HE?
YOU SURE CAUSED HIM A LOT OF TROUBLE...HOW DOES IT MAKE YOU FEEL KNOWING THAT YOU'VE MADE HIM GO THROUGH ALL THAT GRIEF AND ANGUISH?
6-29
DOES IT BOTHER YOU, LUCY?
BUGS ARE FASCINATING..I COULD WATCH THEM FOR HOURS...
NO, I GUESS IT DOESN'T...
SCHULZ

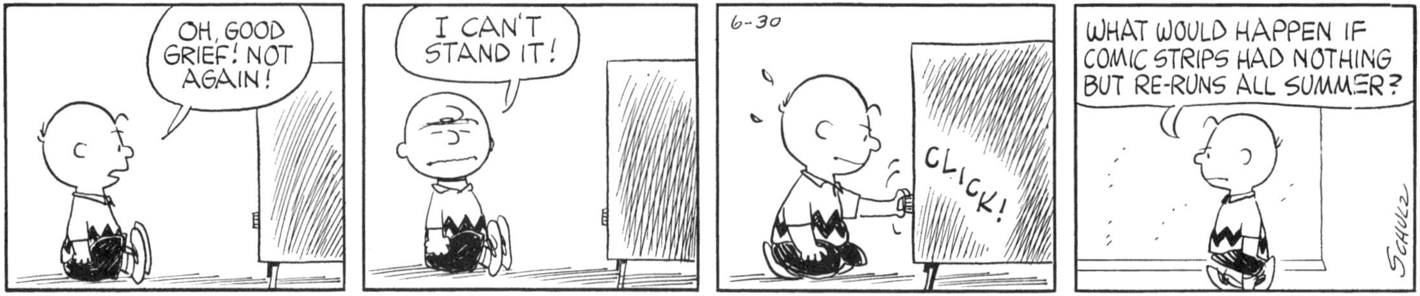
OH, GOOD GRIEF! NOT AGAIN!
I CAN'T STAND IT!
6-30
CLICK!
WHAT WOULD HAPPEN IF COMIC STRIPS HAD NOTHING BUT RE-RUNS ALL SUMMER?
SCHULZ

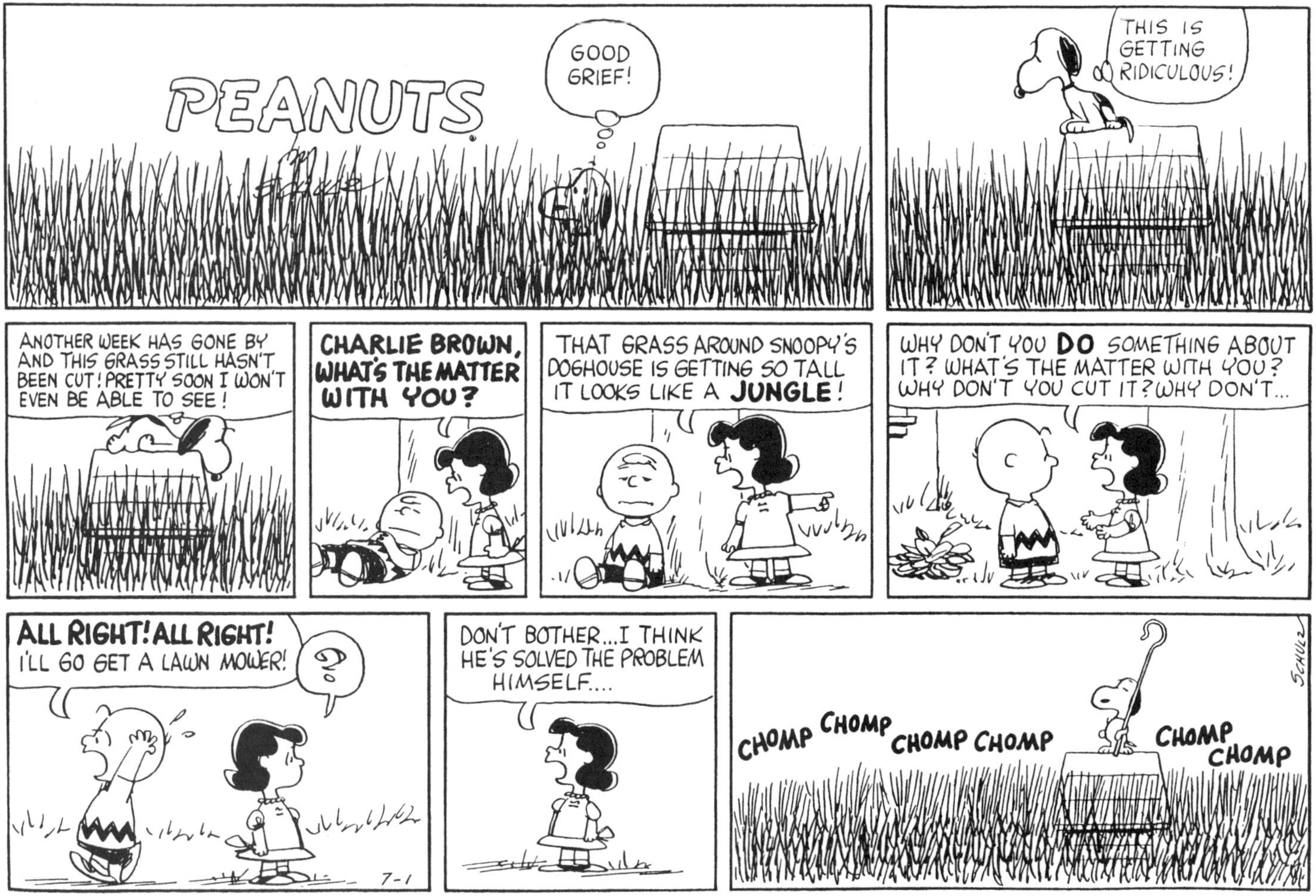
PEANUTS
GOOD GRIEF!
THIS IS GETTING RIDICULOUS!
ANOTHER WEEK HAS GONE BY AND THIS GRASS STILL HASN'T BEEN CUT! PRETTY SOON I WON'T EVEN BE ABLE TO SEE!
CHARLIE BROWN, WHAT'S THE MATTER WITH YOU?
THAT GRASS AROUND SNOOPY'S DOGHOUSE IS GETTING SO TALL IT LOOKS LIKE A JUNGLE!
WHY DON'T YOU DO SOMETHING ABOUT IT? WHAT'S THE MATTER WITH YOU? WHY DON'T YOU CUT IT? WHY DON'T...
ALL RIGHT! ALL RIGHT! I'LL GO GET A LAWN MOWER!
?
DON'T BOTHER...I THINK HE'S SOLVED THE PROBLEM HIMSELF....
CHOMP CHOMP CHOMP CHOMP CHOMP CHOMP
SCHULZ

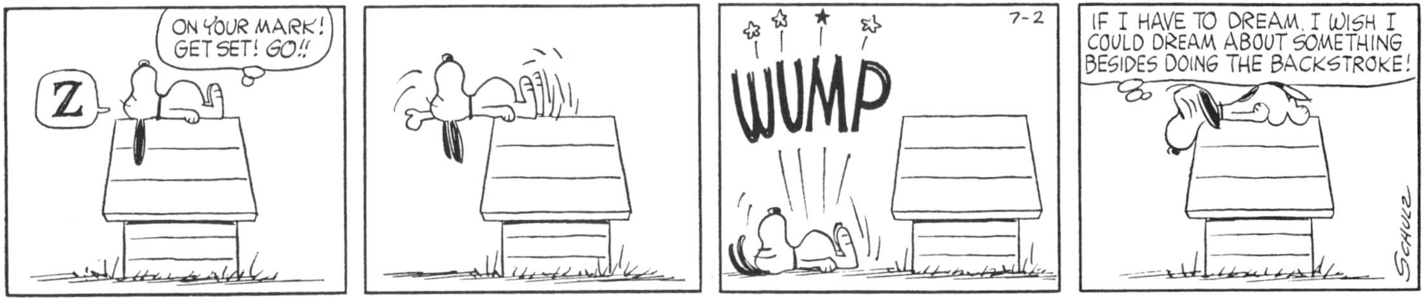
Z
ON YOUR MARK! GET SET! GO!!
7-2
WUMP
IF I HAVE TO DREAM, I WISH I COULD DREAM ABOUT SOMETHING BESIDES DOING THE BACKSTROKE!
SCHULZ

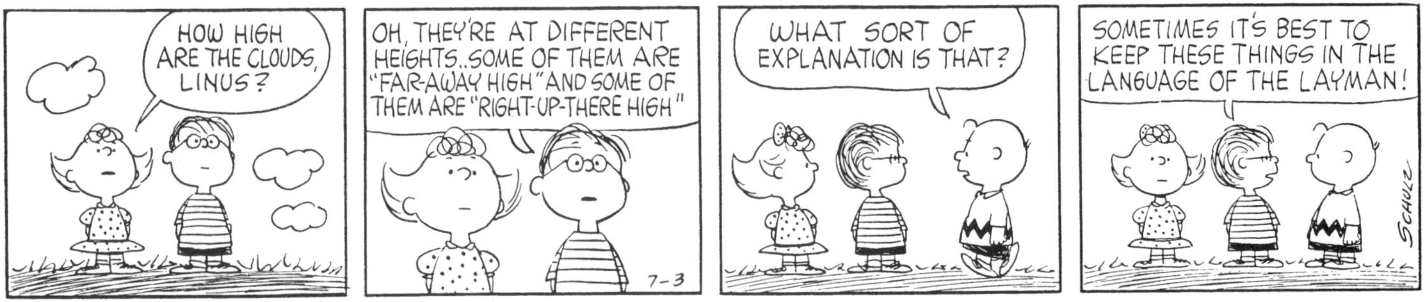
HOW HIGH ARE THE CLOUDS, LINUS?
OH, THEY'RE AT DIFFERENT HEIGHTS..SOME OF THEM ARE "FAR-AWAY HIGH" AND SOME OF THEM ARE "RIGHT-UP-THERE HIGH"
7-3
WHAT SORT OF EXPLANATION IS THAT?
SOMETIMES IT'S BEST TO KEEP THESE THINGS IN THE LANGUAGE OF THE LAYMAN!
SCHULZ

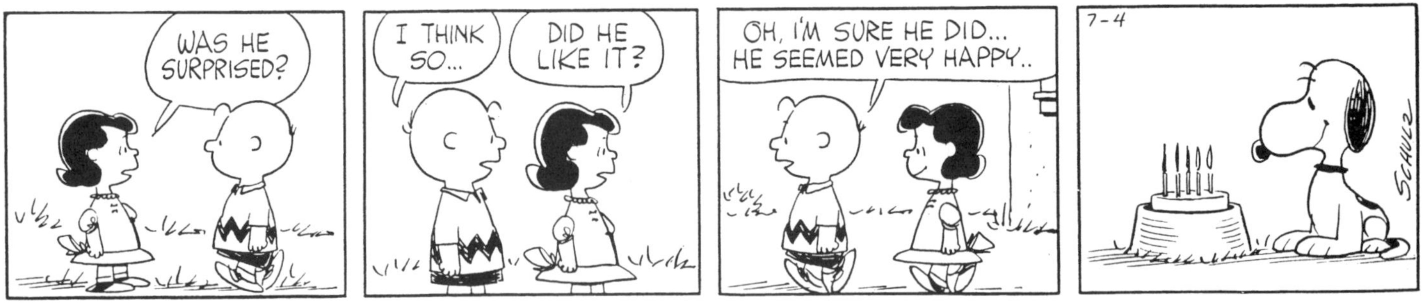
WAS HE SURPRISED?
I THINK SO...
DID HE LIKE IT?
OH, I'M SURE HE DID... HE SEEMED VERY HAPPY..
7-4
SCHULZ

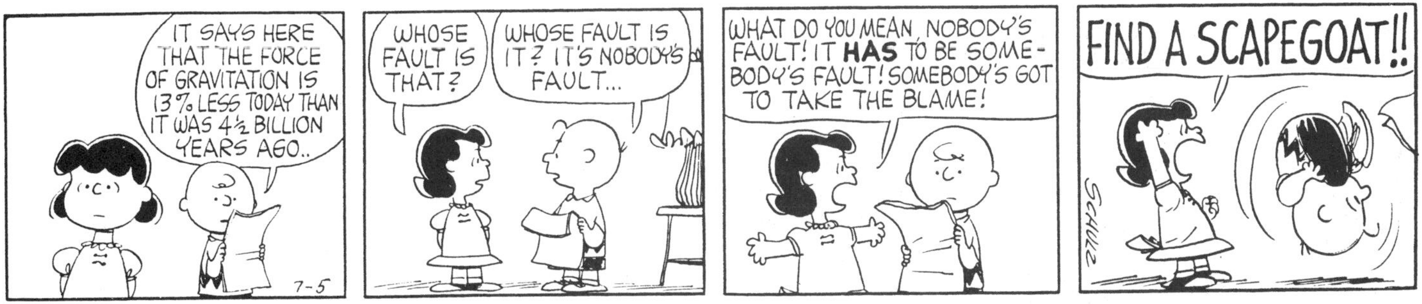
IT SAYS HERE THAT THE FORCE OF GRAVITATION IS 13% LESS TODAY THAN IT WAS 4½ BILLION YEARS AGO..
7-5
WHOSE FAULT IS THAT?
WHOSE FAULT IS IT? IT'S NOBODY'S FAULT...
WHAT DO YOU MEAN, NOBODY'S FAULT! IT **HAS** TO BE SOMEBODY'S FAULT! SOMEBODY'S GOT TO TAKE THE BLAME!
FIND A SCAPEGOAT!!
SCHULZ

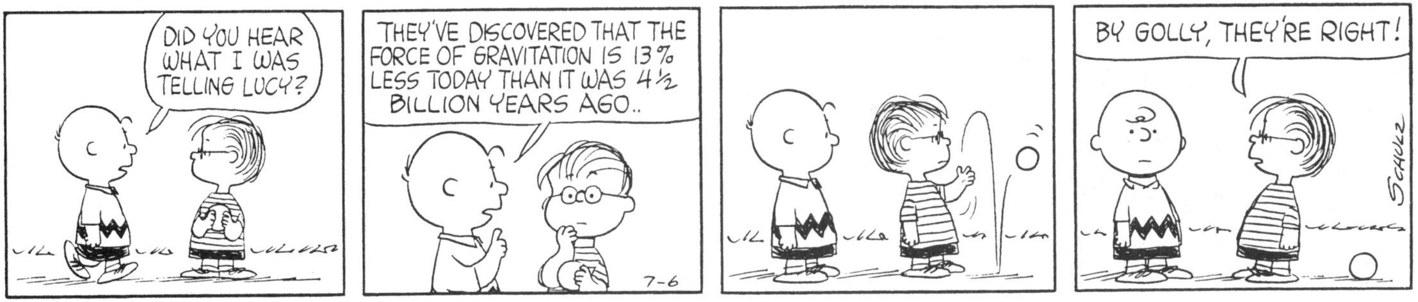
DID YOU HEAR WHAT I WAS TELLING LUCY?
THEY'VE DISCOVERED THAT THE FORCE OF GRAVITATION IS 13% LESS TODAY THAN IT WAS 4½ BILLION YEARS AGO..
7-6
BY GOLLY, THEY'RE RIGHT!
SCHULZ

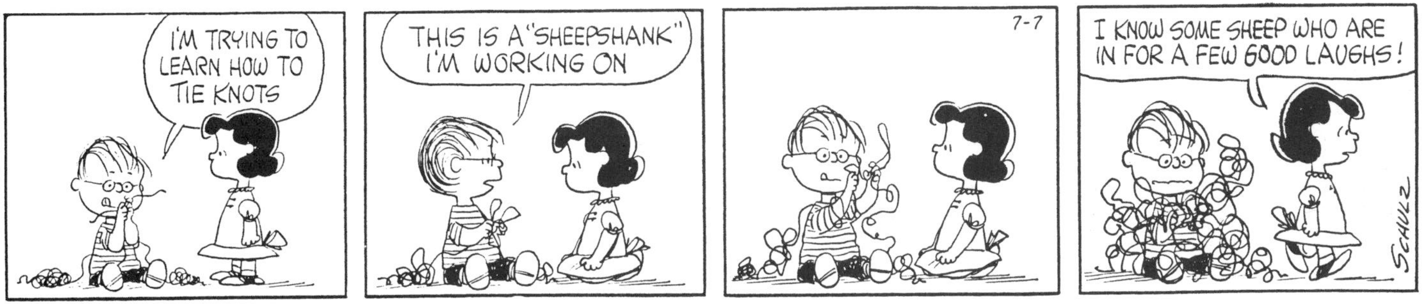
I'M TRYING TO LEARN HOW TO TIE KNOTS
THIS IS A "SHEEPSHANK" I'M WORKING ON
7-7
I KNOW SOME SHEEP WHO ARE IN FOR A FEW GOOD LAUGHS!
SCHULZ

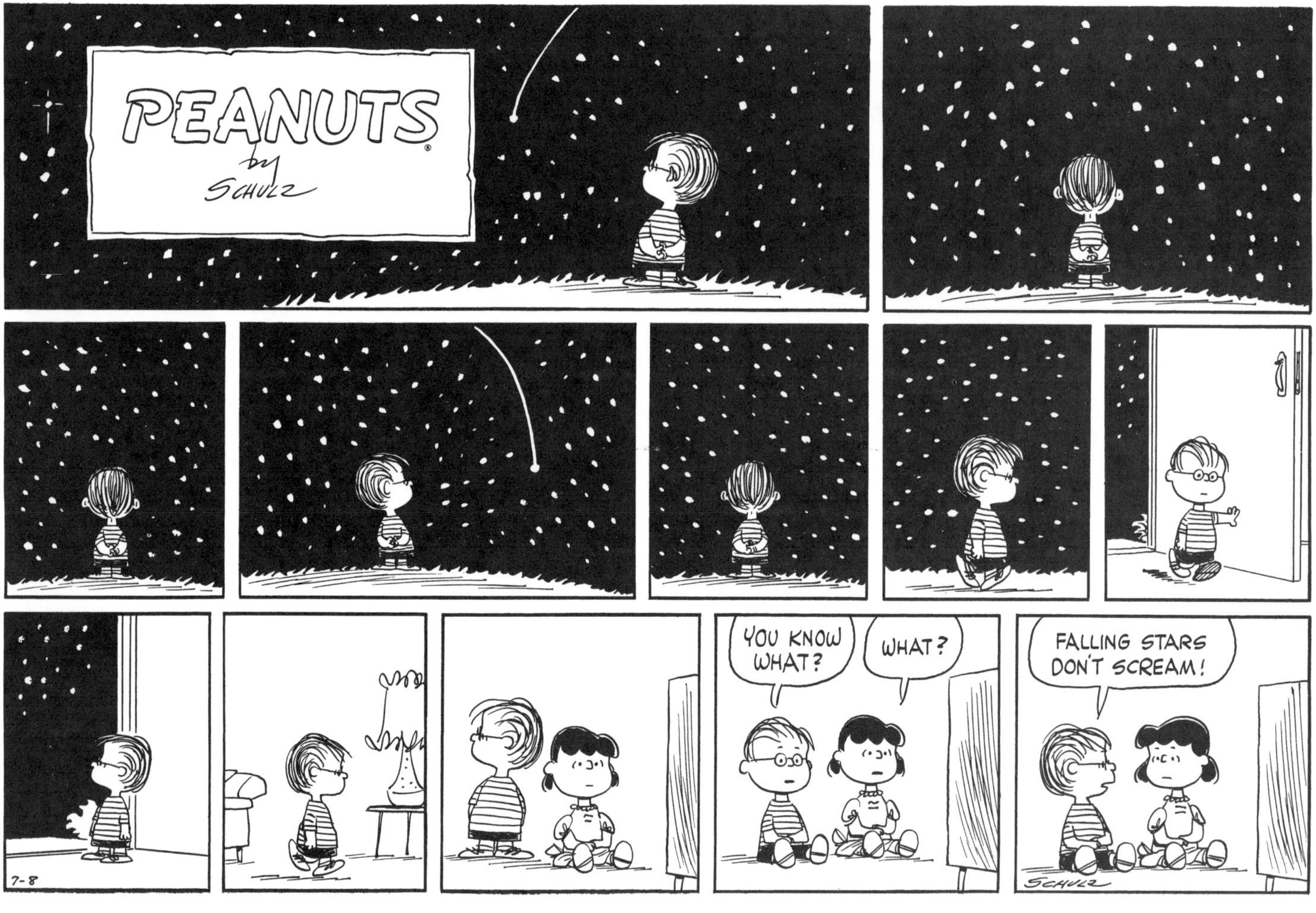
PEANUTS
by SCHULZ
7-8
YOU KNOW WHAT?
WHAT?
FALLING STARS DON'T SCREAM!
SCHULZ

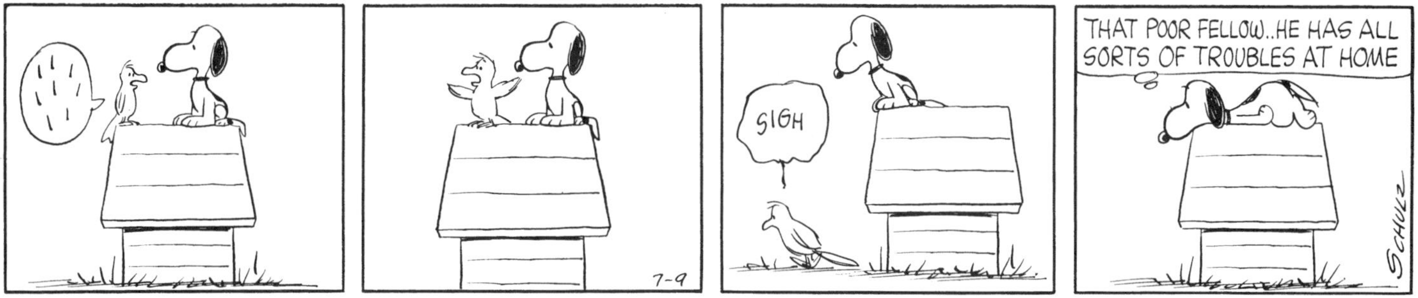
SIGH
THAT POOR FELLOW..HE HAS ALL SORTS OF TROUBLES AT HOME

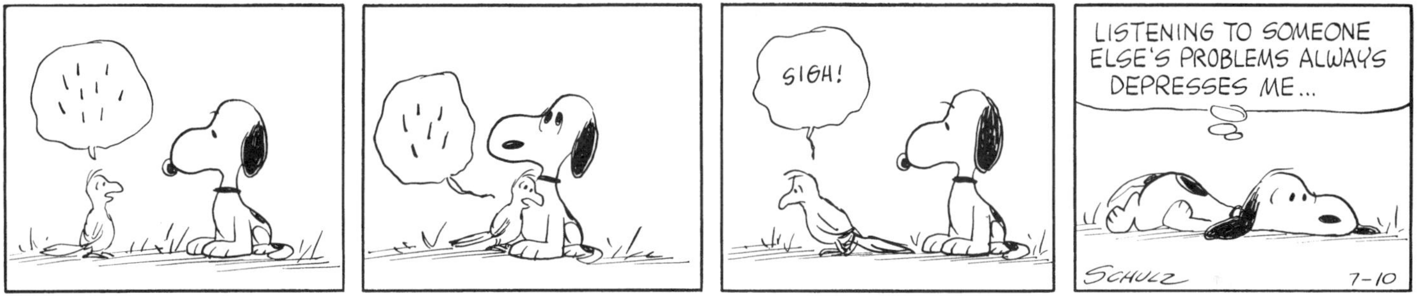
SIGH!
LISTENING TO SOMEONE ELSE'S PROBLEMS ALWAYS DEPRESSES ME...

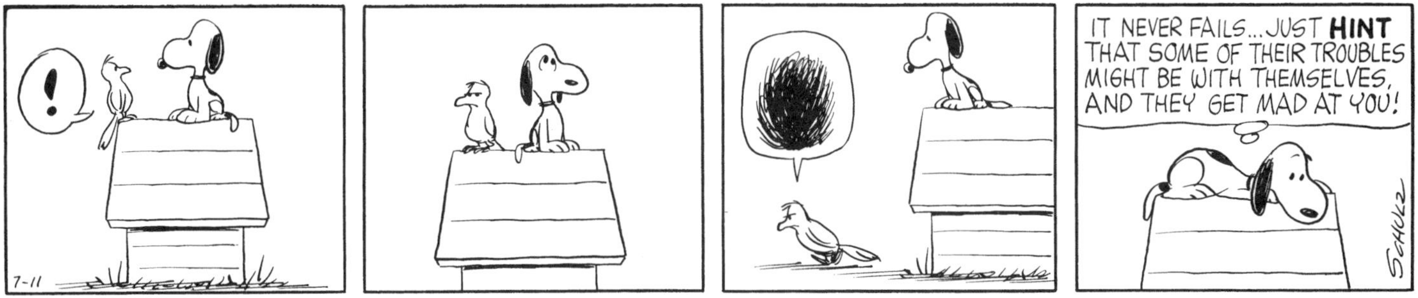
!
IT NEVER FAILS...JUST **HINT** THAT SOME OF THEIR TROUBLES MIGHT BE WITH THEMSELVES, AND THEY GET MAD AT YOU!

Panel 1: MY DAD HAS ALWAYS HAD AMBITIONS TO BE A GREAT GOLFER OR A GREAT BOWLER

Panel 2: HE'S ALWAYS WANTED TO PLAY GOLF LIKE SAM SNEAD AND BOWL LIKE DON CARTER...

Panel 3: 7-12 HAS HE ACHIEVED HIS AMBITION?

Panel 4: NO, HE BOWLS LIKE SAM SNEAD, AND PLAYS GOLF LIKE DON CARTER!

Panel 5: (Snoopy and doghouse labeled SNOOPY)

Panel 6: 7-13 IT DOES NOT! NOW, GET OUT OF HERE!

Panel 7: WHAT AN IMAGINATION..

Panel 8: HE CLAIMS HIS DOG DISH GETS LONESOME WHEN IT DOESN'T HAVE ANY FOOD IN IT!

Panel 9: GET OUT! GET WAY OUT!!

Panel 10: 7-14

Panel 11: (Lucy getting ready to catch)

Panel 12: LET'S TRY TO GET IN ON THOSE!

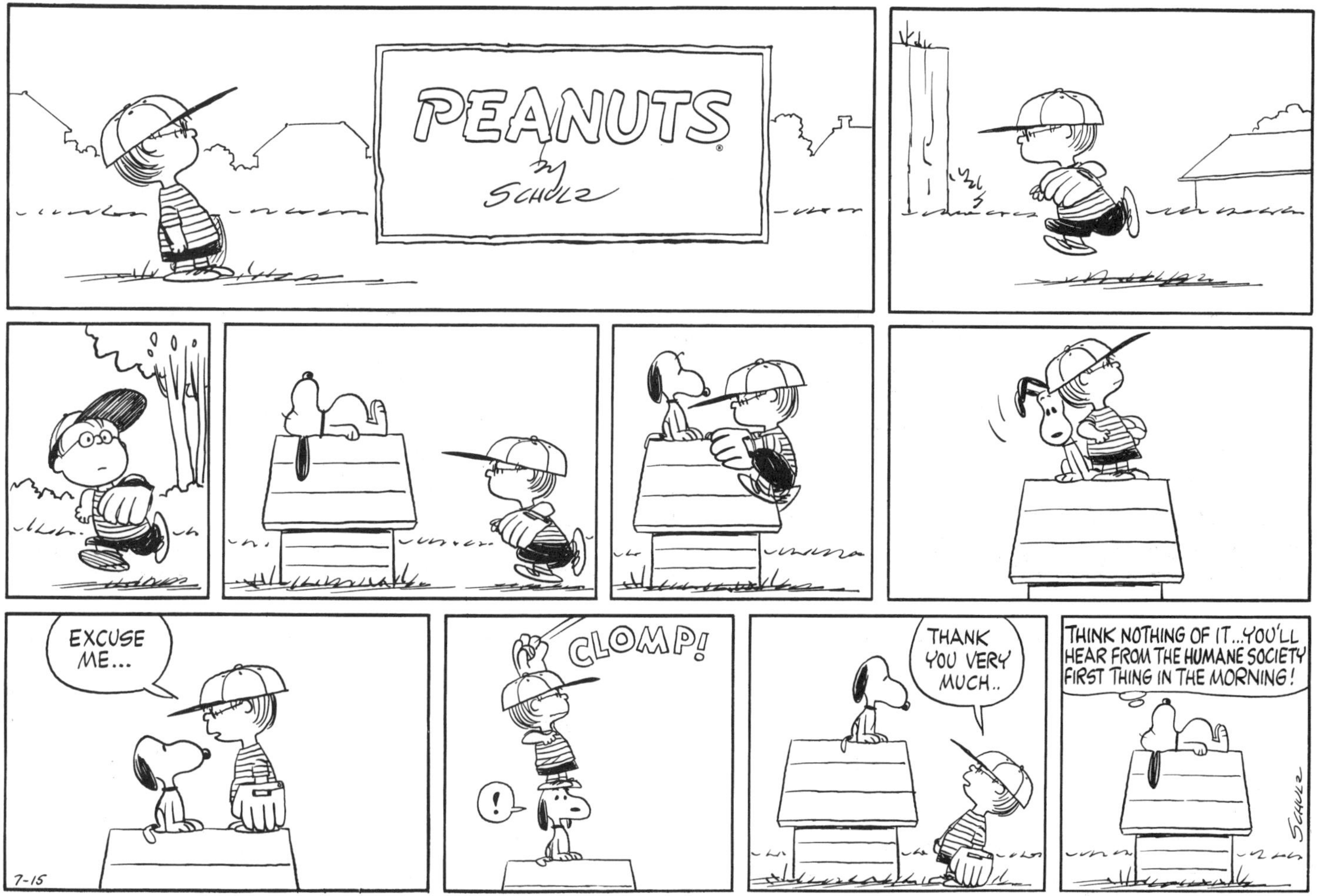
PEANUTS
by SCHULZ
EXCUSE ME...
7-15
CLOMP!
!
THANK YOU VERY MUCH..
THINK NOTHING OF IT...YOU'LL HEAR FROM THE HUMANE SOCIETY FIRST THING IN THE MORNING!
SCHULZ

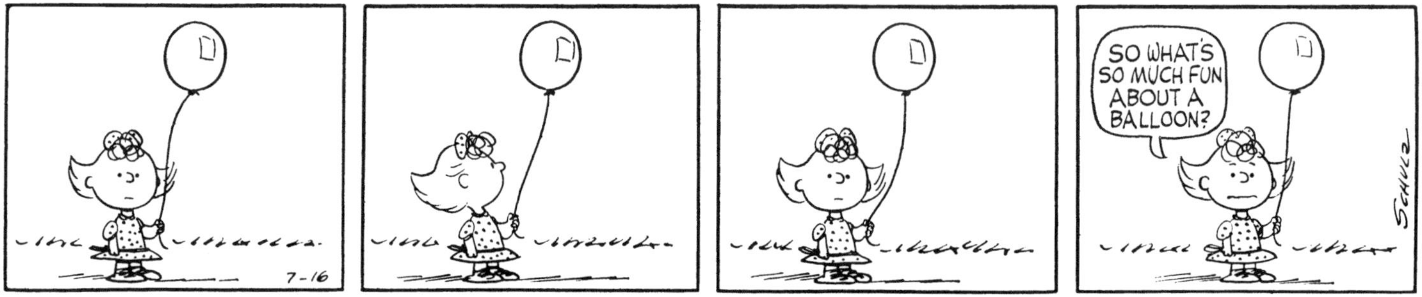
SO WHAT'S SO MUCH FUN ABOUT A BALLOON?

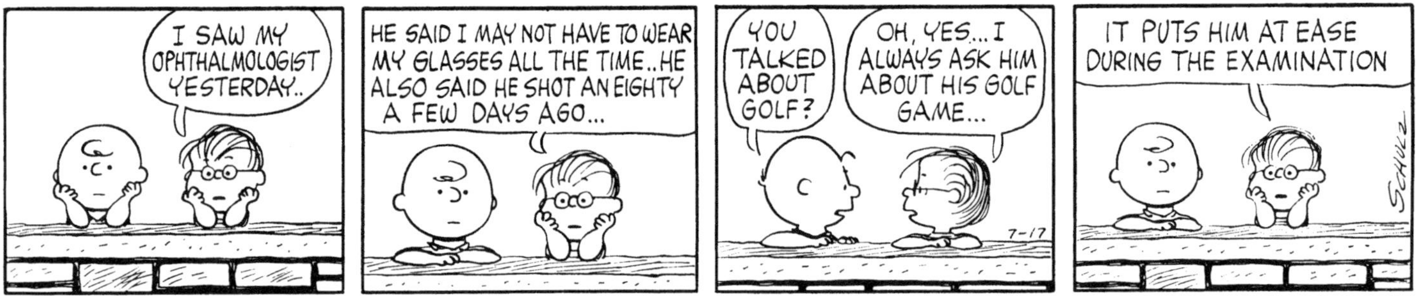
I SAW MY OPHTHALMOLOGIST YESTERDAY..
HE SAID I MAY NOT HAVE TO WEAR MY GLASSES ALL THE TIME..HE ALSO SAID HE SHOT AN EIGHTY A FEW DAYS AGO...
YOU TALKED ABOUT GOLF?
OH, YES... I ALWAYS ASK HIM ABOUT HIS GOLF GAME...
IT PUTS HIM AT EASE DURING THE EXAMINATION

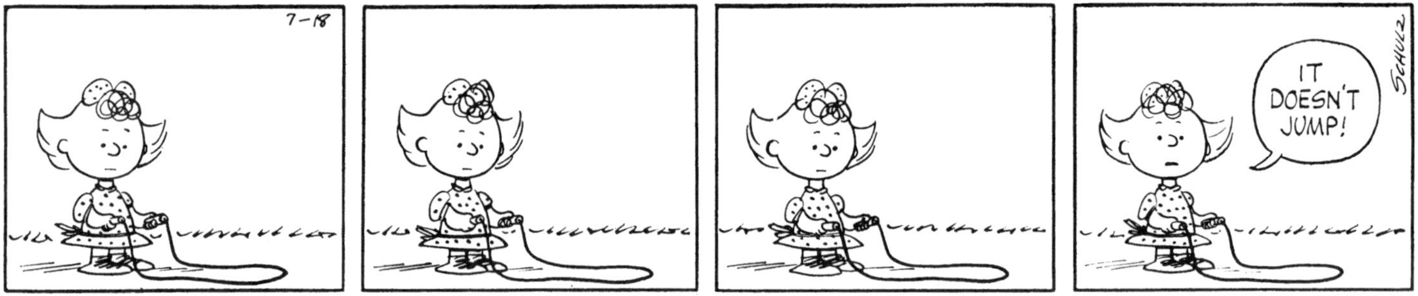
IT DOESN'T JUMP!

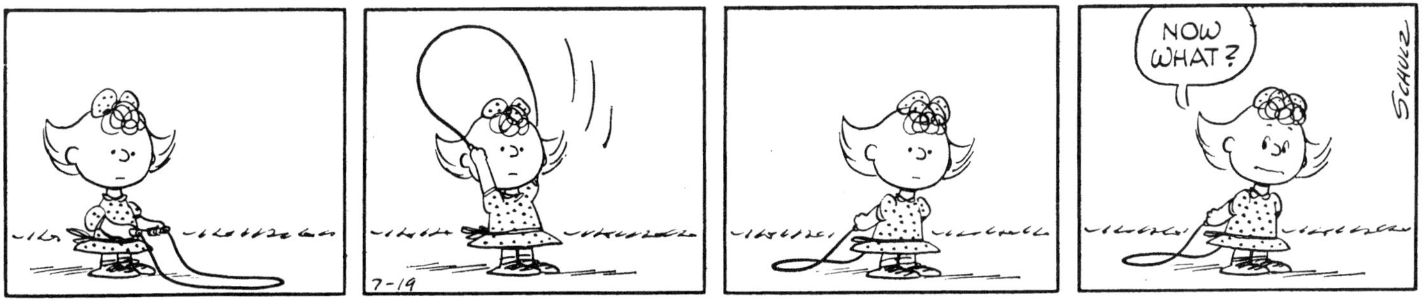
7-19
NOW WHAT?
SCHULZ

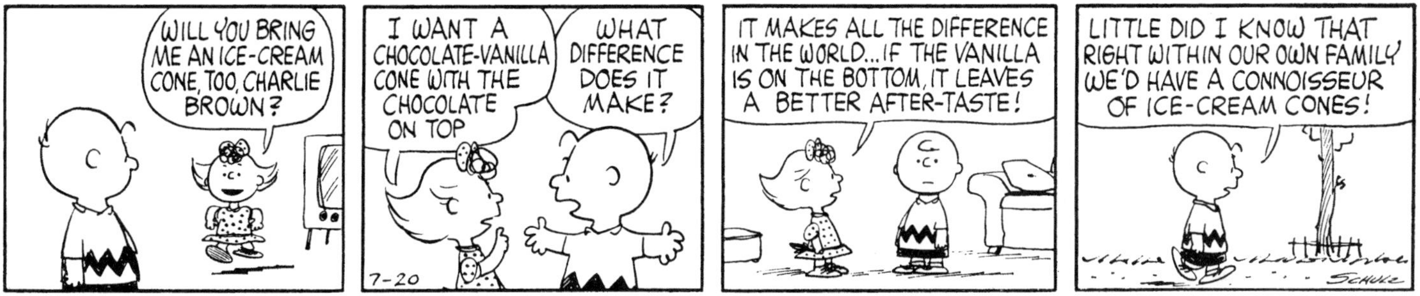
WILL YOU BRING ME AN ICE-CREAM CONE, TOO, CHARLIE BROWN?
7-20
I WANT A CHOCOLATE-VANILLA CONE WITH THE CHOCOLATE ON TOP
WHAT DIFFERENCE DOES IT MAKE?
IT MAKES ALL THE DIFFERENCE IN THE WORLD... IF THE VANILLA IS ON THE BOTTOM, IT LEAVES A BETTER AFTER-TASTE!
LITTLE DID I KNOW THAT RIGHT WITHIN OUR OWN FAMILY WE'D HAVE A CONNOISSEUR OF ICE-CREAM CONES!
SCHULZ

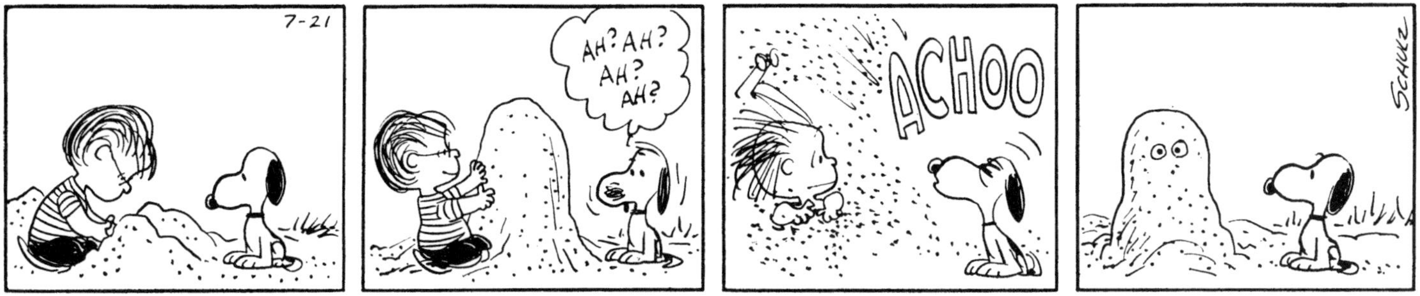
7-21
AH? AH? AH? AH?
ACHOO
SCHULZ

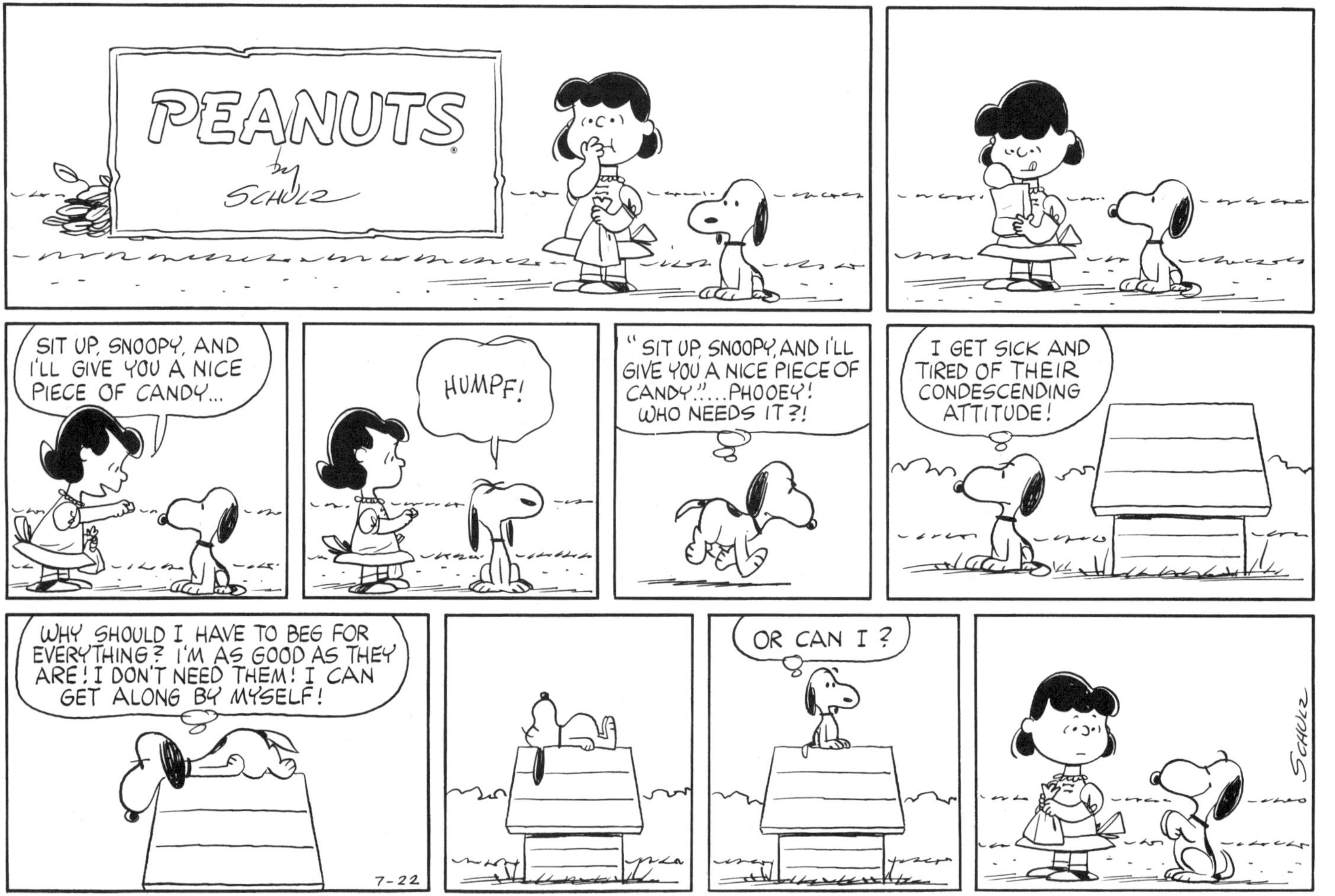
PEANUTS
by SCHULZ
SIT UP, SNOOPY, AND I'LL GIVE YOU A NICE PIECE OF CANDY...
HUMPF!
"SIT UP, SNOOPY, AND I'LL GIVE YOU A NICE PIECE OF CANDY."... PHOOEY! WHO NEEDS IT?!
I GET SICK AND TIRED OF THEIR CONDESCENDING ATTITUDE!
WHY SHOULD I HAVE TO BEG FOR EVERYTHING? I'M AS GOOD AS THEY ARE! I DON'T NEED THEM! I CAN GET ALONG BY MYSELF!
7-22
OR CAN I ?
SCHULZ

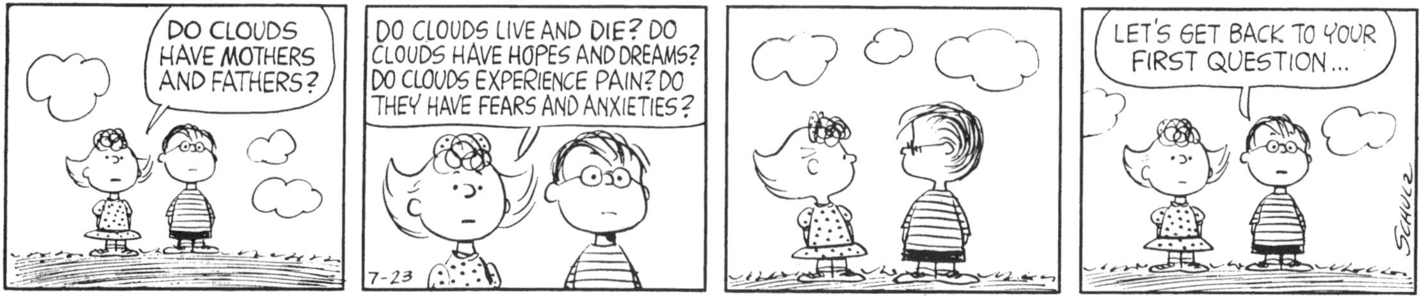
DO CLOUDS HAVE MOTHERS AND FATHERS?
DO CLOUDS LIVE AND DIE? DO CLOUDS HAVE HOPES AND DREAMS? DO CLOUDS EXPERIENCE PAIN? DO THEY HAVE FEARS AND ANXIETIES?
7-23
LET'S GET BACK TO YOUR FIRST QUESTION...
SCHULZ

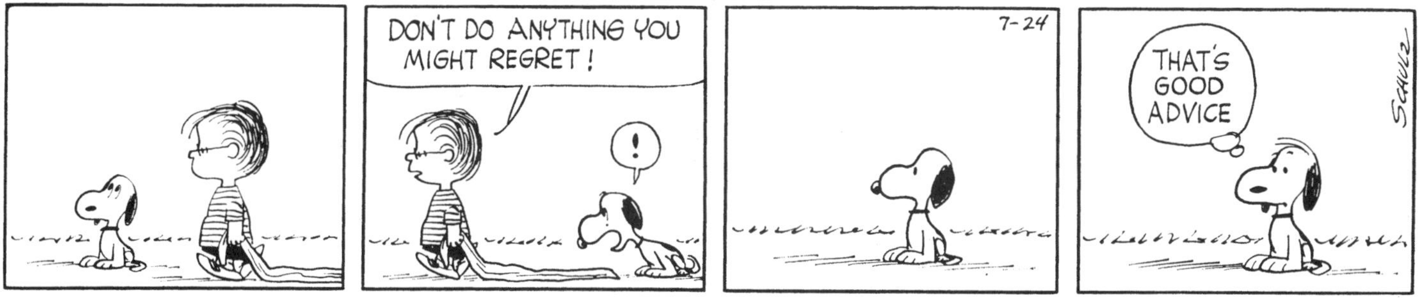
DON'T DO ANYTHING YOU MIGHT REGRET!
!
7-24
THAT'S GOOD ADVICE
SCHULZ

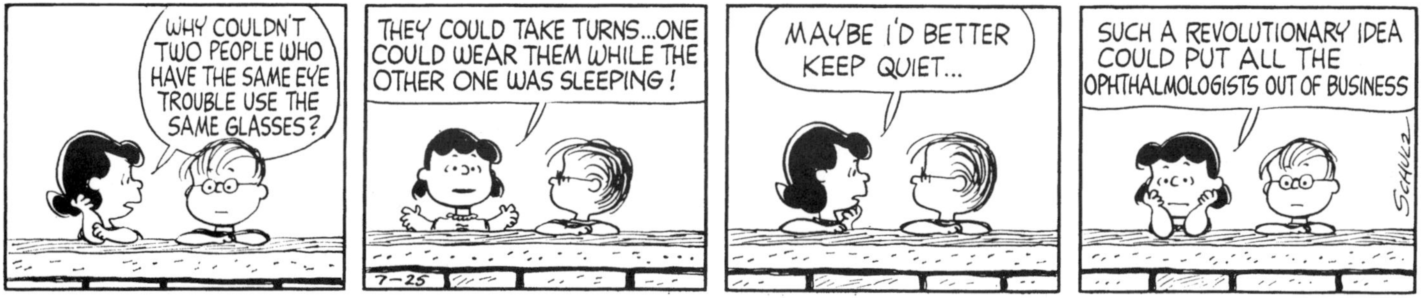
WHY COULDN'T TWO PEOPLE WHO HAVE THE SAME EYE TROUBLE USE THE SAME GLASSES?
THEY COULD TAKE TURNS...ONE COULD WEAR THEM WHILE THE OTHER ONE WAS SLEEPING!
7-25
MAYBE I'D BETTER KEEP QUIET...
SUCH A REVOLUTIONARY IDEA COULD PUT ALL THE OPHTHALMOLOGISTS OUT OF BUSINESS
SCHULZ

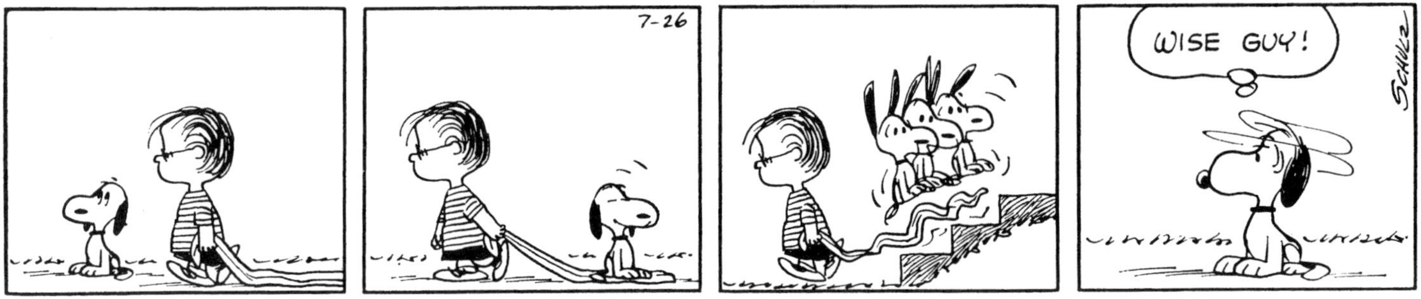
7-26
WISE GUY!
SCHULZ

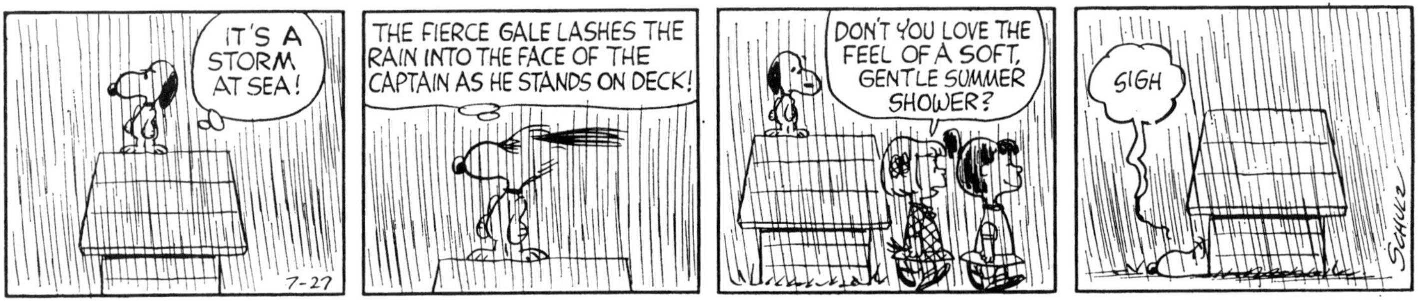
IT'S A STORM AT SEA!
7-27
THE FIERCE GALE LASHES THE RAIN INTO THE FACE OF THE CAPTAIN AS HE STANDS ON DECK!
DON'T YOU LOVE THE FEEL OF A SOFT, GENTLE SUMMER SHOWER?
SIGH
SCHULZ

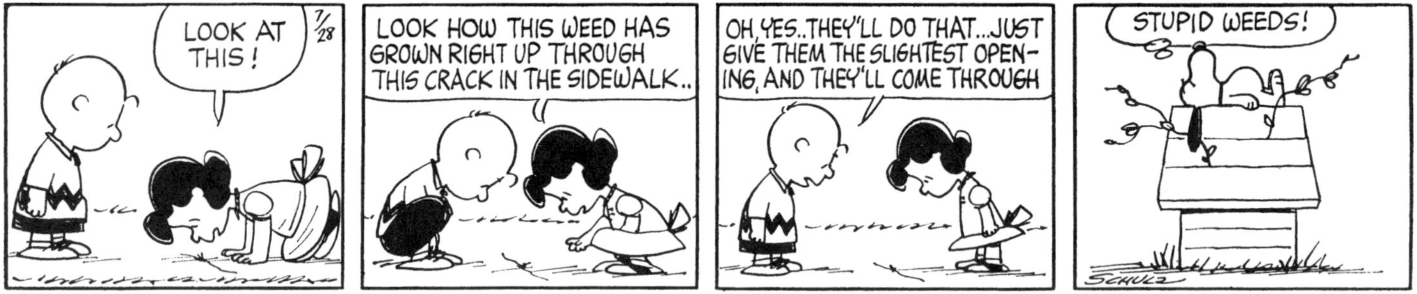
LOOK AT THIS!
7/28
LOOK HOW THIS WEED HAS GROWN RIGHT UP THROUGH THIS CRACK IN THE SIDEWALK..
OH, YES..THEY'LL DO THAT...JUST GIVE THEM THE SLIGHTEST OPENING, AND THEY'LL COME THROUGH
STUPID WEEDS!
SCHULZ

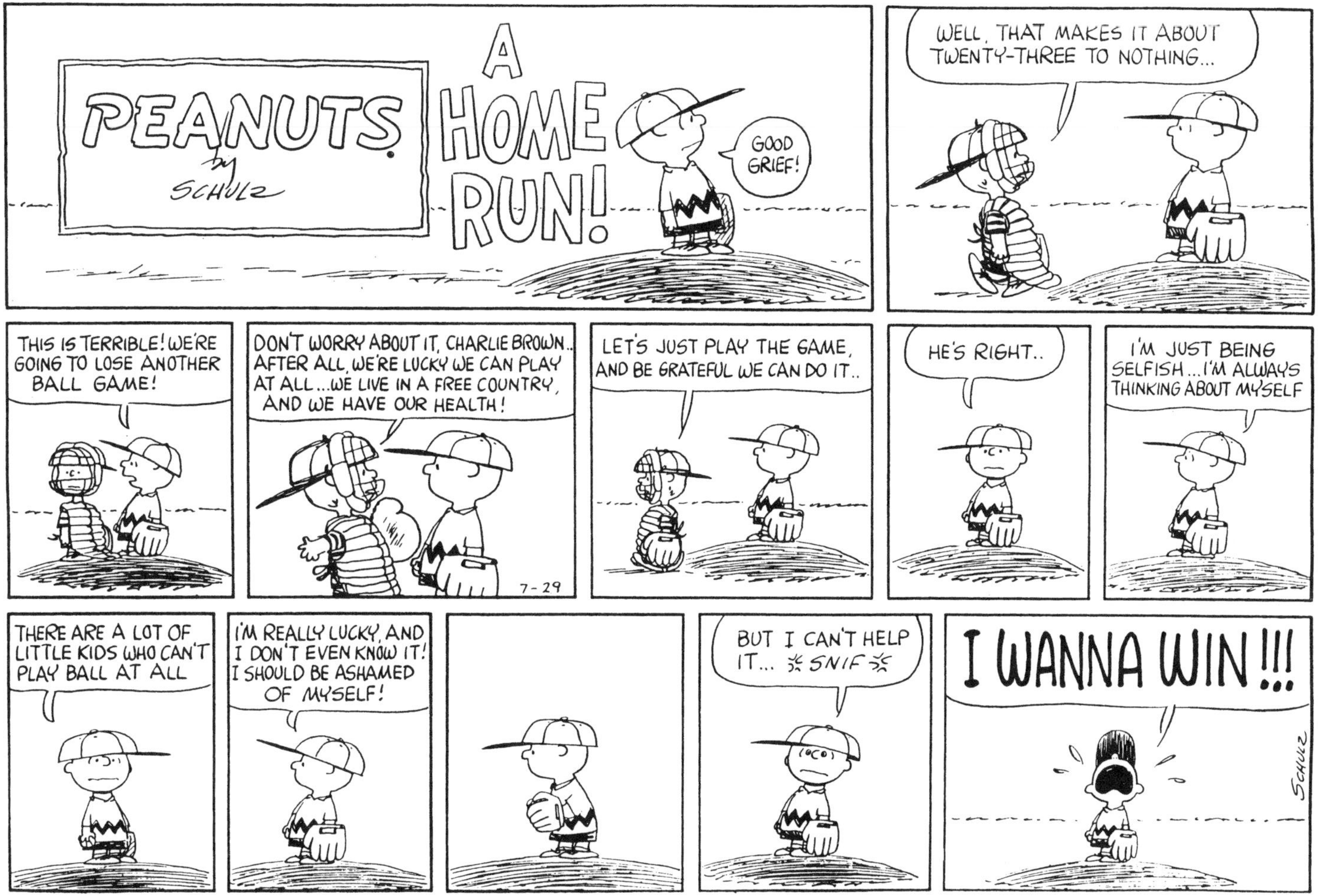
PEANUTS
by SCHULZ
A HOME RUN!
GOOD GRIEF!
WELL, THAT MAKES IT ABOUT TWENTY-THREE TO NOTHING...
THIS IS TERRIBLE! WE'RE GOING TO LOSE ANOTHER BALL GAME!
DON'T WORRY ABOUT IT, CHARLIE BROWN.. AFTER ALL, WE'RE LUCKY WE CAN PLAY AT ALL...WE LIVE IN A FREE COUNTRY, AND WE HAVE OUR HEALTH!
7-29
LET'S JUST PLAY THE GAME, AND BE GRATEFUL WE CAN DO IT..
HE'S RIGHT..
I'M JUST BEING SELFISH...I'M ALWAYS THINKING ABOUT MYSELF
THERE ARE A LOT OF LITTLE KIDS WHO CAN'T PLAY BALL AT ALL
I'M REALLY LUCKY, AND I DON'T EVEN KNOW IT! I SHOULD BE ASHAMED OF MYSELF!
BUT I CAN'T HELP IT... SNIF
I WANNA WIN!!!
SCHULZ

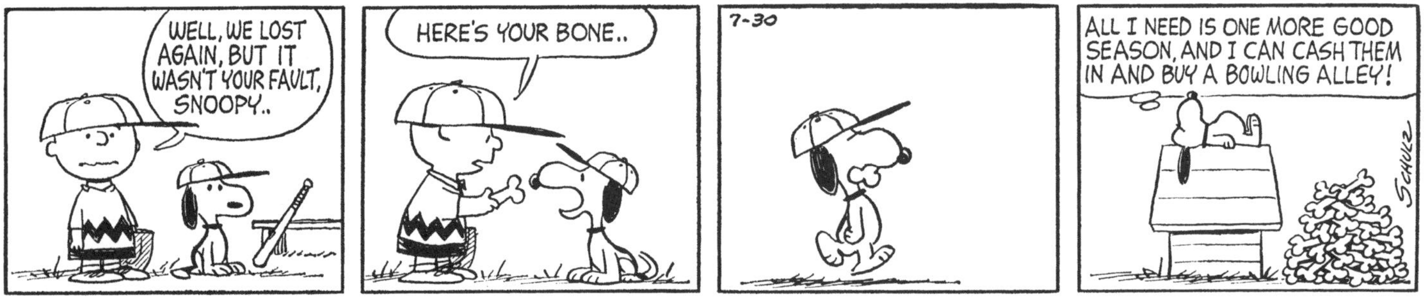
WELL, WE LOST AGAIN, BUT IT WASN'T YOUR FAULT, SNOOPY..
HERE'S YOUR BONE..
7-30
ALL I NEED IS ONE MORE GOOD SEASON, AND I CAN CASH THEM IN AND BUY A BOWLING ALLEY!
SCHULZ

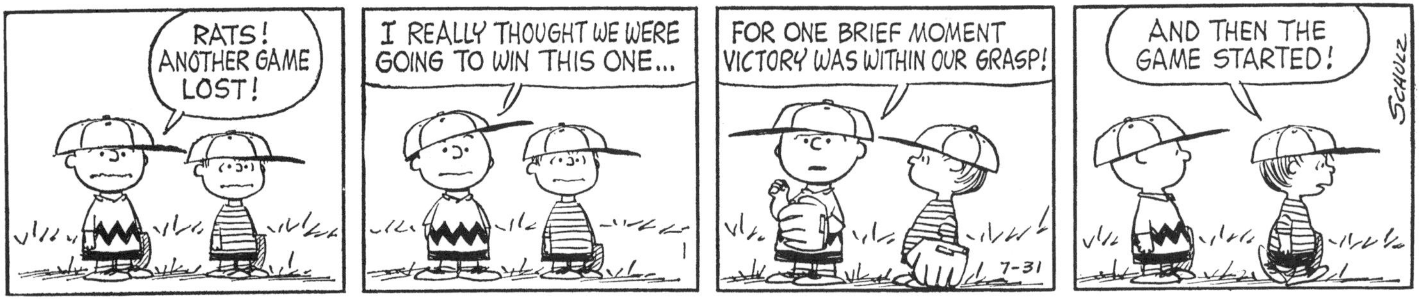
RATS! ANOTHER GAME LOST!
I REALLY THOUGHT WE WERE GOING TO WIN THIS ONE...
FOR ONE BRIEF MOMENT VICTORY WAS WITHIN OUR GRASP!
7-31
AND THEN THE GAME STARTED!
SCHULZ

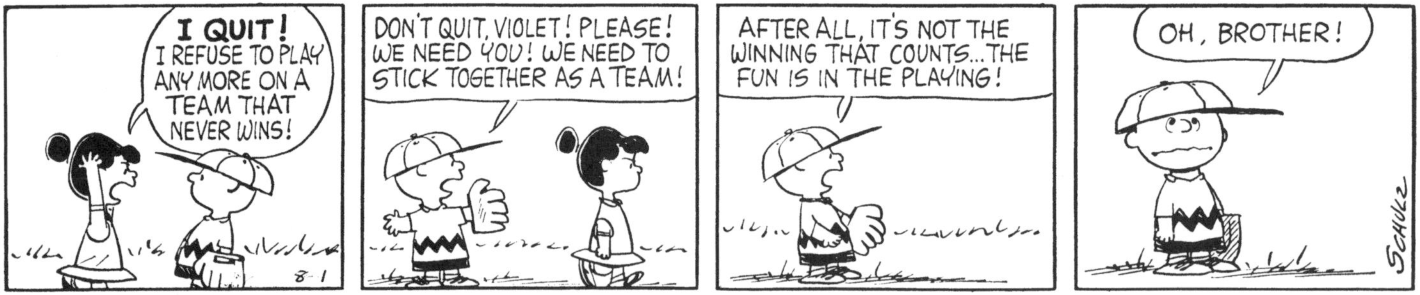
I QUIT! I REFUSE TO PLAY ANY MORE ON A TEAM THAT NEVER WINS!
8-1
DON'T QUIT, VIOLET! PLEASE! WE NEED YOU! WE NEED TO STICK TOGETHER AS A TEAM!
AFTER ALL, IT'S NOT THE WINNING THAT COUNTS...THE FUN IS IN THE PLAYING!
OH, BROTHER!
SCHULZ

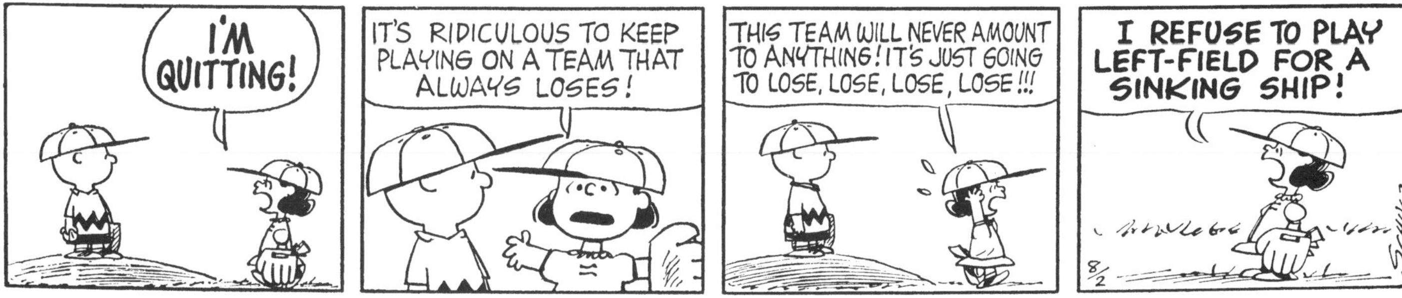
I'M QUITTING!
IT'S RIDICULOUS TO KEEP PLAYING ON A TEAM THAT ALWAYS LOSES!
THIS TEAM WILL NEVER AMOUNT TO ANYTHING! IT'S JUST GOING TO LOSE, LOSE, LOSE, LOSE!!!
I REFUSE TO PLAY LEFT-FIELD FOR A SINKING SHIP!

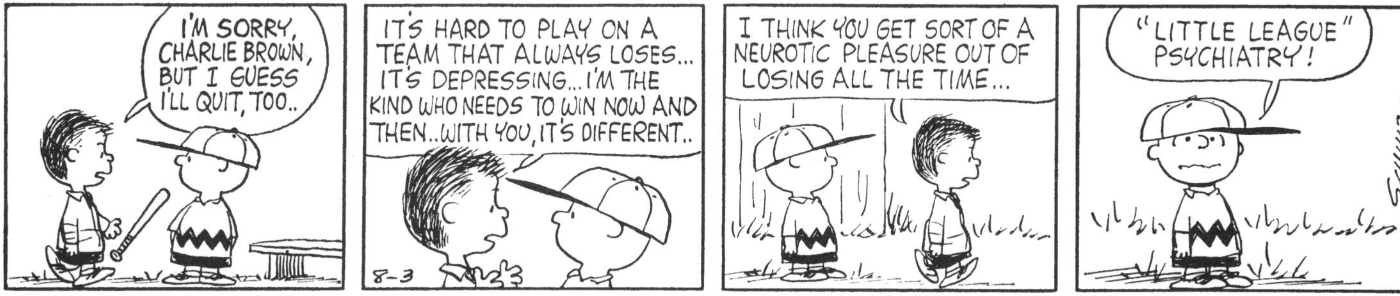
I'M SORRY, CHARLIE BROWN, BUT I GUESS I'LL QUIT, TOO..
IT'S HARD TO PLAY ON A TEAM THAT ALWAYS LOSES... IT'S DEPRESSING... I'M THE KIND WHO NEEDS TO WIN NOW AND THEN.. WITH YOU, IT'S DIFFERENT..
I THINK YOU GET SORT OF A NEUROTIC PLEASURE OUT OF LOSING ALL THE TIME...
"LITTLE LEAGUE" PSYCHIATRY!

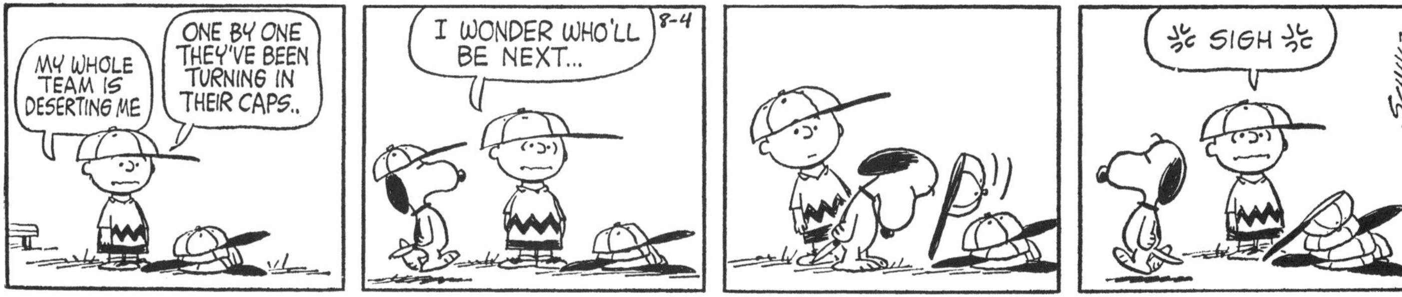
MY WHOLE TEAM IS DESERTING ME
ONE BY ONE THEY'VE BEEN TURNING IN THEIR CAPS..
I WONDER WHO'LL BE NEXT...
SIGH

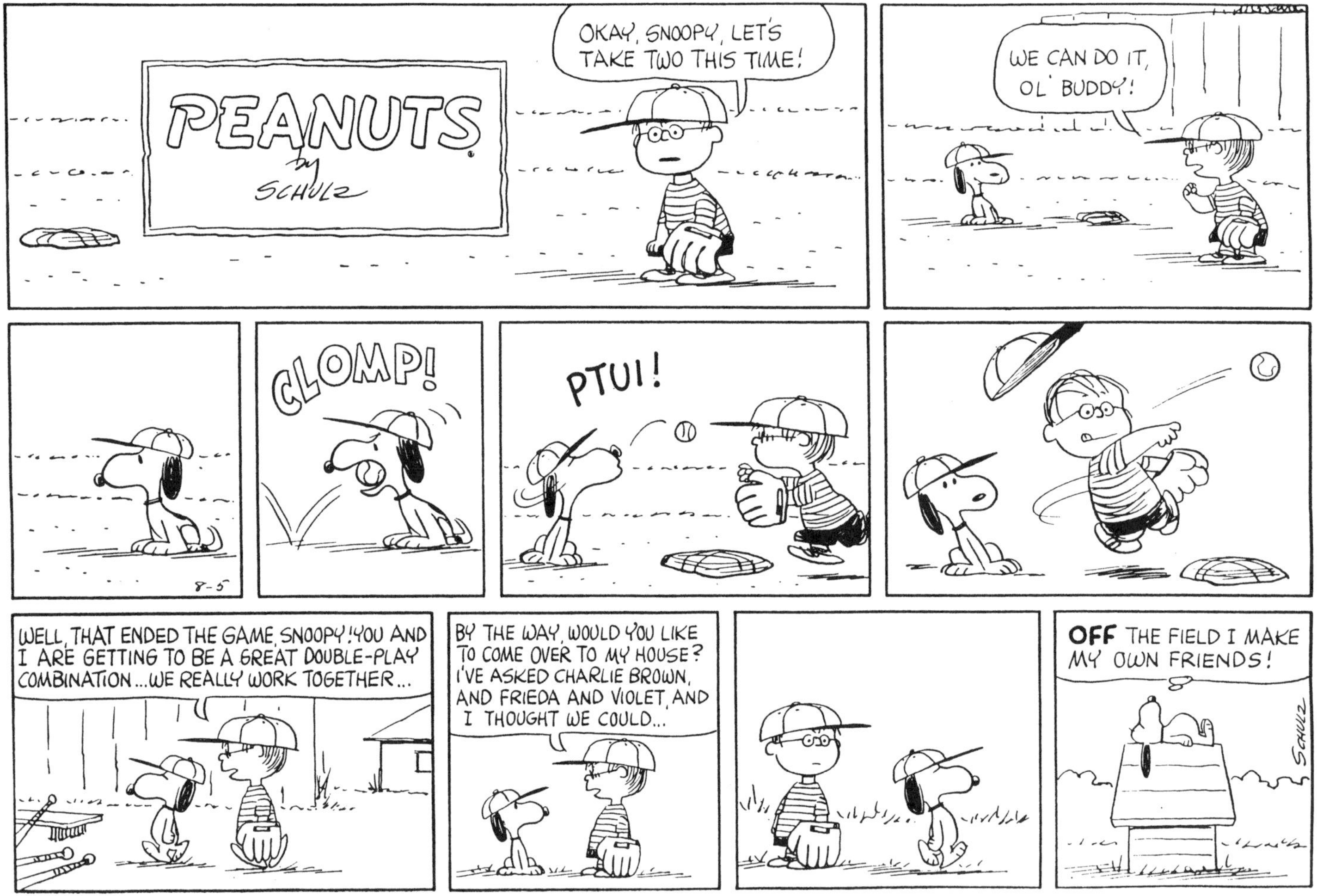
PEANUTS
by SCHULZ
OKAY, SNOOPY, LET'S TAKE TWO THIS TIME!
WE CAN DO IT, OL' BUDDY!
CLOMP!
PTUI!
WELL, THAT ENDED THE GAME, SNOOPY! YOU AND I ARE GETTING TO BE A GREAT DOUBLE-PLAY COMBINATION...WE REALLY WORK TOGETHER...
BY THE WAY, WOULD YOU LIKE TO COME OVER TO MY HOUSE? I'VE ASKED CHARLIE BROWN, AND FRIEDA AND VIOLET, AND I THOUGHT WE COULD...
OFF THE FIELD I MAKE MY OWN FRIENDS!

Panel 1: MY WHOLE TEAM HAS DESERTED ME!

Panel 2: ALL I'M LEFT WITH IS BAD MEMORIES AND A PILE OF EMPTY BASEBALL CAPS...

Panel 4: EVEN CASEY STENGEL COULDN'T DO **THAT**!

Panel 5: IN A WAY THIS IS KIND OF INTERESTING...

Panel 6: THIS IS MY CHANCE TO OBSERVE AT FIRST HAND WHAT HAPPENS TO A BASEBALL MANAGER WHEN HIS TEAM DESERTS HIM...

Panel 7: HERE IS A MAN DEDICATED TO HIS JOB...SUDDENLY HE IS WITHOUT A TEAM..WHAT DOES HE DO? WHERE DOES HE GO?

Panel 8: HE GOES HOME! ☆ SIGH ☆

Panel 9: LOOK, HOW DO YOU EXPECT ME TO PRACTICE WITH YOU HANGING AROUND ALL THE TIME?

Panel 10: I'M SORRY..I SHOULD HAVE KNOWN...I APOLOGIZE...

Panel 11: I'LL GO AWAY, AND LEAVE YOU ALONE...I UNDERSTAND YOUR PROBLEM COMPLETELY...

Panel 12: IT'S HARD TO CONCENTRATE IN THE PRESENCE OF A PRETTY FACE!

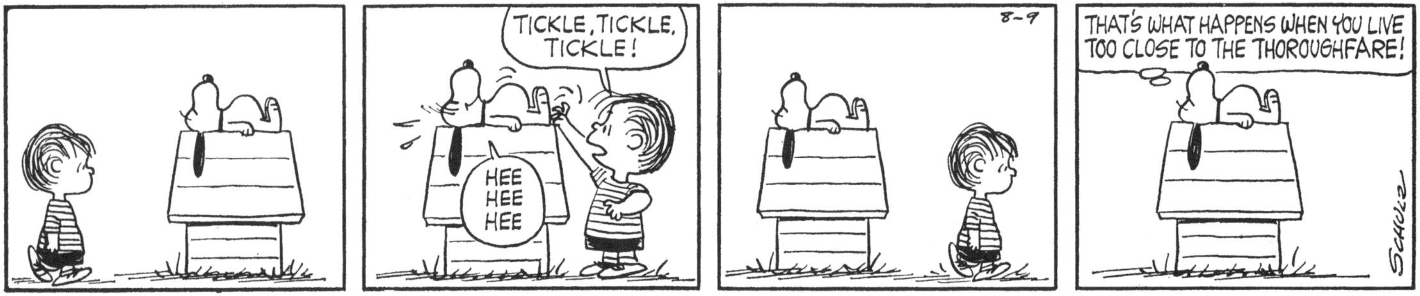
TICKLE, TICKLE, TICKLE!
HEE HEE HEE
8-9
THAT'S WHAT HAPPENS WHEN YOU LIVE TOO CLOSE TO THE THOROUGHFARE!
SCHULZ

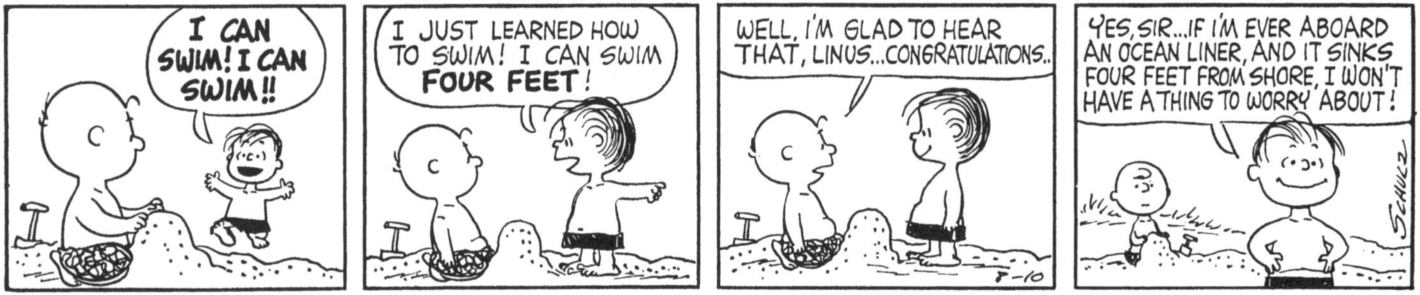
I CAN SWIM! I CAN SWIM!!
I JUST LEARNED HOW TO SWIM! I CAN SWIM FOUR FEET!
WELL, I'M GLAD TO HEAR THAT, LINUS...CONGRATULATIONS..
8-10
YES, SIR...IF I'M EVER ABOARD AN OCEAN LINER, AND IT SINKS FOUR FEET FROM SHORE, I WON'T HAVE A THING TO WORRY ABOUT!
SCHULZ

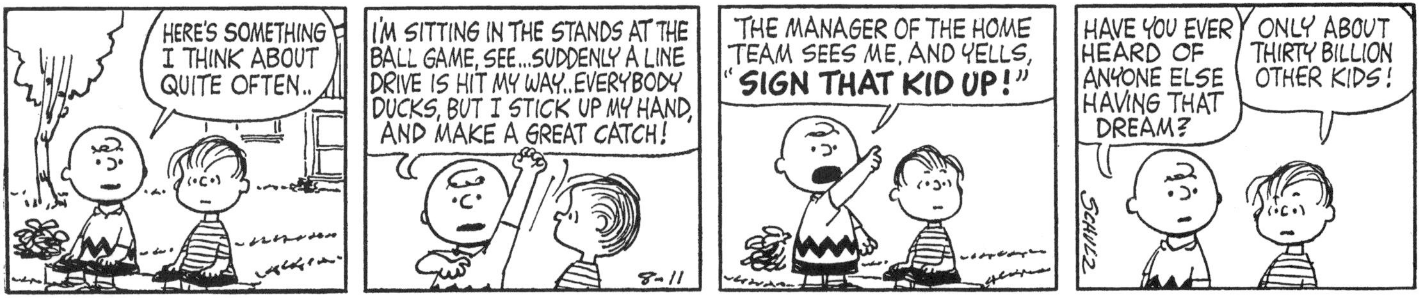
HERE'S SOMETHING I THINK ABOUT QUITE OFTEN..
I'M SITTING IN THE STANDS AT THE BALL GAME, SEE...SUDDENLY A LINE DRIVE IS HIT MY WAY..EVERYBODY DUCKS, BUT I STICK UP MY HAND, AND MAKE A GREAT CATCH!
8-11
THE MANAGER OF THE HOME TEAM SEES ME, AND YELLS, "SIGN THAT KID UP!"
HAVE YOU EVER HEARD OF ANYONE ELSE HAVING THAT DREAM?
ONLY ABOUT THIRTY BILLION OTHER KIDS!
SCHULZ

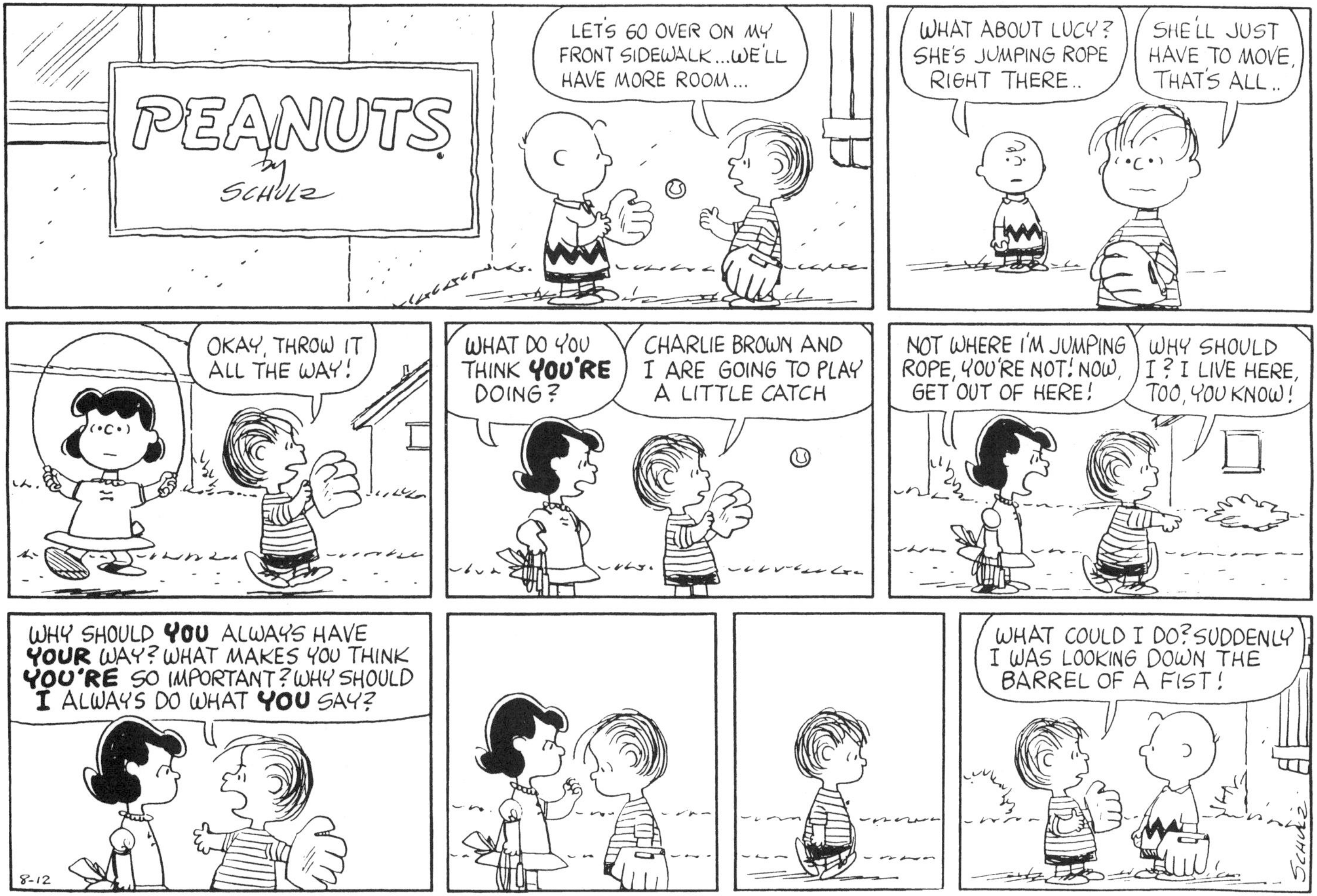
PEANUTS
by SCHULZ
LET'S GO OVER ON MY FRONT SIDEWALK...WE'LL HAVE MORE ROOM...
WHAT ABOUT LUCY? SHE'S JUMPING ROPE RIGHT THERE..
SHE'LL JUST HAVE TO MOVE, THAT'S ALL..
OKAY, THROW IT ALL THE WAY!
WHAT DO YOU THINK **YOU'RE** DOING?
CHARLIE BROWN AND I ARE GOING TO PLAY A LITTLE CATCH
NOT WHERE I'M JUMPING ROPE, YOU'RE NOT! NOW, GET OUT OF HERE!
WHY SHOULD I? I LIVE HERE, TOO, YOU KNOW!
WHY SHOULD **YOU** ALWAYS HAVE **YOUR** WAY? WHAT MAKES YOU THINK **YOU'RE** SO IMPORTANT? WHY SHOULD **I** ALWAYS DO WHAT **YOU** SAY?
8-12
WHAT COULD I DO? SUDDENLY I WAS LOOKING DOWN THE BARREL OF A FIST!
SCHULZ

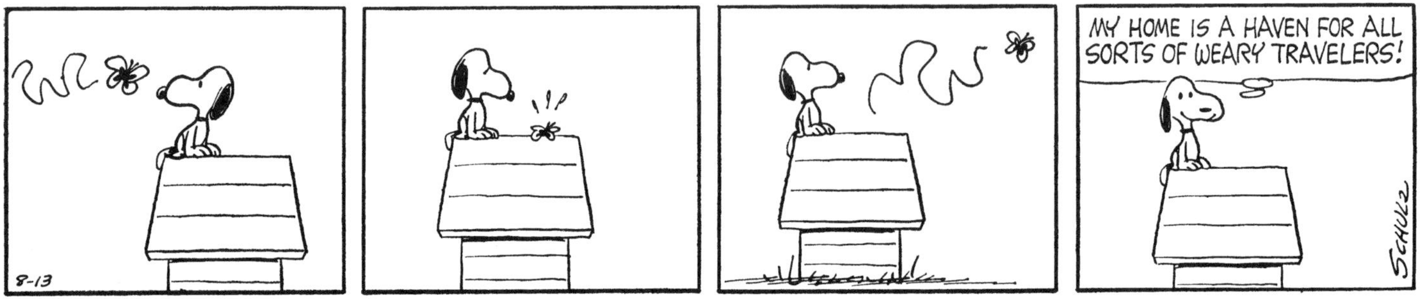
8-13
MY HOME IS A HAVEN FOR ALL SORTS OF WEARY TRAVELERS!
SCHULZ

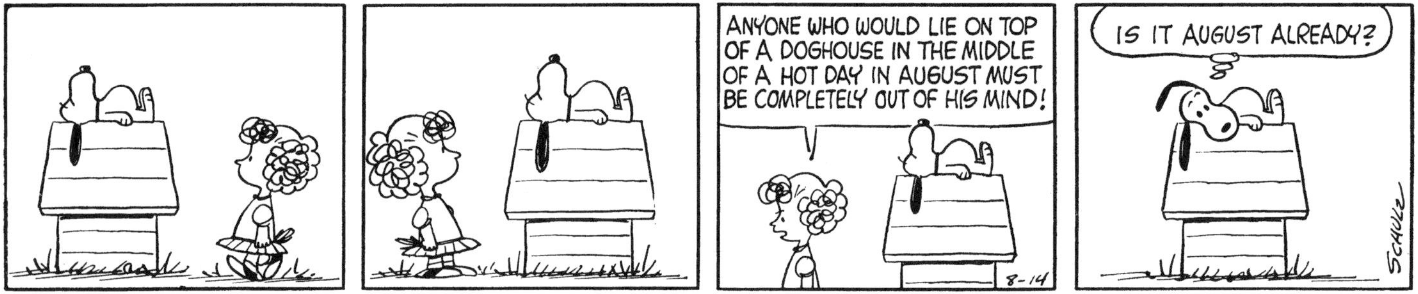
ANYONE WHO WOULD LIE ON TOP OF A DOGHOUSE IN THE MIDDLE OF A HOT DAY IN AUGUST MUST BE COMPLETELY OUT OF HIS MIND!
8-14
IS IT AUGUST ALREADY?
SCHULZ

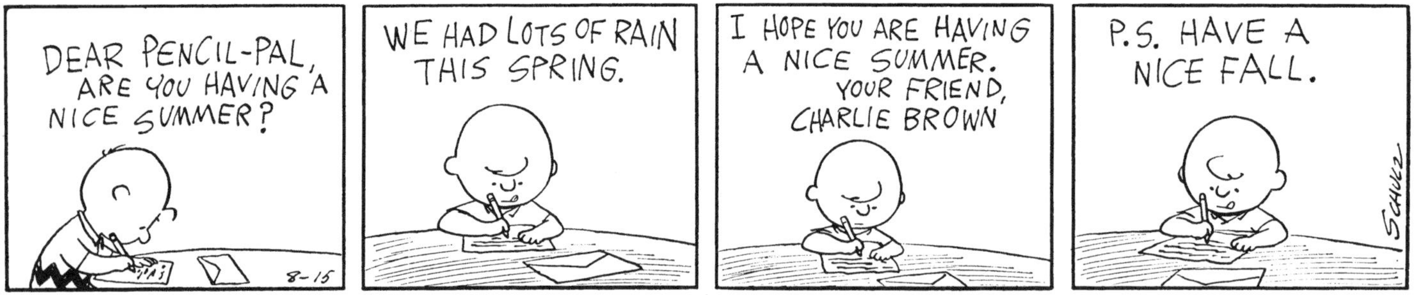
DEAR PENCIL-PAL, ARE YOU HAVING A NICE SUMMER?
8-15
WE HAD LOTS OF RAIN THIS SPRING.
I HOPE YOU ARE HAVING A NICE SUMMER. YOUR FRIEND, CHARLIE BROWN
P.S. HAVE A NICE FALL.
SCHULZ

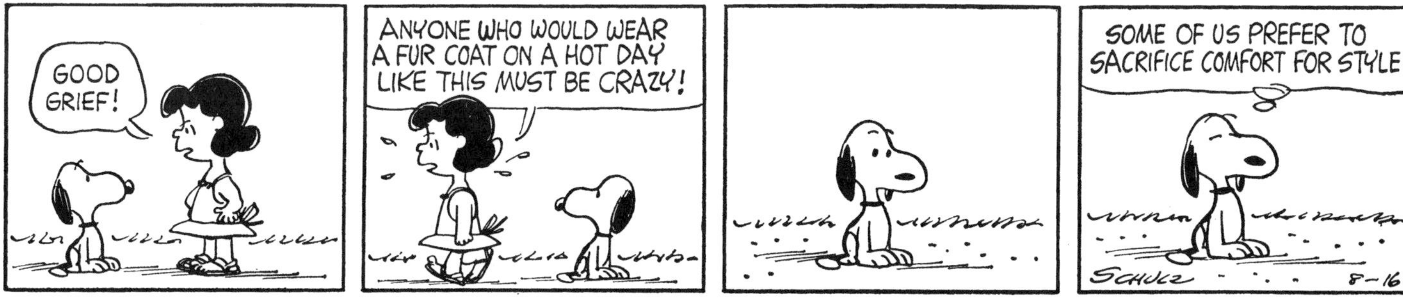
GOOD GRIEF!
ANYONE WHO WOULD WEAR A FUR COAT ON A HOT DAY LIKE THIS MUST BE CRAZY!
SOME OF US PREFER TO SACRIFICE COMFORT FOR STYLE!
SCHULZ
8-16

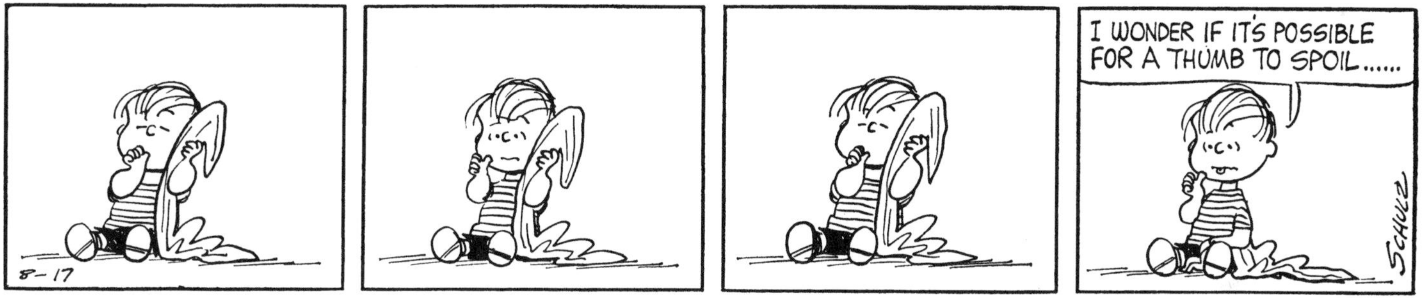
8-17
I WONDER IF IT'S POSSIBLE FOR A THUMB TO SPOIL......
SCHULZ

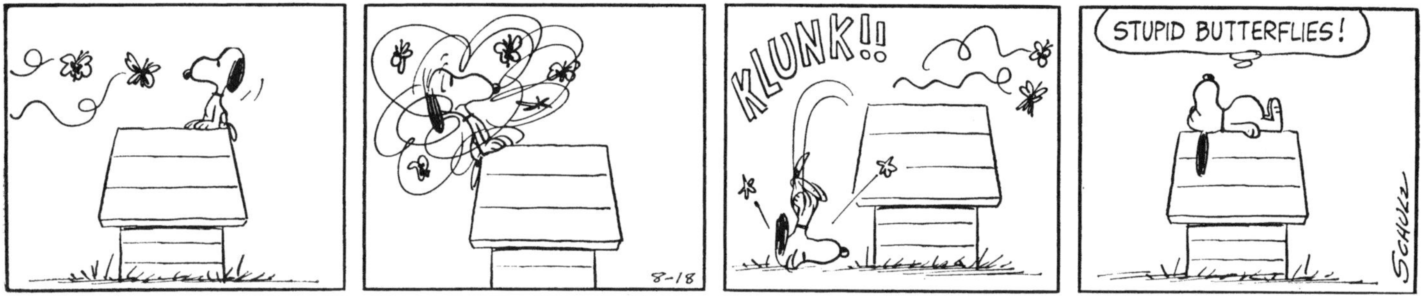
8-18
KLUNK!!
STUPID BUTTERFLIES!
SCHULZ

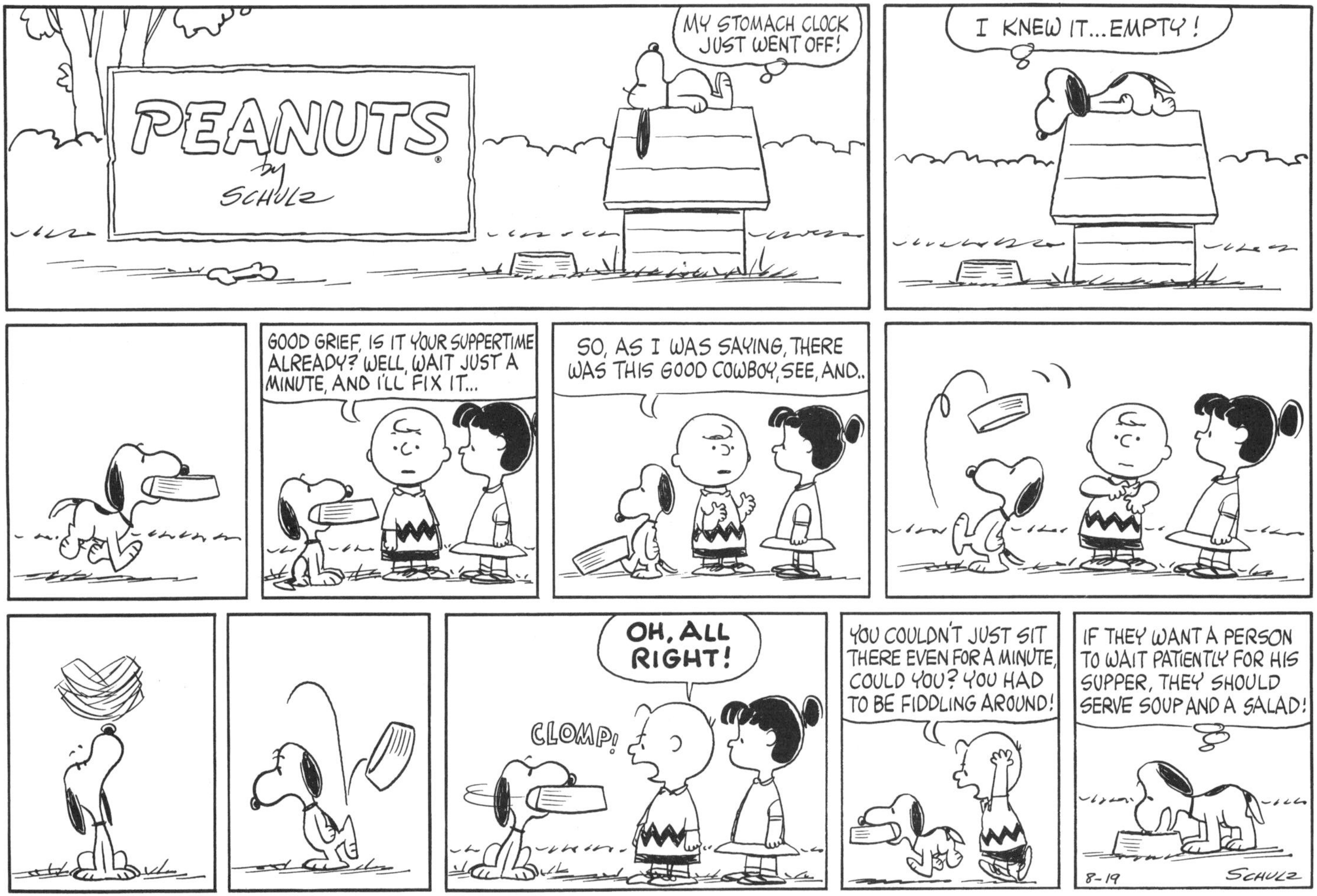
PEANUTS
by SCHULZ
MY STOMACH CLOCK JUST WENT OFF!
I KNEW IT...EMPTY!
GOOD GRIEF, IS IT YOUR SUPPERTIME ALREADY? WELL, WAIT JUST A MINUTE, AND I'LL FIX IT...
SO, AS I WAS SAYING, THERE WAS THIS GOOD COWBOY, SEE, AND..
OH, ALL RIGHT!
CLOMP!
YOU COULDN'T JUST SIT THERE EVEN FOR A MINUTE, COULD YOU? YOU HAD TO BE FIDDLING AROUND!
IF THEY WANT A PERSON TO WAIT PATIENTLY FOR HIS SUPPER, THEY SHOULD SERVE SOUP AND A SALAD!
8-19
SCHULZ

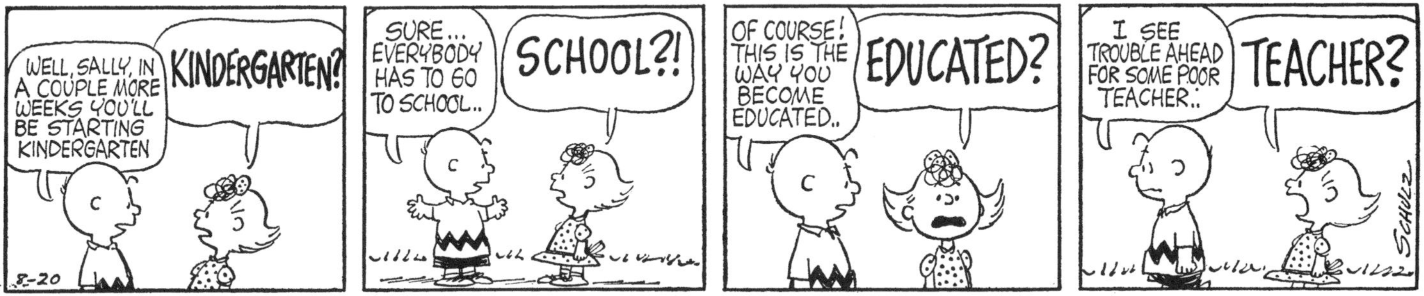
WELL, SALLY, IN A COUPLE MORE WEEKS YOU'LL BE STARTING KINDERGARTEN
KINDERGARTEN?
8-20
SURE... EVERYBODY HAS TO GO TO SCHOOL..
SCHOOL?!
OF COURSE! THIS IS THE WAY YOU BECOME EDUCATED..
EDUCATED?
I SEE TROUBLE AHEAD FOR SOME POOR TEACHER..
TEACHER?
SCHULZ

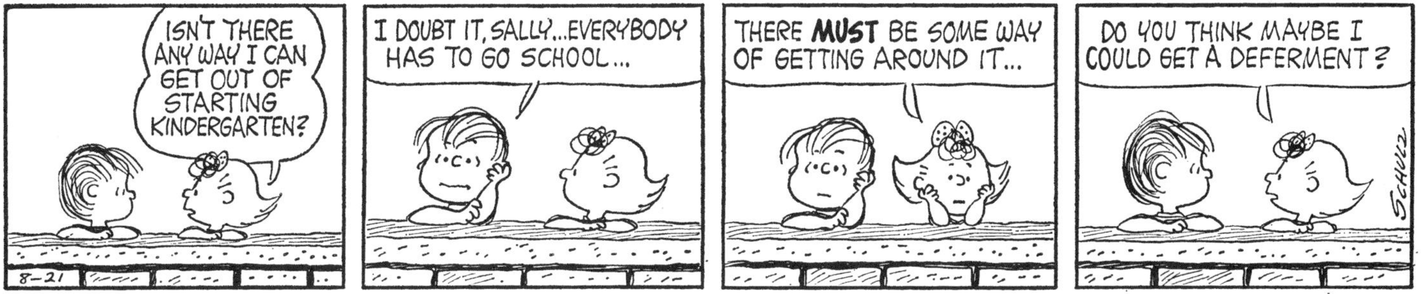
ISN'T THERE ANY WAY I CAN GET OUT OF STARTING KINDERGARTEN?
8-21
I DOUBT IT, SALLY...EVERYBODY HAS TO GO SCHOOL...
THERE MUST BE SOME WAY OF GETTING AROUND IT...
DO YOU THINK MAYBE I COULD GET A DEFERMENT?
SCHULZ

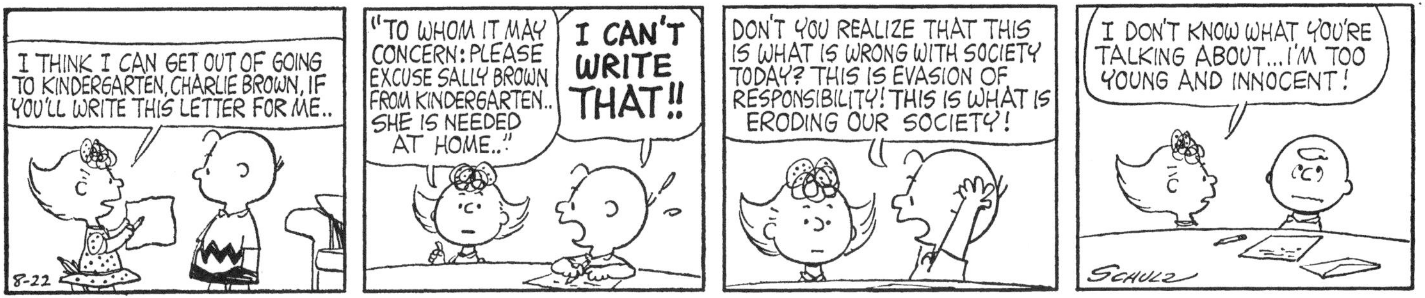
I THINK I CAN GET OUT OF GOING TO KINDERGARTEN, CHARLIE BROWN, IF YOU'LL WRITE THIS LETTER FOR ME..
8-22
"TO WHOM IT MAY CONCERN: PLEASE EXCUSE SALLY BROWN FROM KINDERGARTEN.. SHE IS NEEDED AT HOME.."
I CAN'T WRITE THAT!!
DON'T YOU REALIZE THAT THIS IS WHAT IS WRONG WITH SOCIETY TODAY? THIS IS EVASION OF RESPONSIBILITY! THIS IS WHAT IS ERODING OUR SOCIETY!
I DON'T KNOW WHAT YOU'RE TALKING ABOUT...I'M TOO YOUNG AND INNOCENT!
SCHULZ

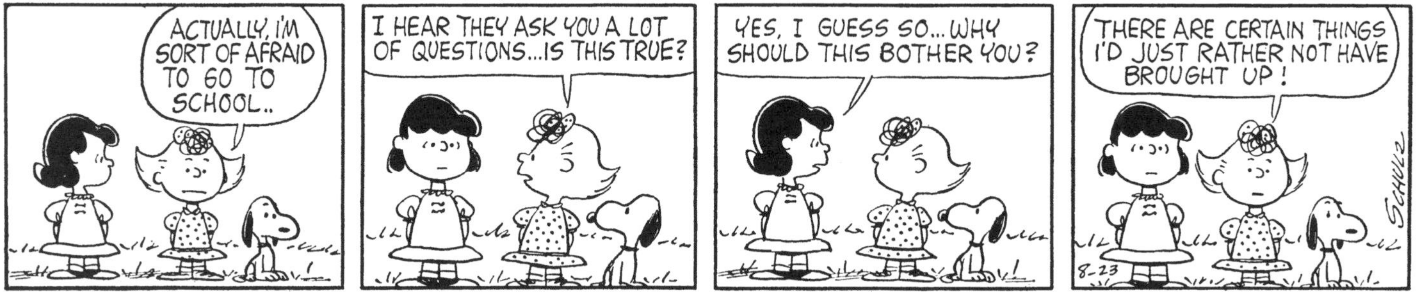
ACTUALLY, I'M SORT OF AFRAID TO GO TO SCHOOL..
I HEAR THEY ASK YOU A LOT OF QUESTIONS...IS THIS TRUE?
YES, I GUESS SO...WHY SHOULD THIS BOTHER YOU?
THERE ARE CERTAIN THINGS I'D JUST RATHER NOT HAVE BROUGHT UP!
SCHULZ
8-23

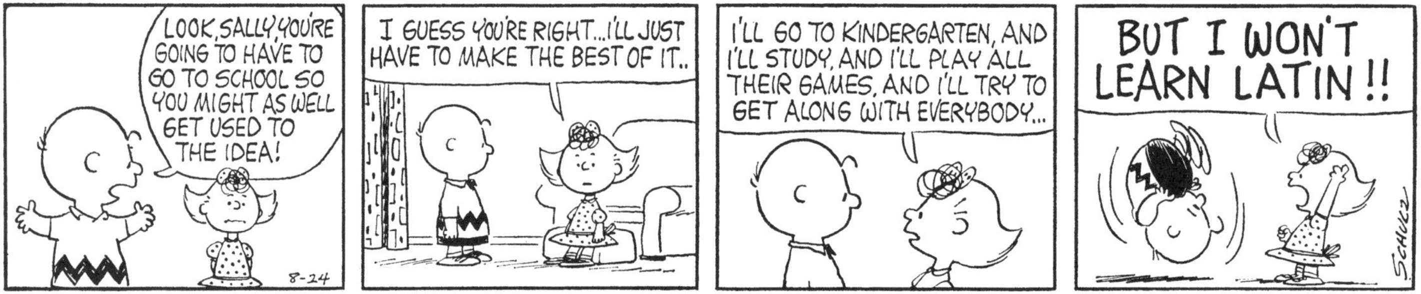
LOOK, SALLY, YOU'RE GOING TO HAVE TO GO TO SCHOOL SO YOU MIGHT AS WELL GET USED TO THE IDEA!
8-24
I GUESS YOU'RE RIGHT...I'LL JUST HAVE TO MAKE THE BEST OF IT..
I'LL GO TO KINDERGARTEN, AND I'LL STUDY, AND I'LL PLAY ALL THEIR GAMES, AND I'LL TRY TO GET ALONG WITH EVERYBODY...
BUT I WON'T LEARN LATIN!!
SCHULZ

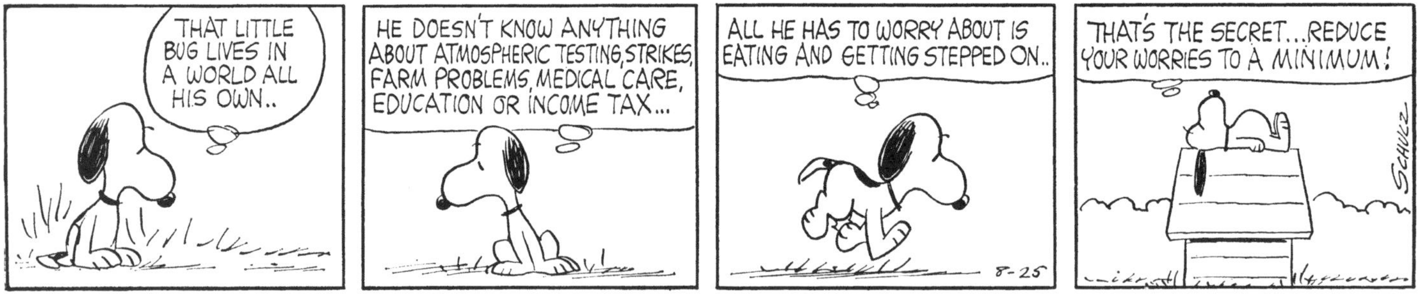
THAT LITTLE BUG LIVES IN A WORLD ALL HIS OWN..
HE DOESN'T KNOW ANYTHING ABOUT ATMOSPHERIC TESTING, STRIKES, FARM PROBLEMS, MEDICAL CARE, EDUCATION OR INCOME TAX...
ALL HE HAS TO WORRY ABOUT IS EATING AND GETTING STEPPED ON..
8-25
THAT'S THE SECRET...REDUCE YOUR WORRIES TO A MINIMUM!
SCHULZ

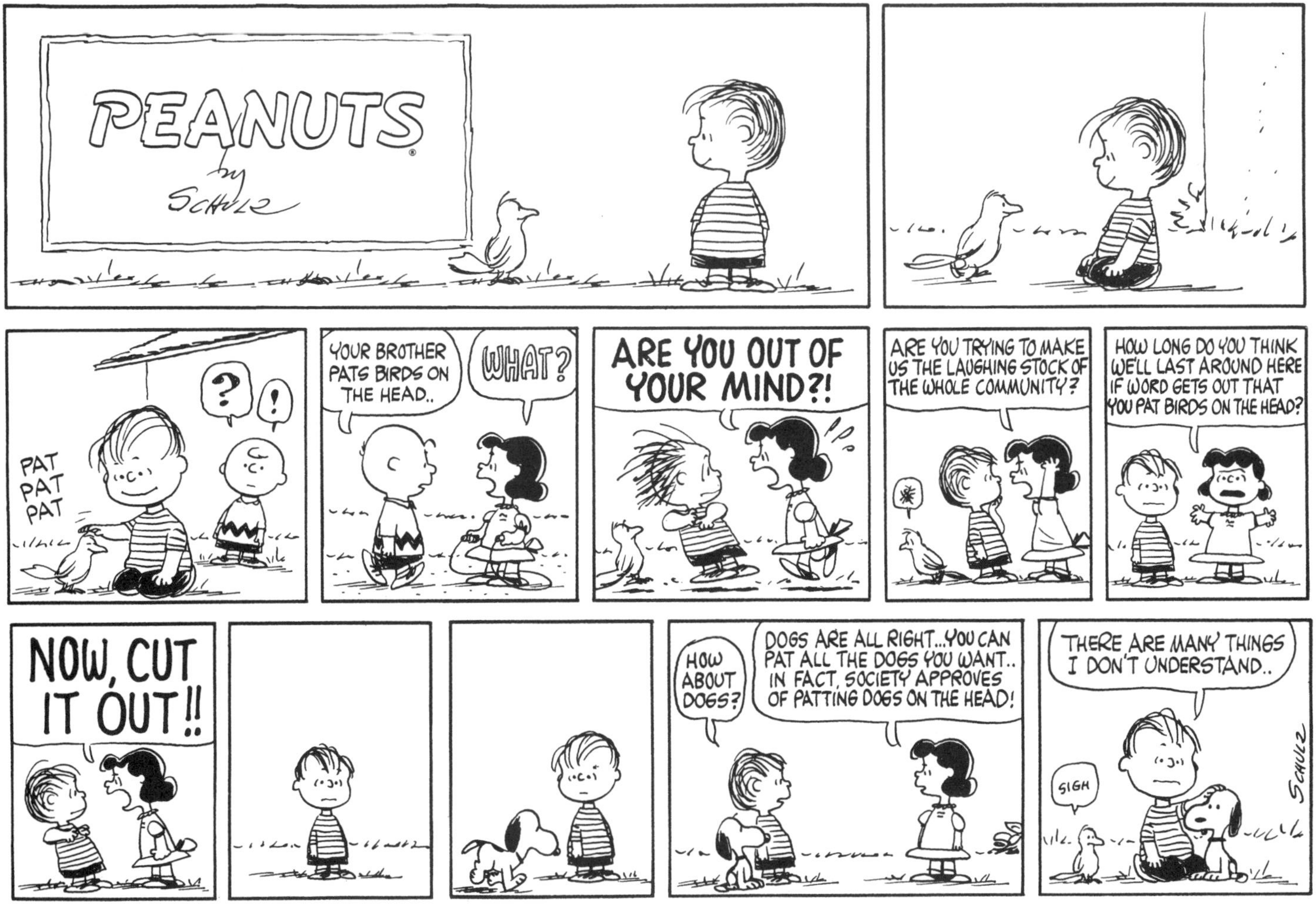
PEANUTS
by SCHULZ
PAT PAT PAT
?
!
YOUR BROTHER PATS BIRDS ON THE HEAD..
WHAT?
ARE YOU OUT OF YOUR MIND?!
ARE YOU TRYING TO MAKE US THE LAUGHING STOCK OF THE WHOLE COMMUNITY?
HOW LONG DO YOU THINK WE'LL LAST AROUND HERE IF WORD GETS OUT THAT YOU PAT BIRDS ON THE HEAD?
NOW, CUT IT OUT!!
HOW ABOUT DOGS?
DOGS ARE ALL RIGHT...YOU CAN PAT ALL THE DOGS YOU WANT.. IN FACT, SOCIETY APPROVES OF PATTING DOGS ON THE HEAD!
THERE ARE MANY THINGS I DON'T UNDERSTAND..
SIGH
SCHULZ

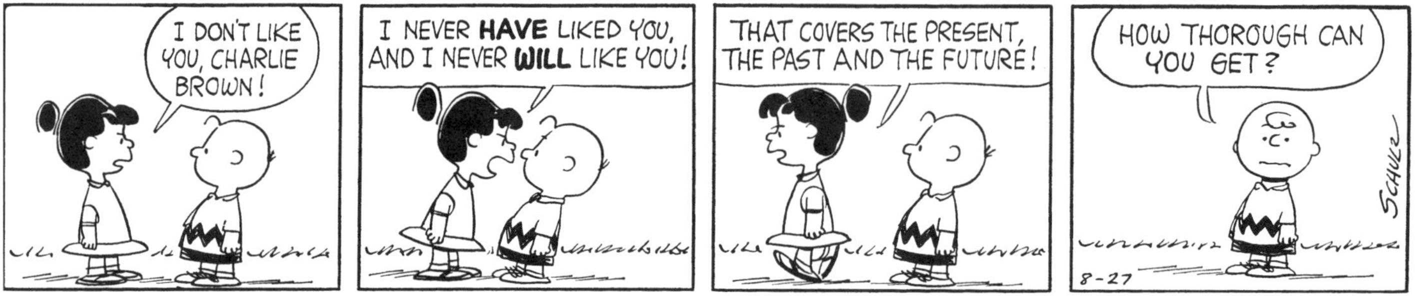
I DON'T LIKE YOU, CHARLIE BROWN!
I NEVER **HAVE** LIKED YOU, AND I NEVER **WILL** LIKE YOU!
THAT COVERS THE PRESENT, THE PAST AND THE FUTURE!
HOW THOROUGH CAN YOU GET?
SCHULZ
8-27

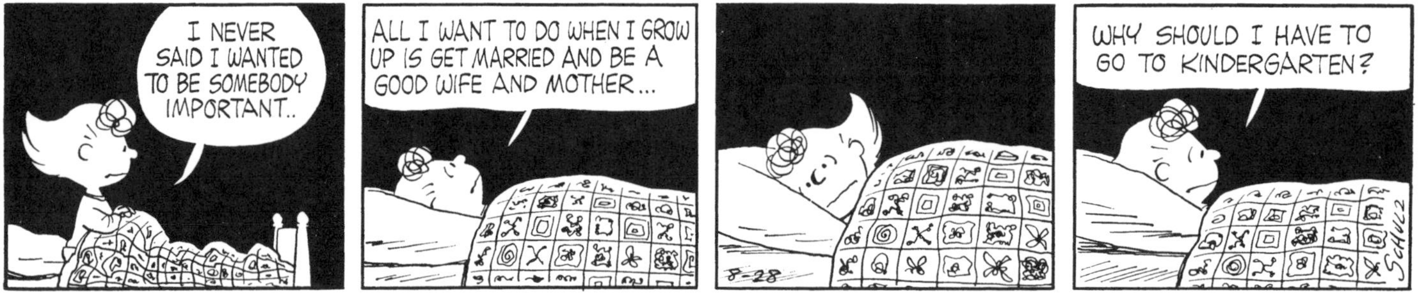
I NEVER SAID I WANTED TO BE SOMEBODY IMPORTANT..
ALL I WANT TO DO WHEN I GROW UP IS GET MARRIED AND BE A GOOD WIFE AND MOTHER...
8-28
WHY SHOULD I HAVE TO GO TO KINDERGARTEN?
SCHULZ

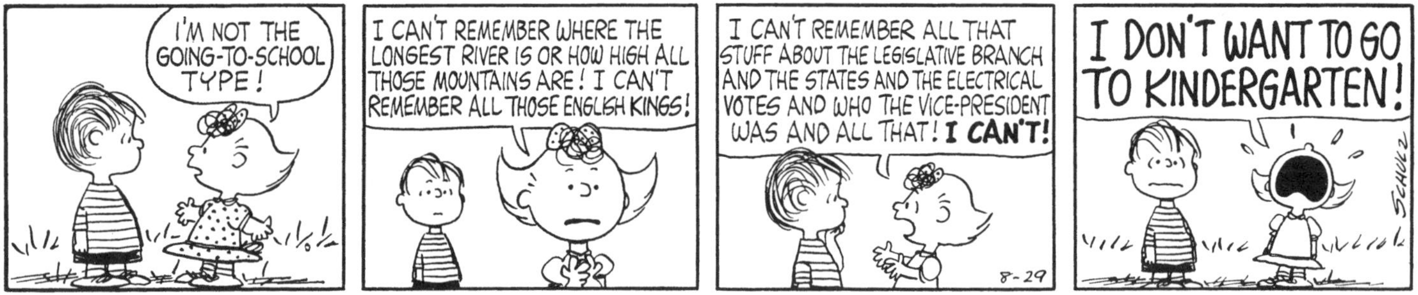
I'M NOT THE GOING-TO-SCHOOL TYPE!
I CAN'T REMEMBER WHERE THE LONGEST RIVER IS OR HOW HIGH ALL THOSE MOUNTAINS ARE! I CAN'T REMEMBER ALL THOSE ENGLISH KINGS!
I CAN'T REMEMBER ALL THAT STUFF ABOUT THE LEGISLATIVE BRANCH AND THE STATES AND THE ELECTRICAL VOTES AND WHO THE VICE-PRESIDENT WAS AND ALL THAT! **I CAN'T!**
8-29
I DON'T WANT TO GO TO KINDERGARTEN!
SCHULZ

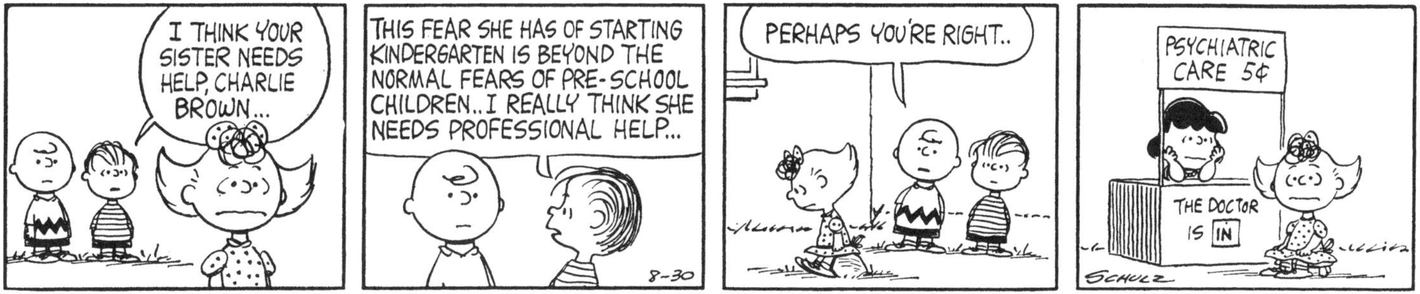
I THINK YOUR SISTER NEEDS HELP, CHARLIE BROWN...
THIS FEAR SHE HAS OF STARTING KINDERGARTEN IS BEYOND THE NORMAL FEARS OF PRE-SCHOOL CHILDREN.. I REALLY THINK SHE NEEDS PROFESSIONAL HELP...
8-30
PERHAPS YOU'RE RIGHT..
PSYCHIATRIC CARE 5¢
THE DOCTOR IS IN
SCHULZ

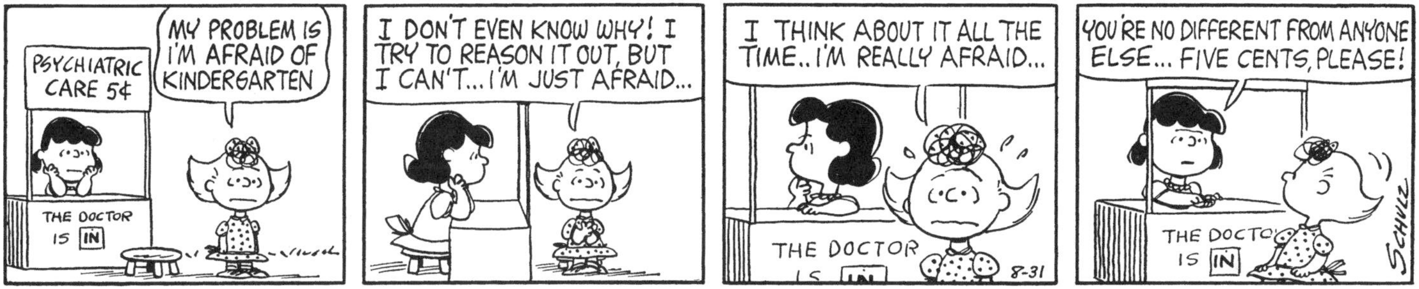
PSYCHIATRIC CARE 5¢
MY PROBLEM IS I'M AFRAID OF KINDERGARTEN
THE DOCTOR IS IN
I DON'T EVEN KNOW WHY! I TRY TO REASON IT OUT, BUT I CAN'T... I'M JUST AFRAID...
I THINK ABOUT IT ALL THE TIME.. I'M REALLY AFRAID...
THE DOCTOR
8-31
YOU'RE NO DIFFERENT FROM ANYONE ELSE... FIVE CENTS, PLEASE!
IS IN
SCHULZ

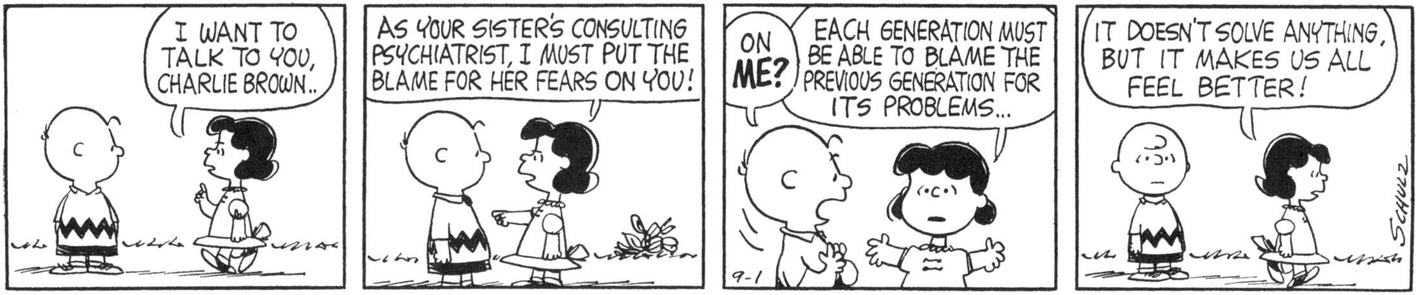
I WANT TO TALK TO YOU, CHARLIE BROWN..
AS YOUR SISTER'S CONSULTING PSYCHIATRIST, I MUST PUT THE BLAME FOR HER FEARS ON YOU!
ON ME?
EACH GENERATION MUST BE ABLE TO BLAME THE PREVIOUS GENERATION FOR ITS PROBLEMS...
9-1
IT DOESN'T SOLVE ANYTHING, BUT IT MAKES US ALL FEEL BETTER!
SCHULZ

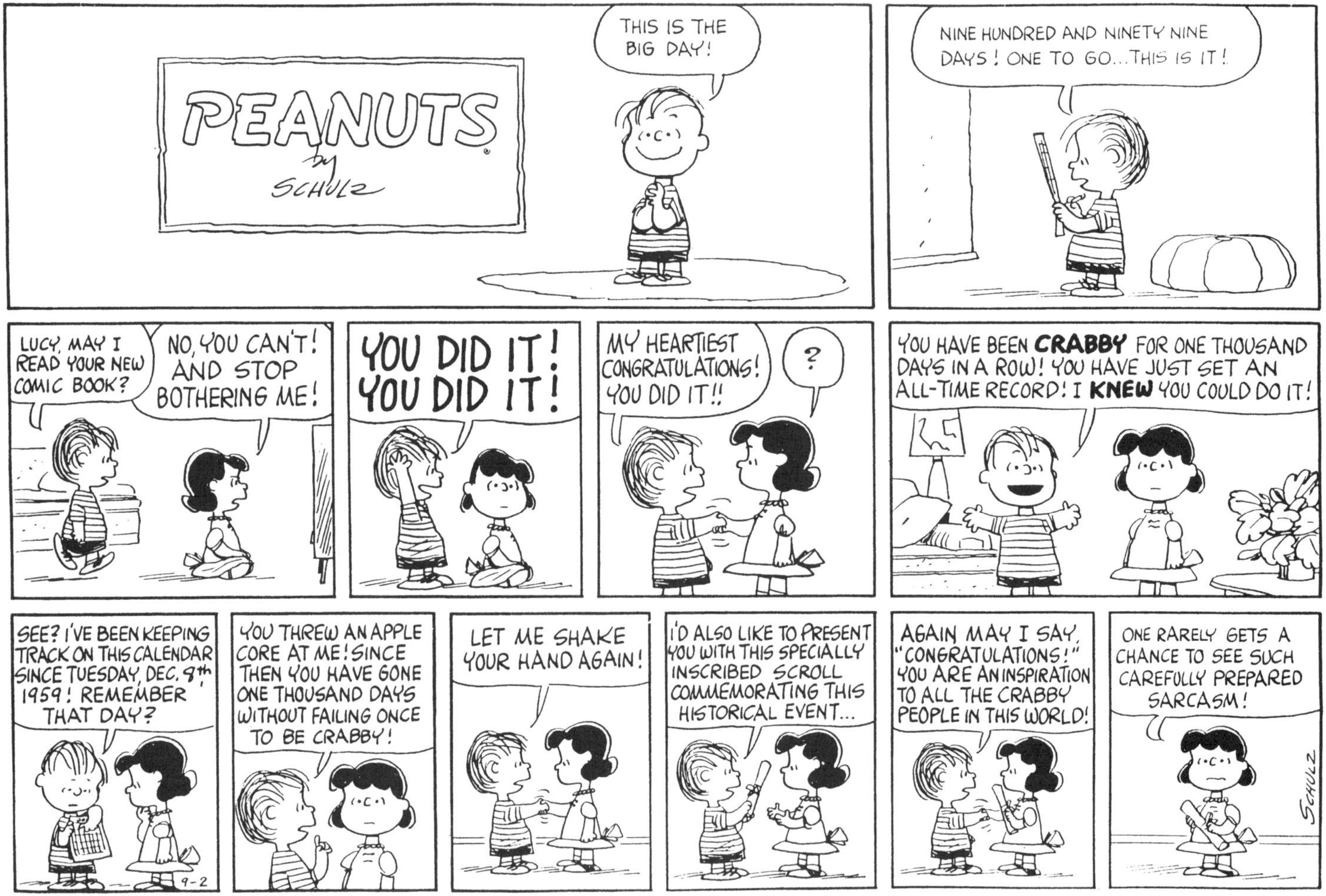
PEANUTS
by SCHULZ
THIS IS THE BIG DAY!
NINE HUNDRED AND NINETY NINE DAYS! ONE TO GO...THIS IS IT!
LUCY, MAY I READ YOUR NEW COMIC BOOK?
NO, YOU CAN'T! AND STOP BOTHERING ME!
YOU DID IT! YOU DID IT!
MY HEARTIEST CONGRATULATIONS! YOU DID IT!!
?
YOU HAVE BEEN CRABBY FOR ONE THOUSAND DAYS IN A ROW! YOU HAVE JUST SET AN ALL-TIME RECORD! I KNEW YOU COULD DO IT!
SEE? I'VE BEEN KEEPING TRACK ON THIS CALENDAR SINCE TUESDAY, DEC. 8th, 1959! REMEMBER THAT DAY?
9-2
YOU THREW AN APPLE CORE AT ME! SINCE THEN YOU HAVE GONE ONE THOUSAND DAYS WITHOUT FAILING ONCE TO BE CRABBY!
LET ME SHAKE YOUR HAND AGAIN!
I'D ALSO LIKE TO PRESENT YOU WITH THIS SPECIALLY INSCRIBED SCROLL COMMEMORATING THIS HISTORICAL EVENT...
AGAIN MAY I SAY, "CONGRATULATIONS!" YOU ARE AN INSPIRATION TO ALL THE CRABBY PEOPLE IN THIS WORLD!
ONE RARELY GETS A CHANCE TO SEE SUCH CAREFULLY PREPARED SARCASM!
SCHULZ

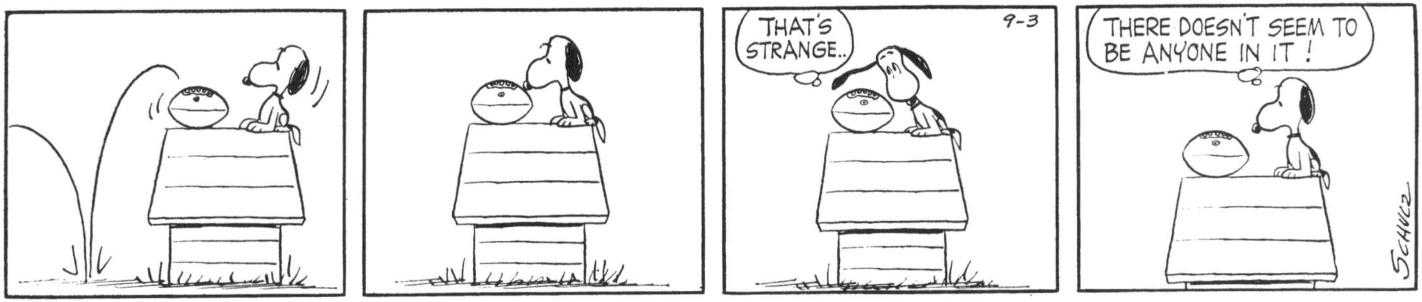
THAT'S STRANGE..
9-3
THERE DOESN'T SEEM TO BE ANYONE IN IT!
SCHULZ

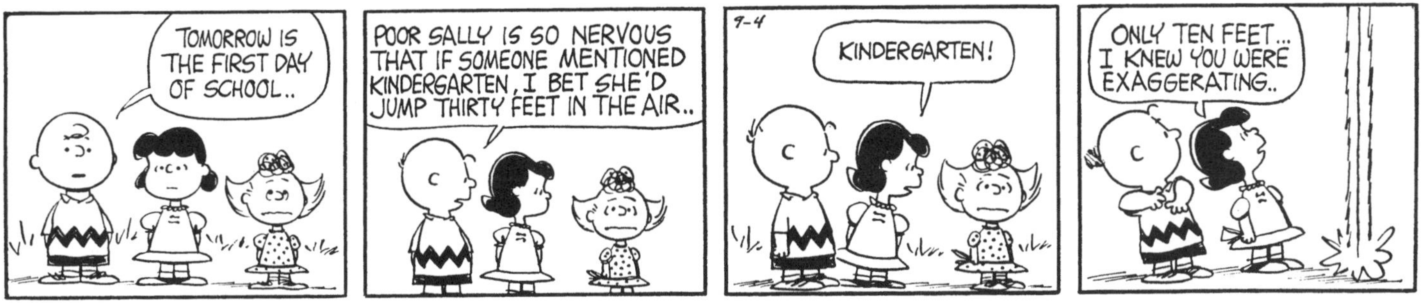
TOMORROW IS THE FIRST DAY OF SCHOOL..
POOR SALLY IS SO NERVOUS THAT IF SOMEONE MENTIONED KINDERGARTEN, I BET SHE'D JUMP THIRTY FEET IN THE AIR..
9-4
KINDERGARTEN!
ONLY TEN FEET... I KNEW YOU WERE EXAGGERATING..

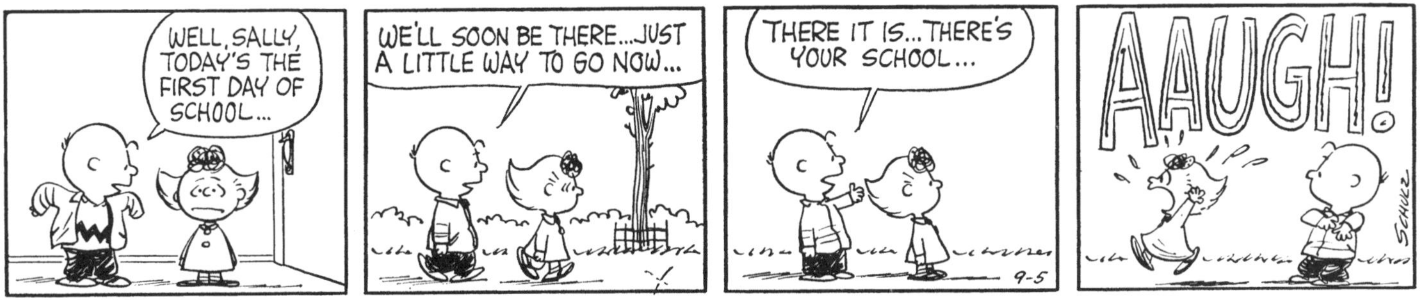
WELL, SALLY, TODAY'S THE FIRST DAY OF SCHOOL...
WE'LL SOON BE THERE...JUST A LITTLE WAY TO GO NOW...
THERE IT IS...THERE'S YOUR SCHOOL...
9-5
AAUGH!
SCHULZ

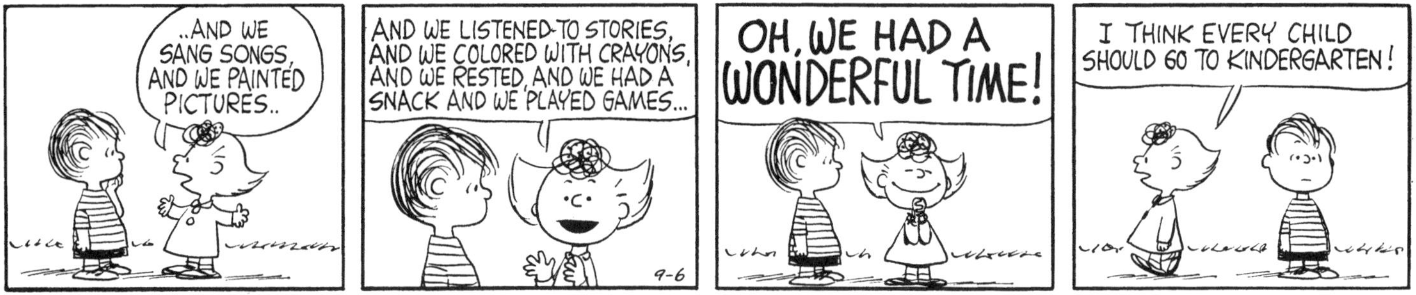
..AND WE SANG SONGS, AND WE PAINTED PICTURES..
AND WE LISTENED TO STORIES, AND WE COLORED WITH CRAYONS, AND WE RESTED, AND WE HAD A SNACK AND WE PLAYED GAMES...
9-6
OH, WE HAD A WONDERFUL TIME!
I THINK EVERY CHILD SHOULD GO TO KINDERGARTEN!

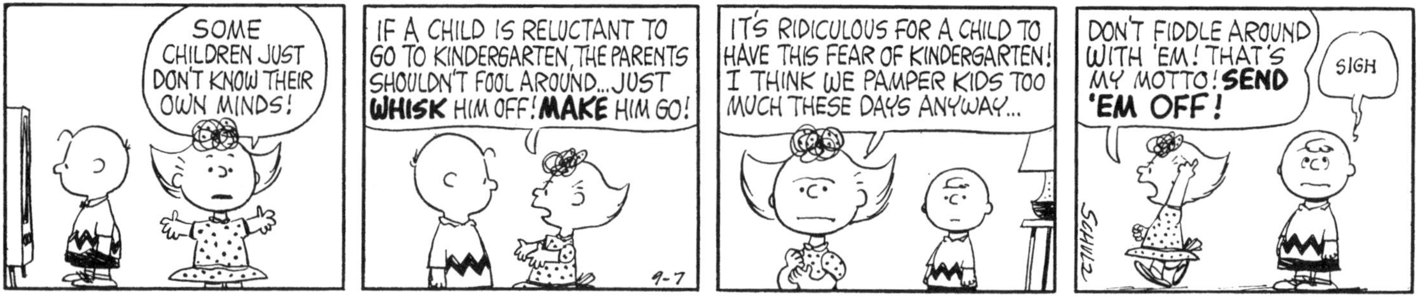
SOME CHILDREN JUST DON'T KNOW THEIR OWN MINDS!
IF A CHILD IS RELUCTANT TO GO TO KINDERGARTEN, THE PARENTS SHOULDN'T FOOL AROUND...JUST **WHISK** HIM OFF! **MAKE** HIM GO!
9-7
IT'S RIDICULOUS FOR A CHILD TO HAVE THIS FEAR OF KINDERGARTEN! I THINK WE PAMPER KIDS TOO MUCH THESE DAYS ANYWAY...
DON'T FIDDLE AROUND WITH 'EM! THAT'S MY MOTTO! **SEND 'EM OFF!**
SIGH
SCHULZ

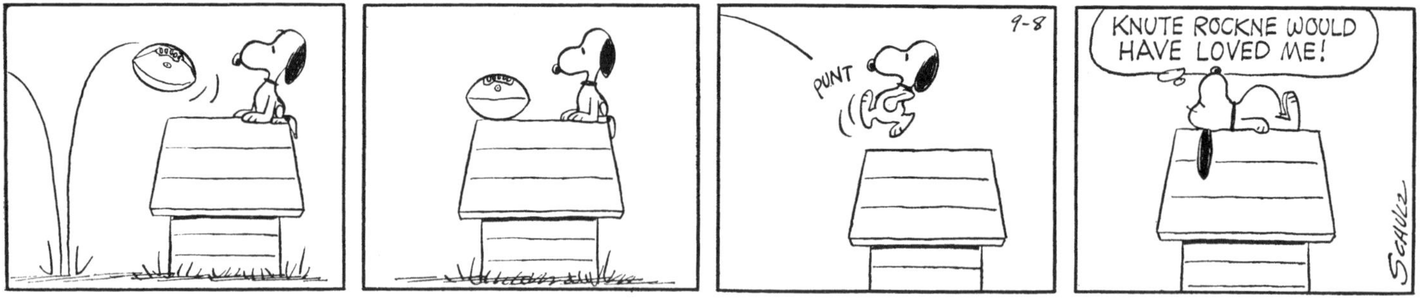
9-8
PUNT
KNUTE ROCKNE WOULD HAVE LOVED ME!
SCHULZ

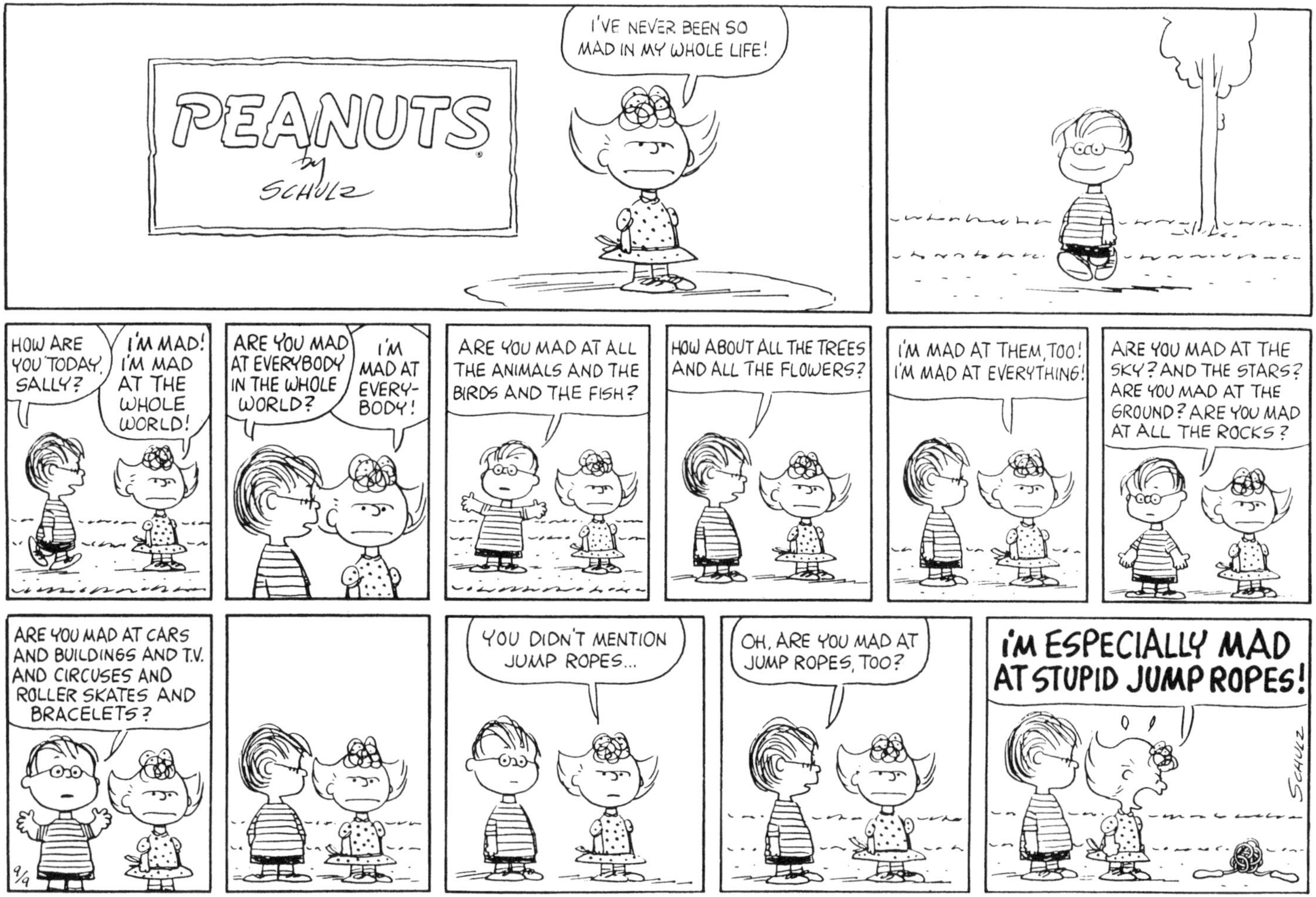
PEANUTS
by SCHULZ
I'VE NEVER BEEN SO MAD IN MY WHOLE LIFE!
HOW ARE YOU TODAY, SALLY?
I'M MAD! I'M MAD AT THE WHOLE WORLD!
ARE YOU MAD AT EVERYBODY IN THE WHOLE WORLD?
I'M MAD AT EVERYBODY!
ARE YOU MAD AT ALL THE ANIMALS AND THE BIRDS AND THE FISH?
HOW ABOUT ALL THE TREES AND ALL THE FLOWERS?
I'M MAD AT THEM, TOO! I'M MAD AT EVERYTHING!
ARE YOU MAD AT THE SKY? AND THE STARS? ARE YOU MAD AT THE GROUND? ARE YOU MAD AT ALL THE ROCKS?
ARE YOU MAD AT CARS AND BUILDINGS AND T.V. AND CIRCUSES AND ROLLER SKATES AND BRACELETS?
9/9
YOU DIDN'T MENTION JUMP ROPES...
OH, ARE YOU MAD AT JUMP ROPES, TOO?
I'M ESPECIALLY MAD AT STUPID JUMP ROPES!
SCHULZ

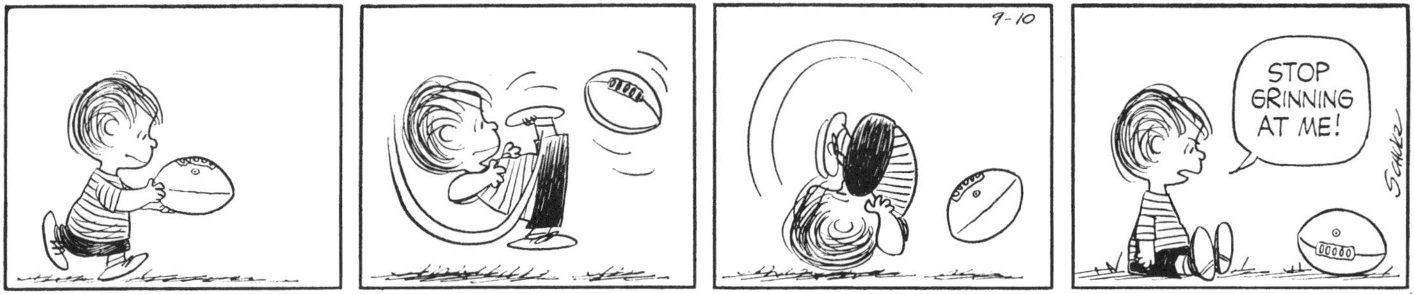
9-10
STOP GRINNING AT ME!
SCHULZ

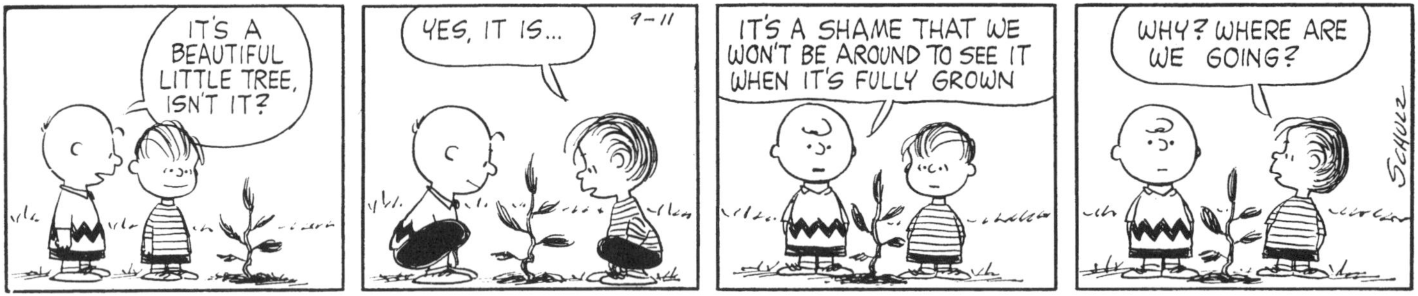
IT'S A BEAUTIFUL LITTLE TREE, ISN'T IT?
YES, IT IS...
9-11
IT'S A SHAME THAT WE WON'T BE AROUND TO SEE IT WHEN IT'S FULLY GROWN
WHY? WHERE ARE WE GOING?
SCHULZ

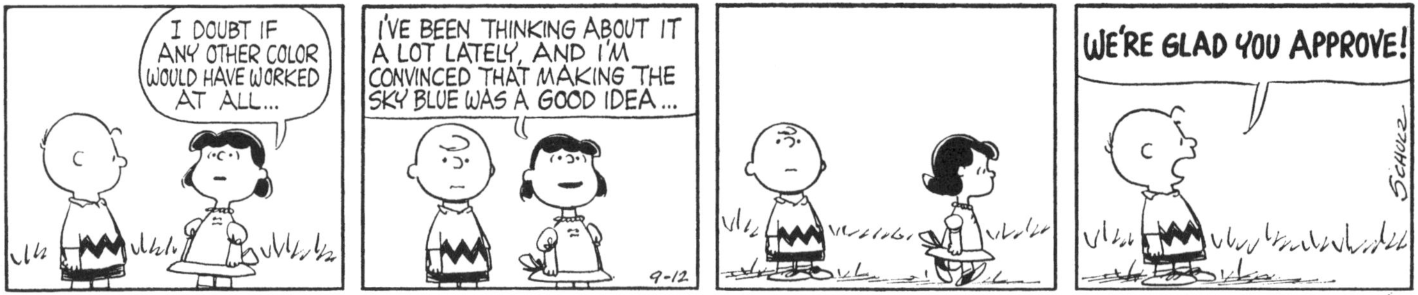
I DOUBT IF ANY OTHER COLOR WOULD HAVE WORKED AT ALL...
I'VE BEEN THINKING ABOUT IT A LOT LATELY, AND I'M CONVINCED THAT MAKING THE SKY BLUE WAS A GOOD IDEA...
9-12
WE'RE GLAD YOU APPROVE!
SCHULZ

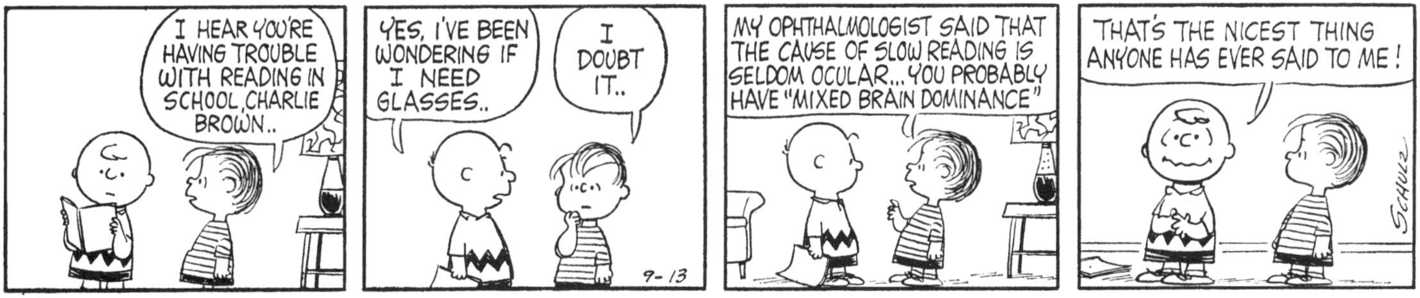
I HEAR YOU'RE HAVING TROUBLE WITH READING IN SCHOOL, CHARLIE BROWN..
YES, I'VE BEEN WONDERING IF I NEED GLASSES..
I DOUBT IT..
9-13
MY OPHTHALMOLOGIST SAID THAT THE CAUSE OF SLOW READING IS SELDOM OCULAR... YOU PROBABLY HAVE "MIXED BRAIN DOMINANCE"
THAT'S THE NICEST THING ANYONE HAS EVER SAID TO ME!
SCHULZ

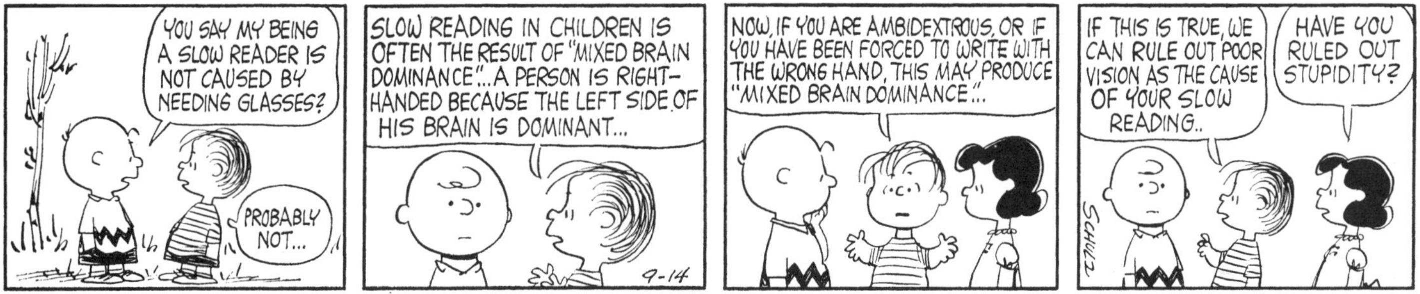
YOU SAY MY BEING A SLOW READER IS NOT CAUSED BY NEEDING GLASSES?
PROBABLY NOT...
SLOW READING IN CHILDREN IS OFTEN THE RESULT OF "MIXED BRAIN DOMINANCE"... A PERSON IS RIGHT-HANDED BECAUSE THE LEFT SIDE OF HIS BRAIN IS DOMINANT...
9-14
NOW, IF YOU ARE AMBIDEXTROUS, OR IF YOU HAVE BEEN FORCED TO WRITE WITH THE WRONG HAND, THIS MAY PRODUCE "MIXED BRAIN DOMINANCE"...
IF THIS IS TRUE, WE CAN RULE OUT POOR VISION AS THE CAUSE OF YOUR SLOW READING..
HAVE YOU RULED OUT STUPIDITY?
SCHULZ

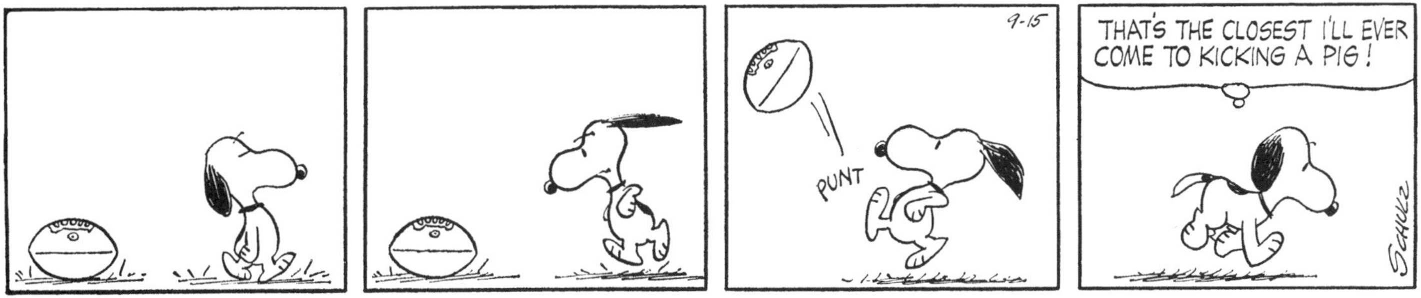
9-15
PUNT
THAT'S THE CLOSEST I'LL EVER COME TO KICKING A PIG!
SCHULZ

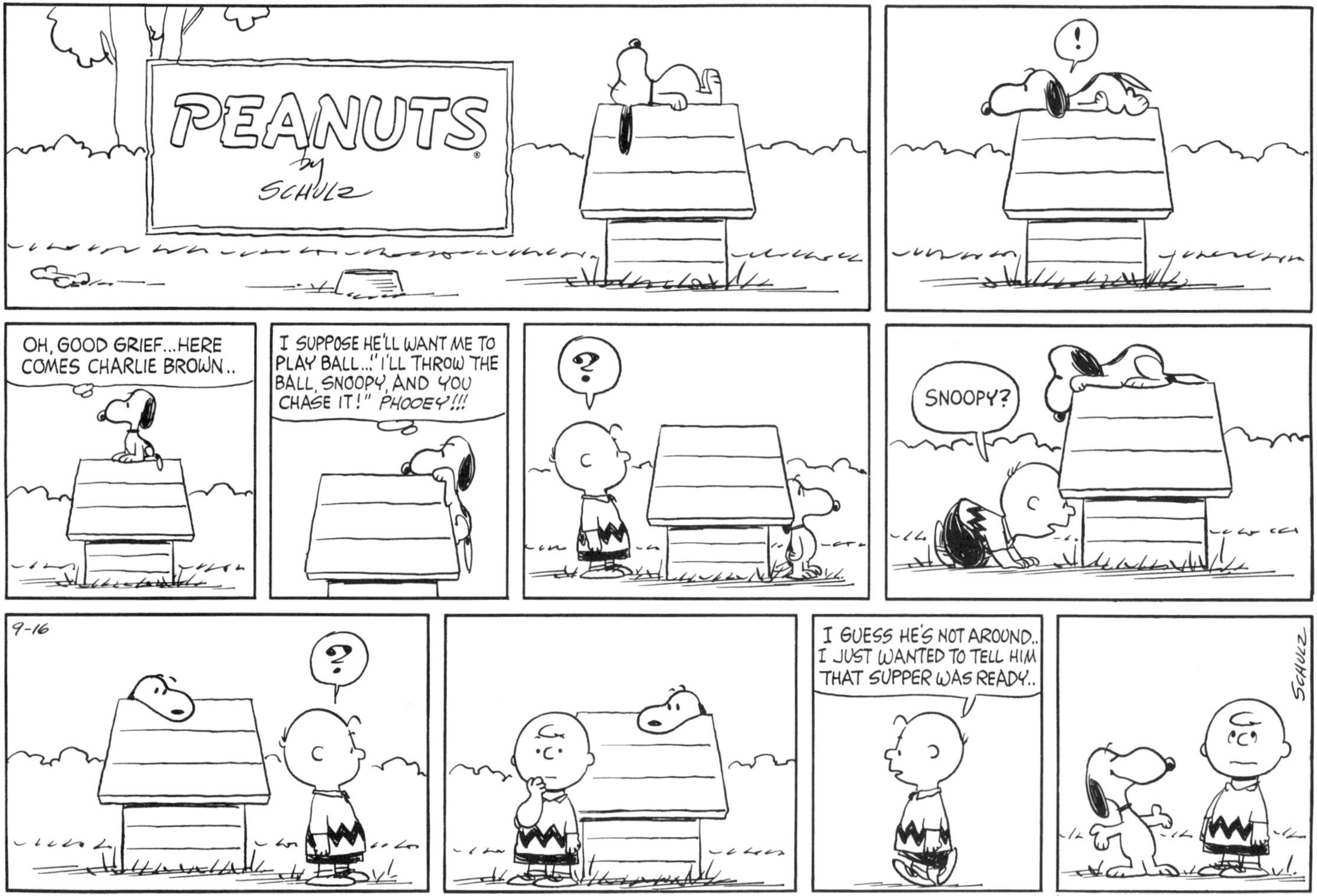
PEANUTS
by
SCHULZ
!
OH, GOOD GRIEF...HERE COMES CHARLIE BROWN..
I SUPPOSE HE'LL WANT ME TO PLAY BALL..."I'LL THROW THE BALL, SNOOPY, AND YOU CHASE IT!" PHOOEY!!!
?
SNOOPY?
9-16
?
I GUESS HE'S NOT AROUND.. I JUST WANTED TO TELL HIM THAT SUPPER WAS READY..
SCHULZ

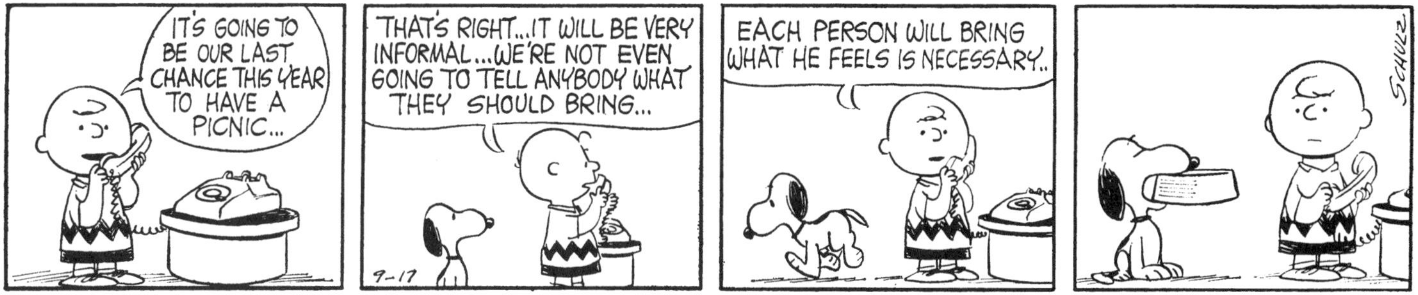
IT'S GOING TO BE OUR LAST CHANCE THIS YEAR TO HAVE A PICNIC...
THAT'S RIGHT...IT WILL BE VERY INFORMAL...WE'RE NOT EVEN GOING TO TELL ANYBODY WHAT THEY SHOULD BRING...
9-17
EACH PERSON WILL BRING WHAT HE FEELS IS NECESSARY..
SCHULZ

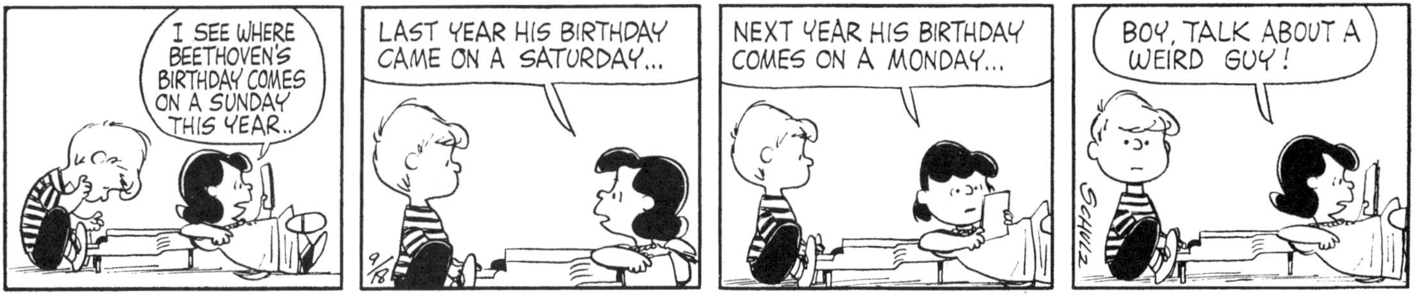
I SEE WHERE BEETHOVEN'S BIRTHDAY COMES ON A SUNDAY THIS YEAR..
LAST YEAR HIS BIRTHDAY CAME ON A SATURDAY...
9/18
NEXT YEAR HIS BIRTHDAY COMES ON A MONDAY...
BOY, TALK ABOUT A WEIRD GUY!
SCHULZ

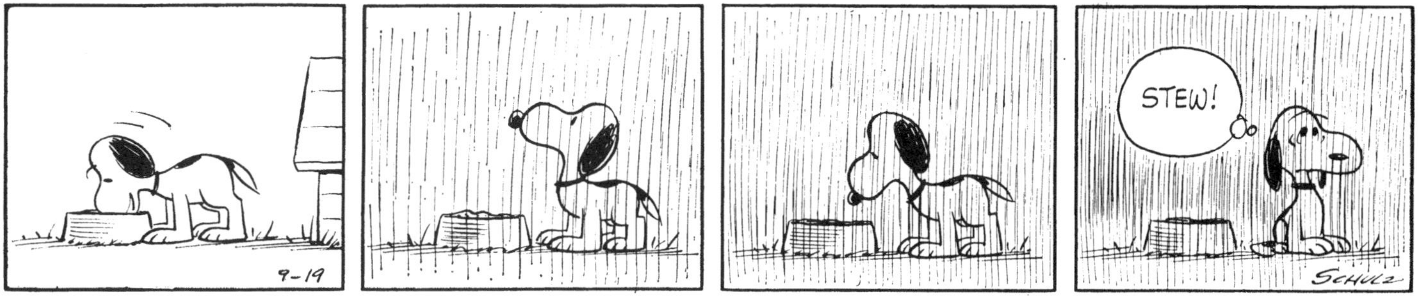
9-19
STEW!
SCHULZ

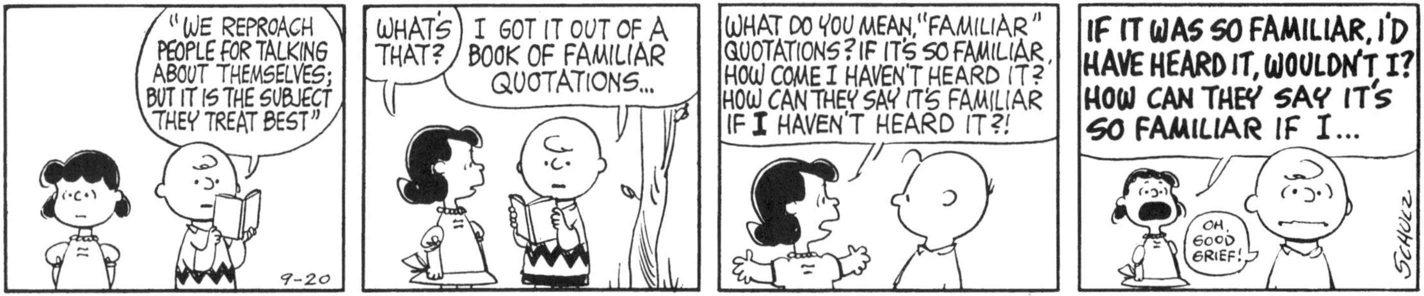
"WE REPROACH PEOPLE FOR TALKING ABOUT THEMSELVES; BUT IT IS THE SUBJECT THEY TREAT BEST"
9-20
WHAT'S THAT?
I GOT IT OUT OF A BOOK OF FAMILIAR QUOTATIONS...
WHAT DO YOU MEAN, "FAMILIAR" QUOTATIONS? IF IT'S SO FAMILIAR, HOW COME I HAVEN'T HEARD IT? HOW CAN THEY SAY IT'S FAMILIAR IF I HAVEN'T HEARD IT?!
IF IT WAS SO FAMILIAR, I'D HAVE HEARD IT, WOULDN'T I? HOW CAN THEY SAY IT'S SO FAMILIAR IF I...
OH, GOOD GRIEF!
SCHULZ

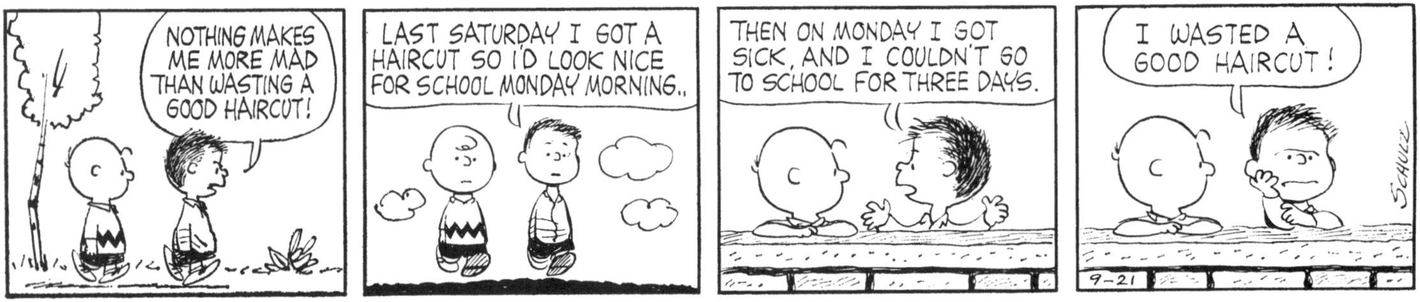
NOTHING MAKES ME MORE MAD THAN WASTING A GOOD HAIRCUT!
LAST SATURDAY I GOT A HAIRCUT SO I'D LOOK NICE FOR SCHOOL MONDAY MORNING..
THEN ON MONDAY I GOT SICK, AND I COULDN'T GO TO SCHOOL FOR THREE DAYS.
I WASTED A GOOD HAIRCUT!
SCHULZ
9-21

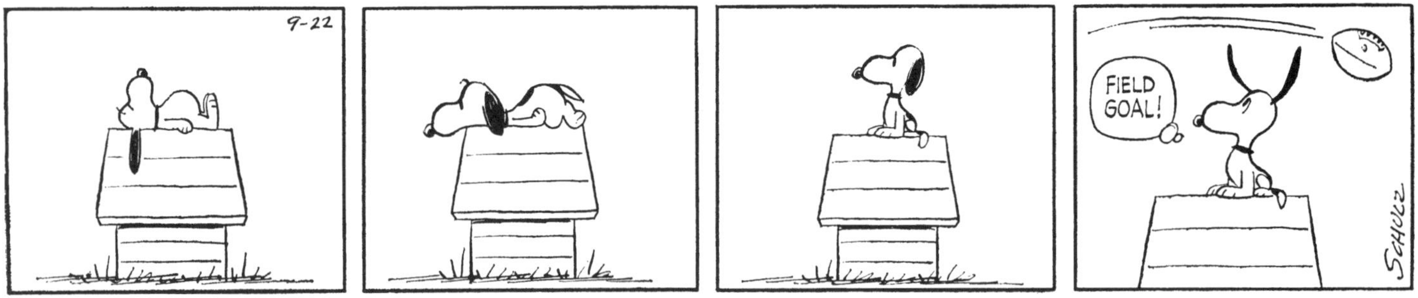
9-22
FIELD GOAL!
SCHULZ

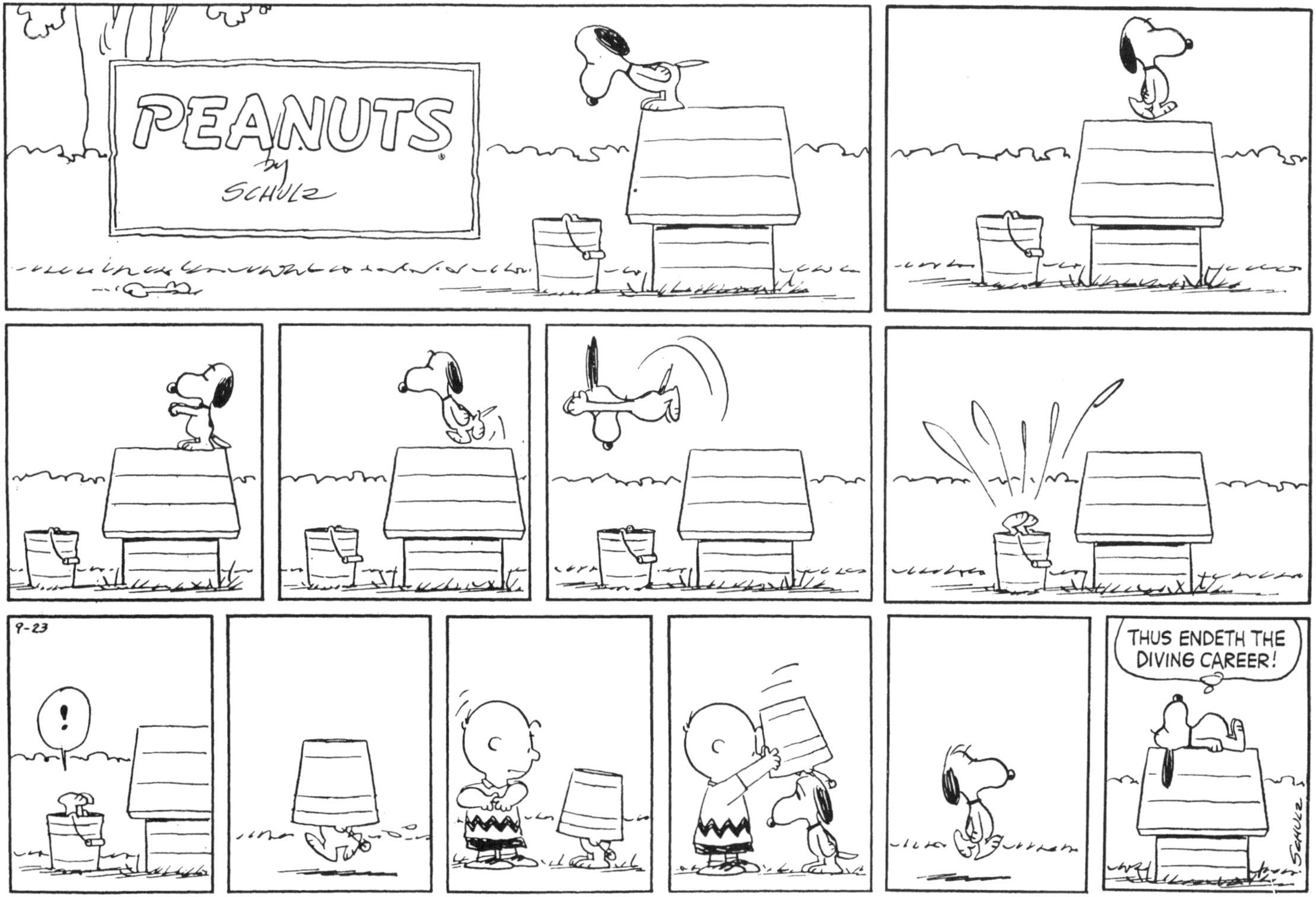
PEANUTS
by
SCHULZ
9-23
!
THUS ENDETH THE DIVING CAREER!
SCHULZ

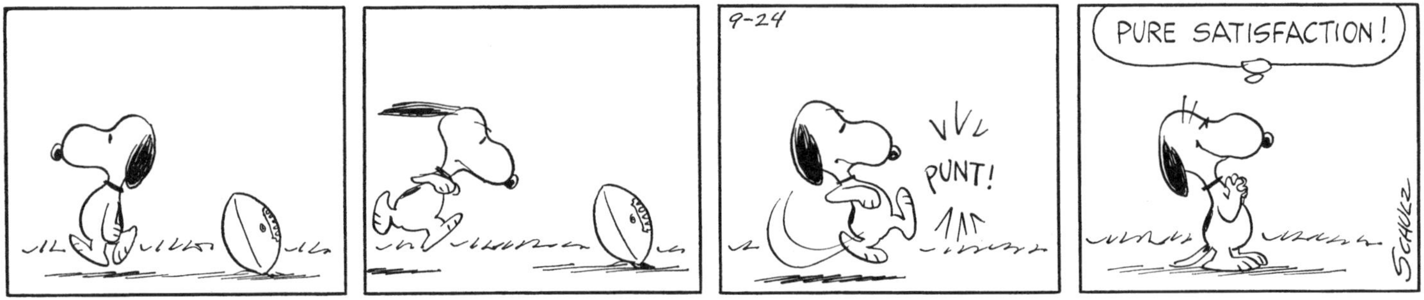
9-24
PUNT!
PURE SATISFACTION!
SCHULZ

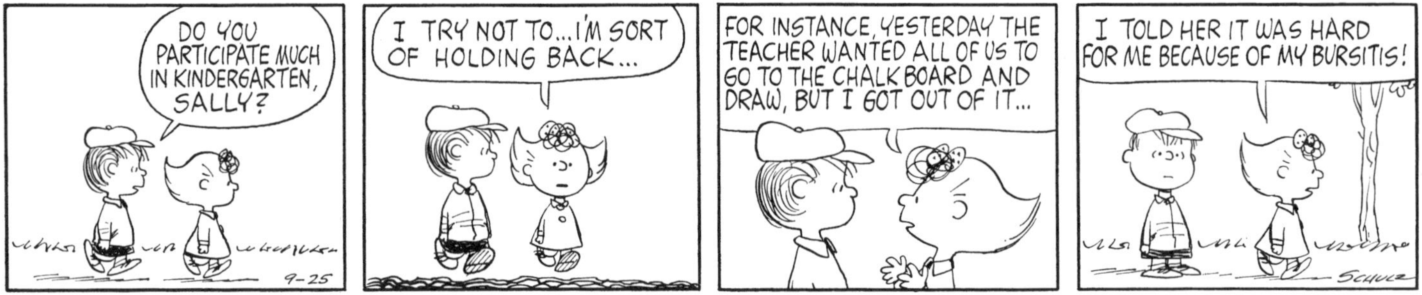
DO YOU PARTICIPATE MUCH IN KINDERGARTEN, SALLY?
9-25
I TRY NOT TO...I'M SORT OF HOLDING BACK...
FOR INSTANCE, YESTERDAY THE TEACHER WANTED ALL OF US TO GO TO THE CHALK BOARD AND DRAW, BUT I GOT OUT OF IT...
I TOLD HER IT WAS HARD FOR ME BECAUSE OF MY BURSITIS!
SCHULZ

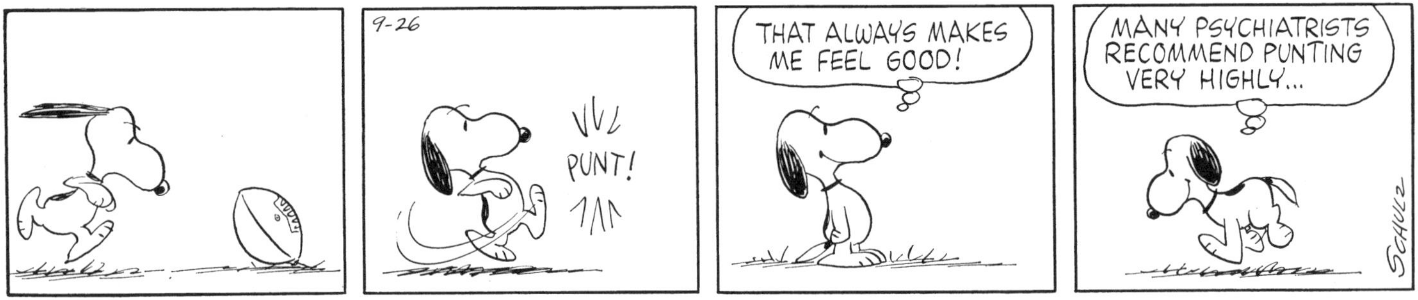
9-26
PUNT!
THAT ALWAYS MAKES ME FEEL GOOD!
MANY PSYCHIATRISTS RECOMMEND PUNTING VERY HIGHLY...
SCHULZ

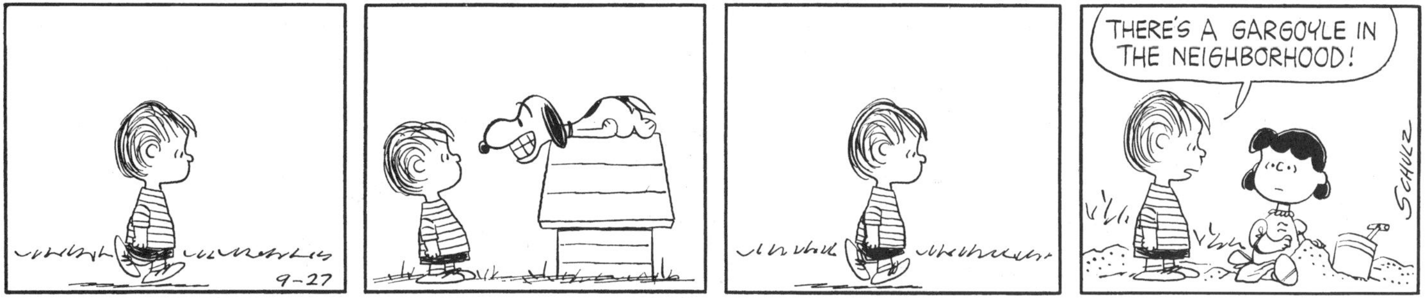
9-27
THERE'S A GARGOYLE IN THE NEIGHBORHOOD!
SCHULZ

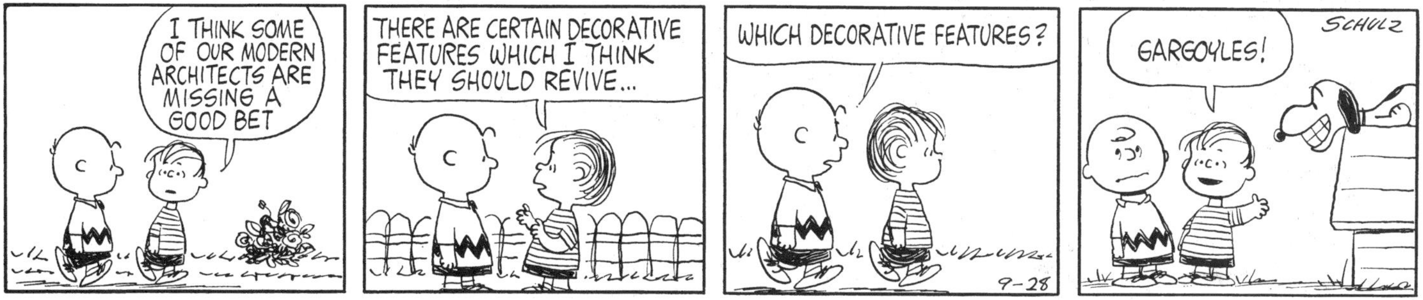
I THINK SOME OF OUR MODERN ARCHITECTS ARE MISSING A GOOD BET
THERE ARE CERTAIN DECORATIVE FEATURES WHICH I THINK THEY SHOULD REVIVE...
WHICH DECORATIVE FEATURES?
9-28
SCHULZ
GARGOYLES!

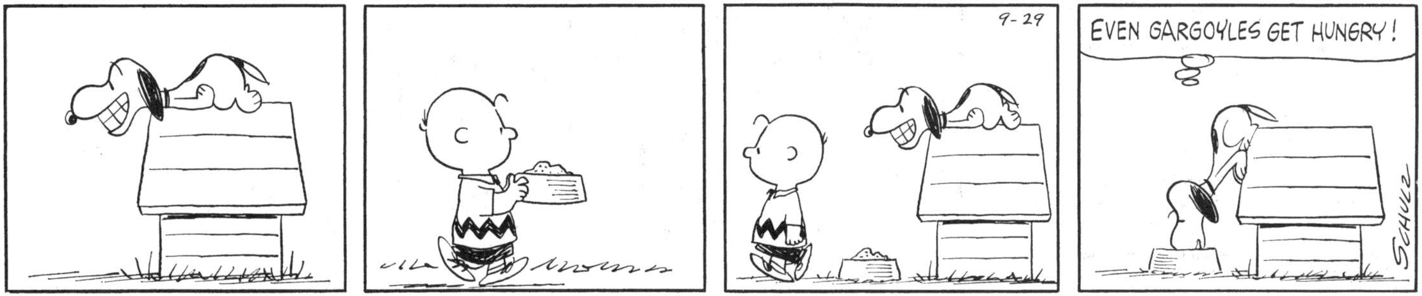
9-29
EVEN GARGOYLES GET HUNGRY!
SCHULZ

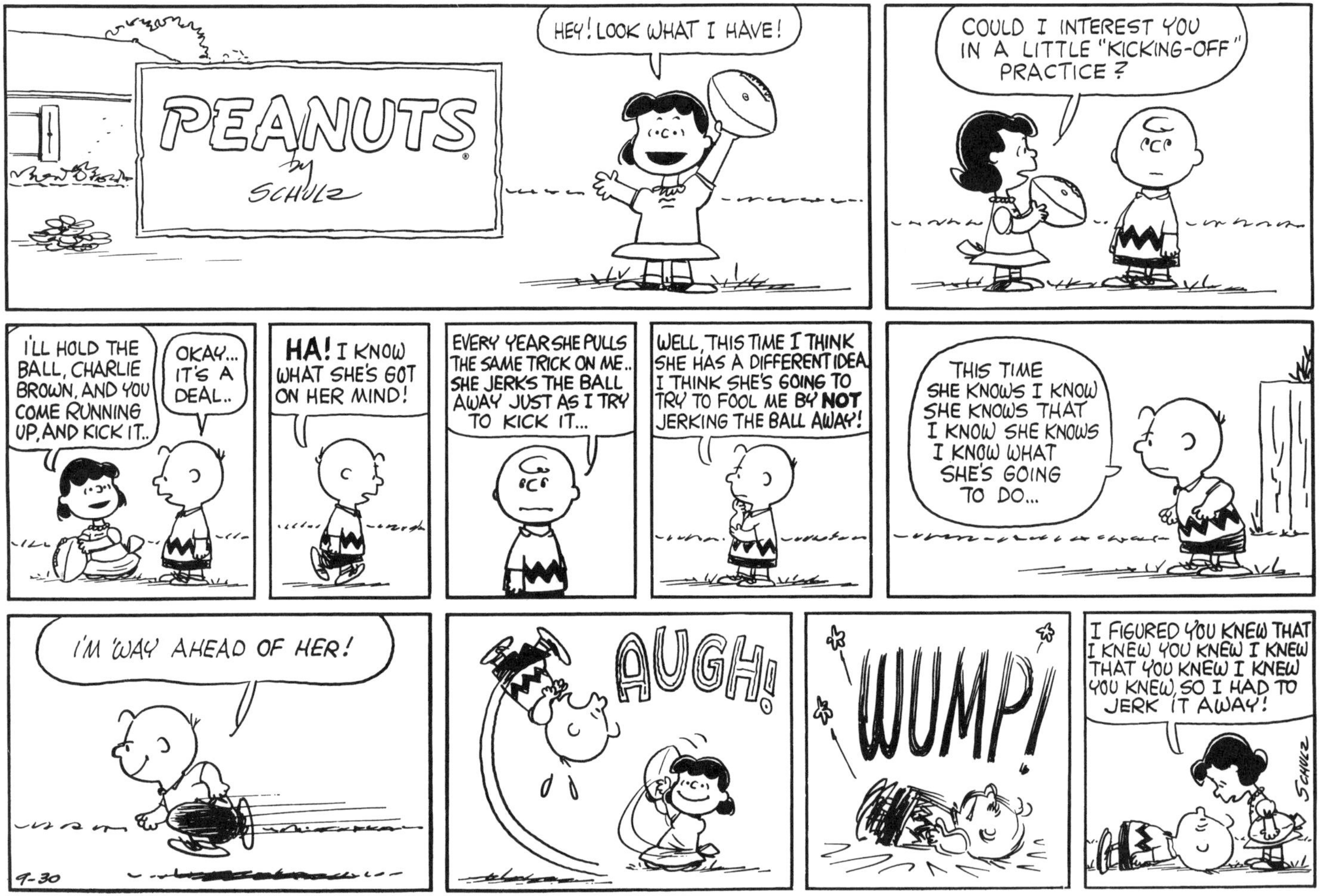
PEANUTS
by SCHULZ
HEY! LOOK WHAT I HAVE!
COULD I INTEREST YOU IN A LITTLE "KICKING-OFF" PRACTICE?
I'LL HOLD THE BALL, CHARLIE BROWN, AND YOU COME RUNNING UP, AND KICK IT..
OKAY... IT'S A DEAL..
HA! I KNOW WHAT SHE'S GOT ON HER MIND!
EVERY YEAR SHE PULLS THE SAME TRICK ON ME.. SHE JERKS THE BALL AWAY JUST AS I TRY TO KICK IT...
WELL, THIS TIME I THINK SHE HAS A DIFFERENT IDEA. I THINK SHE'S GOING TO TRY TO FOOL ME BY NOT JERKING THE BALL AWAY!
THIS TIME SHE KNOWS I KNOW SHE KNOWS THAT I KNOW SHE KNOWS I KNOW WHAT SHE'S GOING TO DO...
I'M 'WAY AHEAD OF HER!
9-30
AUGH!
WUMP!
I FIGURED YOU KNEW THAT I KNEW YOU KNEW I KNEW THAT YOU KNEW I KNEW YOU KNEW, SO I HAD TO JERK IT AWAY!
SCHULZ

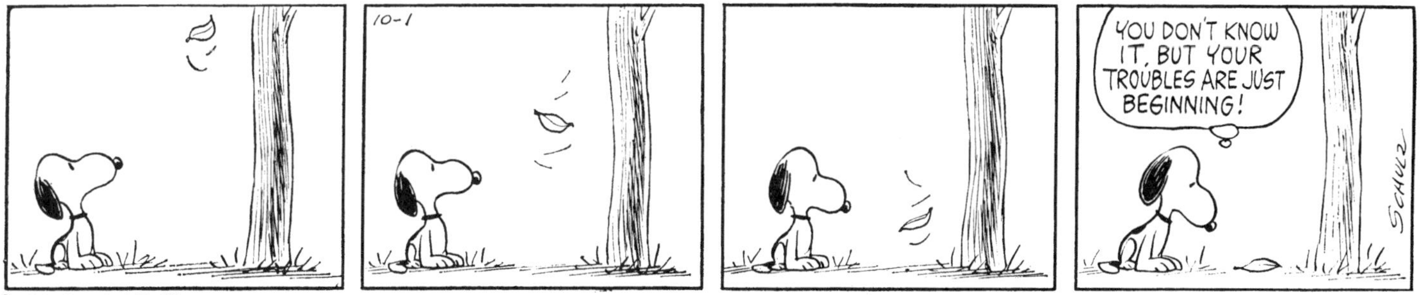
10-1
YOU DON'T KNOW IT, BUT YOUR TROUBLES ARE JUST BEGINNING!
SCHULZ

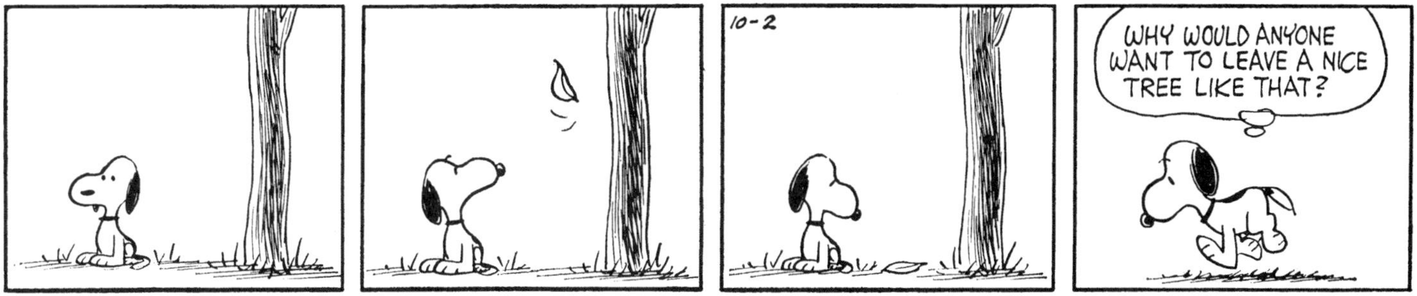
10-2
WHY WOULD ANYONE WANT TO LEAVE A NICE TREE LIKE THAT?

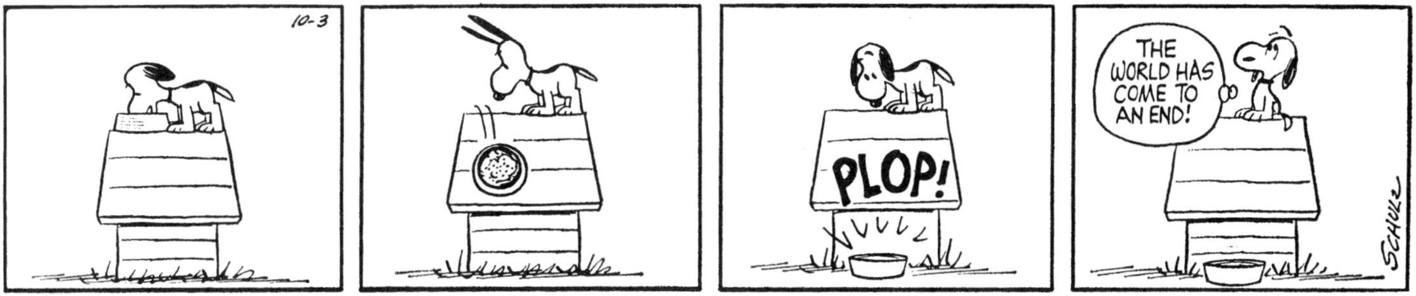
10-3
PLOP!
THE WORLD HAS COME TO AN END!
SCHULZ

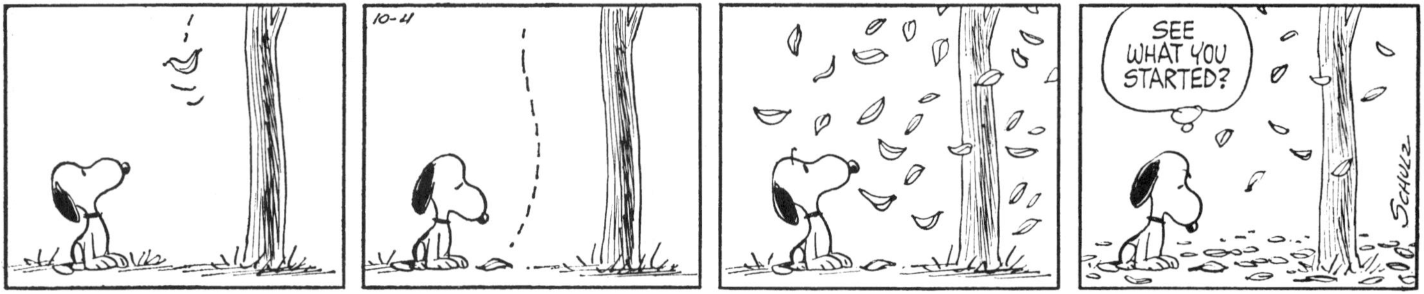
10-4
SEE WHAT YOU STARTED?
SCHULZ

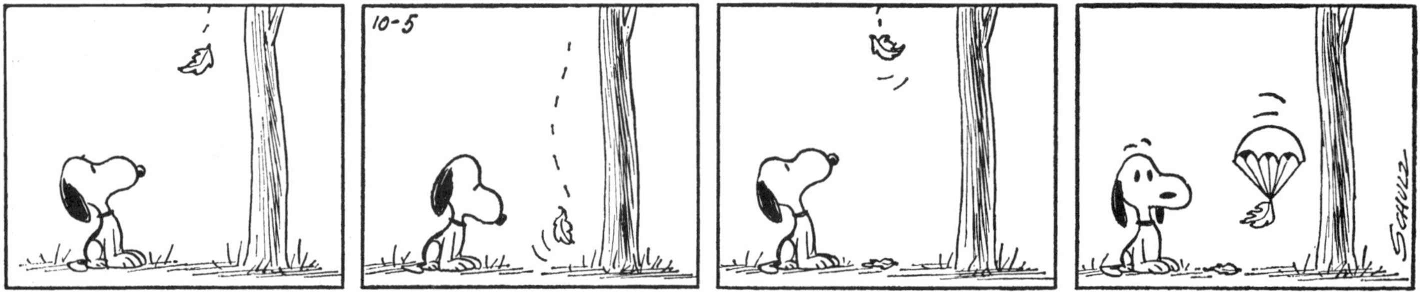
10-5
SCHULZ

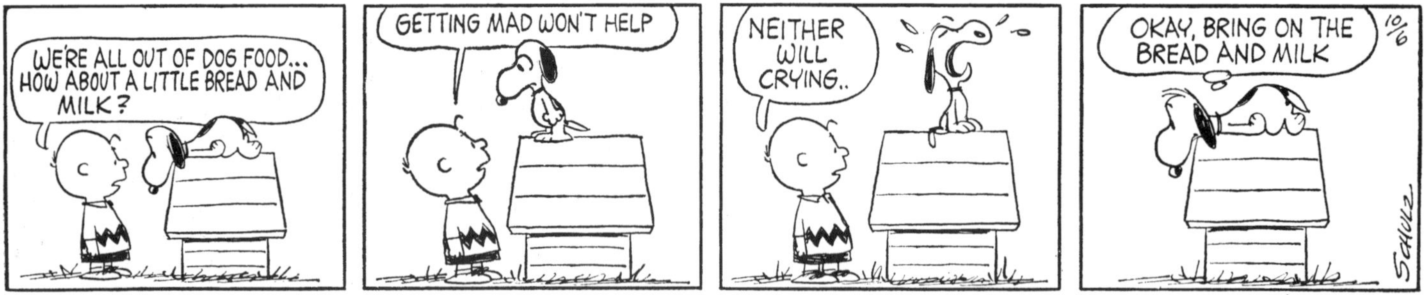
WE'RE ALL OUT OF DOG FOOD... HOW ABOUT A LITTLE BREAD AND MILK?
GETTING MAD WON'T HELP
NEITHER WILL CRYING..
OKAY, BRING ON THE BREAD AND MILK
10/6
SCHULZ

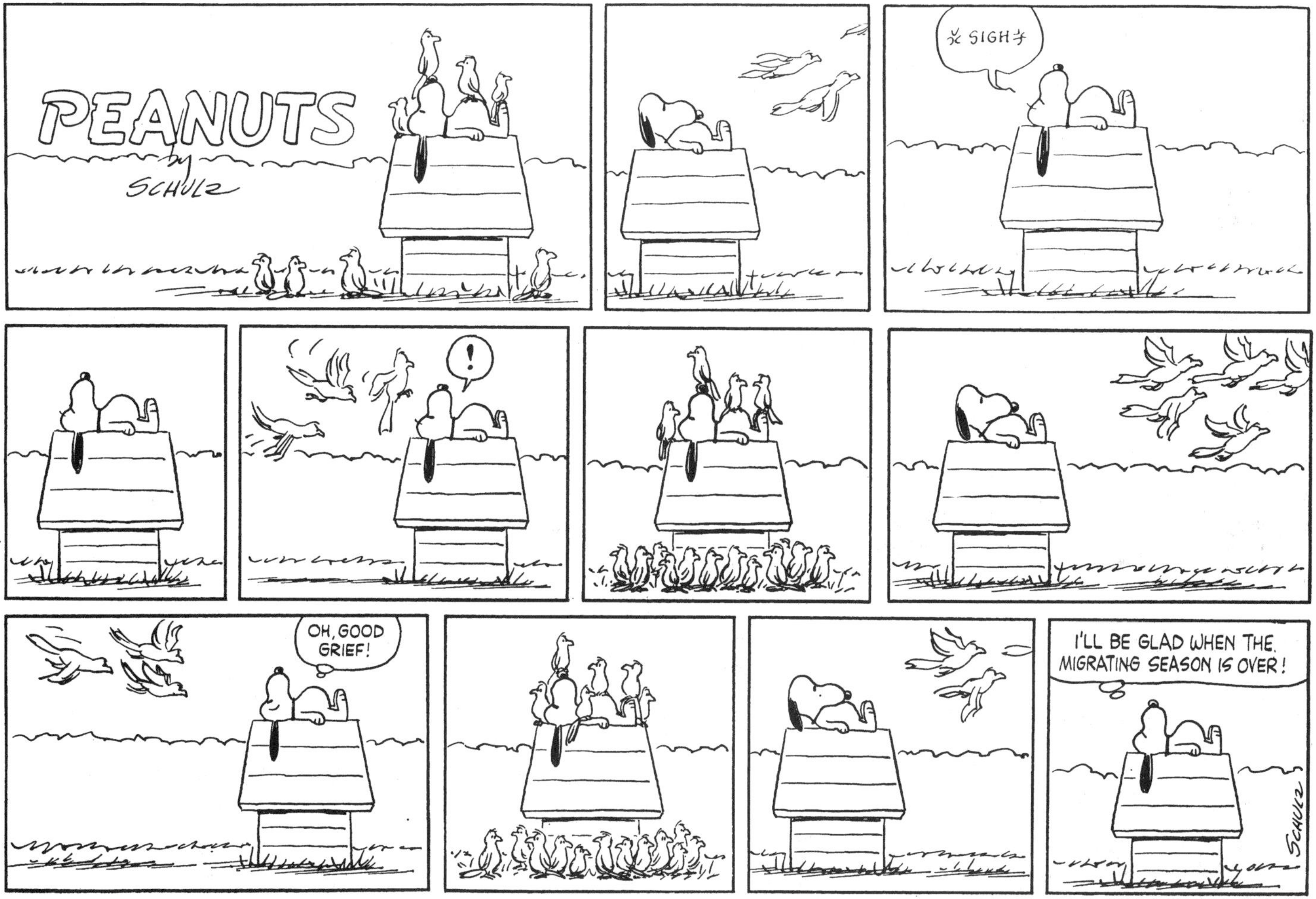
PEANUTS
by
SCHULZ
SIGH
!
OH, GOOD GRIEF!
I'LL BE GLAD WHEN THE MIGRATING SEASON IS OVER!
SCHULZ

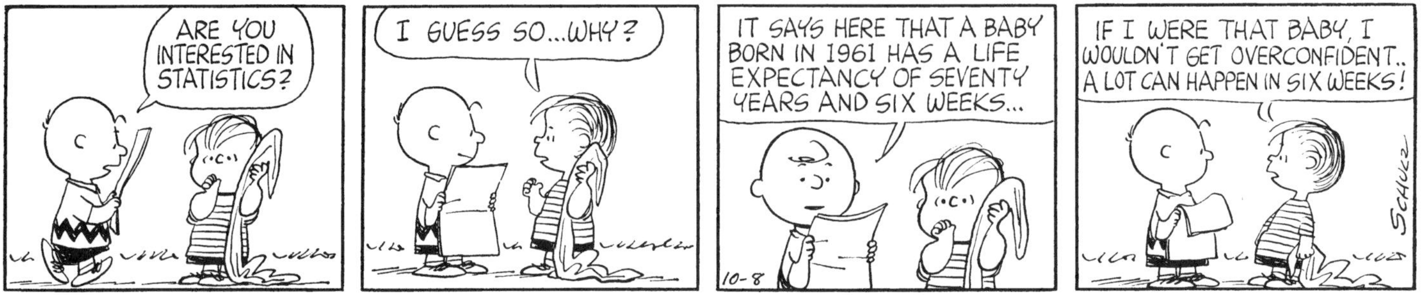
ARE YOU INTERESTED IN STATISTICS?
I GUESS SO...WHY?
IT SAYS HERE THAT A BABY BORN IN 1961 HAS A LIFE EXPECTANCY OF SEVENTY YEARS AND SIX WEEKS...
10-8
IF I WERE THAT BABY, I WOULDN'T GET OVERCONFIDENT.. A LOT CAN HAPPEN IN SIX WEEKS!
SCHULZ

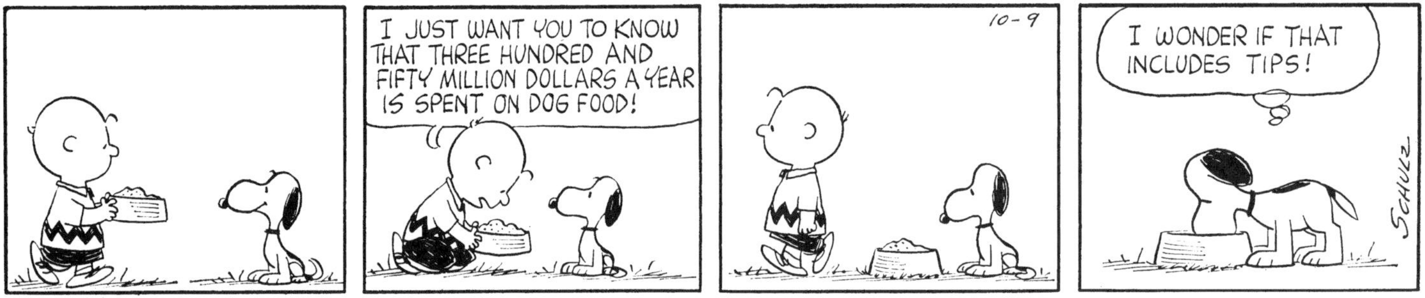
I JUST WANT YOU TO KNOW THAT THREE HUNDRED AND FIFTY MILLION DOLLARS A YEAR IS SPENT ON DOG FOOD!
10-9
I WONDER IF THAT INCLUDES TIPS!
SCHULZ

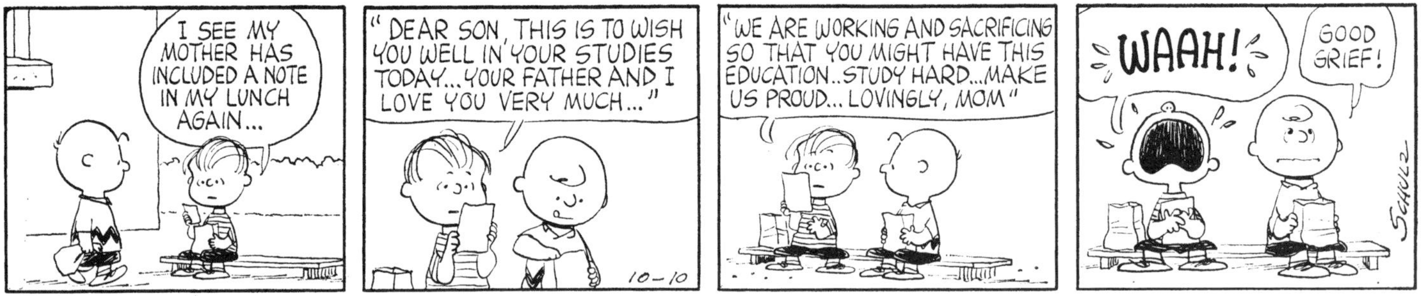
I SEE MY MOTHER HAS INCLUDED A NOTE IN MY LUNCH AGAIN...
" DEAR SON, THIS IS TO WISH YOU WELL IN YOUR STUDIES TODAY...YOUR FATHER AND I LOVE YOU VERY MUCH..."
10-10
"WE ARE WORKING AND SACRIFICING SO THAT YOU MIGHT HAVE THIS EDUCATION..STUDY HARD...MAKE US PROUD... LOVINGLY, MOM"
WAAH!
GOOD GRIEF!
SCHULZ

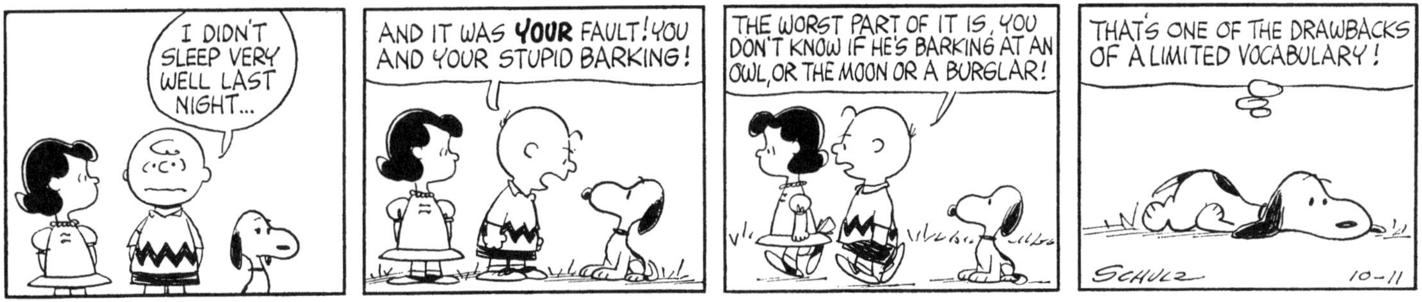
I DIDN'T SLEEP VERY WELL LAST NIGHT...
AND IT WAS YOUR FAULT! YOU AND YOUR STUPID BARKING!
THE WORST PART OF IT IS, YOU DON'T KNOW IF HE'S BARKING AT AN OWL, OR THE MOON OR A BURGLAR!
THAT'S ONE OF THE DRAWBACKS OF A LIMITED VOCABULARY!
SCHULZ
10-11

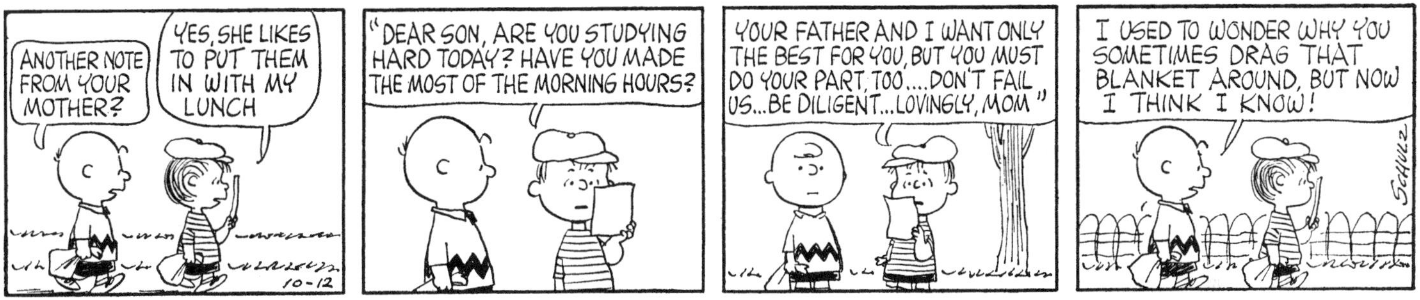
ANOTHER NOTE FROM YOUR MOTHER?
YES, SHE LIKES TO PUT THEM IN WITH MY LUNCH
10-12
"DEAR SON, ARE YOU STUDYING HARD TODAY? HAVE YOU MADE THE MOST OF THE MORNING HOURS?
YOUR FATHER AND I WANT ONLY THE BEST FOR YOU, BUT YOU MUST DO YOUR PART, TOO.... DON'T FAIL US... BE DILIGENT... LOVINGLY, MOM"
I USED TO WONDER WHY YOU SOMETIMES DRAG THAT BLANKET AROUND, BUT NOW I THINK I KNOW!
SCHULZ

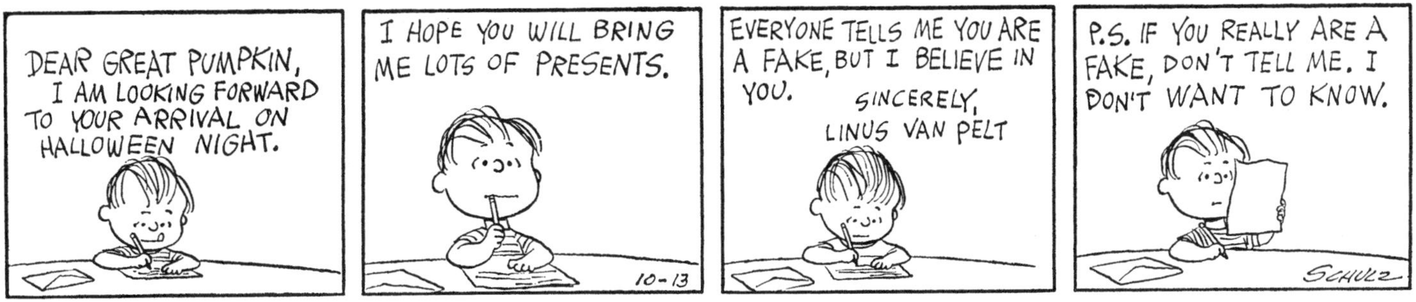
DEAR GREAT PUMPKIN, I AM LOOKING FORWARD TO YOUR ARRIVAL ON HALLOWEEN NIGHT.
I HOPE YOU WILL BRING ME LOTS OF PRESENTS.
10-13
EVERYONE TELLS ME YOU ARE A FAKE, BUT I BELIEVE IN YOU.
SINCERELY, LINUS VAN PELT
P.S. IF YOU REALLY ARE A FAKE, DON'T TELL ME. I DON'T WANT TO KNOW.
SCHULZ

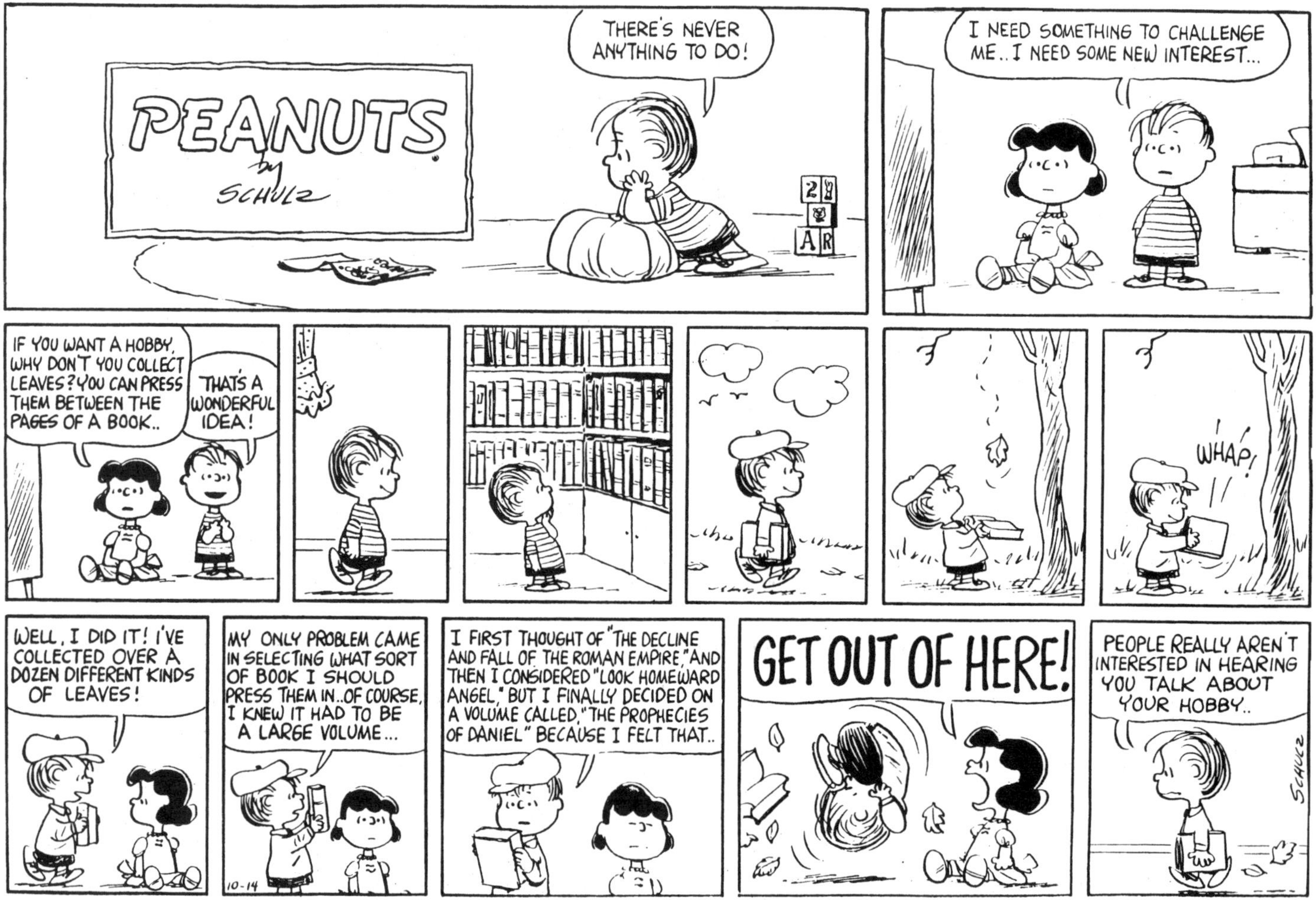
PEANUTS
by SCHULZ
THERE'S NEVER ANYTHING TO DO!
I NEED SOMETHING TO CHALLENGE ME.. I NEED SOME NEW INTEREST...
IF YOU WANT A HOBBY, WHY DON'T YOU COLLECT LEAVES? YOU CAN PRESS THEM BETWEEN THE PAGES OF A BOOK..
THAT'S A WONDERFUL IDEA!
WHAP!
WELL, I DID IT! I'VE COLLECTED OVER A DOZEN DIFFERENT KINDS OF LEAVES!
MY ONLY PROBLEM CAME IN SELECTING WHAT SORT OF BOOK I SHOULD PRESS THEM IN..OF COURSE, I KNEW IT HAD TO BE A LARGE VOLUME...
10-14
I FIRST THOUGHT OF "THE DECLINE AND FALL OF THE ROMAN EMPIRE," AND THEN I CONSIDERED "LOOK HOMEWARD ANGEL," BUT I FINALLY DECIDED ON A VOLUME CALLED, "THE PROPHECIES OF DANIEL" BECAUSE I FELT THAT..
GET OUT OF HERE!
SCHULZ
PEOPLE REALLY AREN'T INTERESTED IN HEARING YOU TALK ABOUT YOUR HOBBY..

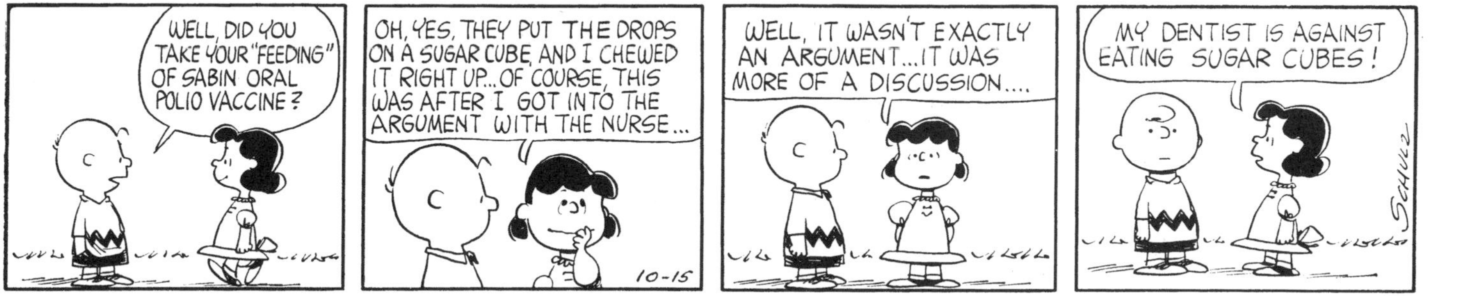
WELL, DID YOU TAKE YOUR "FEEDING" OF SABIN ORAL POLIO VACCINE?
OH, YES, THEY PUT THE DROPS ON A SUGAR CUBE, AND I CHEWED IT RIGHT UP...OF COURSE, THIS WAS AFTER I GOT INTO THE ARGUMENT WITH THE NURSE...
10-15
WELL, IT WASN'T EXACTLY AN ARGUMENT...IT WAS MORE OF A DISCUSSION....
MY DENTIST IS AGAINST EATING SUGAR CUBES!
SCHULZ

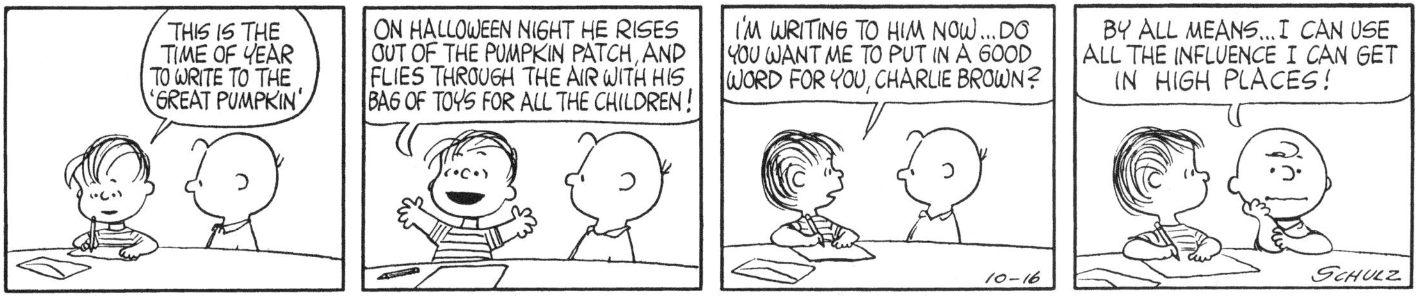
THIS IS THE TIME OF YEAR TO WRITE TO THE 'GREAT PUMPKIN'
ON HALLOWEEN NIGHT HE RISES OUT OF THE PUMPKIN PATCH, AND FLIES THROUGH THE AIR WITH HIS BAG OF TOYS FOR ALL THE CHILDREN!
I'M WRITING TO HIM NOW...DO YOU WANT ME TO PUT IN A GOOD WORD FOR YOU, CHARLIE BROWN?
10-16
BY ALL MEANS...I CAN USE ALL THE INFLUENCE I CAN GET IN HIGH PLACES!
SCHULZ

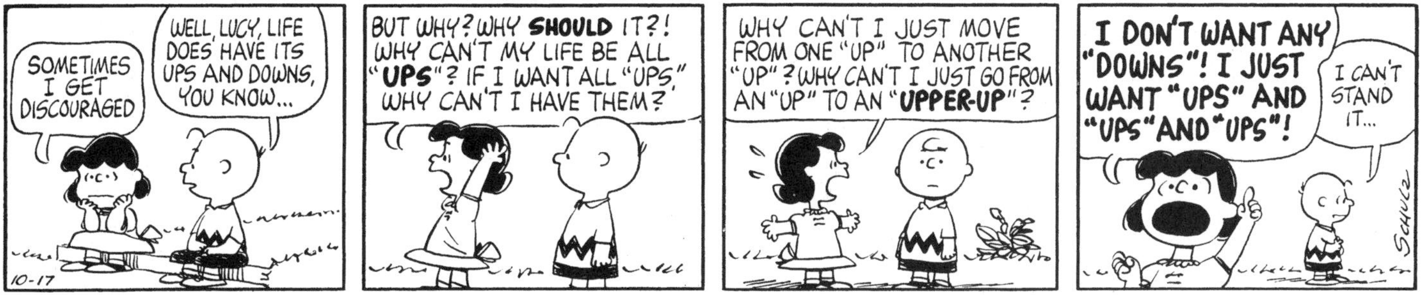
SOMETIMES I GET DISCOURAGED
WELL, LUCY, LIFE DOES HAVE ITS UPS AND DOWNS, YOU KNOW...
10-17
BUT WHY? WHY **SHOULD** IT?! WHY CAN'T MY LIFE BE ALL "**UPS**"? IF I WANT ALL "UPS," WHY CAN'T I HAVE THEM?
WHY CAN'T I JUST MOVE FROM ONE "UP" TO ANOTHER "UP"? WHY CAN'T I JUST GO FROM AN "UP" TO AN "**UPPER-UP**"?
I DON'T WANT ANY "DOWNS"! I JUST WANT "UPS" AND "UPS" AND "UPS"!
I CAN'T STAND IT...
SCHULZ

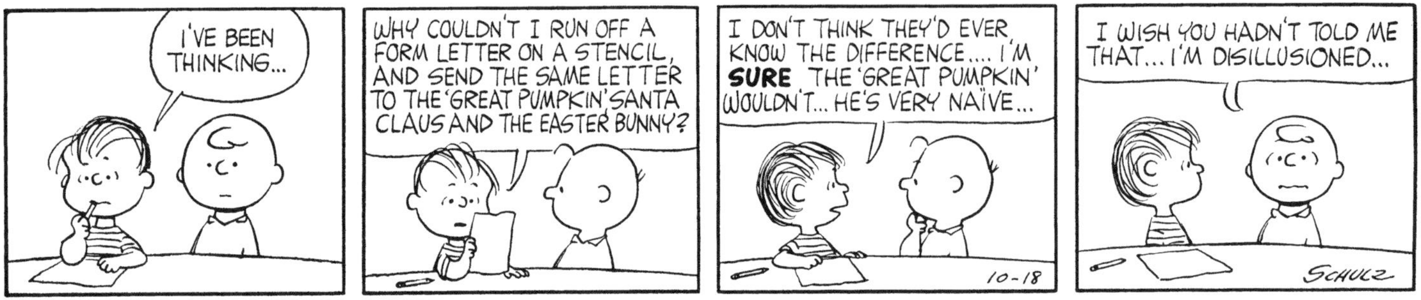
I'VE BEEN THINKING...
WHY COULDN'T I RUN OFF A FORM LETTER ON A STENCIL, AND SEND THE SAME LETTER TO THE 'GREAT PUMPKIN' SANTA CLAUS AND THE EASTER BUNNY?
I DON'T THINK THEY'D EVER KNOW THE DIFFERENCE.... I'M SURE THE 'GREAT PUMPKIN' WOULDN'T... HE'S VERY NAÏVE...
10-18
I WISH YOU HADN'T TOLD ME THAT... I'M DISILLUSIONED...
SCHULZ

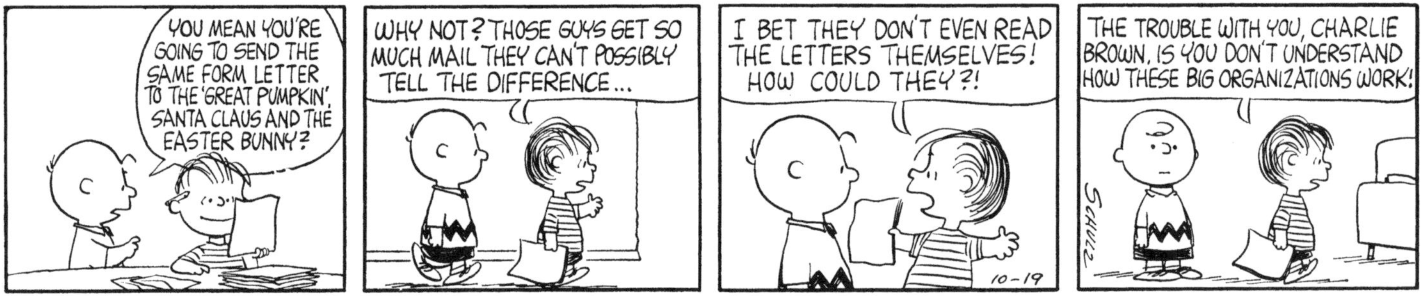
YOU MEAN YOU'RE GOING TO SEND THE SAME FORM LETTER TO THE 'GREAT PUMPKIN', SANTA CLAUS AND THE EASTER BUNNY?
WHY NOT? THOSE GUYS GET SO MUCH MAIL THEY CAN'T POSSIBLY TELL THE DIFFERENCE...
I BET THEY DON'T EVEN READ THE LETTERS THEMSELVES! HOW COULD THEY?!
10-19
THE TROUBLE WITH YOU, CHARLIE BROWN, IS YOU DON'T UNDERSTAND HOW THESE BIG ORGANIZATIONS WORK!
SCHULZ

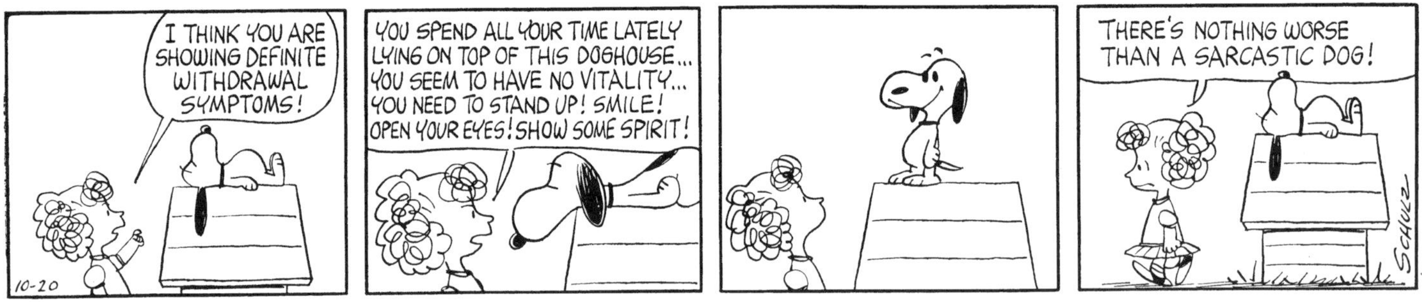
I THINK YOU ARE SHOWING DEFINITE WITHDRAWAL SYMPTOMS!
10-20
YOU SPEND ALL YOUR TIME LATELY LYING ON TOP OF THIS DOGHOUSE... YOU SEEM TO HAVE NO VITALITY... YOU NEED TO STAND UP! SMILE! OPEN YOUR EYES! SHOW SOME SPIRIT!
THERE'S NOTHING WORSE THAN A SARCASTIC DOG!
SCHULZ

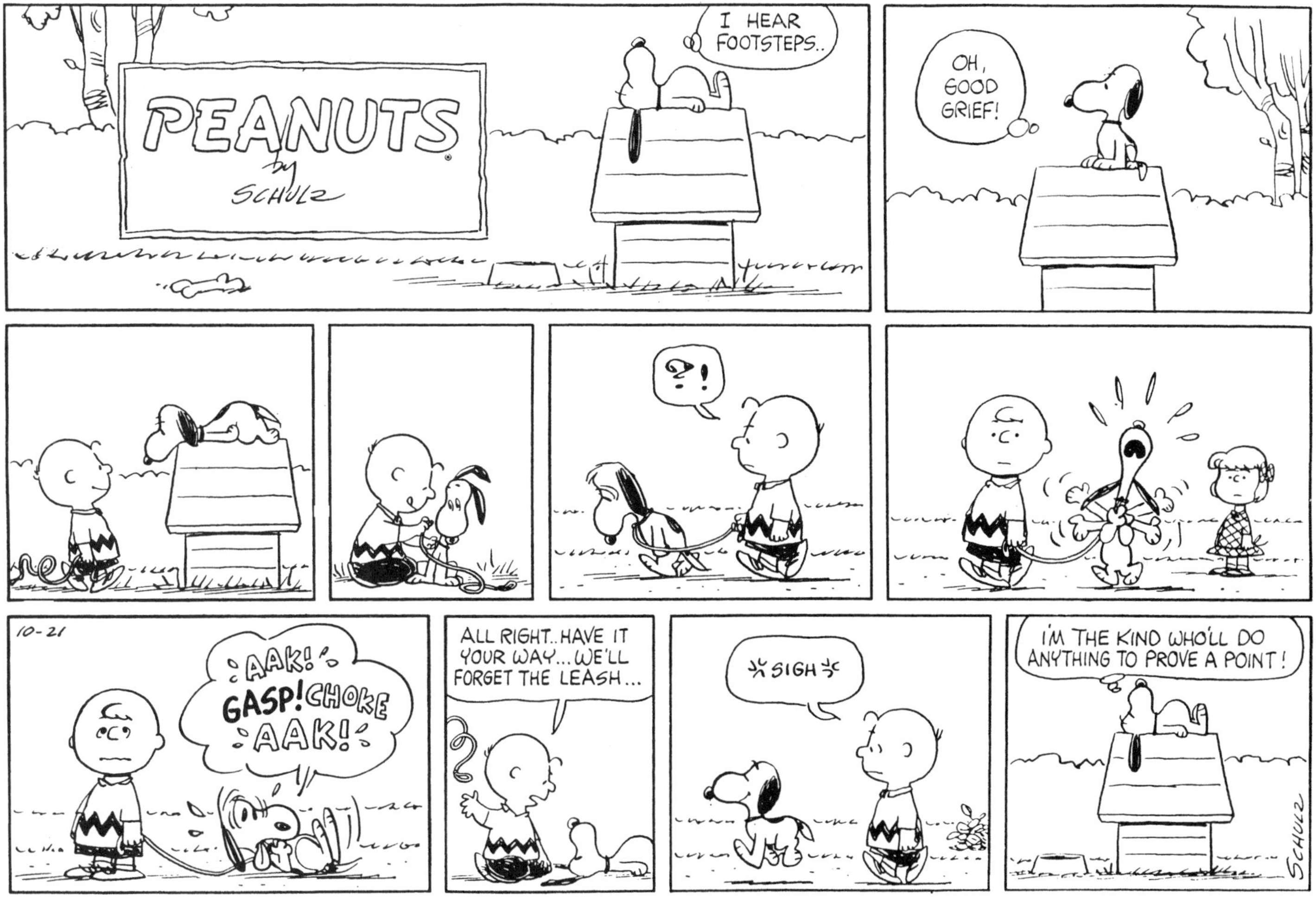
PEANUTS
by SCHULZ
I HEAR FOOTSTEPS..
OH, GOOD GRIEF!
?!
10-21
AAK! GASP! CHOKE AAK!
ALL RIGHT.. HAVE IT YOUR WAY... WE'LL FORGET THE LEASH...
SIGH
I'M THE KIND WHO'LL DO ANYTHING TO PROVE A POINT!
SCHULZ

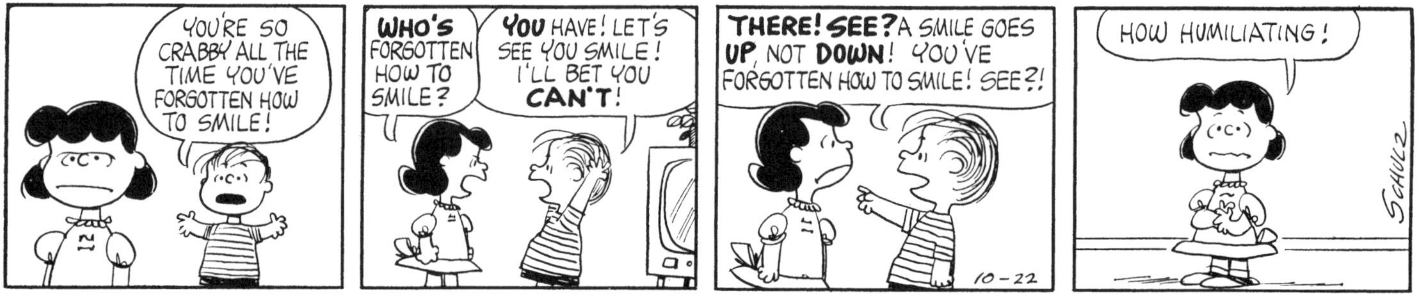
YOU'RE SO CRABBY ALL THE TIME YOU'VE FORGOTTEN HOW TO SMILE!
WHO'S FORGOTTEN HOW TO SMILE?
YOU HAVE! LET'S SEE YOU SMILE! I'LL BET YOU CAN'T!
THERE! SEE? A SMILE GOES UP, NOT DOWN! YOU'VE FORGOTTEN HOW TO SMILE! SEE?!
10-22
HOW HUMILIATING!
SCHULZ

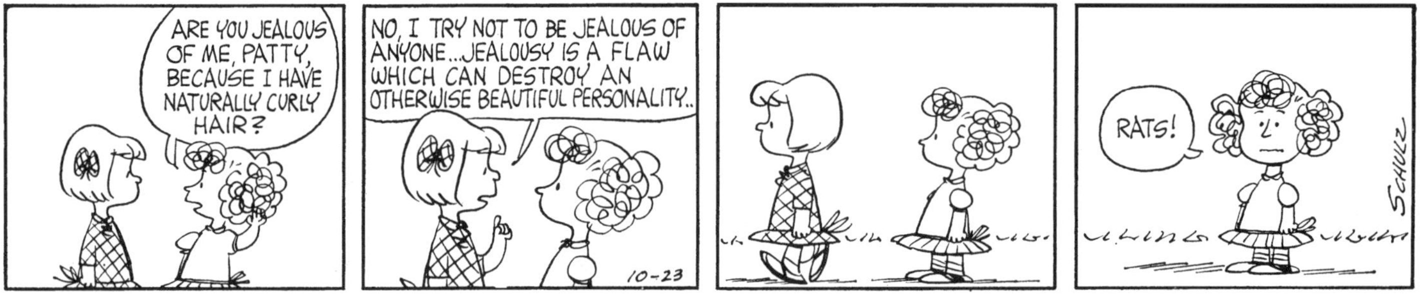
ARE YOU JEALOUS OF ME, PATTY, BECAUSE I HAVE NATURALLY CURLY HAIR?
NO, I TRY NOT TO BE JEALOUS OF ANYONE...JEALOUSY IS A FLAW WHICH CAN DESTROY AN OTHERWISE BEAUTIFUL PERSONALITY..
10-23
RATS!
SCHULZ

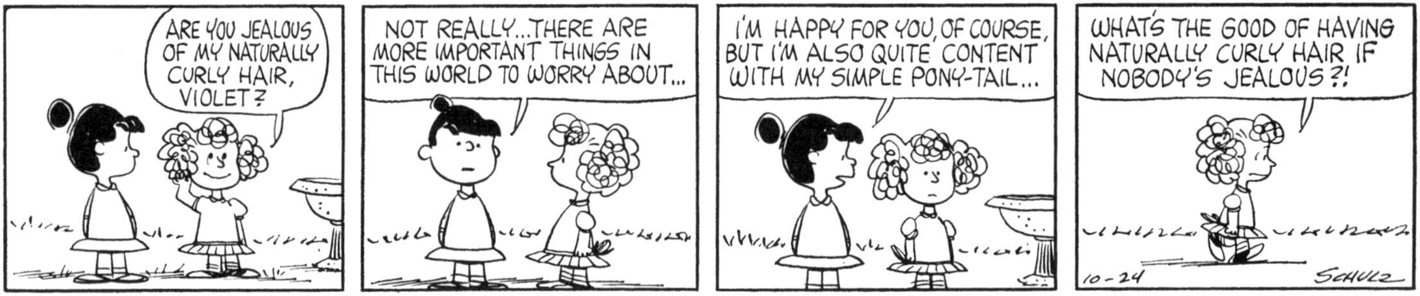
ARE YOU JEALOUS OF MY NATURALLY CURLY HAIR, VIOLET?
NOT REALLY...THERE ARE MORE IMPORTANT THINGS IN THIS WORLD TO WORRY ABOUT...
I'M HAPPY FOR YOU, OF COURSE, BUT I'M ALSO QUITE CONTENT WITH MY SIMPLE PONY-TAIL...
WHAT'S THE GOOD OF HAVING NATURALLY CURLY HAIR IF NOBODY'S JEALOUS?!
10-24
SCHULZ

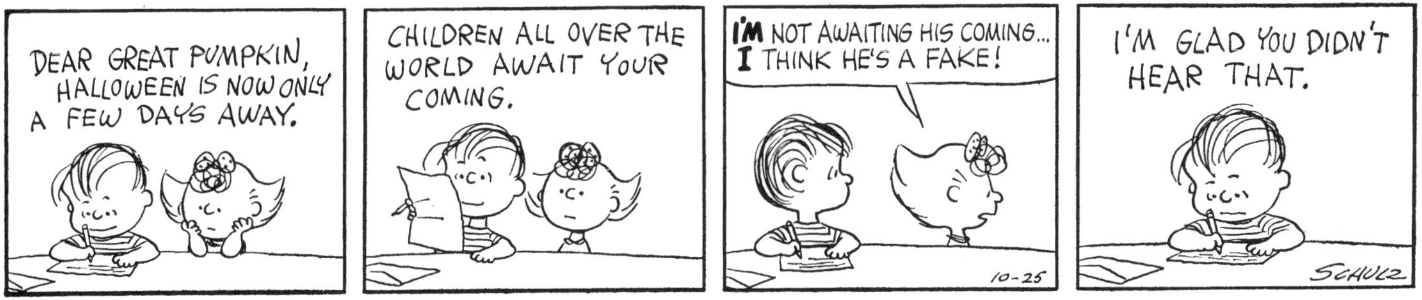
DEAR GREAT PUMPKIN, HALLOWEEN IS NOW ONLY A FEW DAYS AWAY.
CHILDREN ALL OVER THE WORLD AWAIT YOUR COMING.
I'M NOT AWAITING HIS COMING... I THINK HE'S A FAKE!
10-25
I'M GLAD YOU DIDN'T HEAR THAT.
SCHULZ

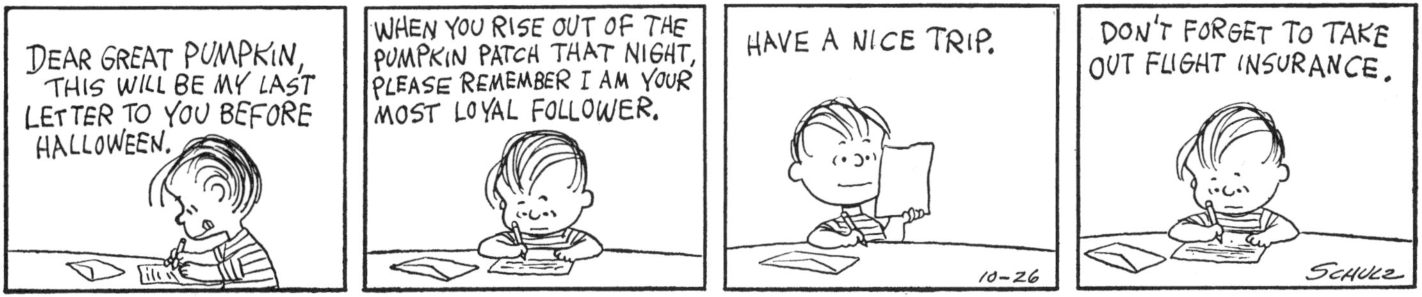
DEAR GREAT PUMPKIN, THIS WILL BE MY LAST LETTER TO YOU BEFORE HALLOWEEN.
WHEN YOU RISE OUT OF THE PUMPKIN PATCH THAT NIGHT, PLEASE REMEMBER I AM YOUR MOST LOYAL FOLLOWER.
HAVE A NICE TRIP.
10-26
DON'T FORGET TO TAKE OUT FLIGHT INSURANCE.
SCHULZ

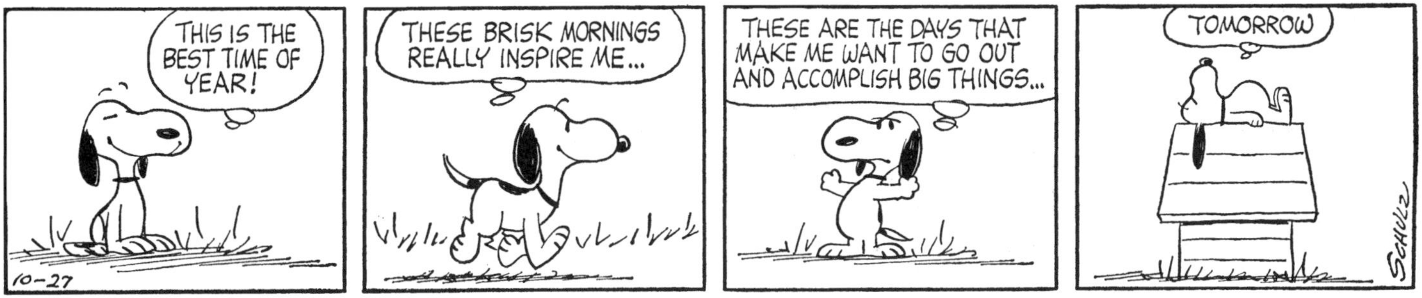
THIS IS THE BEST TIME OF YEAR!
10-27
THESE BRISK MORNINGS REALLY INSPIRE ME...
THESE ARE THE DAYS THAT MAKE ME WANT TO GO OUT AND ACCOMPLISH BIG THINGS...
TOMORROW
SCHULZ

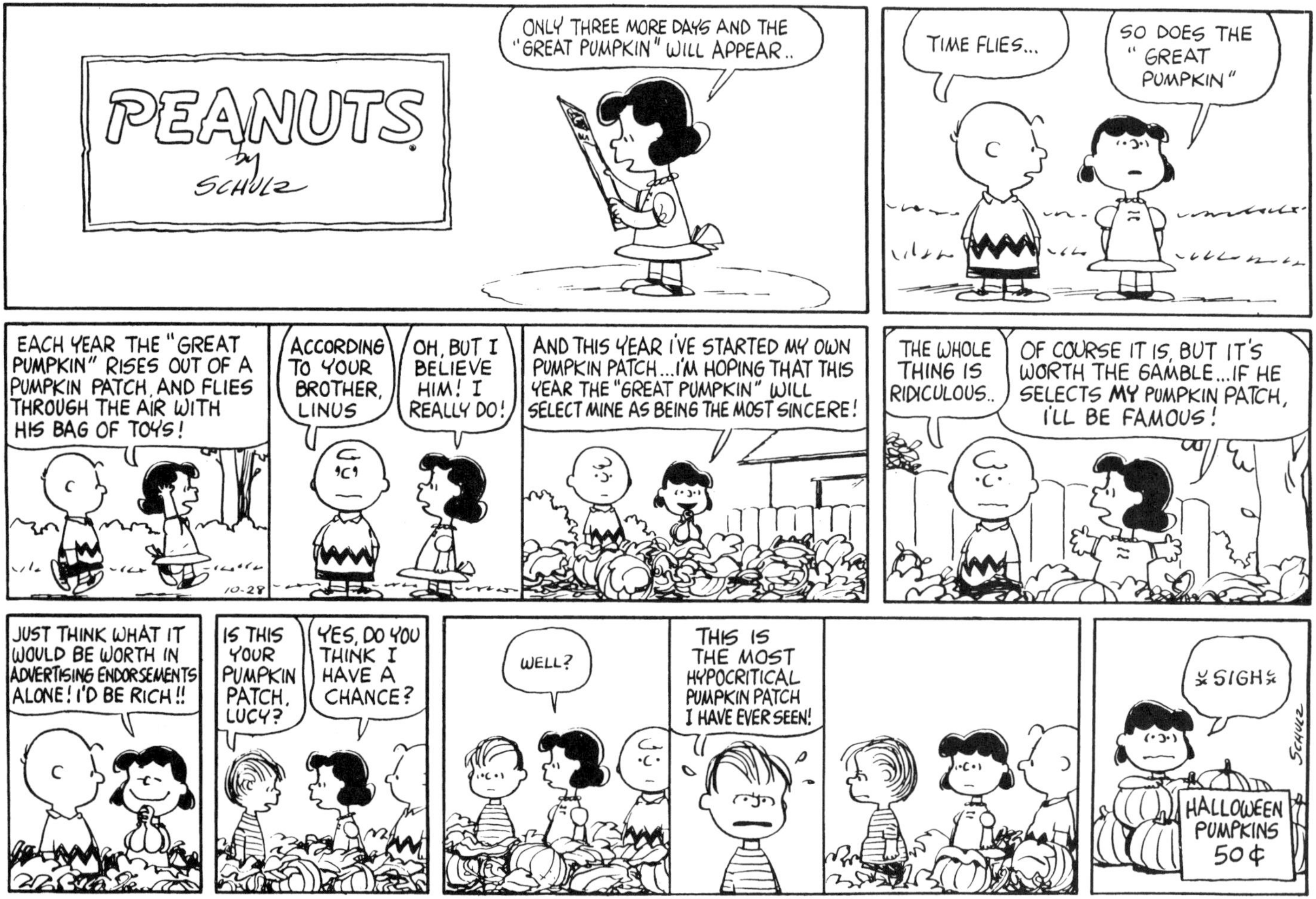
PEANUTS
by SCHULZ
ONLY THREE MORE DAYS AND THE "GREAT PUMPKIN" WILL APPEAR..
TIME FLIES...
SO DOES THE "GREAT PUMPKIN"
EACH YEAR THE "GREAT PUMPKIN" RISES OUT OF A PUMPKIN PATCH, AND FLIES THROUGH THE AIR WITH HIS BAG OF TOYS!
10-28
ACCORDING TO YOUR BROTHER, LINUS
OH, BUT I BELIEVE HIM! I REALLY DO!
AND THIS YEAR I'VE STARTED MY OWN PUMPKIN PATCH...I'M HOPING THAT THIS YEAR THE "GREAT PUMPKIN" WILL SELECT MINE AS BEING THE MOST SINCERE!
THE WHOLE THING IS RIDICULOUS..
OF COURSE IT IS, BUT IT'S WORTH THE GAMBLE...IF HE SELECTS MY PUMPKIN PATCH, I'LL BE FAMOUS!
JUST THINK WHAT IT WOULD BE WORTH IN ADVERTISING ENDORSEMENTS ALONE! I'D BE RICH!!
IS THIS YOUR PUMPKIN PATCH, LUCY?
YES, DO YOU THINK I HAVE A CHANCE?
WELL?
THIS IS THE MOST HYPOCRITICAL PUMPKIN PATCH I HAVE EVER SEEN!
SCHULZ
SIGH
HALLOWEEN PUMPKINS 50¢

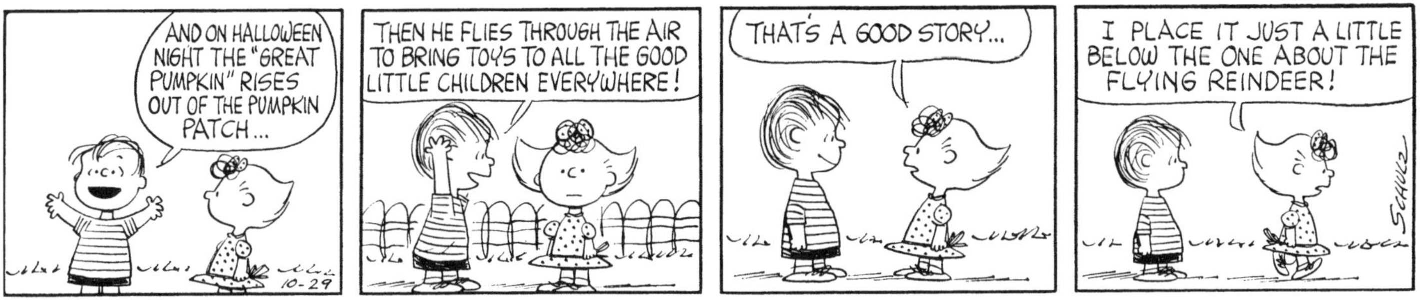
AND ON HALLOWEEN NIGHT THE "GREAT PUMPKIN" RISES OUT OF THE PUMPKIN PATCH...
10-29
THEN HE FLIES THROUGH THE AIR TO BRING TOYS TO ALL THE GOOD LITTLE CHILDREN EVERYWHERE!
THAT'S A GOOD STORY...
I PLACE IT JUST A LITTLE BELOW THE ONE ABOUT THE FLYING REINDEER!
SCHULZ

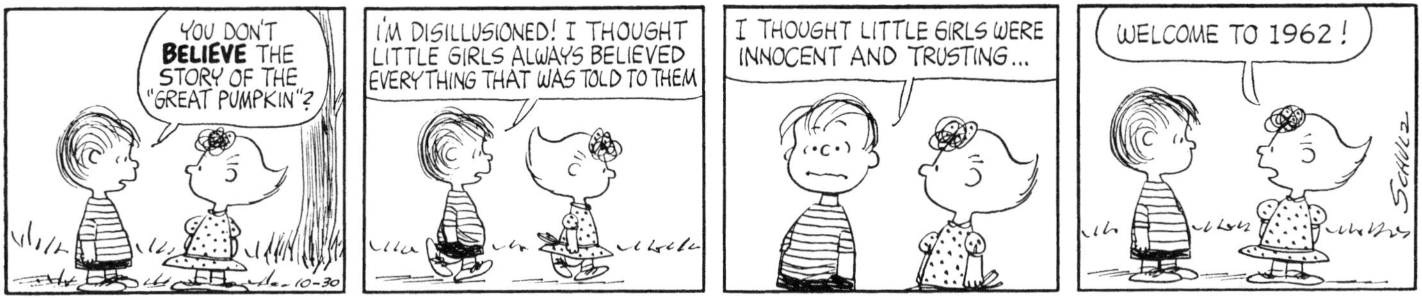
YOU DON'T **BELIEVE** THE STORY OF THE "GREAT PUMPKIN"?
10-30
I'M DISILLUSIONED! I THOUGHT LITTLE GIRLS ALWAYS BELIEVED EVERYTHING THAT WAS TOLD TO THEM
I THOUGHT LITTLE GIRLS WERE INNOCENT AND TRUSTING...
WELCOME TO 1962!
SCHULZ

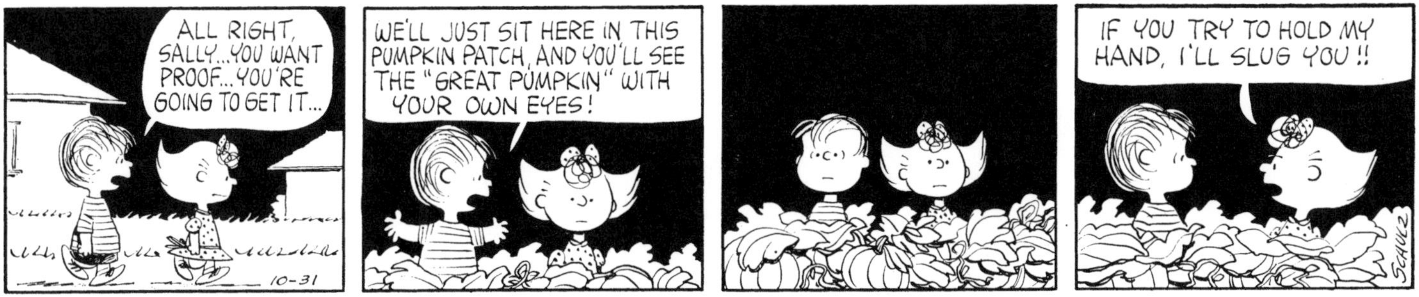
ALL RIGHT, SALLY...YOU WANT PROOF...YOU'RE GOING TO GET IT...
10-31
WE'LL JUST SIT HERE IN THIS PUMPKIN PATCH, AND YOU'LL SEE THE "GREAT PUMPKIN" WITH YOUR OWN EYES!
IF YOU TRY TO HOLD MY HAND, I'LL SLUG YOU!!
SCHULZ

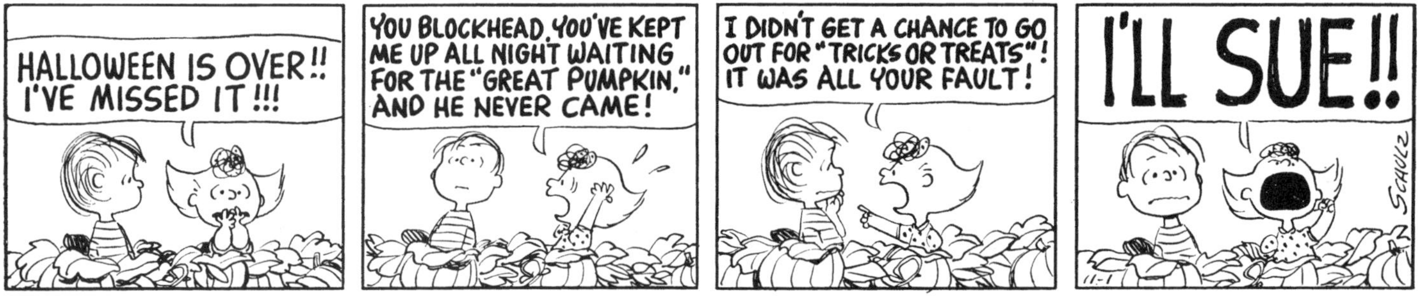
HALLOWEEN IS OVER!! I'VE MISSED IT!!!
YOU BLOCKHEAD, YOU'VE KEPT ME UP ALL NIGHT WAITING FOR THE "GREAT PUMPKIN," AND HE NEVER CAME!
I DIDN'T GET A CHANCE TO GO OUT FOR "TRICKS OR TREATS"! IT WAS ALL YOUR FAULT!
I'LL SUE!!
SCHULZ
11-1

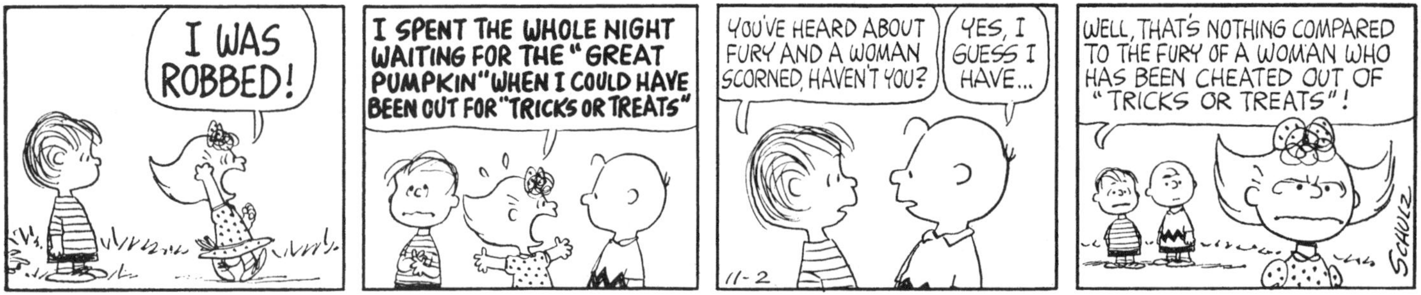
I WAS ROBBED!
I SPENT THE WHOLE NIGHT WAITING FOR THE "GREAT PUMPKIN" WHEN I COULD HAVE BEEN OUT FOR "TRICKS OR TREATS"
YOU'VE HEARD ABOUT FURY AND A WOMAN SCORNED, HAVEN'T YOU?
YES, I GUESS I HAVE...
11-2
WELL, THAT'S NOTHING COMPARED TO THE FURY OF A WOMAN WHO HAS BEEN CHEATED OUT OF "TRICKS OR TREATS"!
SCHULZ

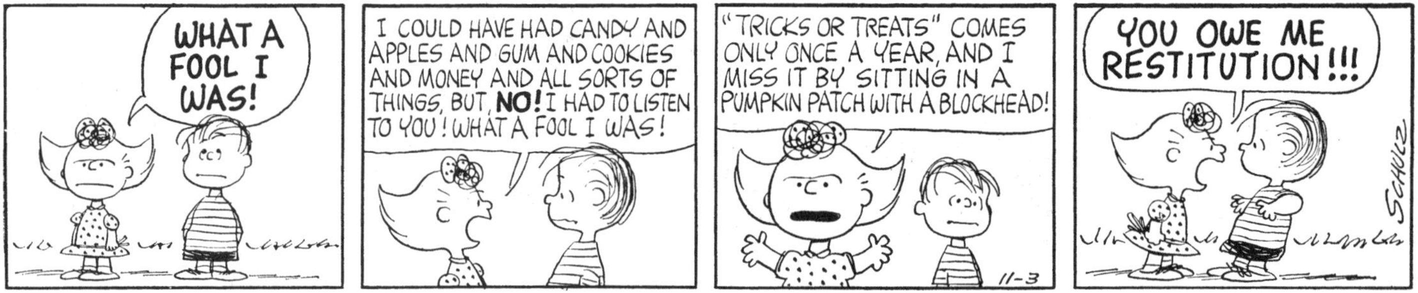
WHAT A FOOL I WAS!
I COULD HAVE HAD CANDY AND APPLES AND GUM AND COOKIES AND MONEY AND ALL SORTS OF THINGS, BUT, NO! I HAD TO LISTEN TO YOU! WHAT A FOOL I WAS!
"TRICKS OR TREATS" COMES ONLY ONCE A YEAR, AND I MISS IT BY SITTING IN A PUMPKIN PATCH WITH A BLOCKHEAD!
11-3
YOU OWE ME RESTITUTION!!!
SCHULZ

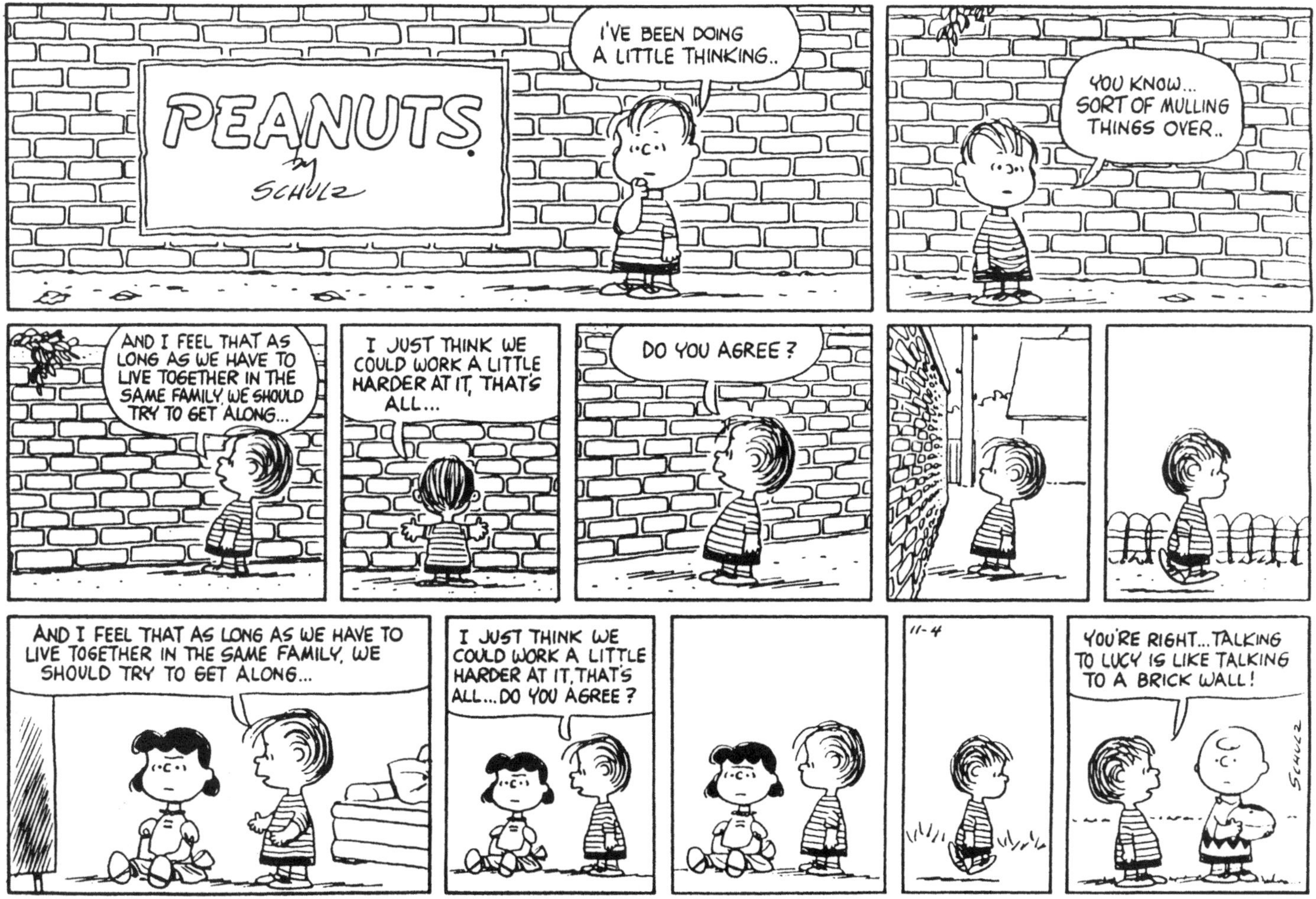
PEANUTS
by SCHULZ
I'VE BEEN DOING A LITTLE THINKING..
YOU KNOW... SORT OF MULLING THINGS OVER..
AND I FEEL THAT AS LONG AS WE HAVE TO LIVE TOGETHER IN THE SAME FAMILY, WE SHOULD TRY TO GET ALONG...
I JUST THINK WE COULD WORK A LITTLE HARDER AT IT, THAT'S ALL...
DO YOU AGREE ?
AND I FEEL THAT AS LONG AS WE HAVE TO LIVE TOGETHER IN THE SAME FAMILY, WE SHOULD TRY TO GET ALONG...
I JUST THINK WE COULD WORK A LITTLE HARDER AT IT, THAT'S ALL... DO YOU AGREE ?
11-4
YOU'RE RIGHT... TALKING TO LUCY IS LIKE TALKING TO A BRICK WALL!
SCHULZ

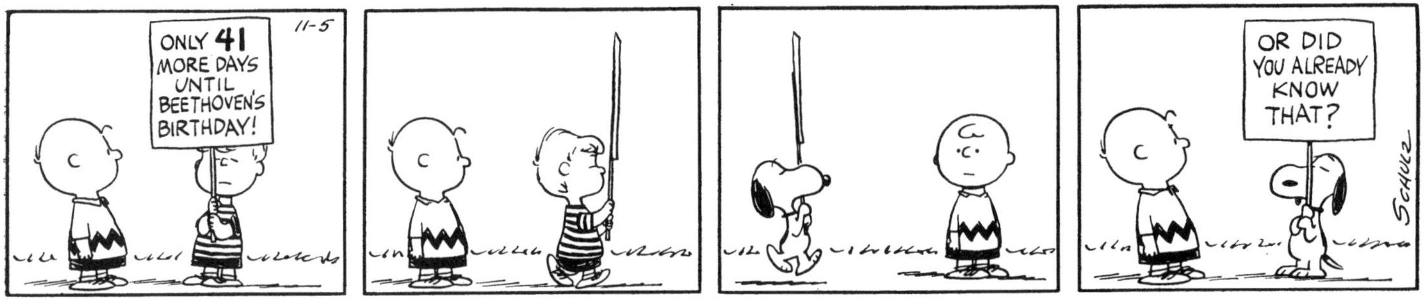
ONLY 41 MORE DAYS UNTIL BEETHOVEN'S BIRTHDAY!
OR DID YOU ALREADY KNOW THAT?

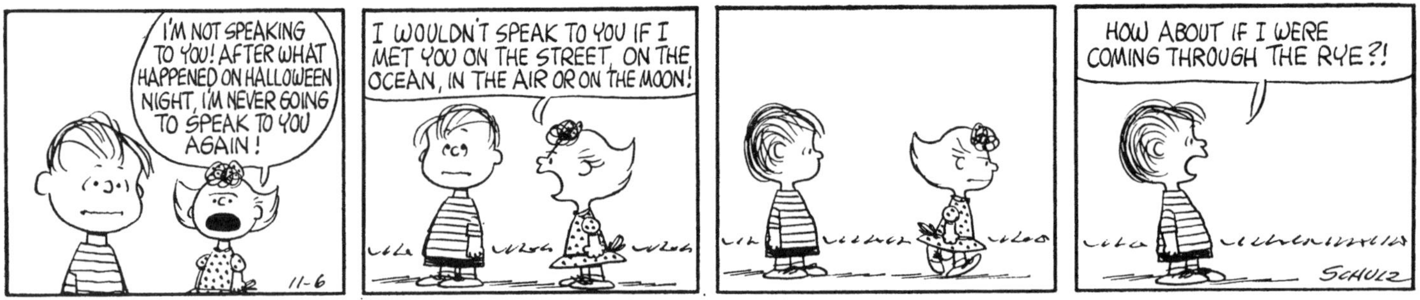
I'M NOT SPEAKING TO YOU! AFTER WHAT HAPPENED ON HALLOWEEN NIGHT, I'M NEVER GOING TO SPEAK TO YOU AGAIN!
I WOULDN'T SPEAK TO YOU IF I MET YOU ON THE STREET, ON THE OCEAN, IN THE AIR OR ON THE MOON!
HOW ABOUT IF I WERE COMING THROUGH THE RYE?!

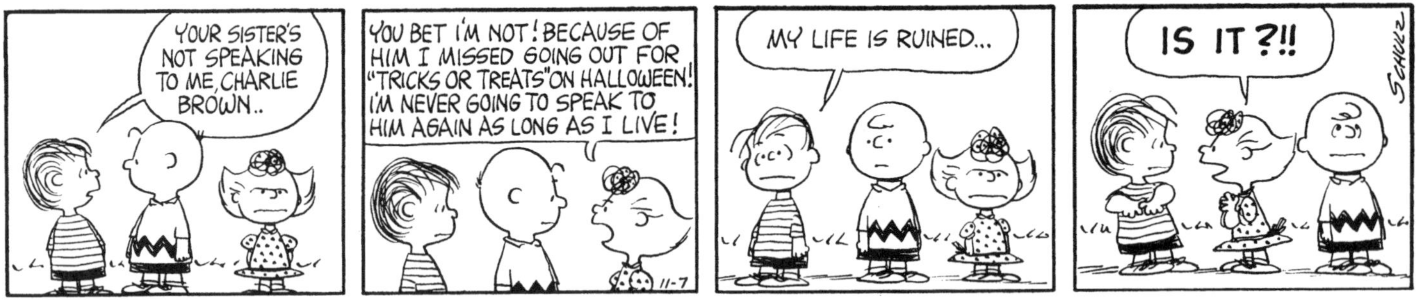
YOUR SISTER'S NOT SPEAKING TO ME, CHARLIE BROWN..
YOU BET I'M NOT! BECAUSE OF HIM I MISSED GOING OUT FOR "TRICKS OR TREATS" ON HALLOWEEN! I'M NEVER GOING TO SPEAK TO HIM AGAIN AS LONG AS I LIVE!
MY LIFE IS RUINED...
IS IT?!!

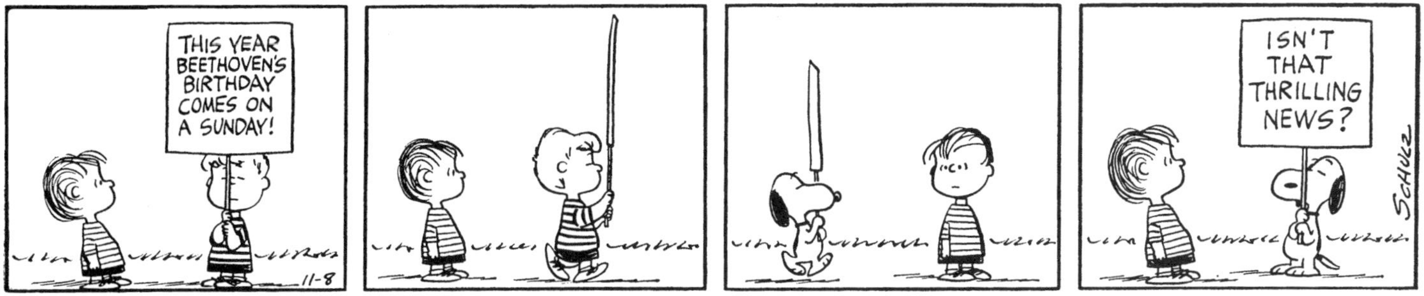
THIS YEAR BEETHOVEN'S BIRTHDAY COMES ON A SUNDAY!
ISN'T THAT THRILLING NEWS?

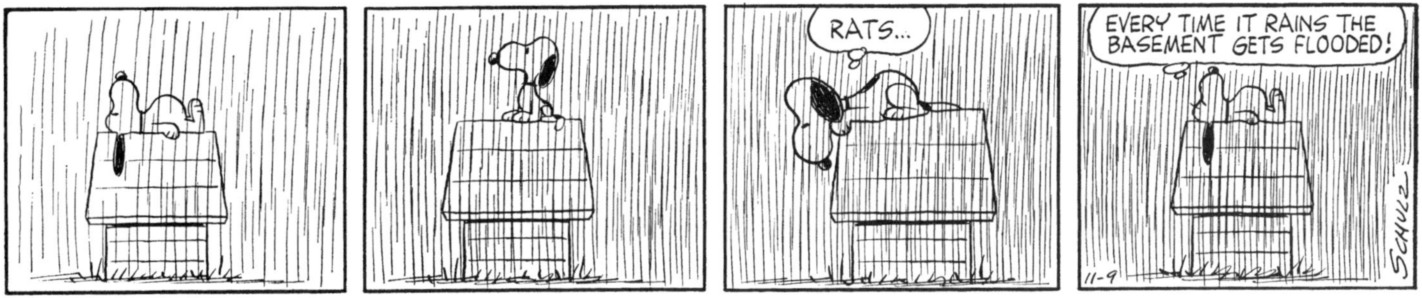
RATS...
EVERY TIME IT RAINS THE BASEMENT GETS FLOODED!

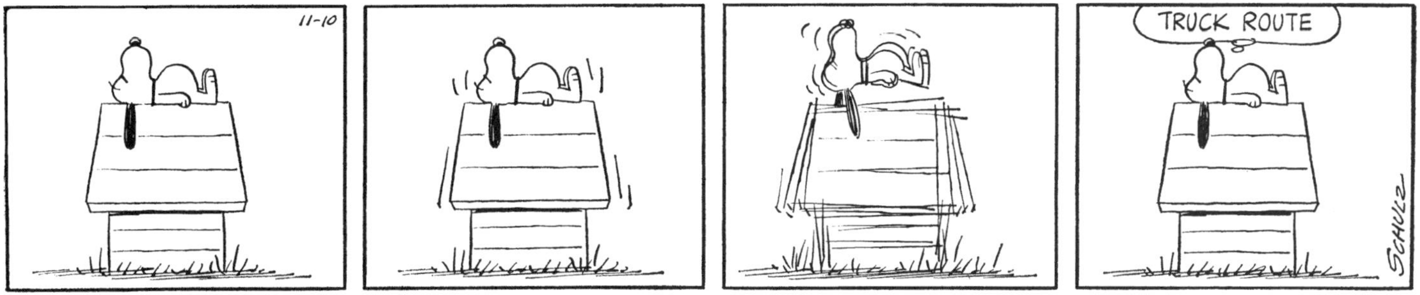
TRUCK ROUTE

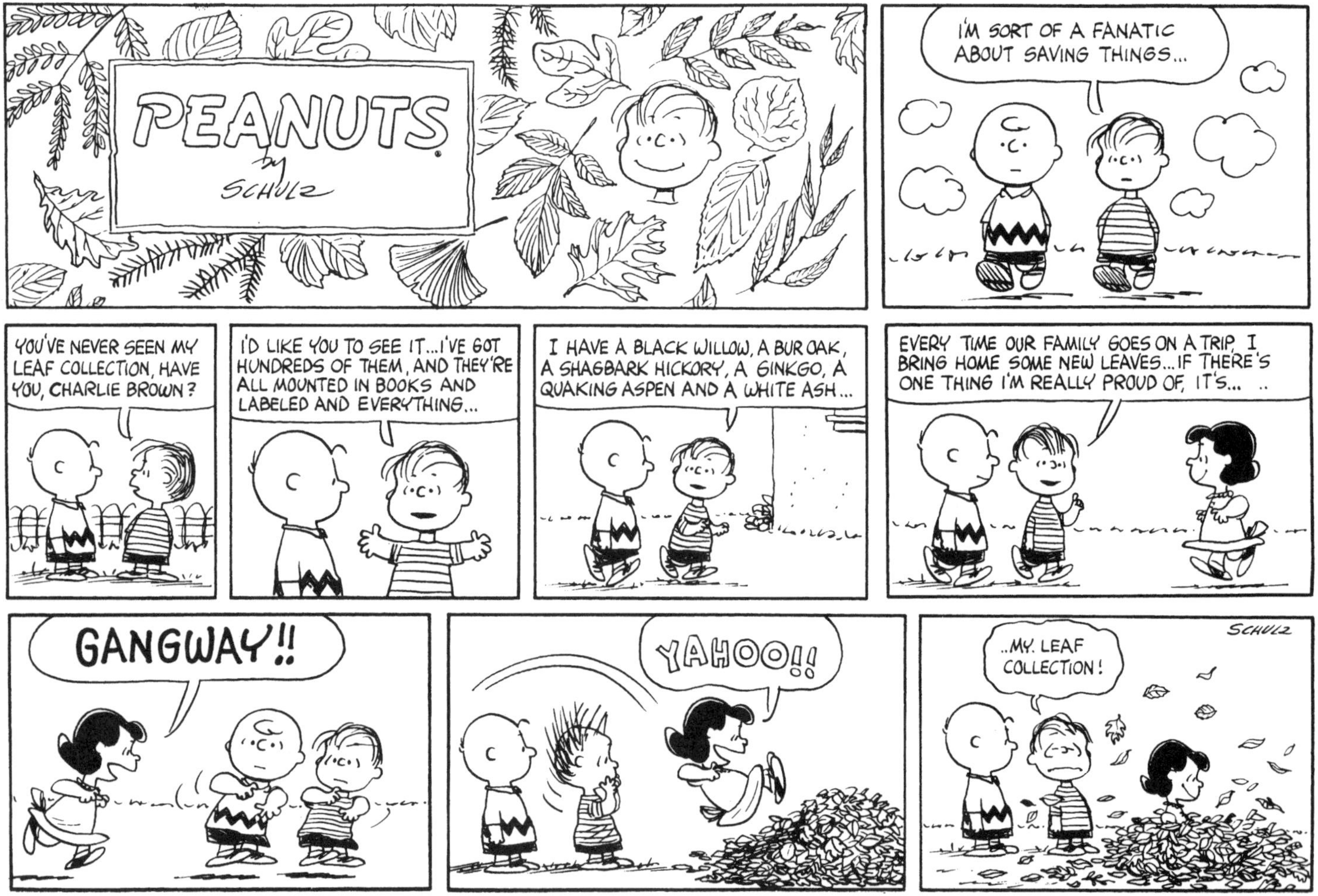
PEANUTS
by SCHULZ
I'M SORT OF A FANATIC ABOUT SAVING THINGS...
YOU'VE NEVER SEEN MY LEAF COLLECTION, HAVE YOU, CHARLIE BROWN?
I'D LIKE YOU TO SEE IT...I'VE GOT HUNDREDS OF THEM, AND THEY'RE ALL MOUNTED IN BOOKS AND LABELED AND EVERYTHING...
I HAVE A BLACK WILLOW, A BUR OAK, A SHAGBARK HICKORY, A GINKGO, A QUAKING ASPEN AND A WHITE ASH...
EVERY TIME OUR FAMILY GOES ON A TRIP, I BRING HOME SOME NEW LEAVES...IF THERE'S ONE THING I'M REALLY PROUD OF, IT'S... ..
GANGWAY!!
YAHOO!!
..MY. LEAF COLLECTION!
SCHULZ

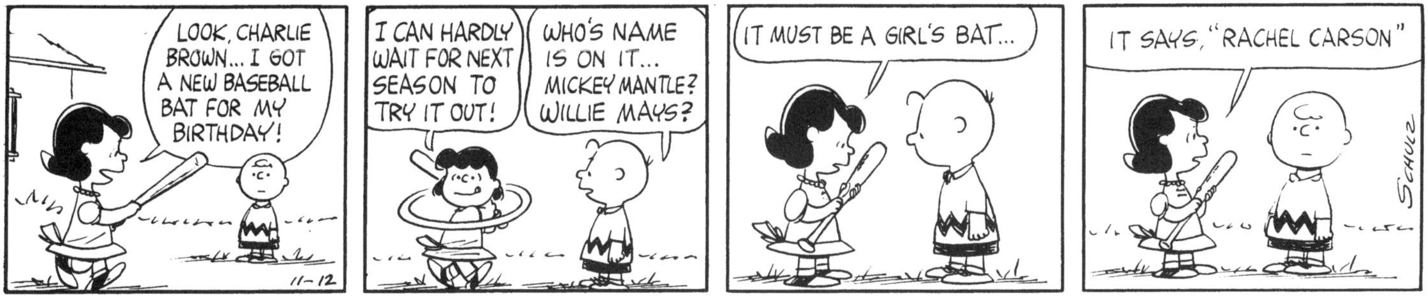
LOOK, CHARLIE BROWN... I GOT A NEW BASEBALL BAT FOR MY BIRTHDAY!
11-12
I CAN HARDLY WAIT FOR NEXT SEASON TO TRY IT OUT!
WHO'S NAME IS ON IT... MICKEY MANTLE? WILLIE MAYS?
IT MUST BE A GIRL'S BAT...
IT SAYS, "RACHEL CARSON"
SCHULZ

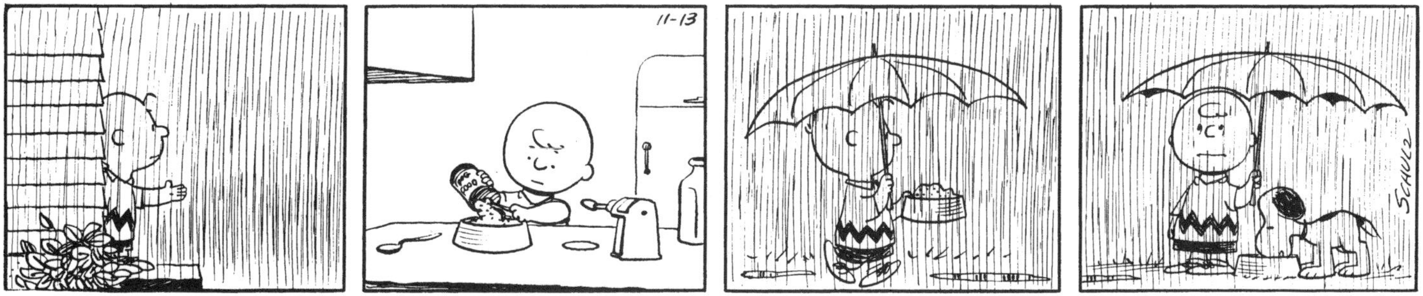
11-13
SCHULZ

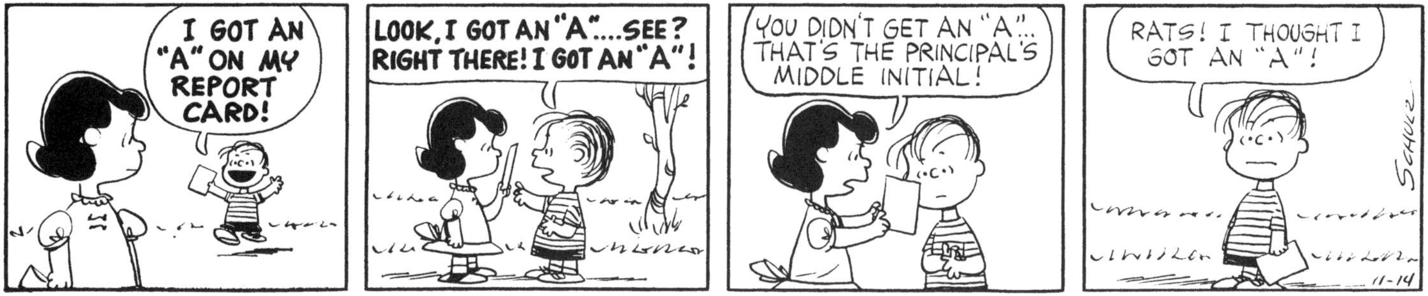
I GOT AN "A" ON MY REPORT CARD!
LOOK, I GOT AN "A"....SEE? RIGHT THERE! I GOT AN "A"!
YOU DIDN'T GET AN "A"... THAT'S THE PRINCIPAL'S MIDDLE INITIAL!
RATS! I THOUGHT I GOT AN "A"!
SCHULZ
11-14

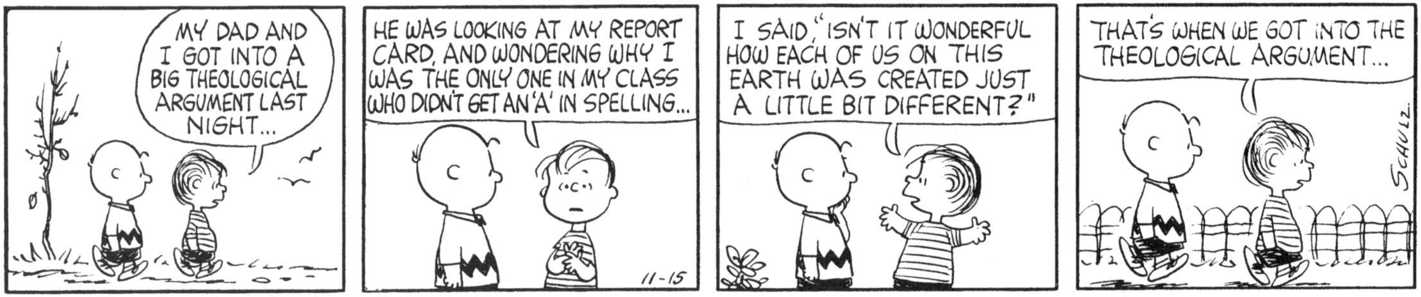
MY DAD AND I GOT INTO A BIG THEOLOGICAL ARGUMENT LAST NIGHT...
HE WAS LOOKING AT MY REPORT CARD, AND WONDERING WHY I WAS THE ONLY ONE IN MY CLASS WHO DIDN'T GET AN 'A' IN SPELLING...
11-15
I SAID, "ISN'T IT WONDERFUL HOW EACH OF US ON THIS EARTH WAS CREATED JUST A LITTLE BIT DIFFERENT?"
THAT'S WHEN WE GOT INTO THE THEOLOGICAL ARGUMENT...
SCHULZ

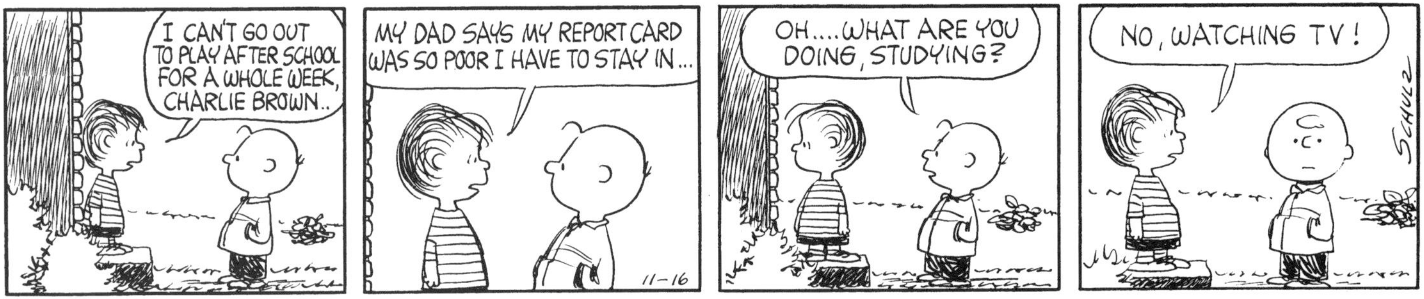
I CAN'T GO OUT TO PLAY AFTER SCHOOL FOR A WHOLE WEEK, CHARLIE BROWN..
MY DAD SAYS MY REPORT CARD WAS SO POOR I HAVE TO STAY IN...
11-16
OH....WHAT ARE YOU DOING, STUDYING?
NO, WATCHING TV!
SCHULZ

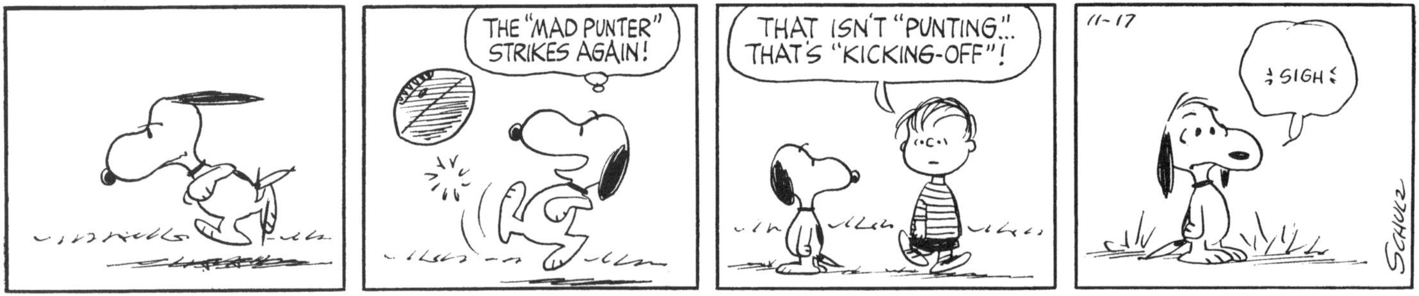
THE "MAD PUNTER" STRIKES AGAIN!
THAT ISN'T "PUNTING".. THAT'S "KICKING-OFF"!
11-17
SIGH
SCHULZ

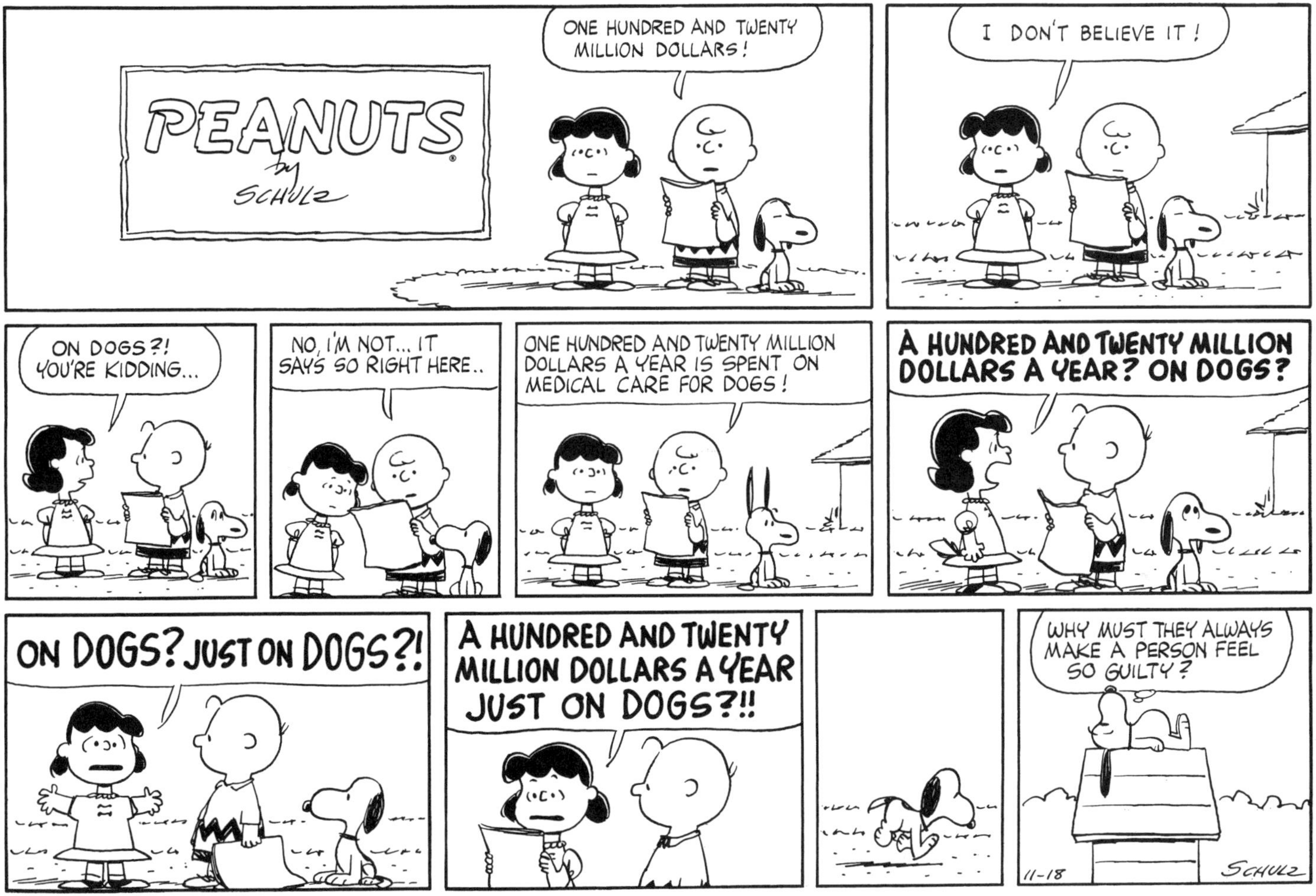
PEANUTS
by SCHULZ
ONE HUNDRED AND TWENTY MILLION DOLLARS!
I DON'T BELIEVE IT!
ON DOGS?! YOU'RE KIDDING...
NO, I'M NOT... IT SAYS SO RIGHT HERE..
ONE HUNDRED AND TWENTY MILLION DOLLARS A YEAR IS SPENT ON MEDICAL CARE FOR DOGS!
A HUNDRED AND TWENTY MILLION DOLLARS A YEAR? ON DOGS?
ON DOGS? JUST ON DOGS?!
A HUNDRED AND TWENTY MILLION DOLLARS A YEAR JUST ON DOGS?!!
WHY MUST THEY ALWAYS MAKE A PERSON FEEL SO GUILTY?
11-18
SCHULZ

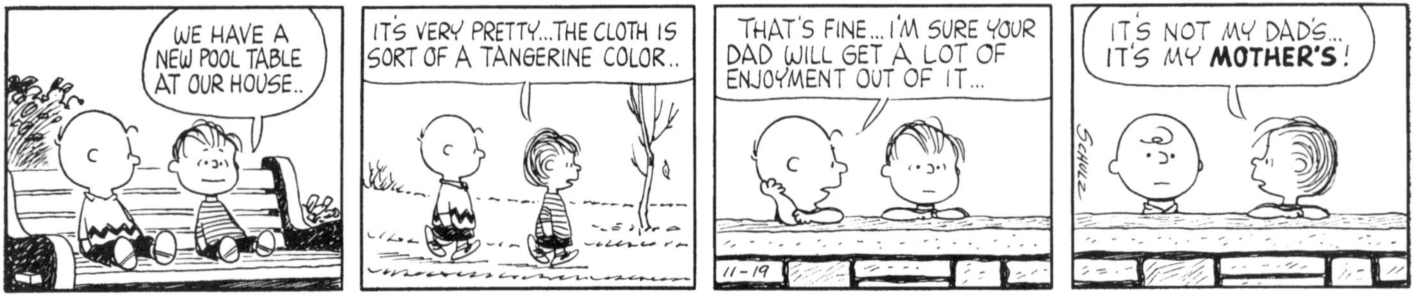
WE HAVE A NEW POOL TABLE AT OUR HOUSE..
IT'S VERY PRETTY...THE CLOTH IS SORT OF A TANGERINE COLOR..
THAT'S FINE... I'M SURE YOUR DAD WILL GET A LOT OF ENJOYMENT OUT OF IT...
11-19
IT'S NOT MY DAD'S... IT'S MY **MOTHER'S**!
SCHULZ

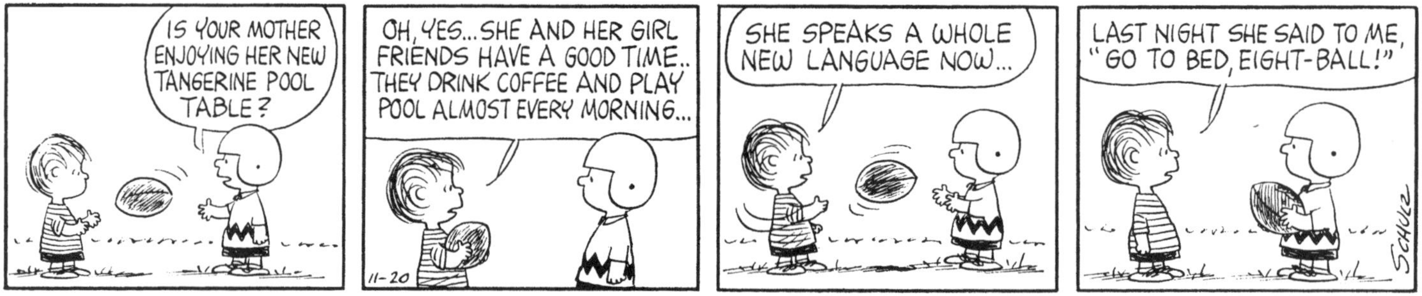
IS YOUR MOTHER ENJOYING HER NEW TANGERINE POOL TABLE?
OH, YES...SHE AND HER GIRL FRIENDS HAVE A GOOD TIME.. THEY DRINK COFFEE AND PLAY POOL ALMOST EVERY MORNING...
11-20
SHE SPEAKS A WHOLE NEW LANGUAGE NOW...
LAST NIGHT SHE SAID TO ME, "GO TO BED, EIGHT-BALL!"
SCHULZ

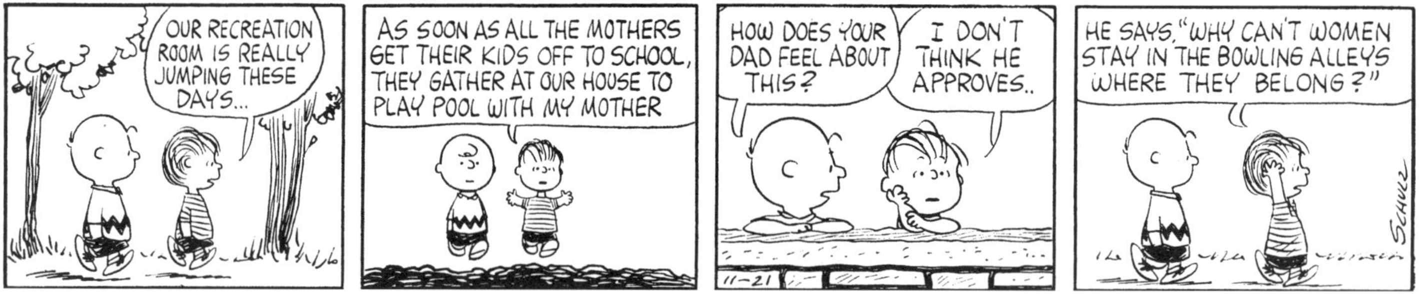
OUR RECREATION ROOM IS REALLY JUMPING THESE DAYS...
AS SOON AS ALL THE MOTHERS GET THEIR KIDS OFF TO SCHOOL, THEY GATHER AT OUR HOUSE TO PLAY POOL WITH MY MOTHER
HOW DOES YOUR DAD FEEL ABOUT THIS?
I DON'T THINK HE APPROVES..
11-21
HE SAYS, "WHY CAN'T WOMEN STAY IN THE BOWLING ALLEYS WHERE THEY BELONG?"
SCHULZ

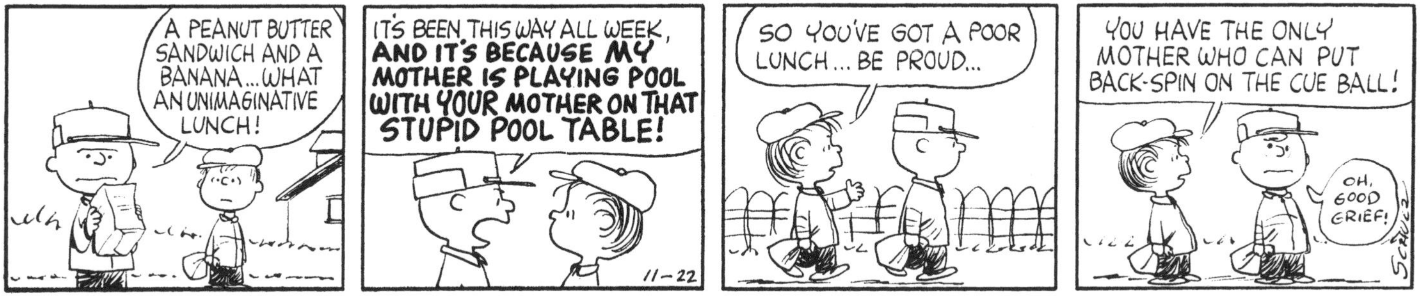
A PEANUT BUTTER SANDWICH AND A BANANA...WHAT AN UNIMAGINATIVE LUNCH!
IT'S BEEN THIS WAY ALL WEEK, AND IT'S BECAUSE MY MOTHER IS PLAYING POOL WITH YOUR MOTHER ON THAT STUPID POOL TABLE!
11-22
SO YOU'VE GOT A POOR LUNCH... BE PROUD...
YOU HAVE THE ONLY MOTHER WHO CAN PUT BACK-SPIN ON THE CUE BALL!
OH, GOOD GRIEF!
SCHULZ

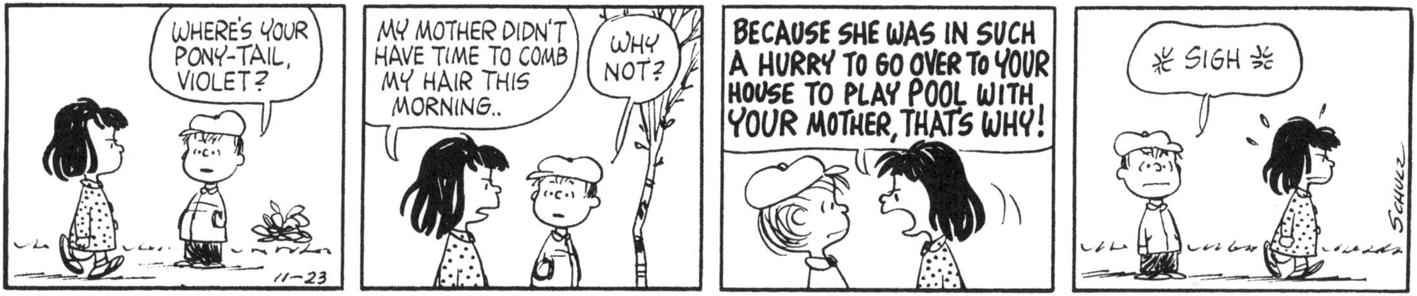
WHERE'S YOUR PONY-TAIL, VIOLET?
11-23
MY MOTHER DIDN'T HAVE TIME TO COMB MY HAIR THIS MORNING..
WHY NOT?
BECAUSE SHE WAS IN SUCH A HURRY TO GO OVER TO YOUR HOUSE TO PLAY POOL WITH YOUR MOTHER, THAT'S WHY!
SIGH
SCHULZ

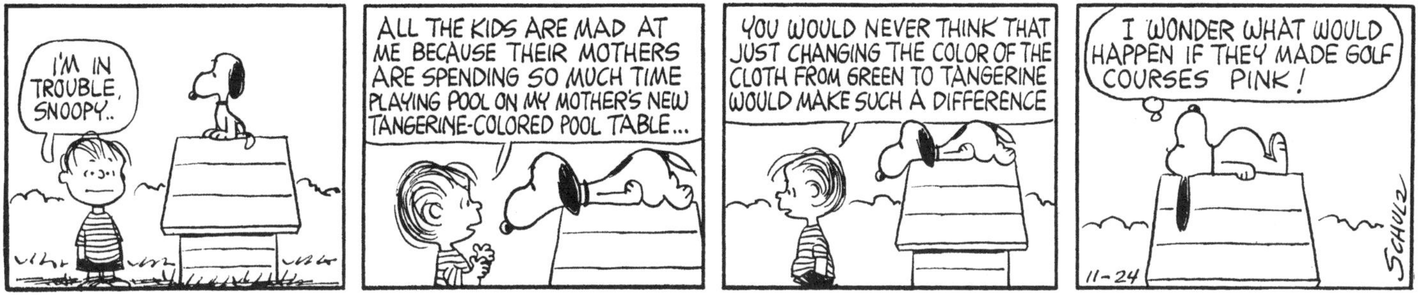
I'M IN TROUBLE, SNOOPY..
ALL THE KIDS ARE MAD AT ME BECAUSE THEIR MOTHERS ARE SPENDING SO MUCH TIME PLAYING POOL ON MY MOTHER'S NEW TANGERINE-COLORED POOL TABLE...
YOU WOULD NEVER THINK THAT JUST CHANGING THE COLOR OF THE CLOTH FROM GREEN TO TANGERINE WOULD MAKE SUCH A DIFFERENCE
I WONDER WHAT WOULD HAPPEN IF THEY MADE GOLF COURSES PINK!
11-24
SCHULZ

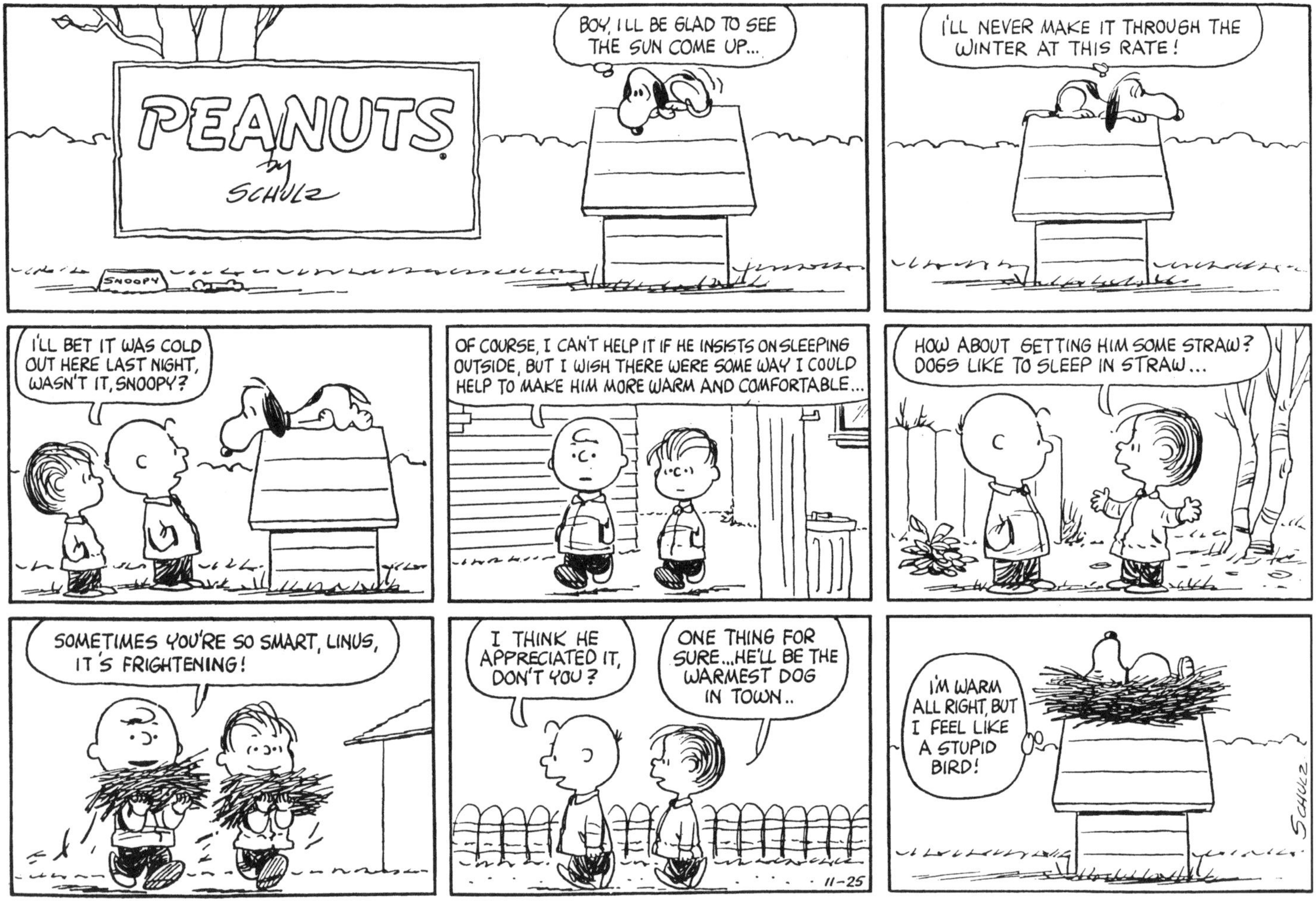
PEANUTS
by SCHULZ
SNOOPY
BOY, I'LL BE GLAD TO SEE THE SUN COME UP...
I'LL NEVER MAKE IT THROUGH THE WINTER AT THIS RATE!
I'LL BET IT WAS COLD OUT HERE LAST NIGHT, WASN'T IT, SNOOPY?
OF COURSE, I CAN'T HELP IT IF HE INSISTS ON SLEEPING OUTSIDE, BUT I WISH THERE WERE SOME WAY I COULD HELP TO MAKE HIM MORE WARM AND COMFORTABLE...
HOW ABOUT GETTING HIM SOME STRAW? DOGS LIKE TO SLEEP IN STRAW...
SOMETIMES YOU'RE SO SMART, LINUS, IT'S FRIGHTENING!
I THINK HE APPRECIATED IT, DON'T YOU?
ONE THING FOR SURE...HE'LL BE THE WARMEST DOG IN TOWN..
11-25
I'M WARM ALL RIGHT, BUT I FEEL LIKE A STUPID BIRD!
SCHULZ

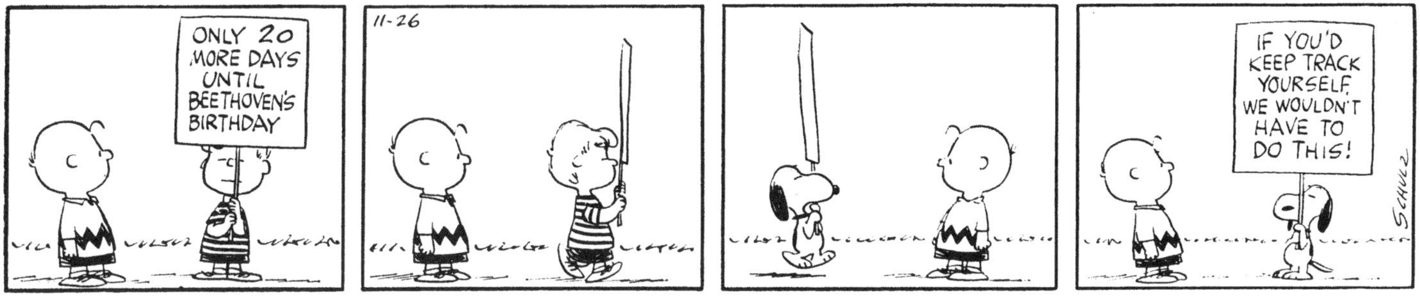
ONLY 20 MORE DAYS UNTIL BEETHOVEN'S BIRTHDAY
11-26
IF YOU'D KEEP TRACK YOURSELF, WE WOULDN'T HAVE TO DO THIS!
SCHULZ

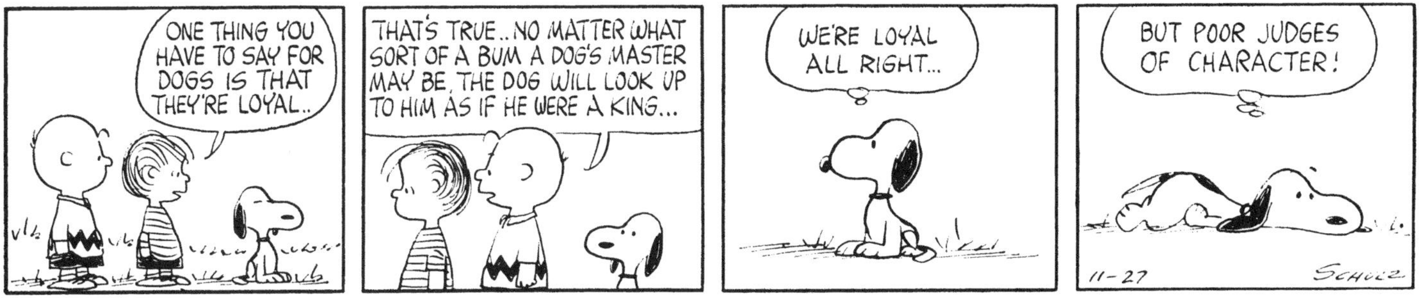
ONE THING YOU HAVE TO SAY FOR DOGS IS THAT THEY'RE LOYAL..
THAT'S TRUE.. NO MATTER WHAT SORT OF A BUM A DOG'S MASTER MAY BE, THE DOG WILL LOOK UP TO HIM AS IF HE WERE A KING...
WE'RE LOYAL ALL RIGHT...
BUT POOR JUDGES OF CHARACTER!
11-27
SCHULZ

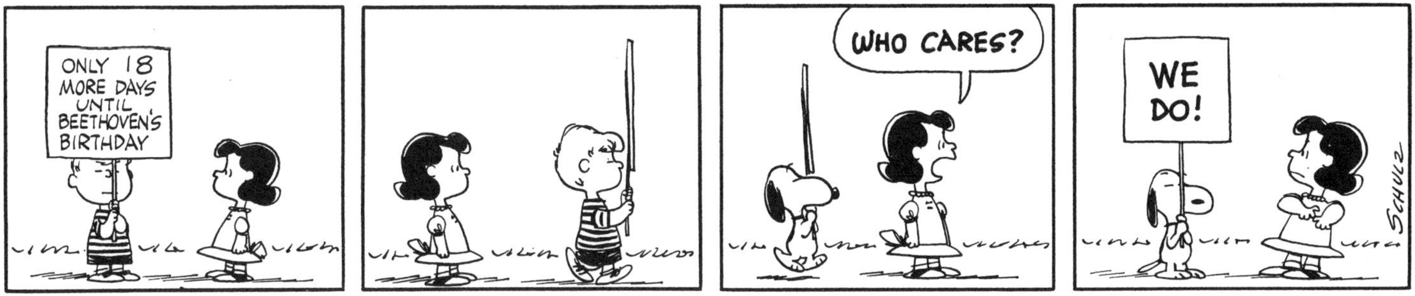
ONLY 18 MORE DAYS UNTIL BEETHOVEN'S BIRTHDAY
WHO CARES?
WE DO!
SCHULZ

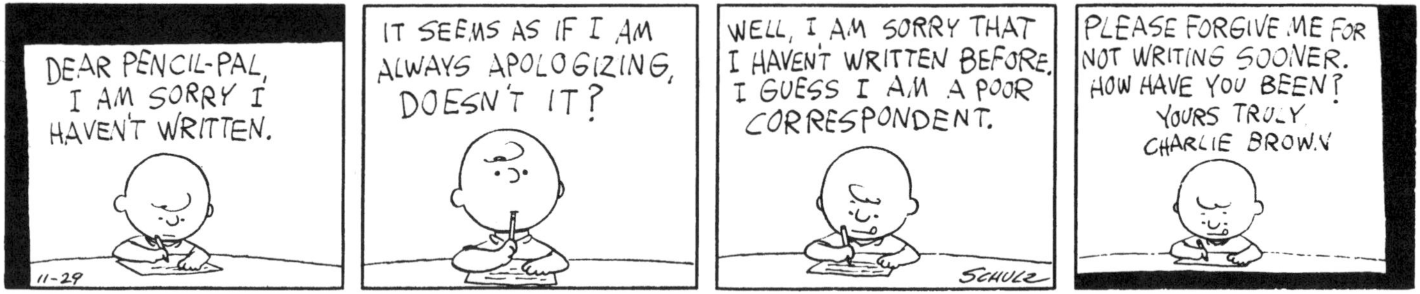
DEAR PENCIL-PAL, I AM SORRY I HAVEN'T WRITTEN.
IT SEEMS AS IF I AM ALWAYS APOLOGIZING, DOESN'T IT?
WELL, I AM SORRY THAT I HAVEN'T WRITTEN BEFORE. I GUESS I AM A POOR CORRESPONDENT.
PLEASE FORGIVE ME FOR NOT WRITING SOONER. HOW HAVE YOU BEEN? YOURS TRULY, CHARLIE BROWN
11-29
SCHULZ

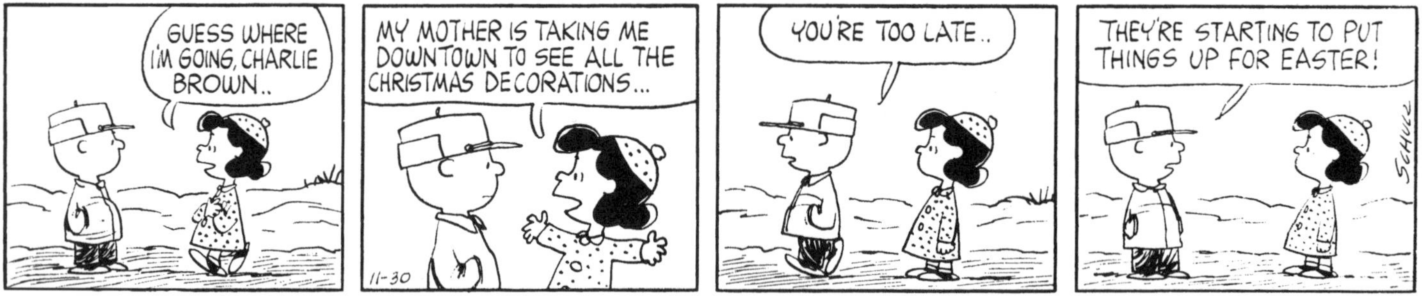
GUESS WHERE I'M GOING, CHARLIE BROWN..
MY MOTHER IS TAKING ME DOWNTOWN TO SEE ALL THE CHRISTMAS DECORATIONS...
11-30
YOU'RE TOO LATE..
THEY'RE STARTING TO PUT THINGS UP FOR EASTER!
SCHULZ

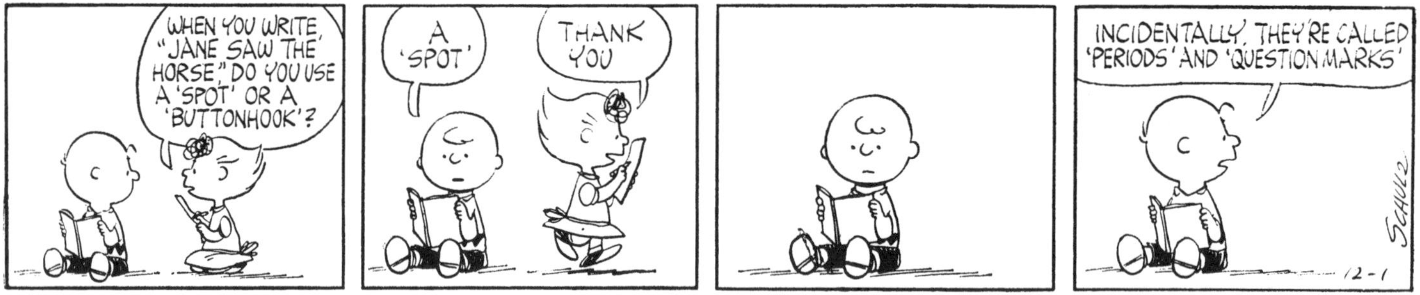
WHEN YOU WRITE, "JANE SAW THE HORSE," DO YOU USE A 'SPOT' OR A 'BUTTONHOOK'?
A 'SPOT'
THANK YOU
INCIDENTALLY, THEY'RE CALLED 'PERIODS' AND 'QUESTION MARKS'
SCHULZ
12-1

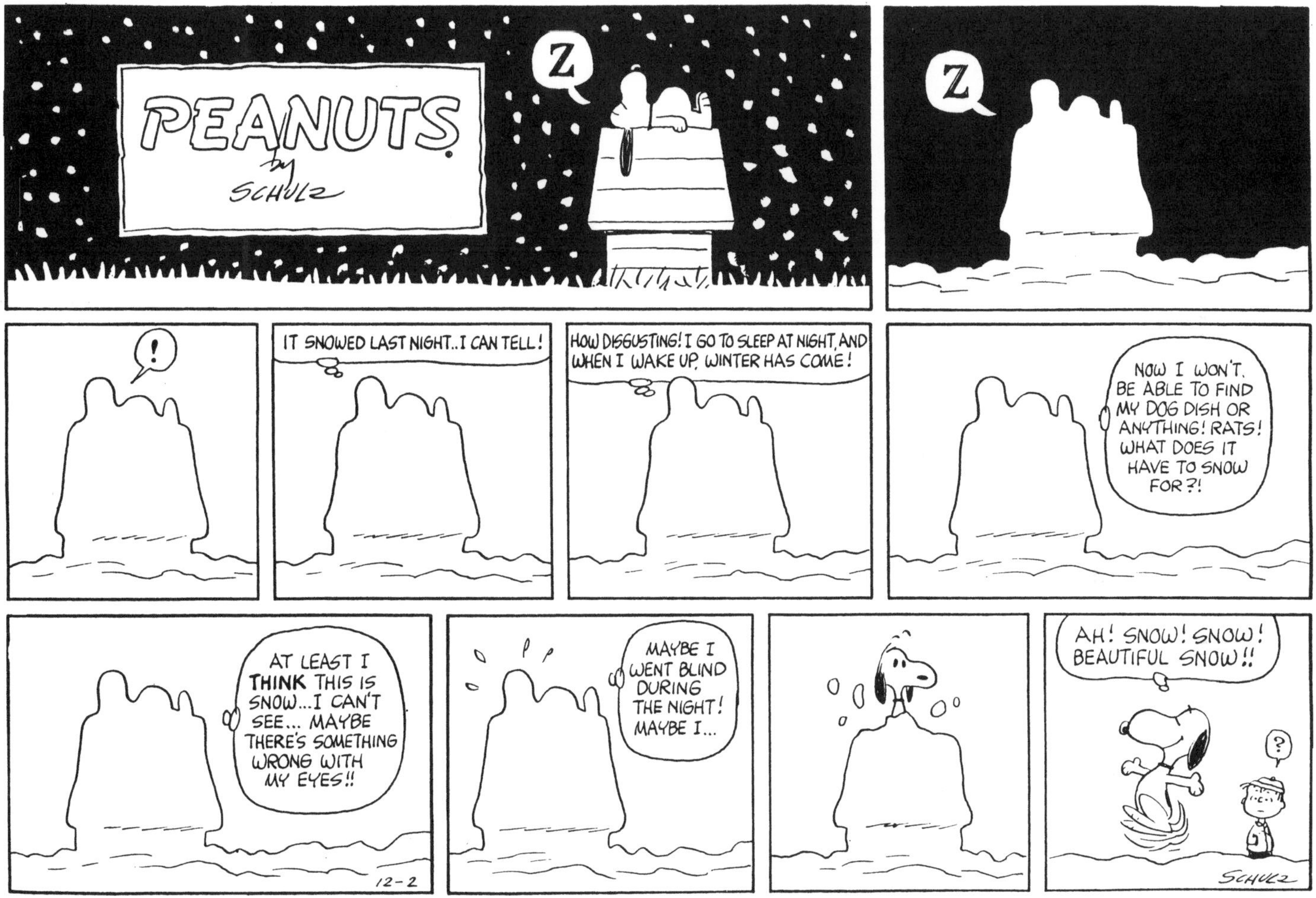
PEANUTS
by SCHULZ
Z
Z
!
IT SNOWED LAST NIGHT..I CAN TELL!
HOW DISGUSTING! I GO TO SLEEP AT NIGHT, AND WHEN I WAKE UP, WINTER HAS COME!
NOW I WON'T BE ABLE TO FIND MY DOG DISH OR ANYTHING! RATS! WHAT DOES IT HAVE TO SNOW FOR?!
AT LEAST I **THINK** THIS IS SNOW...I CAN'T SEE... MAYBE THERE'S SOMETHING WRONG WITH MY EYES!!
12-2
MAYBE I WENT BLIND DURING THE NIGHT! MAYBE I...
AH! SNOW! SNOW! BEAUTIFUL SNOW!!
?
SCHULZ

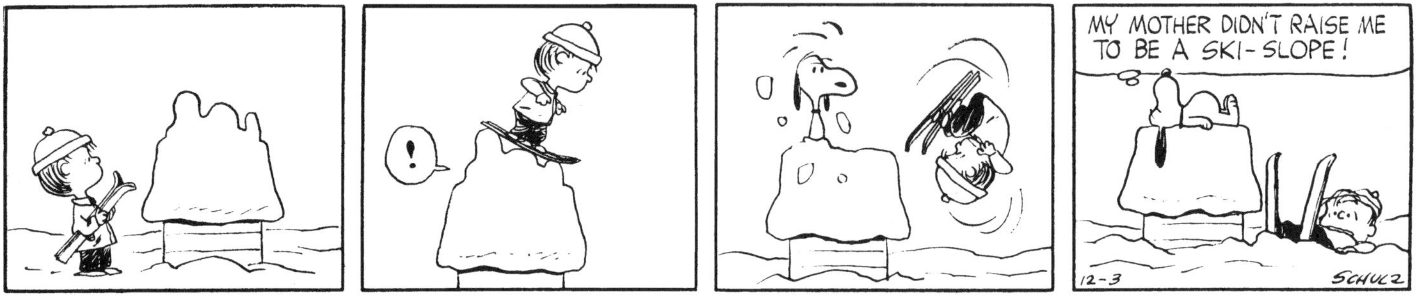
!
MY MOTHER DIDN'T RAISE ME TO BE A SKI-SLOPE!
12-3
SCHULZ

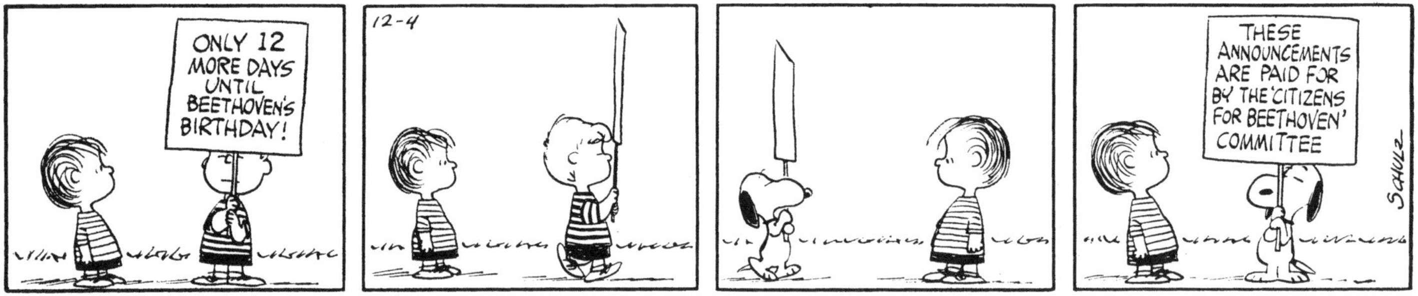
ONLY 12 MORE DAYS UNTIL BEETHOVEN'S BIRTHDAY!
12-4
THESE ANNOUNCEMENTS ARE PAID FOR BY THE 'CITIZENS FOR BEETHOVEN' COMMITTEE
SCHULZ

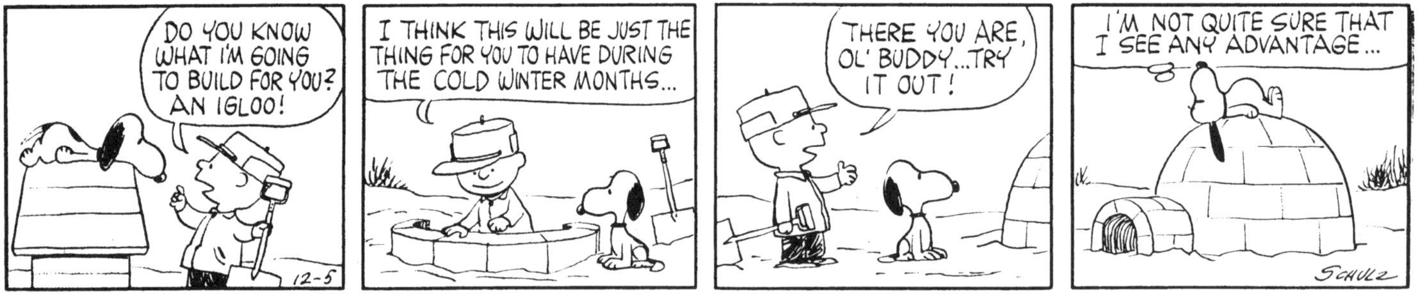
DO YOU KNOW WHAT I'M GOING TO BUILD FOR YOU? AN IGLOO!
12-5
I THINK THIS WILL BE JUST THE THING FOR YOU TO HAVE DURING THE COLD WINTER MONTHS...
THERE YOU ARE, OL' BUDDY...TRY IT OUT!
I'M NOT QUITE SURE THAT I SEE ANY ADVANTAGE...
SCHULZ

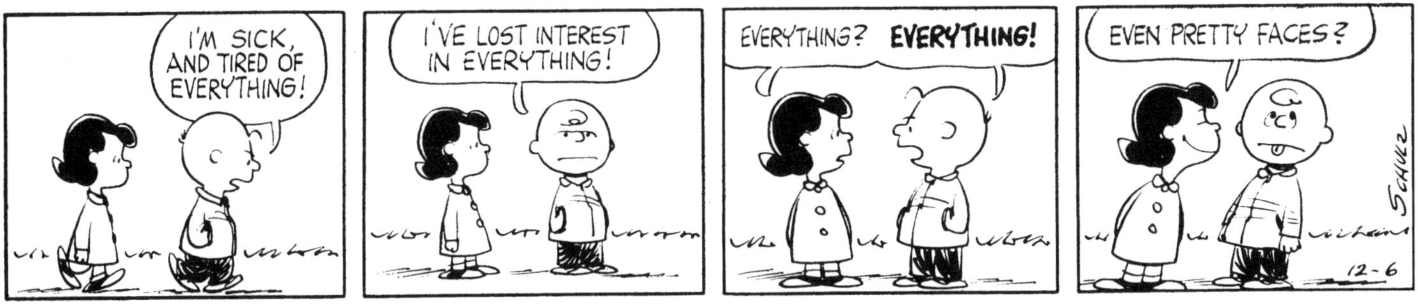
I'M SICK, AND TIRED OF EVERYTHING!
I'VE LOST INTEREST IN EVERYTHING!
EVERYTHING? EVERYTHING!
EVEN PRETTY FACES?
SCHULZ
12-6

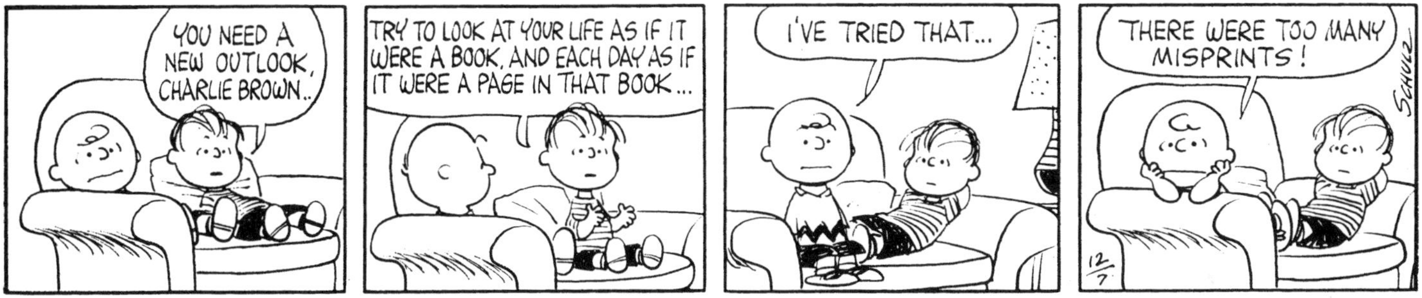
YOU NEED A NEW OUTLOOK, CHARLIE BROWN..
TRY TO LOOK AT YOUR LIFE AS IF IT WERE A BOOK, AND EACH DAY AS IF IT WERE A PAGE IN THAT BOOK...
I'VE TRIED THAT...
THERE WERE TOO MANY MISPRINTS!
SCHULZ
12/7

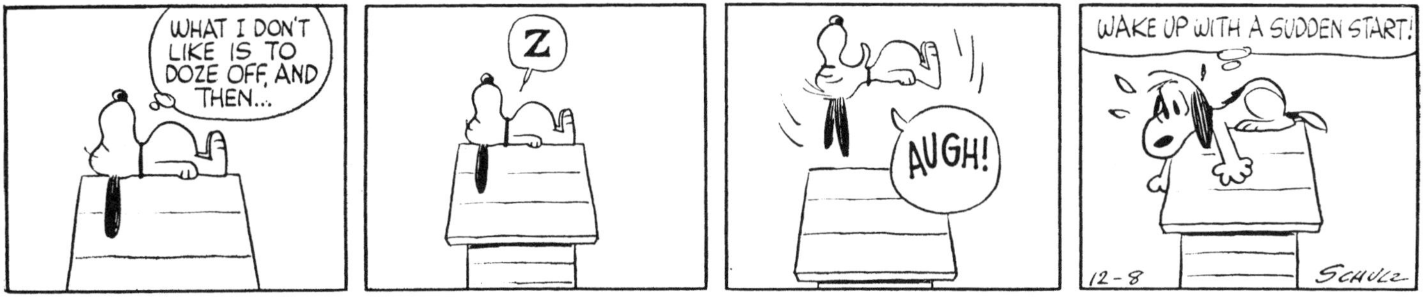
WHAT I DON'T LIKE IS TO DOZE OFF, AND THEN...
Z
AUGH!
WAKE UP WITH A SUDDEN START!
12-8
SCHULZ

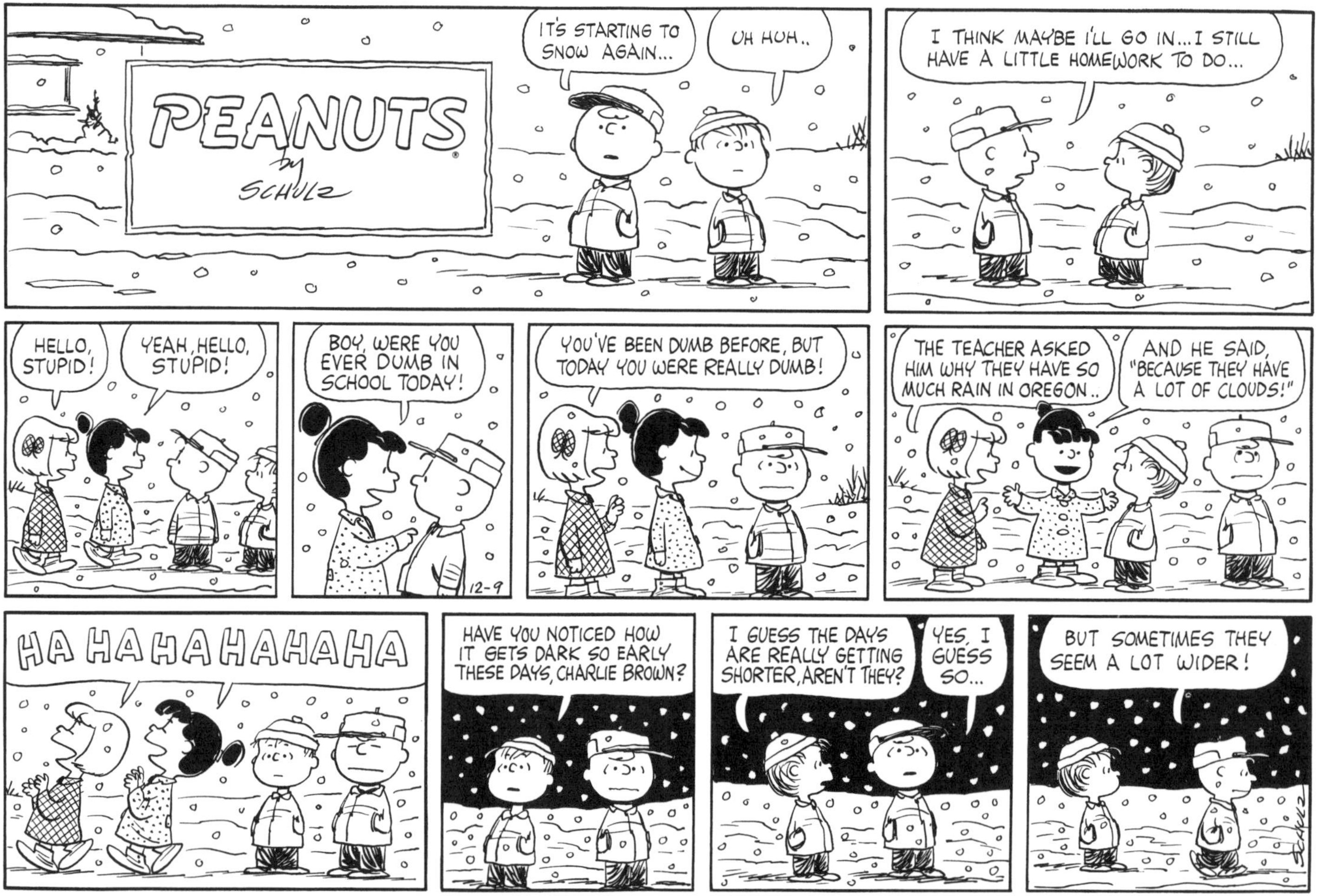
PEANUTS
by SCHULZ
IT'S STARTING TO SNOW AGAIN...
UH HUH..
I THINK MAYBE I'LL GO IN... I STILL HAVE A LITTLE HOMEWORK TO DO...
HELLO, STUPID!
YEAH, HELLO, STUPID!
BOY, WERE YOU EVER DUMB IN SCHOOL TODAY!
12-9
YOU'VE BEEN DUMB BEFORE, BUT TODAY YOU WERE REALLY DUMB!
THE TEACHER ASKED HIM WHY THEY HAVE SO MUCH RAIN IN OREGON..
AND HE SAID, "BECAUSE THEY HAVE A LOT OF CLOUDS!"
HA HA HA HA HA HA HA HA HA
HAVE YOU NOTICED HOW IT GETS DARK SO EARLY THESE DAYS, CHARLIE BROWN?
I GUESS THE DAYS ARE REALLY GETTING SHORTER, AREN'T THEY?
YES, I GUESS SO...
BUT SOMETIMES THEY SEEM A LOT WIDER!
SCHULZ

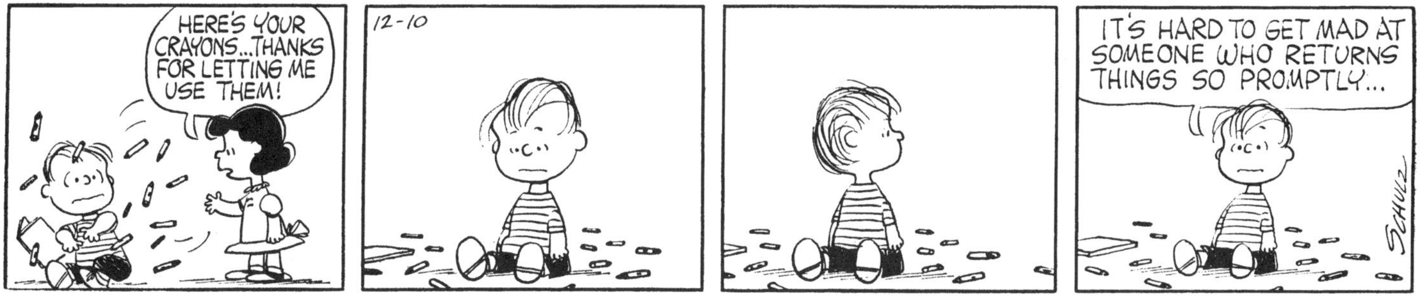
HERE'S YOUR CRAYONS...THANKS FOR LETTING ME USE THEM!
12-10
IT'S HARD TO GET MAD AT SOMEONE WHO RETURNS THINGS SO PROMPTLY...
SCHULZ

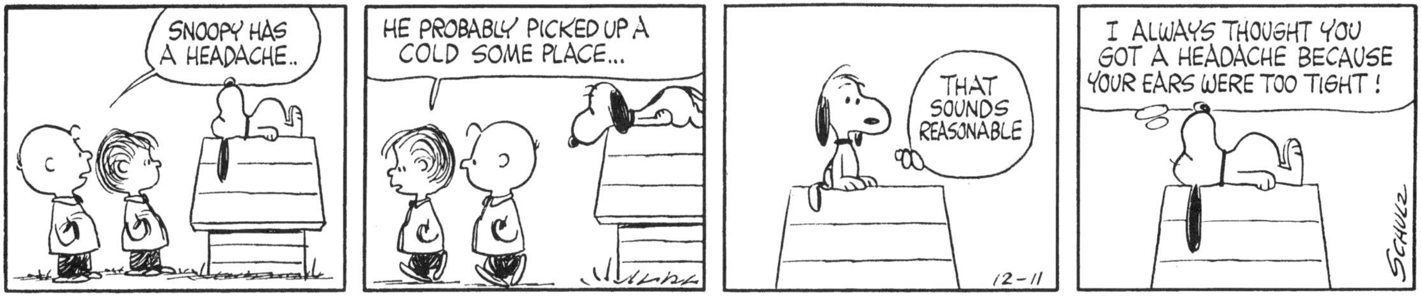
SNOOPY HAS A HEADACHE..
HE PROBABLY PICKED UP A COLD SOME PLACE...
THAT SOUNDS REASONABLE
12-11
I ALWAYS THOUGHT YOU GOT A HEADACHE BECAUSE YOUR EARS WERE TOO TIGHT!
SCHULZ

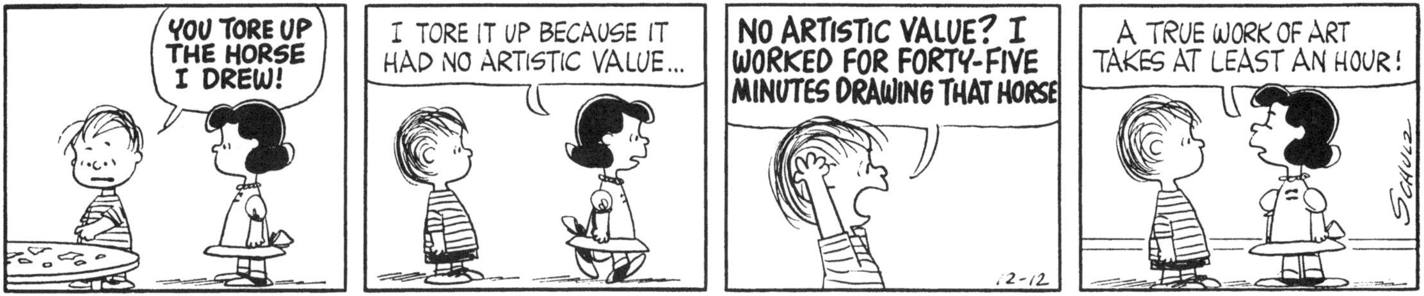
YOU TORE UP THE HORSE I DREW!
I TORE IT UP BECAUSE IT HAD NO ARTISTIC VALUE...
NO ARTISTIC VALUE? I WORKED FOR FORTY-FIVE MINUTES DRAWING THAT HORSE
12-12
A TRUE WORK OF ART TAKES AT LEAST AN HOUR!
SCHULZ

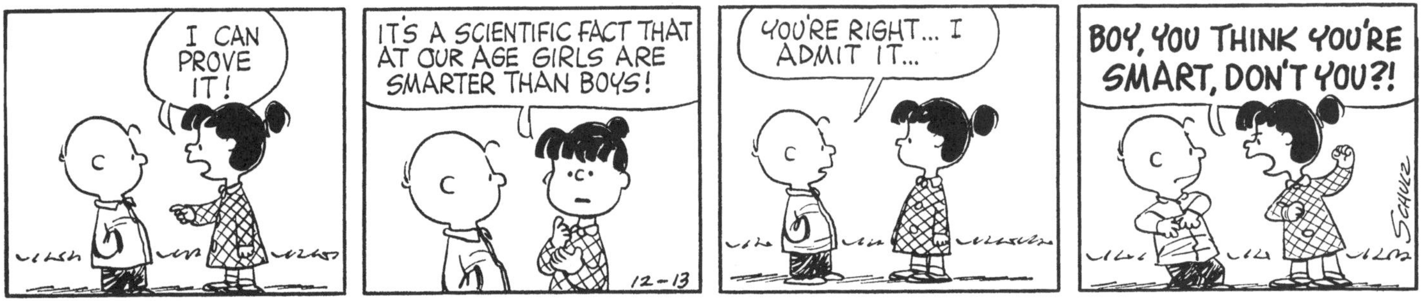
I CAN PROVE IT!
IT'S A SCIENTIFIC FACT THAT AT OUR AGE GIRLS ARE SMARTER THAN BOYS!
12-13
YOU'RE RIGHT... I ADMIT IT...
BOY, YOU THINK YOU'RE SMART, DON'T YOU?!

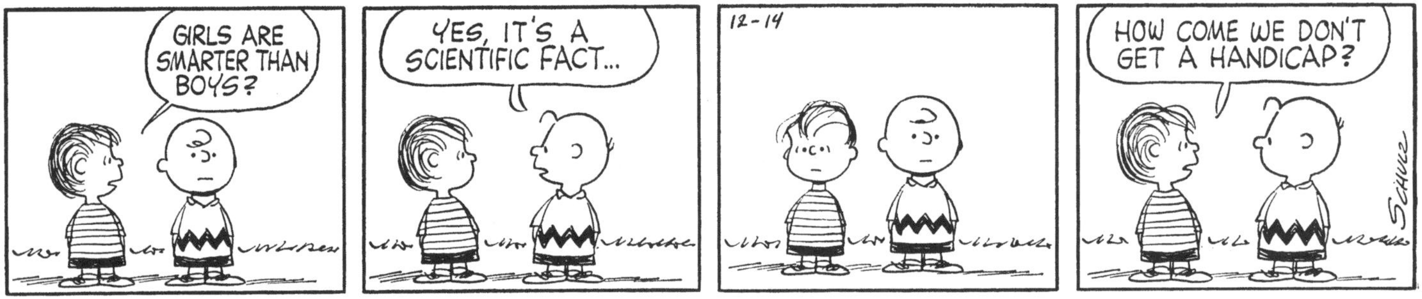
GIRLS ARE SMARTER THAN BOYS?
YES, IT'S A SCIENTIFIC FACT...
12-14
HOW COME WE DON'T GET A HANDICAP?

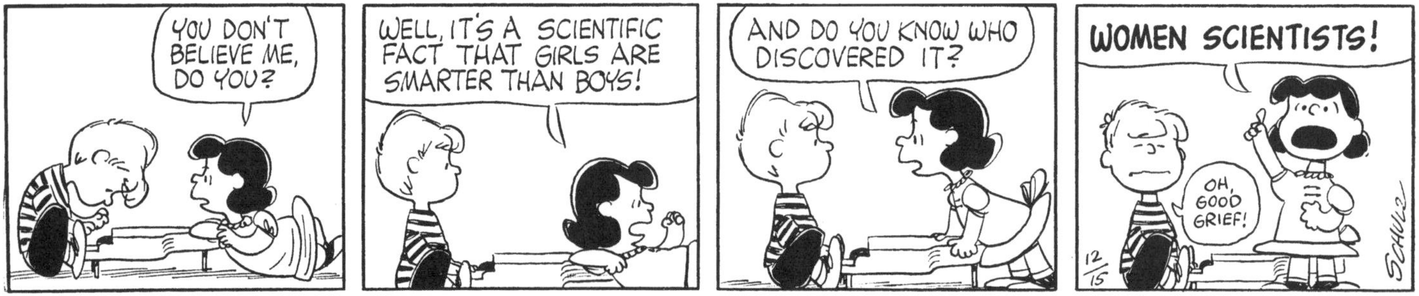
YOU DON'T BELIEVE ME, DO YOU?
WELL, IT'S A SCIENTIFIC FACT THAT GIRLS ARE SMARTER THAN BOYS!
AND DO YOU KNOW WHO DISCOVERED IT?
WOMEN SCIENTISTS!
OH, GOOD GRIEF!
12/15

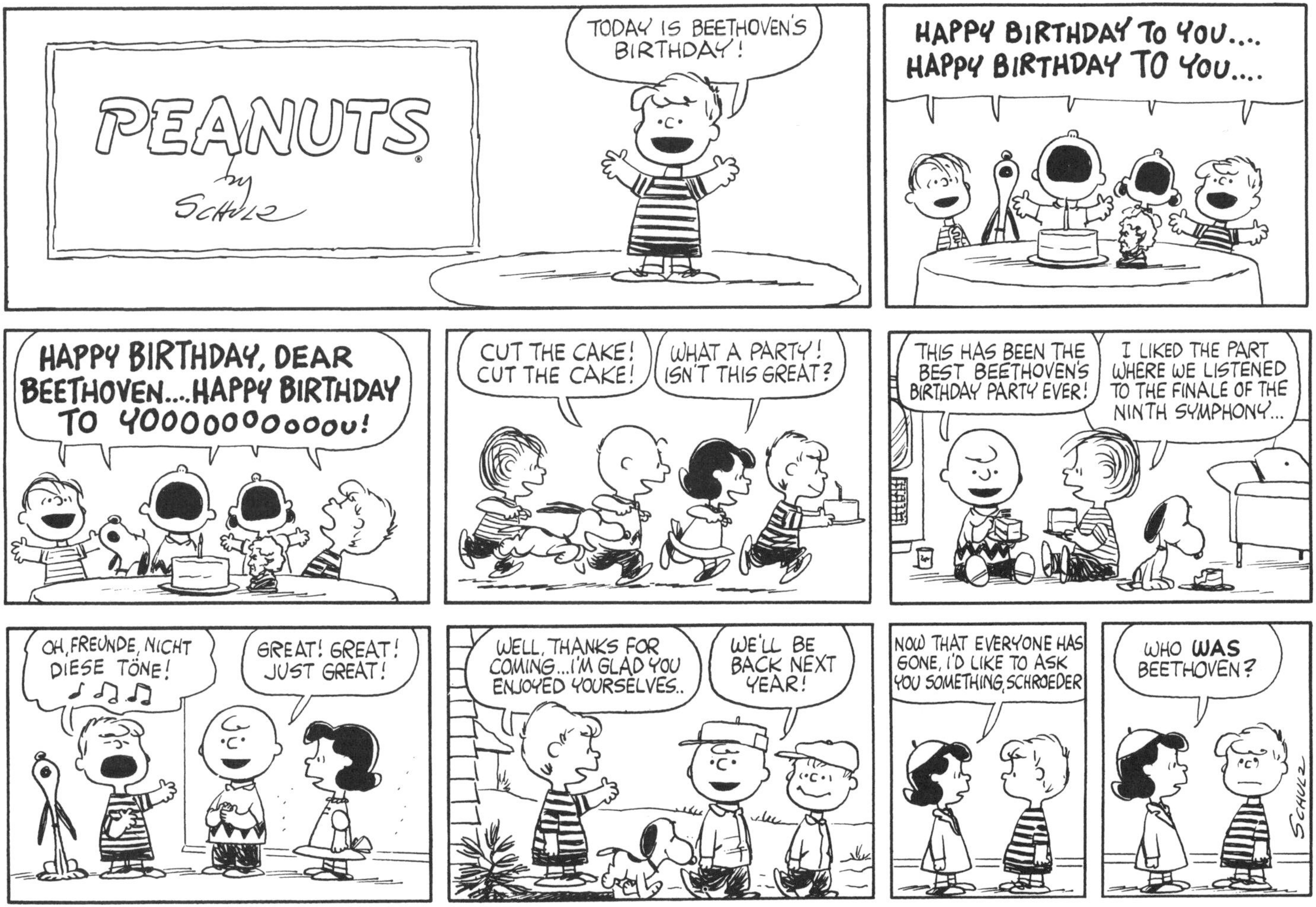
PEANUTS
by Schulz
TODAY IS BEETHOVEN'S BIRTHDAY!
HAPPY BIRTHDAY TO YOU.... HAPPY BIRTHDAY TO YOU....
HAPPY BIRTHDAY, DEAR BEETHOVEN....HAPPY BIRTHDAY TO YOOOOOOOooooU!
CUT THE CAKE! CUT THE CAKE!
WHAT A PARTY! ISN'T THIS GREAT?
THIS HAS BEEN THE BEST BEETHOVEN'S BIRTHDAY PARTY EVER!
I LIKED THE PART WHERE WE LISTENED TO THE FINALE OF THE NINTH SYMPHONY...
OH, FREUNDE, NICHT DIESE TÖNE!
GREAT! GREAT! JUST GREAT!
WELL, THANKS FOR COMING...I'M GLAD YOU ENJOYED YOURSELVES..
WE'LL BE BACK NEXT YEAR!
NOW THAT EVERYONE HAS GONE, I'D LIKE TO ASK YOU SOMETHING, SCHROEDER
WHO **WAS** BEETHOVEN?
SCHULZ

Panel 1: TELL MOM I DON'T THINK I'LL GO TO SCHOOL TODAY..TELL HER I'M EMOTIONALLY EXHAUSTED...

Panel 2: SHE SAYS TO GET OUT OF BED THIS VERY MINUTE!

Panel 3: 12-17

Panel 4: NICE TRY!

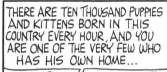

Panel 5: YOU DON'T KNOW HOW LUCKY YOU ARE!

Panel 6: THERE ARE TEN THOUSAND PUPPIES AND KITTENS BORN IN THIS COUNTRY EVERY HOUR, AND YOU ARE ONE OF THE VERY FEW WHO HAS HIS OWN HOME...

Panel 7: 12-18

Panel 8: HOW CAN YOU ENJOY IT WHEN THEY MAKE YOU FEEL GUILTY?

Panel 9: MISS OTHMAR IS RETIRING FROM TEACHING...

Panel 10: SHE SAID IT'S ABOUT TIME SHE STARTED TO RAISE A FAMILY OF HER OWN...

Panel 11: I ASKED HER IF SHE CONSIDERED THIS A STEP FORWARD OR A STEP BACKWARD, BUT JUST THEN THE BELL RANG, AND I NEVER GOT AN ANSWER   12-19

Panel 12: IT WOULD MAKE A GOOD TOPIC FOR A PANEL DISCUSSION

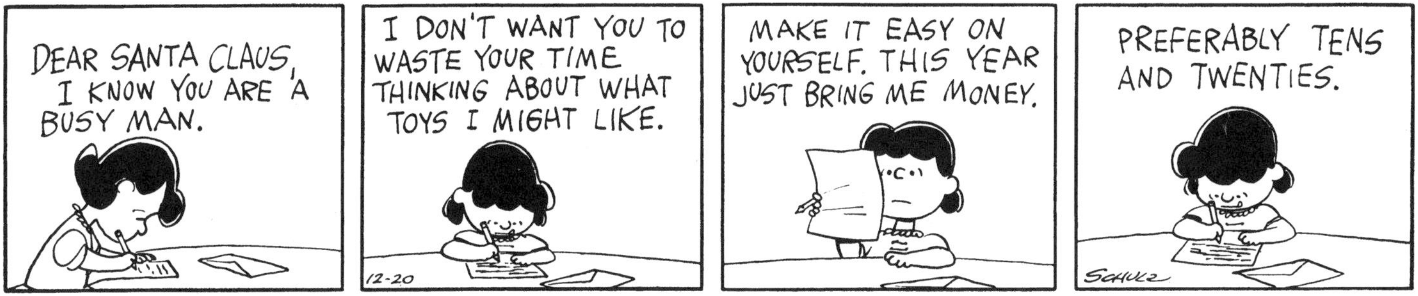
DEAR SANTA CLAUS, I KNOW YOU ARE A BUSY MAN.
I DON'T WANT YOU TO WASTE YOUR TIME THINKING ABOUT WHAT TOYS I MIGHT LIKE.
12-20
MAKE IT EASY ON YOURSELF. THIS YEAR JUST BRING ME MONEY.
PREFERABLY TENS AND TWENTIES.
SCHULZ

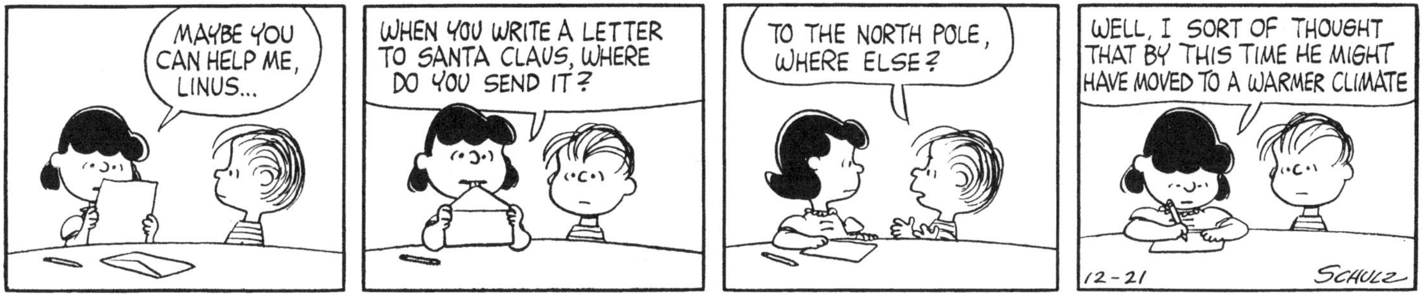
MAYBE YOU CAN HELP ME, LINUS...
WHEN YOU WRITE A LETTER TO SANTA CLAUS, WHERE DO YOU SEND IT?
TO THE NORTH POLE, WHERE ELSE?
WELL, I SORT OF THOUGHT THAT BY THIS TIME HE MIGHT HAVE MOVED TO A WARMER CLIMATE
12-21
SCHULZ

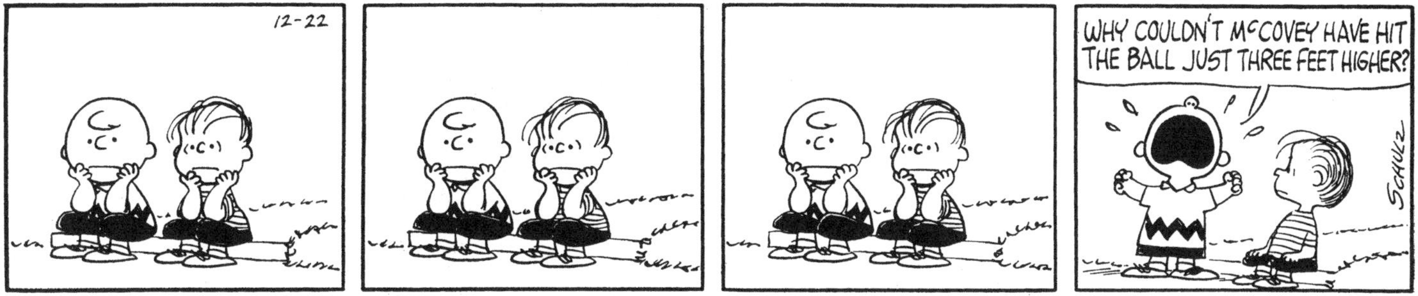
12-22
WHY COULDN'T McCOVEY HAVE HIT THE BALL JUST THREE FEET HIGHER?
SCHULZ

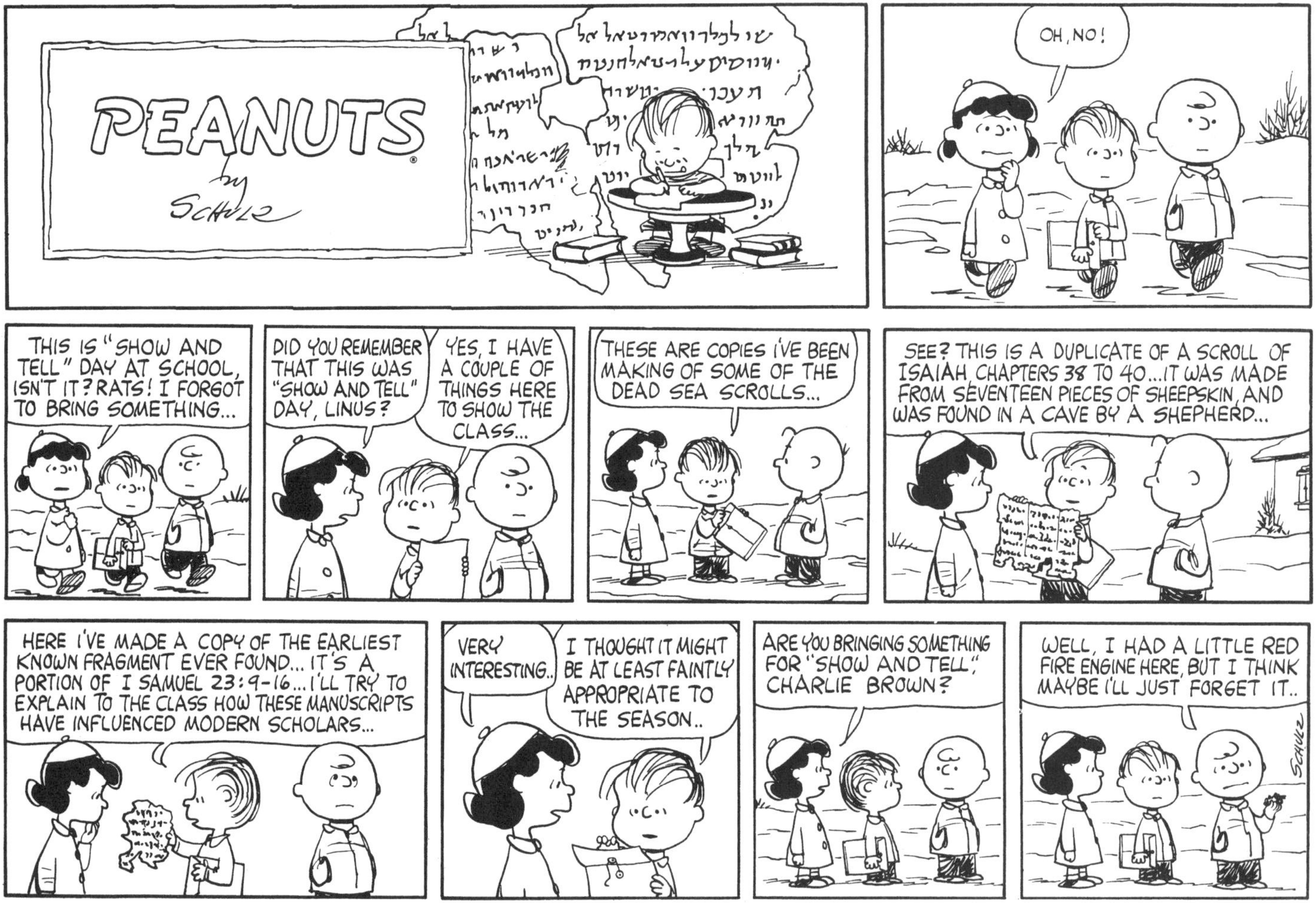
PEANUTS
by Schulz
OH, NO!
THIS IS "SHOW AND TELL" DAY AT SCHOOL, ISN'T IT? RATS! I FORGOT TO BRING SOMETHING...
DID YOU REMEMBER THAT THIS WAS "SHOW AND TELL" DAY, LINUS?
YES, I HAVE A COUPLE OF THINGS HERE TO SHOW THE CLASS...
THESE ARE COPIES I'VE BEEN MAKING OF SOME OF THE DEAD SEA SCROLLS...
SEE? THIS IS A DUPLICATE OF A SCROLL OF ISAIAH, CHAPTERS 38 TO 40...IT WAS MADE FROM SEVENTEEN PIECES OF SHEEPSKIN, AND WAS FOUND IN A CAVE BY A SHEPHERD...
HERE I'VE MADE A COPY OF THE EARLIEST KNOWN FRAGMENT EVER FOUND... IT'S A PORTION OF I SAMUEL 23:9-16...I'LL TRY TO EXPLAIN TO THE CLASS HOW THESE MANUSCRIPTS HAVE INFLUENCED MODERN SCHOLARS...
VERY INTERESTING..
I THOUGHT IT MIGHT BE AT LEAST FAINTLY APPROPRIATE TO THE SEASON..
ARE YOU BRINGING SOMETHING FOR "SHOW AND TELL," CHARLIE BROWN?
WELL, I HAD A LITTLE RED FIRE ENGINE HERE, BUT I THINK MAYBE I'LL JUST FORGET IT..
SCHULZ

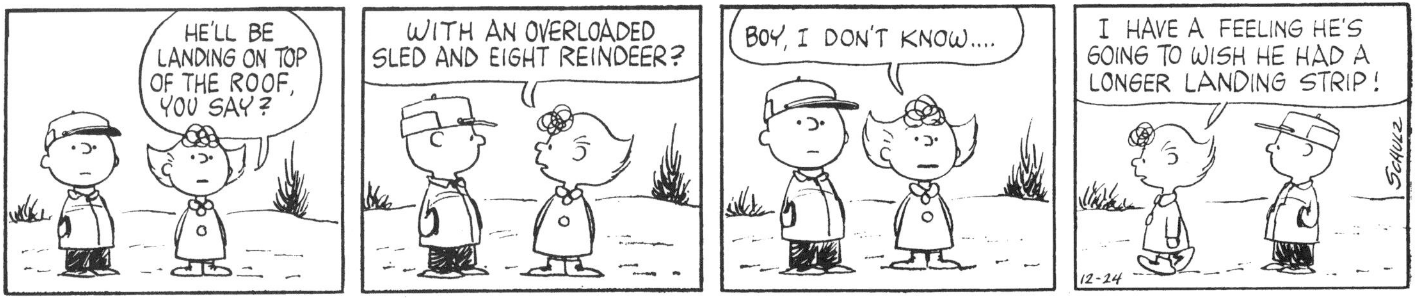
HE'LL BE LANDING ON TOP OF THE ROOF, YOU SAY?
WITH AN OVERLOADED SLED AND EIGHT REINDEER?
BOY, I DON'T KNOW....
I HAVE A FEELING HE'S GOING TO WISH HE HAD A LONGER LANDING STRIP!
SCHULZ
12-24

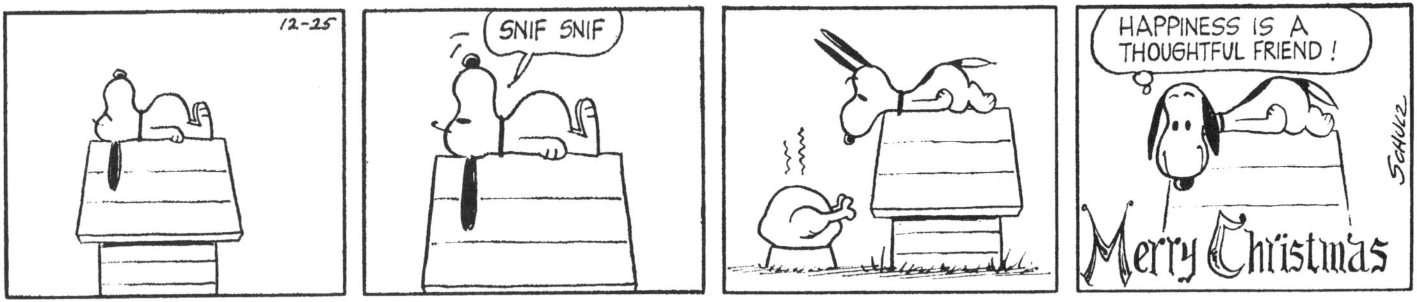
12-25
SNIF SNIF
HAPPINESS IS A THOUGHTFUL FRIEND!
SCHULZ
Merry Christmas

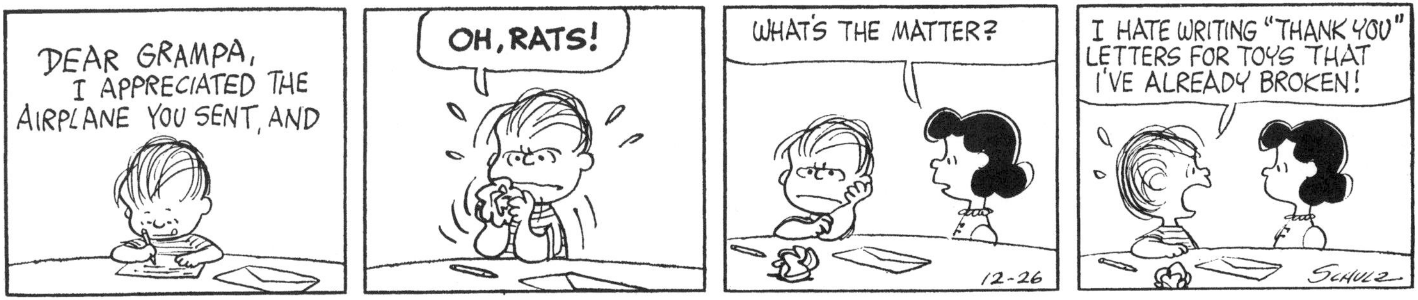
DEAR GRAMPA,
I APPRECIATED THE AIRPLANE YOU SENT, AND
OH, RATS!
WHAT'S THE MATTER?
12-26
I HATE WRITING "THANK YOU" LETTERS FOR TOYS THAT I'VE ALREADY BROKEN!
SCHULZ

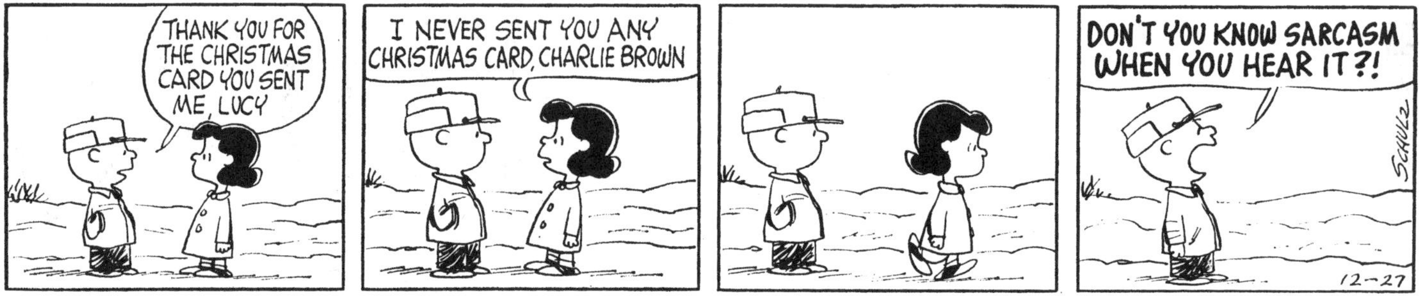
THANK YOU FOR THE CHRISTMAS CARD YOU SENT ME, LUCY
I NEVER SENT YOU ANY CHRISTMAS CARD, CHARLIE BROWN
DON'T YOU KNOW SARCASM WHEN YOU HEAR IT?!
SCHULZ
12-27

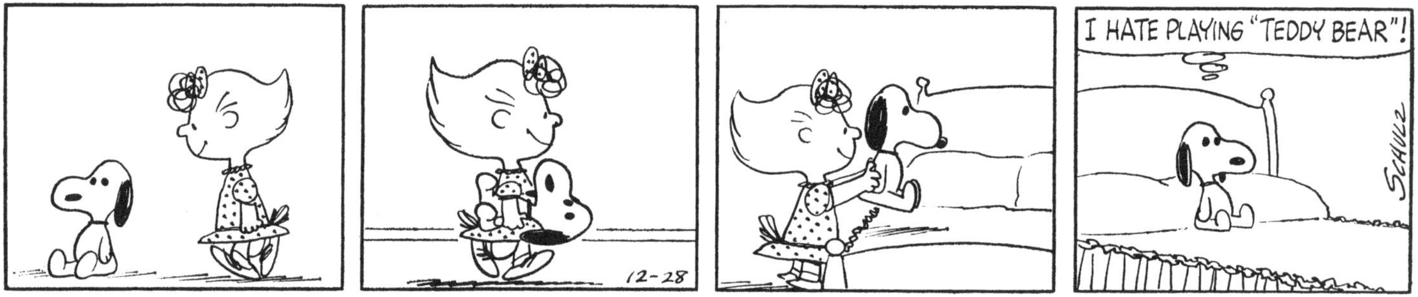
12-28
I HATE PLAYING "TEDDY BEAR"!
SCHULZ

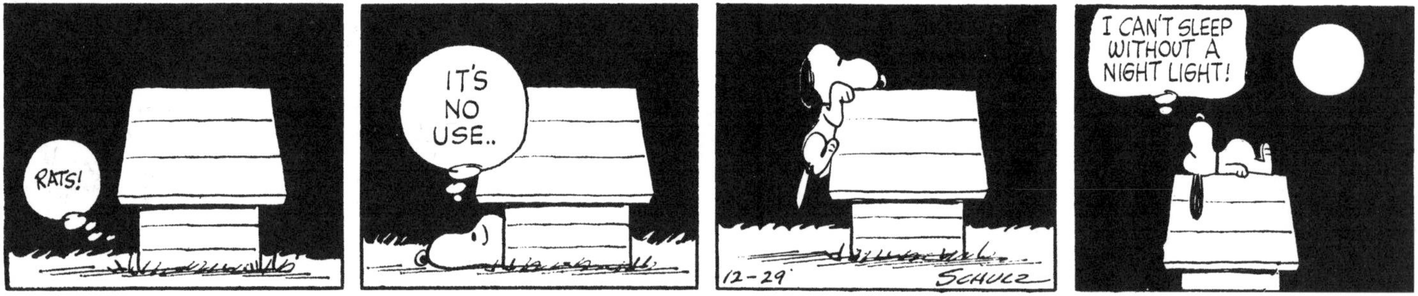
RATS!
IT'S NO USE..
12-29
SCHULZ
I CAN'T SLEEP WITHOUT A NIGHT LIGHT!

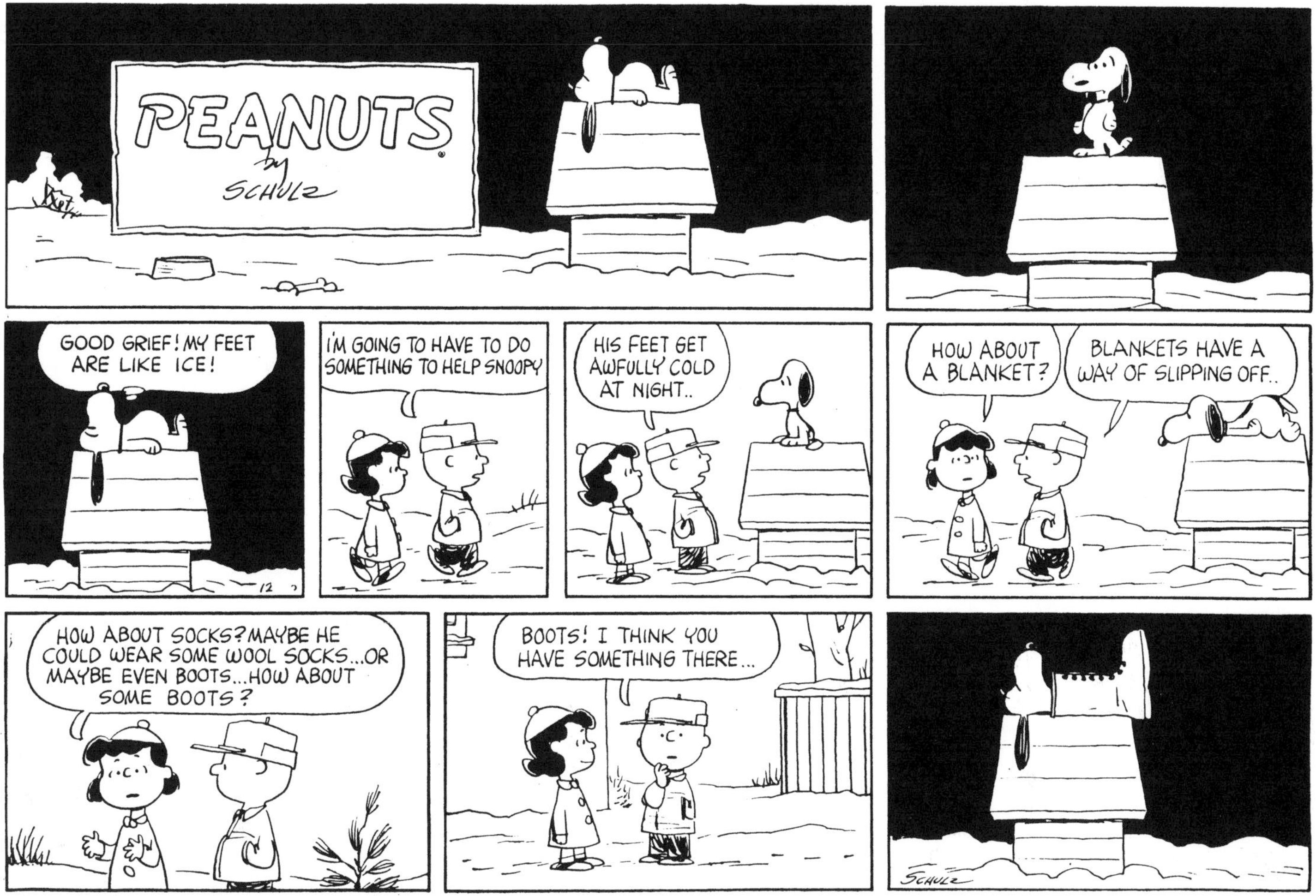
PEANUTS
by SCHULZ
GOOD GRIEF! MY FEET ARE LIKE ICE!
I'M GOING TO HAVE TO DO SOMETHING TO HELP SNOOPY
HIS FEET GET AWFULLY COLD AT NIGHT..
HOW ABOUT A BLANKET?
BLANKETS HAVE A WAY OF SLIPPING OFF..
HOW ABOUT SOCKS? MAYBE HE COULD WEAR SOME WOOL SOCKS...OR MAYBE EVEN BOOTS...HOW ABOUT SOME BOOTS?
BOOTS! I THINK YOU HAVE SOMETHING THERE...
SCHULZ

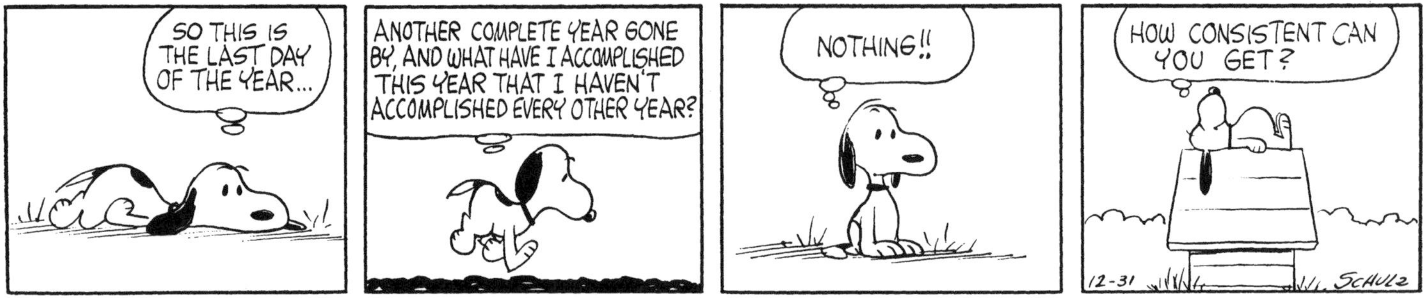
SO THIS IS THE LAST DAY OF THE YEAR...
ANOTHER COMPLETE YEAR GONE BY, AND WHAT HAVE I ACCOMPLISHED THIS YEAR THAT I HAVEN'T ACCOMPLISHED EVERY OTHER YEAR?
NOTHING!!
HOW CONSISTENT CAN YOU GET?
12-31
SCHULZ

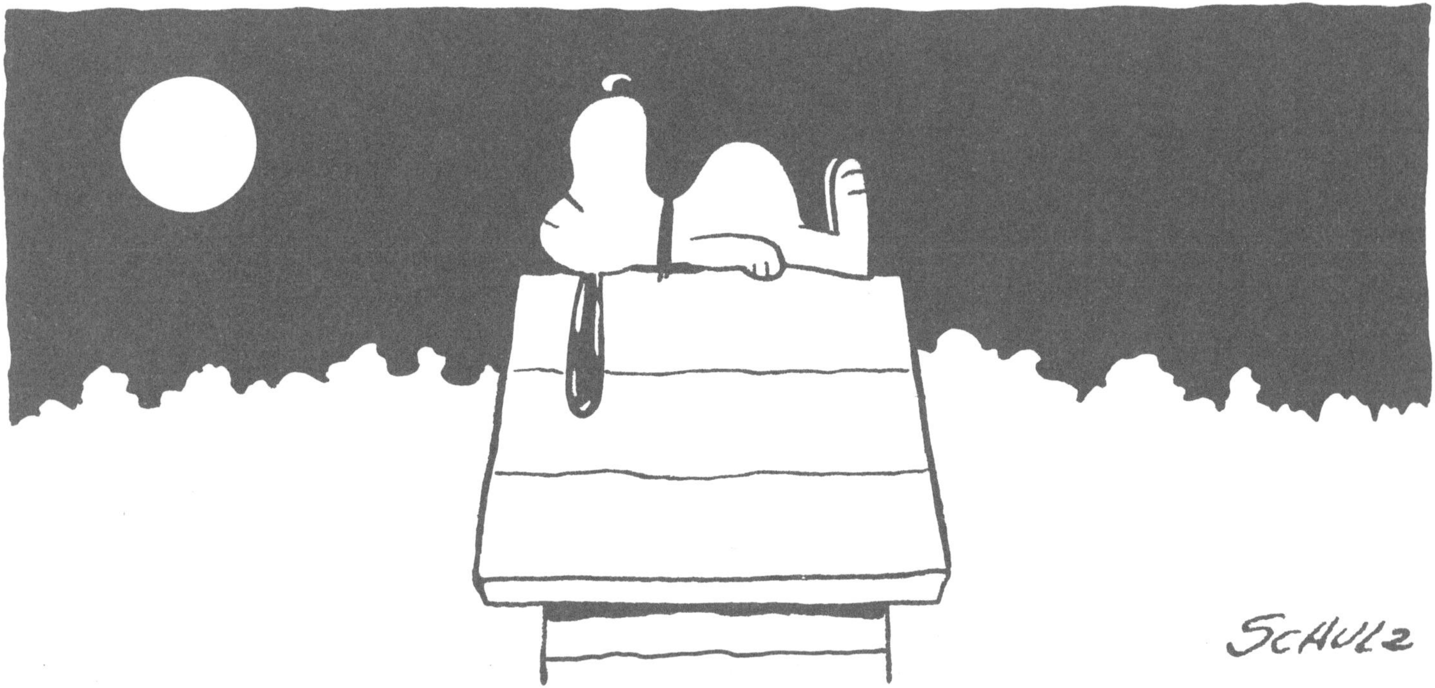
SCHULZ

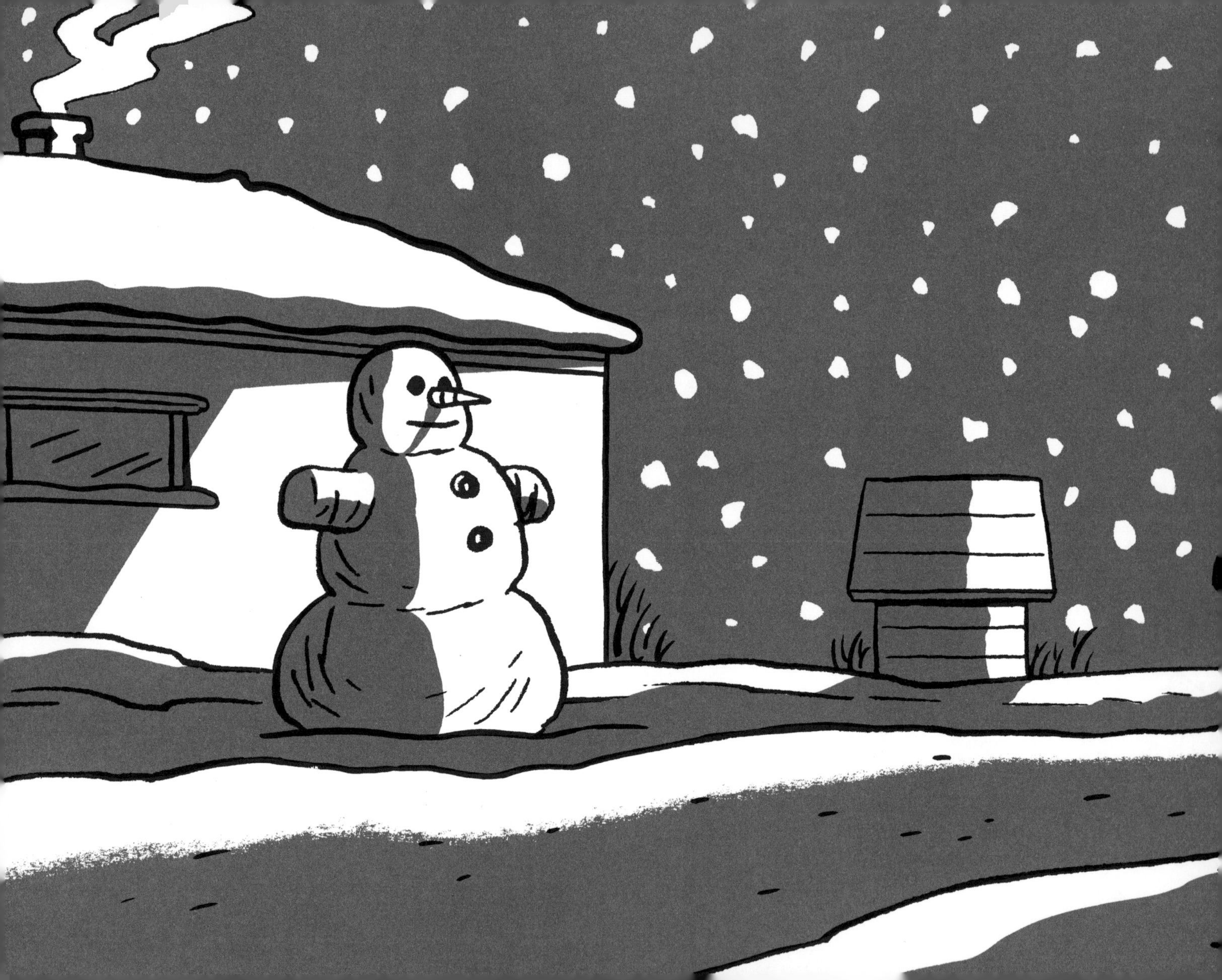

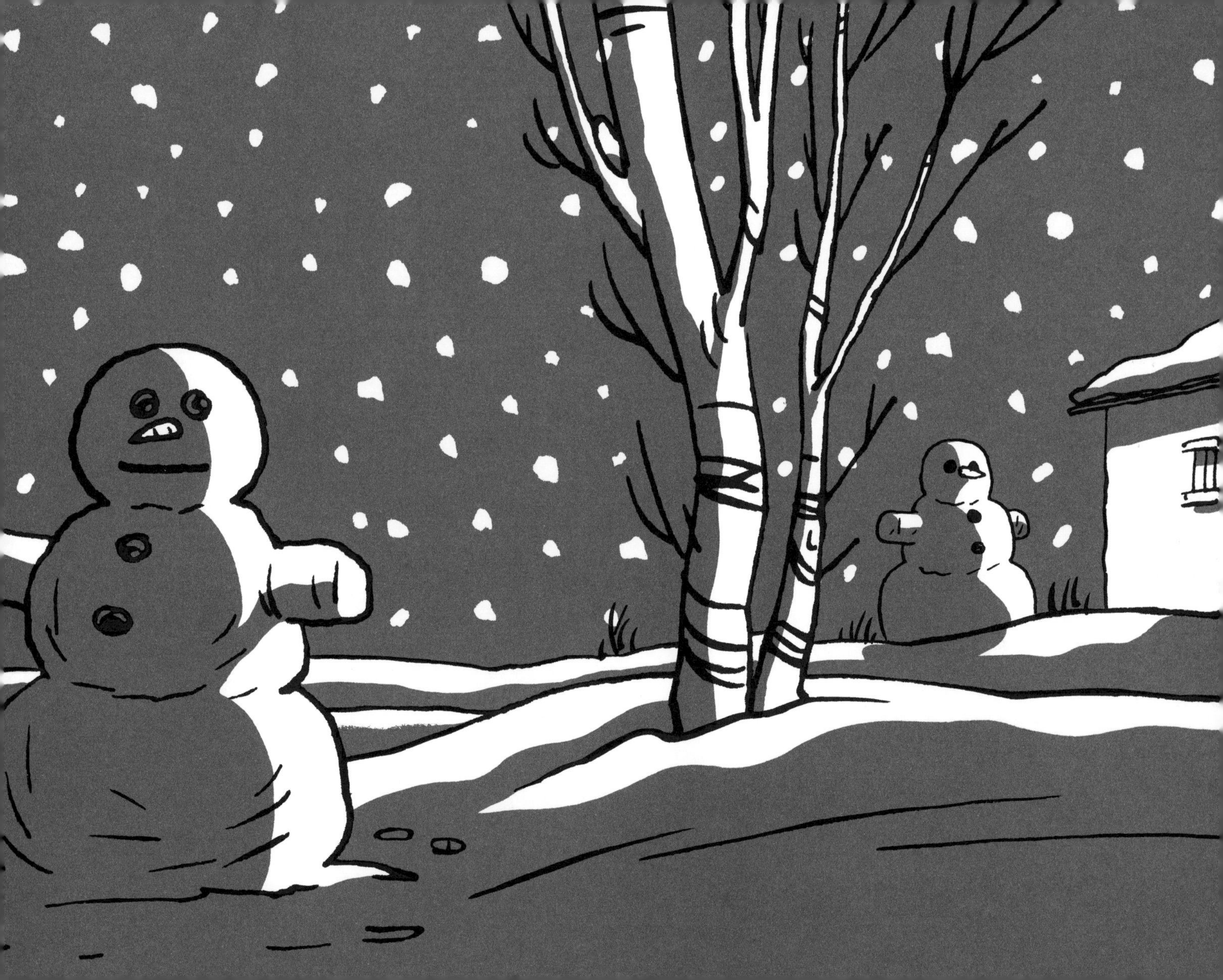

INDEX

I HAVE NATURALLY CURLY HAIR!

OH, GOOD GRIEF!

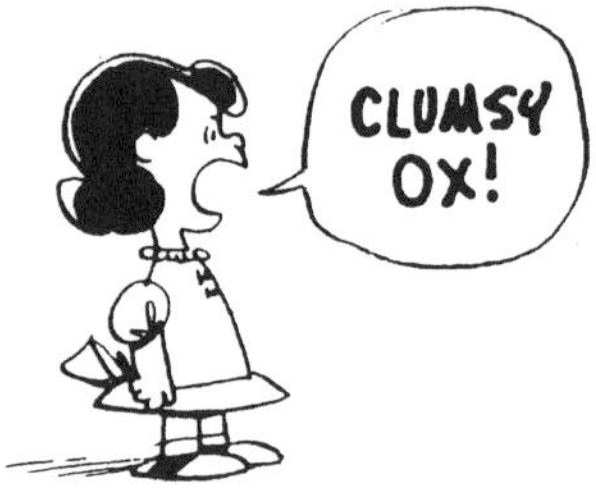
CLUMSY OX!

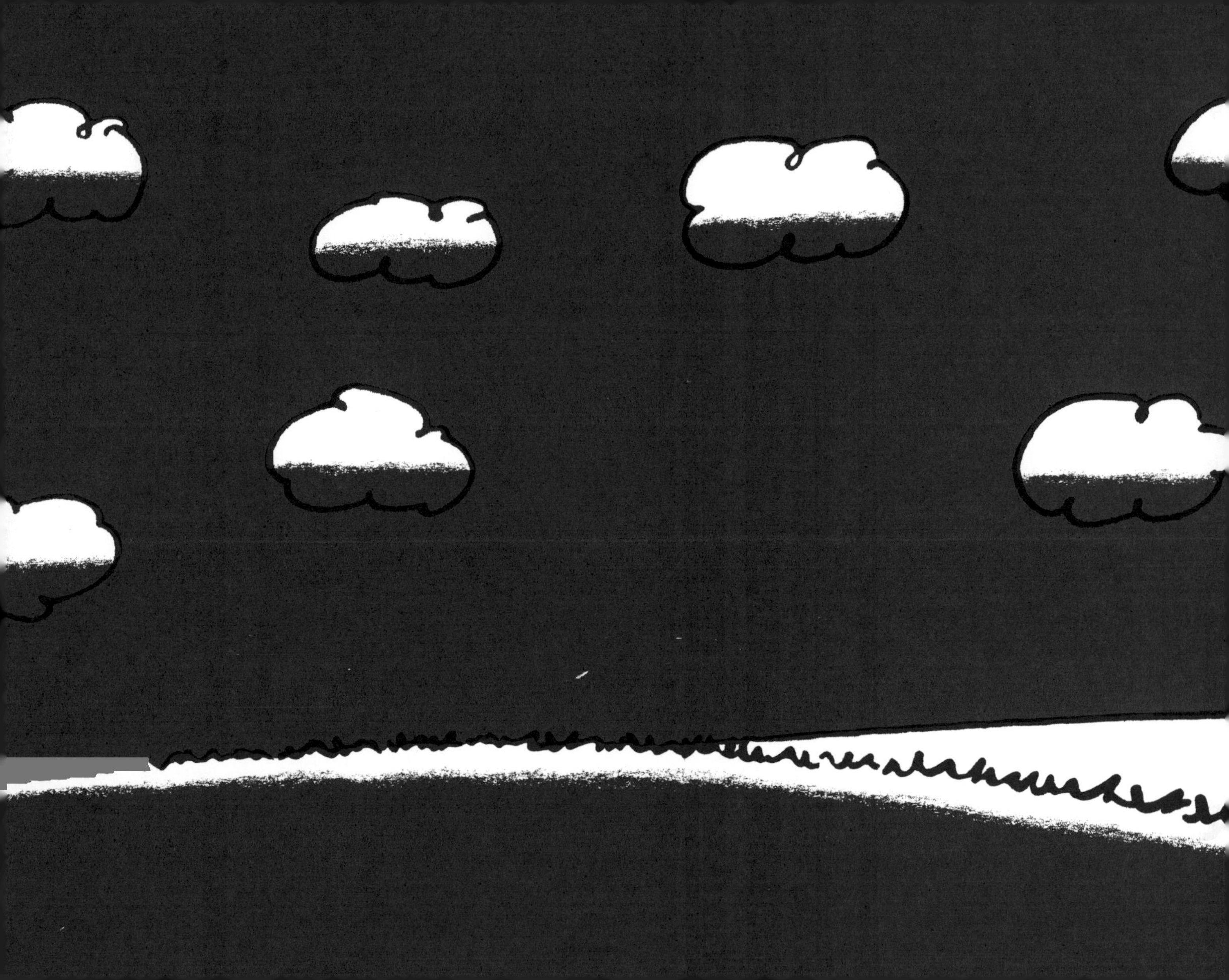

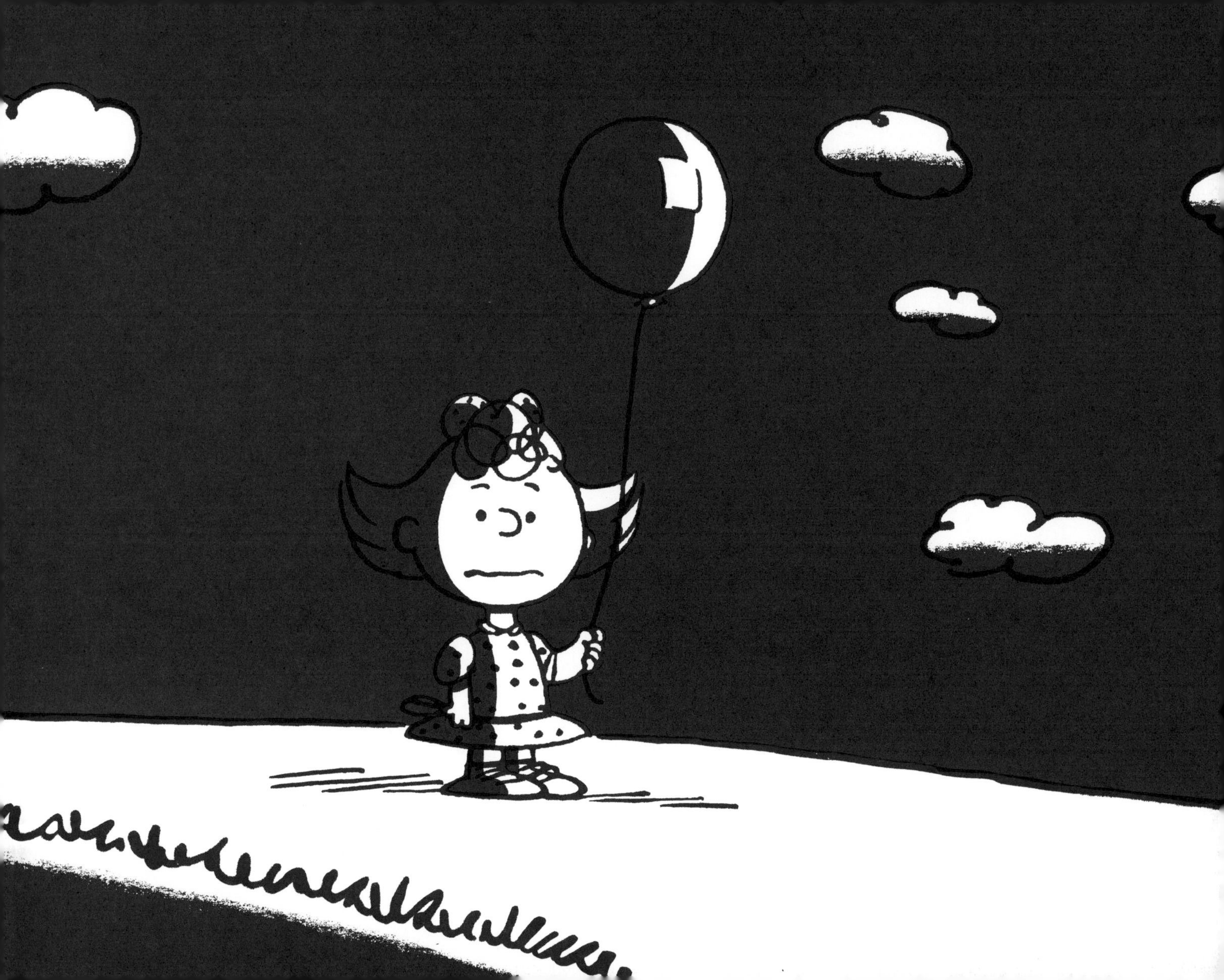

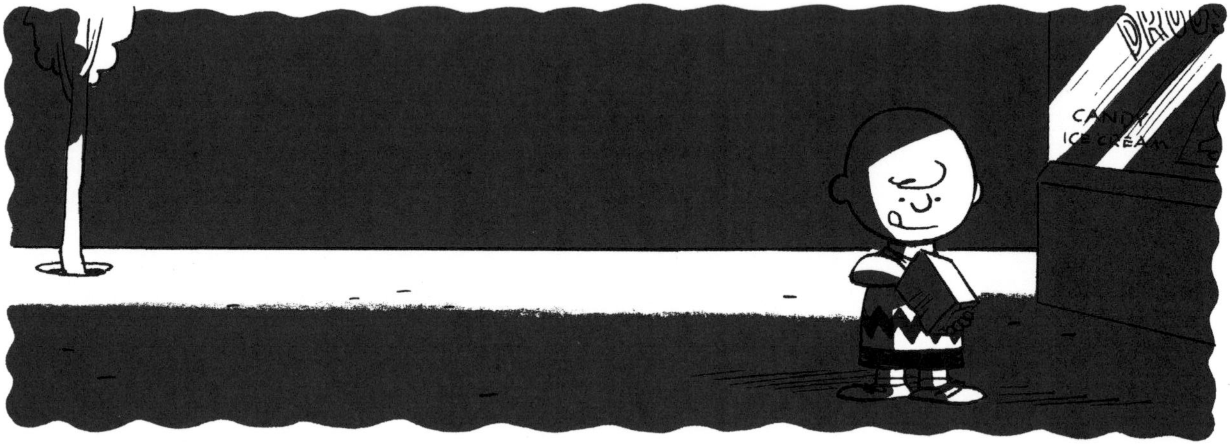

CHARLES M. SCHULZ · 1922 To 2000

Charles M. Schulz was born November 26, 1922 in Minneapolis. His destiny was foreshadowed when an uncle gave him, at the age of two days, the nickname Sparky (after the racehorse Spark Plug in the newspaper strip *Barney Google*).

Schulz grew up in St. Paul. By all accounts, he led an unremarkable, albeit sheltered, childhood. He was an only child, close to both parents, his eventual career path nurtured by his father, who bought four Sunday papers every week — just for the comics.

An outstanding student, he skipped two grades early on, but began to flounder in high school — perhaps not so coincidentally at the same time kids are going through their cruelest, most status-conscious period of socialization. The pain, bitterness, insecurity, and failures chronicled in *Peanuts* appear to have originated from this period of Schulz's life.

Although Schulz enjoyed sports, he also found refuge in solitary activities: reading, drawing, and watching movies. He bought comic books and Big Little Books, pored over the newspaper strips, and copied his favorites — *Buck Rogers*, the Walt Disney characters, *Popeye*, *Tim Tyler's Luck*. He quickly became a connoisseur; his heroes were Milton Caniff, Roy Crane, Hal Foster, and Alex Raymond.

In his senior year in high school, his mother noticed an ad in a local newspaper for a correspondence school, Federal Schools (later called Art

Instruction Schools). Schulz passed the talent test, completed the course and began trying, unsuccessfully, to sell gag cartoons to magazines. (His first published drawing was of his dog, Spike, and appeared in a 1937 Ripley's *Believe It Or Not!* installment.)

After World War II had ended and Schulz was discharged from the army, he started submitting gag cartoons to the various magazines of the time; his first breakthrough, however, came when an editor at Timeless Topix hired him to letter adventure comics. Soon after that, he was hired by his alma mater, Art Instruction, to correct student lessons returned by mail.

Between 1948 and 1950, he succeeded in selling 17 cartoons to the *Saturday Evening Post* — as well as, to the local *St. Paul Pioneer Press*, a weekly comic feature called *Li'l Folks*. It was run in the women's section and paid $10 a week. After writing and drawing the feature for two years, Schulz asked for a better location in the paper or for daily exposure, as well as a raise. When he was turned down on all three counts, he quit.

He started submitting strips to the newspaper syndicates. In the Spring of 1950, he received a letter from the United Feature Syndicate, announcing their interest in his submission, *Li'l Folks*. Schulz boarded a train in June for New York City; more interested in doing a strip than a panel, he also brought along the first installments of what would become *Peanuts* — and that was what sold. (The title, which Schulz loathed to his dying day, was imposed by the syndicate). The first *Peanuts* daily appeared October 2, 1950; the first Sunday, January 6, 1952.

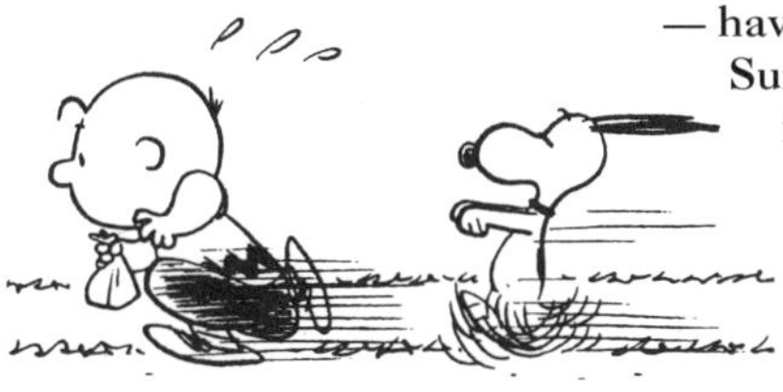

Prior to *Peanuts*, the province of the comics page had been that of gags, social and political observation, domestic comedy, soap opera, and various adventure genres. Although *Peanuts* changed, or evolved, during the 50 years Schulz wrote and drew it, it remained, as it began, an anomaly on the comics page — a comic strip about the interior crises of the cartoonist himself. After a painful divorce in 1973 from which he had not yet recovered, Schulz told a reporter, "Strangely, I've drawn better cartoons in the last six months — or as good as I've ever drawn. I don't know how the human mind works." Surely, it was this kind of humility in the face of profoundly irreducible human question that makes *Peanuts* as universally moving as it is.

Diagnosed with cancer, Schulz retired from *Peanuts* at the end of 1999. He died on February 12th 2000, the day before his last strip was published (and two days before Valentine's Day) — having completed 17,897 daily and Sunday strips, each and every one fully written, drawn, and lettered entirely by his own hand — an unmatched achievement in comics.

—*Gary Groth*

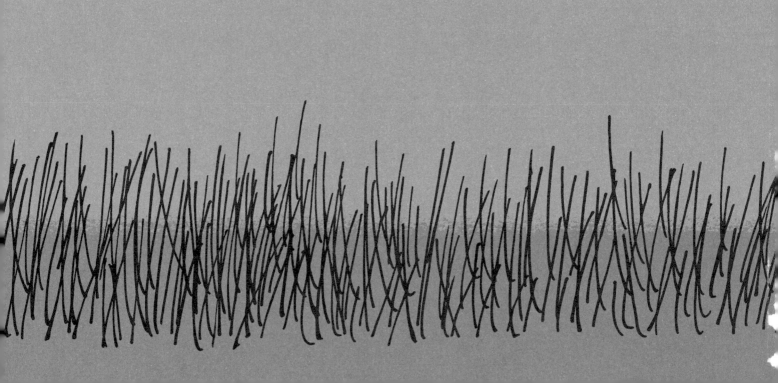

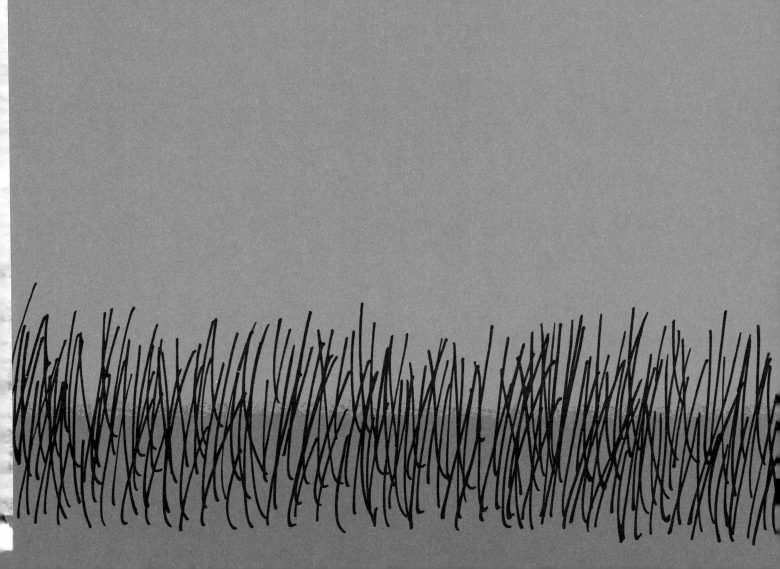

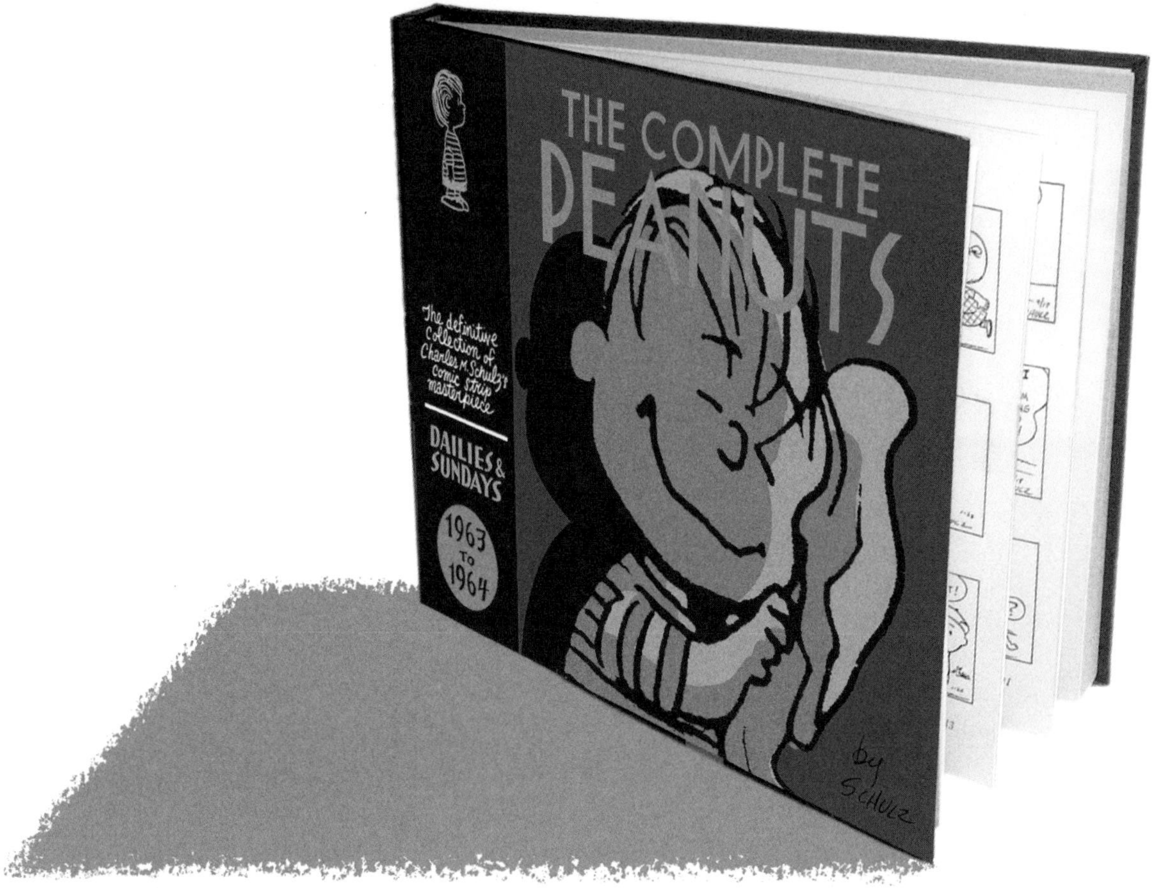
THE COMPLETE PEANUTS
The definitive Collection of Charles M. Schulz's comic strip masterpiece
DAILIES & SUNDAYS
1963 TO 1964
by SCHULZ

COMING IN *THE COMPLETE PEANUTS: 1963-1964*

A new character — in fact, three new characters — appear: the numerically-monikered 555 95472 and his sisters 3 and 4... Charlie Brown blows a baseball match with the little red haired girl in attendance... Snoopy befriends bunnies and birds, and goes for a stay in the hospital ... Linus's run for class president is derailed by his religious beliefs... Plus Sally vs. school, and Lucy's campaign to improve everyone but herself!

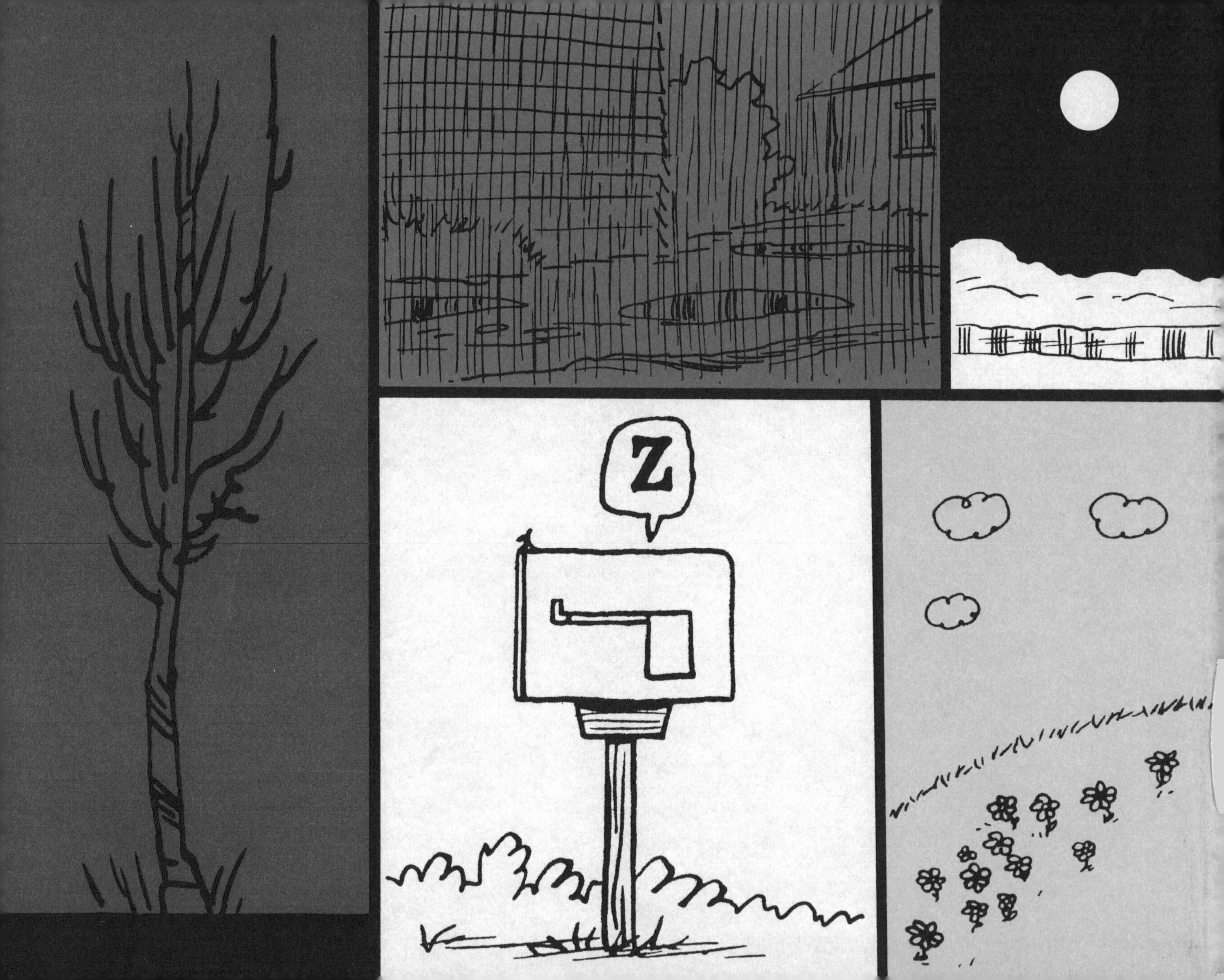
Z